OFISCH

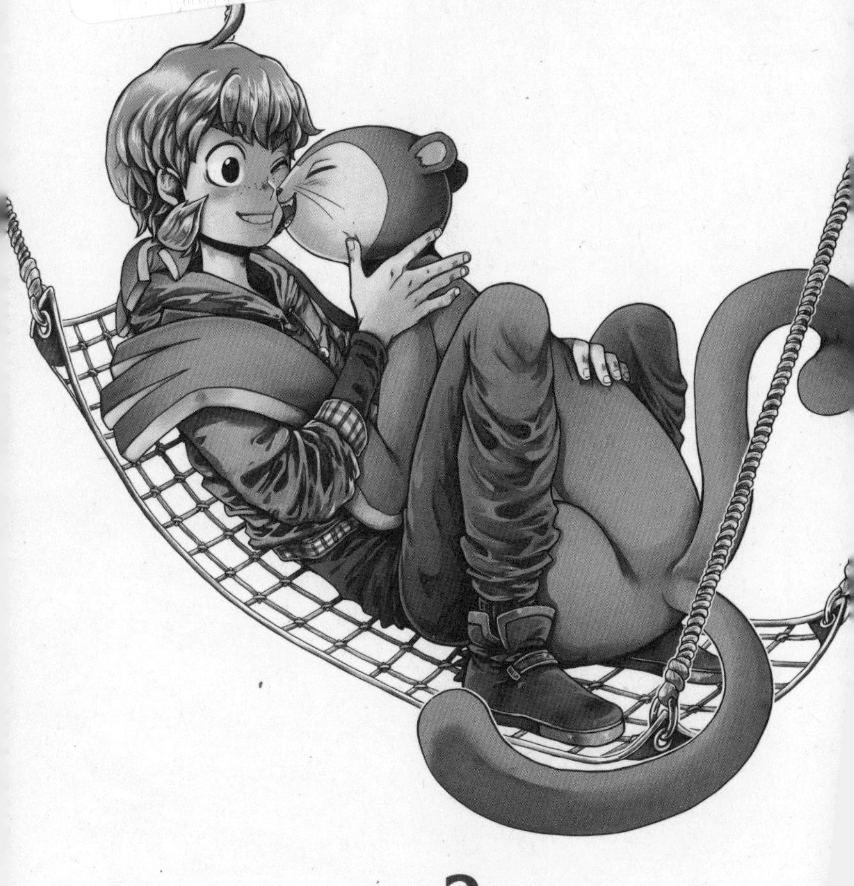

3

Nana Yaa

TOKYOPOP®

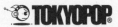

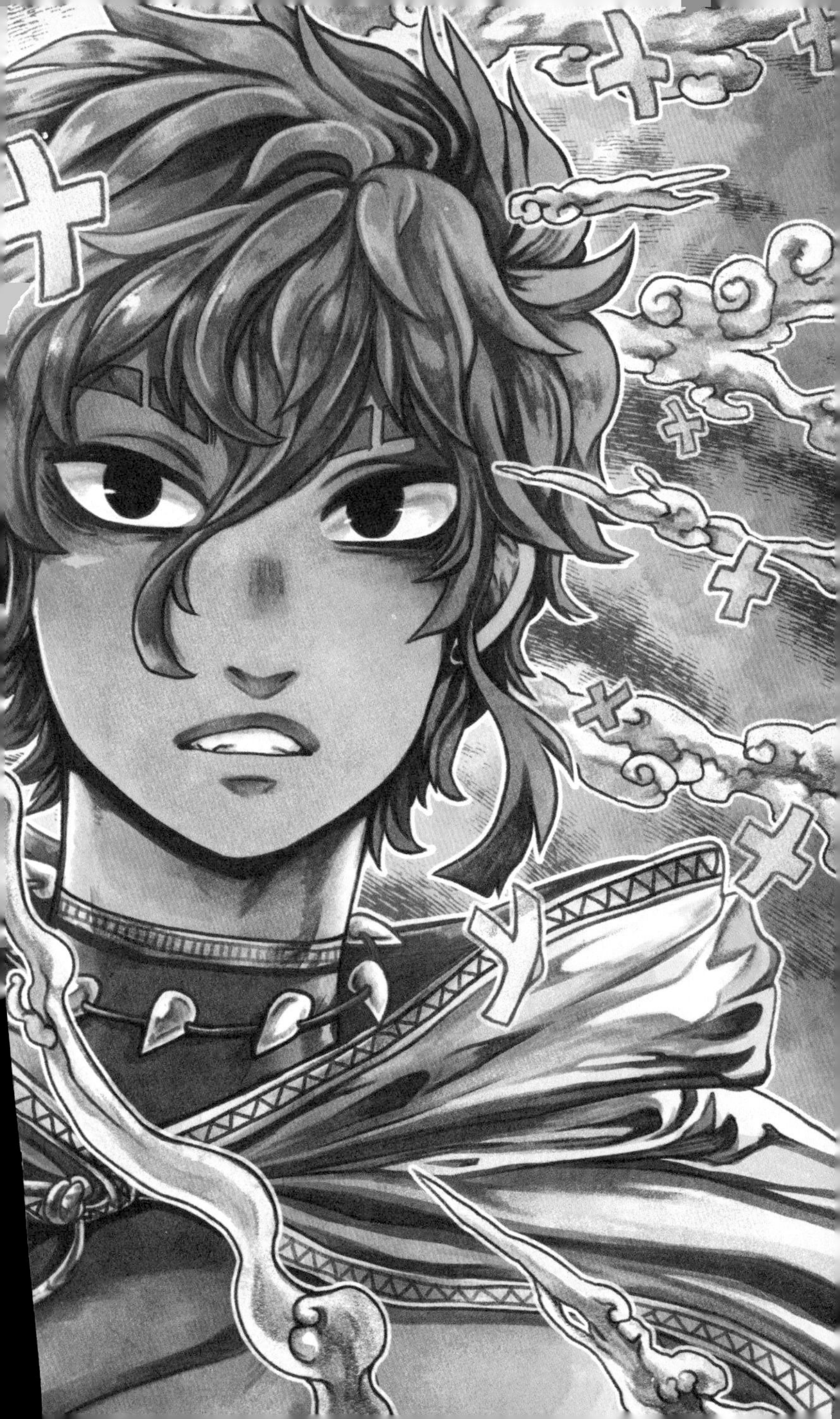

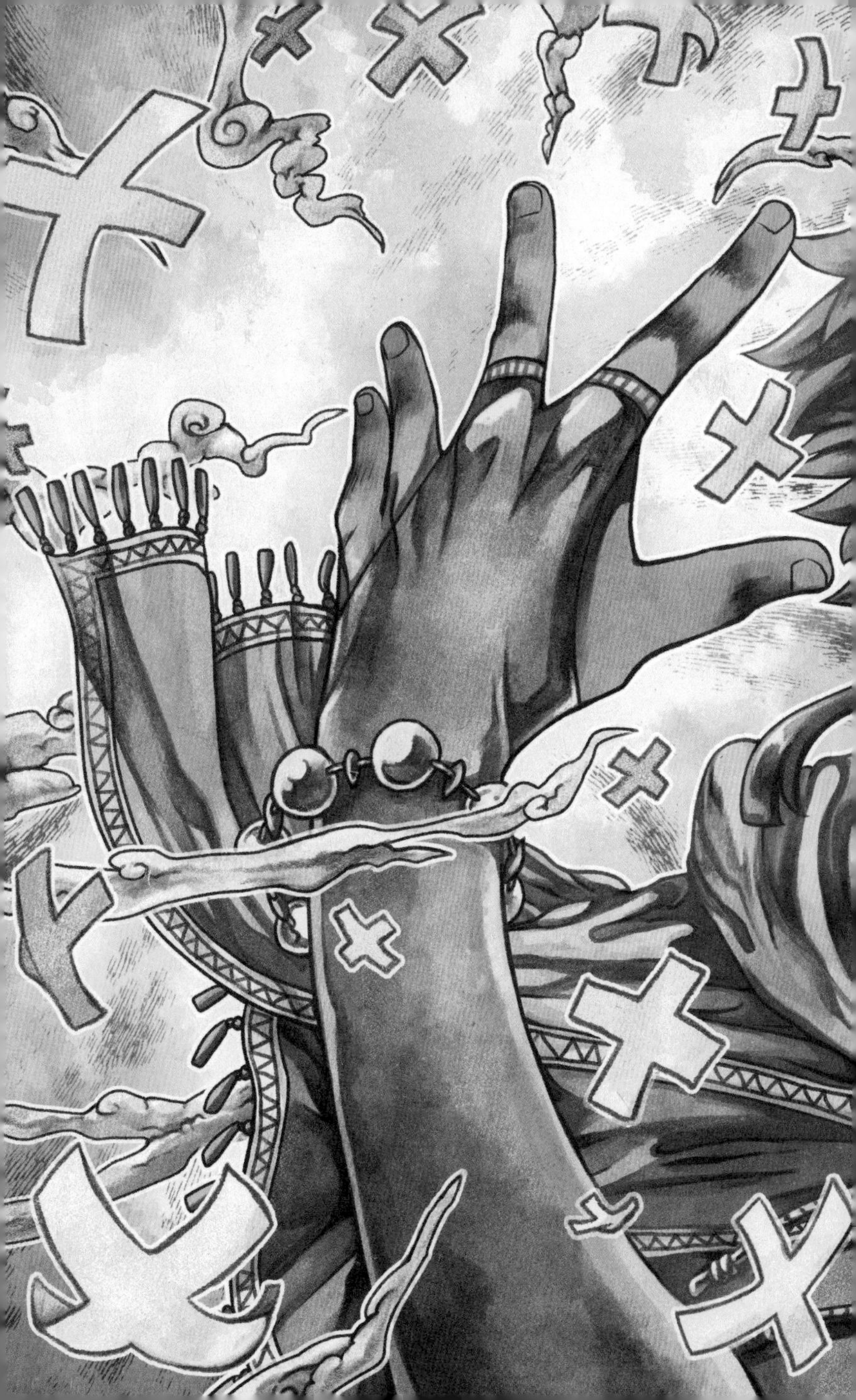

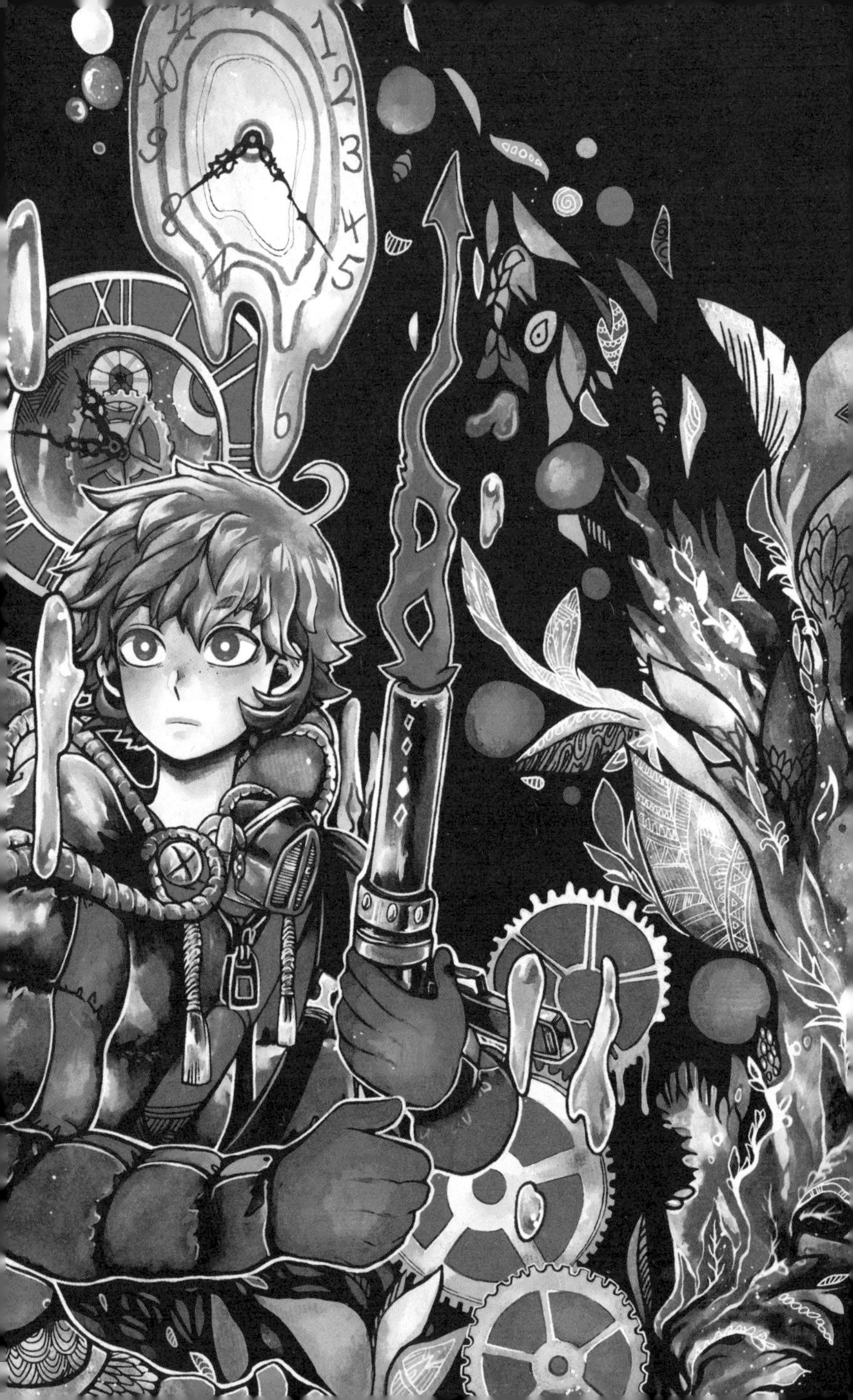

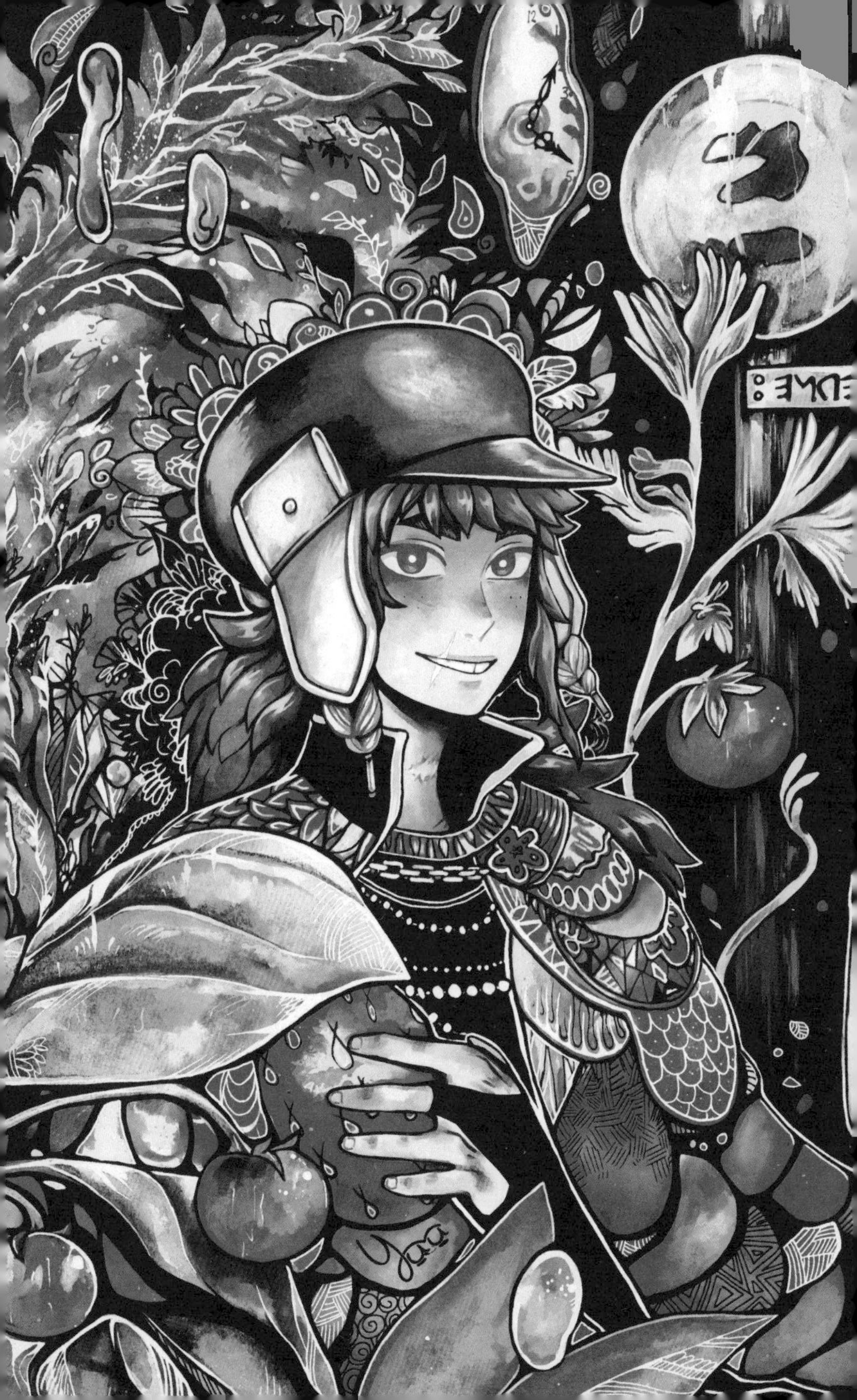

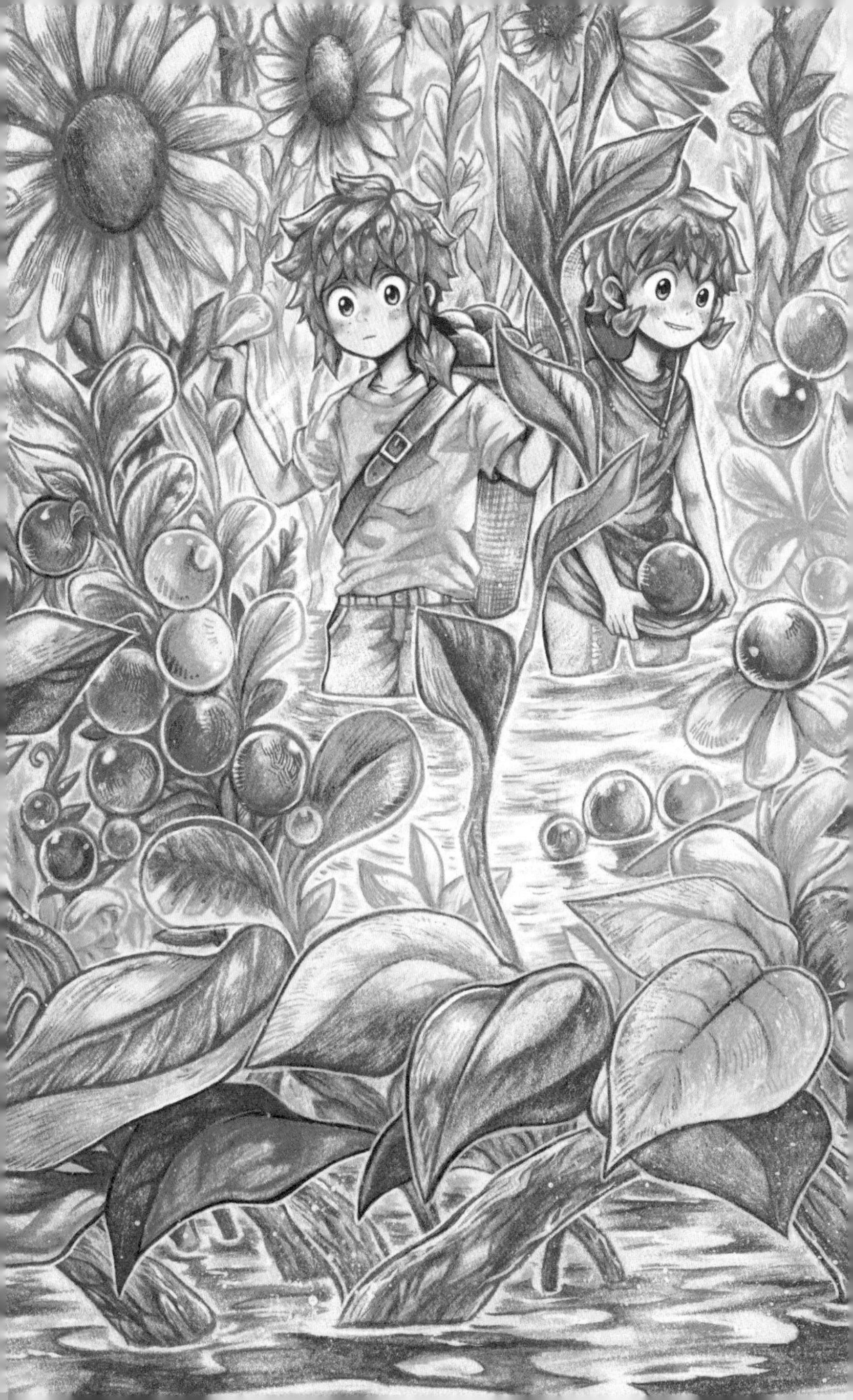

GOLDFISCH

3

Nana Yaa

TOKYOPOP®

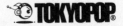

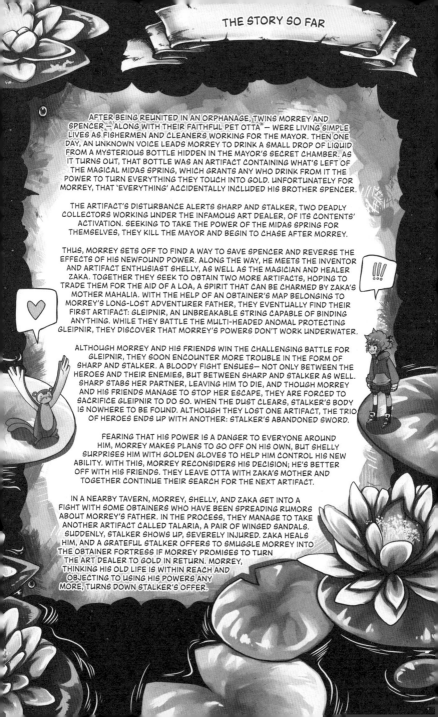

AFTER BEING REUNITED IN AN ORPHANAGE, TWINS MORREY AND SPENCER — ALONG WITH THEIR FAITHFUL PET OTTA — WERE LIVING SIMPLE LIVES AS FISHERMEN AND CLEANERS WORKING FOR THE MAYOR. THEN ONE DAY, AN UNKNOWN VOICE LEADS MORREY TO DRINK A SMALL DROP OF LIQUID FROM A MYSTERIOUS BOTTLE HIDDEN IN THE MAYOR'S SECRET CHAMBER. AS IT TURNS OUT, THAT BOTTLE WAS AN ARTIFACT CONTAINING WHAT'S LEFT OF THE MAGICAL MIDAS SPRING, WHICH GRANTS ANY WHO DRINK FROM IT THE POWER TO TURN EVERYTHING THEY TOUCH INTO GOLD. UNFORTUNATELY FOR MORREY, THAT 'EVERYTHING' ACCIDENTALLY INCLUDED HIS BROTHER SPENCER.

THE ARTIFACT'S DISTURBANCE ALERTS SHARP AND STALKER, TWO DEADLY COLLECTORS WORKING UNDER THE INFAMOUS ART DEALER, OF ITS CONTENTS' ACTIVATION. SEEKING TO TAKE THE POWER OF THE MIDAS SPRING FOR THEMSELVES, THEY KILL THE MAYOR AND BEGIN TO CHASE AFTER MORREY.

THUS, MORREY SETS OFF TO FIND A WAY TO SAVE SPENCER AND REVERSE THE EFFECTS OF HIS NEWFOUND POWER. ALONG THE WAY, HE MEETS THE INVENTOR AND ARTIFACT ENTHUSIAST SHELLY, AS WELL AS THE MAGICIAN AND HEALER ZAKA. TOGETHER THEY SEEK TO OBTAIN TWO MORE ARTIFACTS, HOPING TO TRADE THEM FOR THE AID OF A LOA, A SPIRIT THAT CAN BE CHARMED BY ZAKA'S MOTHER MAHALIA. WITH THE HELP OF AN OBTAINER'S MAP BELONGING TO MORREY'S LONG-LOST ADVENTURER FATHER, THEY EVENTUALLY FIND THEIR FIRST ARTIFACT: GLEIPNIR, AN UNBREAKABLE STRING CAPABLE OF BINDING ANYTHING. WHILE THEY BATTLE THE MULTI-HEADED ANOMAL PROTECTING GLEIPNIR, THEY DISCOVER THAT MORREY'S POWERS DON'T WORK UNDERWATER.

ALTHOUGH MORREY AND HIS FRIENDS WIN THE CHALLENGING BATTLE FOR GLEIPNIR, THEY SOON ENCOUNTER MORE TROUBLE IN THE FORM OF SHARP AND STALKER. A BLOODY FIGHT ENSUES— NOT ONLY BETWEEN THE HEROES AND THEIR ENEMIES, BUT BETWEEN SHARP AND STALKER AS WELL. SHARP STABS HER PARTNER, LEAVING HIM TO DIE, AND THOUGH MORREY AND HIS FRIENDS MANAGE TO STOP HER ESCAPE, THEY ARE FORCED TO SACRIFICE GLEIPNIR TO DO SO. WHEN THE DUST CLEARS, STALKER'S BODY IS NOWHERE TO BE FOUND. ALTHOUGH THEY LOST ONE ARTIFACT, THE TRIO OF HEROES ENDS UP WITH ANOTHER: STALKER'S ABANDONED SWORD.

FEARING THAT HIS POWER IS A DANGER TO EVERYONE AROUND HIM, MORREY MAKES PLANS TO GO OFF ON HIS OWN, BUT SHELLY SURPRISES HIM WITH GOLDEN GLOVES TO HELP HIM CONTROL HIS NEW ABILITY. WITH THIS, MORREY RECONSIDERS HIS DECISION; HE'S BETTER OFF WITH HIS FRIENDS. THEY LEAVE OTTA WITH ZAKA'S MOTHER AND TOGETHER CONTINUE THEIR SEARCH FOR THE NEXT ARTIFACT.

IN A NEARBY TAVERN, MORREY, SHELLY, AND ZAKA GET INTO A FIGHT WITH SOME OBTAINERS WHO HAVE BEEN SPREADING RUMORS ABOUT MORREY'S FATHER. IN THE PROCESS, THEY MANAGE TO TAKE ANOTHER ARTIFACT CALLED TALARIA, A PAIR OF WINGED SANDALS. SUDDENLY, STALKER SHOWS UP, SEVERELY INJURED. ZAKA HEALS HIM, AND A GRATEFUL STALKER OFFERS TO SMUGGLE MORREY INTO THE OBTAINER FORTRESS IF MORREY PROMISES TO TURN THE ART DEALER TO GOLD IN RETURN. MORREY, THINKING HIS OLD LIFE IS WITHIN REACH AND OBJECTING TO USING HIS POWERS ANY MORE, TURNS DOWN STALKER'S OFFER.

OTTA

SPENCER

MORREY

SOBO KESSOU

ZAKA

SHELLY

THE MAYOR/DOLPH

MAHALIA

AGENT RED/CONRAD

THE ART DEALER/?

AGENT SHARP/NIAN

AGENT STALKER/KOLJA

CONTENTS

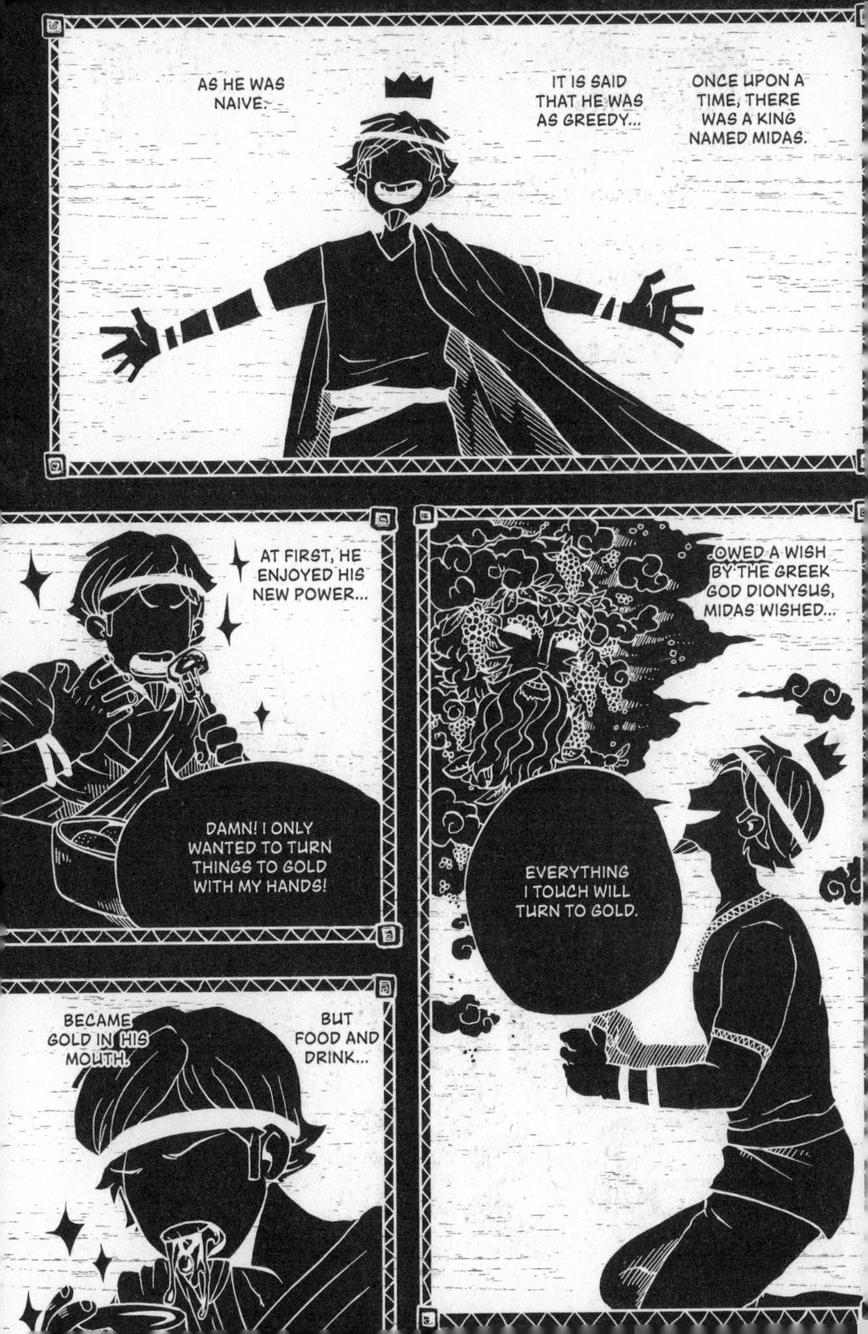
ONCE UPON A TIME, THERE WAS A KING NAMED MIDAS.
IT IS SAID THAT HE WAS AS GREEDY...
AS HE WAS NAIVE.
OWED A WISH BY THE GREEK GOD DIONYSUS, MIDAS WISHED...
EVERYTHING I TOUCH WILL TURN TO GOLD.
AT FIRST, HE ENJOYED HIS NEW POWER...
DAMN! I ONLY WANTED TO TURN THINGS TO GOLD WITH MY HANDS!
BUT FOOD AND DRINK...
BECAME GOLD IN HIS MOUTH.

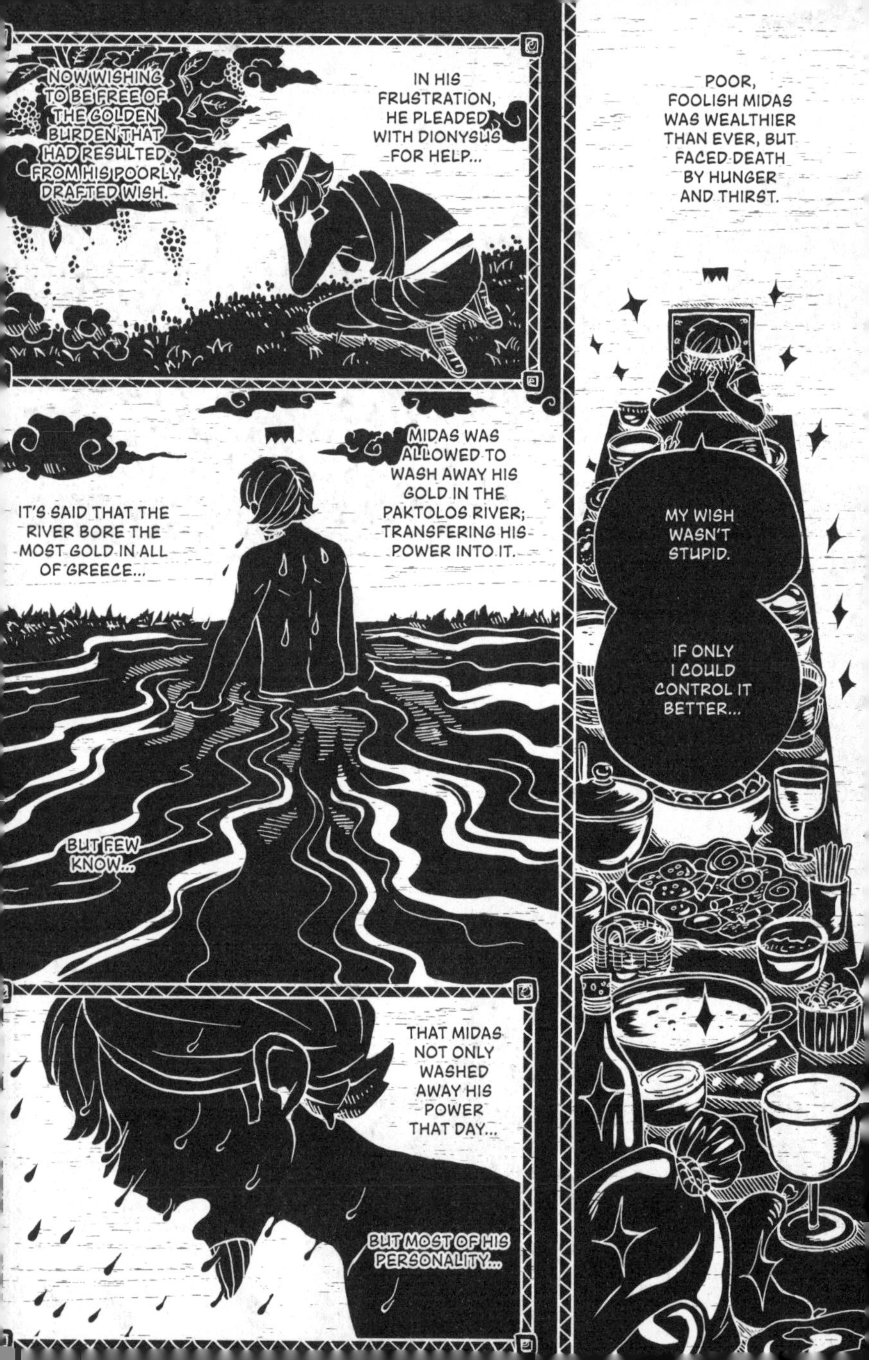
POOR, FOOLISH MIDAS WAS WEALTHIER THAN EVER, BUT FACED DEATH BY HUNGER AND THIRST.
MY WISH WASN'T STUPID.
IF ONLY I COULD CONTROL IT BETTER...
IN HIS FRUSTRATION, HE PLEADED WITH DIONYSUS FOR HELP...
NOW WISHING TO BE FREE OF THE GOLDEN BURDEN THAT HAD RESULTED FROM HIS POORLY DRAFTED WISH.
MIDAS WAS ALLOWED TO WASH AWAY HIS GOLD IN THE PAKTOLOS RIVER; TRANSFERING HIS POWER INTO IT.
IT'S SAID THAT THE RIVER BORE THE MOST GOLD IN ALL OF GREECE...
BUT FEW KNOW...
THAT MIDAS NOT ONLY WASHED AWAY HIS POWER THAT DAY...
BUT MOST OF HIS PERSONALITY...

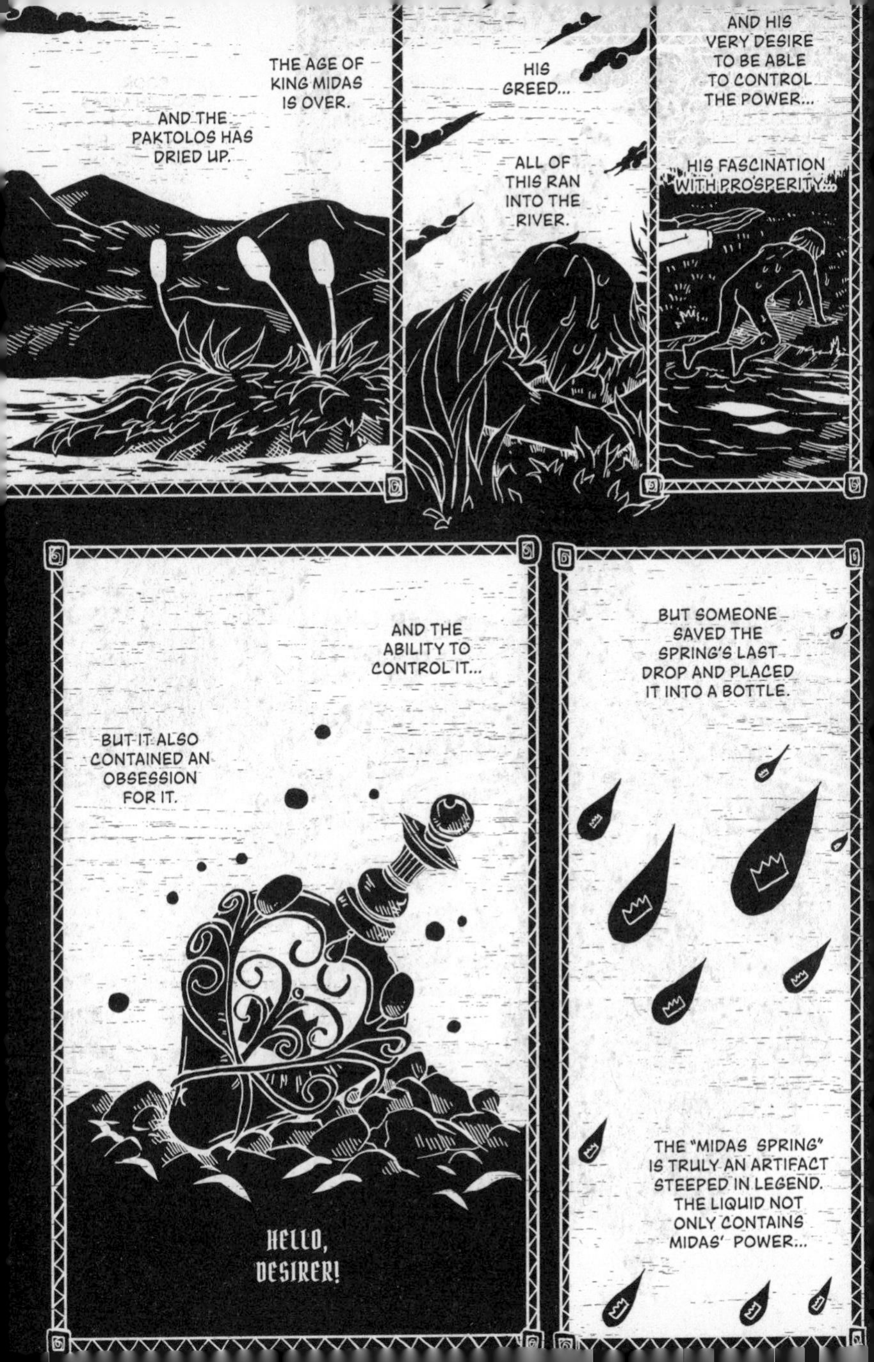
AND HIS VERY DESIRE TO BE ABLE TO CONTROL THE POWER...
HIS FASCINATION WITH PROSPERITY...
HIS GREED...
ALL OF THIS RAN INTO THE RIVER.
THE AGE OF KING MIDAS IS OVER.
AND THE PAKTOLOS HAS DRIED UP.
BUT SOMEONE SAVED THE SPRING'S LAST DROP AND PLACED IT INTO A BOTTLE.
THE "MIDAS SPRING" IS TRULY AN ARTIFACT STEEPED IN LEGEND. THE LIQUID NOT ONLY CONTAINS MIDAS' POWER...
AND THE ABILITY TO CONTROL IT...
BUT IT ALSO CONTAINED AN OBSESSION FOR IT.
HELLO, DESIRER!

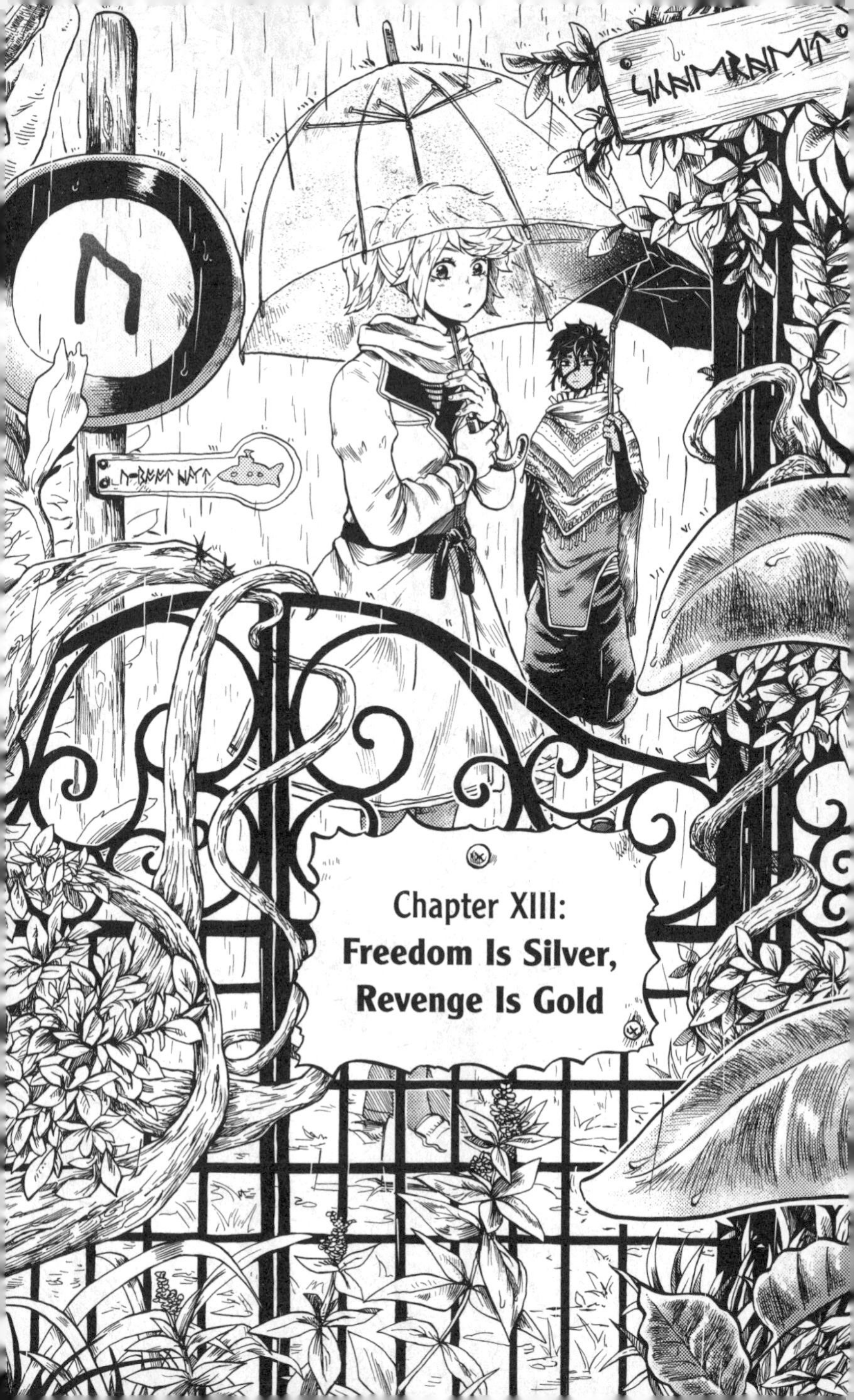
Chapter XIII:
Freedom Is Silver,
Revenge Is Gold

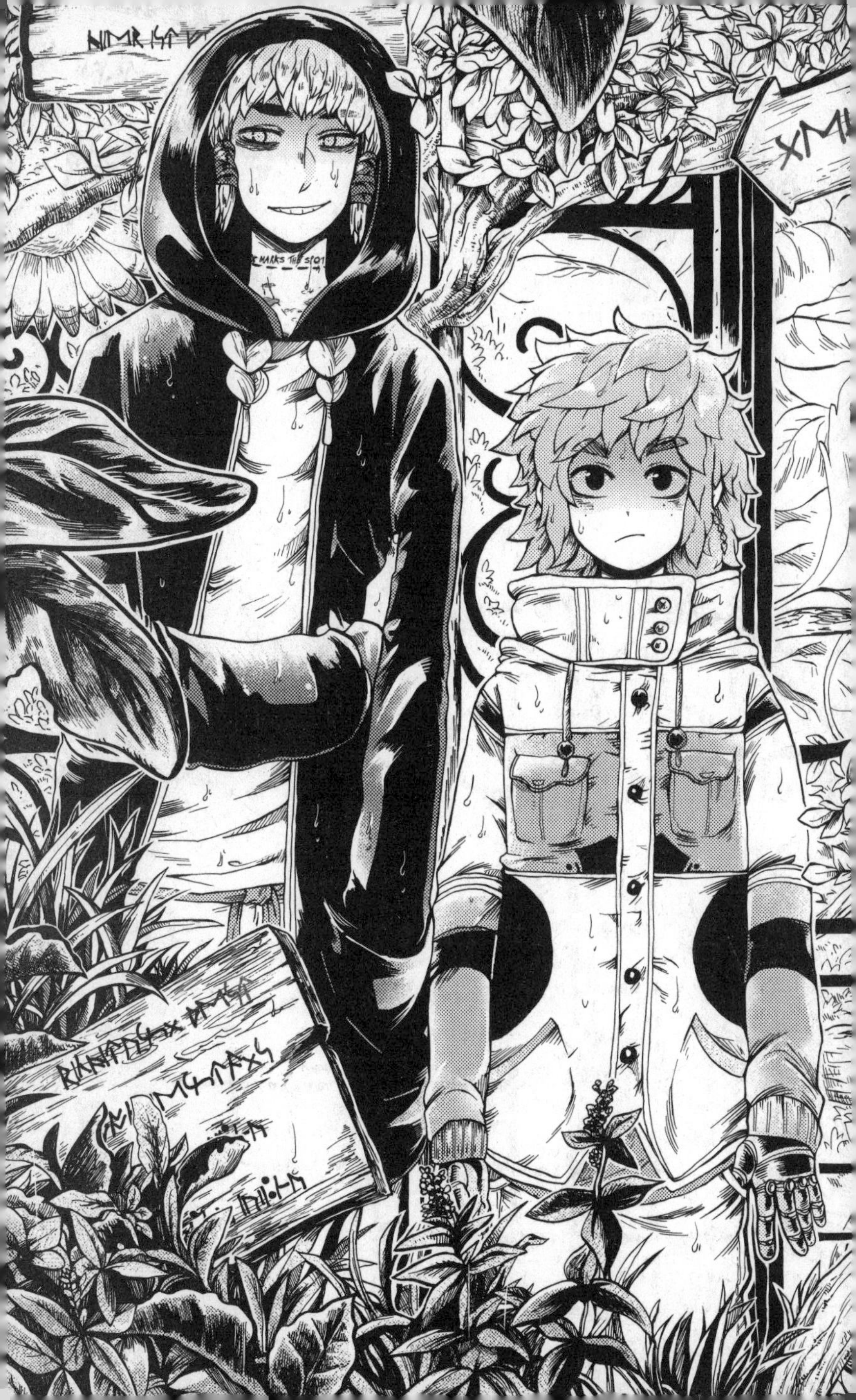
MARKS THE SPOT

URGH...

THAT'S THE SLOGAN OF THE OBTAINER ORGANIZATION...

CHOKE

HELP ME!

SHELLY... PLEASE...

IF YOU'RE READING THIS, IT IS ALREADY TOO LATE.

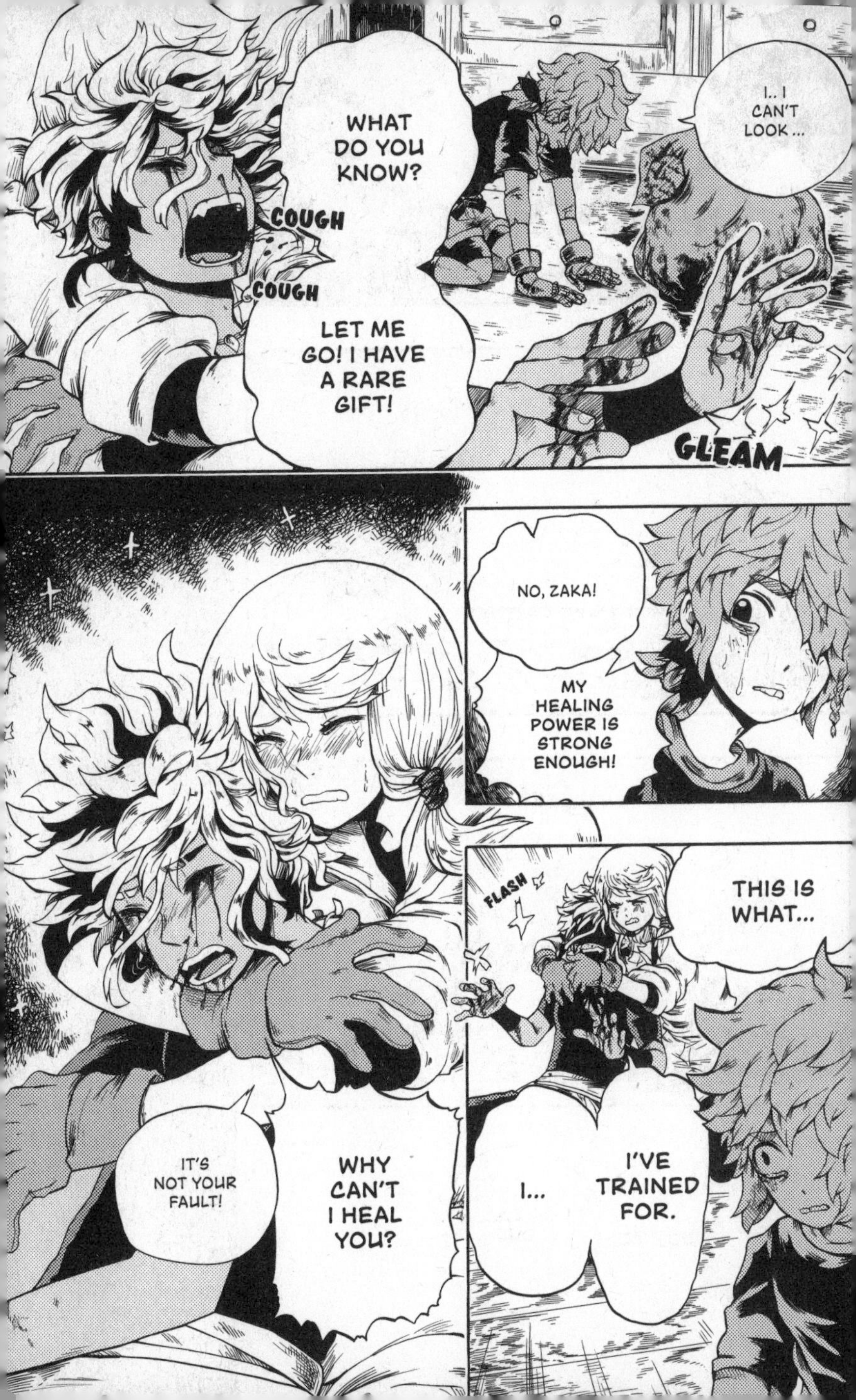
I.. I CAN'T LOOK...
WHAT DO YOU KNOW?
COUGH
COUGH
LET ME GO! I HAVE A RARE GIFT!
GLEAM
NO, ZAKA!
MY HEALING POWER IS STRONG ENOUGH!
THIS IS WHAT...
FLASH
I'VE TRAINED FOR.
I...
WHY CAN'T I HEAL YOU?
IT'S NOT YOUR FAULT!

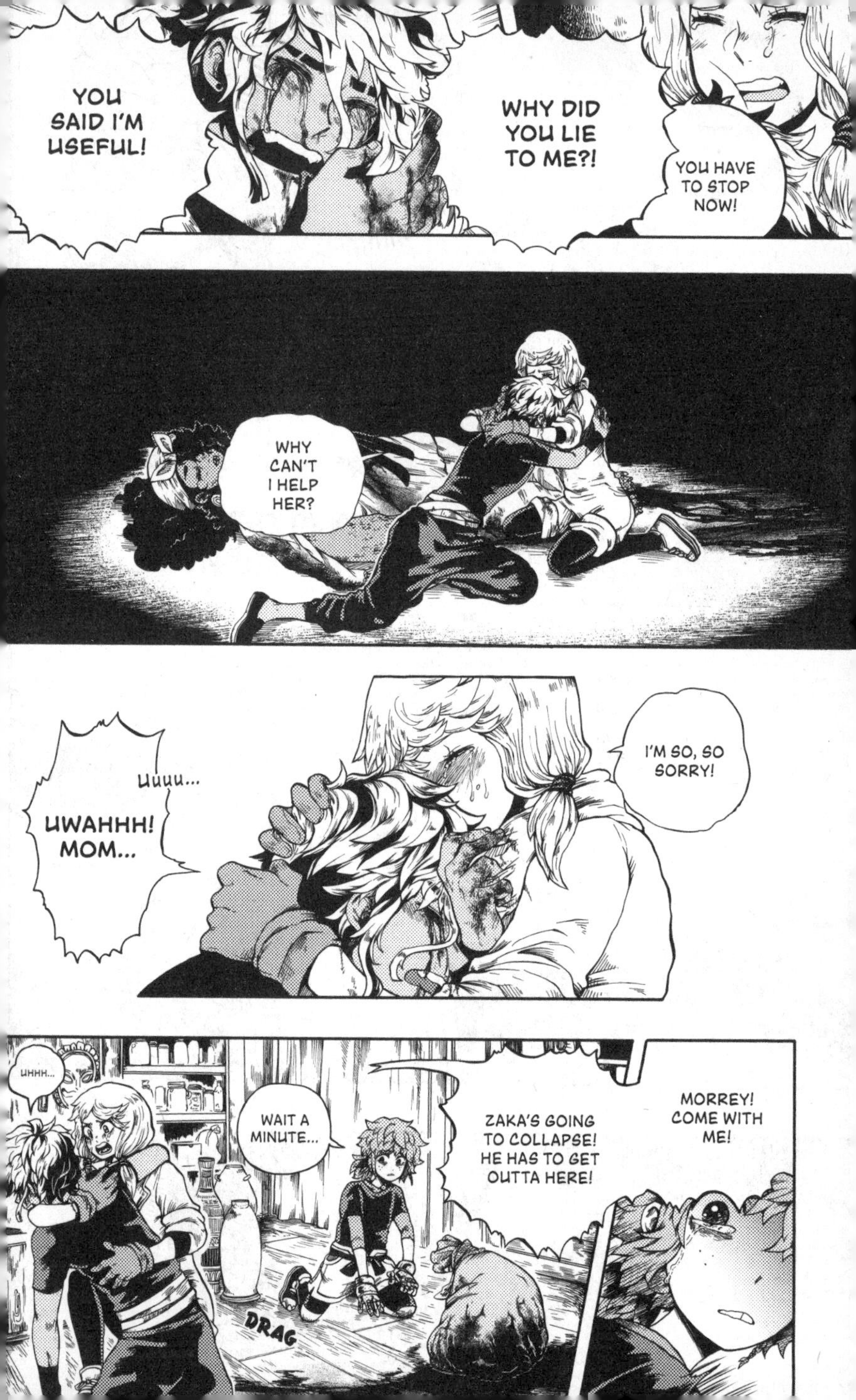
YOU HAVE TO STOP NOW!
WHY DID YOU LIE TO ME?!
YOU SAID I'M USEFUL!
WHY CAN'T I HELP HER?
I'M SO, SO SORRY!
Uuuu...
UWAHHH! MOM...
MORREY! COME WITH ME!
ZAKA'S GOING TO COLLAPSE! HE HAS TO GET OUTTA HERE!
WAIT A MINUTE...
DRAG
UHHH...

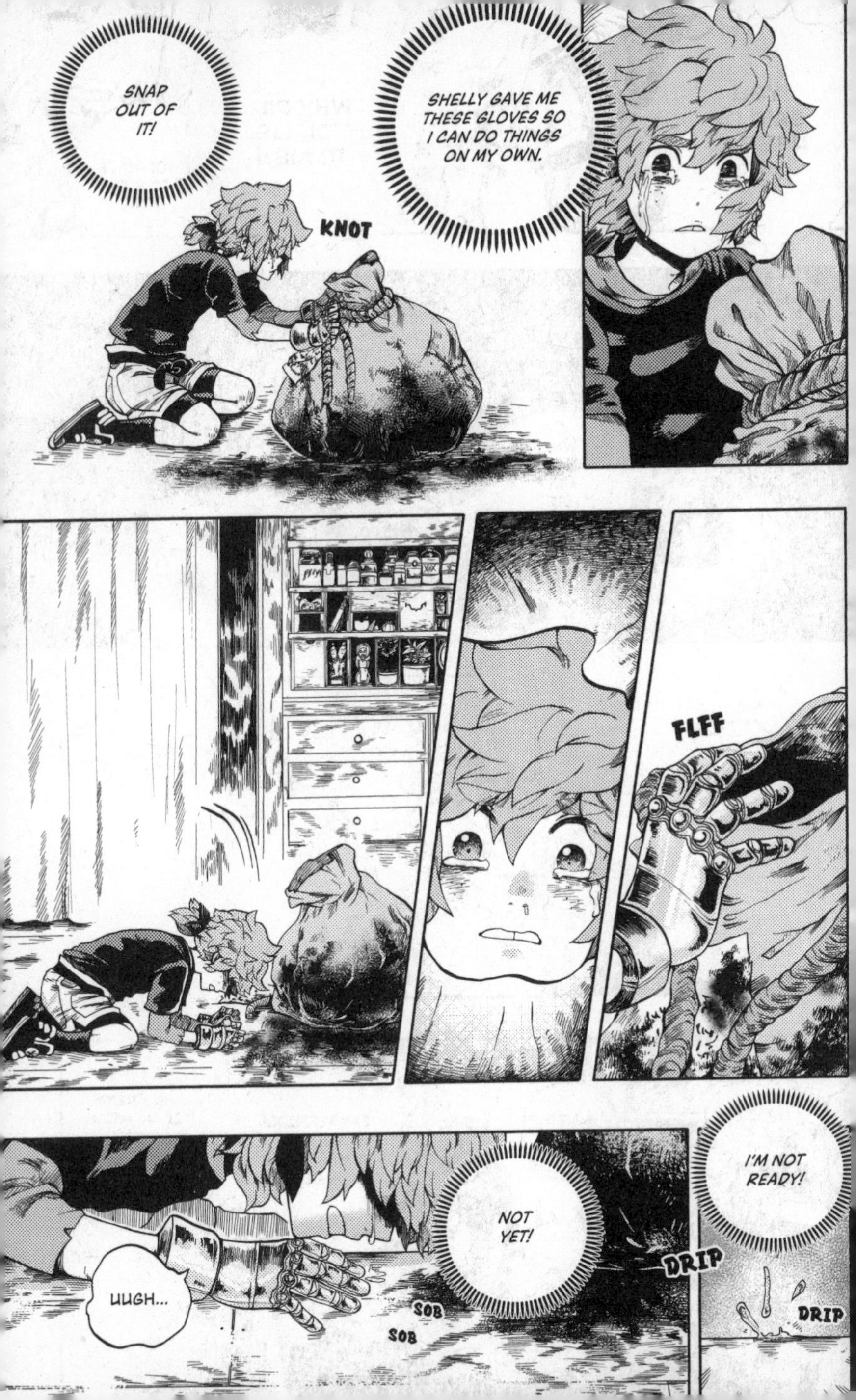
SHELLY GAVE ME THESE GLOVES SO I CAN DO THINGS ON MY OWN.
SNAP OUT OF IT!
KNOT
FLFF
I'M NOT READY!
DRIP
NOT YET!
DRIP
SOB
SOB
UUGH...

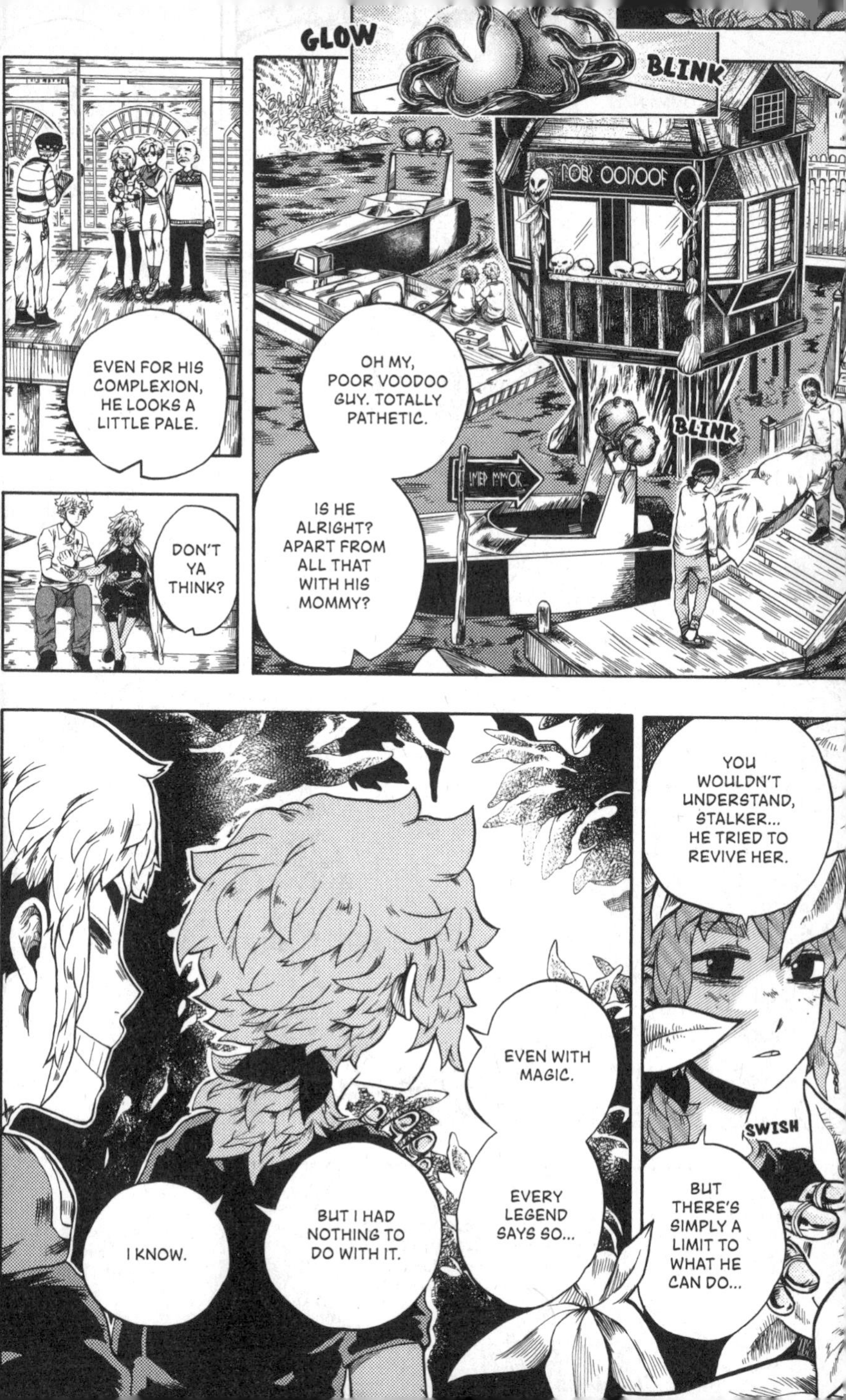
GLOW
BLINK
OH MY, POOR VOODOO GUY. TOTALLY PATHETIC.
IS HE ALRIGHT? APART FROM ALL THAT WITH HIS MOMMY?
BLINK
EVEN FOR HIS COMPLEXION, HE LOOKS A LITTLE PALE.
DON'T YA THINK?
YOU WOULDN'T UNDERSTAND, STALKER... HE TRIED TO REVIVE HER.
SWISH
BUT THERE'S SIMPLY A LIMIT TO WHAT HE CAN DO...
EVEN WITH MAGIC.
EVERY LEGEND SAYS SO...
BUT I HAD NOTHING TO DO WITH IT.
I KNOW.

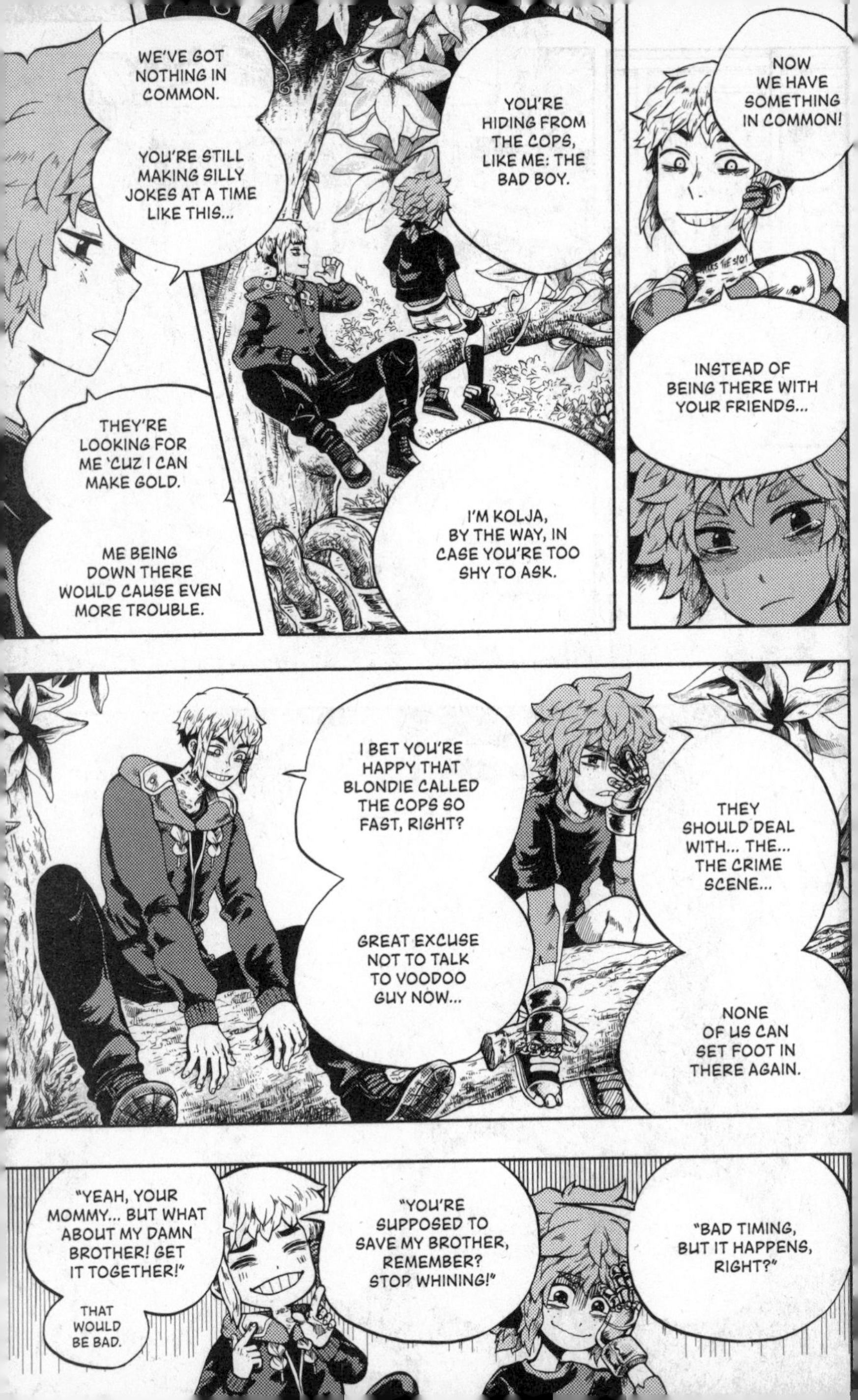
NOW WE HAVE SOMETHING IN COMMON!
INSTEAD OF BEING THERE WITH YOUR FRIENDS...
YOU'RE HIDING FROM THE COPS, LIKE ME: THE BAD BOY.
I'M KOLJA, BY THE WAY, IN CASE YOU'RE TOO SHY TO ASK.
WE'VE GOT NOTHING IN COMMON.
YOU'RE STILL MAKING SILLY JOKES AT A TIME LIKE THIS...
THEY'RE LOOKING FOR ME 'CUZ I CAN MAKE GOLD.
ME BEING DOWN THERE WOULD CAUSE EVEN MORE TROUBLE.
THEY SHOULD DEAL WITH... THE... THE CRIME SCENE...
NONE OF US CAN SET FOOT IN THERE AGAIN.
I BET YOU'RE HAPPY THAT BLONDIE CALLED THE COPS SO FAST, RIGHT?
GREAT EXCUSE NOT TO TALK TO VOODOO GUY NOW...
"BAD TIMING, BUT IT HAPPENS, RIGHT?"
"YOU'RE SUPPOSED TO SAVE MY BROTHER, REMEMBER? STOP WHINING!"
"YEAH, YOUR MOMMY... BUT WHAT ABOUT MY DAMN BROTHER! GET IT TOGETHER!"
THAT WOULD BE BAD.

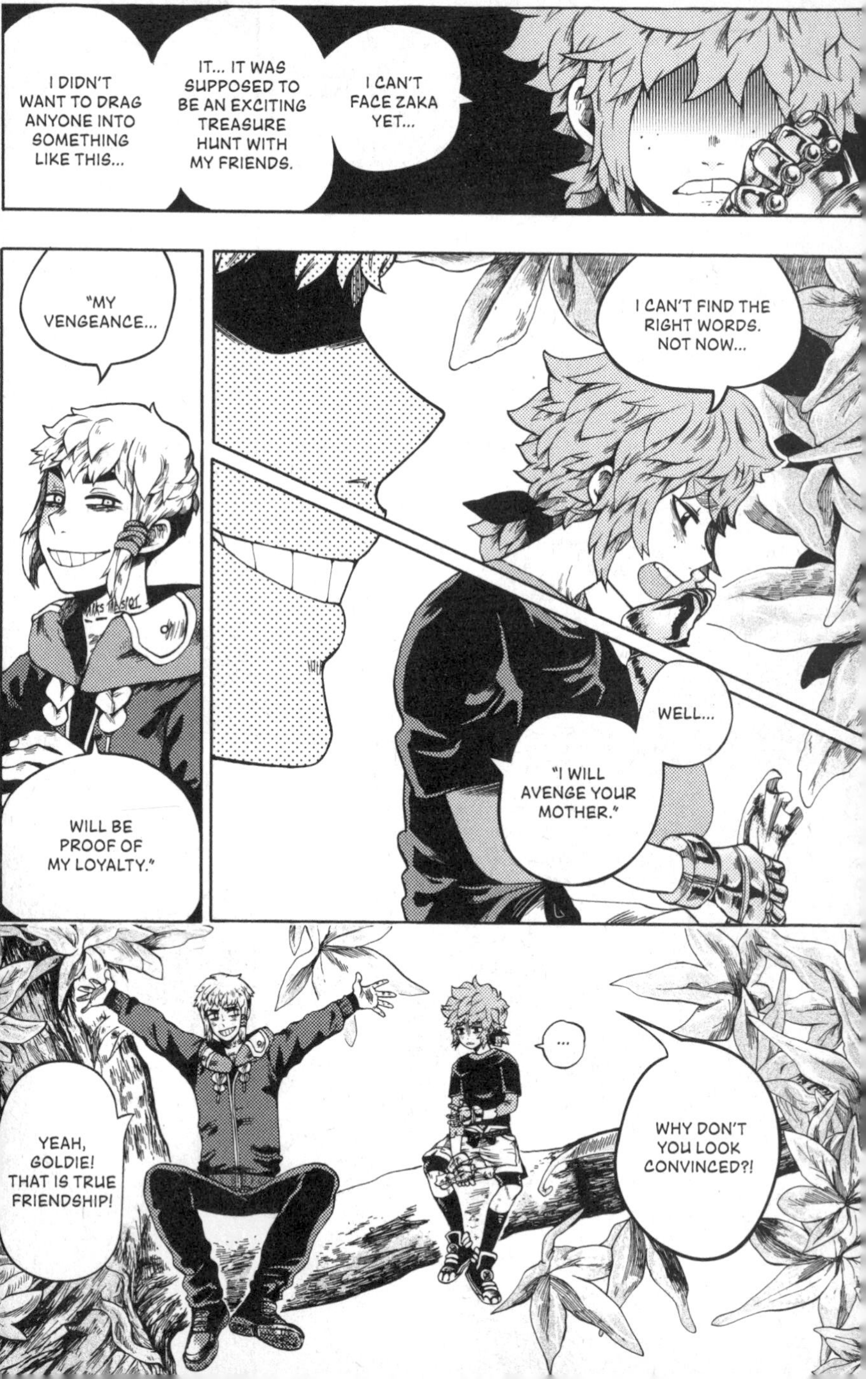
I CAN'T FACE ZAKA YET...
IT... IT WAS SUPPOSED TO BE AN EXCITING TREASURE HUNT WITH MY FRIENDS.
I DIDN'T WANT TO DRAG ANYONE INTO SOMETHING LIKE THIS...
I CAN'T FIND THE RIGHT WORDS. NOT NOW...
WELL...
"I WILL AVENGE YOUR MOTHER."
"MY VENGEANCE...
WILL BE PROOF OF MY LOYALTY."
YEAH, GOLDIE! THAT IS TRUE FRIENDSHIP!
...
WHY DON'T YOU LOOK CONVINCED?!

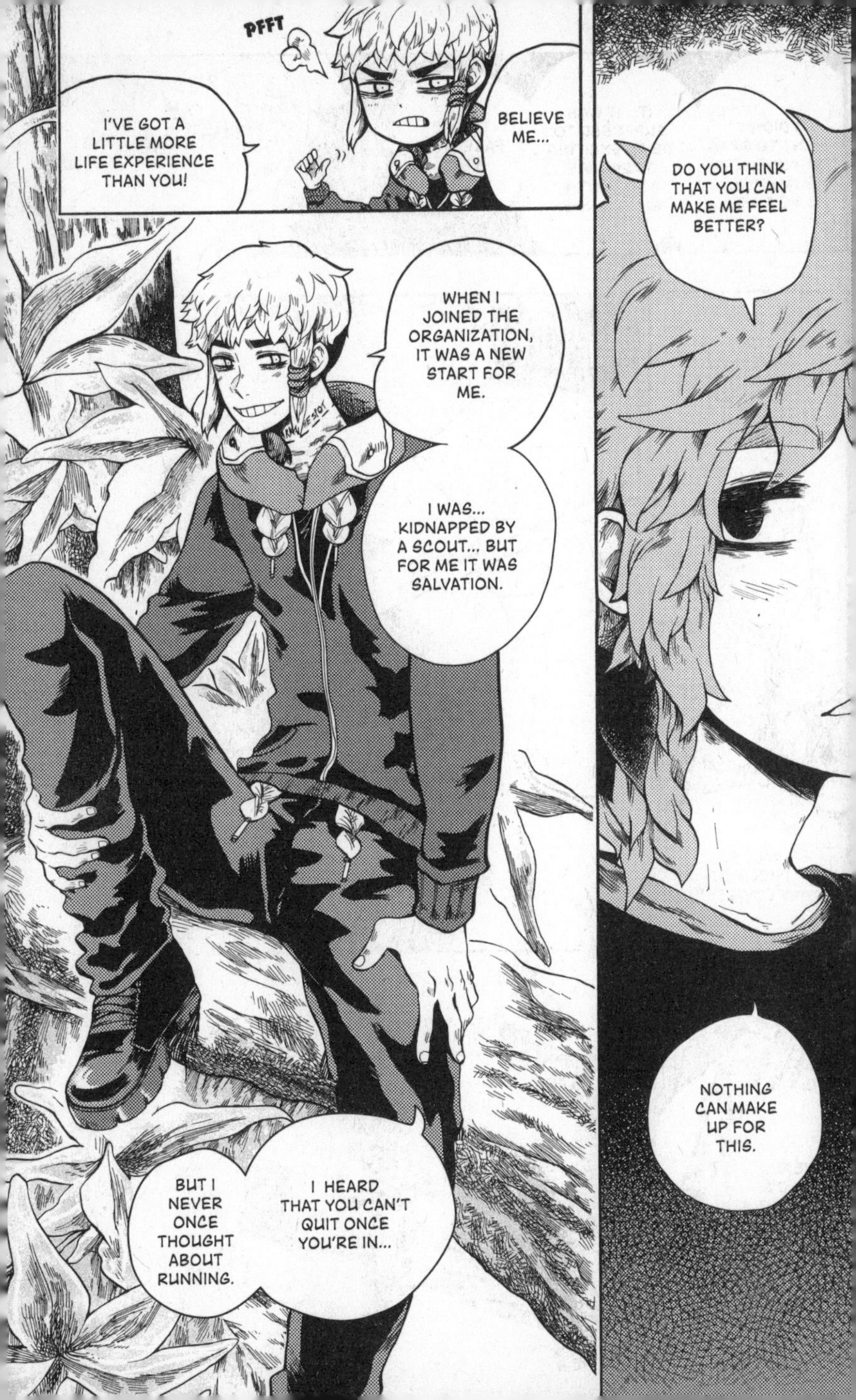
DO YOU THINK THAT YOU CAN MAKE ME FEEL BETTER?
NOTHING CAN MAKE UP FOR THIS.
PFFT
BELIEVE ME...
I'VE GOT A LITTLE MORE LIFE EXPERIENCE THAN YOU!
WHEN I JOINED THE ORGANIZATION, IT WAS A NEW START FOR ME.
I WAS... KIDNAPPED BY A SCOUT... BUT FOR ME IT WAS SALVATION.
I HEARD THAT YOU CAN'T QUIT ONCE YOU'RE IN...
BUT I NEVER ONCE THOUGHT ABOUT RUNNING.

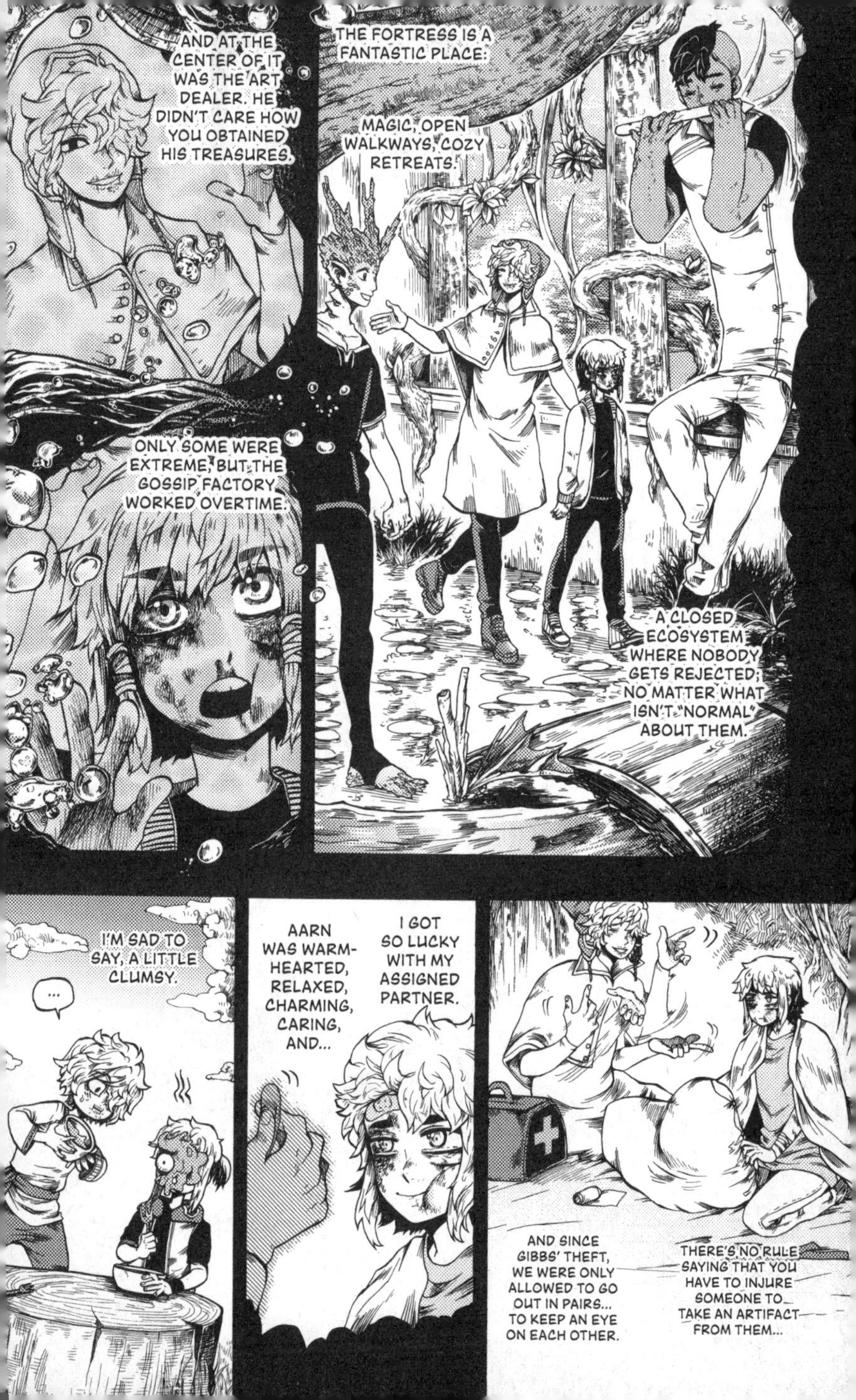
THE FORTRESS IS A FANTASTIC PLACE:
MAGIC, OPEN WALKWAYS, COZY RETREATS.
A CLOSED ECOSYSTEM WHERE NOBODY GETS REJECTED; NO MATTER WHAT ISN'T "NORMAL" ABOUT THEM.
AND AT THE CENTER OF IT WAS THE ART DEALER. HE DIDN'T CARE HOW YOU OBTAINED HIS TREASURES.
ONLY SOME WERE EXTREME, BUT THE GOSSIP FACTORY WORKED OVERTIME.
THERE'S NO RULE SAYING THAT YOU HAVE TO INJURE SOMEONE TO TAKE AN ARTIFACT FROM THEM...
AND SINCE GIBBS' THEFT, WE WERE ONLY ALLOWED TO GO OUT IN PAIRS... TO KEEP AN EYE ON EACH OTHER.
I GOT SO LUCKY WITH MY ASSIGNED PARTNER.
AARN WAS WARM-HEARTED, RELAXED, CHARMING, CARING, AND...
I'M SAD TO SAY, A LITTLE CLUMSY.
...

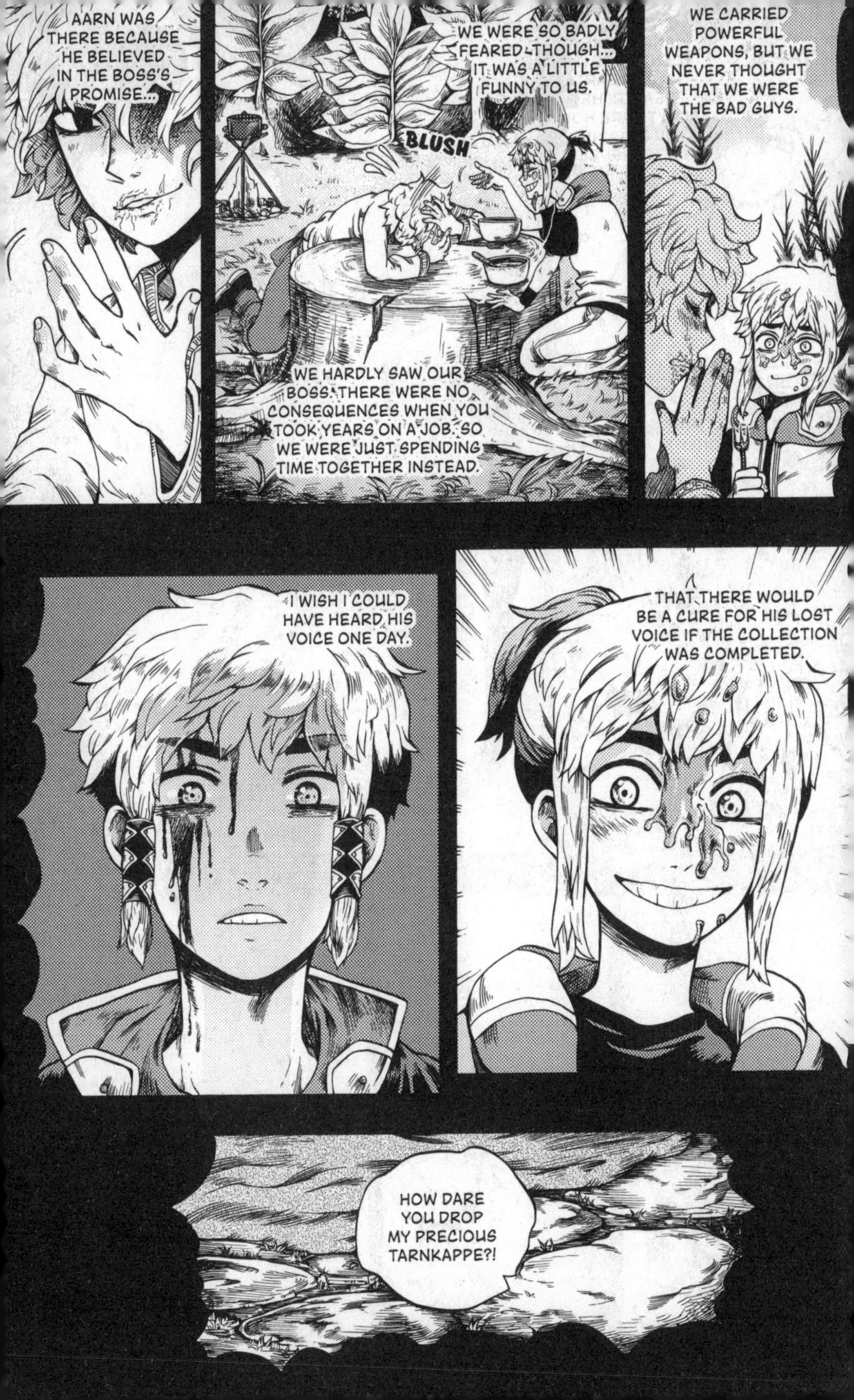
WE CARRIED POWERFUL WEAPONS, BUT WE NEVER THOUGHT THAT WE WERE THE BAD GUYS.
WE WERE SO BADLY FEARED THOUGH... IT WAS A LITTLE FUNNY TO US.
BLUSH
WE HARDLY SAW OUR BOSS. THERE WERE NO CONSEQUENCES WHEN YOU TOOK YEARS ON A JOB. SO WE WERE JUST SPENDING TIME TOGETHER INSTEAD.
AARN WAS THERE BECAUSE HE BELIEVED IN THE BOSS'S PROMISE...
THAT THERE WOULD BE A CURE FOR HIS LOST VOICE IF THE COLLECTION WAS COMPLETED.
I WISH I COULD HAVE HEARD HIS VOICE ONE DAY.
HOW DARE YOU DROP MY PRECIOUS TARNKAPPE?!

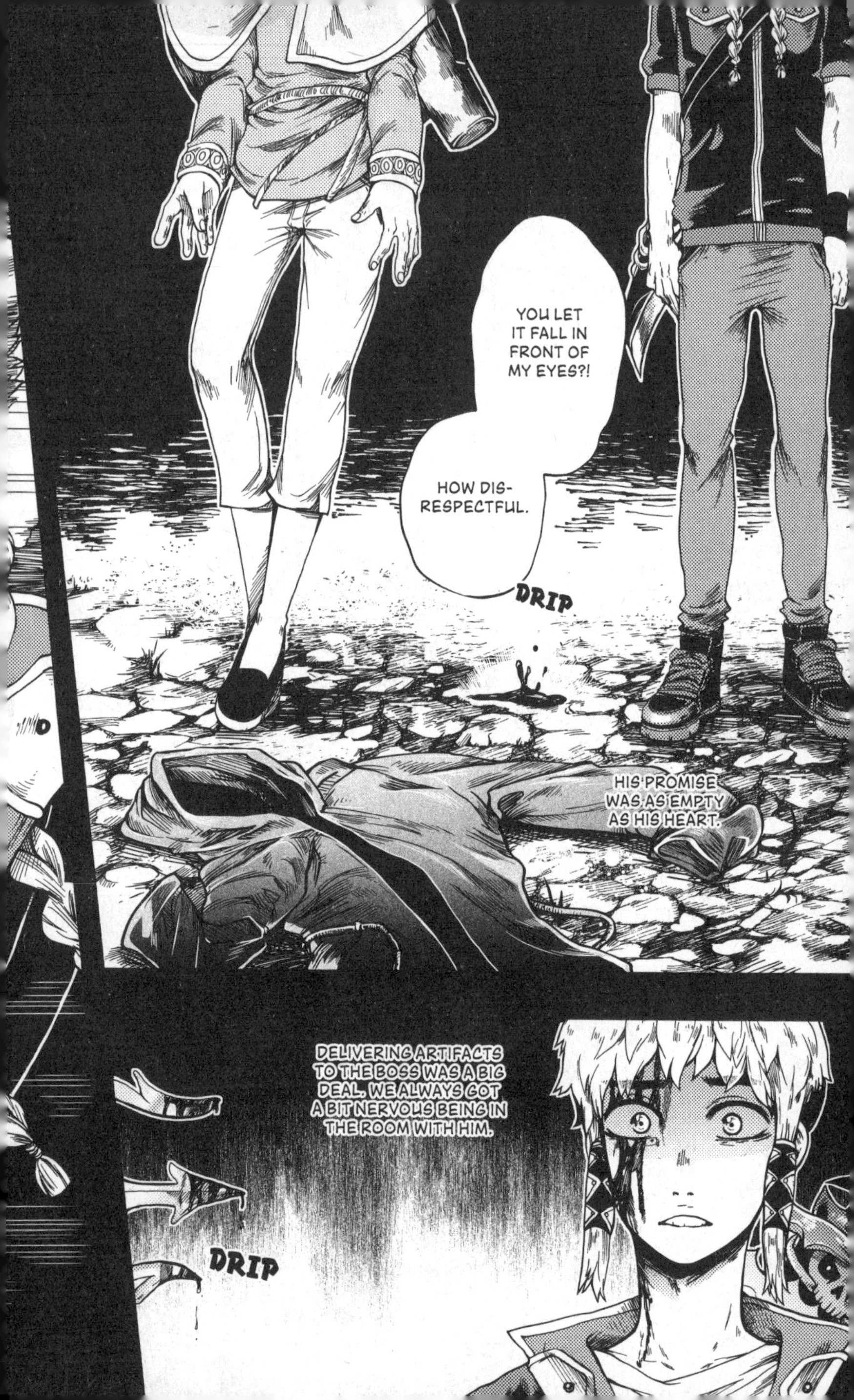
YOU LET IT FALL IN FRONT OF MY EYES?!
HOW DIS-RESPECTFUL.
DRIP
HIS PROMISE WAS AS EMPTY AS HIS HEART.
DELIVERING ARTIFACTS TO THE BOSS WAS A BIG DEAL. WE ALWAYS GOT A BIT NERVOUS BEING IN THE ROOM WITH HIM.
DRIP

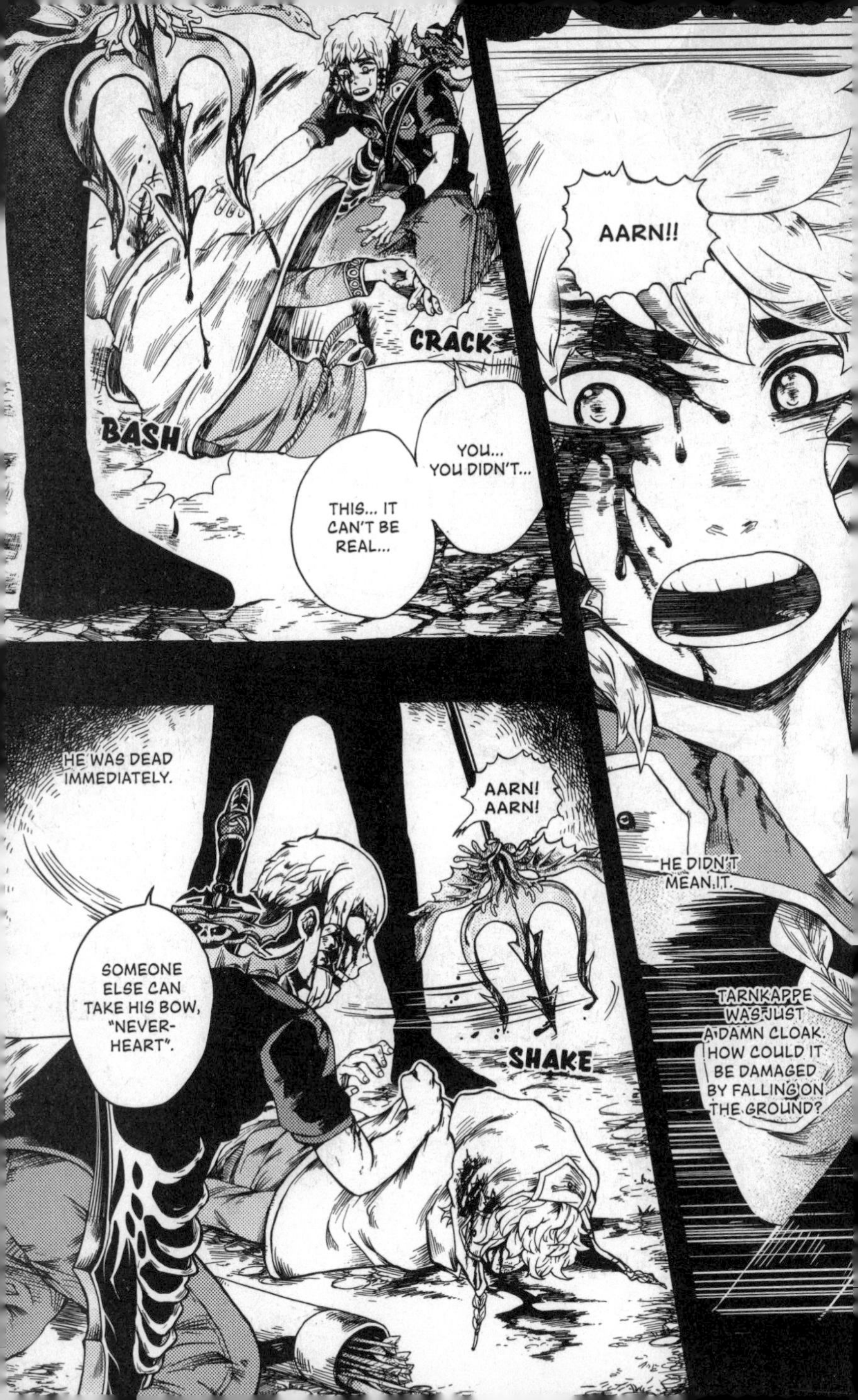
AARN!!
HE DIDN'T MEAN IT.
TARNKAPPE WAS JUST A DAMN CLOAK. HOW COULD IT BE DAMAGED BY FALLING ON THE GROUND?
CRACK
BASH
YOU... YOU DIDN'T...
THIS... IT CAN'T BE REAL...
AARN! AARN!
HE WAS DEAD IMMEDIATELY.
SHAKE
SOMEONE ELSE CAN TAKE HIS BOW, "NEVER-HEART".

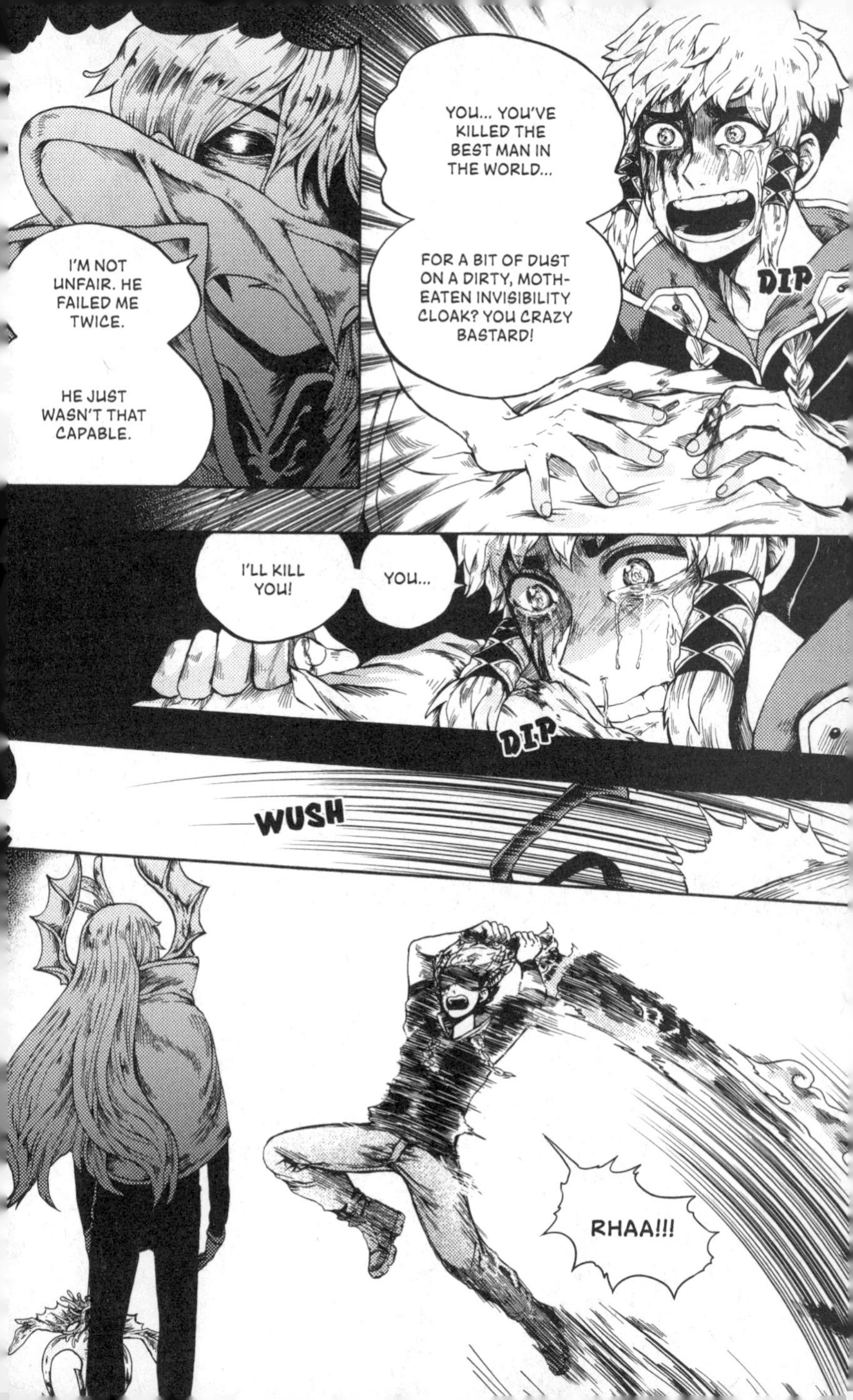
YOU... YOU'VE KILLED THE BEST MAN IN THE WORLD...
FOR A BIT OF DUST ON A DIRTY, MOTH-EATEN INVISIBILITY CLOAK? YOU CRAZY BASTARD!
DIP
I'M NOT UNFAIR. HE FAILED ME TWICE.
HE JUST WASN'T THAT CAPABLE.
YOU...
I'LL KILL YOU!
DIP
WUSH
RHAA!!!

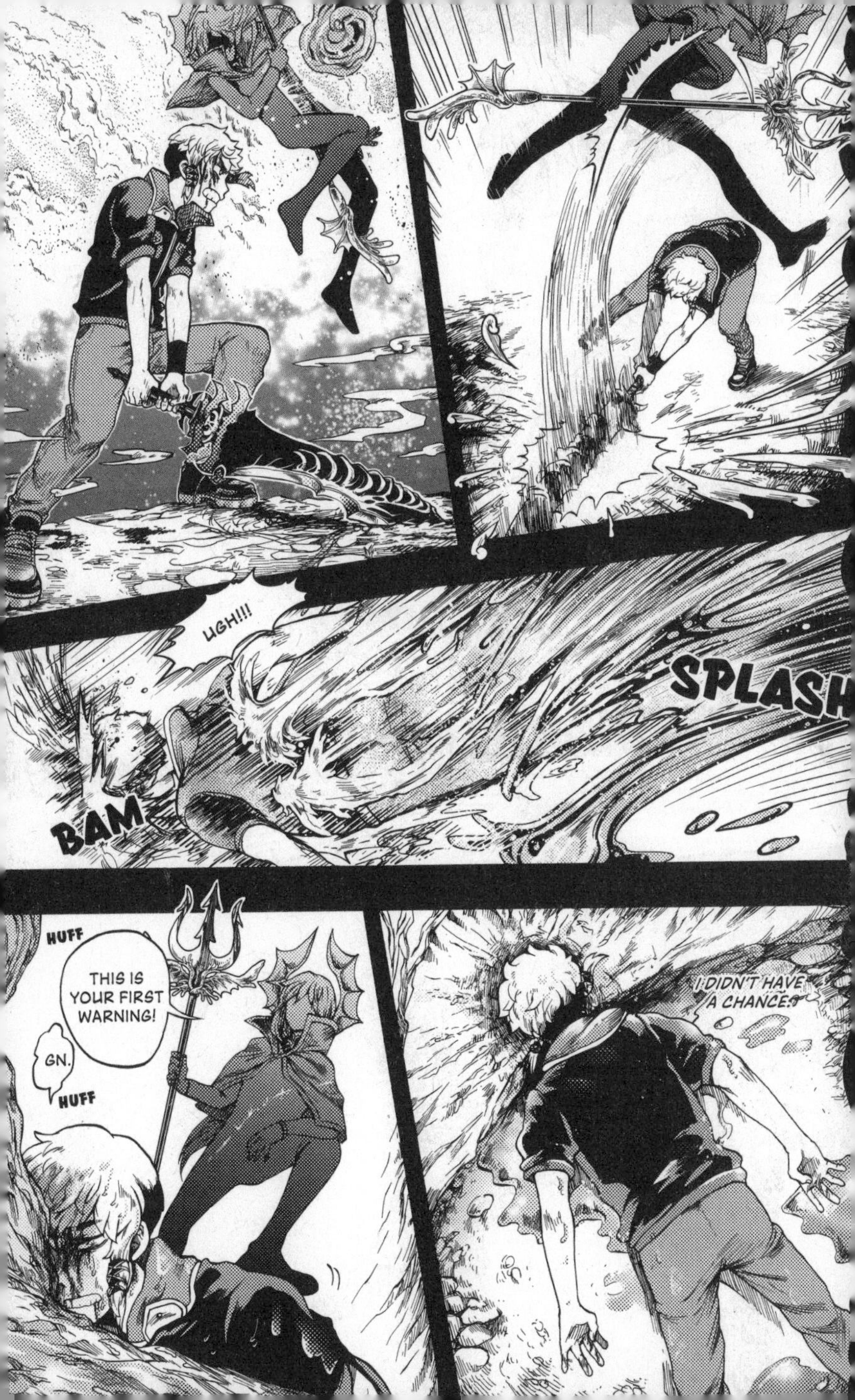
SPLASH
UGH!!!
BAM
I DIDN'T HAVE A CHANCE.
HUFF
THIS IS YOUR FIRST WARNING!
GN.
HUFF

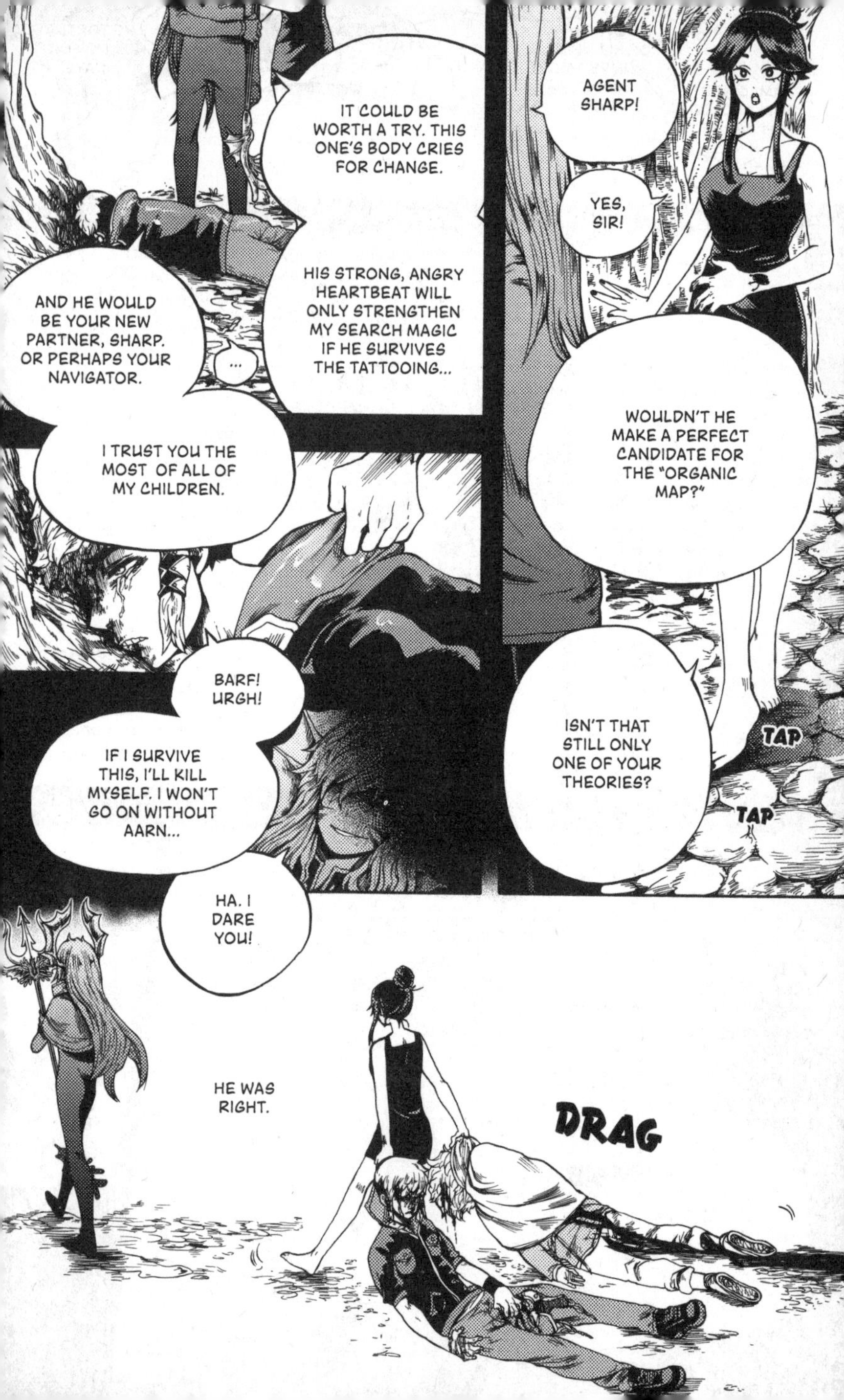
AGENT SHARP!
YES, SIR!
WOULDN'T HE MAKE A PERFECT CANDIDATE FOR THE "ORGANIC MAP?"
ISN'T THAT STILL ONLY ONE OF YOUR THEORIES?
TAP
TAP
IT COULD BE WORTH A TRY. THIS ONE'S BODY CRIES FOR CHANGE.
HIS STRONG, ANGRY HEARTBEAT WILL ONLY STRENGTHEN MY SEARCH MAGIC IF HE SURVIVES THE TATTOOING...
AND HE WOULD BE YOUR NEW PARTNER, SHARP. OR PERHAPS YOUR NAVIGATOR.
...
I TRUST YOU THE MOST OF ALL OF MY CHILDREN.
BARF! URGH!
IF I SURVIVE THIS, I'LL KILL MYSELF. I WON'T GO ON WITHOUT AARN...
HA. I DARE YOU!
HE WAS RIGHT.
DRAG

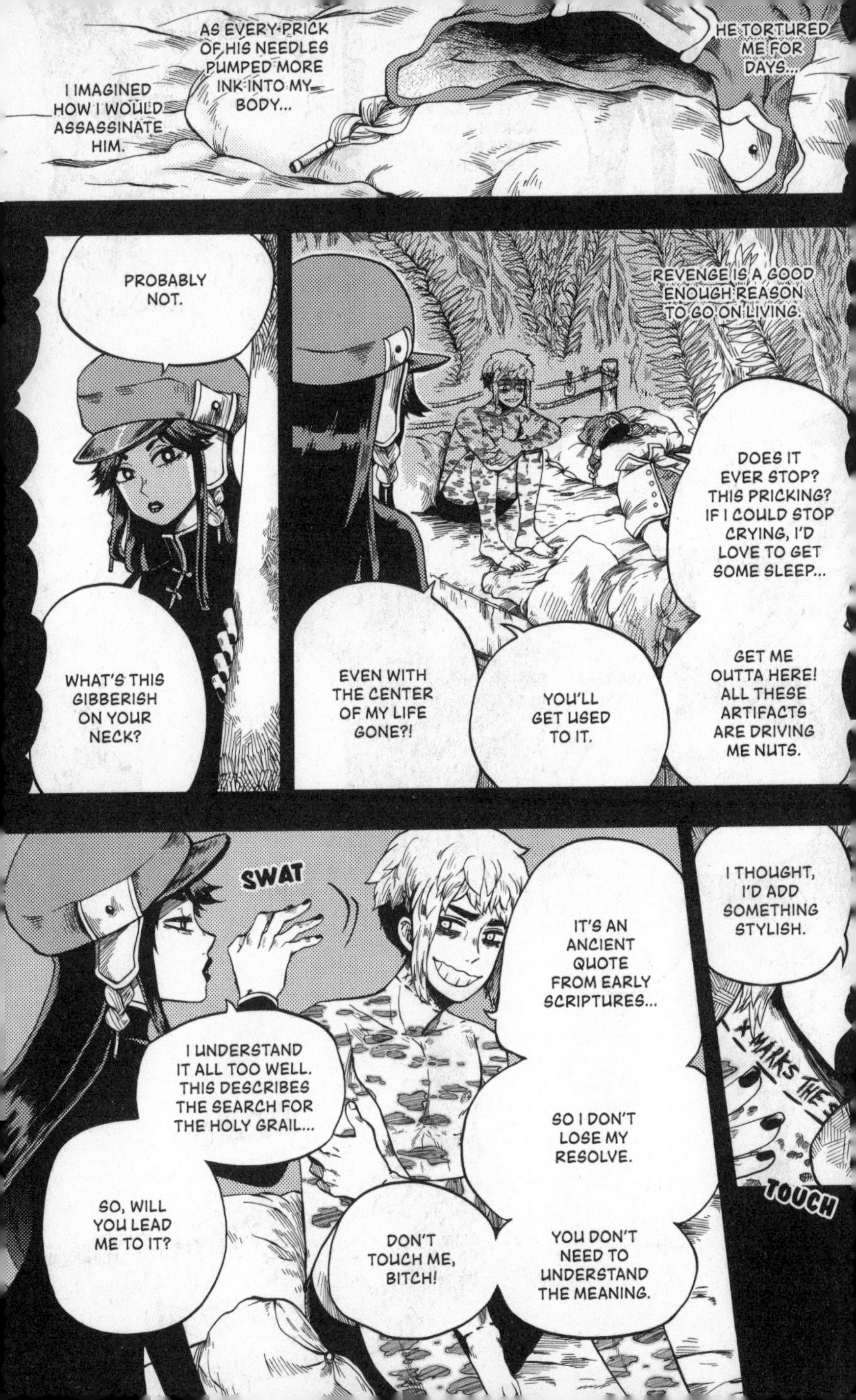
HE TORTURED ME FOR DAYS...
AS EVERY PRICK OF HIS NEEDLES PUMPED MORE INK INTO MY BODY...
I IMAGINED HOW I WOULD ASSASSINATE HIM.
REVENGE IS A GOOD ENOUGH REASON TO GO ON LIVING.
DOES IT EVER STOP? THIS PRICKING? IF I COULD STOP CRYING, I'D LOVE TO GET SOME SLEEP...
GET ME OUTTA HERE! ALL THESE ARTIFACTS ARE DRIVING ME NUTS.
YOU'LL GET USED TO IT.
EVEN WITH THE CENTER OF MY LIFE GONE?!
PROBABLY NOT.
WHAT'S THIS GIBBERISH ON YOUR NECK?
I THOUGHT, I'D ADD SOMETHING STYLISH.
X MARKS THE
TOUCH
IT'S AN ANCIENT QUOTE FROM EARLY SCRIPTURES...
SWAT
SO I DON'T LOSE MY RESOLVE.
I UNDERSTAND IT ALL TOO WELL. THIS DESCRIBES THE SEARCH FOR THE HOLY GRAIL...
YOU DON'T NEED TO UNDERSTAND THE MEANING.
DON'T TOUCH ME, BITCH!
SO, WILL YOU LEAD ME TO IT?

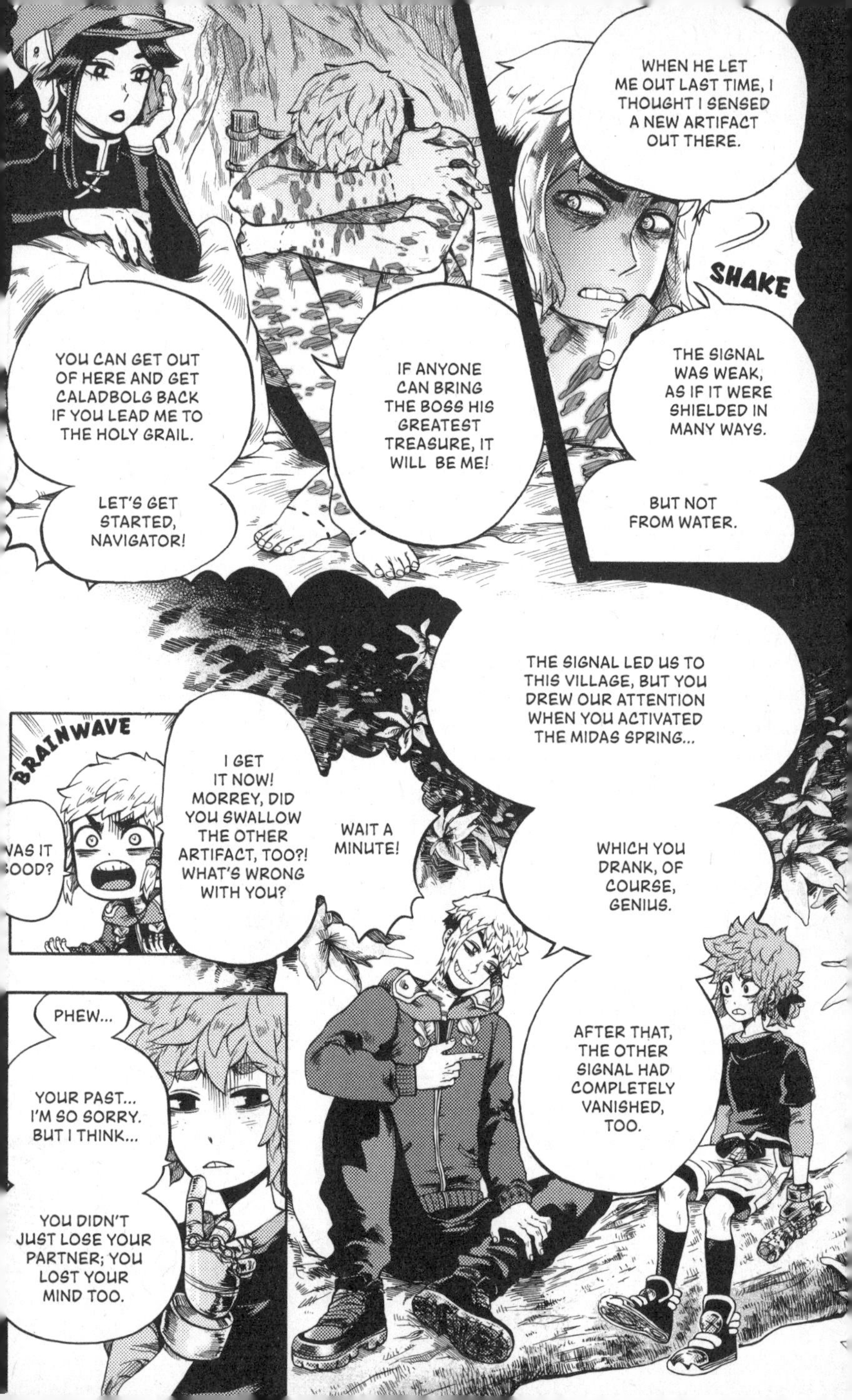
WHEN HE LET ME OUT LAST TIME, I THOUGHT I SENSED A NEW ARTIFACT OUT THERE.
SHAKE
THE SIGNAL WAS WEAK, AS IF IT WERE SHIELDED IN MANY WAYS.
BUT NOT FROM WATER.
IF ANYONE CAN BRING THE BOSS HIS GREATEST TREASURE, IT WILL BE ME!
YOU CAN GET OUT OF HERE AND GET CALADBOLG BACK IF YOU LEAD ME TO THE HOLY GRAIL.
LET'S GET STARTED, NAVIGATOR!
THE SIGNAL LED US TO THIS VILLAGE, BUT YOU DREW OUR ATTENTION WHEN YOU ACTIVATED THE MIDAS SPRING...
WHICH YOU DRANK, OF COURSE, GENIUS.
AFTER THAT, THE OTHER SIGNAL HAD COMPLETELY VANISHED, TOO.
WAIT A MINUTE!
I GET IT NOW! MORREY, DID YOU SWALLOW THE OTHER ARTIFACT, TOO?! WHAT'S WRONG WITH YOU?
BRAINWAVE
VAS IT OOD?
PHEW...
YOUR PAST... I'M SO SORRY. BUT I THINK...
YOU DIDN'T JUST LOSE YOUR PARTNER; YOU LOST YOUR MIND TOO.

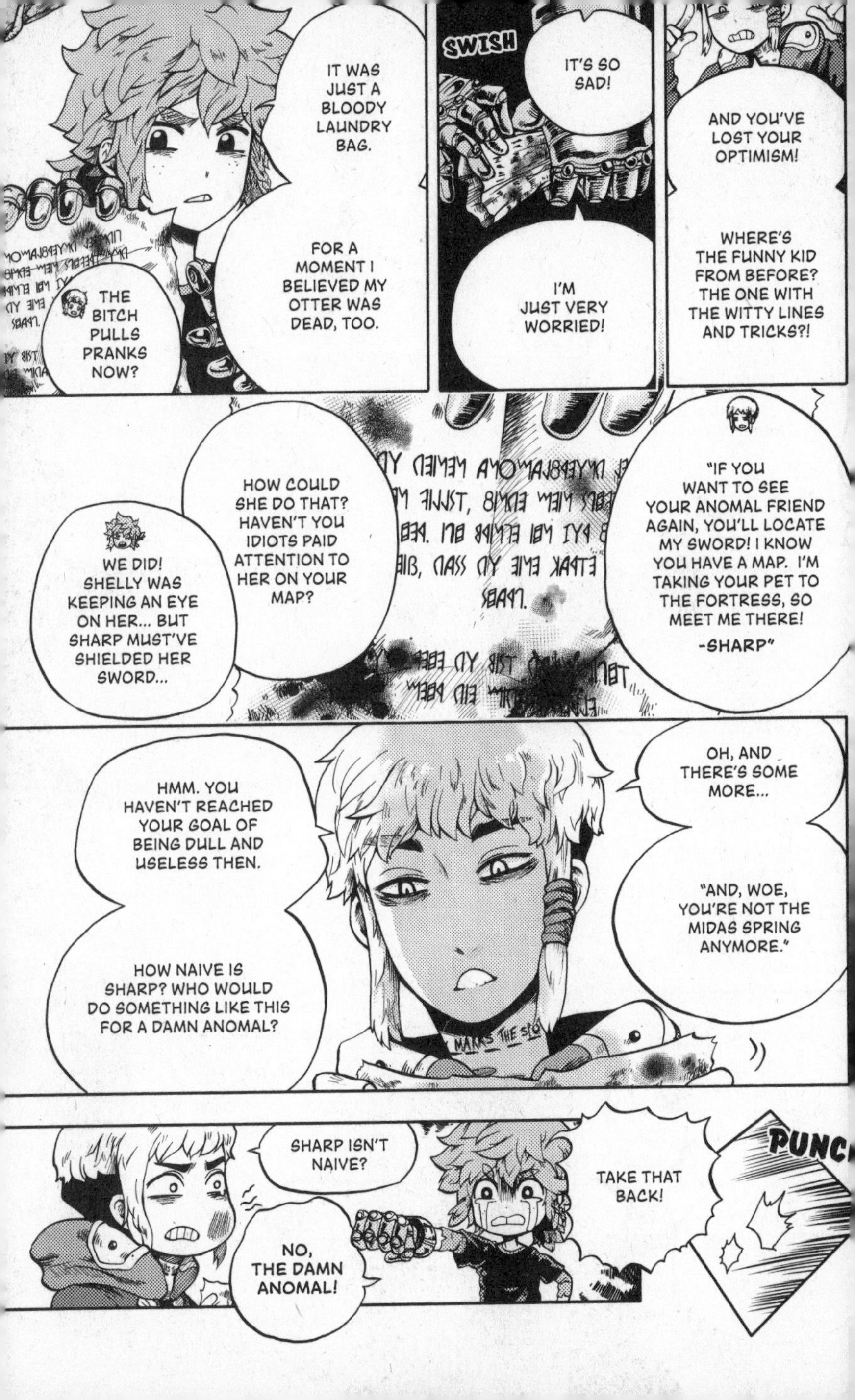
AND YOU'VE LOST YOUR OPTIMISM!
WHERE'S THE FUNNY KID FROM BEFORE? THE ONE WITH THE WITTY LINES AND TRICKS?!
SWISH
IT'S SO SAD!
I'M JUST VERY WORRIED!
IT WAS JUST A BLOODY LAUNDRY BAG.
FOR A MOMENT I BELIEVED MY OTTER WAS DEAD, TOO.
THE BITCH PULLS PRANKS NOW?
"IF YOU WANT TO SEE YOUR ANOMAL FRIEND AGAIN, YOU'LL LOCATE MY SWORD! I KNOW YOU HAVE A MAP. I'M TAKING YOUR PET TO THE FORTRESS, SO MEET ME THERE! -SHARP"
HOW COULD SHE DO THAT? HAVEN'T YOU IDIOTS PAID ATTENTION TO HER ON YOUR MAP?
WE DID! SHELLY WAS KEEPING AN EYE ON HER... BUT SHARP MUST'VE SHIELDED HER SWORD...
OH, AND THERE'S SOME MORE...
"AND, WOE, YOU'RE NOT THE MIDAS SPRING ANYMORE."
HMM. YOU HAVEN'T REACHED YOUR GOAL OF BEING DULL AND USELESS THEN.
HOW NAIVE IS SHARP? WHO WOULD DO SOMETHING LIKE THIS FOR A DAMN ANOMAL?
SHARP ISN'T NAIVE?
NO, THE DAMN ANOMAL!
TAKE THAT BACK!
PUNC

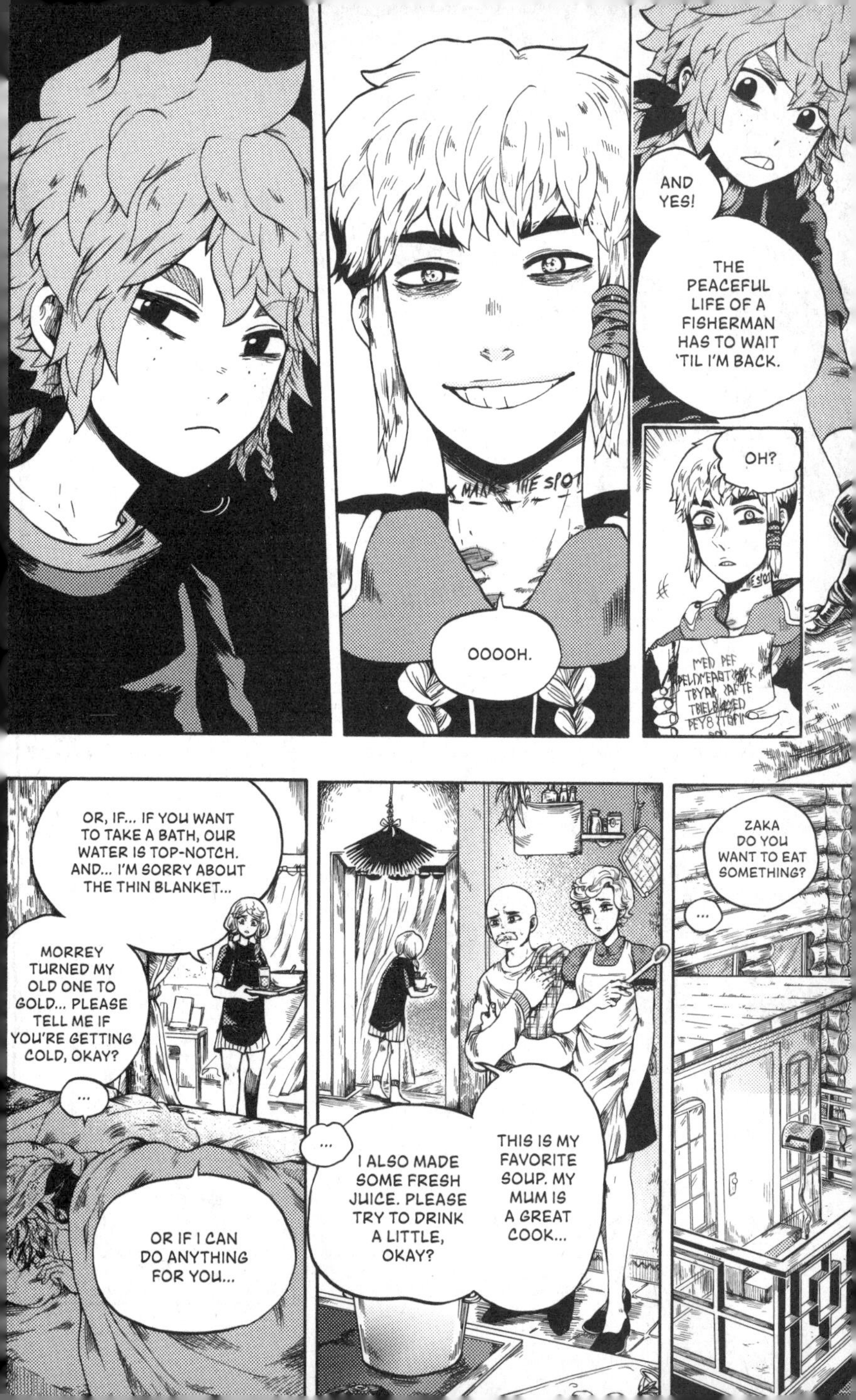
AND YES!
THE PEACEFUL LIFE OF A FISHERMAN HAS TO WAIT 'TIL I'M BACK.
OH?
OOOOH.
ZAKA DO YOU WANT TO EAT SOMETHING?
...
THIS IS MY FAVORITE SOUP. MY MUM IS A GREAT COOK...
I ALSO MADE SOME FRESH JUICE. PLEASE TRY TO DRINK A LITTLE, OKAY?
...
OR, IF... IF YOU WANT TO TAKE A BATH, OUR WATER IS TOP-NOTCH. AND... I'M SORRY ABOUT THE THIN BLANKET...
MORREY TURNED MY OLD ONE TO GOLD... PLEASE TELL ME IF YOU'RE GETTING COLD, OKAY?
...
OR IF I CAN DO ANYTHING FOR YOU...

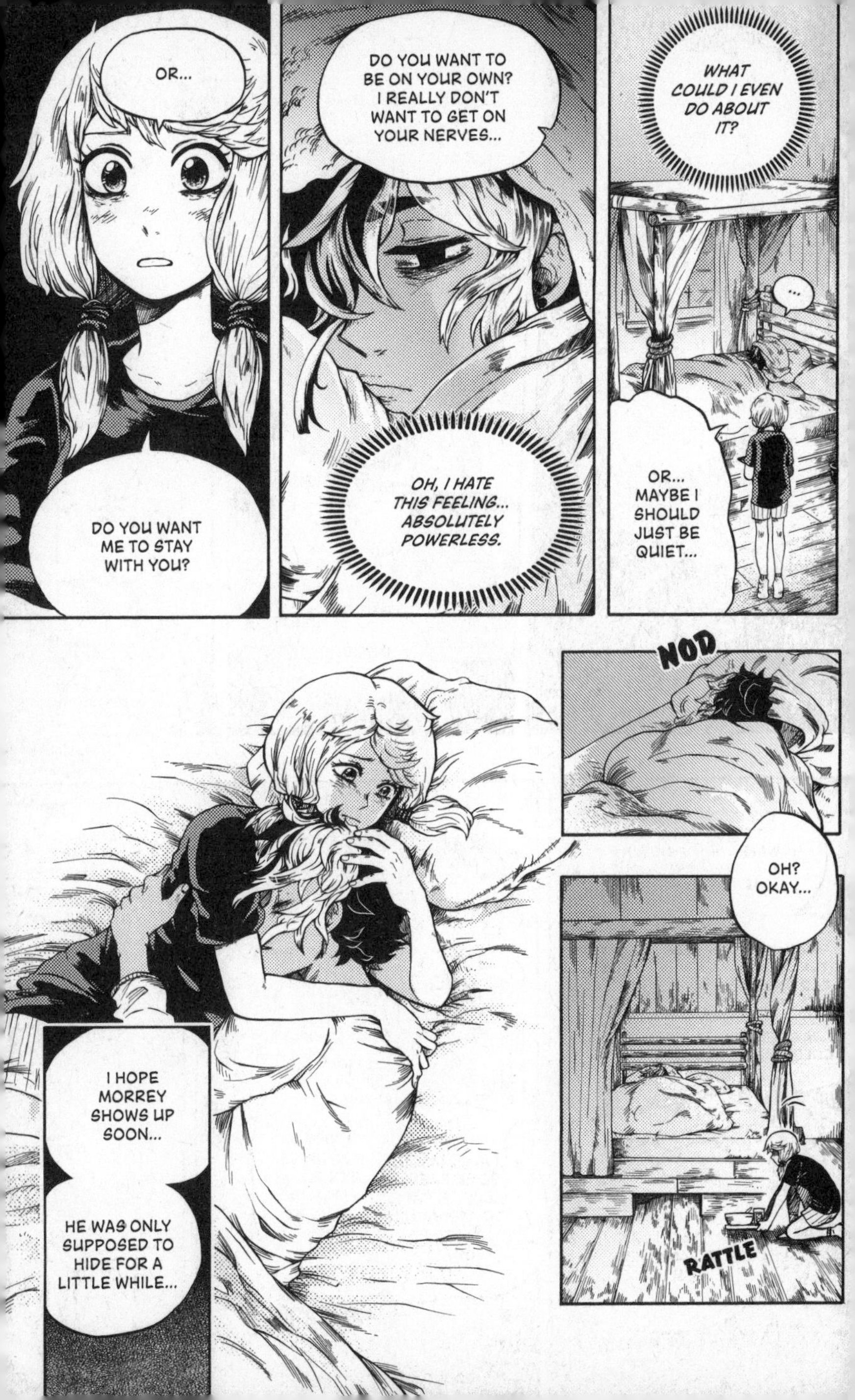
WHAT COULD I EVEN DO ABOUT IT?
...
OR... MAYBE I SHOULD JUST BE QUIET...
DO YOU WANT TO BE ON YOUR OWN? I REALLY DON'T WANT TO GET ON YOUR NERVES...
OH, I HATE THIS FEELING... ABSOLUTELY POWERLESS.
OR...
DO YOU WANT ME TO STAY WITH YOU?
NOD
OH? OKAY...
RATTLE
I HOPE MORREY SHOWS UP SOON...
HE WAS ONLY SUPPOSED TO HIDE FOR A LITTLE WHILE...

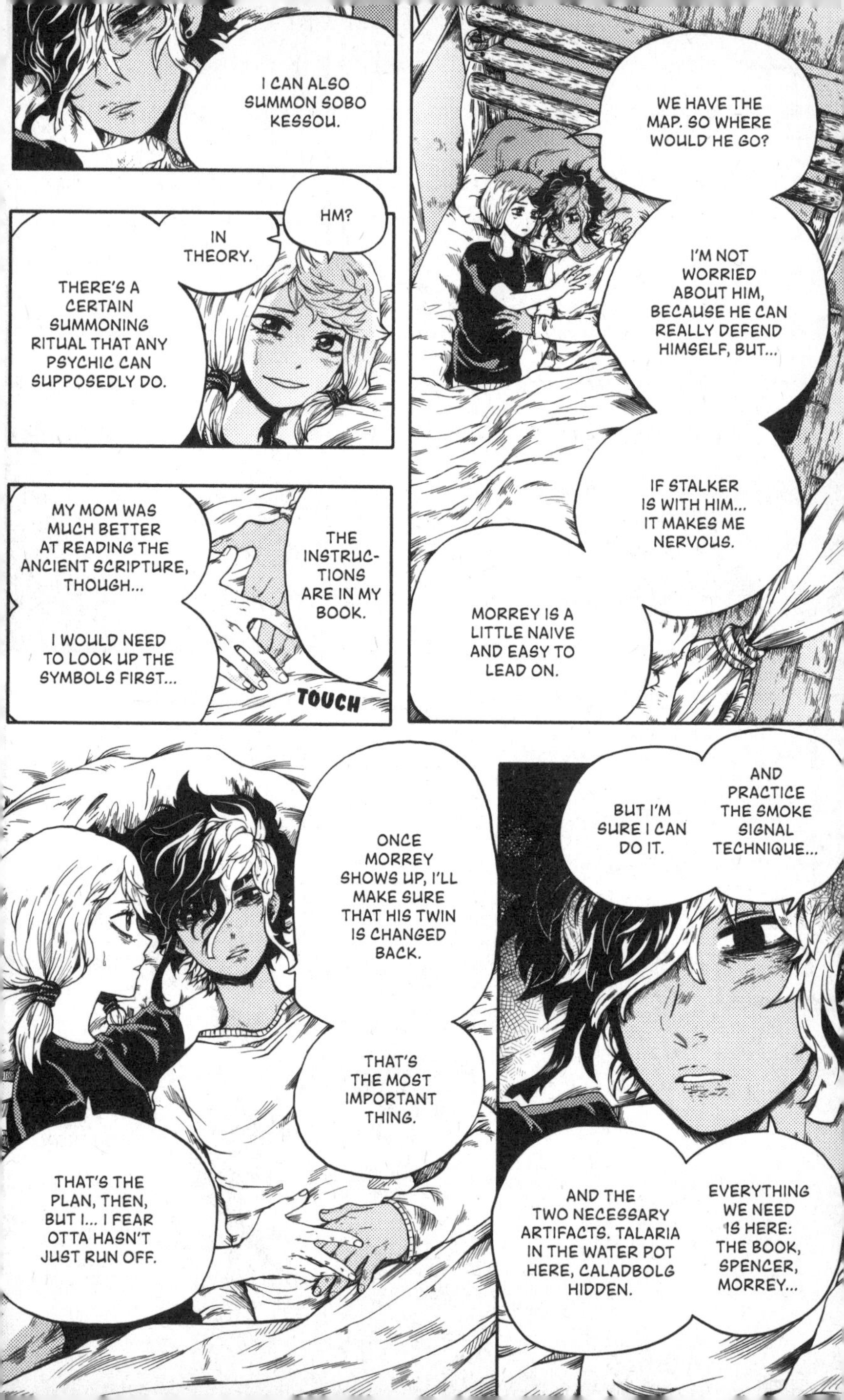
WE HAVE THE MAP. SO WHERE WOULD HE GO?
I'M NOT WORRIED ABOUT HIM, BECAUSE HE CAN REALLY DEFEND HIMSELF, BUT...
IF STALKER IS WITH HIM... IT MAKES ME NERVOUS.
MORREY IS A LITTLE NAIVE AND EASY TO LEAD ON.
I CAN ALSO SUMMON SOBO KESSOU.
HM?
IN THEORY.
THERE'S A CERTAIN SUMMONING RITUAL THAT ANY PSYCHIC CAN SUPPOSEDLY DO.
THE INSTRUCTIONS ARE IN MY BOOK.
MY MOM WAS MUCH BETTER AT READING THE ANCIENT SCRIPTURE, THOUGH...
I WOULD NEED TO LOOK UP THE SYMBOLS FIRST...
TOUCH
AND PRACTICE THE SMOKE SIGNAL TECHNIQUE...
BUT I'M SURE I CAN DO IT.
EVERYTHING WE NEED IS HERE: THE BOOK, SPENCER, MORREY...
AND THE TWO NECESSARY ARTIFACTS. TALARIA IN THE WATER POT HERE, CALADBOLG HIDDEN.
ONCE MORREY SHOWS UP, I'LL MAKE SURE THAT HIS TWIN IS CHANGED BACK.
THAT'S THE MOST IMPORTANT THING.
THAT'S THE PLAN, THEN, BUT I... I FEAR OTTA HASN'T JUST RUN OFF.

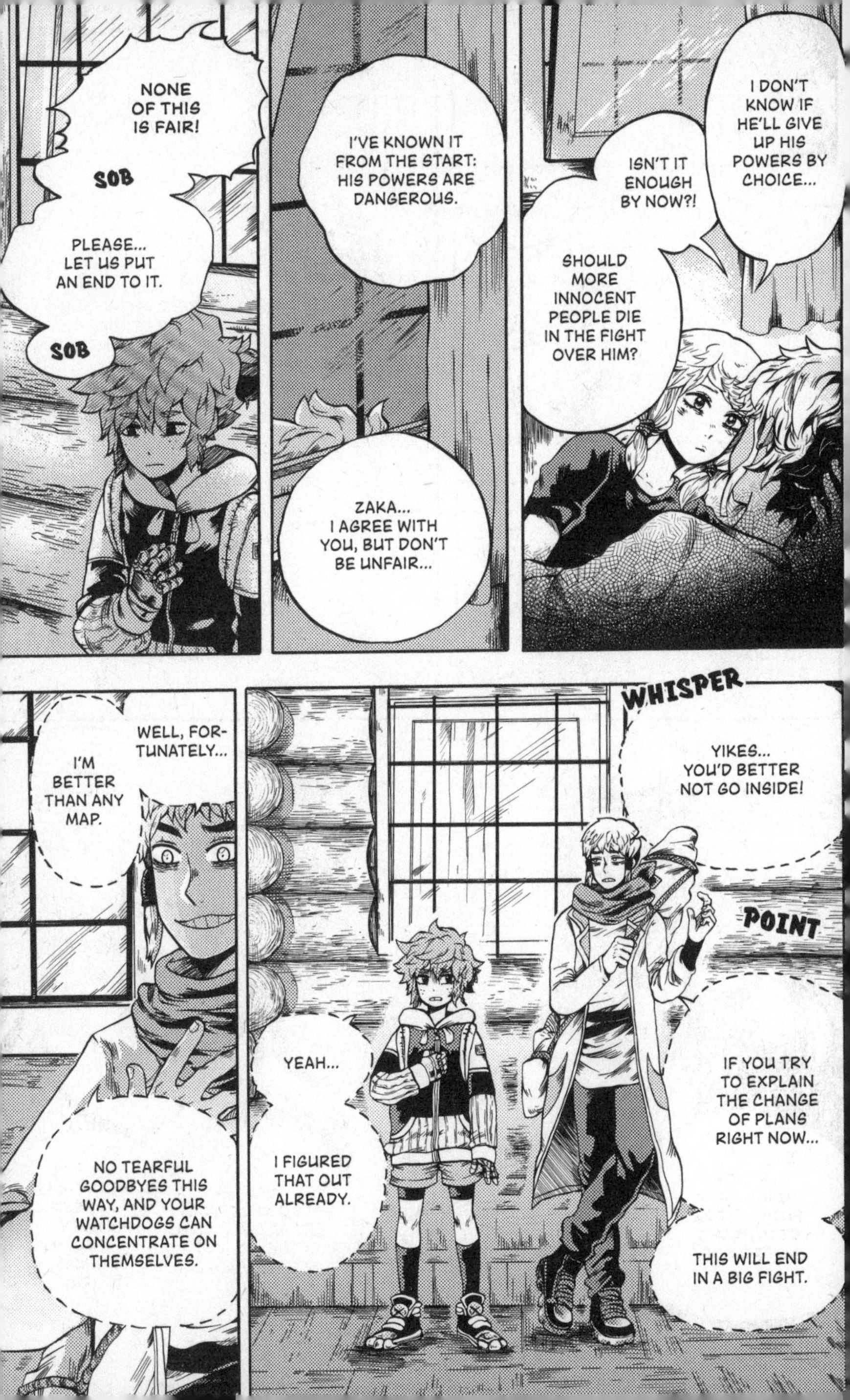
I DON'T KNOW IF HE'LL GIVE UP HIS POWERS BY CHOICE...
ISN'T IT ENOUGH BY NOW?!
SHOULD MORE INNOCENT PEOPLE DIE IN THE FIGHT OVER HIM?
I'VE KNOWN IT FROM THE START: HIS POWERS ARE DANGEROUS.
ZAKA... I AGREE WITH YOU, BUT DON'T BE UNFAIR...
NONE OF THIS IS FAIR!
SOB
PLEASE... LET US PUT AN END TO IT.
SOB
WHISPER
YIKES... YOU'D BETTER NOT GO INSIDE!
POINT
IF YOU TRY TO EXPLAIN THE CHANGE OF PLANS RIGHT NOW...
THIS WILL END IN A BIG FIGHT.
YEAH...
I FIGURED THAT OUT ALREADY.
WELL, FOR-TUNATELY...
I'M BETTER THAN ANY MAP.
NO TEARFUL GOODBYES THIS WAY, AND YOUR WATCHDOGS CAN CONCENTRATE ON THEMSELVES.

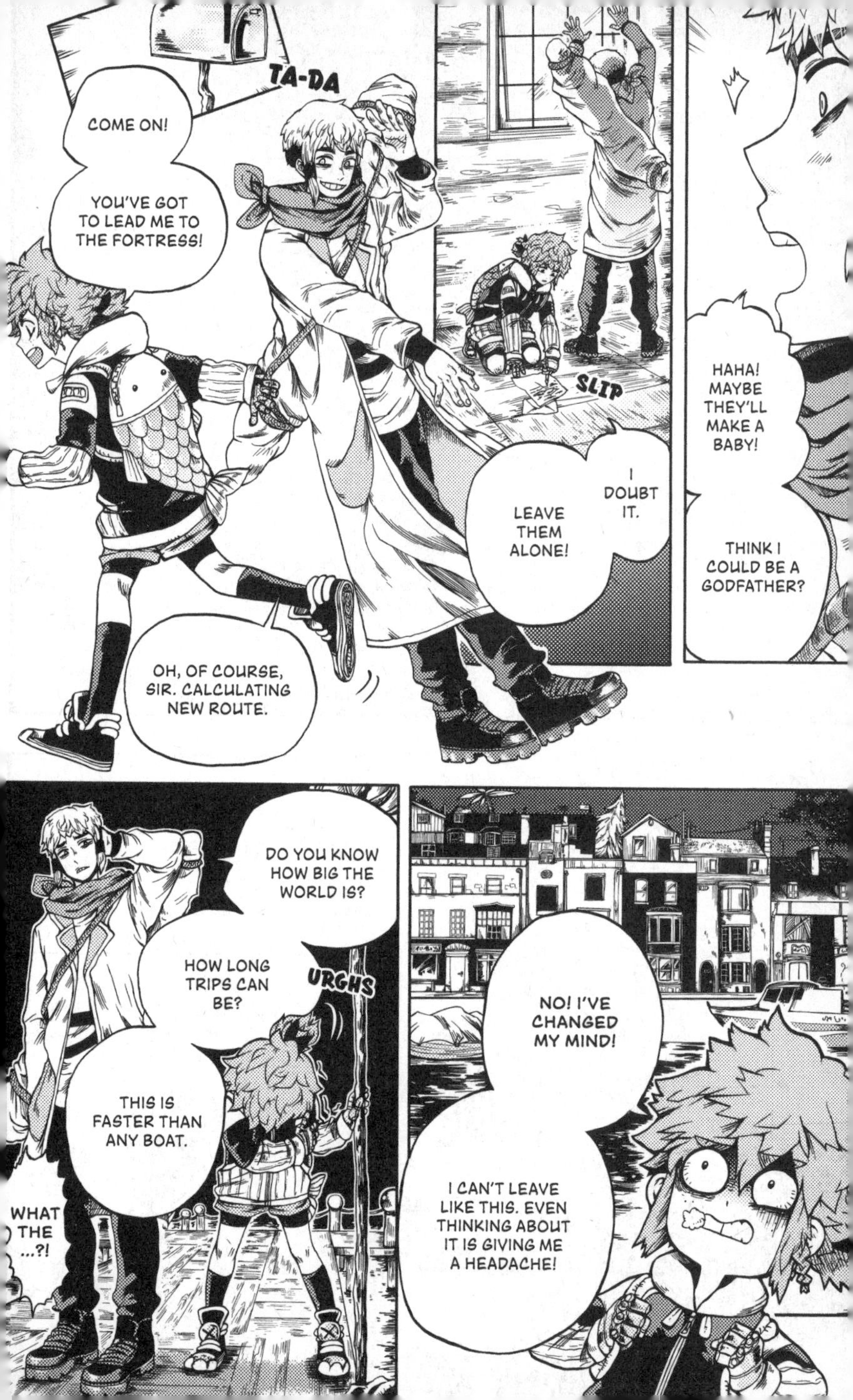
HAHA! MAYBE THEY'LL MAKE A BABY!
THINK I COULD BE A GODFATHER?
SLIP
I DOUBT IT.
LEAVE THEM ALONE!
TA-DA
COME ON!
YOU'VE GOT TO LEAD ME TO THE FORTRESS!
OH, OF COURSE, SIR. CALCULATING NEW ROUTE.
NO! I'VE CHANGED MY MIND!
I CAN'T LEAVE LIKE THIS. EVEN THINKING ABOUT IT IS GIVING ME A HEADACHE!
DO YOU KNOW HOW BIG THE WORLD IS?
HOW LONG TRIPS CAN BE?
URGHS
THIS IS FASTER THAN ANY BOAT.
WHAT THE ...?!

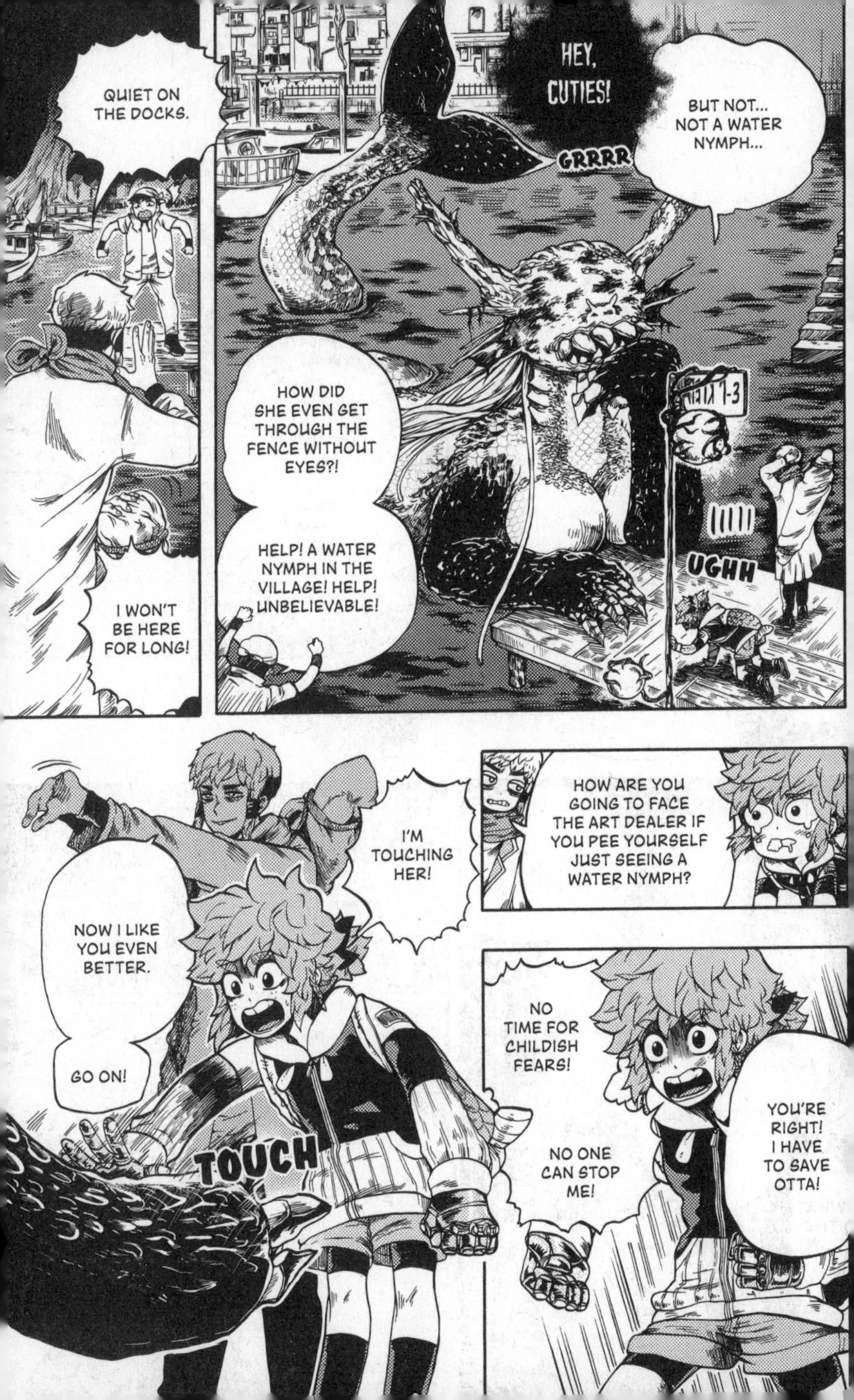
BUT NOT... NOT A WATER NYMPH...
HEY, CUTIES!
GRRRR
UGHH
HOW DID SHE EVEN GET THROUGH THE FENCE WITHOUT EYES?!
HELP! A WATER NYMPH IN THE VILLAGE! HELP! UNBELIEVABLE!
QUIET ON THE DOCKS.
I WON'T BE HERE FOR LONG!
HOW ARE YOU GOING TO FACE THE ART DEALER IF YOU PEE YOURSELF JUST SEEING A WATER NYMPH?
YOU'RE RIGHT! I HAVE TO SAVE OTTA!
NO TIME FOR CHILDISH FEARS!
NO ONE CAN STOP ME!
I'M TOUCHING HER!
NOW I LIKE YOU EVEN BETTER.
GO ON!
TOUCH

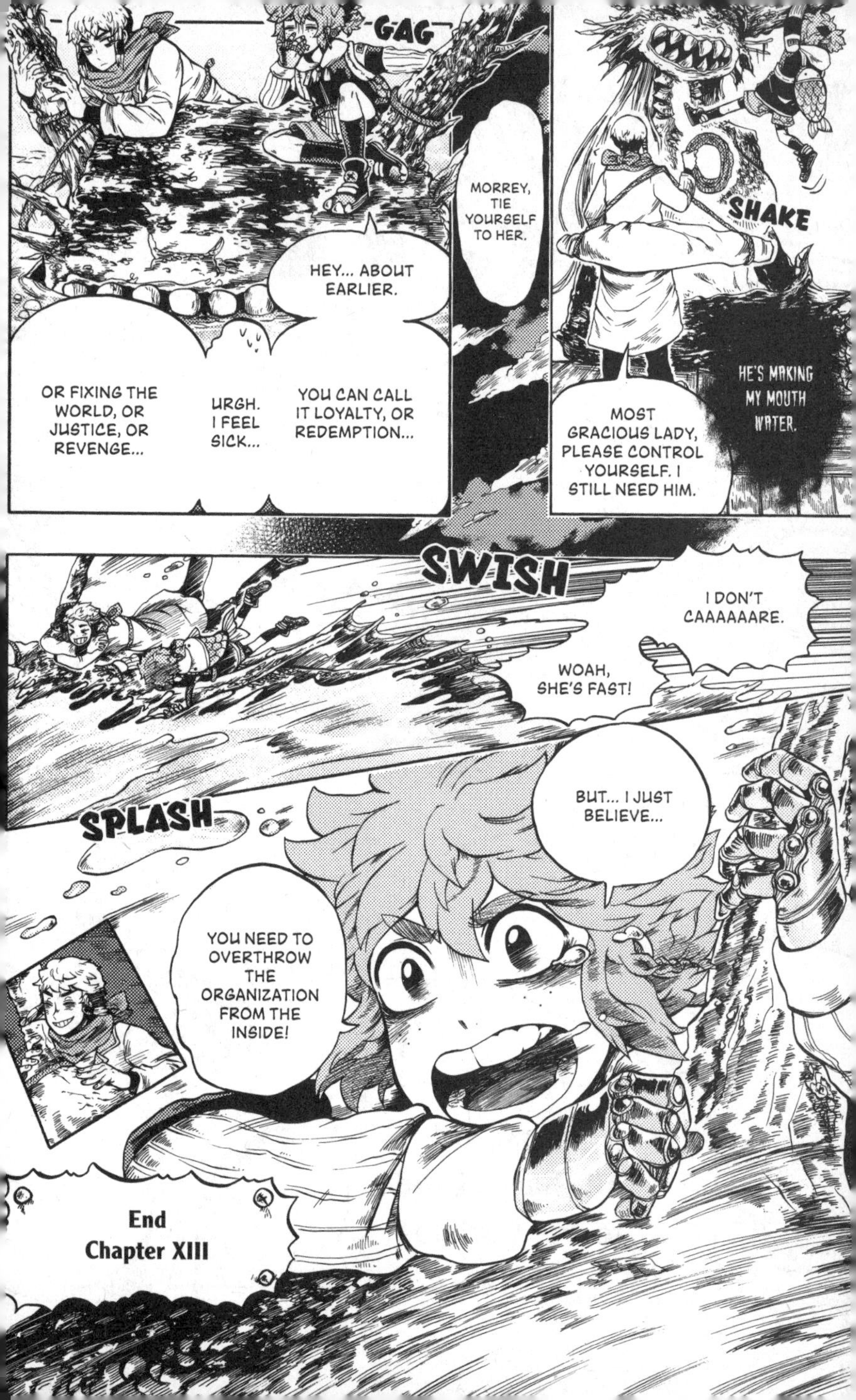
SHAKE
HE'S MAKING MY MOUTH WATER.
MOST GRACIOUS LADY, PLEASE CONTROL YOURSELF. I STILL NEED HIM.
MORREY, TIE YOURSELF TO HER.
GAG
HEY... ABOUT EARLIER.
YOU CAN CALL IT LOYALTY, OR REDEMPTION...
URGH. I FEEL SICK...
OR FIXING THE WORLD, OR JUSTICE, OR REVENGE...
SWISH
I DON'T CAAAAAARE.
WOAH, SHE'S FAST!
BUT... I JUST BELIEVE...
SPLASH
YOU NEED TO OVERTHROW THE ORGANIZATION FROM THE INSIDE!
End Chapter XIII

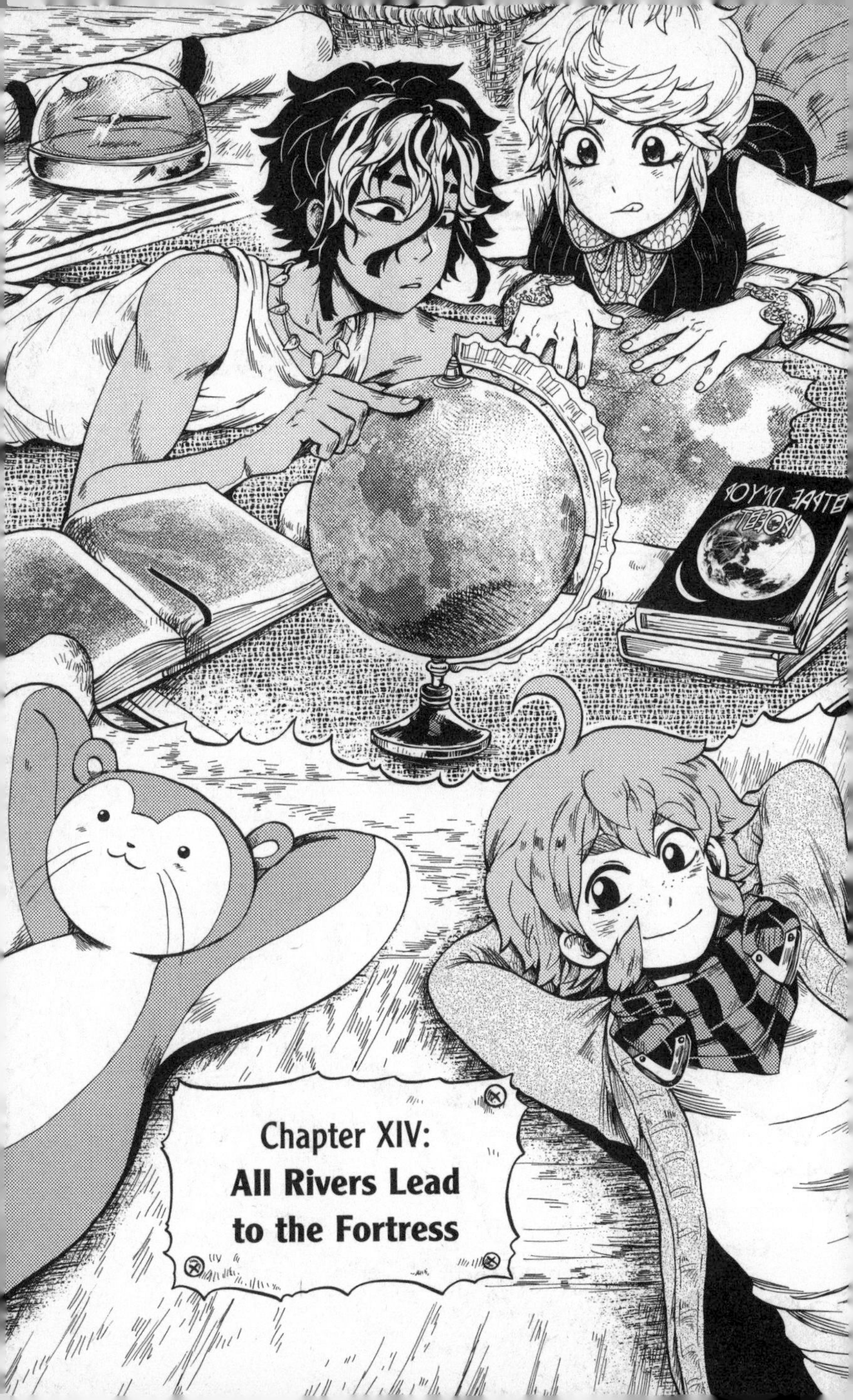
Chapter XIV:
All Rivers Lead
to the Fortress

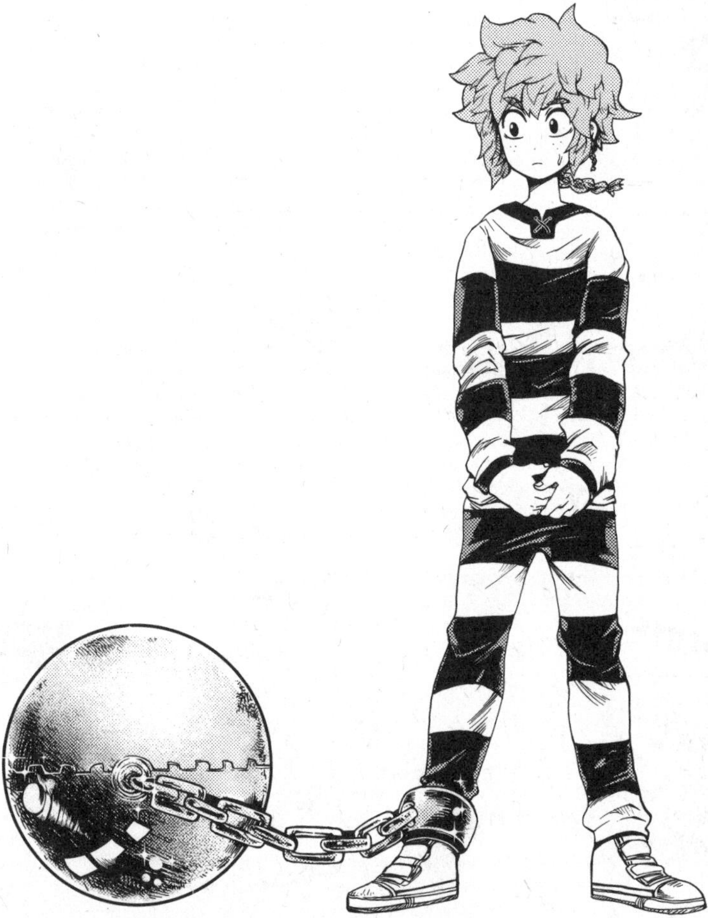

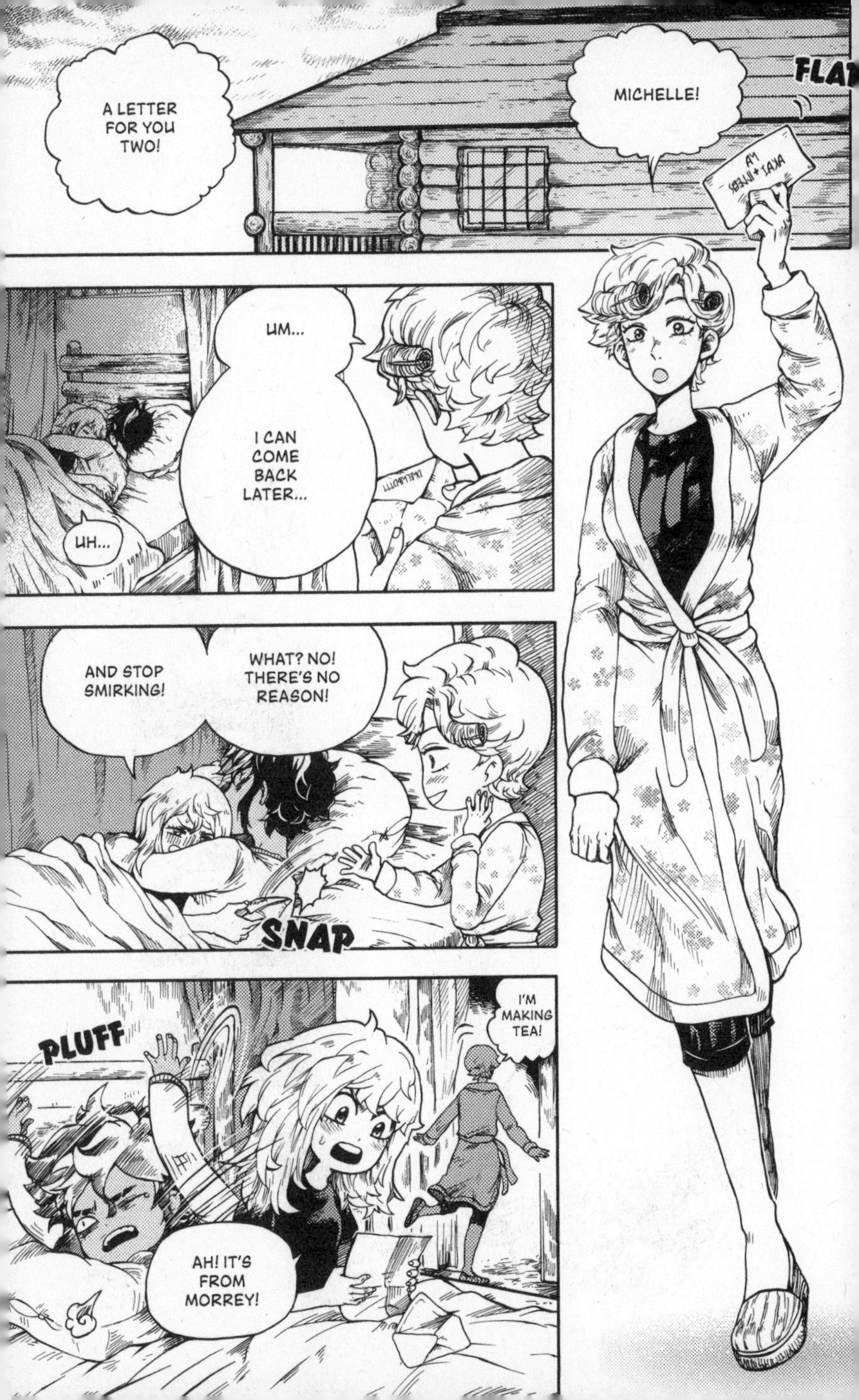
FLAT
MICHELLE!
A LETTER FOR YOU TWO!
UM...
I CAN COME BACK LATER...
UH...
WHAT? NO! THERE'S NO REASON!
AND STOP SMIRKING!
SNAP
I'M MAKING TEA!
PLUFF
AH! IT'S FROM MORREY!

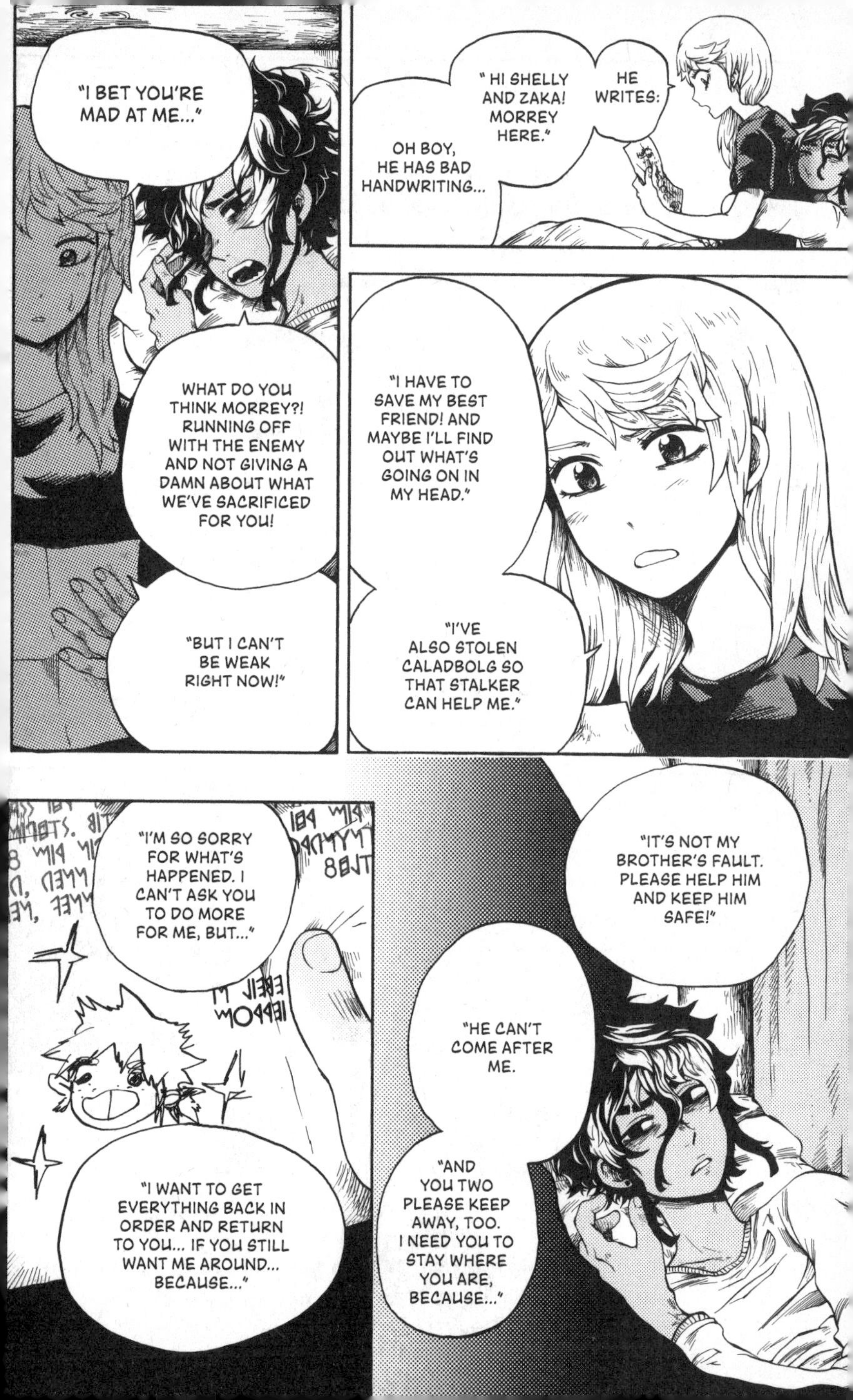
HE WRITES:
" HI SHELLY AND ZAKA! MORREY HERE."
OH BOY, HE HAS BAD HANDWRITING...
"I HAVE TO SAVE MY BEST FRIEND! AND MAYBE I'LL FIND OUT WHAT'S GOING ON IN MY HEAD."
"I'VE ALSO STOLEN CALADBOLG SO THAT STALKER CAN HELP ME."
"I BET YOU'RE MAD AT ME..."
WHAT DO YOU THINK MORREY?! RUNNING OFF WITH THE ENEMY AND NOT GIVING A DAMN ABOUT WHAT WE'VE SACRIFICED FOR YOU!
"BUT I CAN'T BE WEAK RIGHT NOW!"
"IT'S NOT MY BROTHER'S FAULT. PLEASE HELP HIM AND KEEP HIM SAFE!"
"HE CAN'T COME AFTER ME.
"AND YOU TWO PLEASE KEEP AWAY, TOO. I NEED YOU TO STAY WHERE YOU ARE, BECAUSE..."
"I'M SO SORRY FOR WHAT'S HAPPENED. I CAN'T ASK YOU TO DO MORE FOR ME, BUT..."
"I WANT TO GET EVERYTHING BACK IN ORDER AND RETURN TO YOU... IF YOU STILL WANT ME AROUND... BECAUSE..."

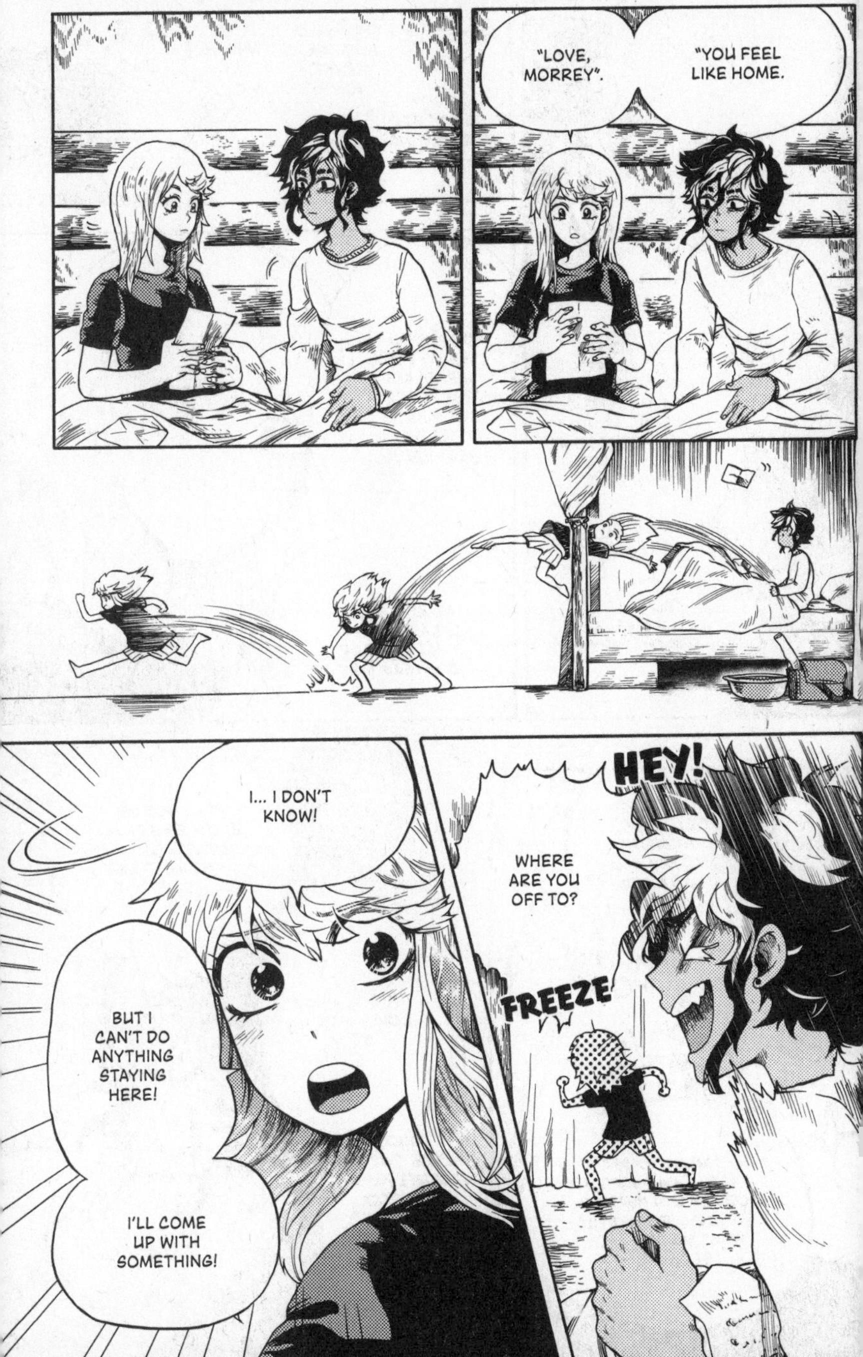
"YOU FEEL LIKE HOME.
"LOVE, MORREY".
HEY!
WHERE ARE YOU OFF TO?
FREEZE
I... I DON'T KNOW!
BUT I CAN'T DO ANYTHING STAYING HERE!
I'LL COME UP WITH SOMETHING!

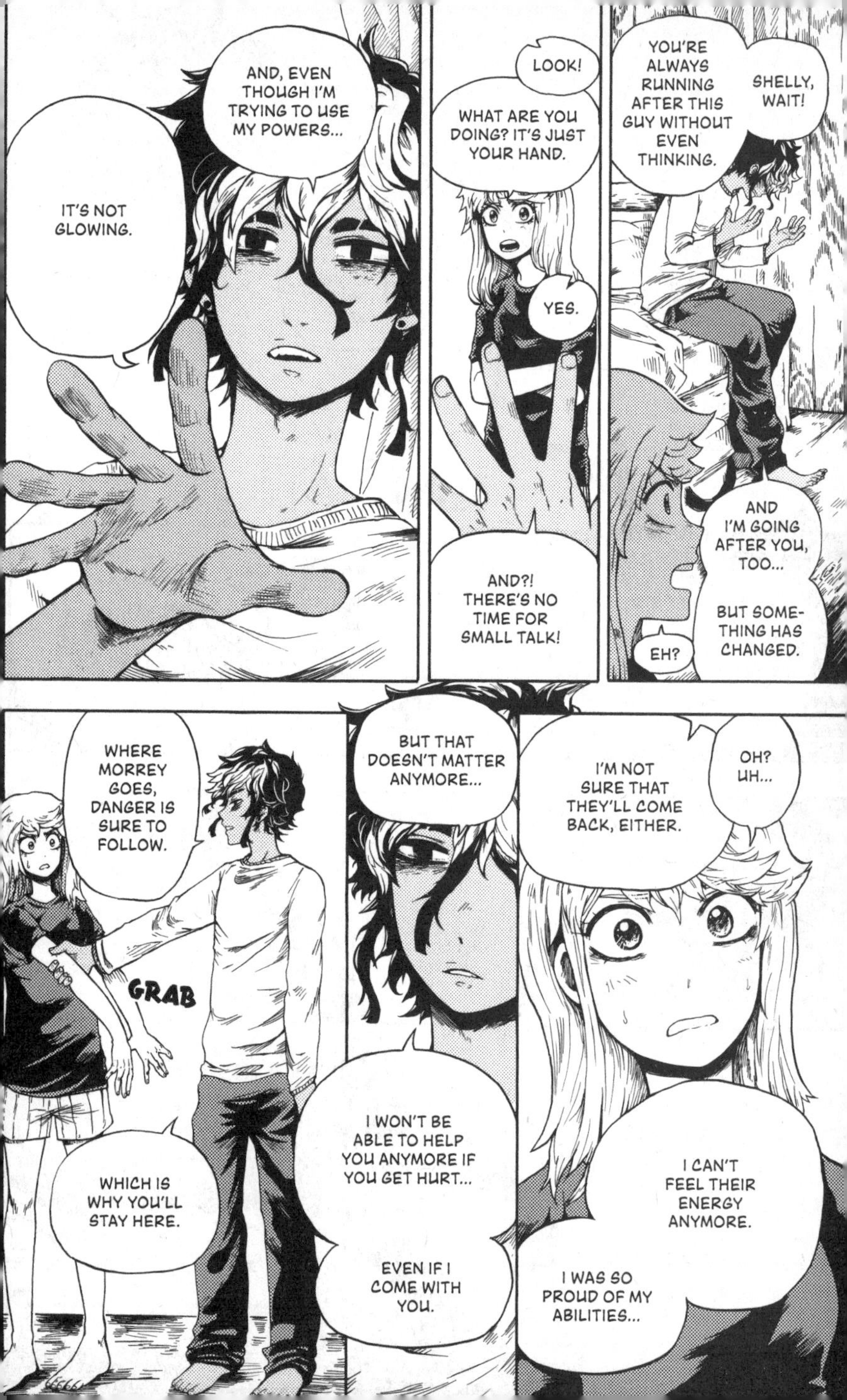
SHELLY, WAIT!
YOU'RE ALWAYS RUNNING AFTER THIS GUY WITHOUT EVEN THINKING.
AND I'M GOING AFTER YOU, TOO...
BUT SOME-THING HAS CHANGED.
EH?
LOOK!
WHAT ARE YOU DOING? IT'S JUST YOUR HAND.
YES.
AND?! THERE'S NO TIME FOR SMALL TALK!
AND, EVEN THOUGH I'M TRYING TO USE MY POWERS...
IT'S NOT GLOWING.
OH? UH...
I'M NOT SURE THAT THEY'LL COME BACK, EITHER.
I CAN'T FEEL THEIR ENERGY ANYMORE.
I WAS SO PROUD OF MY ABILITIES...
BUT THAT DOESN'T MATTER ANYMORE...
I WON'T BE ABLE TO HELP YOU ANYMORE IF YOU GET HURT...
EVEN IF I COME WITH YOU.
WHERE MORREY GOES, DANGER IS SURE TO FOLLOW.
GRAB
WHICH IS WHY YOU'LL STAY HERE.

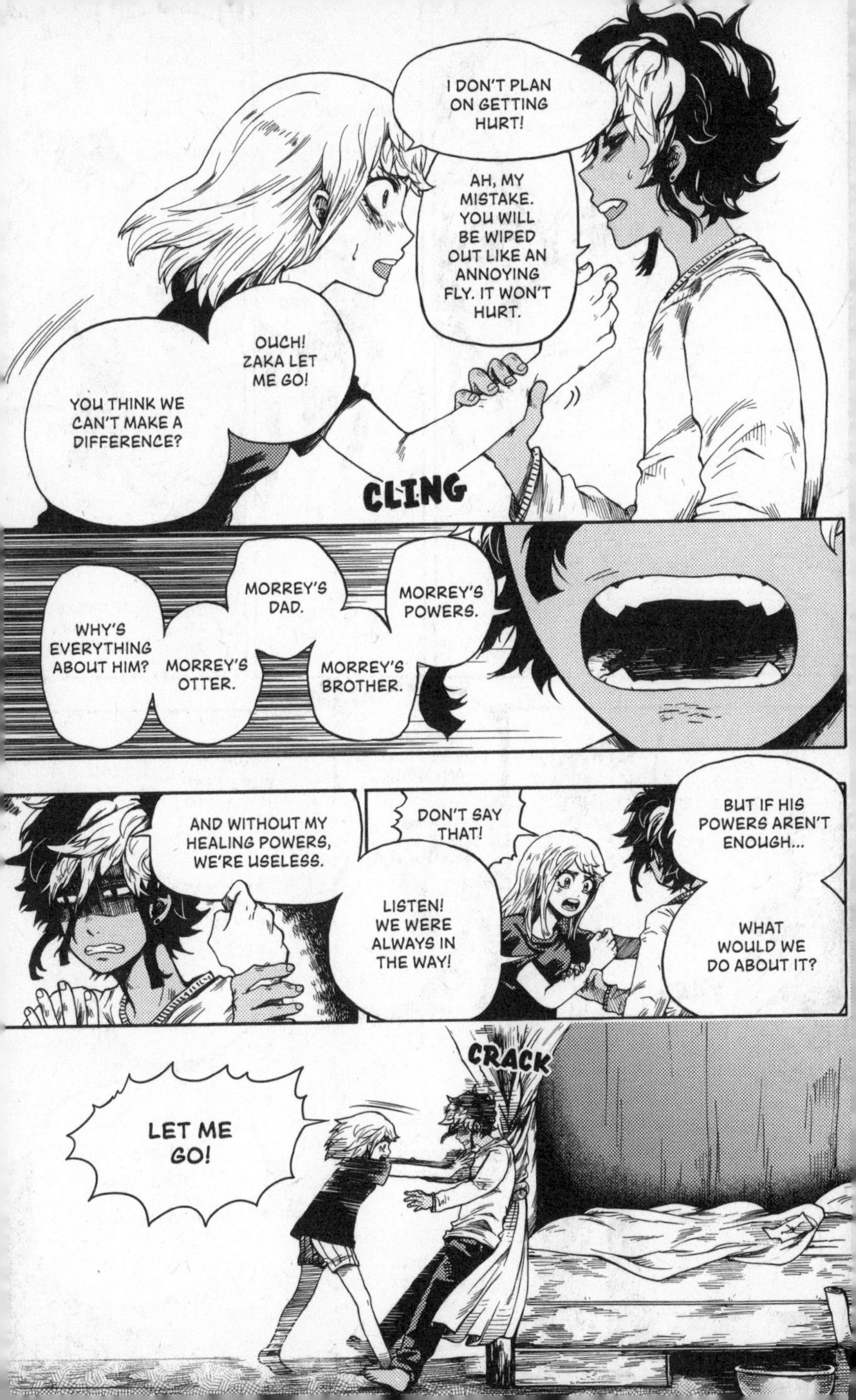
I DON'T PLAN ON GETTING HURT!
AH, MY MISTAKE. YOU WILL BE WIPED OUT LIKE AN ANNOYING FLY. IT WON'T HURT.
OUCH! ZAKA LET ME GO!
YOU THINK WE CAN'T MAKE A DIFFERENCE?
CLING
MORREY'S POWERS.
MORREY'S DAD.
MORREY'S BROTHER.
MORREY'S OTTER.
WHY'S EVERYTHING ABOUT HIM?
BUT IF HIS POWERS AREN'T ENOUGH...
WHAT WOULD WE DO ABOUT IT?
DON'T SAY THAT!
LISTEN! WE WERE ALWAYS IN THE WAY!
AND WITHOUT MY HEALING POWERS, WE'RE USELESS.
CRACK
LET ME GO!

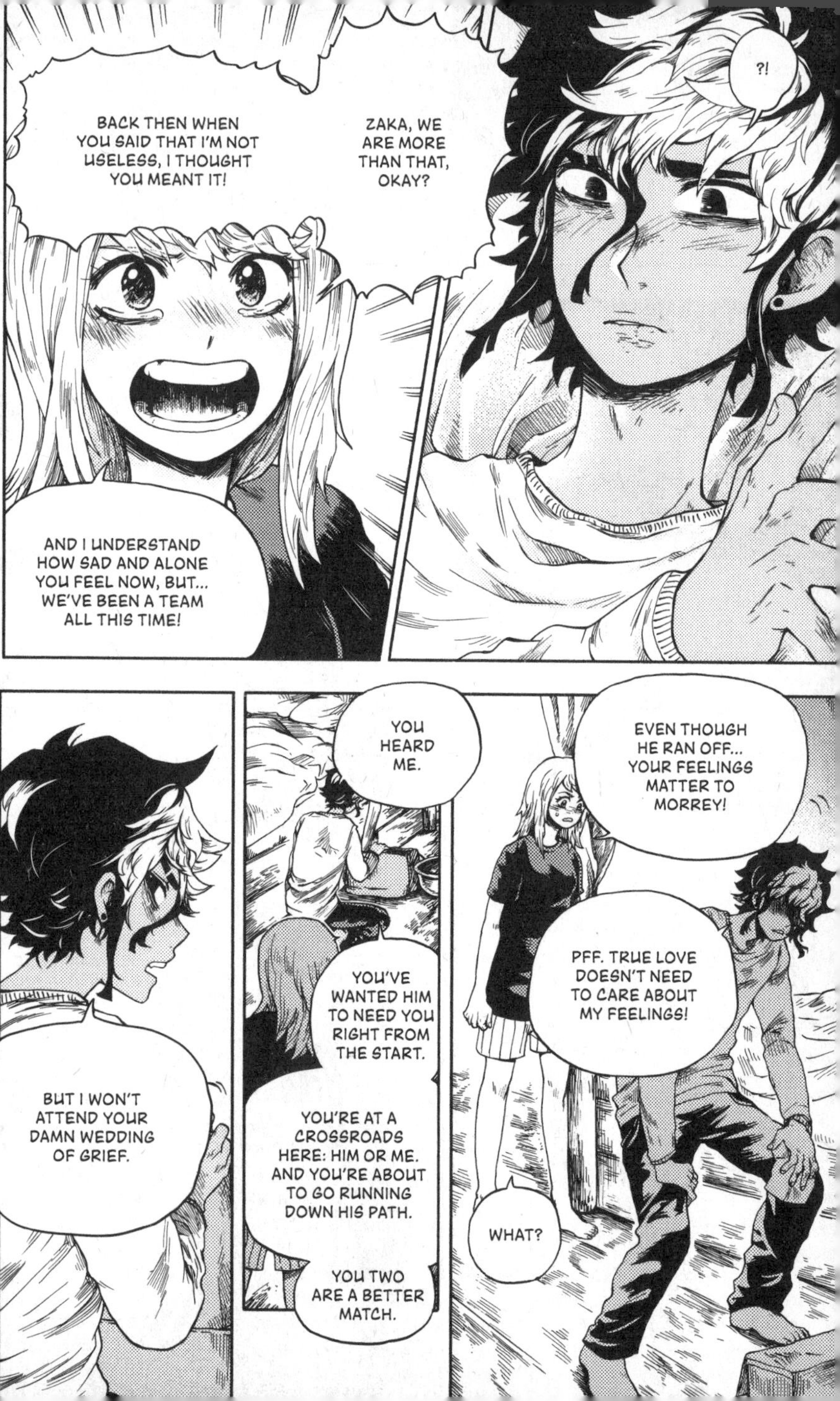
?!
ZAKA, WE ARE MORE THAN THAT, OKAY?
BACK THEN WHEN YOU SAID THAT I'M NOT USELESS, I THOUGHT YOU MEANT IT!
AND I UNDERSTAND HOW SAD AND ALONE YOU FEEL NOW, BUT... WE'VE BEEN A TEAM ALL THIS TIME!
EVEN THOUGH HE RAN OFF... YOUR FEELINGS MATTER TO MORREY!
PFF. TRUE LOVE DOESN'T NEED TO CARE ABOUT MY FEELINGS!
WHAT?
YOU HEARD ME.
YOU'VE WANTED HIM TO NEED YOU RIGHT FROM THE START.
YOU'RE AT A CROSSROADS HERE: HIM OR ME. AND YOU'RE ABOUT TO GO RUNNING DOWN HIS PATH.
YOU TWO ARE A BETTER MATCH.
BUT I WON'T ATTEND YOUR DAMN WEDDING OF GRIEF.

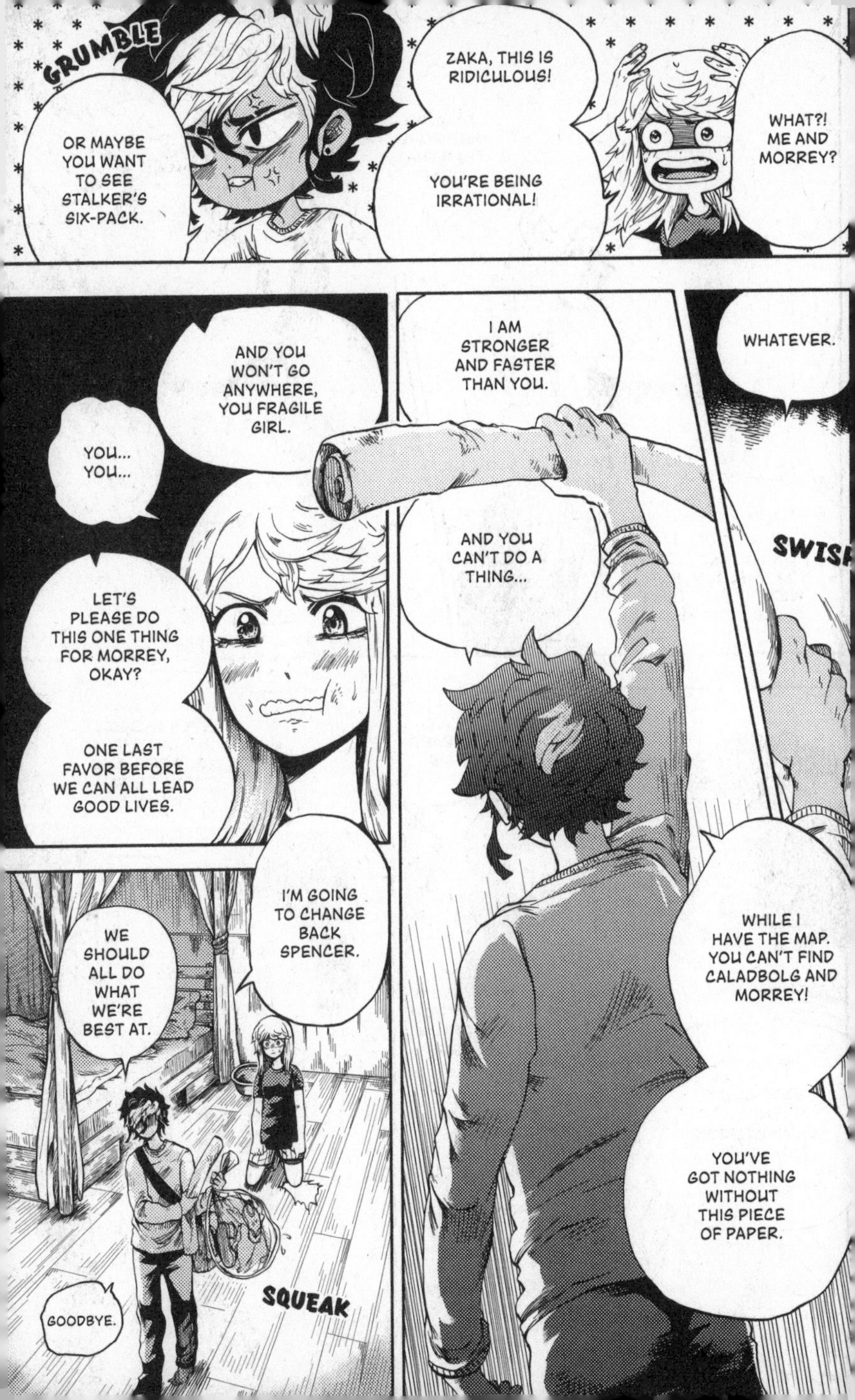
WHAT?! ME AND MORREY?
ZAKA, THIS IS RIDICULOUS!
YOU'RE BEING IRRATIONAL!
GRUMBLE
OR MAYBE YOU WANT TO SEE STALKER'S SIX-PACK.
WHATEVER.
SWISH
WHILE I HAVE THE MAP. YOU CAN'T FIND CALADBOLG AND MORREY!
YOU'VE GOT NOTHING WITHOUT THIS PIECE OF PAPER.
I AM STRONGER AND FASTER THAN YOU.
AND YOU CAN'T DO A THING...
AND YOU WON'T GO ANYWHERE, YOU FRAGILE GIRL.
YOU... YOU...
LET'S PLEASE DO THIS ONE THING FOR MORREY, OKAY?
ONE LAST FAVOR BEFORE WE CAN ALL LEAD GOOD LIVES.
I'M GOING TO CHANGE BACK SPENCER.
WE SHOULD ALL DO WHAT WE'RE BEST AT.
SQUEAK
GOODBYE.

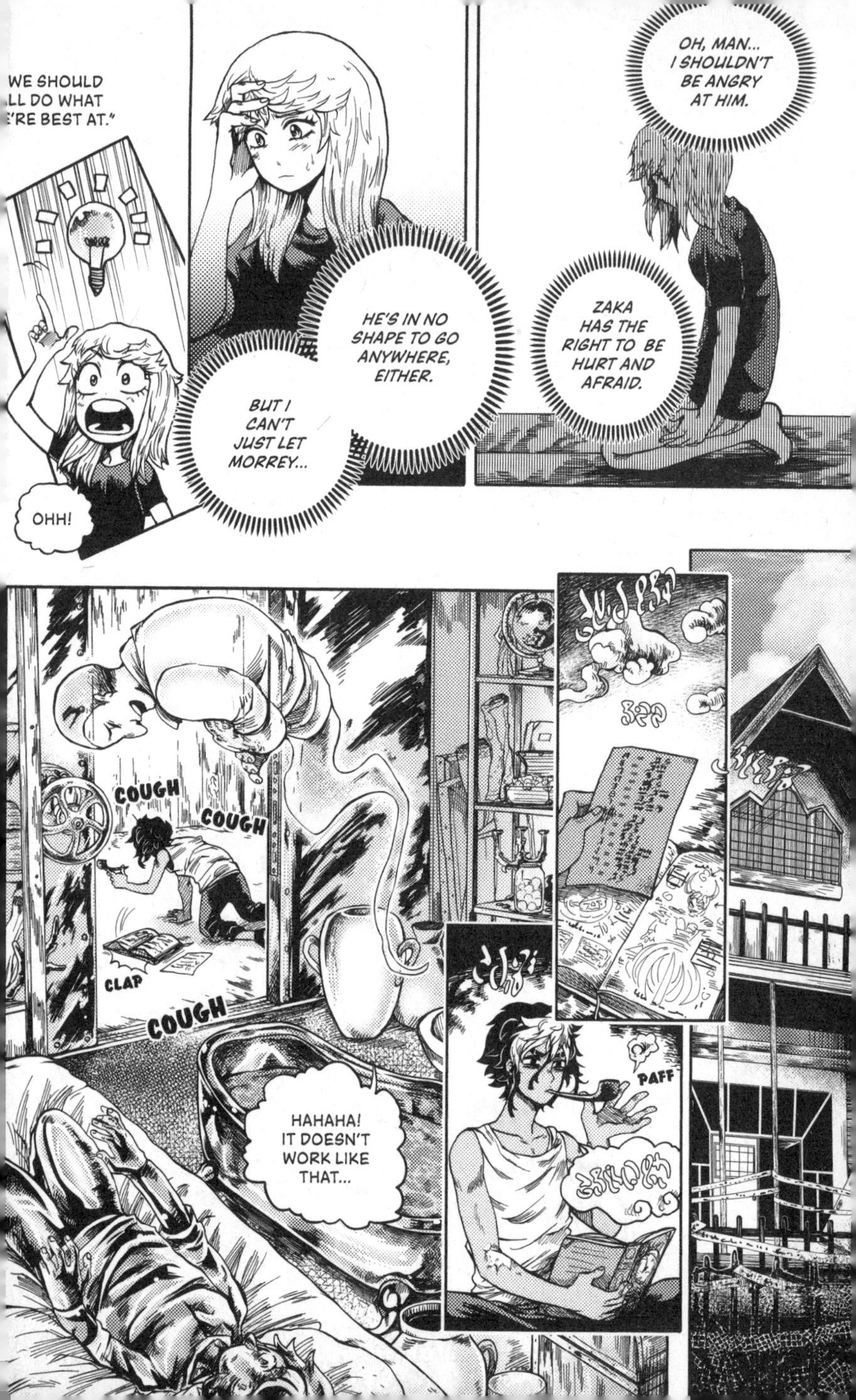
OH, MAN... I SHOULDN'T BE ANGRY AT HIM.
ZAKA HAS THE RIGHT TO BE HURT AND AFRAID.
HE'S IN NO SHAPE TO GO ANYWHERE, EITHER.
BUT I CAN'T JUST LET MORREY...
WE SHOULD LL DO WHAT 'RE BEST AT."
OHH!
PAFF
COUGH
COUGH
CLAP
COUGH
HAHAHA! IT DOESN'T WORK LIKE THAT...

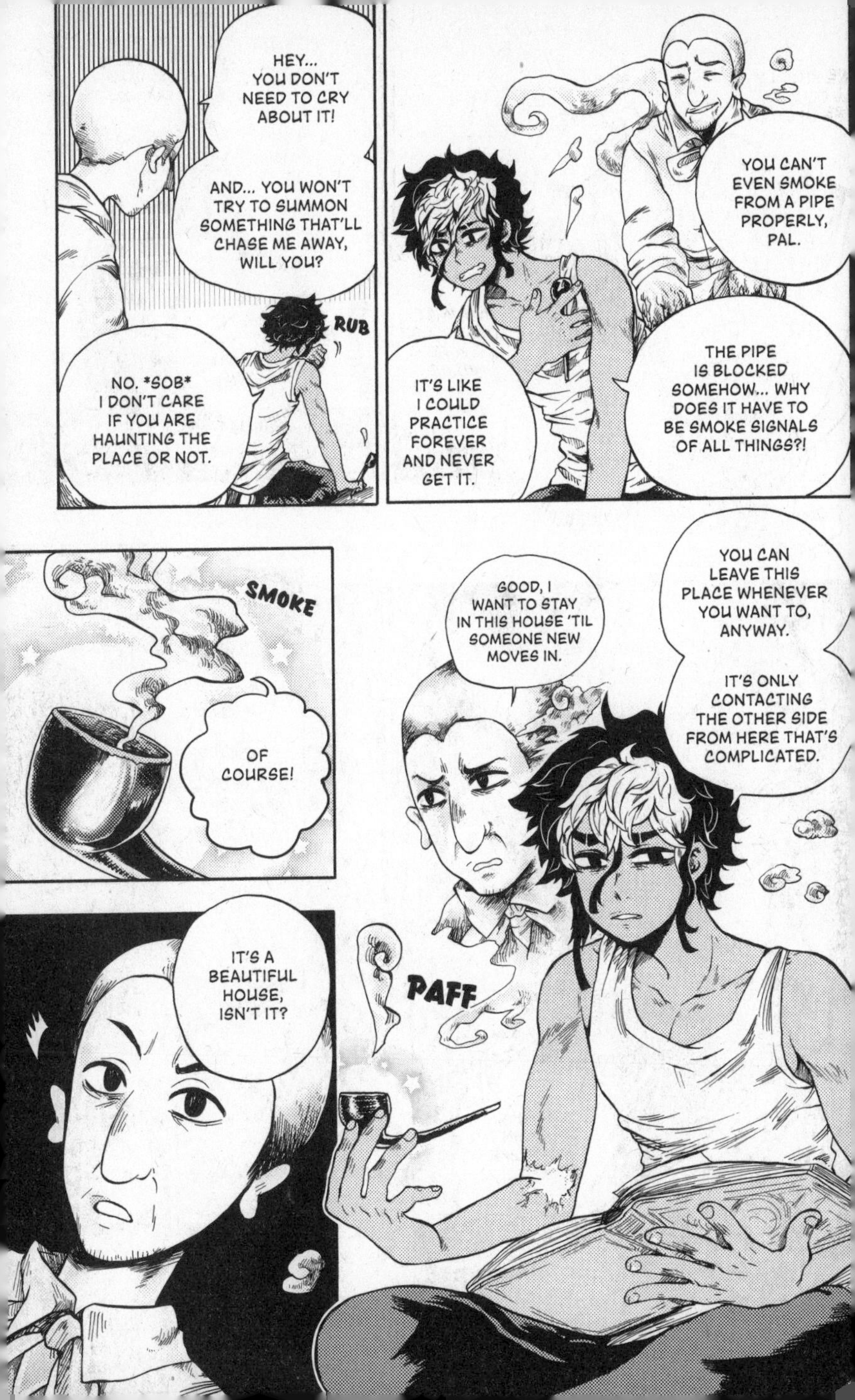
YOU CAN'T EVEN SMOKE FROM A PIPE PROPERLY, PAL.
THE PIPE IS BLOCKED SOMEHOW... WHY DOES IT HAVE TO BE SMOKE SIGNALS OF ALL THINGS?!
IT'S LIKE I COULD PRACTICE FOREVER AND NEVER GET IT.
HEY... YOU DON'T NEED TO CRY ABOUT IT!
AND... YOU WON'T TRY TO SUMMON SOMETHING THAT'LL CHASE ME AWAY, WILL YOU?
RUB
NO. *SOB* I DON'T CARE IF YOU ARE HAUNTING THE PLACE OR NOT.
YOU CAN LEAVE THIS PLACE WHENEVER YOU WANT TO, ANYWAY.
IT'S ONLY CONTACTING THE OTHER SIDE FROM HERE THAT'S COMPLICATED.
GOOD, I WANT TO STAY IN THIS HOUSE 'TIL SOMEONE NEW MOVES IN.
PAFF
SMOKE
OF COURSE!
IT'S A BEAUTIFUL HOUSE, ISN'T IT?

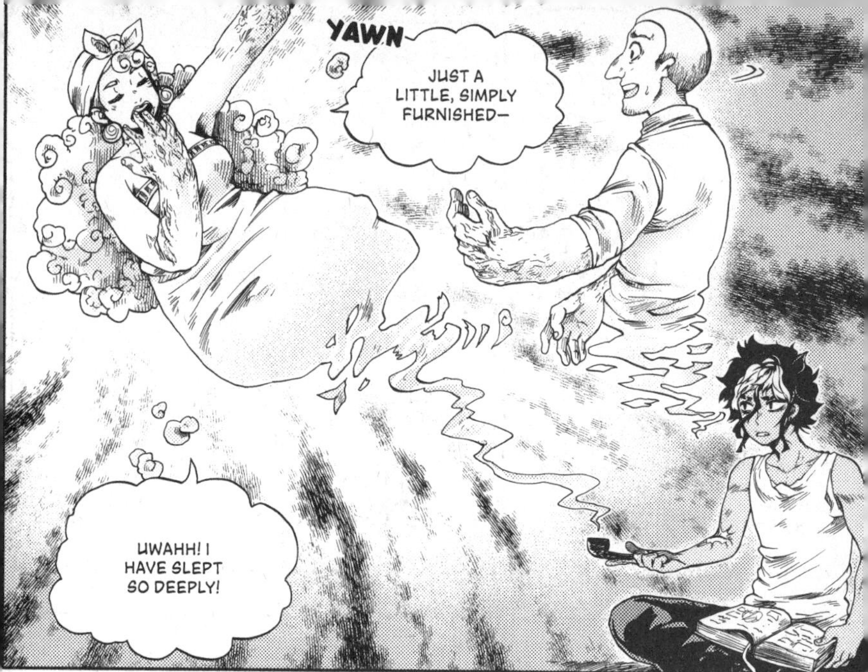
JUST A LITTLE, SIMPLY FURNISHED—
YAWN
UWAHH! I HAVE SLEPT SO DEEPLY!

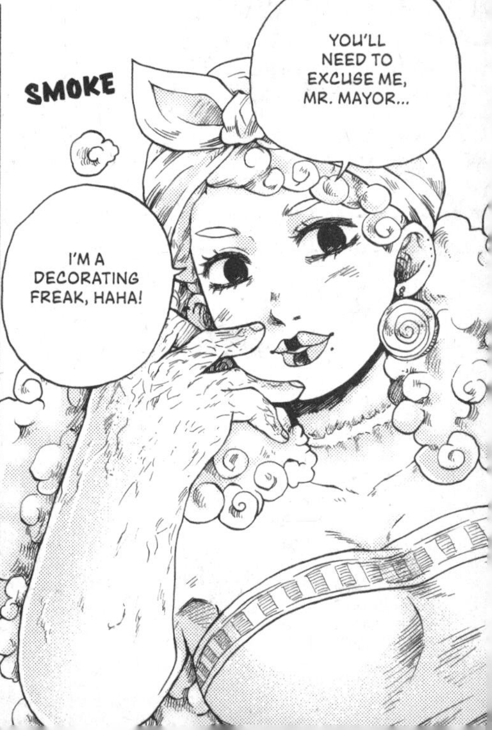
YOU'LL NEED TO EXCUSE ME, MR. MAYOR...
SMOKE
I'M A DECORATING FREAK, HAHA!

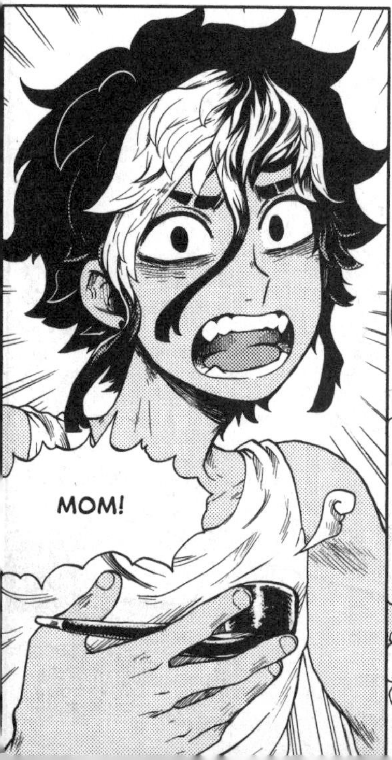
MOM!

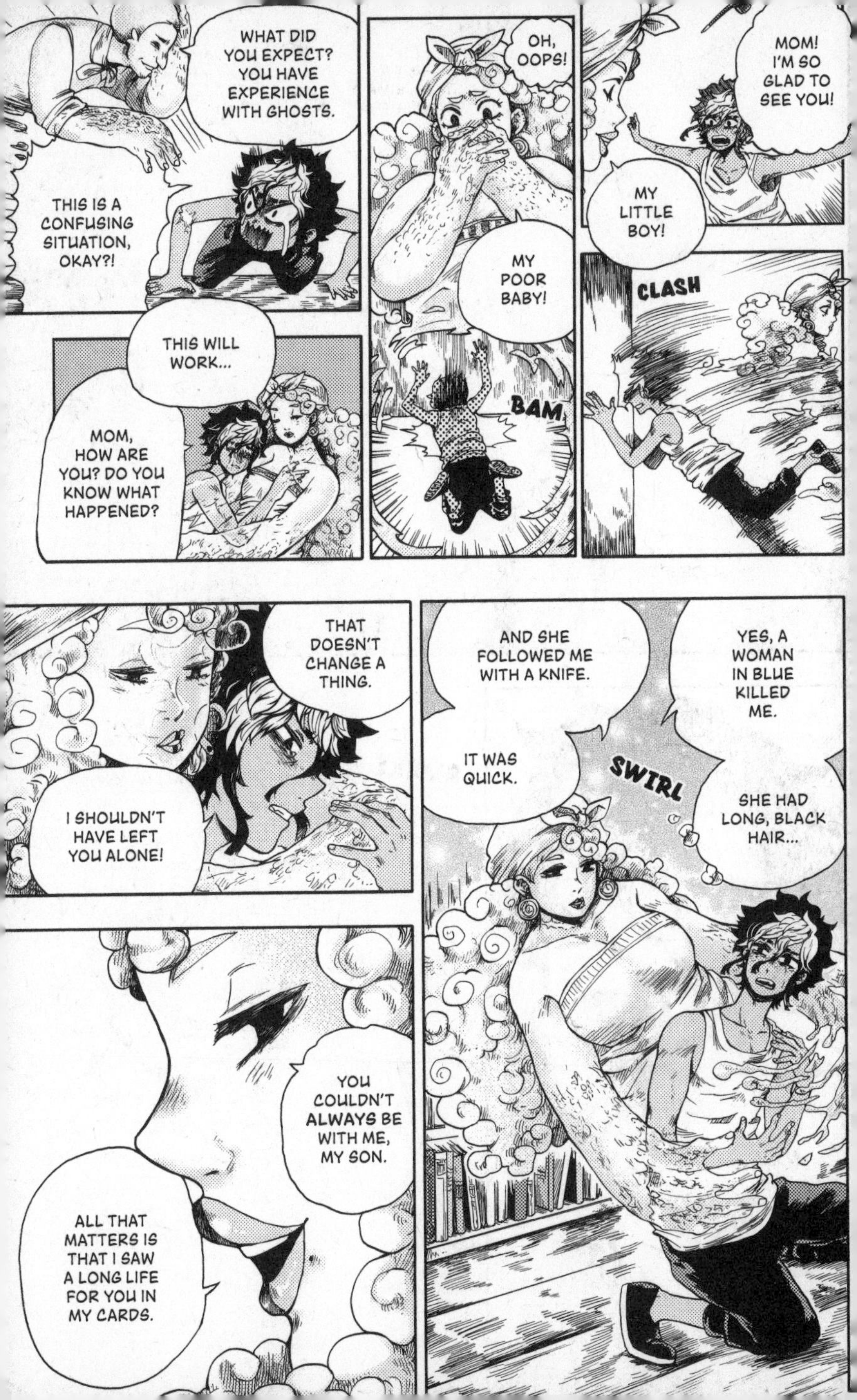
MOM! I'M SO GLAD TO SEE YOU!
MY LITTLE BOY!
CLASH
OH, OOPS!
MY POOR BABY!
BAM
WHAT DID YOU EXPECT? YOU HAVE EXPERIENCE WITH GHOSTS.
THIS IS A CONFUSING SITUATION, OKAY?!
THIS WILL WORK...
MOM, HOW ARE YOU? DO YOU KNOW WHAT HAPPENED?
YES, A WOMAN IN BLUE KILLED ME.
SHE HAD LONG, BLACK HAIR...
SWIRL
AND SHE FOLLOWED ME WITH A KNIFE.
IT WAS QUICK.
THAT DOESN'T CHANGE A THING.
I SHOULDN'T HAVE LEFT YOU ALONE!
YOU COULDN'T ALWAYS BE WITH ME, MY SON.
ALL THAT MATTERS IS THAT I SAW A LONG LIFE FOR YOU IN MY CARDS.

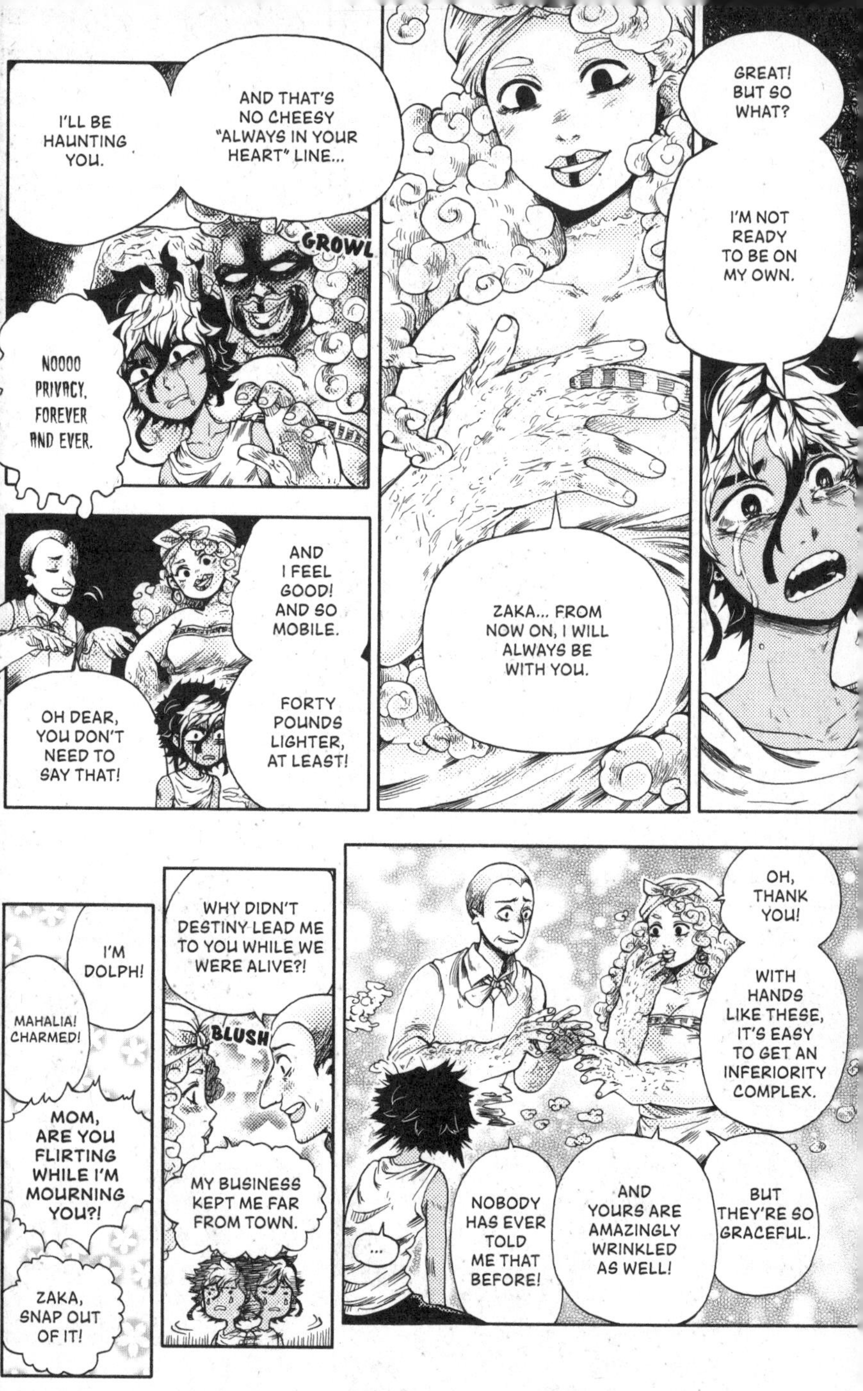
GREAT! BUT SO WHAT?
I'M NOT READY TO BE ON MY OWN.
ZAKA... FROM NOW ON, I WILL ALWAYS BE WITH YOU.
I'LL BE HAUNTING YOU.
AND THAT'S NO CHEESY "ALWAYS IN YOUR HEART" LINE...
GROWL
NOOOO PRIVACY, FOREVER AND EVER.
AND I FEEL GOOD! AND SO MOBILE.
FORTY POUNDS LIGHTER, AT LEAST!
OH DEAR, YOU DON'T NEED TO SAY THAT!
OH, THANK YOU!
WITH HANDS LIKE THESE, IT'S EASY TO GET AN INFERIORITY COMPLEX.
BUT THEY'RE SO GRACEFUL.
AND YOURS ARE AMAZINGLY WRINKLED AS WELL!
NOBODY HAS EVER TOLD ME THAT BEFORE!
...
WHY DIDN'T DESTINY LEAD ME TO YOU WHILE WE WERE ALIVE?!
BLUSH
MY BUSINESS KEPT ME FAR FROM TOWN.
I'M DOLPH!
MAHALIA! CHARMED!
MOM, ARE YOU FLIRTING WHILE I'M MOURNING YOU?!
ZAKA, SNAP OUT OF IT!

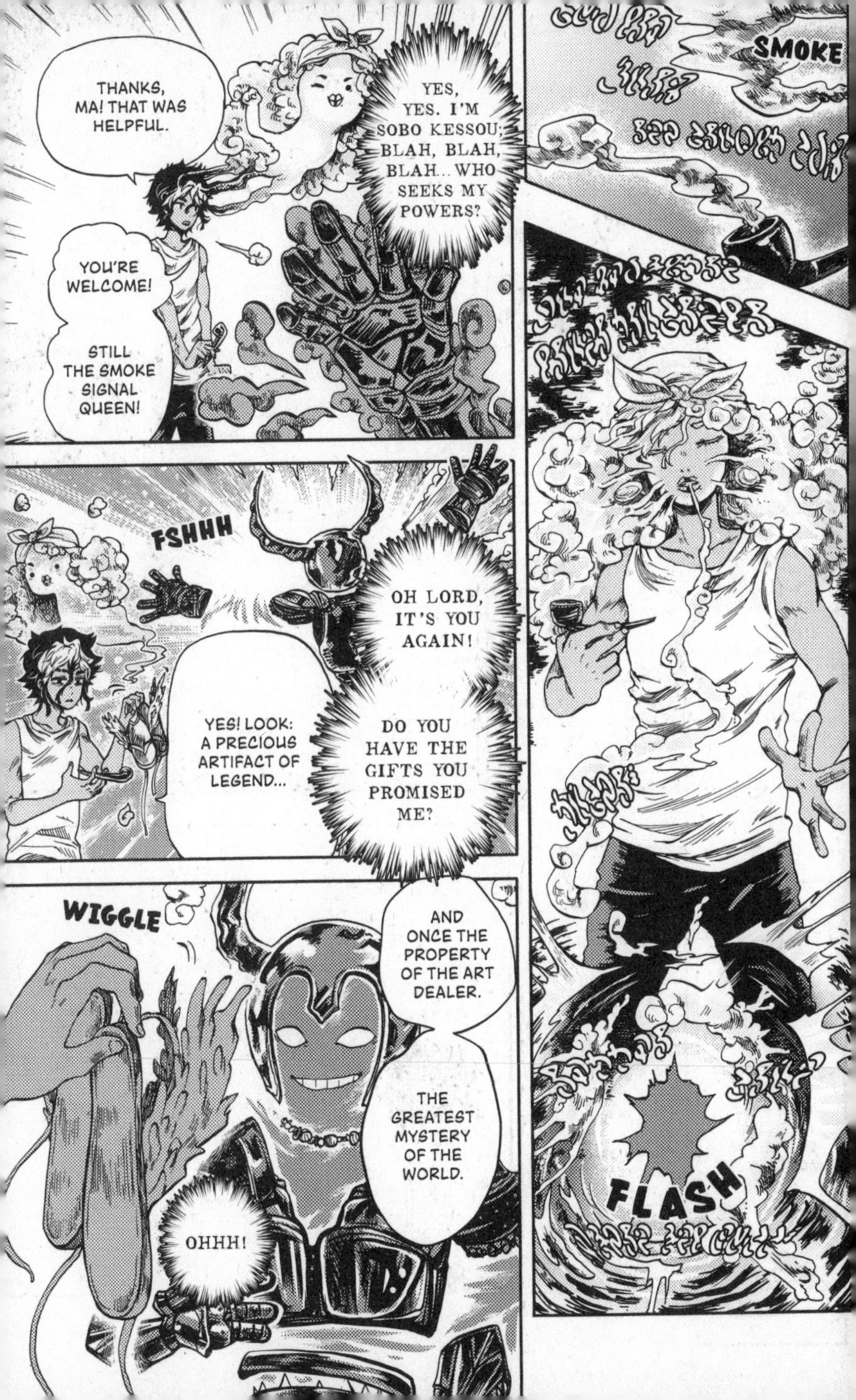
SMOKE
FLASH
YES, YES. I'M SOBO KESSOU; BLAH, BLAH, BLAH... WHO SEEKS MY POWERS?
THANKS, MA! THAT WAS HELPFUL.
YOU'RE WELCOME!
STILL THE SMOKE SIGNAL QUEEN!
OH LORD, IT'S YOU AGAIN!
DO YOU HAVE THE GIFTS YOU PROMISED ME?
FSHHH
YES! LOOK: A PRECIOUS ARTIFACT OF LEGEND...
AND ONCE THE PROPERTY OF THE ART DEALER.
THE GREATEST MYSTERY OF THE WORLD.
WIGGLE
OHHH!

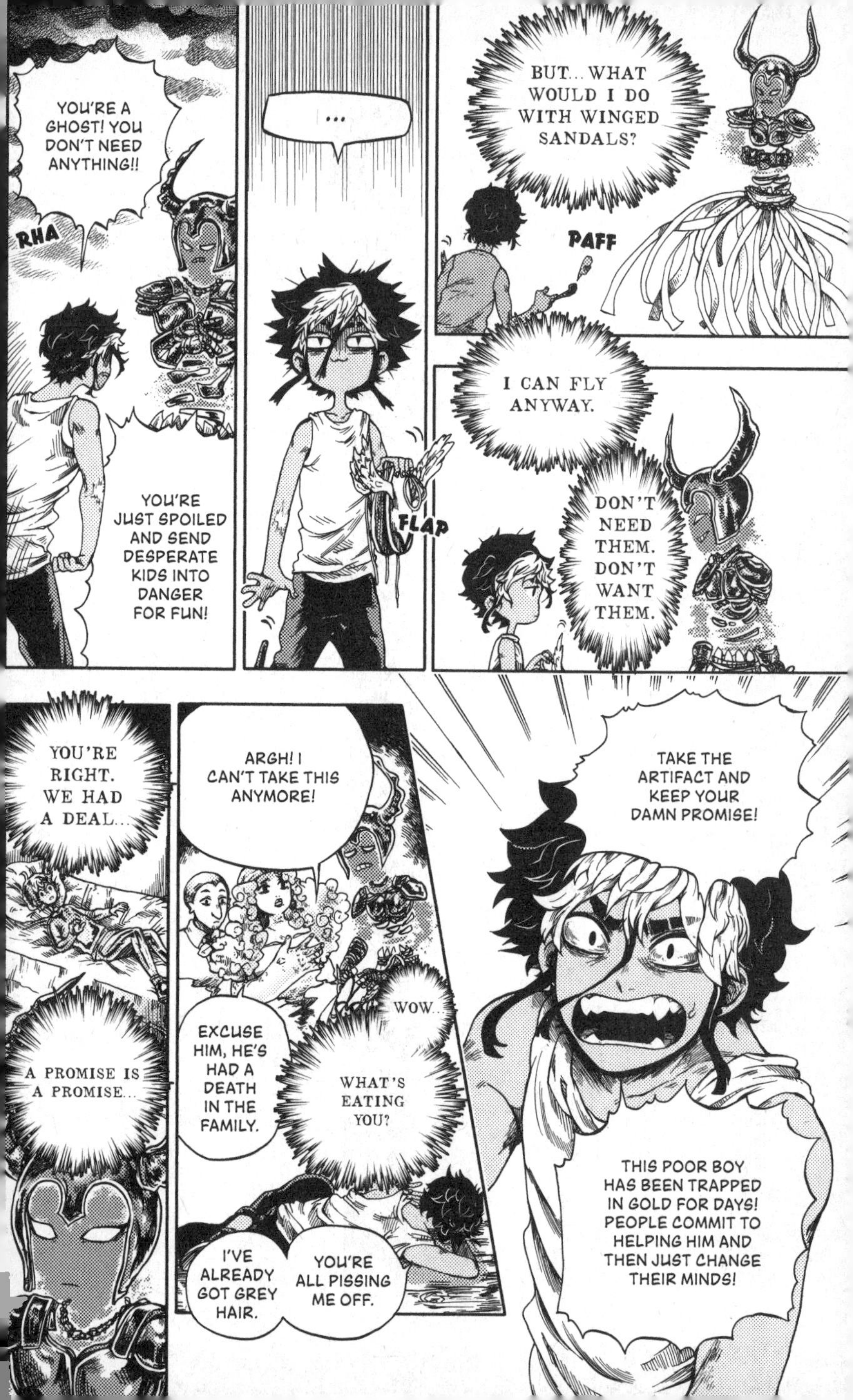
BUT... WHAT WOULD I DO WITH WINGED SANDALS?
PAFF
I CAN FLY ANYWAY.
DON'T NEED THEM. DON'T WANT THEM.
...
FLAP
YOU'RE A GHOST! YOU DON'T NEED ANYTHING!!
RHA
YOU'RE JUST SPOILED AND SEND DESPERATE KIDS INTO DANGER FOR FUN!
TAKE THE ARTIFACT AND KEEP YOUR DAMN PROMISE!
THIS POOR BOY HAS BEEN TRAPPED IN GOLD FOR DAYS! PEOPLE COMMIT TO HELPING HIM AND THEN JUST CHANGE THEIR MINDS!
ARGH! I CAN'T TAKE THIS ANYMORE!
WOW...
WHAT'S EATING YOU?
EXCUSE HIM, HE'S HAD A DEATH IN THE FAMILY.
YOU'RE ALL PISSING ME OFF.
I'VE ALREADY GOT GREY HAIR.
YOU'RE RIGHT. WE HAD A DEAL...
A PROMISE IS A PROMISE...

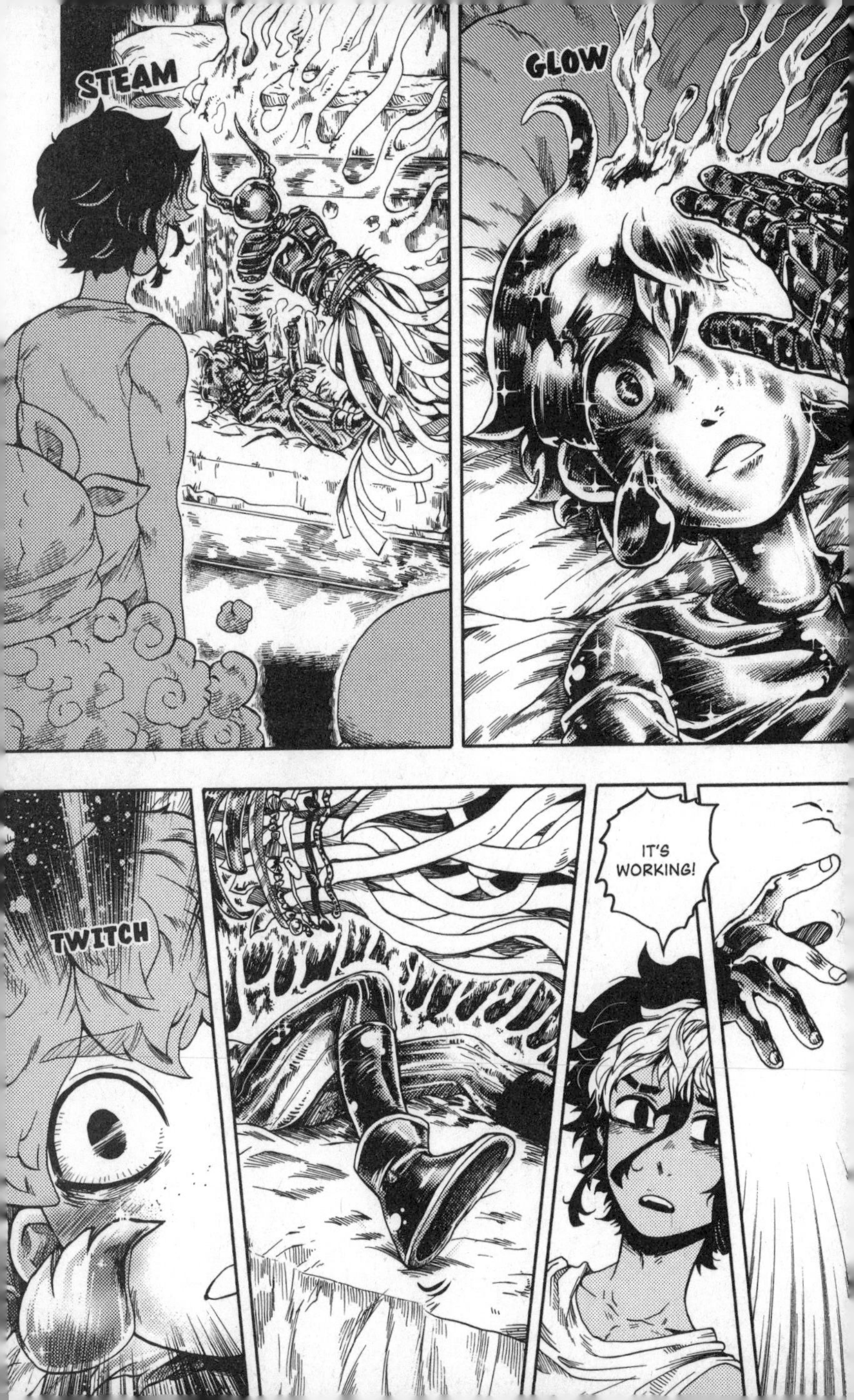
GLOW
STEAM
IT'S WORKING!
TWITCH

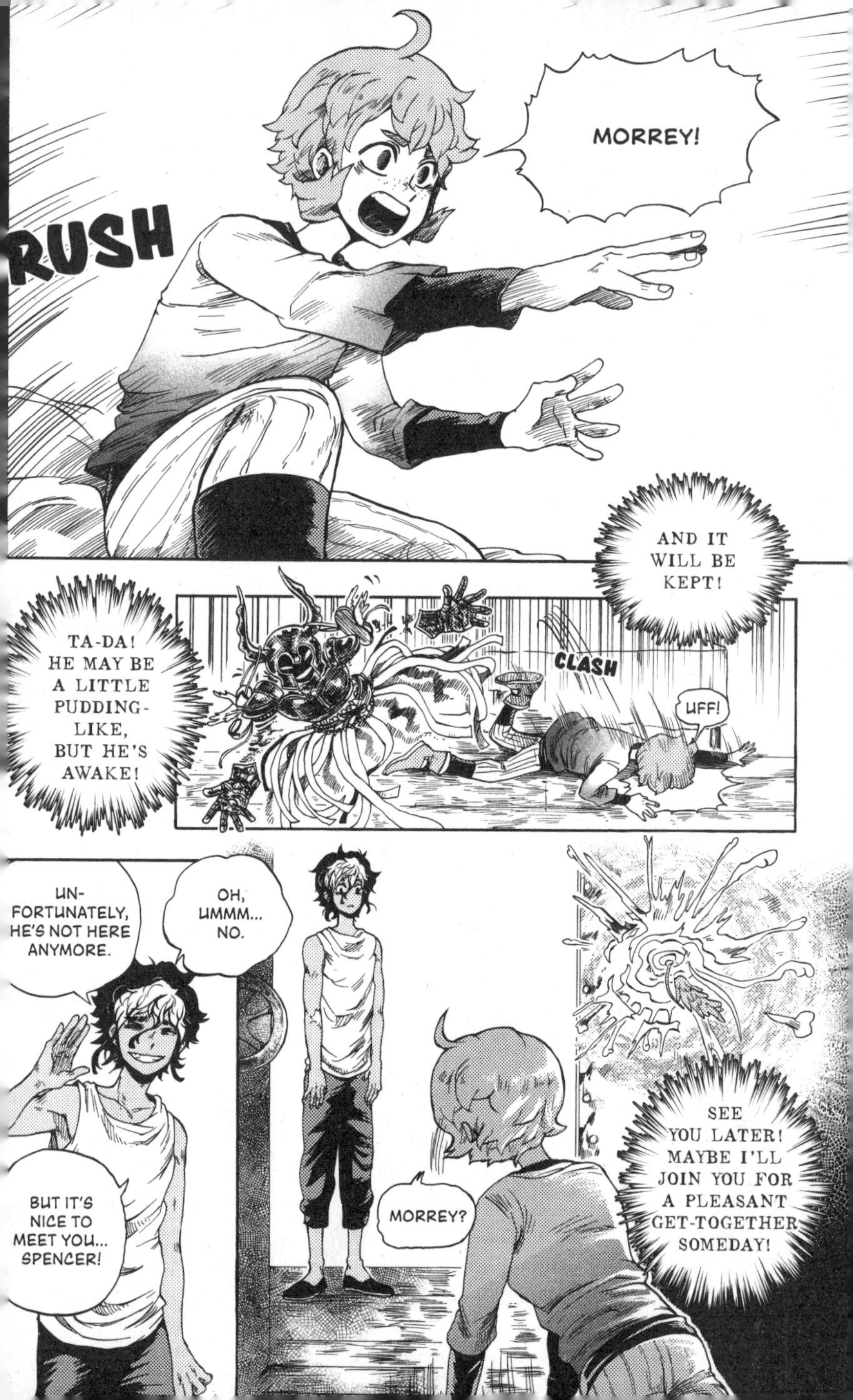
MORREY!
RUSH
AND IT WILL BE KEPT!
CLASH
UFF!
TA-DA! HE MAY BE A LITTLE PUDDING-LIKE, BUT HE'S AWAKE!
SEE YOU LATER! MAYBE I'LL JOIN YOU FOR A PLEASANT GET-TOGETHER SOMEDAY!
OH, UMMM... NO.
MORREY?
UN-FORTUNATELY, HE'S NOT HERE ANYMORE.
BUT IT'S NICE TO MEET YOU... SPENCER!

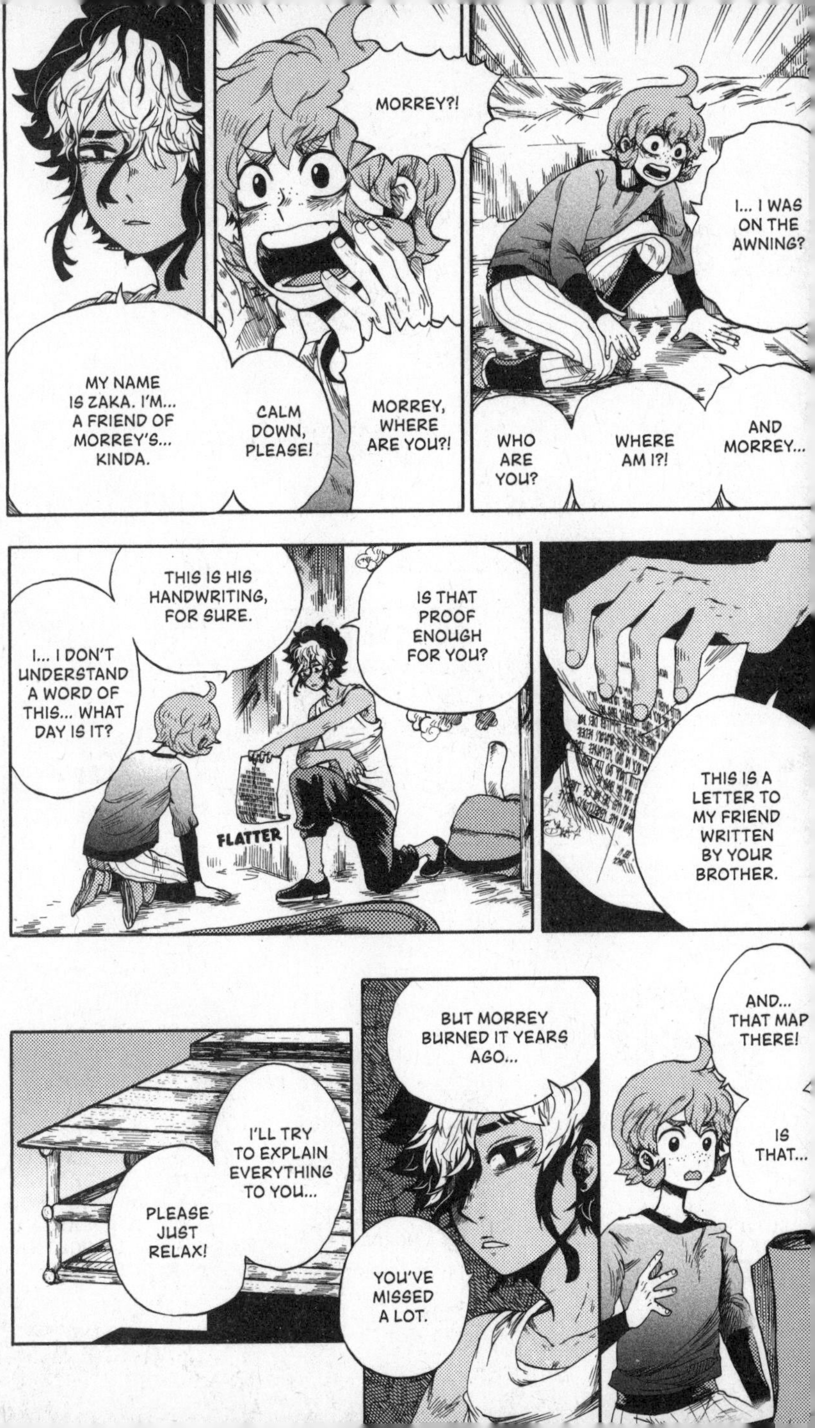
I... I WAS ON THE AWNING?
AND MORREY...
WHERE AM I?!
WHO ARE YOU?
MORREY?!
MORREY, WHERE ARE YOU?!
CALM DOWN, PLEASE!
MY NAME IS ZAKA. I'M... A FRIEND OF MORREY'S... KINDA.
THIS IS A LETTER TO MY FRIEND WRITTEN BY YOUR BROTHER.
IS THAT PROOF ENOUGH FOR YOU?
THIS IS HIS HANDWRITING, FOR SURE.
I... I DON'T UNDERSTAND A WORD OF THIS... WHAT DAY IS IT?
FLATTER
AND... THAT MAP THERE!
IS THAT...
BUT MORREY BURNED IT YEARS AGO...
YOU'VE MISSED A LOT.
I'LL TRY TO EXPLAIN EVERYTHING TO YOU...
PLEASE JUST RELAX!

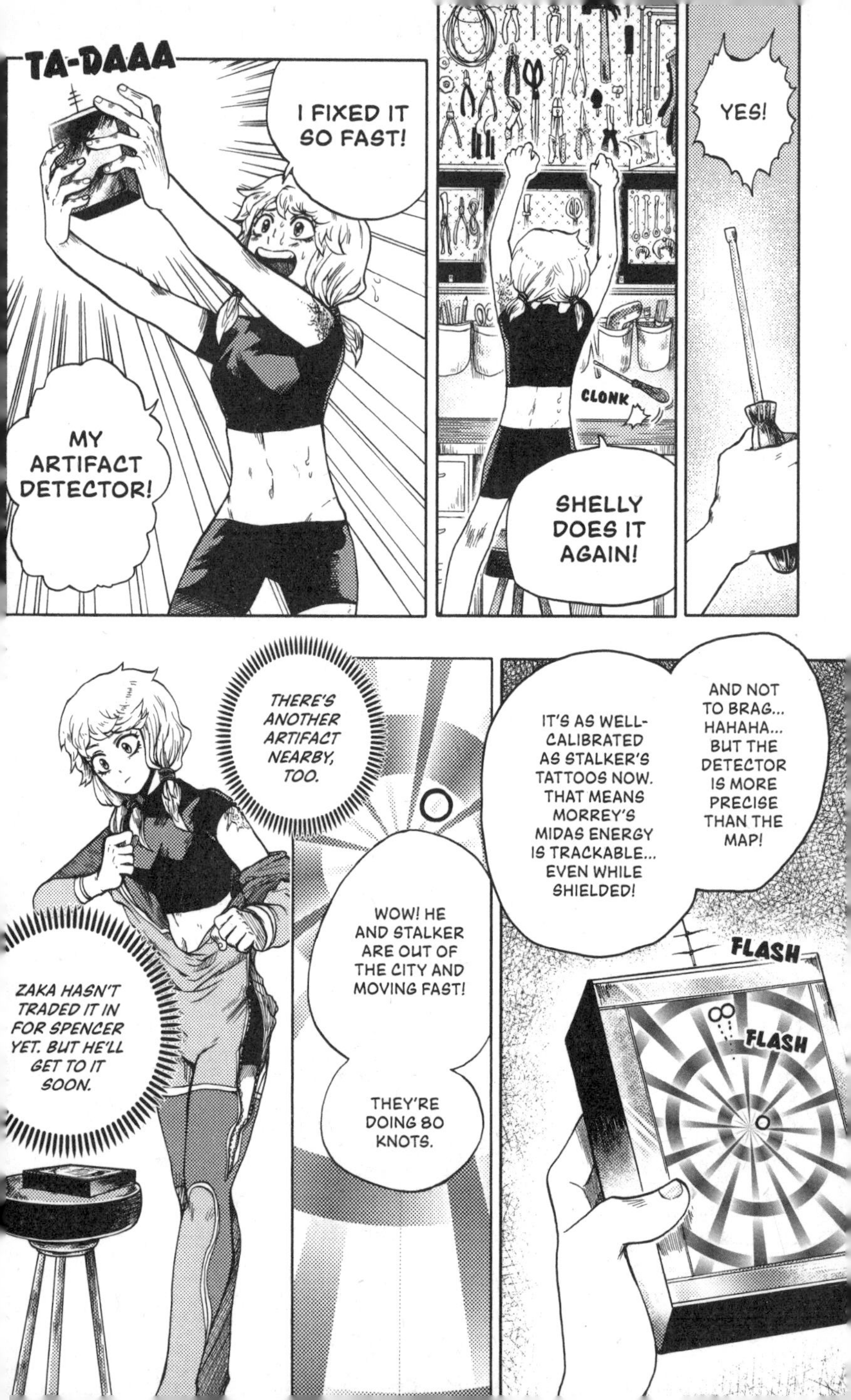
YES!
CLONK
SHELLY DOES IT AGAIN!
TA-DAAA
I FIXED IT SO FAST!
MY ARTIFACT DETECTOR!
AND NOT TO BRAG... HAHAHA... BUT THE DETECTOR IS MORE PRECISE THAN THE MAP!
IT'S AS WELL-CALIBRATED AS STALKER'S TATTOOS NOW. THAT MEANS MORREY'S MIDAS ENERGY IS TRACKABLE... EVEN WHILE SHIELDED!
FLASH
FLASH
THERE'S ANOTHER ARTIFACT NEARBY, TOO.
WOW! HE AND STALKER ARE OUT OF THE CITY AND MOVING FAST!
THEY'RE DOING 80 KNOTS.
ZAKA HASN'T TRADED IT IN FOR SPENCER YET. BUT HE'LL GET TO IT SOON.

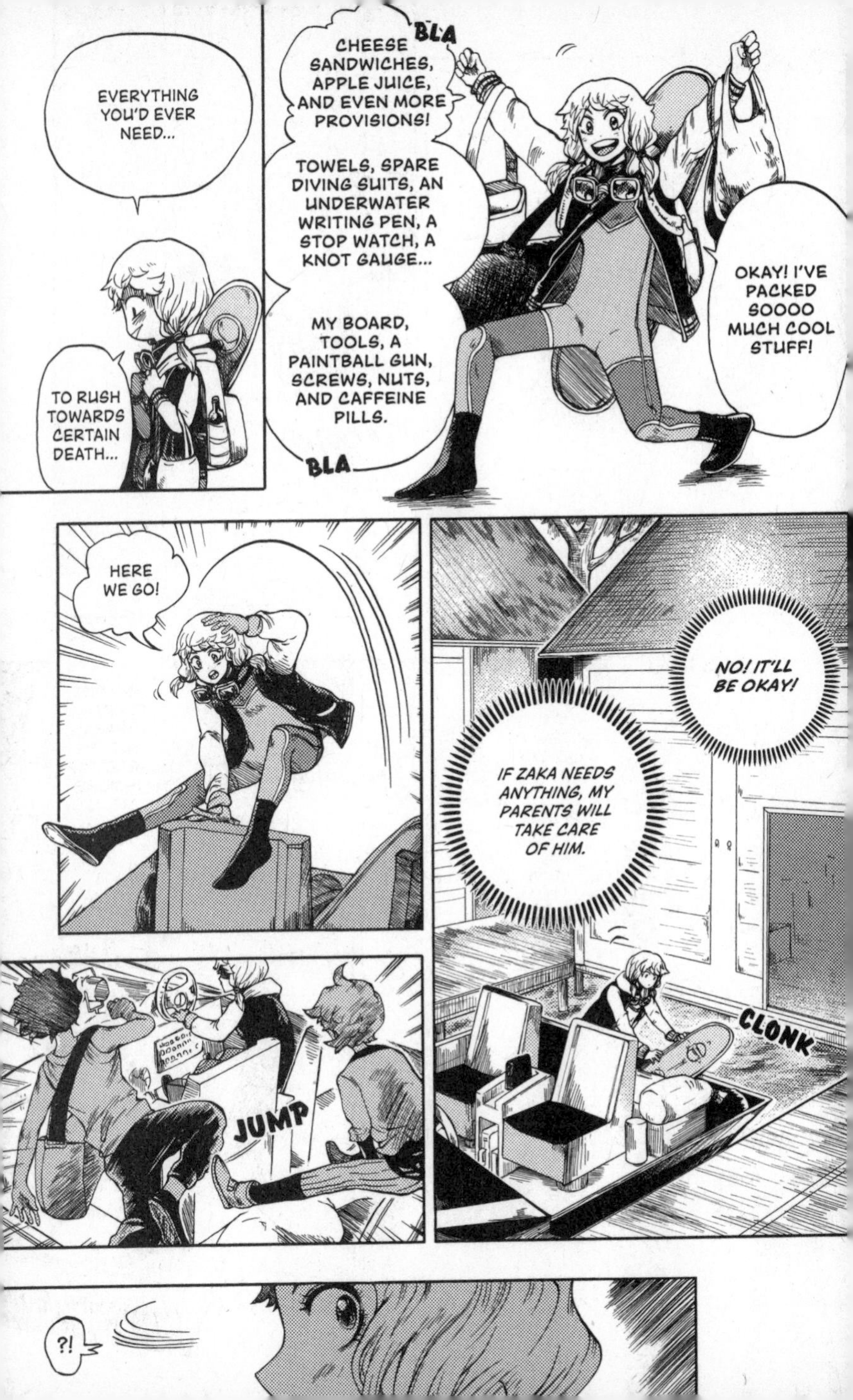
OKAY! I'VE PACKED SOOOO MUCH COOL STUFF!
BLA
CHEESE SANDWICHES, APPLE JUICE, AND EVEN MORE PROVISIONS!
TOWELS, SPARE DIVING SUITS, AN UNDERWATER WRITING PEN, A STOP WATCH, A KNOT GAUGE...
MY BOARD, TOOLS, A PAINTBALL GUN, SCREWS, NUTS, AND CAFFEINE PILLS.
BLA
EVERYTHING YOU'D EVER NEED...
TO RUSH TOWARDS CERTAIN DEATH...
NO! IT'LL BE OKAY!
IF ZAKA NEEDS ANYTHING, MY PARENTS WILL TAKE CARE OF HIM.
CLONK
HERE WE GO!
JUMP
?!

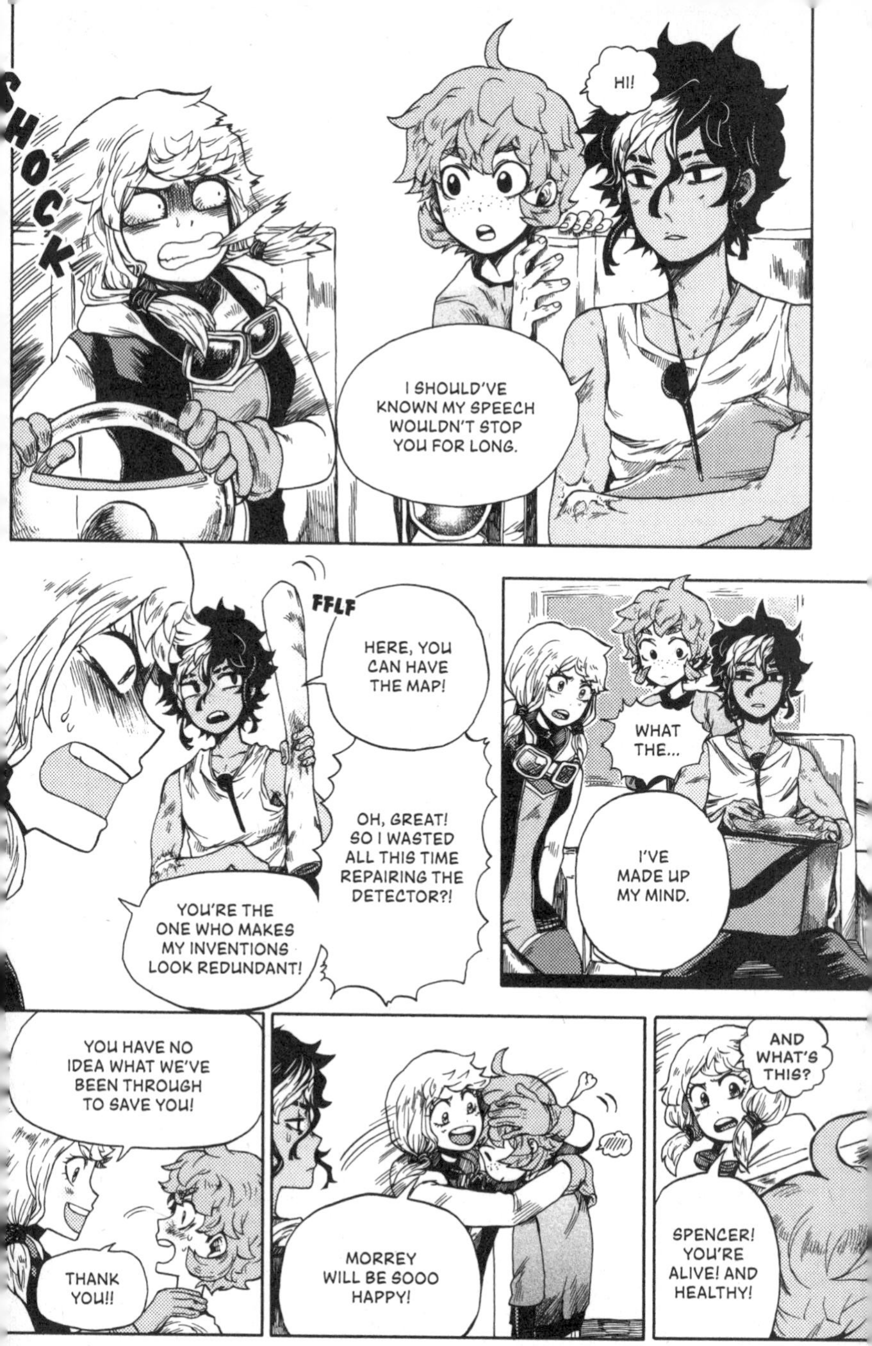
HI!
I SHOULD'VE KNOWN MY SPEECH WOULDN'T STOP YOU FOR LONG.
SHOCK
WHAT THE...
I'VE MADE UP MY MIND.
FFLF
HERE, YOU CAN HAVE THE MAP!
OH, GREAT! SO I WASTED ALL THIS TIME REPAIRING THE DETECTOR?!
YOU'RE THE ONE WHO MAKES MY INVENTIONS LOOK REDUNDANT!
AND WHAT'S THIS?
SPENCER! YOU'RE ALIVE! AND HEALTHY!
MORREY WILL BE SOOO HAPPY!
YOU HAVE NO IDEA WHAT WE'VE BEEN THROUGH TO SAVE YOU!
THANK YOU!!

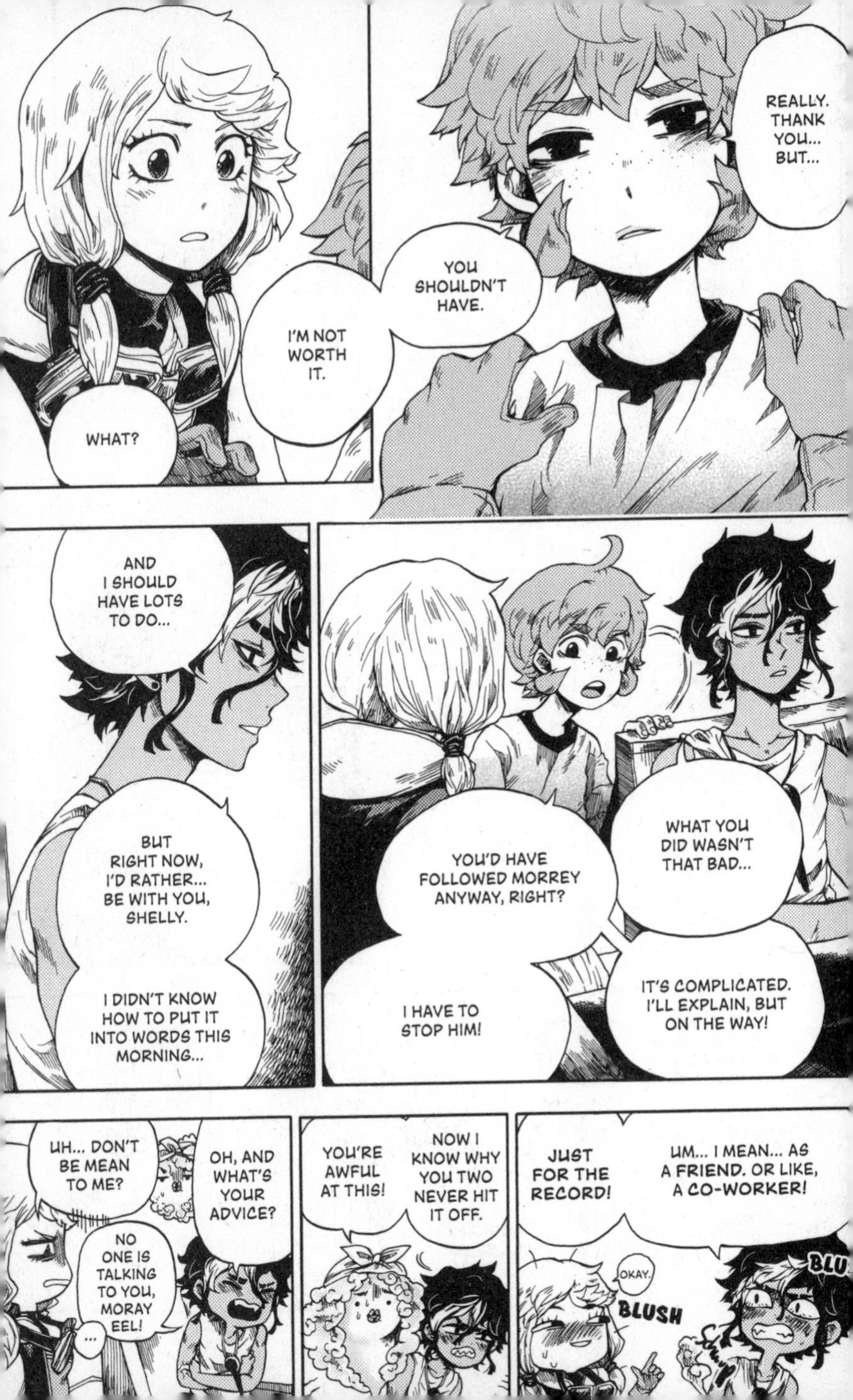
REALLY. THANK YOU... BUT...
YOU SHOULDN'T HAVE.
I'M NOT WORTH IT.
WHAT?
WHAT YOU DID WASN'T THAT BAD...
YOU'D HAVE FOLLOWED MORREY ANYWAY, RIGHT?
IT'S COMPLICATED. I'LL EXPLAIN, BUT ON THE WAY!
I HAVE TO STOP HIM!
AND I SHOULD HAVE LOTS TO DO...
BUT RIGHT NOW, I'D RATHER... BE WITH YOU, SHELLY.
I DIDN'T KNOW HOW TO PUT IT INTO WORDS THIS MORNING...
UM... I MEAN... AS A FRIEND. OR LIKE, A CO-WORKER!
JUST FOR THE RECORD!
BLU
OKAY.
BLUSH
NOW I KNOW WHY YOU TWO NEVER HIT IT OFF.
YOU'RE AWFUL AT THIS!
OH, AND WHAT'S YOUR ADVICE?
UH... DON'T BE MEAN TO ME?
NO ONE IS TALKING TO YOU, MORAY EEL!
...

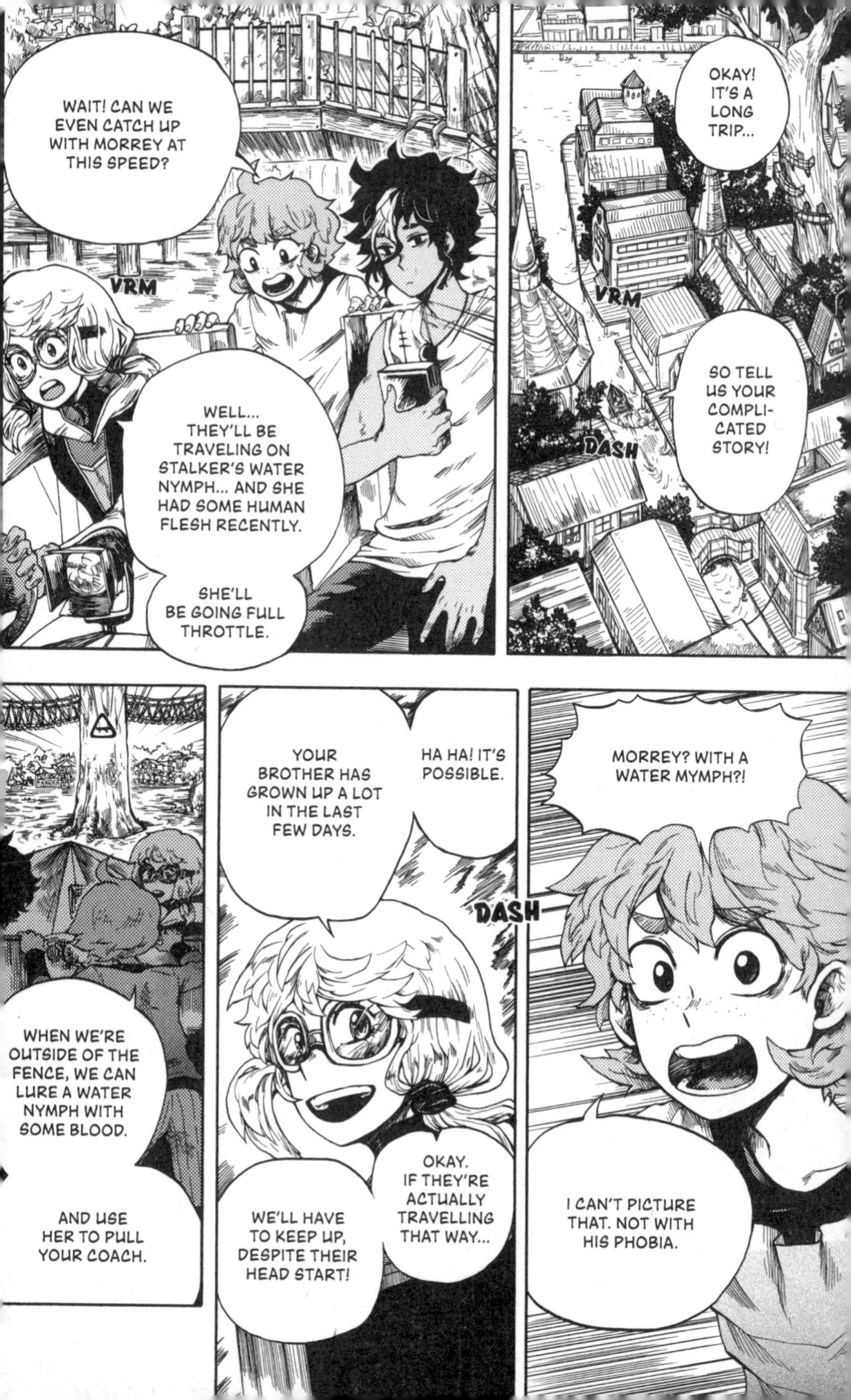
OKAY! IT'S A LONG TRIP...
VRM
SO TELL US YOUR COMPLICATED STORY!
DASH
WAIT! CAN WE EVEN CATCH UP WITH MORREY AT THIS SPEED?
VRM
WELL... THEY'LL BE TRAVELING ON STALKER'S WATER NYMPH... AND SHE HAD SOME HUMAN FLESH RECENTLY.
SHE'LL BE GOING FULL THROTTLE.
MORREY? WITH A WATER MYMPH?!
DASH
I CAN'T PICTURE THAT. NOT WITH HIS PHOBIA.
HA HA! IT'S POSSIBLE.
YOUR BROTHER HAS GROWN UP A LOT IN THE LAST FEW DAYS.
OKAY. IF THEY'RE ACTUALLY TRAVELLING THAT WAY...
WE'LL HAVE TO KEEP UP, DESPITE THEIR HEAD START!
WHEN WE'RE OUTSIDE OF THE FENCE, WE CAN LURE A WATER NYMPH WITH SOME BLOOD.
AND USE HER TO PULL YOUR COACH.

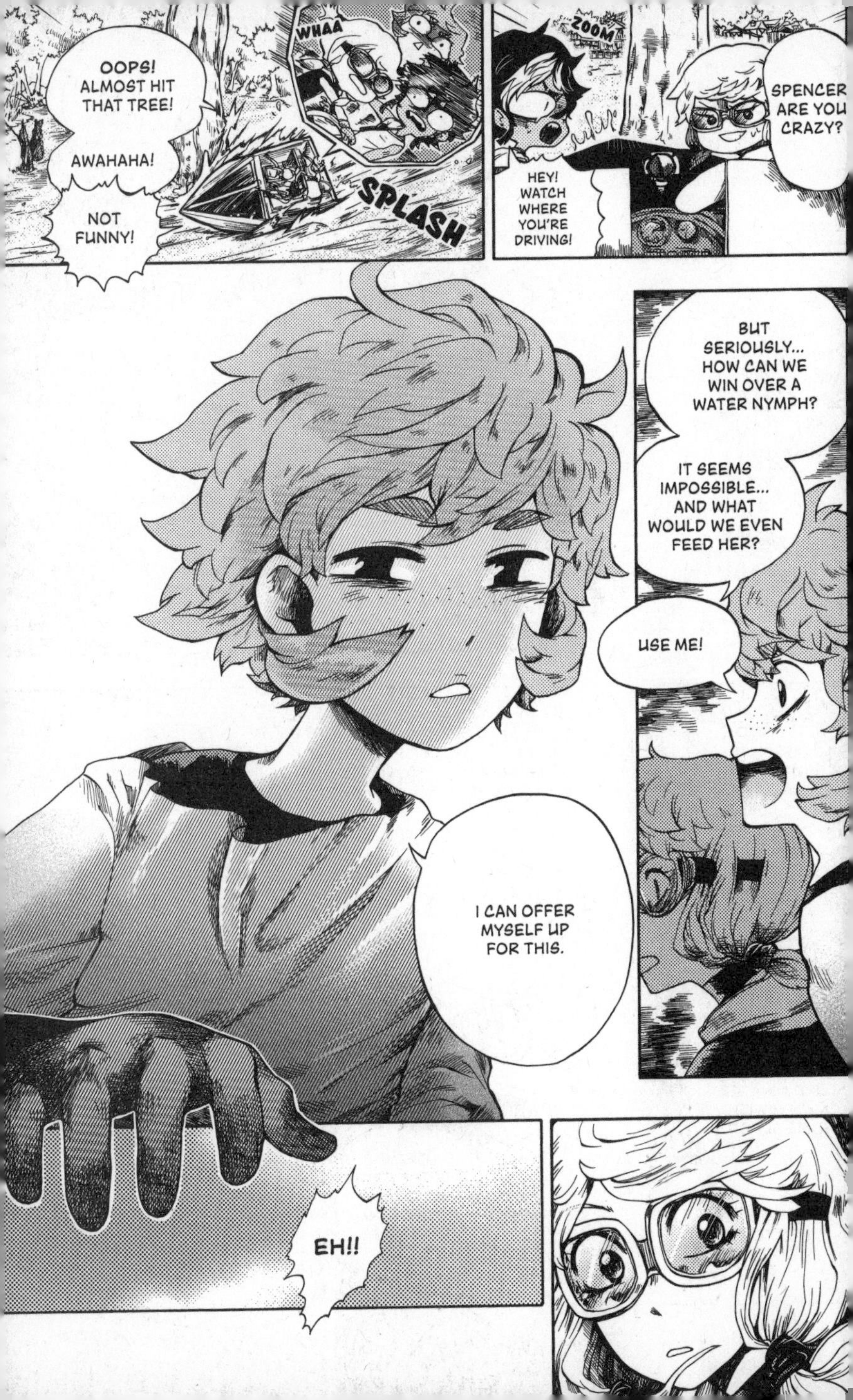
ZOOM
SPENCER ARE YOU CRAZY?
HEY! WATCH WHERE YOU'RE DRIVING!
WHAA
OOPS! ALMOST HIT THAT TREE!
AWAHAHA!
SPLASH
NOT FUNNY!
BUT SERIOUSLY... HOW CAN WE WIN OVER A WATER NYMPH?
IT SEEMS IMPOSSIBLE... AND WHAT WOULD WE EVEN FEED HER?
USE ME!
I CAN OFFER MYSELF UP FOR THIS.
EH!!

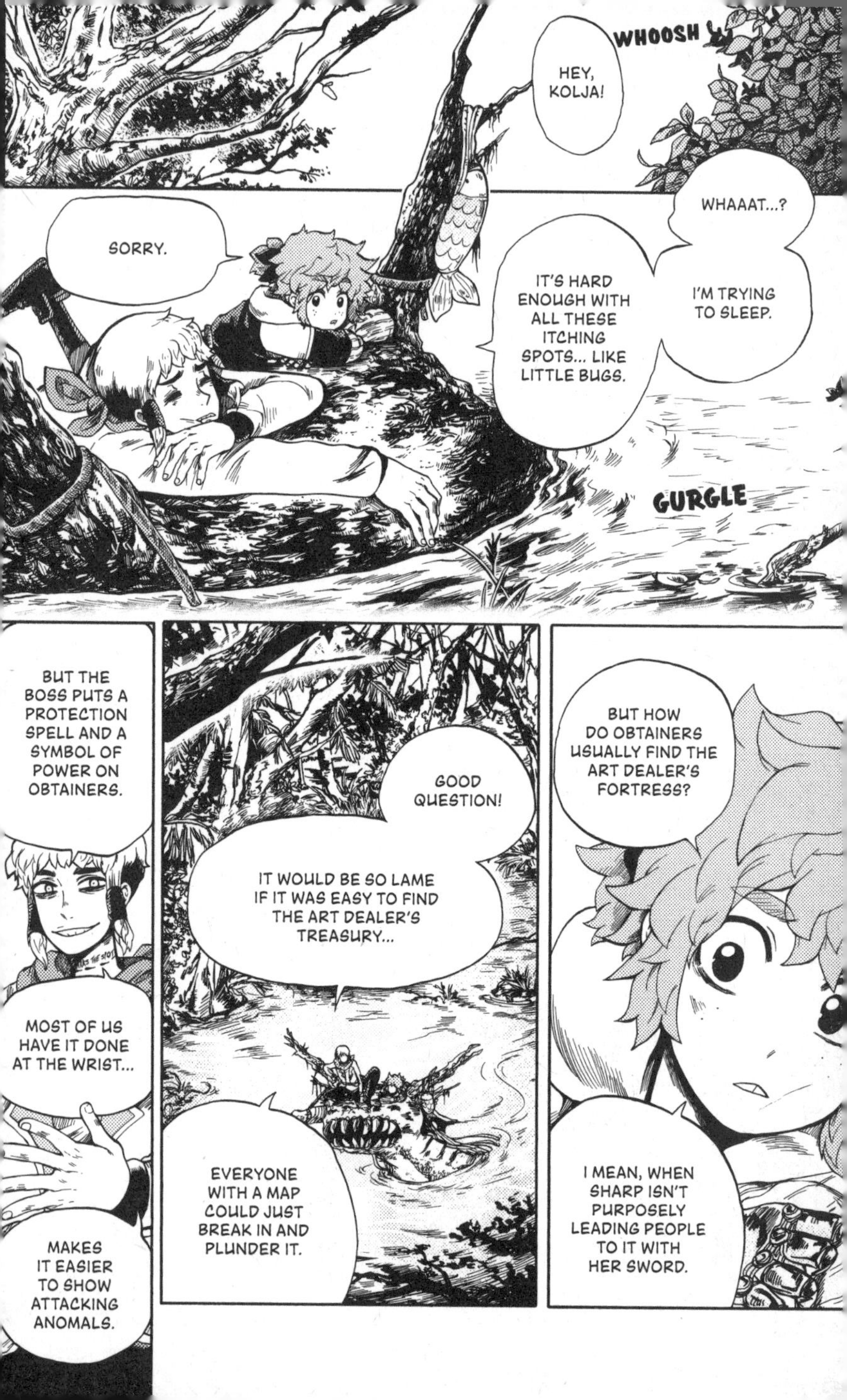
WHOOSH
HEY, KOLJA!
WHAAAT...?
I'M TRYING TO SLEEP.
IT'S HARD ENOUGH WITH ALL THESE ITCHING SPOTS... LIKE LITTLE BUGS.
SORRY.
GURGLE
BUT HOW DO OBTAINERS USUALLY FIND THE ART DEALER'S FORTRESS?
I MEAN, WHEN SHARP ISN'T PURPOSELY LEADING PEOPLE TO IT WITH HER SWORD.
GOOD QUESTION!
IT WOULD BE SO LAME IF IT WAS EASY TO FIND THE ART DEALER'S TREASURY...
EVERYONE WITH A MAP COULD JUST BREAK IN AND PLUNDER IT.
BUT THE BOSS PUTS A PROTECTION SPELL AND A SYMBOL OF POWER ON OBTAINERS.
MOST OF US HAVE IT DONE AT THE WRIST...
MAKES IT EASIER TO SHOW ATTACKING ANOMALS.

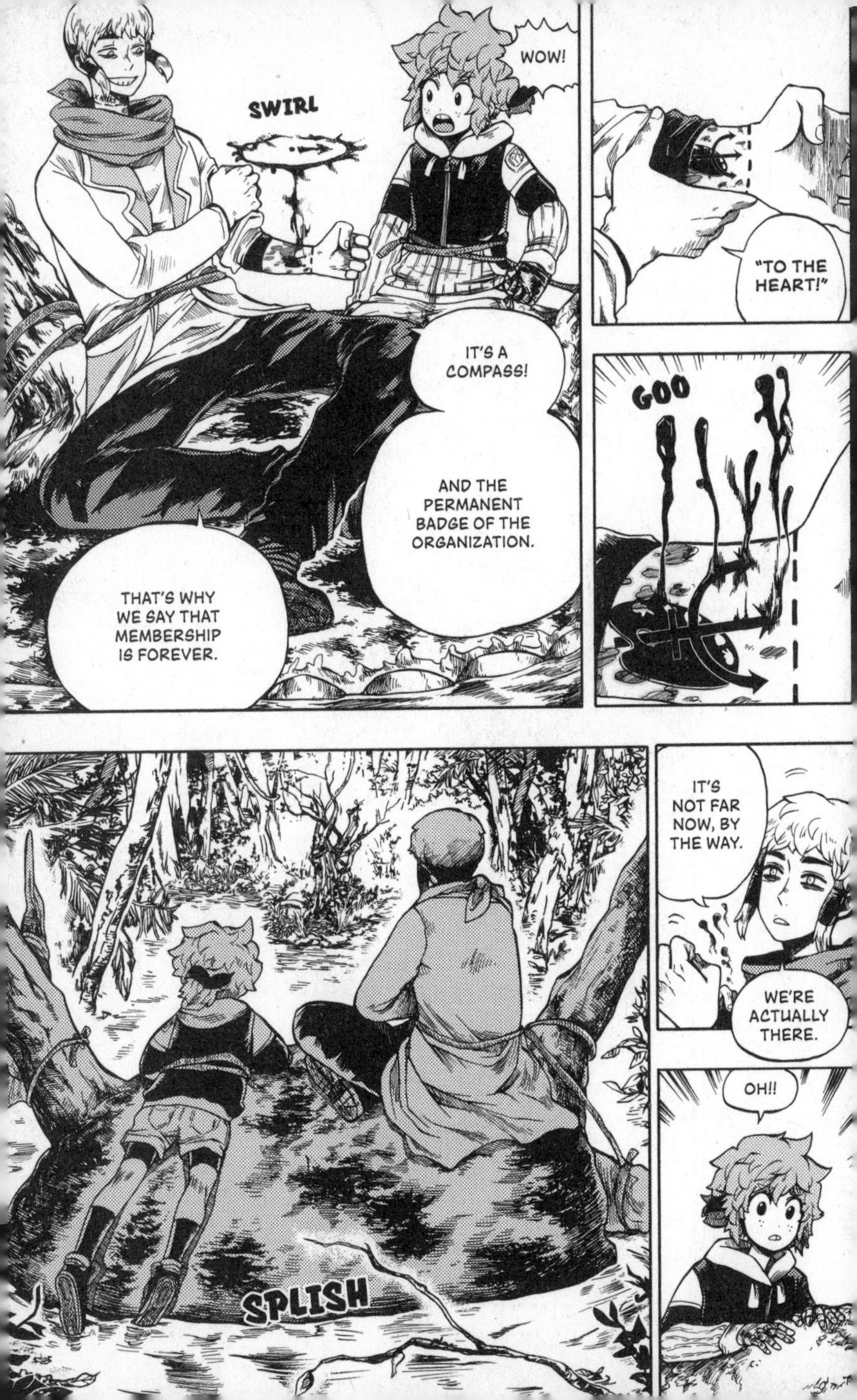
"TO THE HEART!"
GOO
WOW!
SWIRL
IT'S A COMPASS!
AND THE PERMANENT BADGE OF THE ORGANIZATION.
THAT'S WHY WE SAY THAT MEMBERSHIP IS FOREVER.
IT'S NOT FAR NOW, BY THE WAY.
WE'RE ACTUALLY THERE.
OH!!
SPLISH

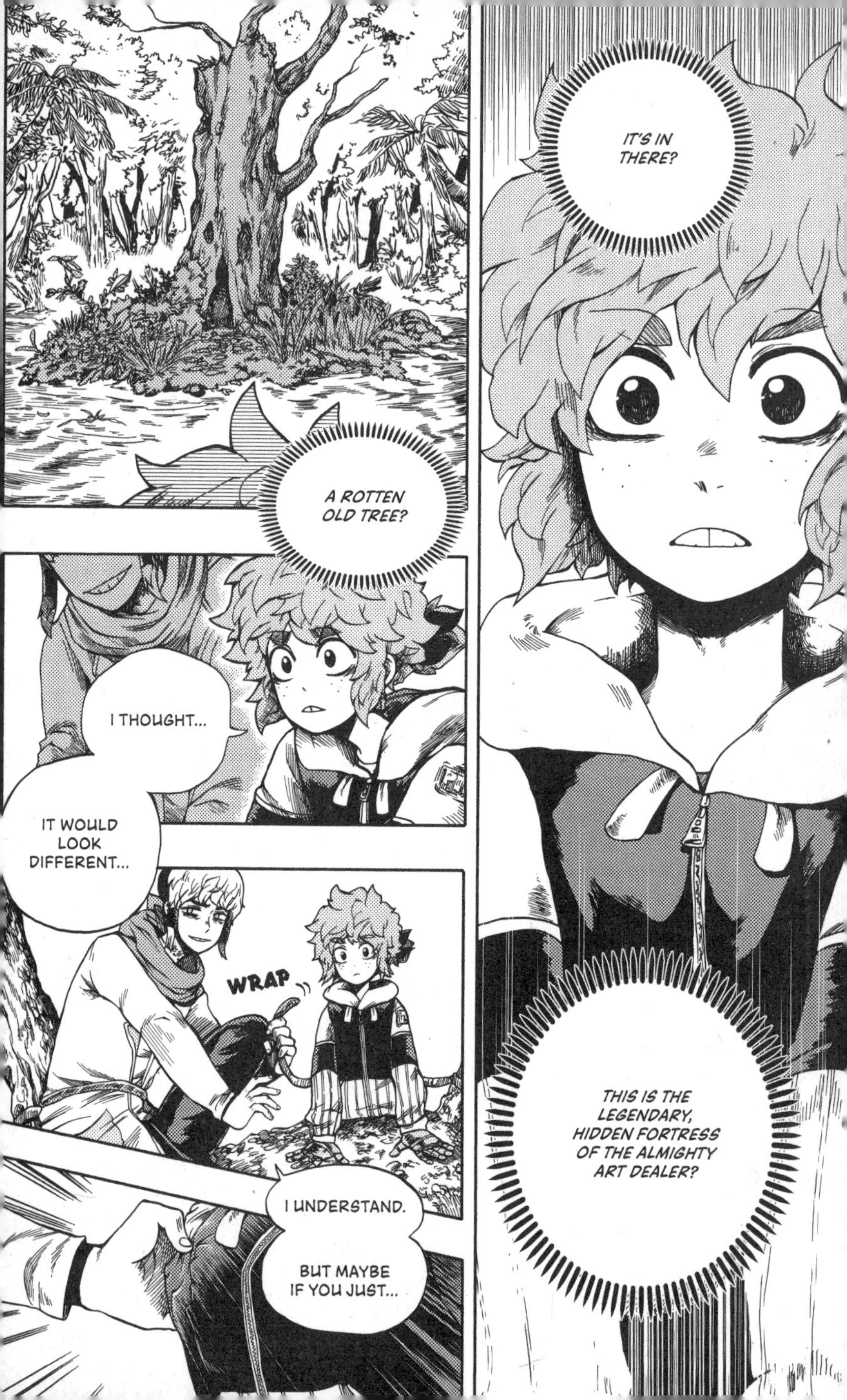
IT'S IN THERE?
THIS IS THE LEGENDARY, HIDDEN FORTRESS OF THE ALMIGHTY ART DEALER?
A ROTTEN OLD TREE?
I THOUGHT...
IT WOULD LOOK DIFFERENT...
WRAP
I UNDERSTAND.
BUT MAYBE IF YOU JUST...

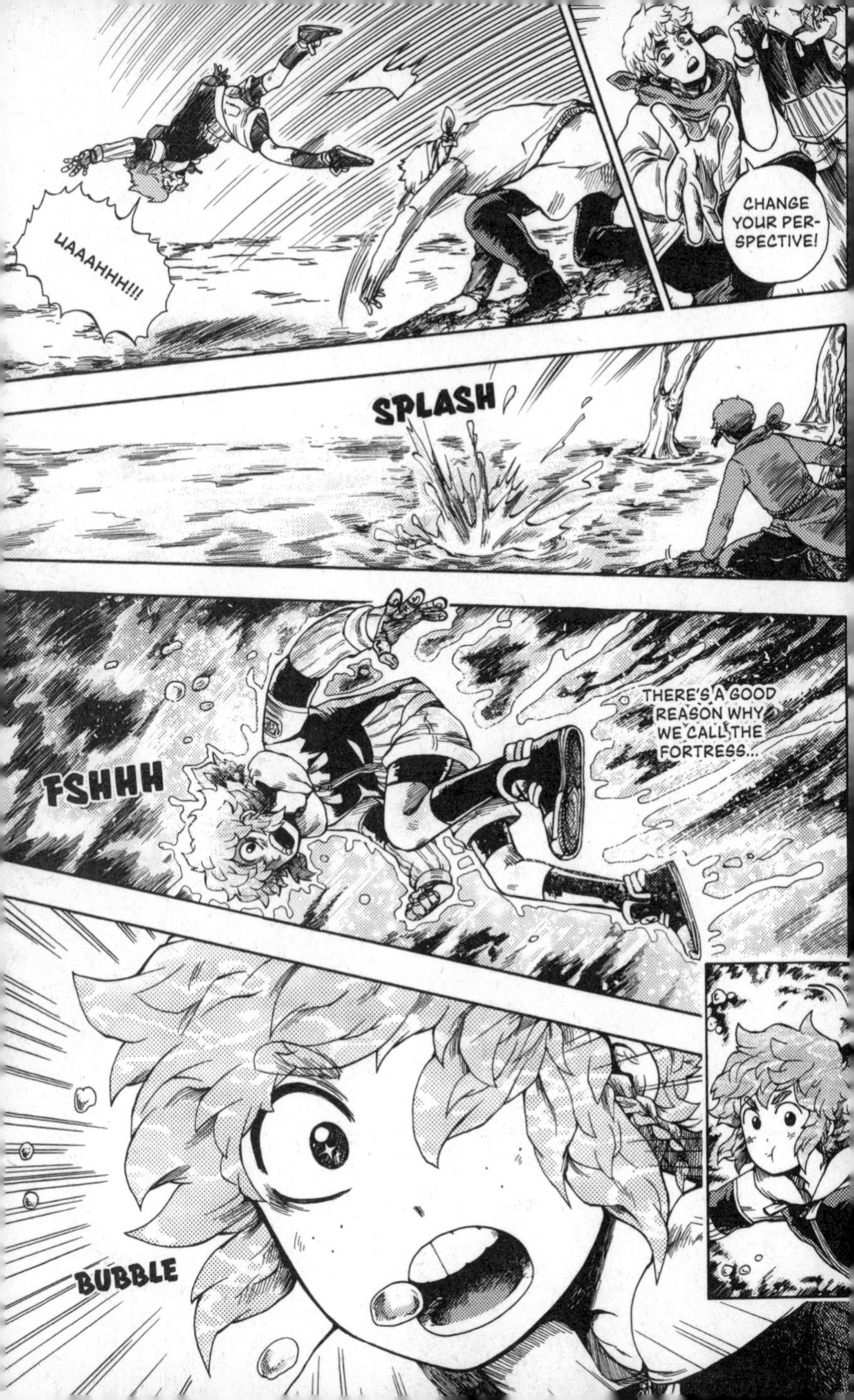

CHANGE YOUR PER-SPECTIVE!
UAAAHHH!!!
SPLASH
THERE'S A GOOD REASON WHY WE CALL THE FORTRESS...
FSHHH
BUBBLE

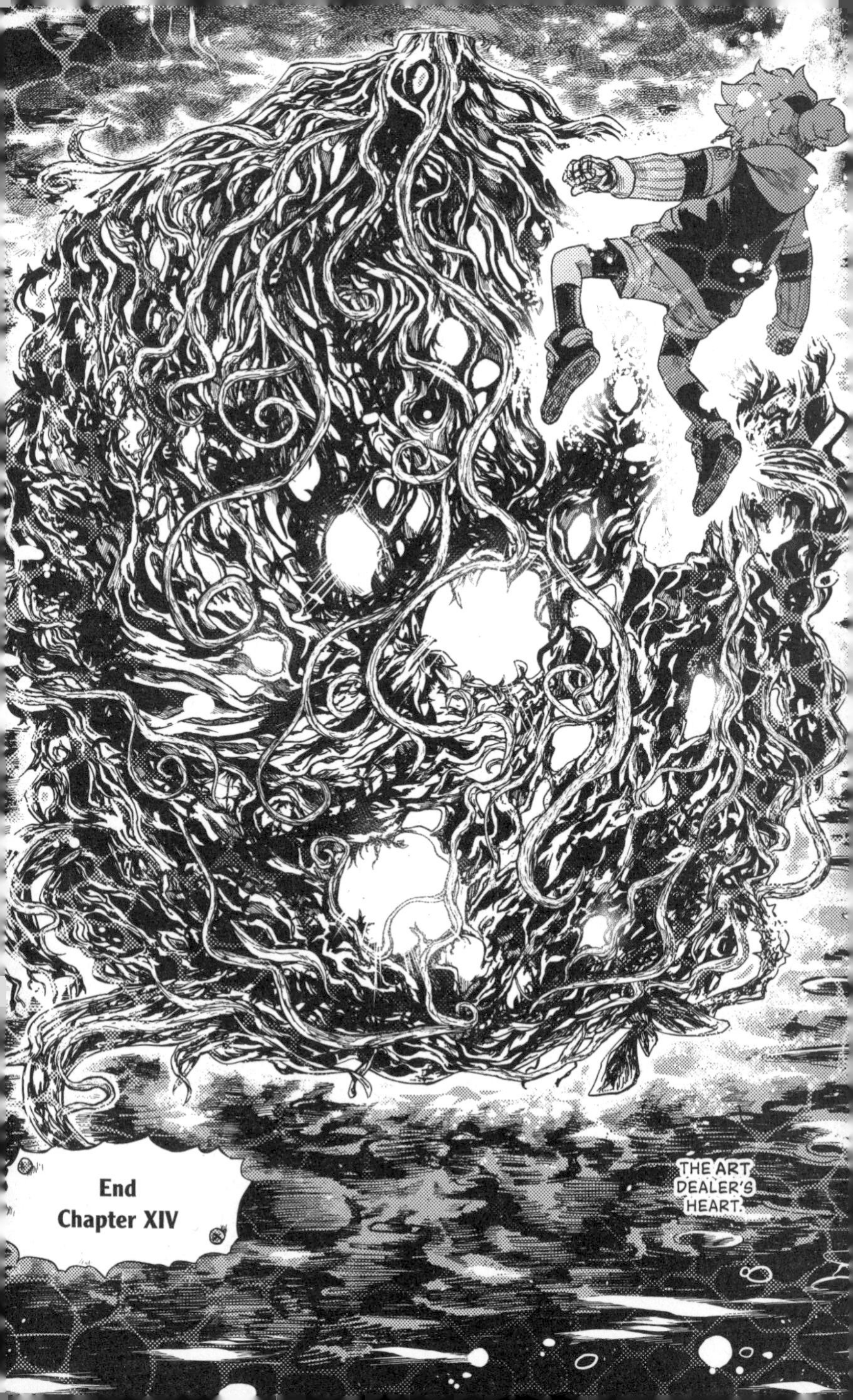
THE ART DEALER'S HEART.
End
Chapter XIV

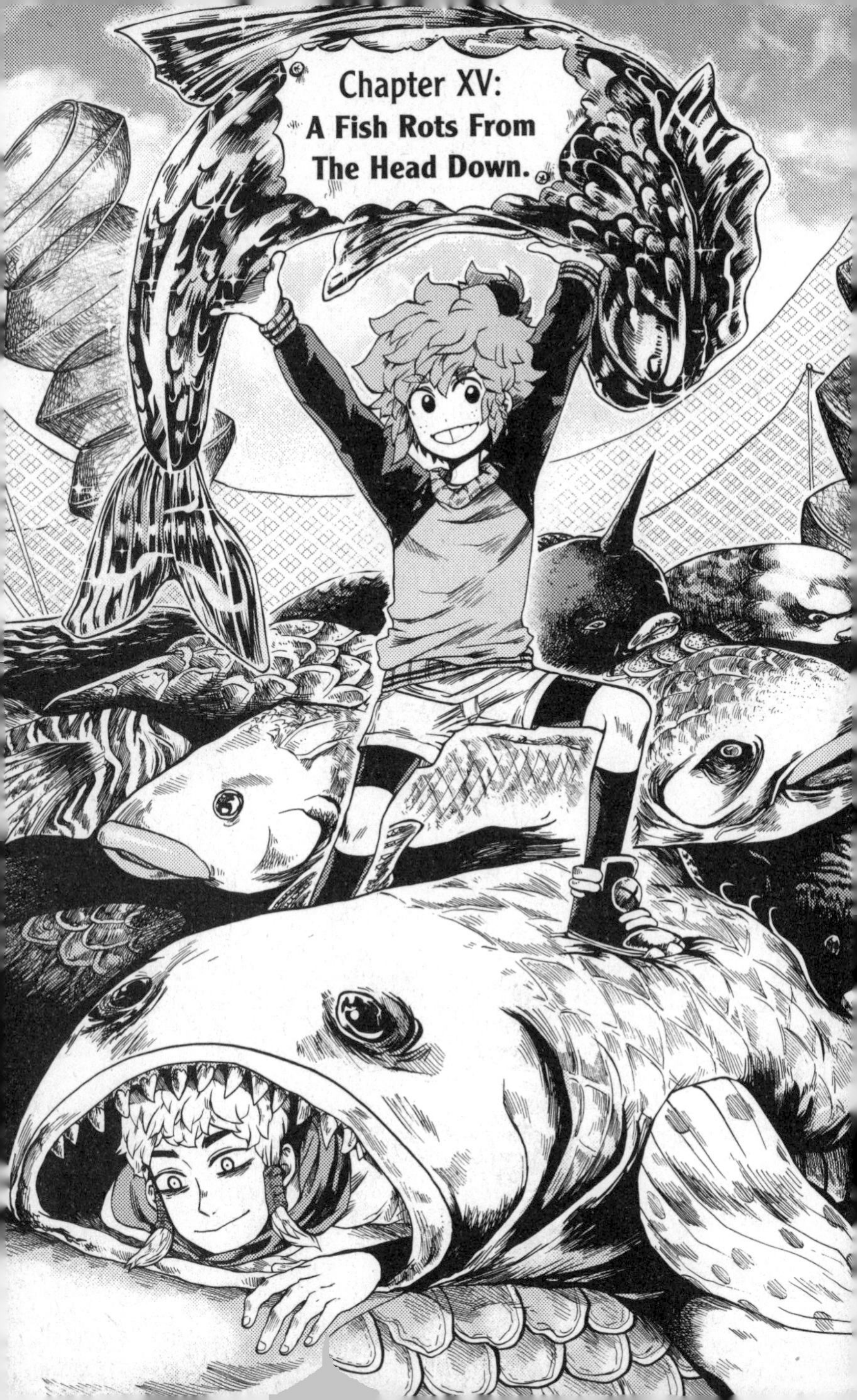
Chapter XV:
A Fish Rots From
The Head Down.

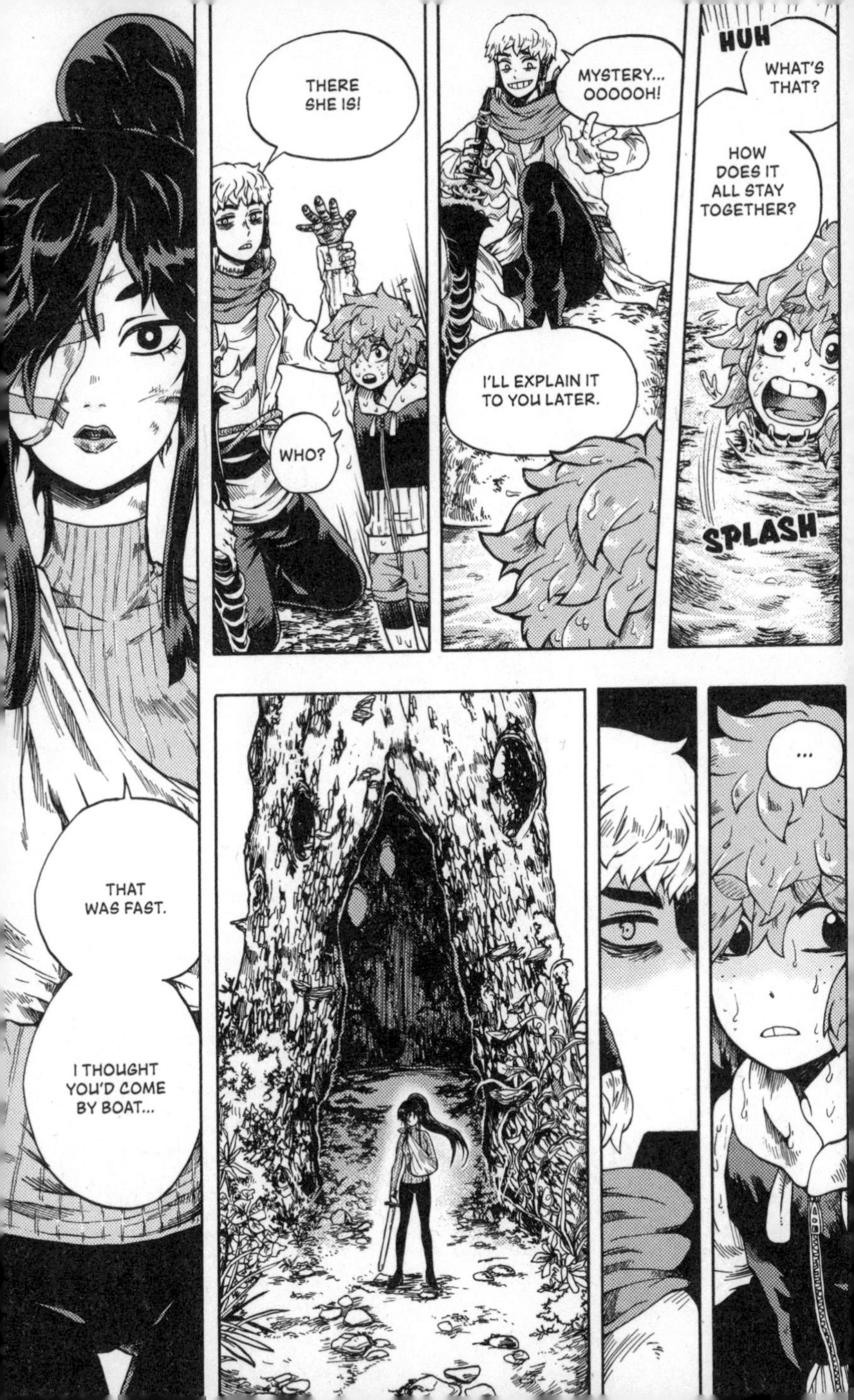
HUH
WHAT'S THAT?
HOW DOES IT ALL STAY TOGETHER?
SPLASH
MYSTERY... OOOOOH!
I'LL EXPLAIN IT TO YOU LATER.
THERE SHE IS!
WHO?
...
THAT WAS FAST.
I THOUGHT YOU'D COME BY BOAT...

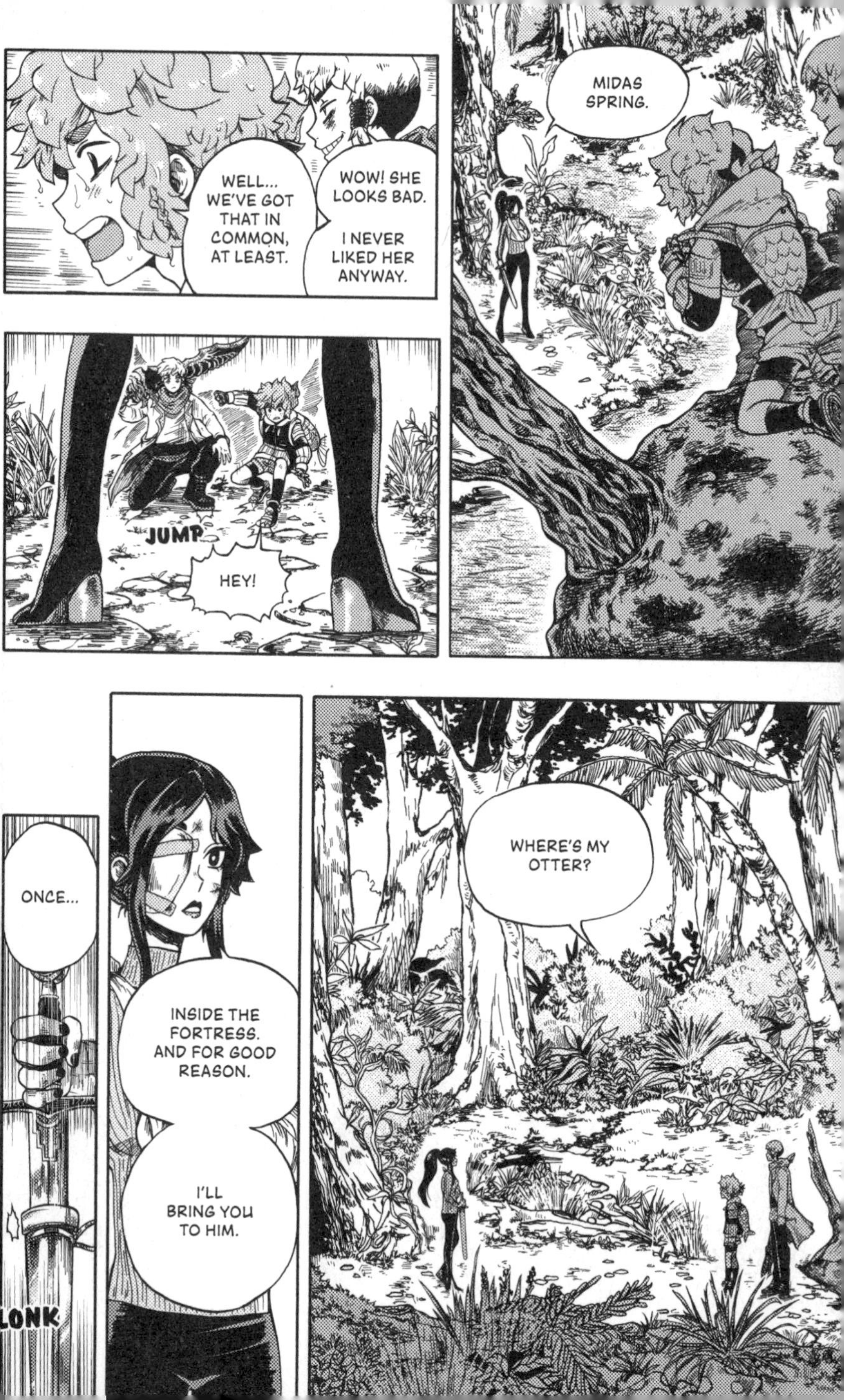
MIDAS SPRING.
WOW! SHE LOOKS BAD.
I NEVER LIKED HER ANYWAY.
WELL... WE'VE GOT THAT IN COMMON, AT LEAST.
JUMP
HEY!
WHERE'S MY OTTER?
INSIDE THE FORTRESS. AND FOR GOOD REASON.
I'LL BRING YOU TO HIM.
ONCE...
LONK

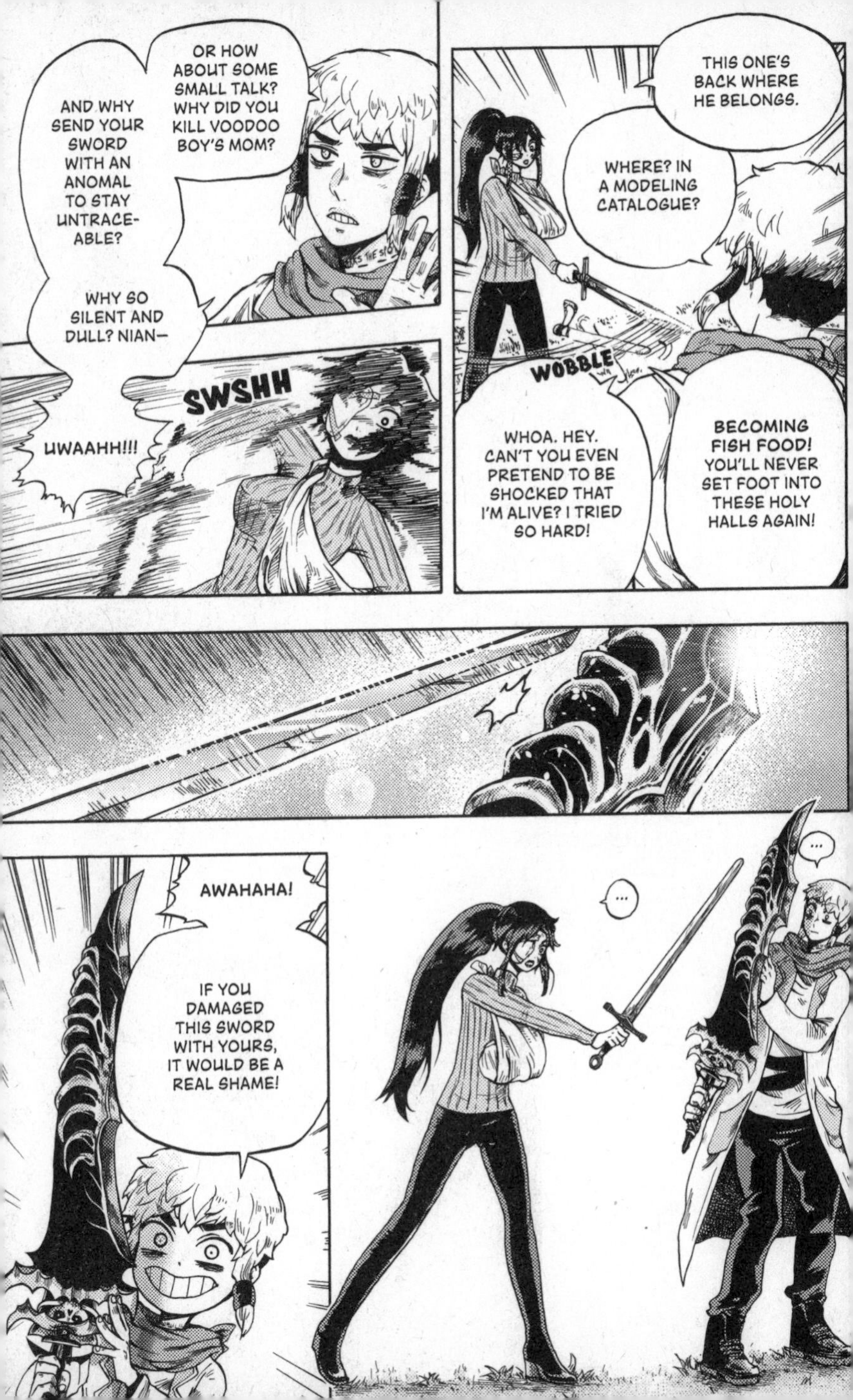
THIS ONE'S BACK WHERE HE BELONGS.
WHERE? IN A MODELING CATALOGUE?
BECOMING FISH FOOD! YOU'LL NEVER SET FOOT INTO THESE HOLY HALLS AGAIN!
WOBBLE
WHOA. HEY. CAN'T YOU EVEN PRETEND TO BE SHOCKED THAT I'M ALIVE? I TRIED SO HARD!
OR HOW ABOUT SOME SMALL TALK? WHY DID YOU KILL VOODOO BOY'S MOM?
AND WHY SEND YOUR SWORD WITH AN ANOMAL TO STAY UNTRACE-ABLE?
WHY SO SILENT AND DULL? NIAN—
SWSHH
UWAAHH!!!
...
...
AWAHAHA!
IF YOU DAMAGED THIS SWORD WITH YOURS, IT WOULD BE A REAL SHAME!

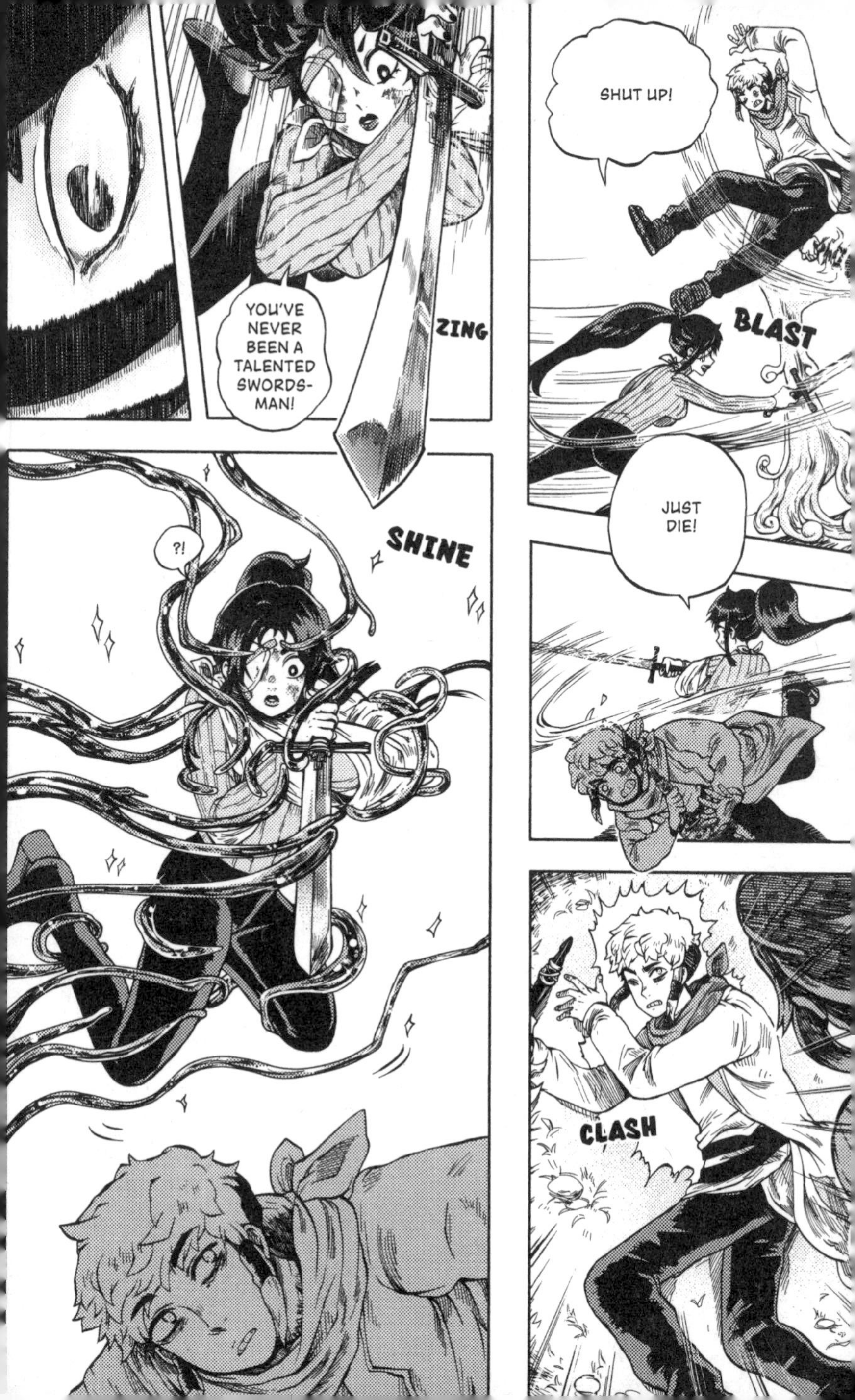
SHUT UP!
BLAST
JUST DIE!
CLASH
YOU'VE NEVER BEEN A TALENTED SWORDS-MAN!
ZING
?!
SHINE

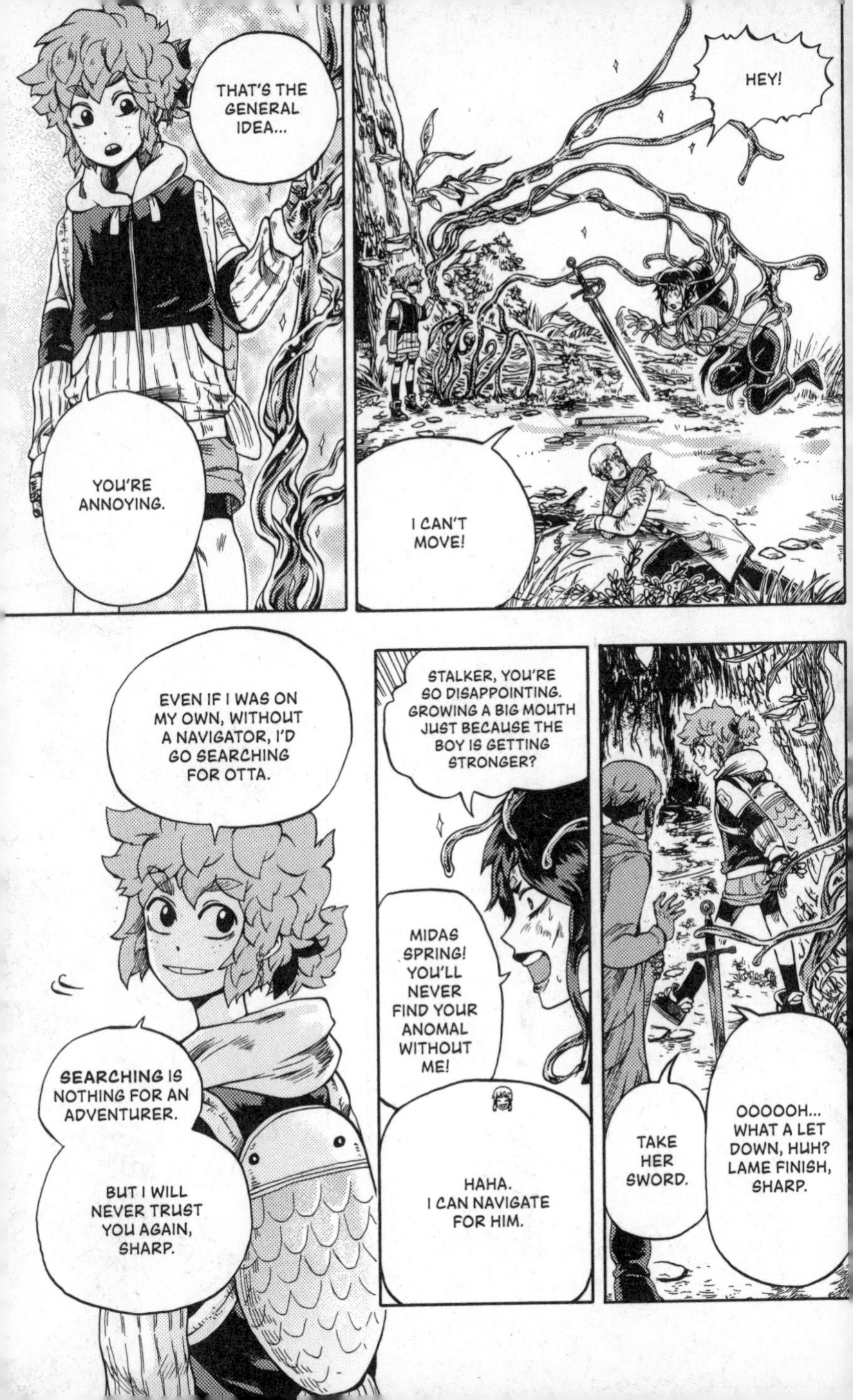
HEY!
I CAN'T MOVE!
THAT'S THE GENERAL IDEA...
YOU'RE ANNOYING.
OOOOOH... WHAT A LET DOWN, HUH? LAME FINISH, SHARP.
TAKE HER SWORD.
STALKER, YOU'RE SO DISAPPOINTING. GROWING A BIG MOUTH JUST BECAUSE THE BOY IS GETTING STRONGER?
MIDAS SPRING! YOU'LL NEVER FIND YOUR ANOMAL WITHOUT ME!
HAHA. I CAN NAVIGATE FOR HIM.
EVEN IF I WAS ON MY OWN, WITHOUT A NAVIGATOR, I'D GO SEARCHING FOR OTTA.
SEARCHING IS NOTHING FOR AN ADVENTURER.
BUT I WILL NEVER TRUST YOU AGAIN, SHARP.

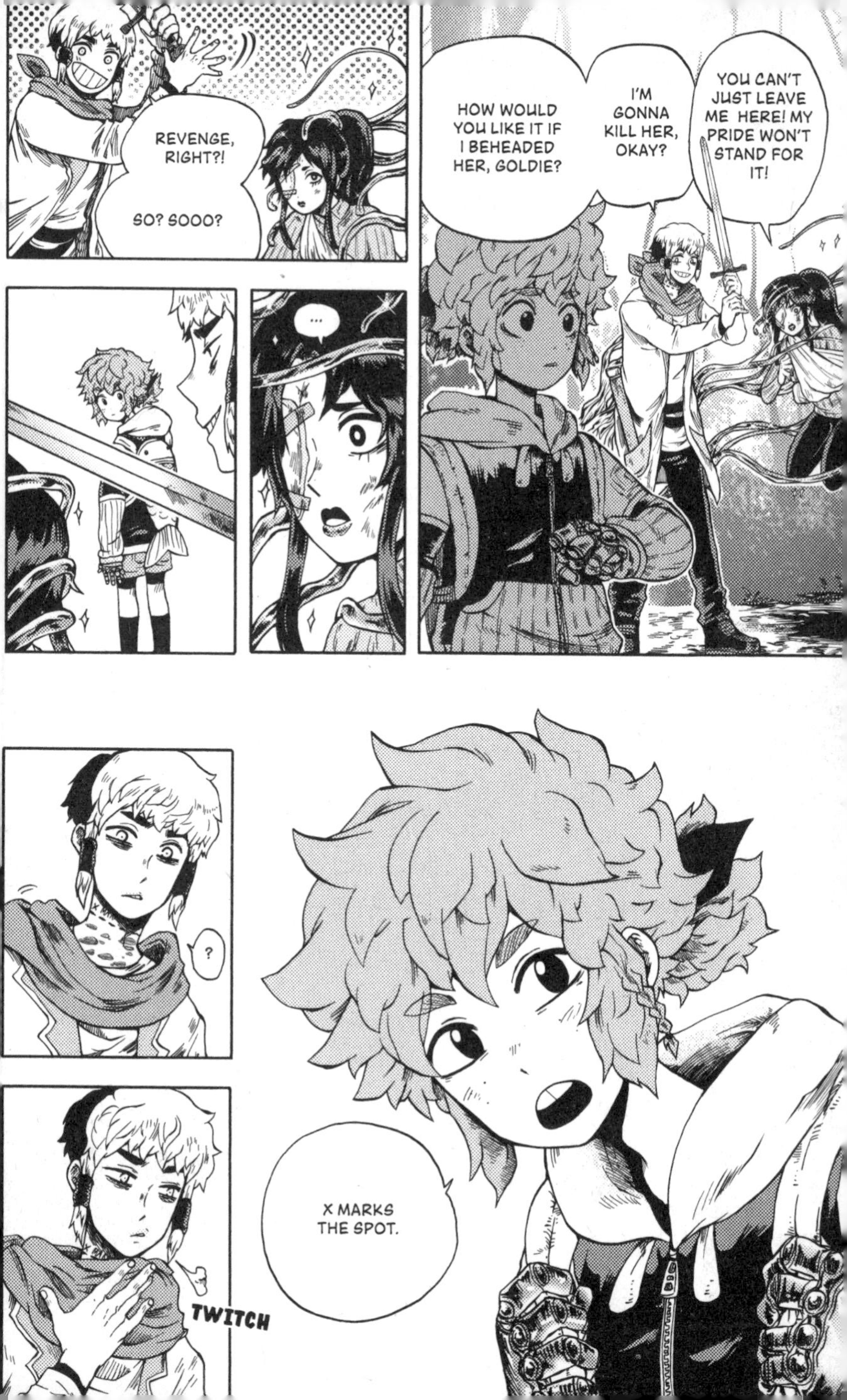
YOU CAN'T JUST LEAVE ME HERE! MY PRIDE WON'T STAND FOR IT!
I'M GONNA KILL HER, OKAY?
HOW WOULD YOU LIKE IT IF I BEHEADED HER, GOLDIE?
REVENGE, RIGHT?!
SO? SOOO?
...
X MARKS THE SPOT.
?
TWITCH

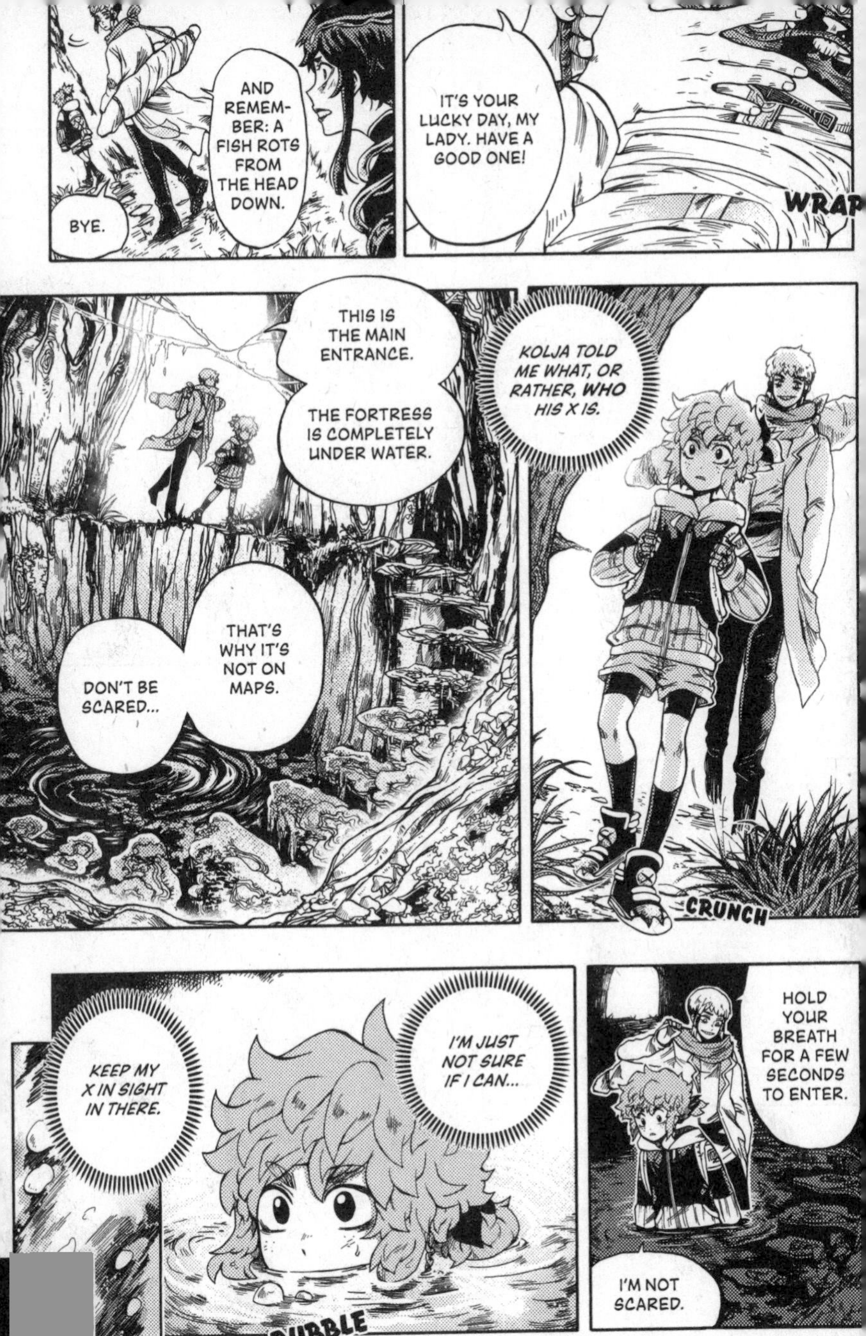
IT'S YOUR LUCKY DAY, MY LADY. HAVE A GOOD ONE!
WRAP
AND REMEMBER: A FISH ROTS FROM THE HEAD DOWN.
BYE.
KOLJA TOLD ME WHAT, OR RATHER, WHO HIS X IS.
CRUNCH
THIS IS THE MAIN ENTRANCE.
THE FORTRESS IS COMPLETELY UNDER WATER.
THAT'S WHY IT'S NOT ON MAPS.
DON'T BE SCARED...
HOLD YOUR BREATH FOR A FEW SECONDS TO ENTER.
I'M NOT SCARED.
I'M JUST NOT SURE IF I CAN...
KEEP MY X IN SIGHT IN THERE.
BUBBLE

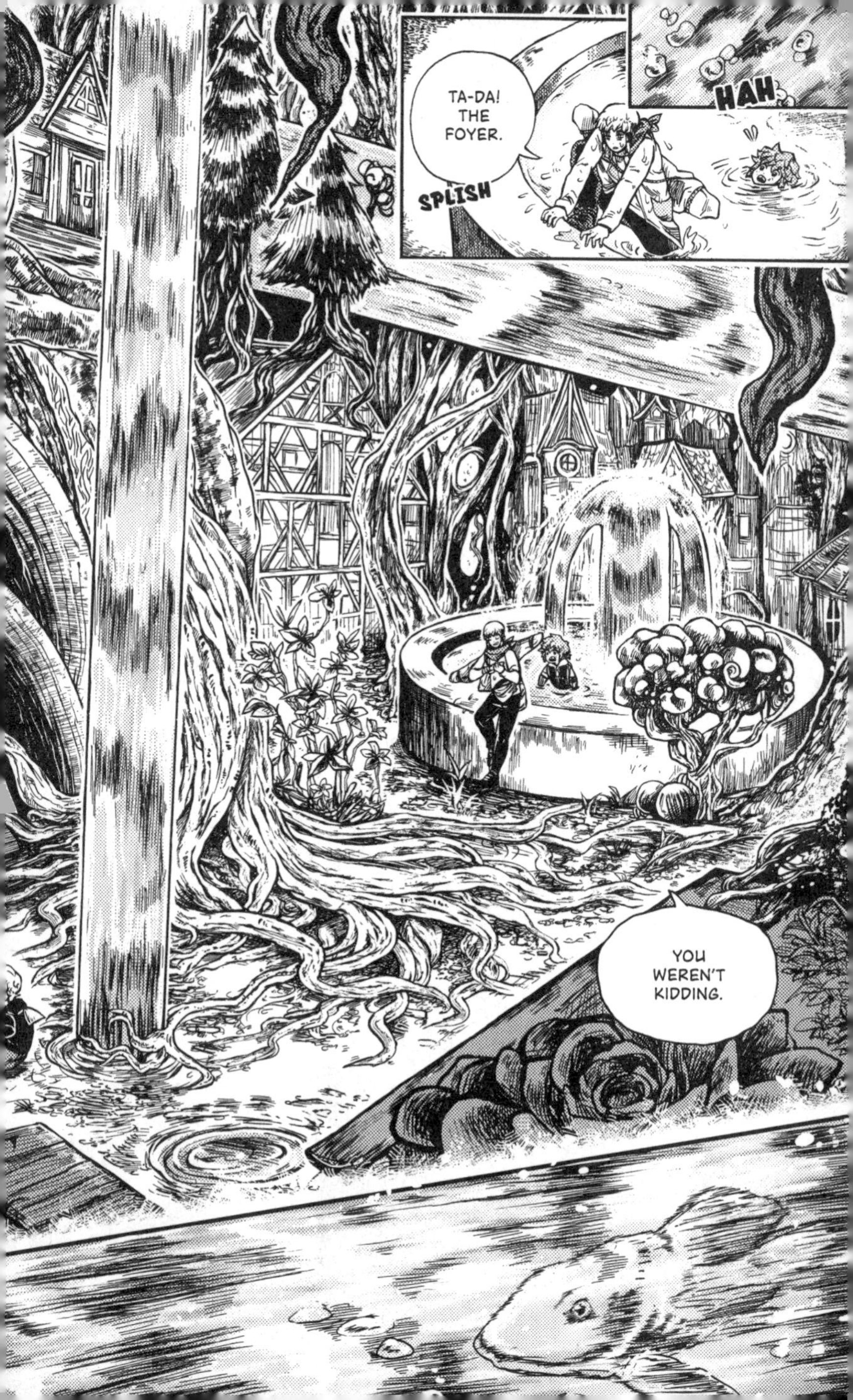
HAH
TA-DA! THE FOYER.
SPLISH
YOU WEREN'T KIDDING.

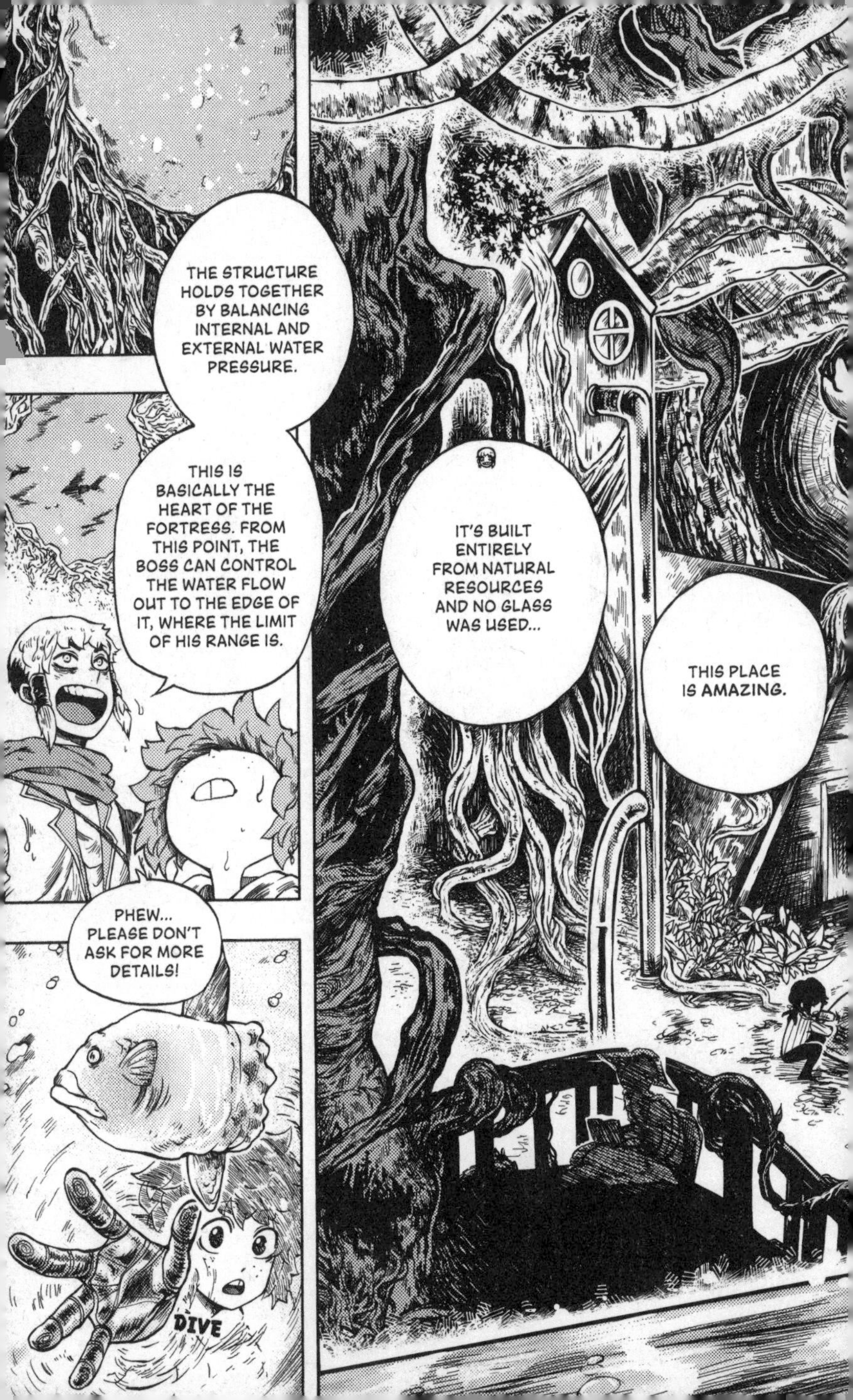
THIS PLACE IS AMAZING.
IT'S BUILT ENTIRELY FROM NATURAL RESOURCES AND NO GLASS WAS USED...
THE STRUCTURE HOLDS TOGETHER BY BALANCING INTERNAL AND EXTERNAL WATER PRESSURE.
THIS IS BASICALLY THE HEART OF THE FORTRESS. FROM THIS POINT, THE BOSS CAN CONTROL THE WATER FLOW OUT TO THE EDGE OF IT, WHERE THE LIMIT OF HIS RANGE IS.
PHEW... PLEASE DON'T ASK FOR MORE DETAILS!
DIVE

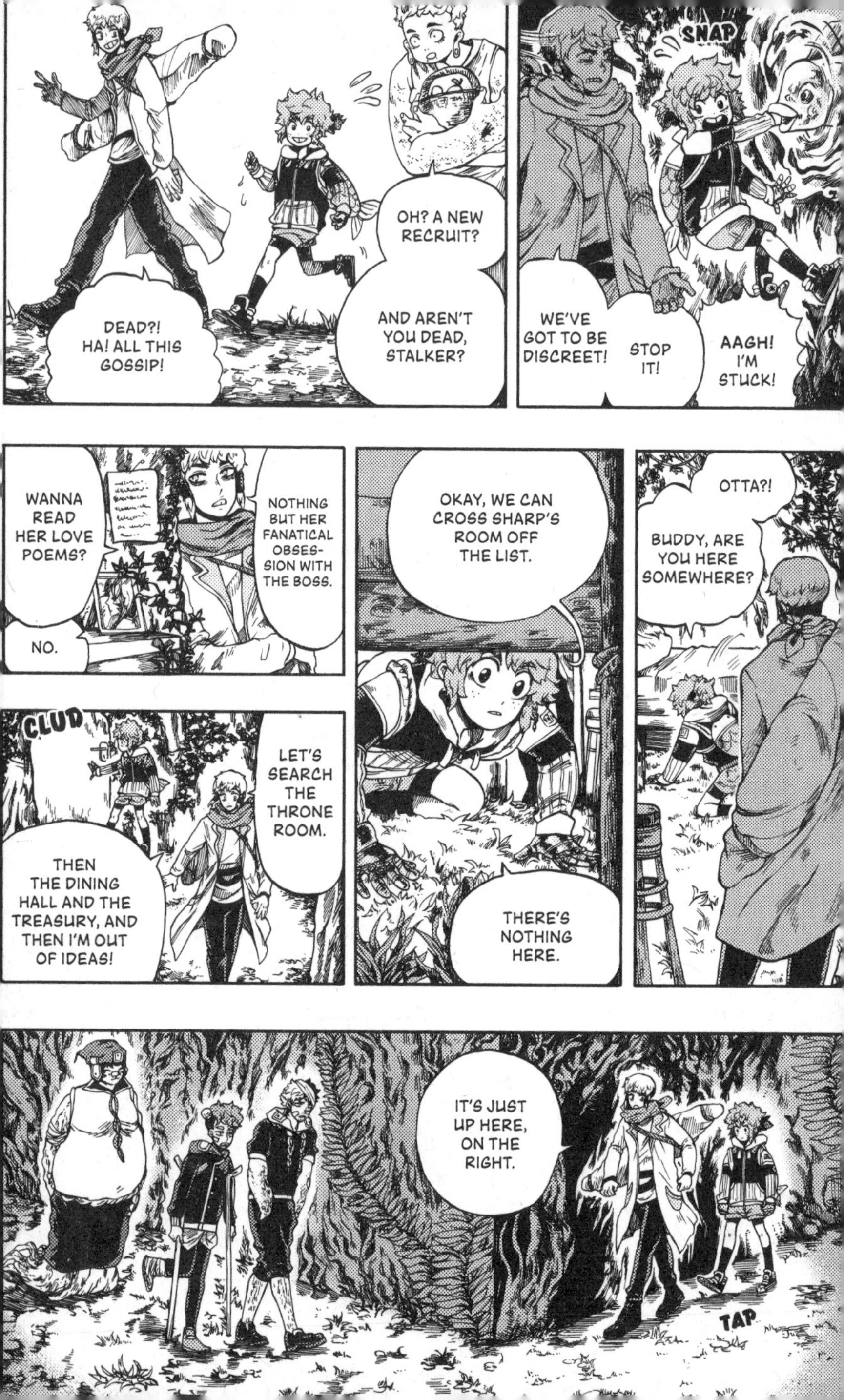
SNAP
AAGH! I'M STUCK!
STOP IT!
WE'VE GOT TO BE DISCREET!
OH? A NEW RECRUIT?
AND AREN'T YOU DEAD, STALKER?
DEAD?! HA! ALL THIS GOSSIP!
OTTA?!
BUDDY, ARE YOU HERE SOMEWHERE?
OKAY, WE CAN CROSS SHARP'S ROOM OFF THE LIST.
THERE'S NOTHING HERE.
NOTHING BUT HER FANATICAL OBSES-SION WITH THE BOSS.
WANNA READ HER LOVE POEMS?
NO.
LET'S SEARCH THE THRONE ROOM.
CLUD
THEN THE DINING HALL AND THE TREASURY, AND THEN I'M OUT OF IDEAS!
IT'S JUST UP HERE, ON THE RIGHT.
TAP

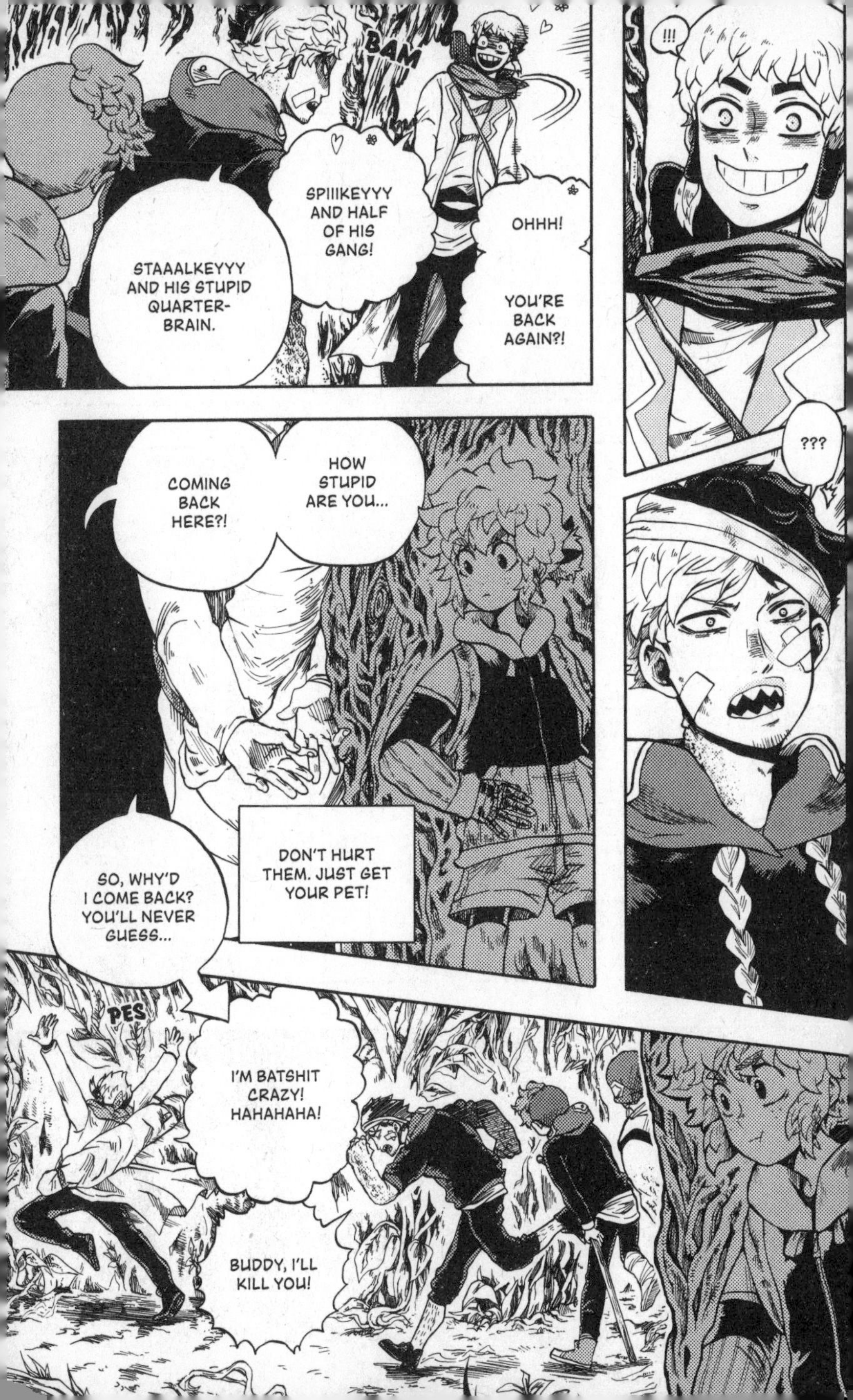
!!!
BAM
SPIIIKEYYY AND HALF OF HIS GANG!
OHHH!
YOU'RE BACK AGAIN?!
STAAALKEYYY AND HIS STUPID QUARTER-BRAIN.
???
HOW STUPID ARE YOU...
COMING BACK HERE?!
DON'T HURT THEM. JUST GET YOUR PET!
SO, WHY'D I COME BACK? YOU'LL NEVER GUESS...
PES
I'M BATSHIT CRAZY! HAHAHAHA!
BUDDY, I'LL KILL YOU!

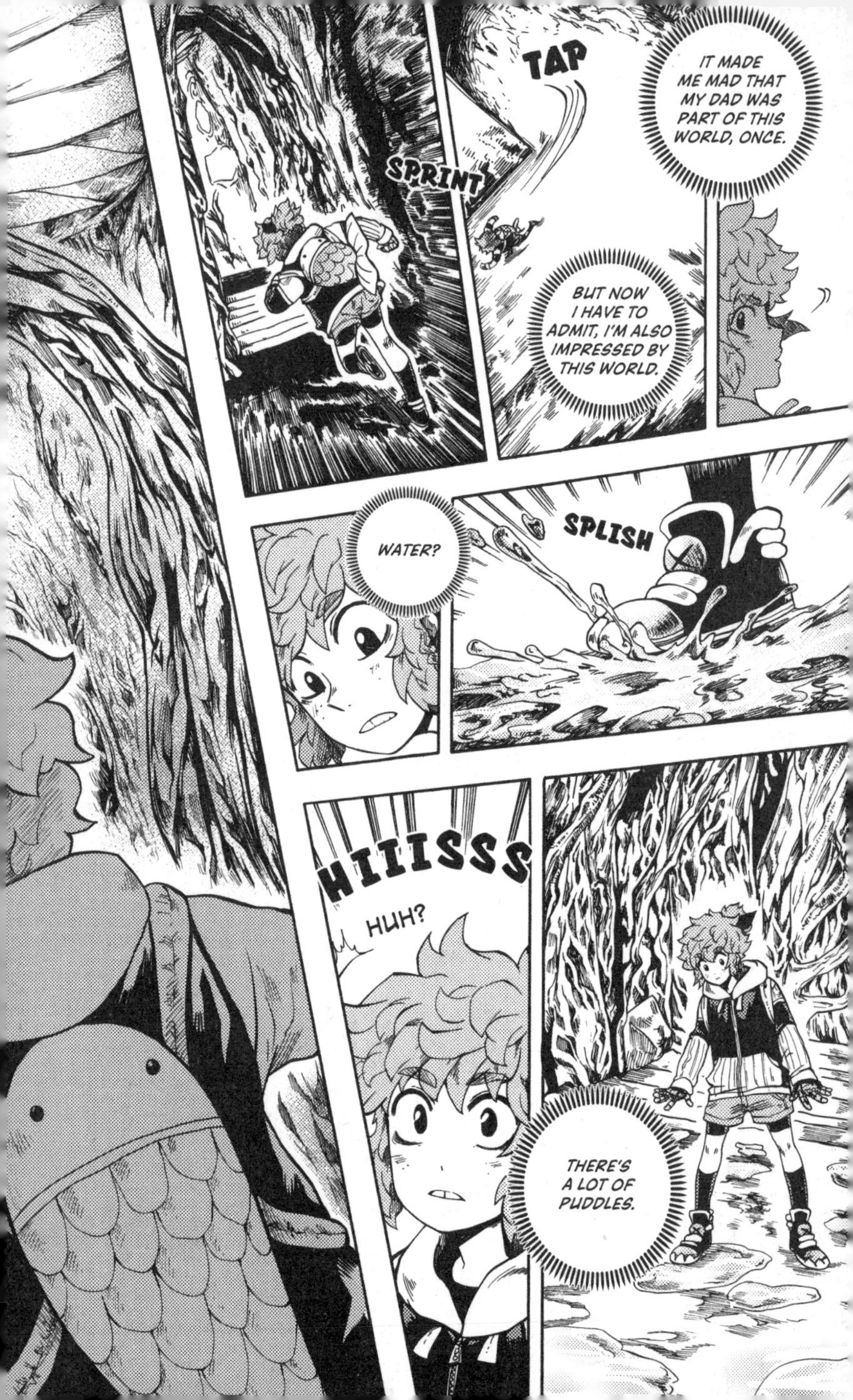
IT MADE ME MAD THAT MY DAD WAS PART OF THIS WORLD, ONCE.
TAP
BUT NOW I HAVE TO ADMIT, I'M ALSO IMPRESSED BY THIS WORLD.
SPRINT
SPLISH
WATER?
THERE'S A LOT OF PUDDLES.
HIIISSS
HUH?

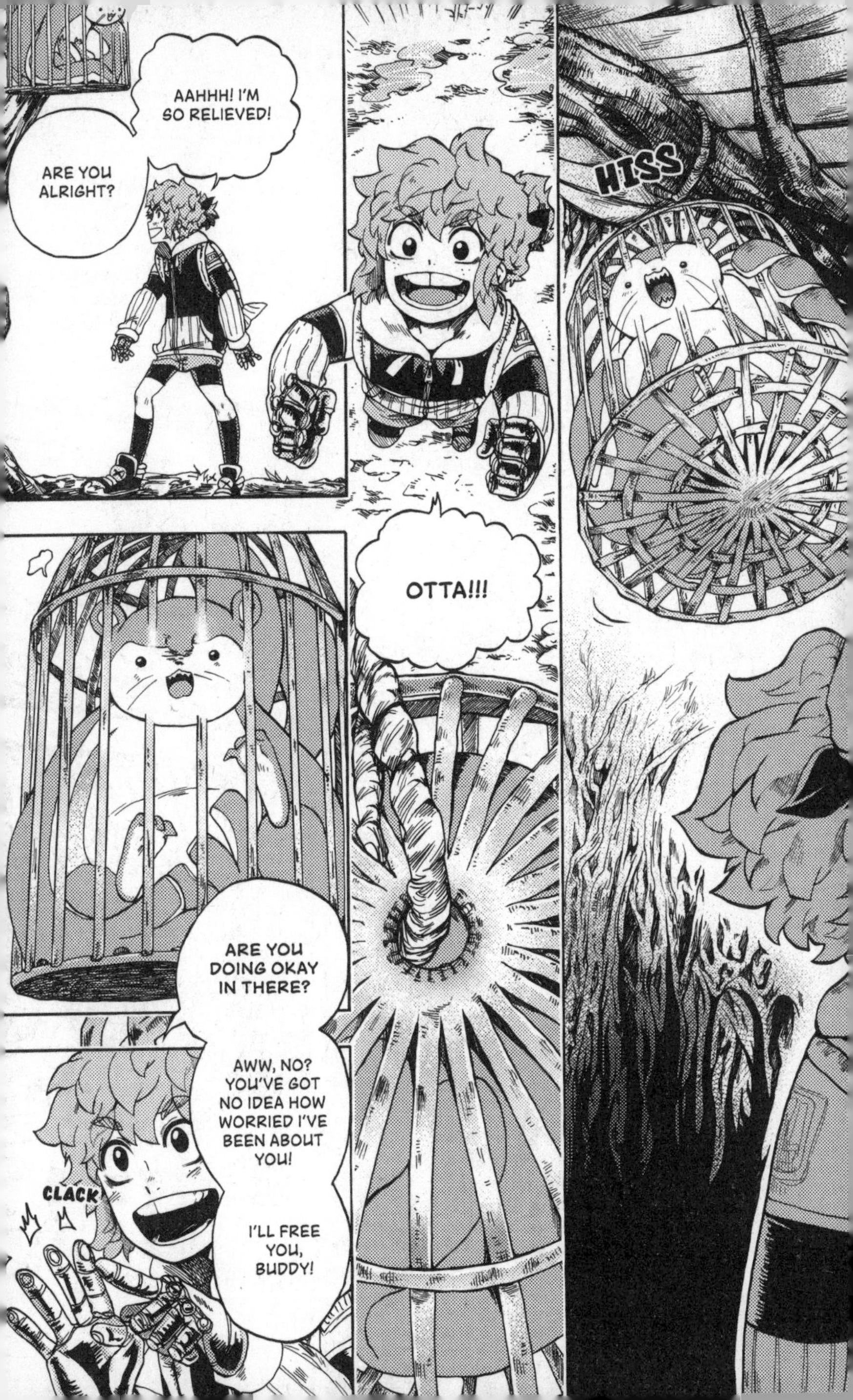
HISS
AAHHH! I'M SO RELIEVED!
ARE YOU ALRIGHT?
OTTA!!!
ARE YOU DOING OKAY IN THERE?
AWW, NO? YOU'VE GOT NO IDEA HOW WORRIED I'VE BEEN ABOUT YOU!
I'LL FREE YOU, BUDDY!
CLACK

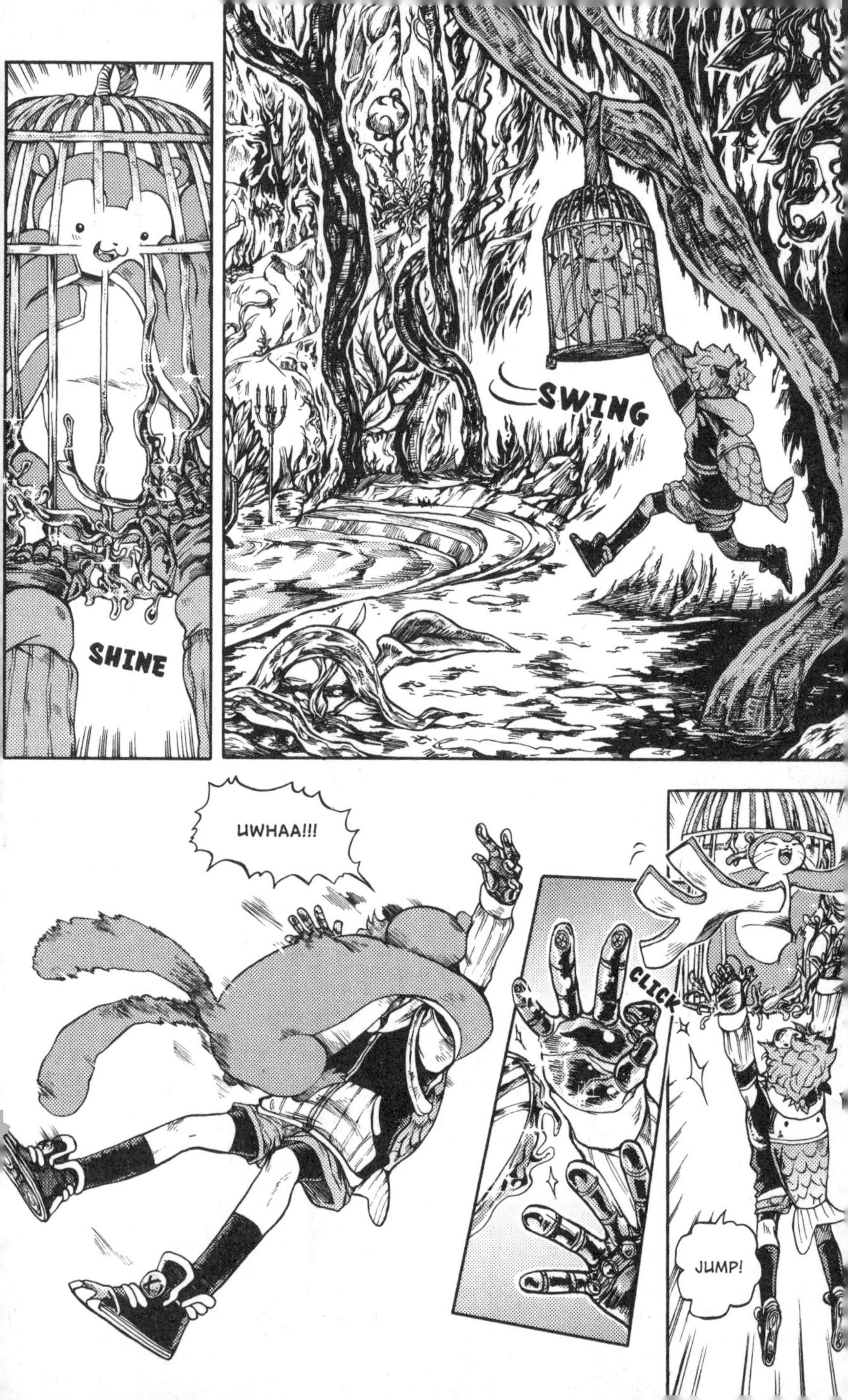
SWING
SHINE
JUMP!
CLICK
UWHAA!!!

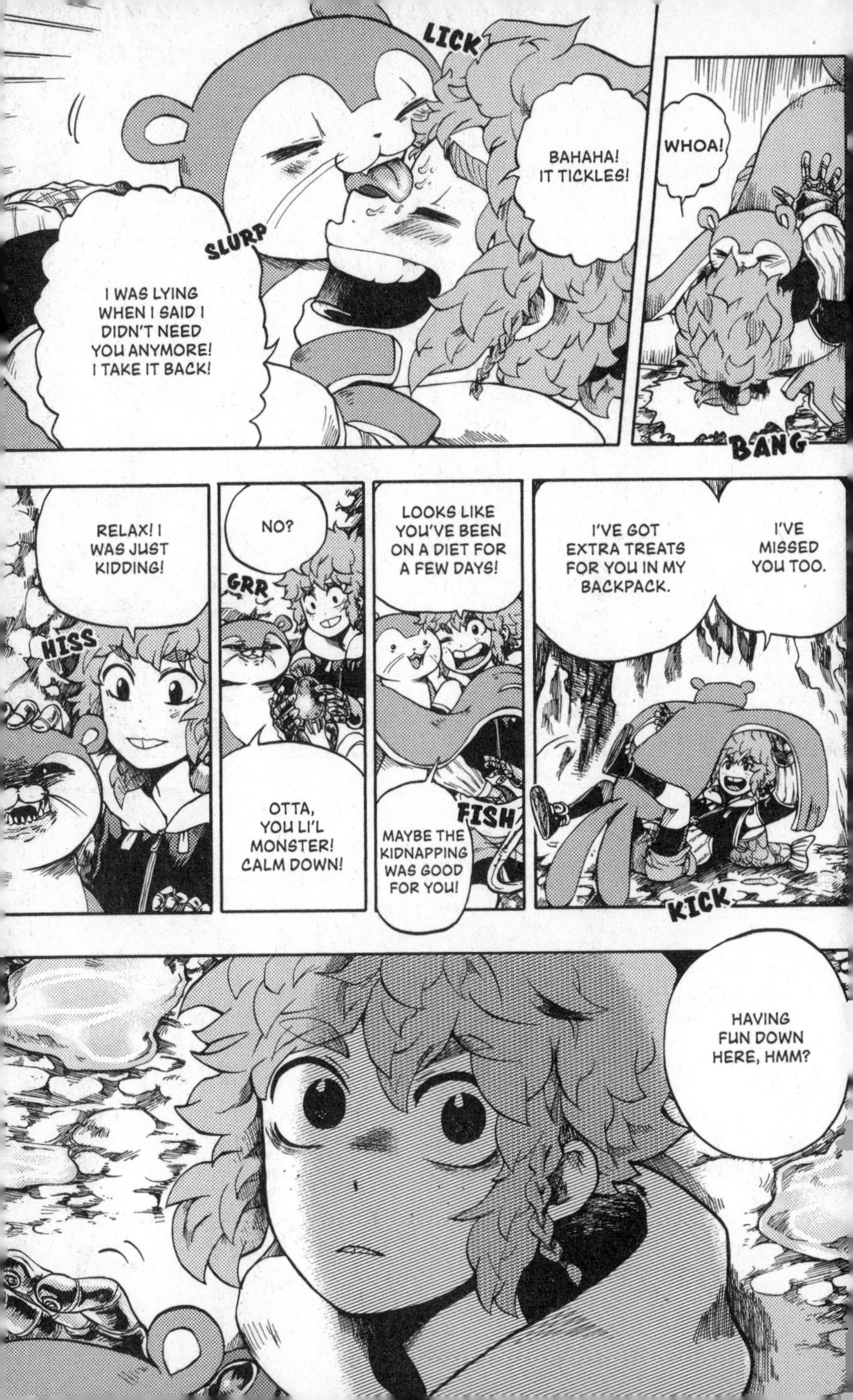
WHOA!
BANG
LICK
BAHAHA! IT TICKLES!
SLURP
I WAS LYING WHEN I SAID I DIDN'T NEED YOU ANYMORE! I TAKE IT BACK!
I'VE MISSED YOU TOO.
I'VE GOT EXTRA TREATS FOR YOU IN MY BACKPACK.
KICK
LOOKS LIKE YOU'VE BEEN ON A DIET FOR A FEW DAYS!
FISH
MAYBE THE KIDNAPPING WAS GOOD FOR YOU!
NO?
GRR
OTTA, YOU LI'L MONSTER! CALM DOWN!
RELAX! I WAS JUST KIDDING!
HISS
HAVING FUN DOWN HERE, HMM?

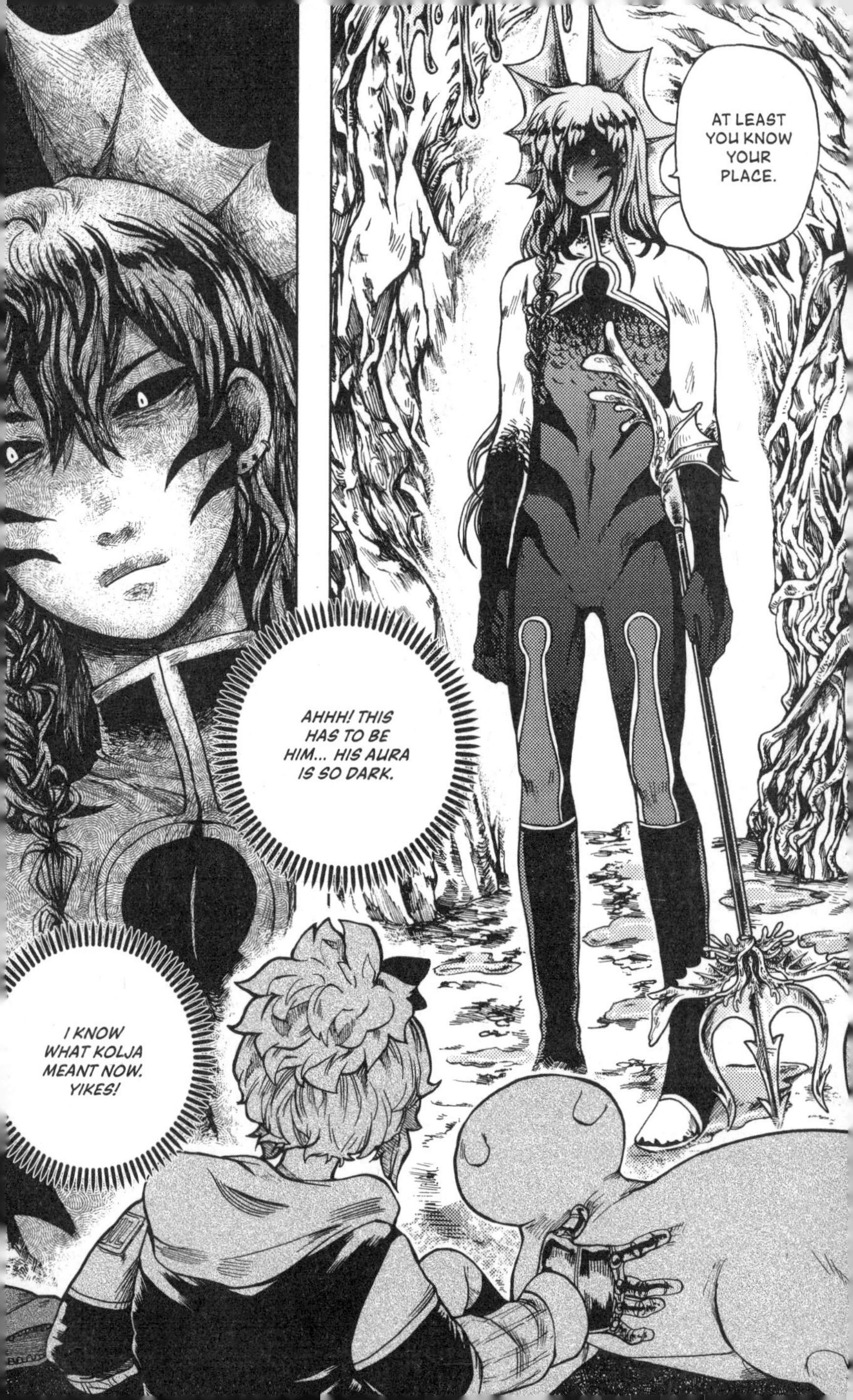
AT LEAST YOU KNOW YOUR PLACE.
AHHH! THIS HAS TO BE HIM... HIS AURA IS SO DARK.
I KNOW WHAT KOLJA MEANT NOW. YIKES!

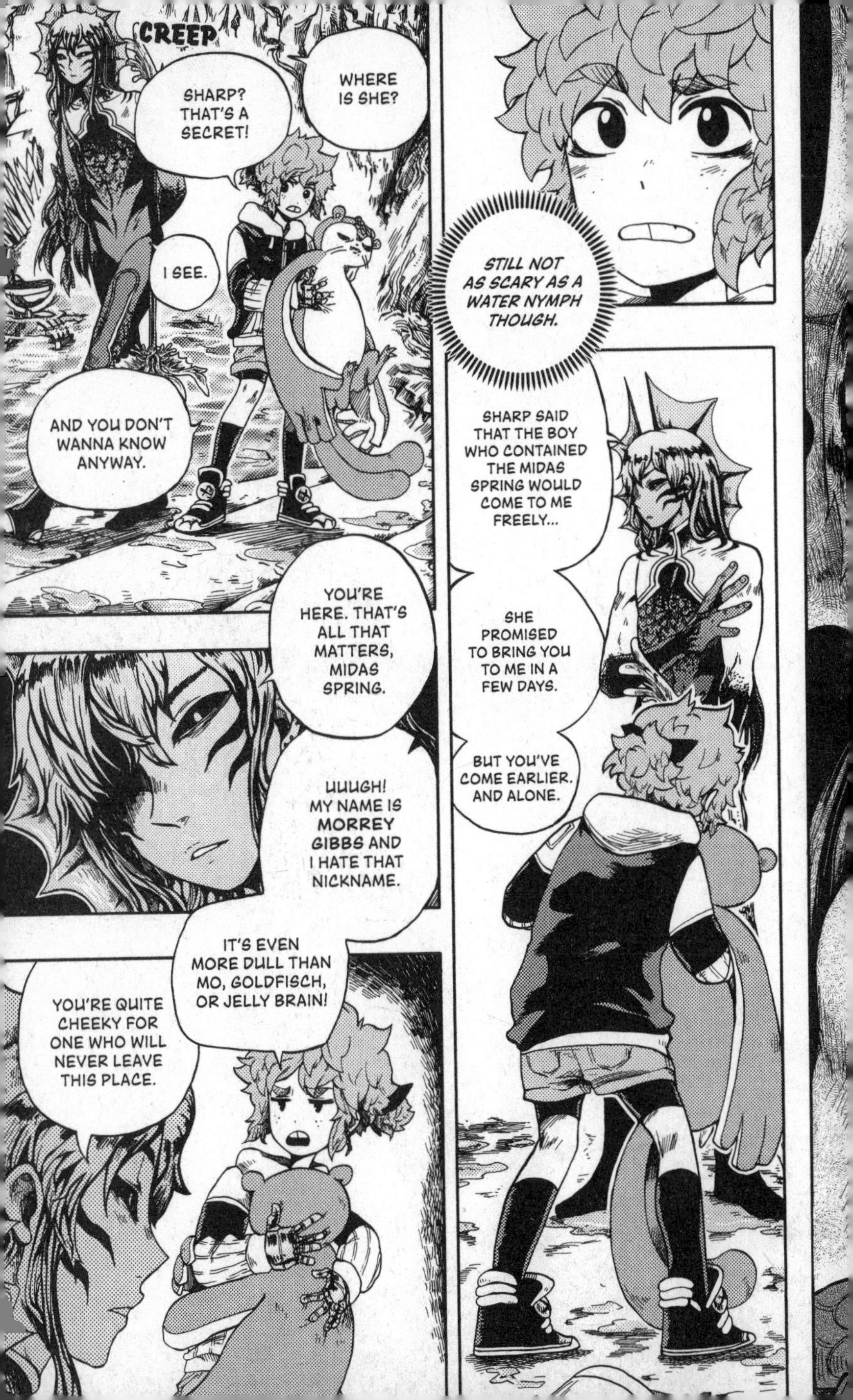
STILL NOT AS SCARY AS A WATER NYMPH THOUGH.
CREEP
WHERE IS SHE?
SHARP? THAT'S A SECRET!
I SEE.
AND YOU DON'T WANNA KNOW ANYWAY.
SHARP SAID THAT THE BOY WHO CONTAINED THE MIDAS SPRING WOULD COME TO ME FREELY...
SHE PROMISED TO BRING YOU TO ME IN A FEW DAYS.
BUT YOU'VE COME EARLIER. AND ALONE.
YOU'RE HERE. THAT'S ALL THAT MATTERS, MIDAS SPRING.
UUUGH! MY NAME IS MORREY GIBBS AND I HATE THAT NICKNAME.
IT'S EVEN MORE DULL THAN MO, GOLDFISCH, OR JELLY BRAIN!
YOU'RE QUITE CHEEKY FOR ONE WHO WILL NEVER LEAVE THIS PLACE.

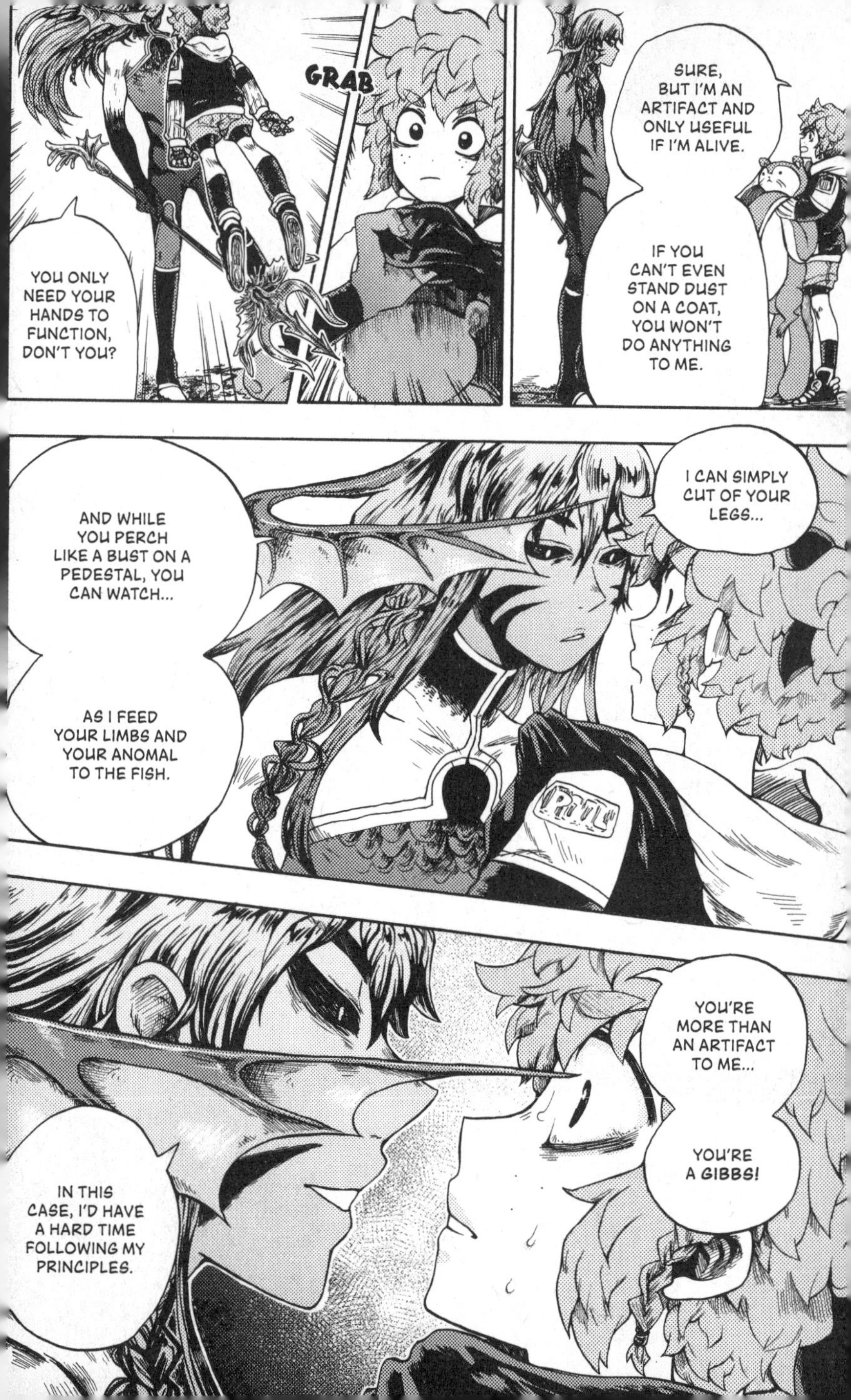
SURE, BUT I'M AN ARTIFACT AND ONLY USEFUL IF I'M ALIVE.
IF YOU CAN'T EVEN STAND DUST ON A COAT, YOU WON'T DO ANYTHING TO ME.
GRAB
YOU ONLY NEED YOUR HANDS TO FUNCTION, DON'T YOU?
I CAN SIMPLY CUT OF YOUR LEGS...
AND WHILE YOU PERCH LIKE A BUST ON A PEDESTAL, YOU CAN WATCH...
AS I FEED YOUR LIMBS AND YOUR ANOMAL TO THE FISH.
YOU'RE MORE THAN AN ARTIFACT TO ME...
YOU'RE A GIBBS!
IN THIS CASE, I'D HAVE A HARD TIME FOLLOWING MY PRINCIPLES.

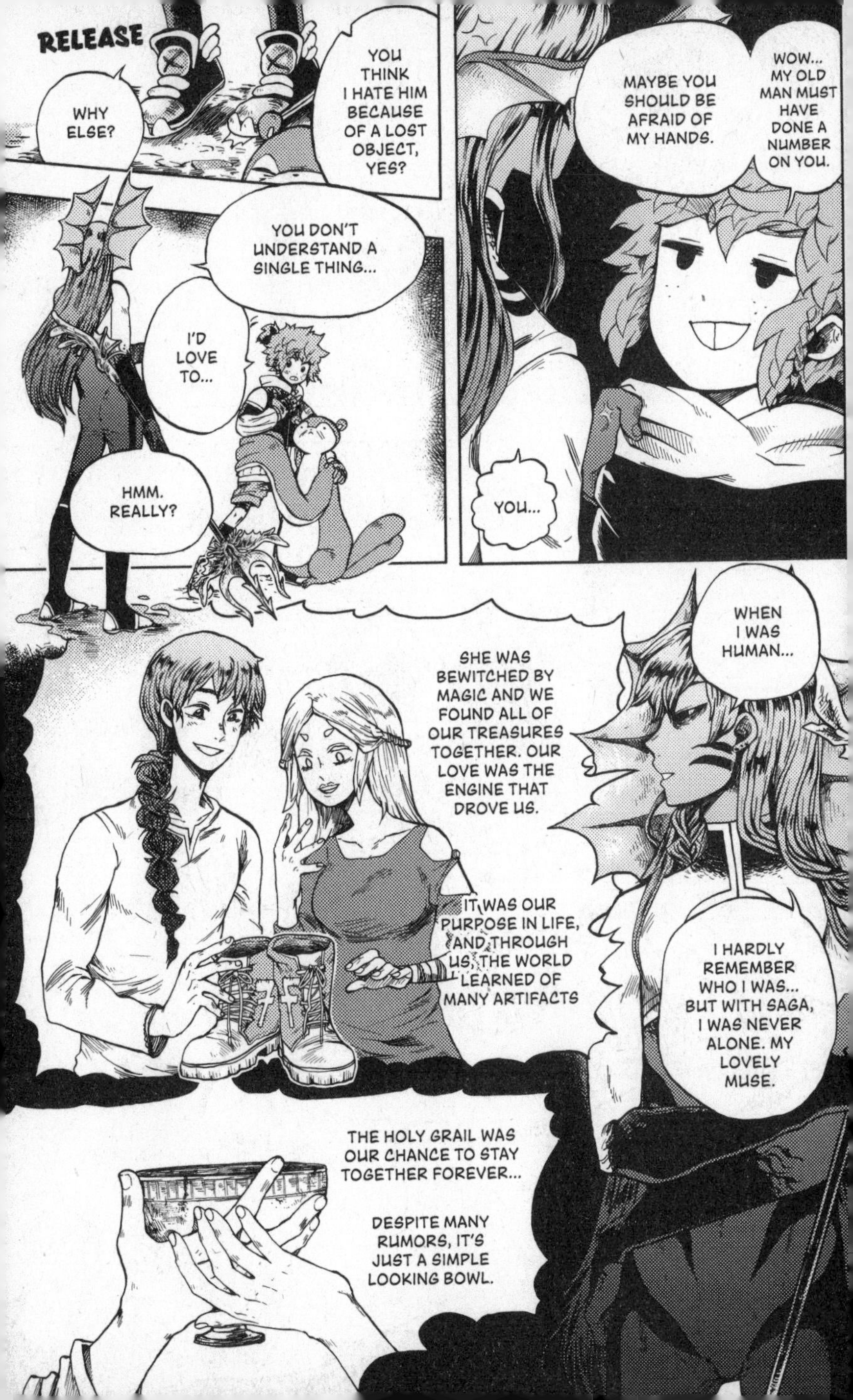
WOW... MY OLD MAN MUST HAVE DONE A NUMBER ON YOU.
MAYBE YOU SHOULD BE AFRAID OF MY HANDS.
YOU...
RELEASE
YOU THINK I HATE HIM BECAUSE OF A LOST OBJECT, YES?
WHY ELSE?
YOU DON'T UNDERSTAND A SINGLE THING...
I'D LOVE TO...
HMM. REALLY?
WHEN I WAS HUMAN...
SHE WAS BEWITCHED BY MAGIC AND WE FOUND ALL OF OUR TREASURES TOGETHER. OUR LOVE WAS THE ENGINE THAT DROVE US.
IT WAS OUR PURPOSE IN LIFE, AND THROUGH US, THE WORLD LEARNED OF MANY ARTIFACTS
I HARDLY REMEMBER WHO I WAS... BUT WITH SAGA, I WAS NEVER ALONE. MY LOVELY MUSE.
THE HOLY GRAIL WAS OUR CHANCE TO STAY TOGETHER FOREVER...
DESPITE MANY RUMORS, IT'S JUST A SIMPLE LOOKING BOWL.

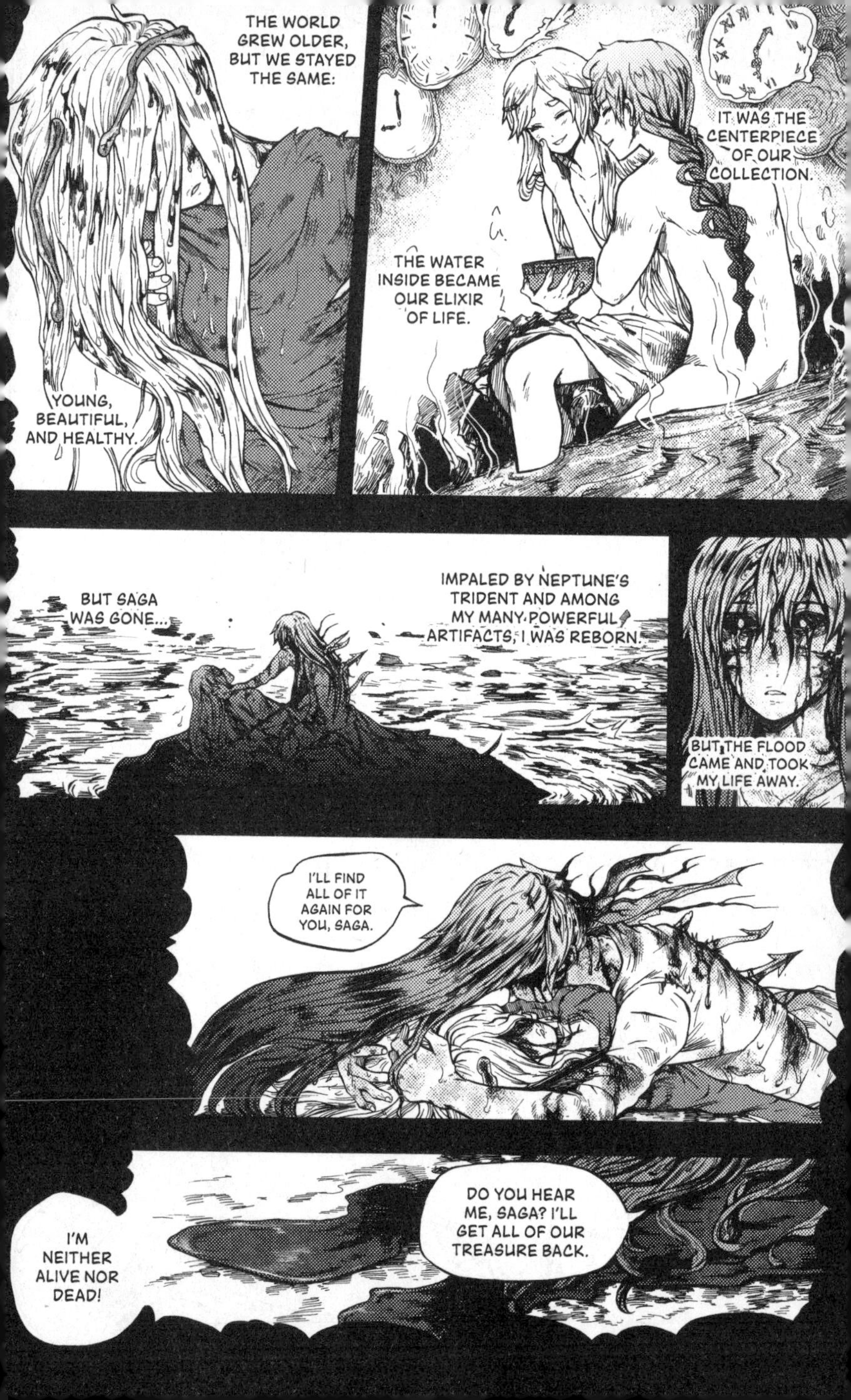
IT WAS THE CENTERPIECE OF OUR COLLECTION.
THE WATER INSIDE BECAME OUR ELIXIR OF LIFE.
THE WORLD GREW OLDER, BUT WE STAYED THE SAME:
YOUNG, BEAUTIFUL, AND HEALTHY.
BUT THE FLOOD CAME AND TOOK MY LIFE AWAY.
IMPALED BY NEPTUNE'S TRIDENT AND AMONG MY MANY POWERFUL ARTIFACTS, I WAS REBORN.
BUT SAGA WAS GONE...
I'LL FIND ALL OF IT AGAIN FOR YOU, SAGA.
DO YOU HEAR ME, SAGA? I'LL GET ALL OF OUR TREASURE BACK.
I'M NEITHER ALIVE NOR DEAD!

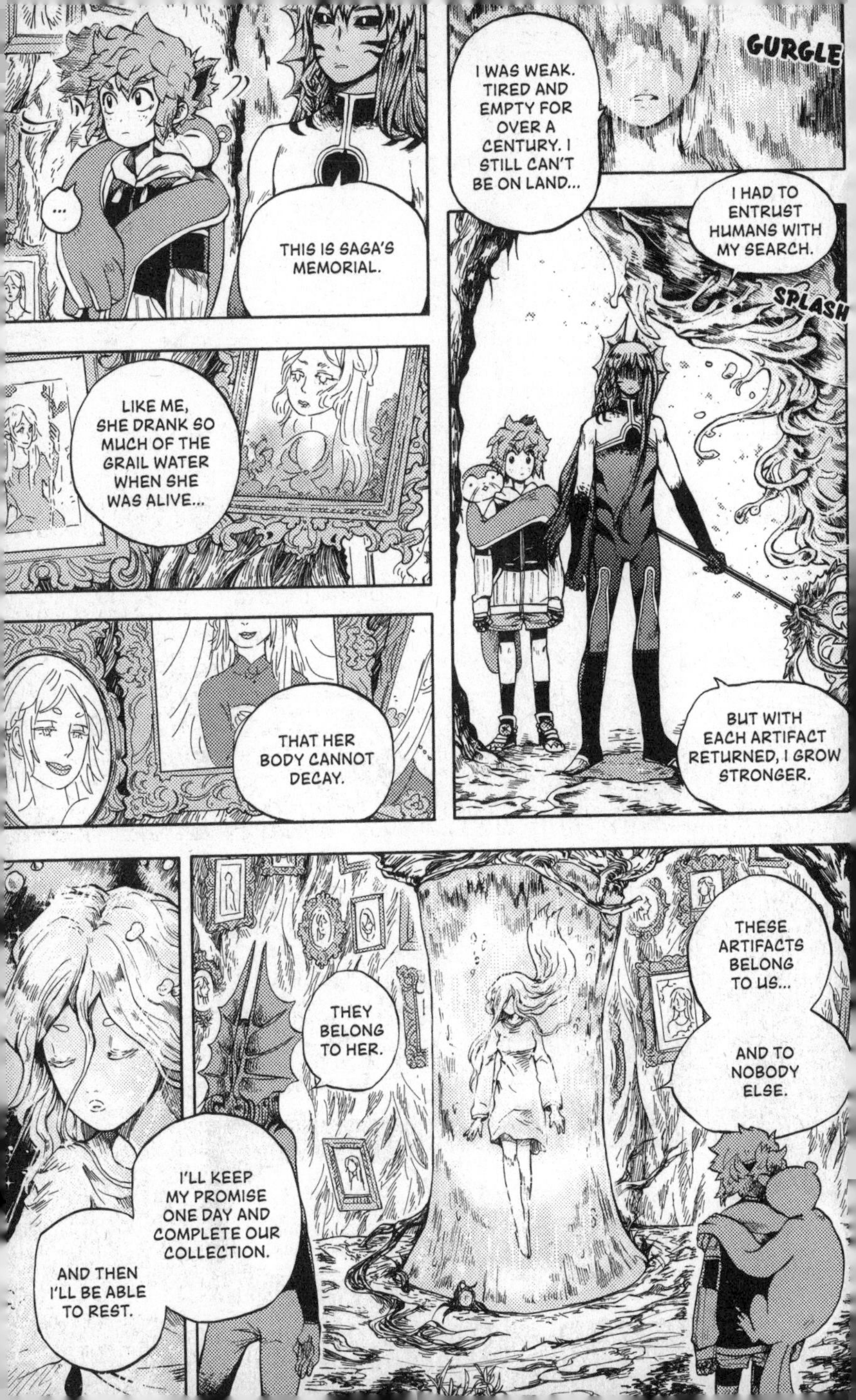
GURGLE
I WAS WEAK. TIRED AND EMPTY FOR OVER A CENTURY. I STILL CAN'T BE ON LAND...
I HAD TO ENTRUST HUMANS WITH MY SEARCH.
SPLASH
BUT WITH EACH ARTIFACT RETURNED, I GROW STRONGER.
THIS IS SAGA'S MEMORIAL.
...
LIKE ME, SHE DRANK SO MUCH OF THE GRAIL WATER WHEN SHE WAS ALIVE...
THAT HER BODY CANNOT DECAY.
THESE ARTIFACTS BELONG TO US...
AND TO NOBODY ELSE.
THEY BELONG TO HER.
I'LL KEEP MY PROMISE ONE DAY AND COMPLETE OUR COLLECTION.
AND THEN I'LL BE ABLE TO REST.

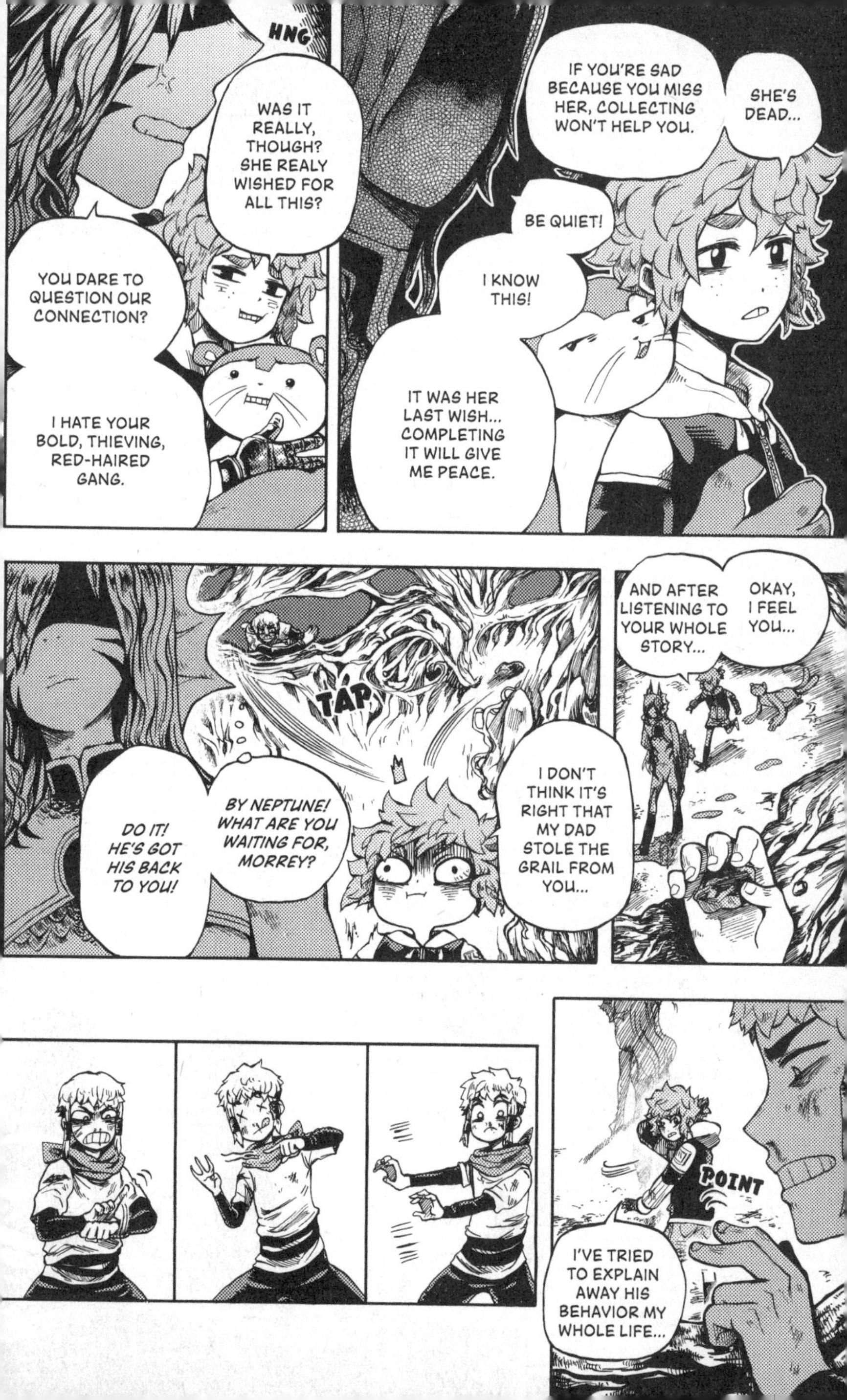

SHE'S DEAD...
IF YOU'RE SAD BECAUSE YOU MISS HER, COLLECTING WON'T HELP YOU.
BE QUIET!
I KNOW THIS!
IT WAS HER LAST WISH... COMPLETING IT WILL GIVE ME PEACE.
HNG
WAS IT REALLY, THOUGH? SHE REALY WISHED FOR ALL THIS?
YOU DARE TO QUESTION OUR CONNECTION?
I HATE YOUR BOLD, THIEVING, RED-HAIRED GANG.
OKAY, I FEEL YOU...
AND AFTER LISTENING TO YOUR WHOLE STORY...
TAP
I DON'T THINK IT'S RIGHT THAT MY DAD STOLE THE GRAIL FROM YOU...
BY NEPTUNE! WHAT ARE YOU WAITING FOR, MORREY?
DO IT! HE'S GOT HIS BACK TO YOU!
POINT
I'VE TRIED TO EXPLAIN AWAY HIS BEHAVIOR MY WHOLE LIFE...

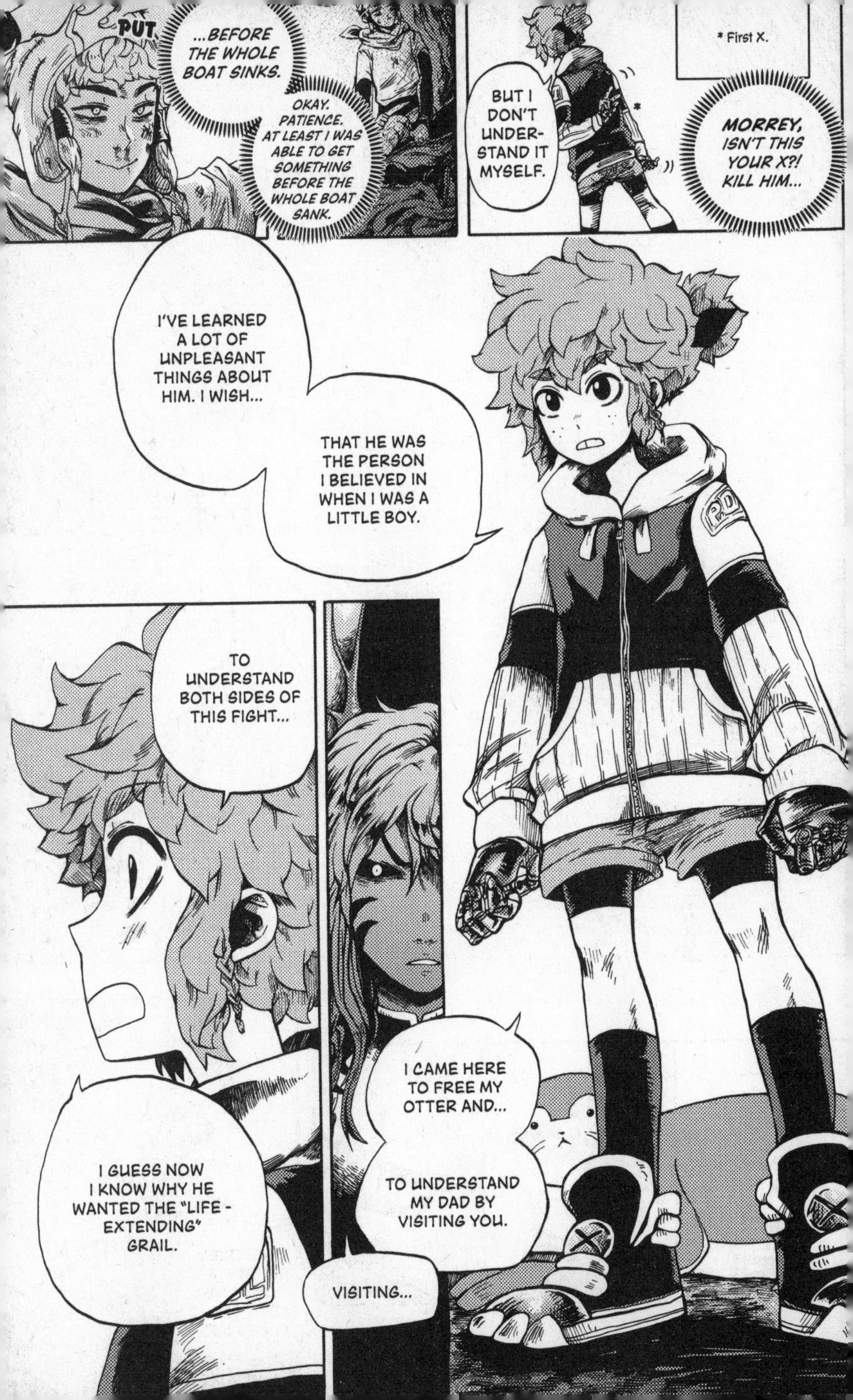
* First X.
MORREY, ISN'T THIS YOUR X?! KILL HIM...
BUT I DON'T UNDERSTAND IT MYSELF.
PUT
...BEFORE THE WHOLE BOAT SINKS.
OKAY. PATIENCE. AT LEAST I WAS ABLE TO GET SOMETHING BEFORE THE WHOLE BOAT SANK.
I'VE LEARNED A LOT OF UNPLEASANT THINGS ABOUT HIM. I WISH...
THAT HE WAS THE PERSON I BELIEVED IN WHEN I WAS A LITTLE BOY.
I CAME HERE TO FREE MY OTTER AND...
TO UNDERSTAND MY DAD BY VISITING YOU.
VISITING...
TO UNDERSTAND BOTH SIDES OF THIS FIGHT...
I GUESS NOW I KNOW WHY HE WANTED THE "LIFE-EXTENDING" GRAIL.

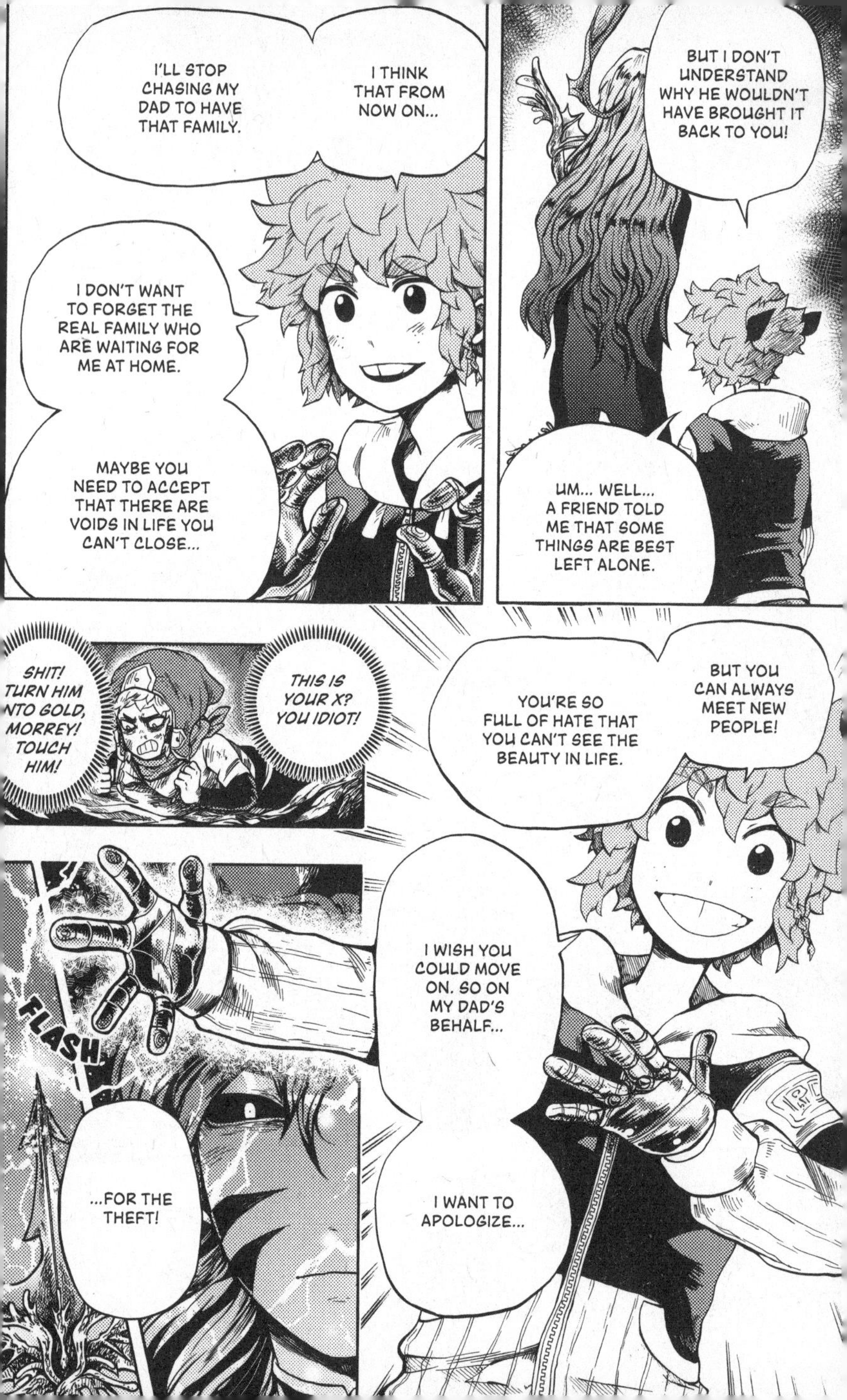
BUT I DON'T UNDERSTAND WHY HE WOULDN'T HAVE BROUGHT IT BACK TO YOU!
UM... WELL... A FRIEND TOLD ME THAT SOME THINGS ARE BEST LEFT ALONE.
I THINK THAT FROM NOW ON...
I'LL STOP CHASING MY DAD TO HAVE THAT FAMILY.
I DON'T WANT TO FORGET THE REAL FAMILY WHO ARE WAITING FOR ME AT HOME.
MAYBE YOU NEED TO ACCEPT THAT THERE ARE VOIDS IN LIFE YOU CAN'T CLOSE...
BUT YOU CAN ALWAYS MEET NEW PEOPLE!
YOU'RE SO FULL OF HATE THAT YOU CAN'T SEE THE BEAUTY IN LIFE.
I WISH YOU COULD MOVE ON. SO ON MY DAD'S BEHALF...
I WANT TO APOLOGIZE...
THIS IS YOUR X? YOU IDIOT!
SHIT! TURN HIM NTO GOLD, MORREY! TOUCH HIM!
FLASH
...FOR THE THEFT!

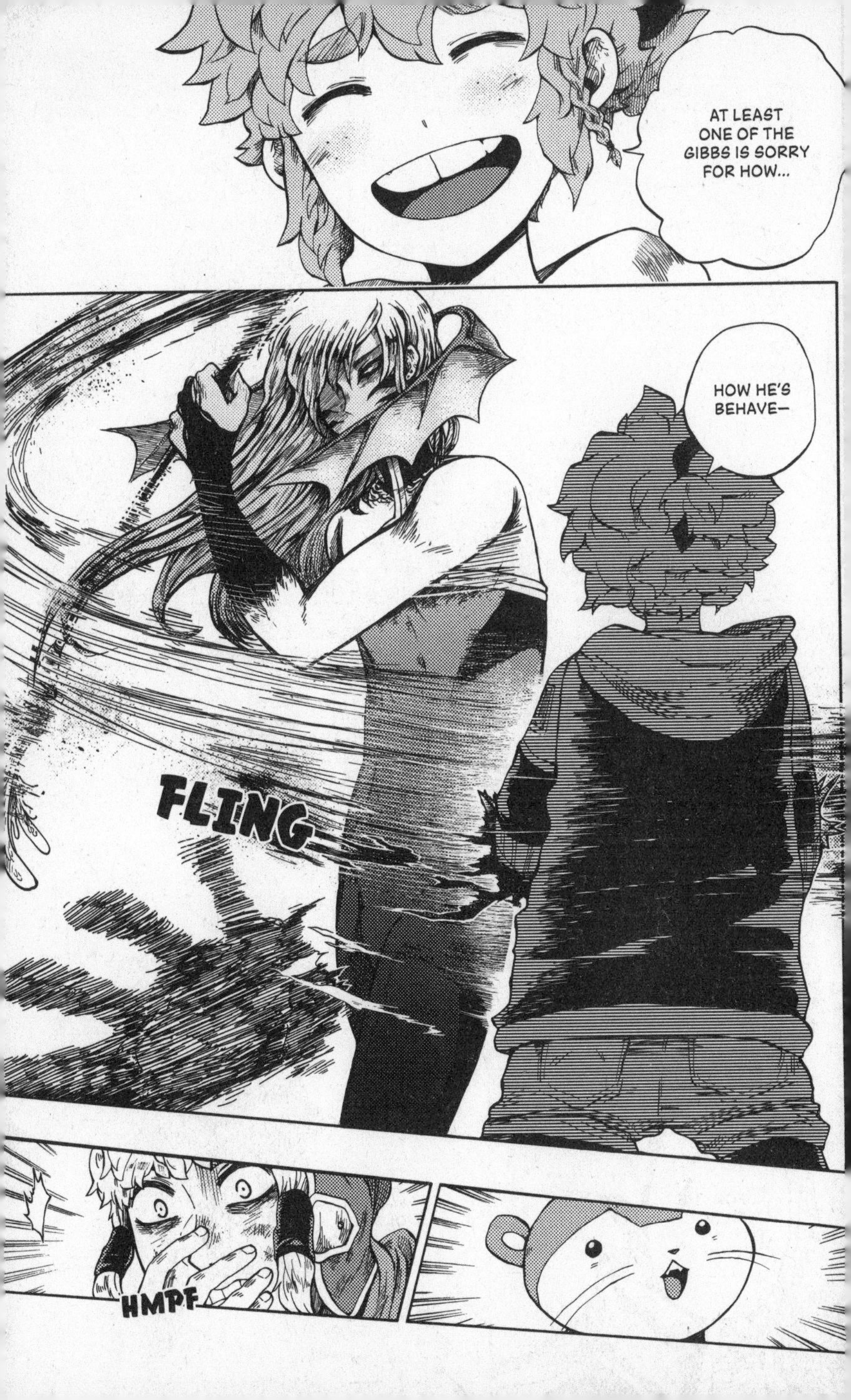
AT LEAST ONE OF THE GIBBS IS SORRY FOR HOW...
HOW HE'S BEHAVE—
FLING
HMPF

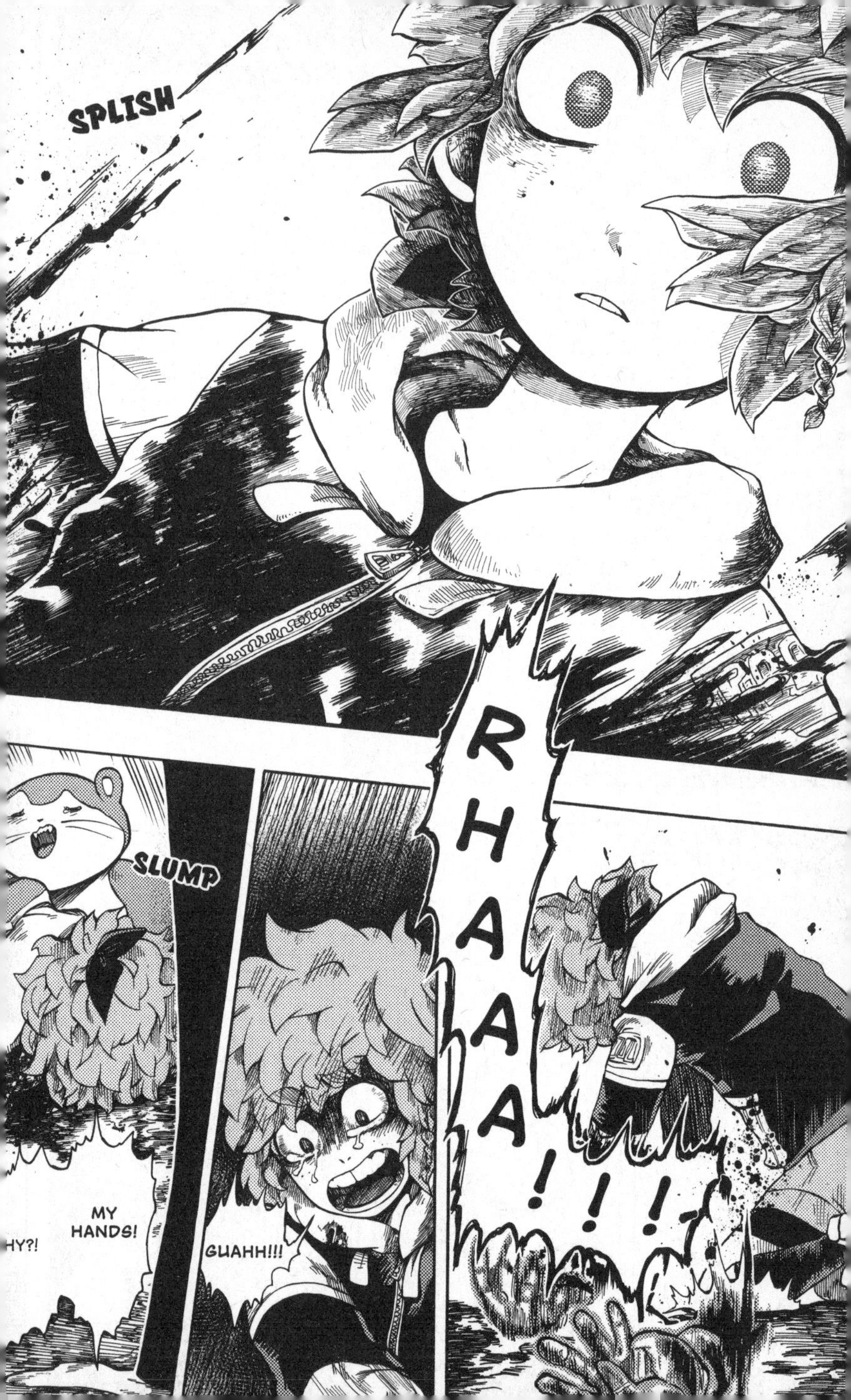
SPLISH
RHAAA!!!!
GUAHH!!!
SLUMP
MY HANDS!
HY?!

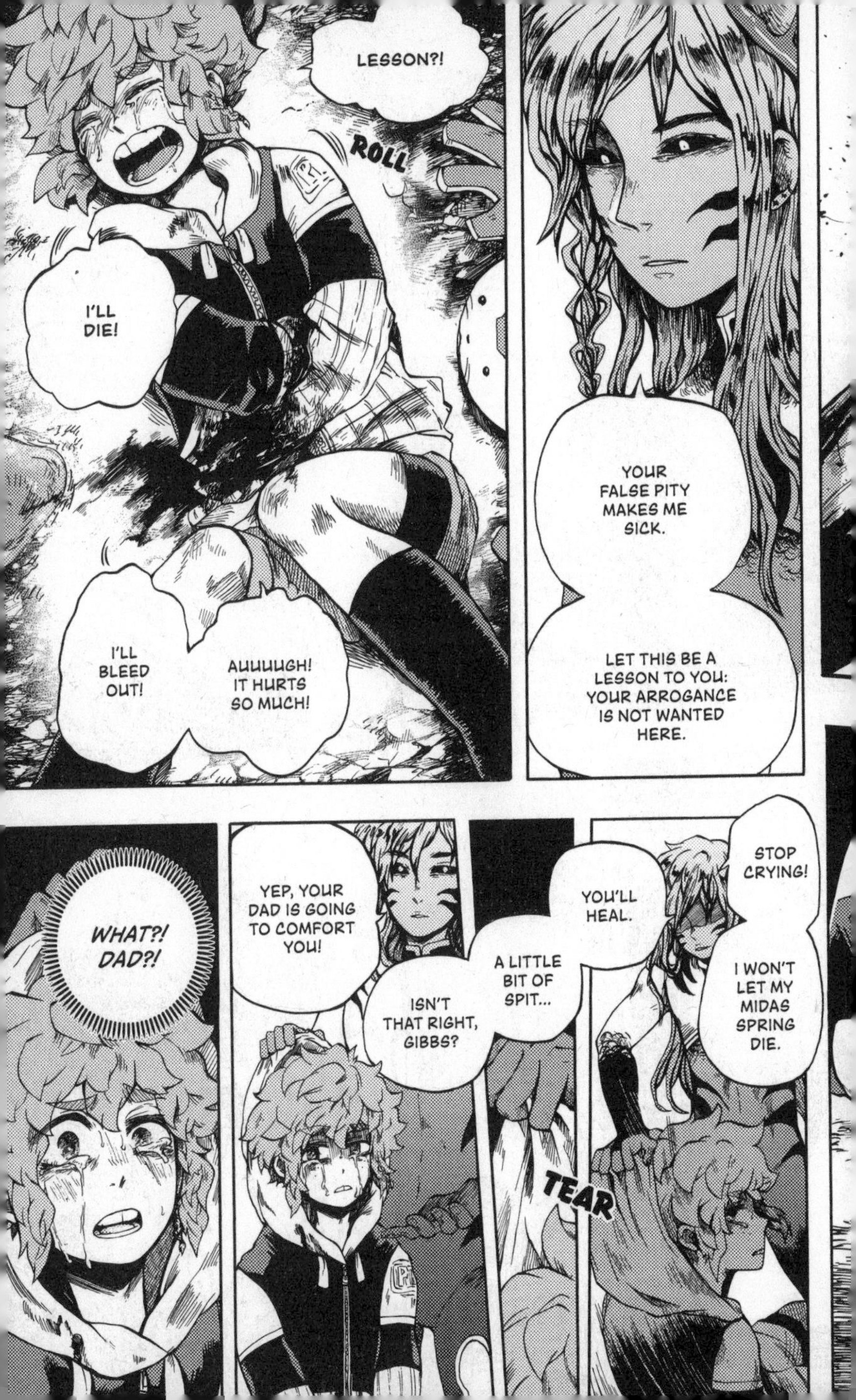
YOUR FALSE PITY MAKES ME SICK.
LET THIS BE A LESSON TO YOU: YOUR ARROGANCE IS NOT WANTED HERE.
LESSON?!
ROLL
I'LL DIE!
AUUUUGH! IT HURTS SO MUCH!
I'LL BLEED OUT!
STOP CRYING!
YOU'LL HEAL.
I WON'T LET MY MIDAS SPRING DIE.
A LITTLE BIT OF SPIT...
TEAR
YEP, YOUR DAD IS GOING TO COMFORT YOU!
ISN'T THAT RIGHT, GIBBS?
WHAT?! DAD?!

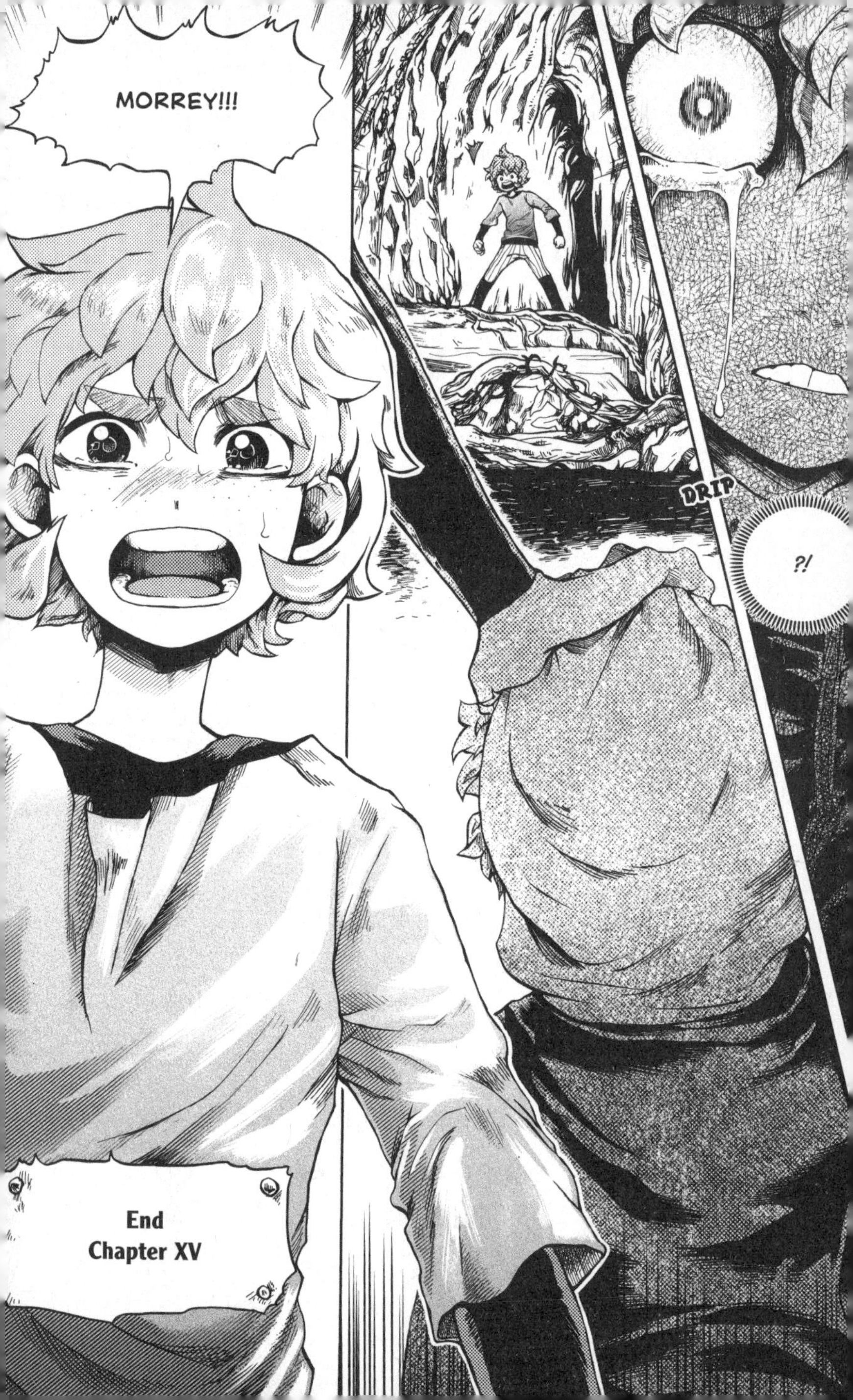
DRIP
?!
MORREY!!!
End
Chapter XV

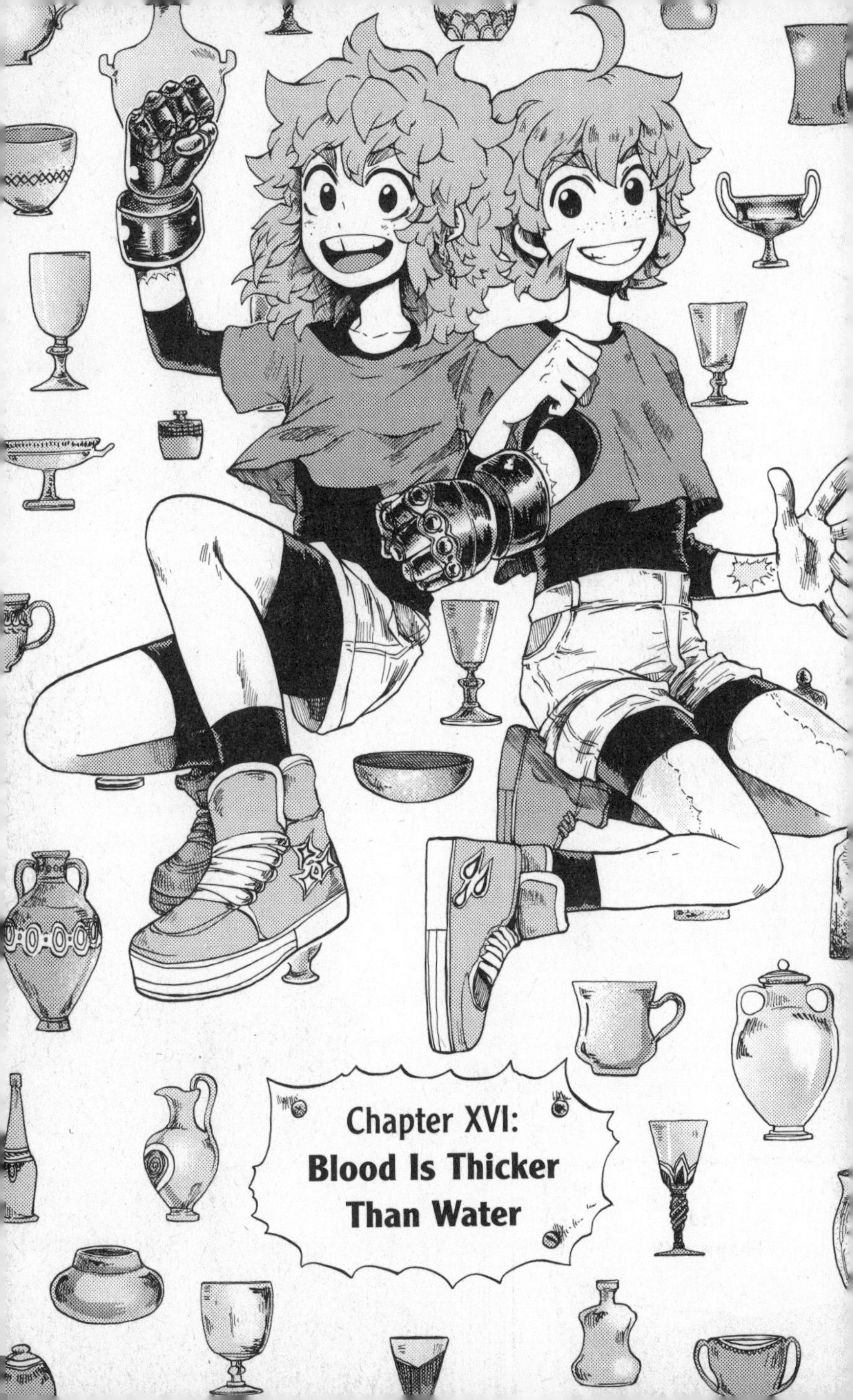
Chapter XVI:
Blood Is Thicker
Than Water

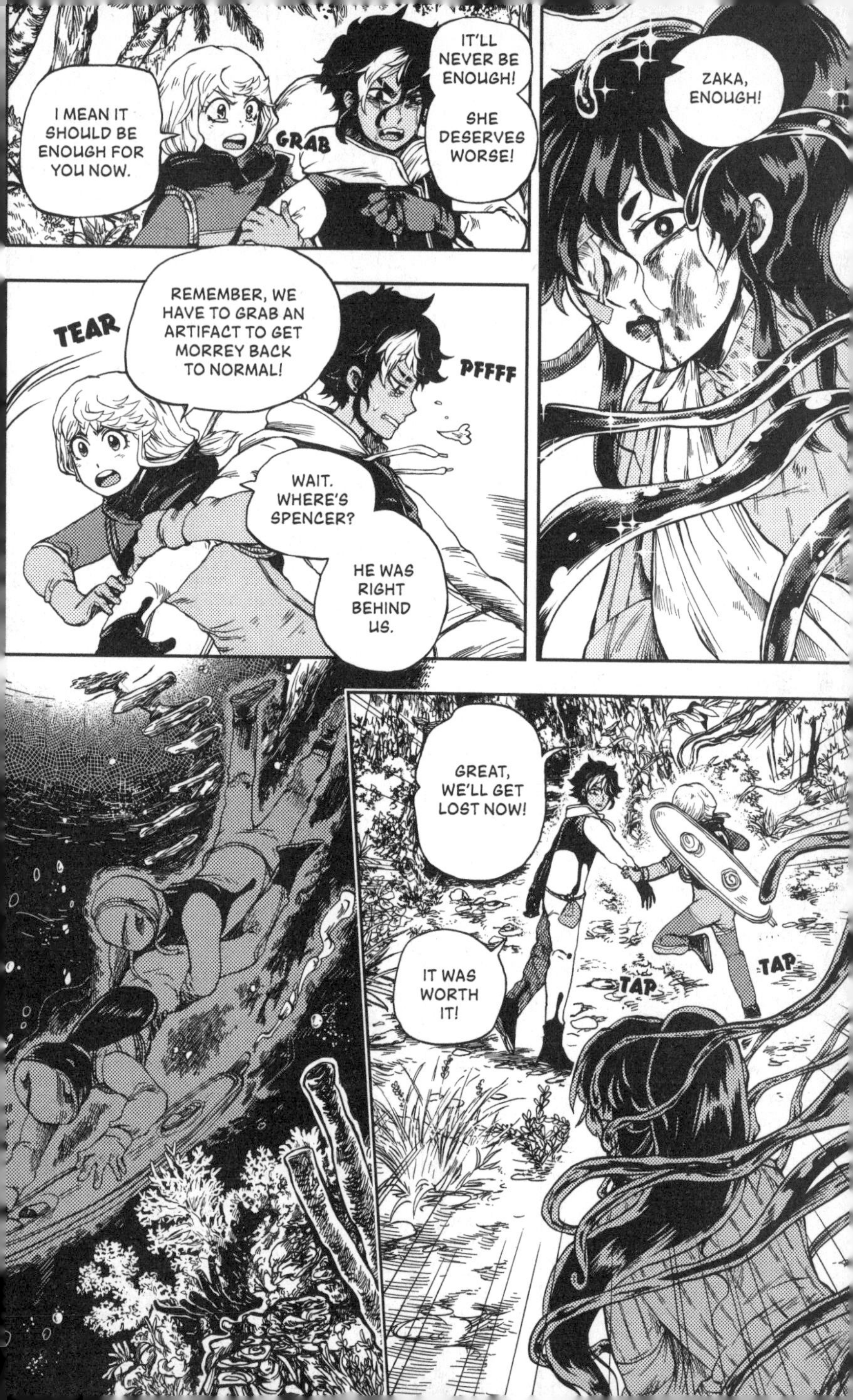
ZAKA, ENOUGH!
IT'LL NEVER BE ENOUGH!
SHE DESERVES WORSE!
GRAB
I MEAN IT SHOULD BE ENOUGH FOR YOU NOW.
REMEMBER, WE HAVE TO GRAB AN ARTIFACT TO GET MORREY BACK TO NORMAL!
PFFFF
TEAR
WAIT. WHERE'S SPENCER?
HE WAS RIGHT BEHIND US.
GREAT, WE'LL GET LOST NOW!
TAP
TAP
IT WAS WORTH IT!

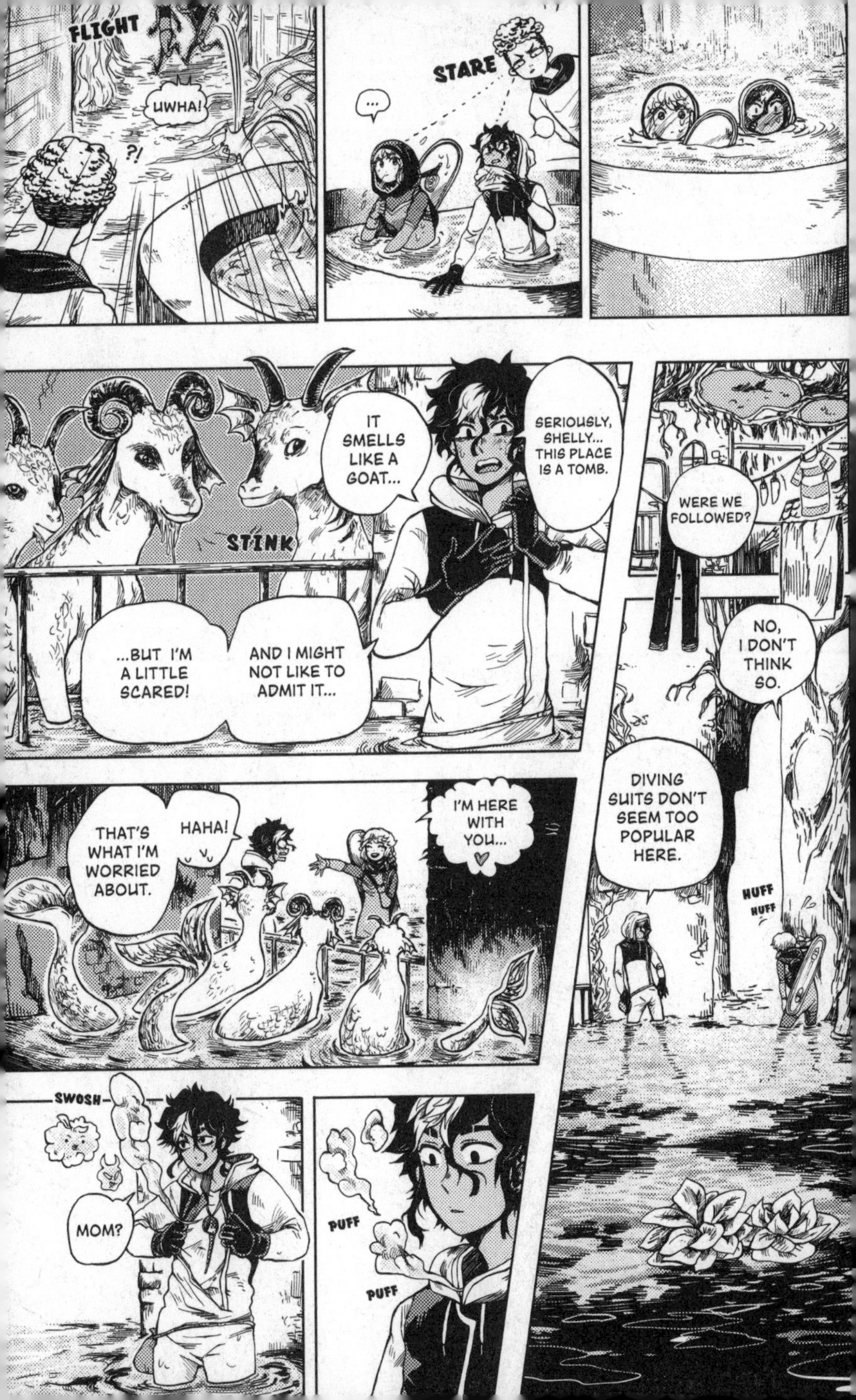
STARE
...
FLIGHT
UWHA!
?!
WERE WE FOLLOWED?
NO, I DON'T THINK SO.
DIVING SUITS DON'T SEEM TOO POPULAR HERE.
HUFF
HUFF
SERIOUSLY, SHELLY... THIS PLACE IS A TOMB.
IT SMELLS LIKE A GOAT...
STINK
AND I MIGHT NOT LIKE TO ADMIT IT...
...BUT I'M A LITTLE SCARED!
I'M HERE WITH YOU... ♥
HAHA!
THAT'S WHAT I'M WORRIED ABOUT.
PUFF
PUFF
SWOSH
MOM?

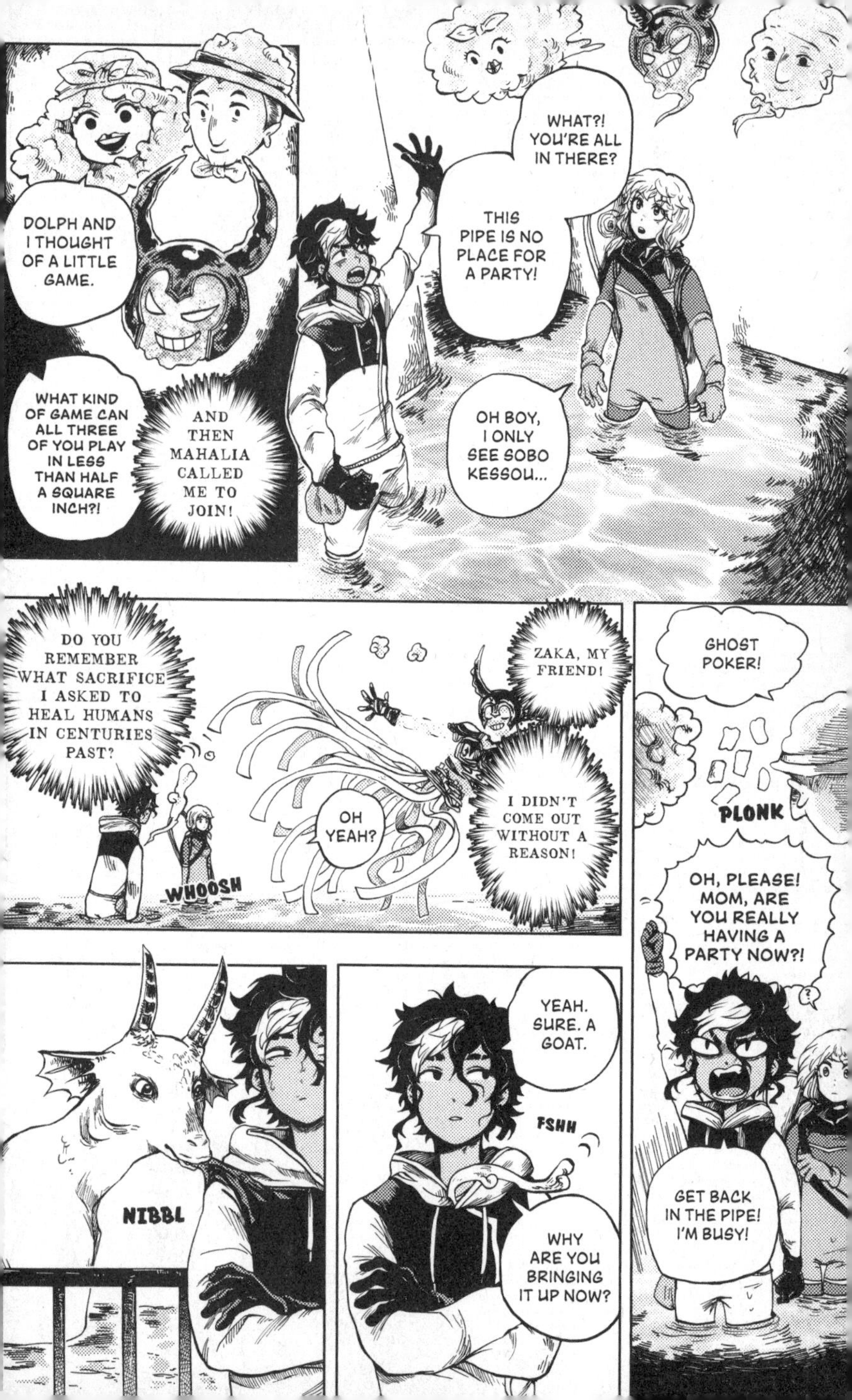
WHAT?! YOU'RE ALL IN THERE?
THIS PIPE IS NO PLACE FOR A PARTY!
OH BOY, I ONLY SEE SOBO KESSOU...
DOLPH AND I THOUGHT OF A LITTLE GAME.
AND THEN MAHALIA CALLED ME TO JOIN!
WHAT KIND OF GAME CAN ALL THREE OF YOU PLAY IN LESS THAN HALF A SQUARE INCH?!
GHOST POKER!
PLONK
OH, PLEASE! MOM, ARE YOU REALLY HAVING A PARTY NOW?!
GET BACK IN THE PIPE! I'M BUSY!
ZAKA, MY FRIEND!
I DIDN'T COME OUT WITHOUT A REASON!
OH YEAH?
DO YOU REMEMBER WHAT SACRIFICE I ASKED TO HEAL HUMANS IN CENTURIES PAST?
WHOOSH
YEAH. SURE. A GOAT.
FSHH
WHY ARE YOU BRINGING IT UP NOW?
NIBBL

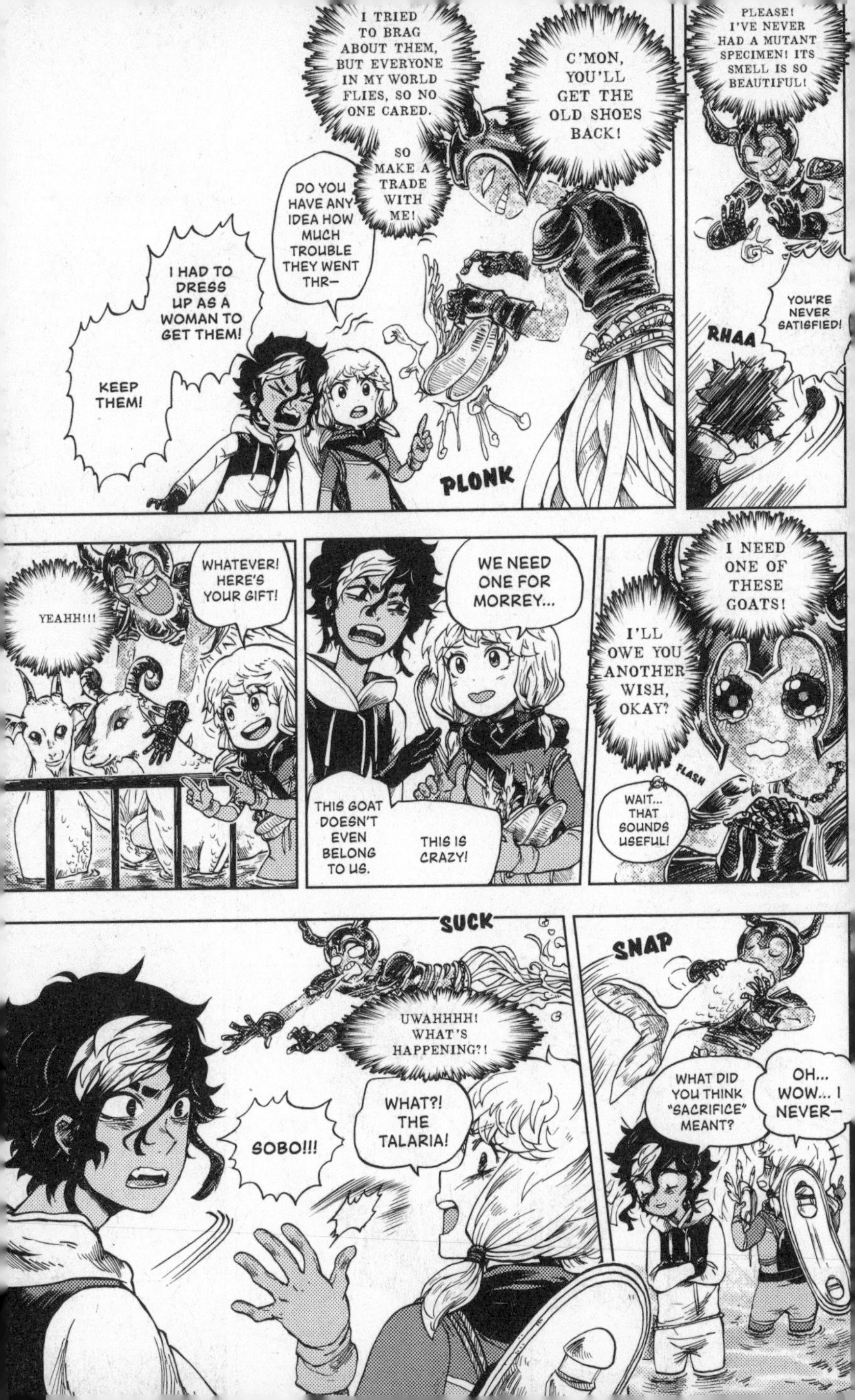

PLEASE! I'VE NEVER HAD A MUTANT SPECIMEN! ITS SMELL IS SO BEAUTIFUL!
YOU'RE NEVER SATISFIED!
RHAA
C'MON, YOU'LL GET THE OLD SHOES BACK!
I TRIED TO BRAG ABOUT THEM, BUT EVERYONE IN MY WORLD FLIES, SO NO ONE CARED.
SO MAKE A TRADE WITH ME!
DO YOU HAVE ANY IDEA HOW MUCH TROUBLE THEY WENT THR—
I HAD TO DRESS UP AS A WOMAN TO GET THEM!
KEEP THEM!
PLONK
I NEED ONE OF THESE GOATS!
I'LL OWE YOU ANOTHER WISH, OKAY?
FLASH
WAIT... THAT SOUNDS USEFUL!
WE NEED ONE FOR MORREY...
THIS IS CRAZY!
THIS GOAT DOESN'T EVEN BELONG TO US.
WHATEVER! HERE'S YOUR GIFT!
YEAHH!!!
SNAP
OH... WOW... I NEVER—
WHAT DID YOU THINK "SACRIFICE" MEANT?
SUCK
UWAHHHH! WHAT'S HAPPENING?!
WHAT?! THE TALARIA!
SOBO!!!

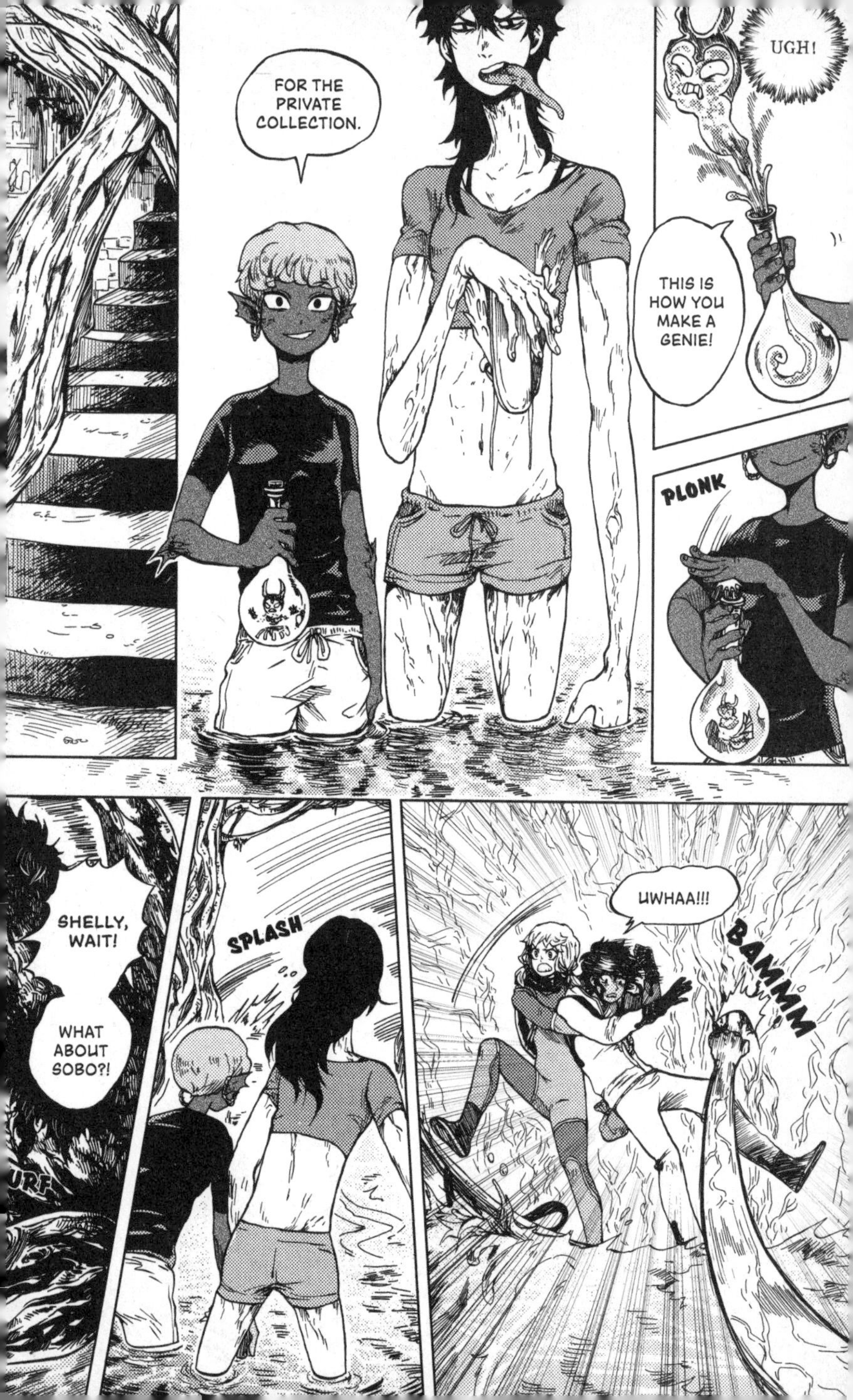
UGH!
THIS IS HOW YOU MAKE A GENIE!
PLONK
FOR THE PRIVATE COLLECTION.
UWHAA!!!
BAMMMM
SPLASH
SHELLY, WAIT!
WHAT ABOUT SOBO?!

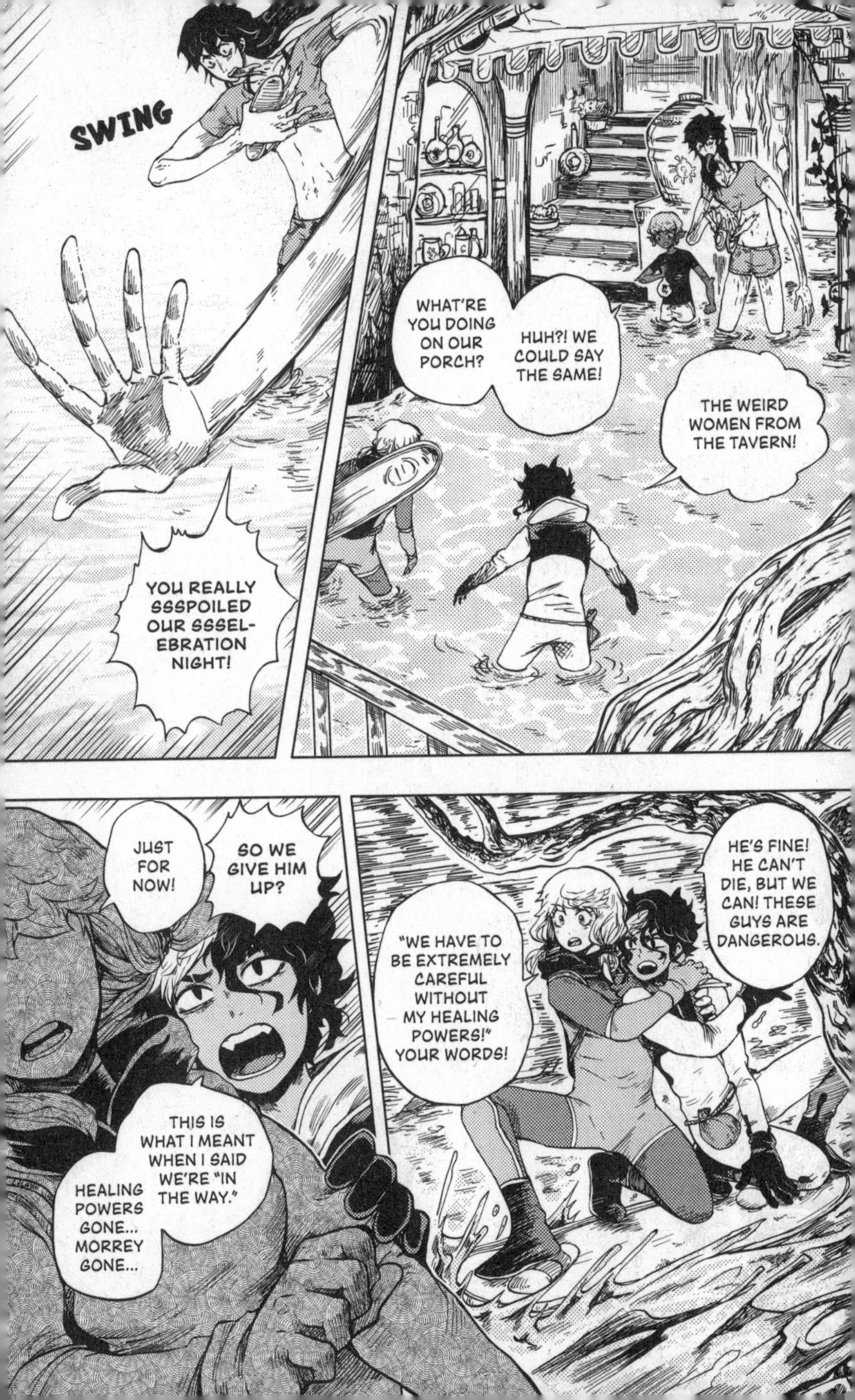
WHAT'RE YOU DOING ON OUR PORCH?
HUH?! WE COULD SAY THE SAME!
THE WEIRD WOMEN FROM THE TAVERN!
SWING
YOU REALLY SSSPOILED OUR SSSEL-EBRATION NIGHT!
HE'S FINE! HE CAN'T DIE, BUT WE CAN! THESE GUYS ARE DANGEROUS.
"WE HAVE TO BE EXTREMELY CAREFUL WITHOUT MY HEALING POWERS!" YOUR WORDS!
SO WE GIVE HIM UP?
JUST FOR NOW!
THIS IS WHAT I MEANT WHEN I SAID WE'RE "IN THE WAY."
HEALING POWERS GONE... MORREY GONE...

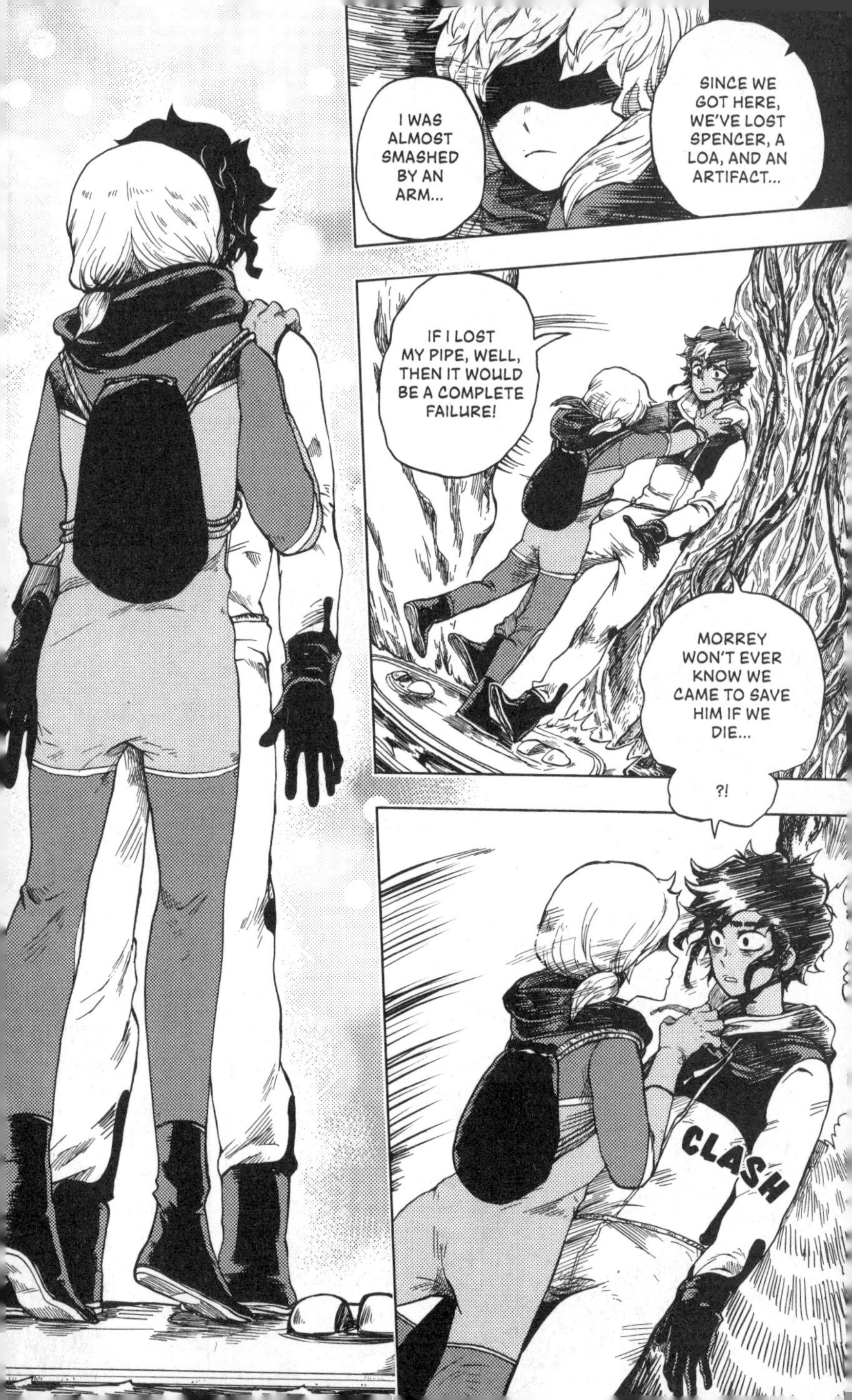
SINCE WE GOT HERE, WE'VE LOST SPENCER, A LOA, AND AN ARTIFACT...
I WAS ALMOST SMASHED BY AN ARM...
IF I LOST MY PIPE, WELL, THEN IT WOULD BE A COMPLETE FAILURE!
MORREY WON'T EVER KNOW WE CAME TO SAVE HIM IF WE DIE...
?!
CLASH

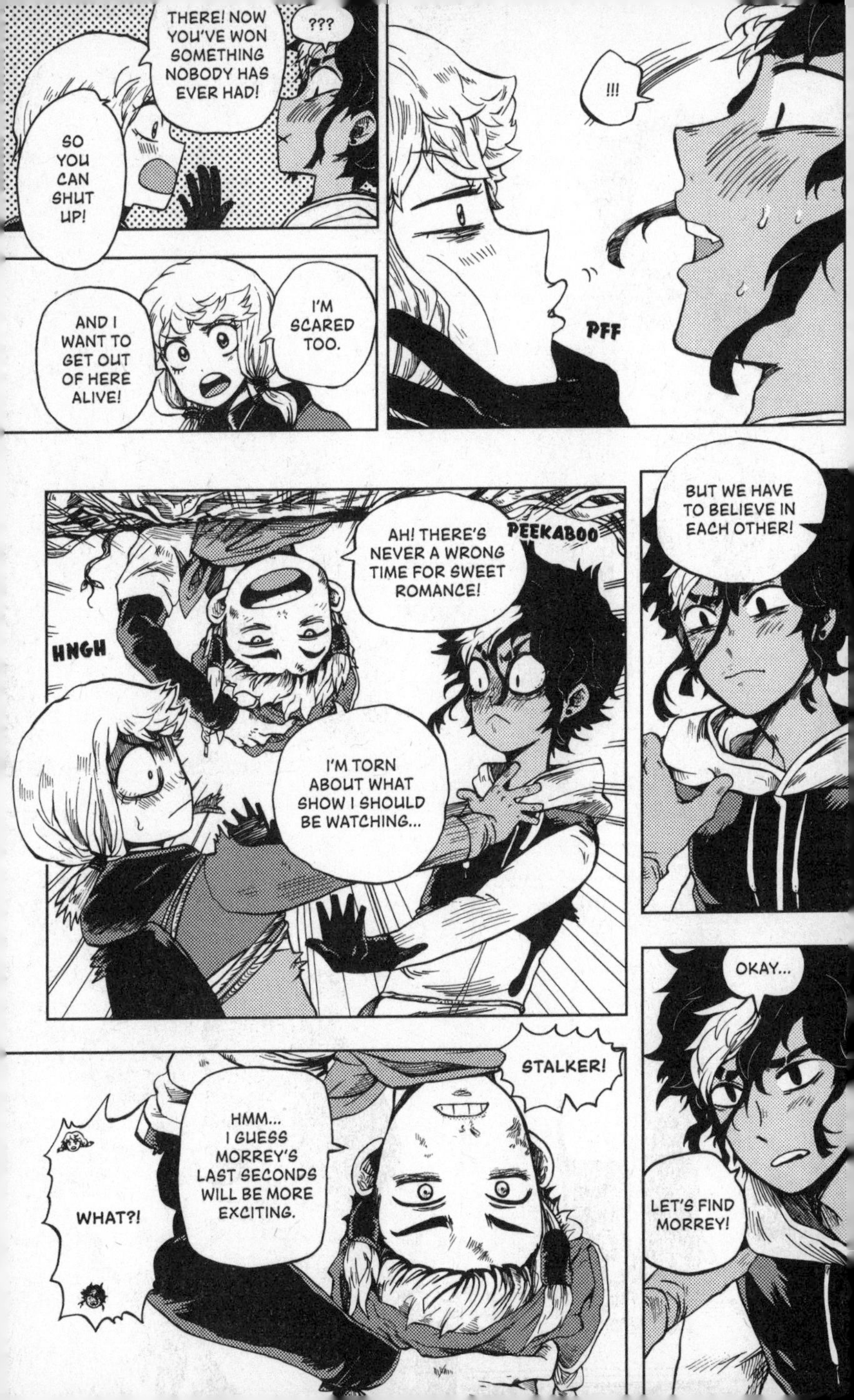
!!!
PFF
???
THERE! NOW YOU'VE WON SOMETHING NOBODY HAS EVER HAD!
SO YOU CAN SHUT UP!
I'M SCARED TOO.
AND I WANT TO GET OUT OF HERE ALIVE!
BUT WE HAVE TO BELIEVE IN EACH OTHER!
OKAY...
LET'S FIND MORREY!
PEEKABOO
AH! THERE'S NEVER A WRONG TIME FOR SWEET ROMANCE!
HNGH
I'M TORN ABOUT WHAT SHOW I SHOULD BE WATCHING...
STALKER!
HMM... I GUESS MORREY'S LAST SECONDS WILL BE MORE EXCITING.
WHAT?!

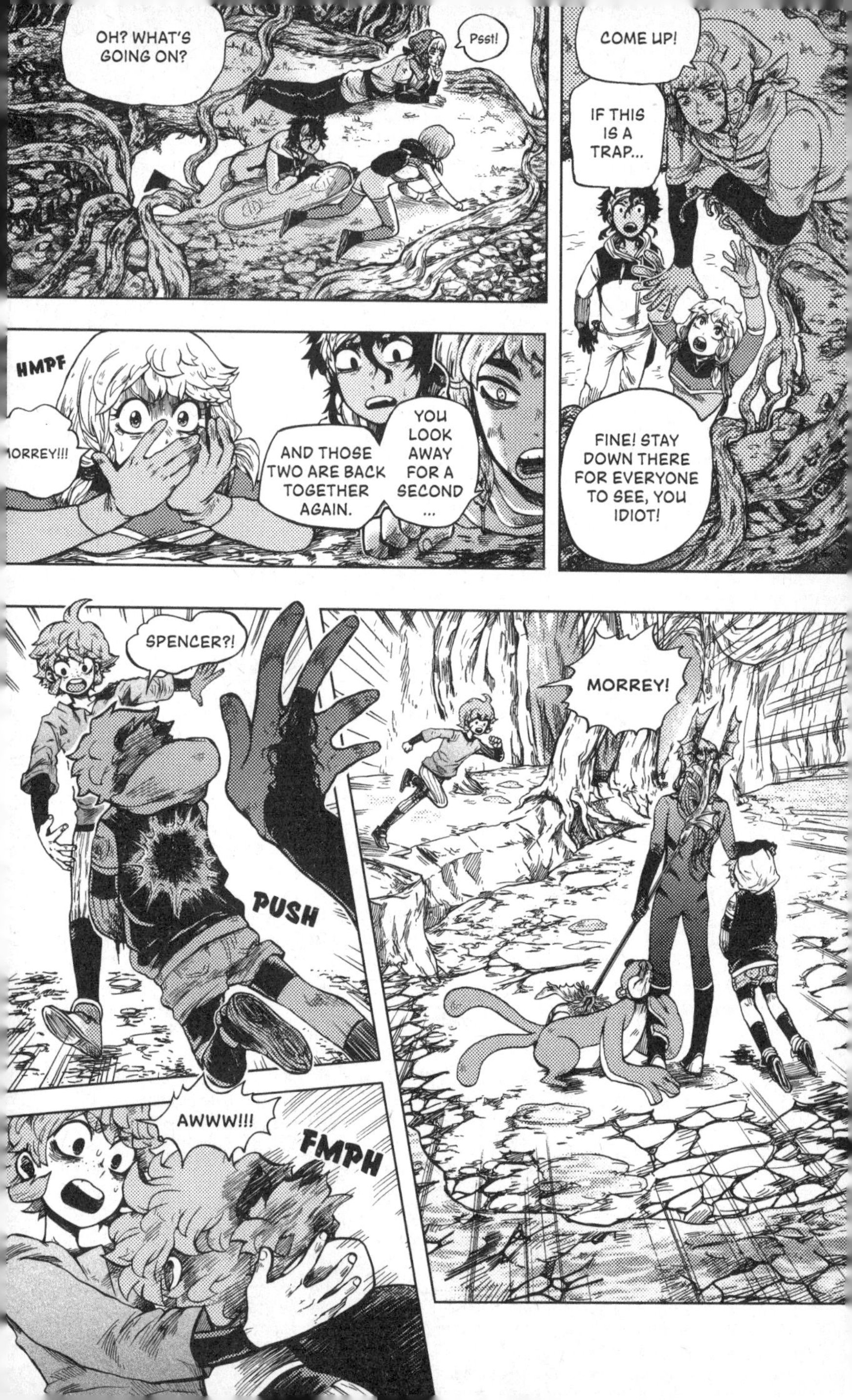
COME UP!
IF THIS IS A TRAP...
FINE! STAY DOWN THERE FOR EVERYONE TO SEE, YOU IDIOT!
Psst!
OH? WHAT'S GOING ON?
YOU LOOK AWAY FOR A SECOND ...
AND THOSE TWO ARE BACK TOGETHER AGAIN.
HMPF
MORREY!!!
MORREY!
SPENCER?!
PUSH
FMPH
AWWW!!!

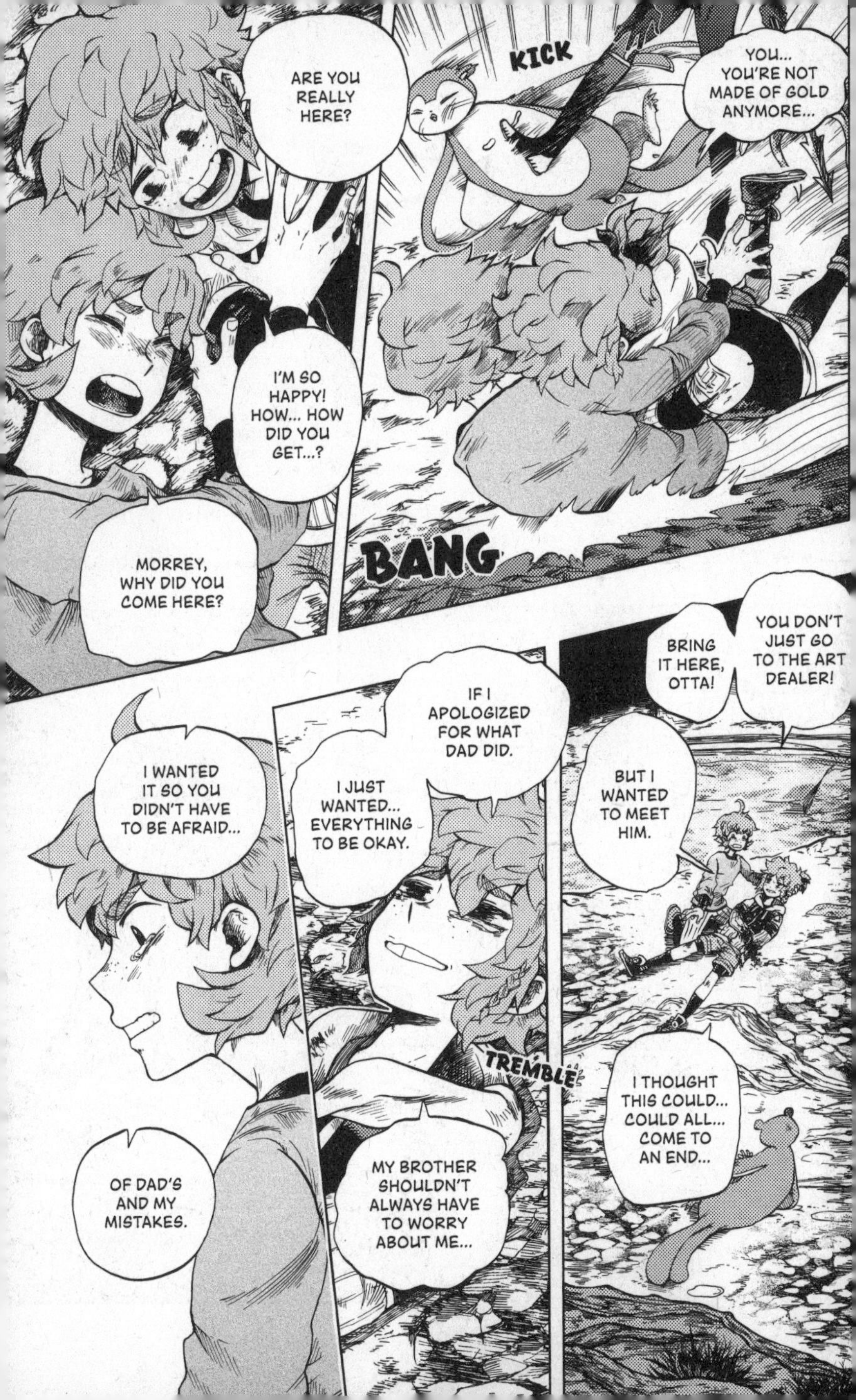
YOU... YOU'RE NOT MADE OF GOLD ANYMORE...
KICK
BANG
ARE YOU REALLY HERE?
I'M SO HAPPY! HOW... HOW DID YOU GET...?
MORREY, WHY DID YOU COME HERE?
YOU DON'T JUST GO TO THE ART DEALER!
BRING IT HERE, OTTA!
BUT I WANTED TO MEET HIM.
I THOUGHT THIS COULD... COULD ALL... COME TO AN END...
IF I APOLOGIZED FOR WHAT DAD DID.
I JUST WANTED... EVERYTHING TO BE OKAY.
TREMBLE
MY BROTHER SHOULDN'T ALWAYS HAVE TO WORRY ABOUT ME...
I WANTED IT SO YOU DIDN'T HAVE TO BE AFRAID...
OF DAD'S AND MY MISTAKES.

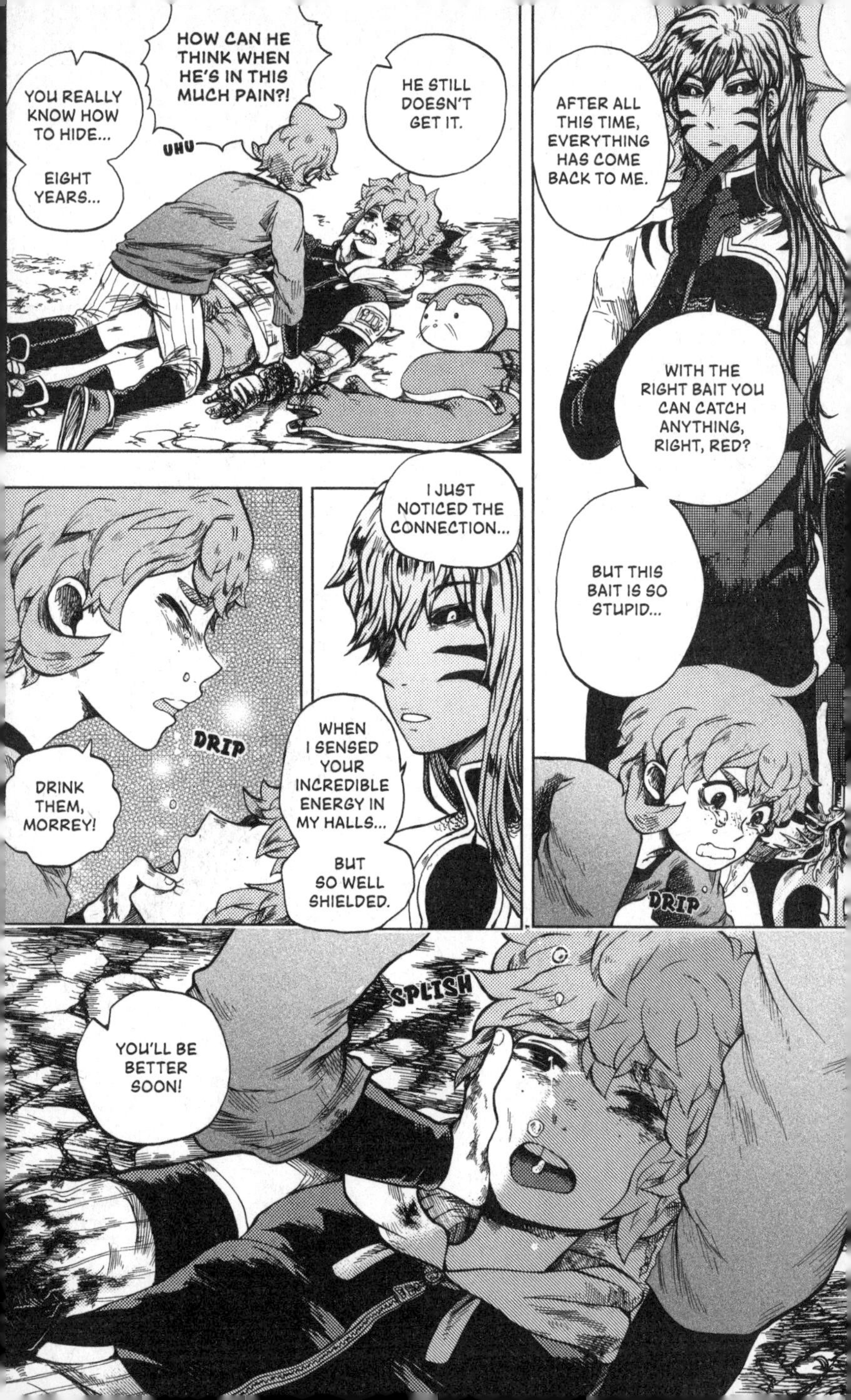
AFTER ALL THIS TIME, EVERYTHING HAS COME BACK TO ME.
WITH THE RIGHT BAIT YOU CAN CATCH ANYTHING, RIGHT, RED?
BUT THIS BAIT IS SO STUPID...
DRIP
HE STILL DOESN'T GET IT.
HOW CAN HE THINK WHEN HE'S IN THIS MUCH PAIN?!
UHU
YOU REALLY KNOW HOW TO HIDE...
EIGHT YEARS...
I JUST NOTICED THE CONNECTION...
WHEN I SENSED YOUR INCREDIBLE ENERGY IN MY HALLS...
BUT SO WELL SHIELDED.
DRIP
DRINK THEM, MORREY!
SPLISH
YOU'LL BE BETTER SOON!

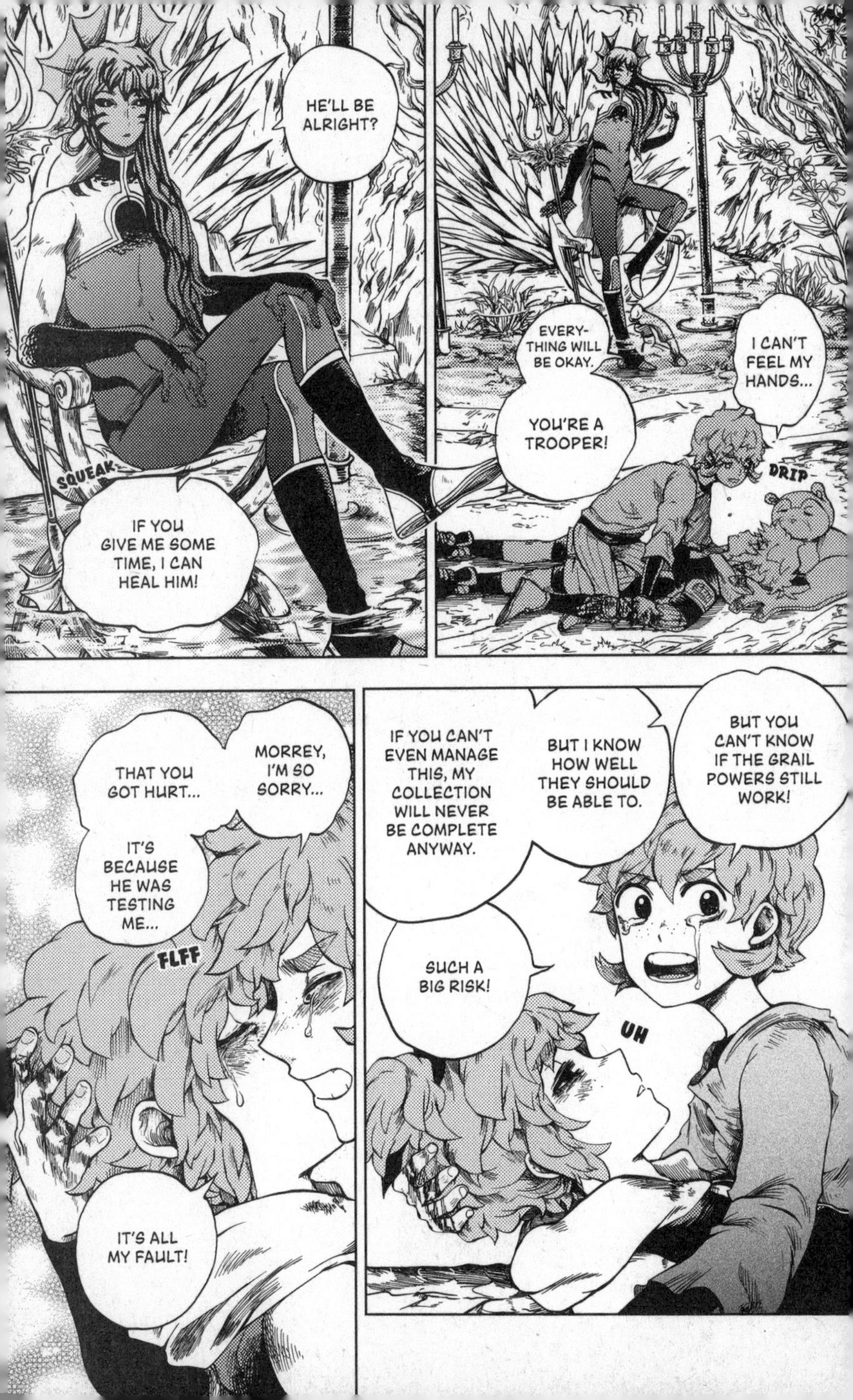
I CAN'T FEEL MY HANDS...
EVERY-THING WILL BE OKAY.
YOU'RE A TROOPER!
DRIP
HE'LL BE ALRIGHT?
SQUEAK
IF YOU GIVE ME SOME TIME, I CAN HEAL HIM!
BUT YOU CAN'T KNOW IF THE GRAIL POWERS STILL WORK!
BUT I KNOW HOW WELL THEY SHOULD BE ABLE TO.
IF YOU CAN'T EVEN MANAGE THIS, MY COLLECTION WILL NEVER BE COMPLETE ANYWAY.
SUCH A BIG RISK!
UH
MORREY, I'M SO SORRY...
THAT YOU GOT HURT...
IT'S BECAUSE HE WAS TESTING ME...
FLFF
IT'S ALL MY FAULT!

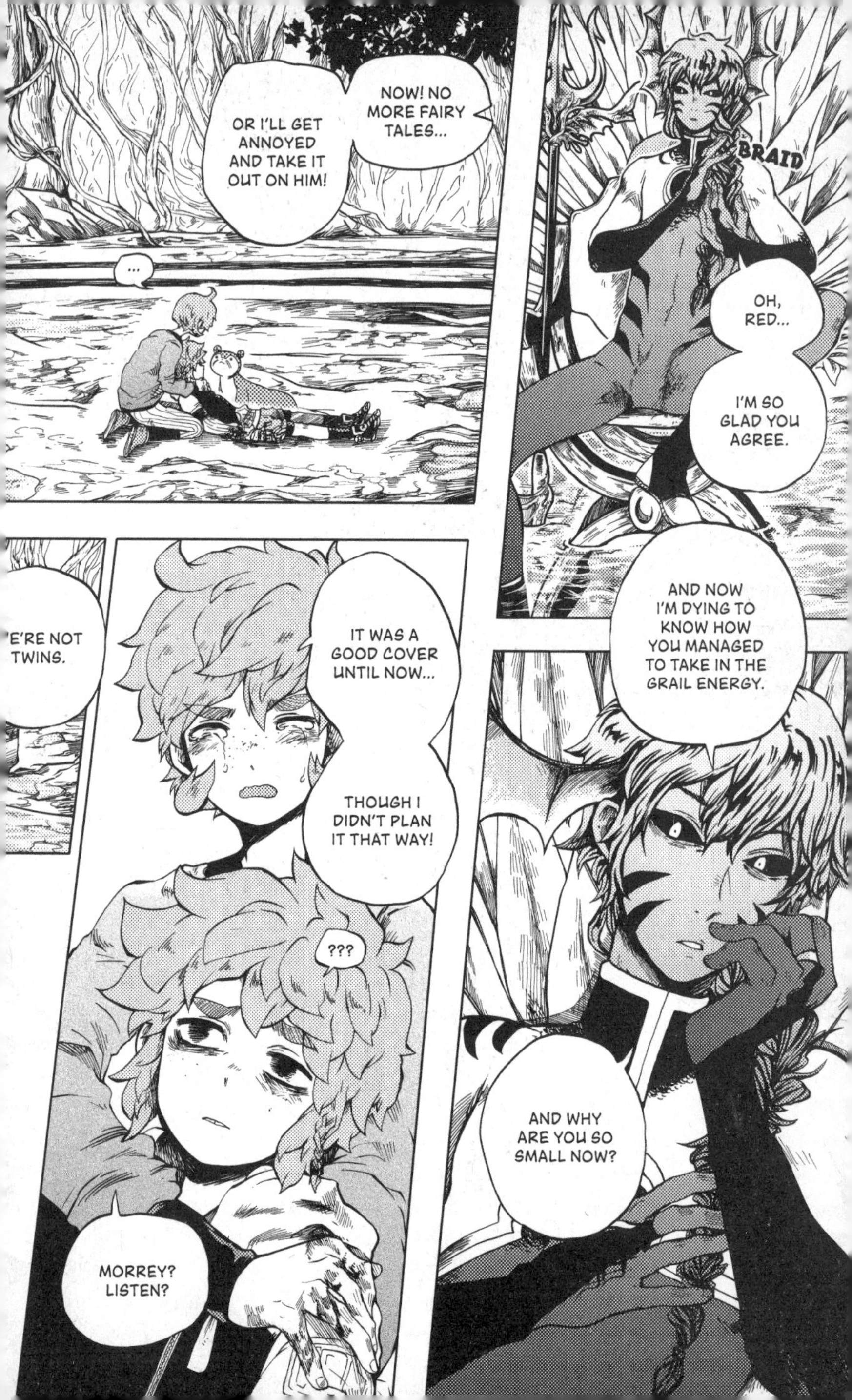
NOW! NO MORE FAIRY TALES...
OR I'LL GET ANNOYED AND TAKE IT OUT ON HIM!
...
BRAID
OH, RED...
I'M SO GLAD YOU AGREE.
'E'RE NOT TWINS.
IT WAS A GOOD COVER UNTIL NOW...
THOUGH I DIDN'T PLAN IT THAT WAY!
???
MORREY? LISTEN?
AND NOW I'M DYING TO KNOW HOW YOU MANAGED TO TAKE IN THE GRAIL ENERGY.
AND WHY ARE YOU SO SMALL NOW?

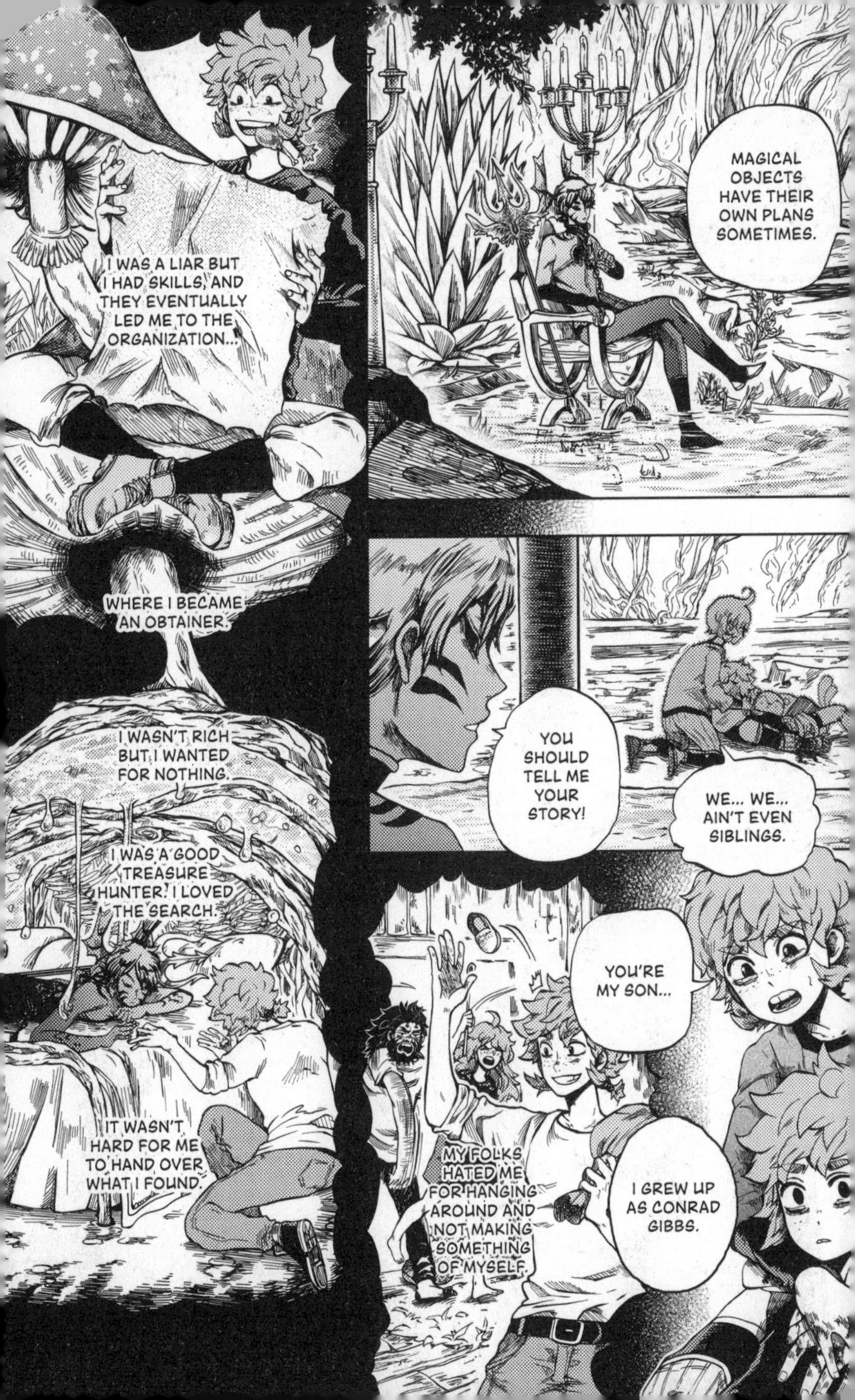
MAGICAL OBJECTS HAVE THEIR OWN PLANS SOMETIMES.
YOU SHOULD TELL ME YOUR STORY!
WE... WE... AIN'T EVEN SIBLINGS.
YOU'RE MY SON...
I GREW UP AS CONRAD GIBBS.
MY FOLKS HATED ME FOR HANGING AROUND AND NOT MAKING SOMETHING OF MYSELF.
I WAS A LIAR BUT I HAD SKILLS, AND THEY EVENTUALLY LED ME TO THE ORGANIZATION...
WHERE I BECAME AN OBTAINER.
I WASN'T RICH BUT I WANTED FOR NOTHING.
I WAS A GOOD TREASURE HUNTER. I LOVED THE SEARCH.
IT WASN'T HARD FOR ME TO HAND OVER WHAT I FOUND.

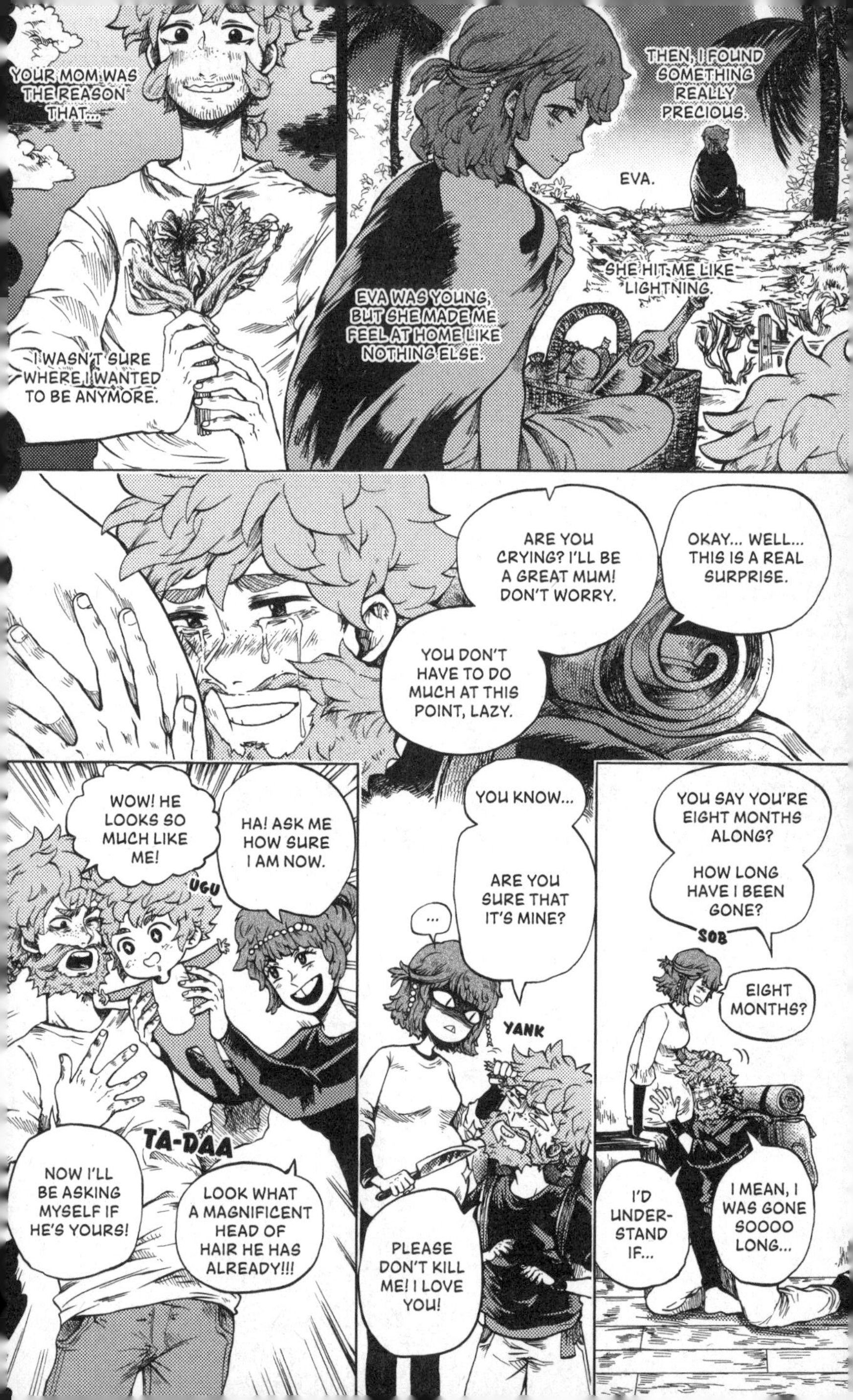
THEN, I FOUND SOMETHING REALLY PRECIOUS.
EVA.
SHE HIT ME LIKE LIGHTNING.
EVA WAS YOUNG, BUT SHE MADE ME FEEL AT HOME LIKE NOTHING ELSE.
YOUR MOM WAS THE REASON THAT...
I WASN'T SURE WHERE I WANTED TO BE ANYMORE.
OKAY... WELL... THIS IS A REAL SURPRISE.
ARE YOU CRYING? I'LL BE A GREAT MUM! DON'T WORRY.
YOU DON'T HAVE TO DO MUCH AT THIS POINT, LAZY.
YOU SAY YOU'RE EIGHT MONTHS ALONG?
HOW LONG HAVE I BEEN GONE?
SOB
EIGHT MONTHS?
I MEAN, I WAS GONE SOOOO LONG...
I'D UNDER-STAND IF...
YOU KNOW...
ARE YOU SURE THAT IT'S MINE?
...
YANK
PLEASE DON'T KILL ME! I LOVE YOU!
HA! ASK ME HOW SURE I AM NOW.
WOW! HE LOOKS SO MUCH LIKE ME!
UGU
TA-DAA
LOOK WHAT A MAGNIFICENT HEAD OF HAIR HE HAS ALREADY!!!
NOW I'LL BE ASKING MYSELF IF HE'S YOURS!

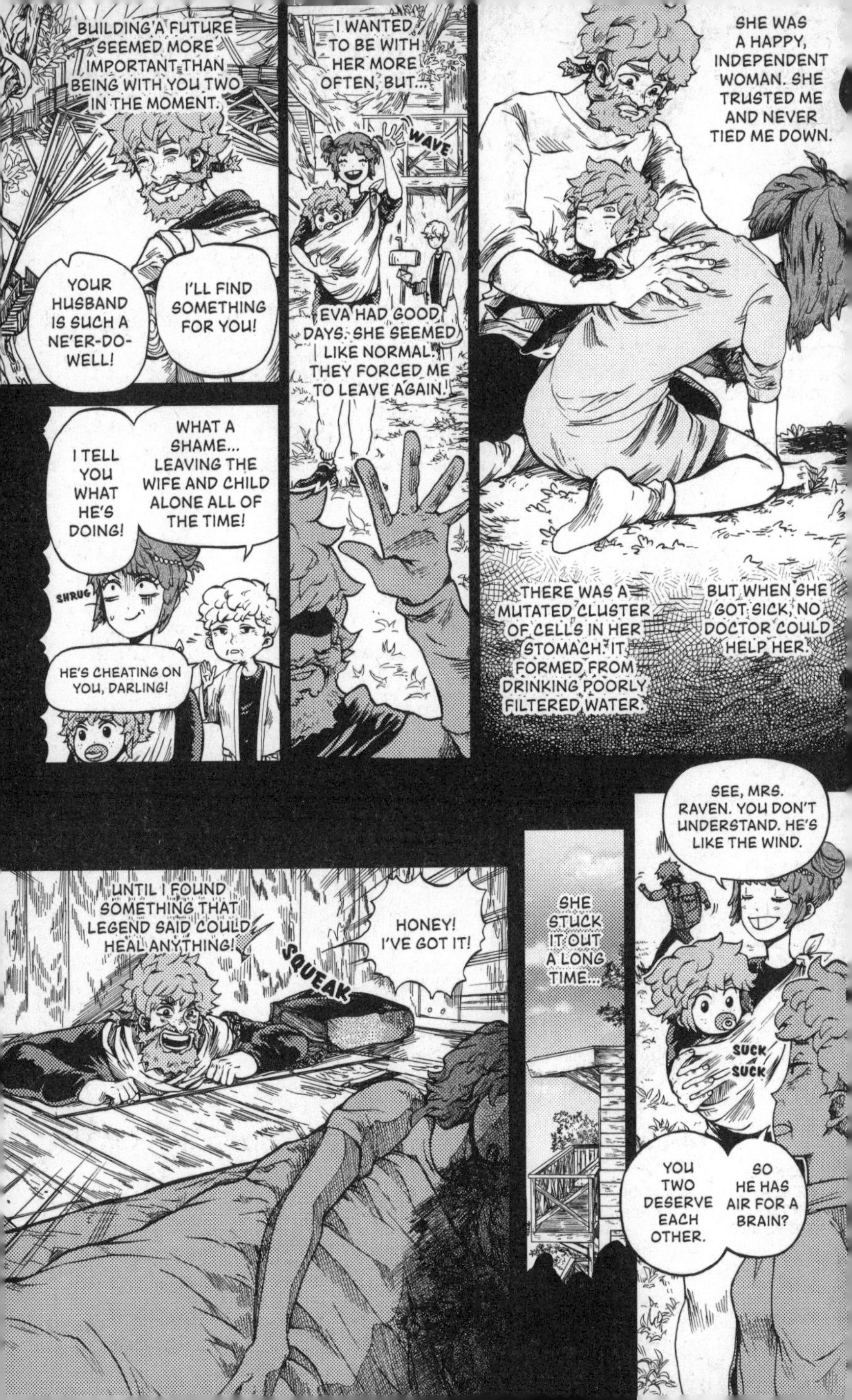
SHE WAS A HAPPY, INDEPENDENT WOMAN. SHE TRUSTED ME AND NEVER TIED ME DOWN.
BUT WHEN SHE GOT SICK, NO DOCTOR COULD HELP HER.
THERE WAS A MUTATED CLUSTER OF CELLS IN HER STOMACH. IT FORMED FROM DRINKING POORLY FILTERED WATER.
I WANTED TO BE WITH HER MORE OFTEN, BUT...
WAVE
EVA HAD GOOD DAYS. SHE SEEMED LIKE NORMAL. THEY FORCED ME TO LEAVE AGAIN.
BUILDING A FUTURE SEEMED MORE IMPORTANT THAN BEING WITH YOU TWO IN THE MOMENT.
I'LL FIND SOMETHING FOR YOU!
YOUR HUSBAND IS SUCH A NE'ER-DO-WELL!
WHAT A SHAME... LEAVING THE WIFE AND CHILD ALONE ALL OF THE TIME!
I TELL YOU WHAT HE'S DOING!
SHRUG
HE'S CHEATING ON YOU, DARLING!
SEE, MRS. RAVEN. YOU DON'T UNDERSTAND. HE'S LIKE THE WIND.
SUCK
SUCK
SO HE HAS AIR FOR A BRAIN?
YOU TWO DESERVE EACH OTHER.
SHE STUCK IT OUT A LONG TIME...
HONEY! I'VE GOT IT!
UNTIL I FOUND SOMETHING THAT LEGEND SAID COULD HEAL ANYTHING!
SQUEAK

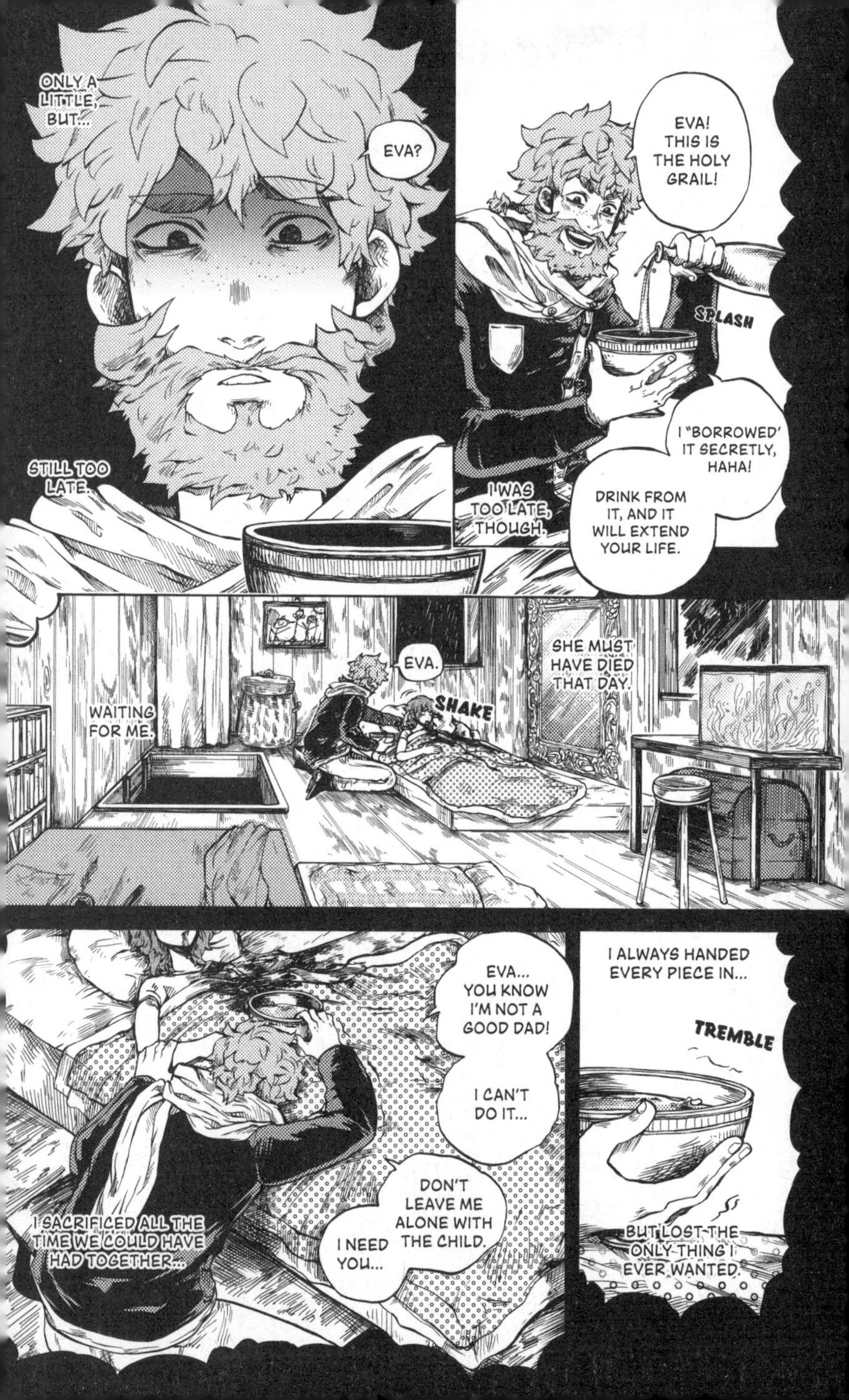
EVA! THIS IS THE HOLY GRAIL!
SPLASH
I "BORROWED' IT SECRETLY, HAHA!
DRINK FROM IT, AND IT WILL EXTEND YOUR LIFE.
I WAS TOO LATE, THOUGH.
EVA?
ONLY A LITTLE, BUT...
STILL TOO LATE.
SHE MUST HAVE DIED THAT DAY.
EVA.
SHAKE
WAITING FOR ME.
I ALWAYS HANDED EVERY PIECE IN...
TREMBLE
BUT LOST THE ONLY THING I EVER WANTED.
EVA... YOU KNOW I'M NOT A GOOD DAD!
I CAN'T DO IT...
DON'T LEAVE ME ALONE WITH THE CHILD.
I NEED YOU...
I SACRIFICED ALL THE TIME WE COULD HAVE HAD TOGETHER...

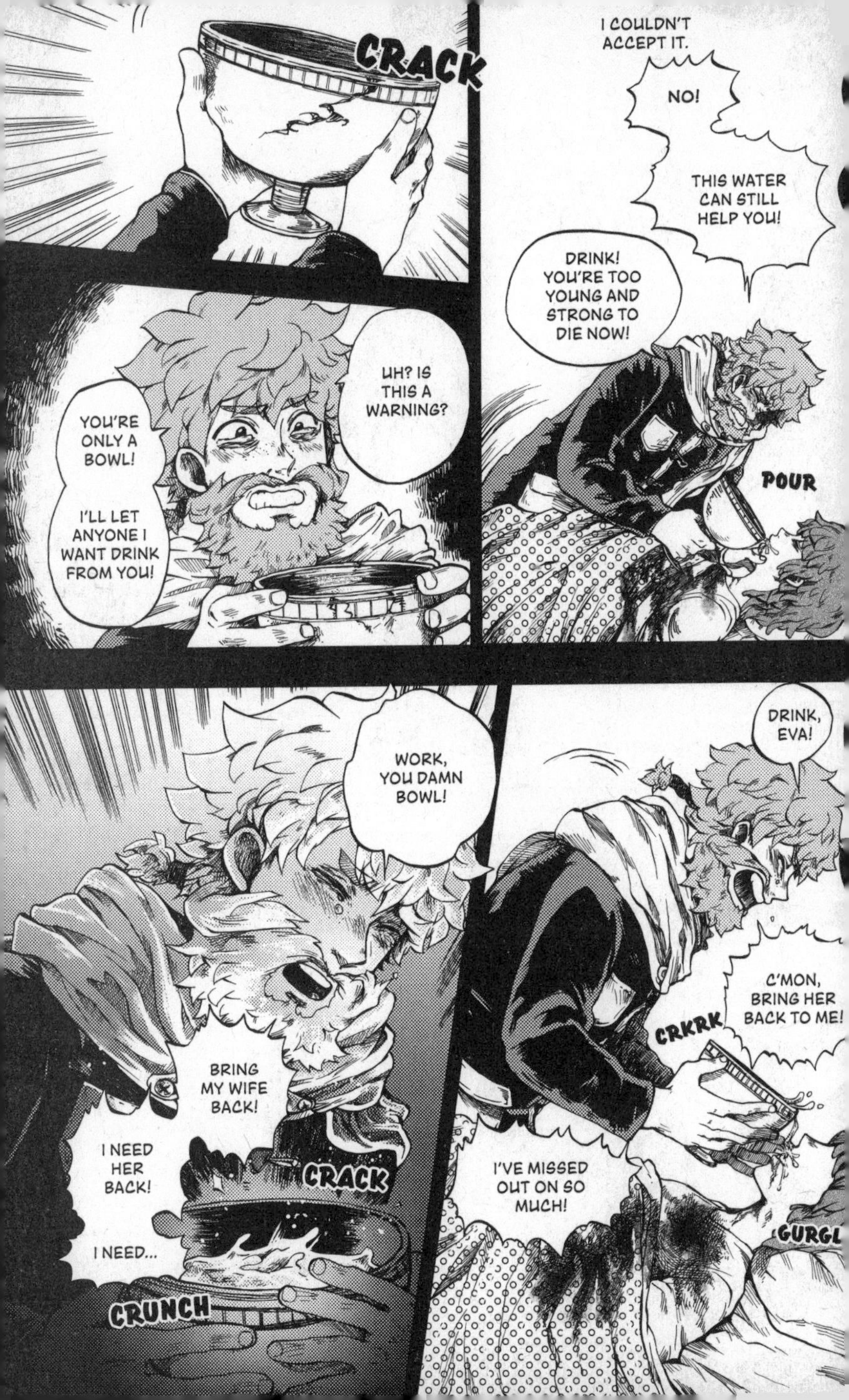
I COULDN'T ACCEPT IT.
NO!
THIS WATER CAN STILL HELP YOU!
DRINK! YOU'RE TOO YOUNG AND STRONG TO DIE NOW!
POUR
CRACK
UH? IS THIS A WARNING?
YOU'RE ONLY A BOWL!
I'LL LET ANYONE I WANT DRINK FROM YOU!
DRINK, EVA!
C'MON, BRING HER BACK TO ME!
CRKRK
I'VE MISSED OUT ON SO MUCH!
GURGL
WORK, YOU DAMN BOWL!
BRING MY WIFE BACK!
I NEED HER BACK!
CRACK
I NEED...
CRUNCH

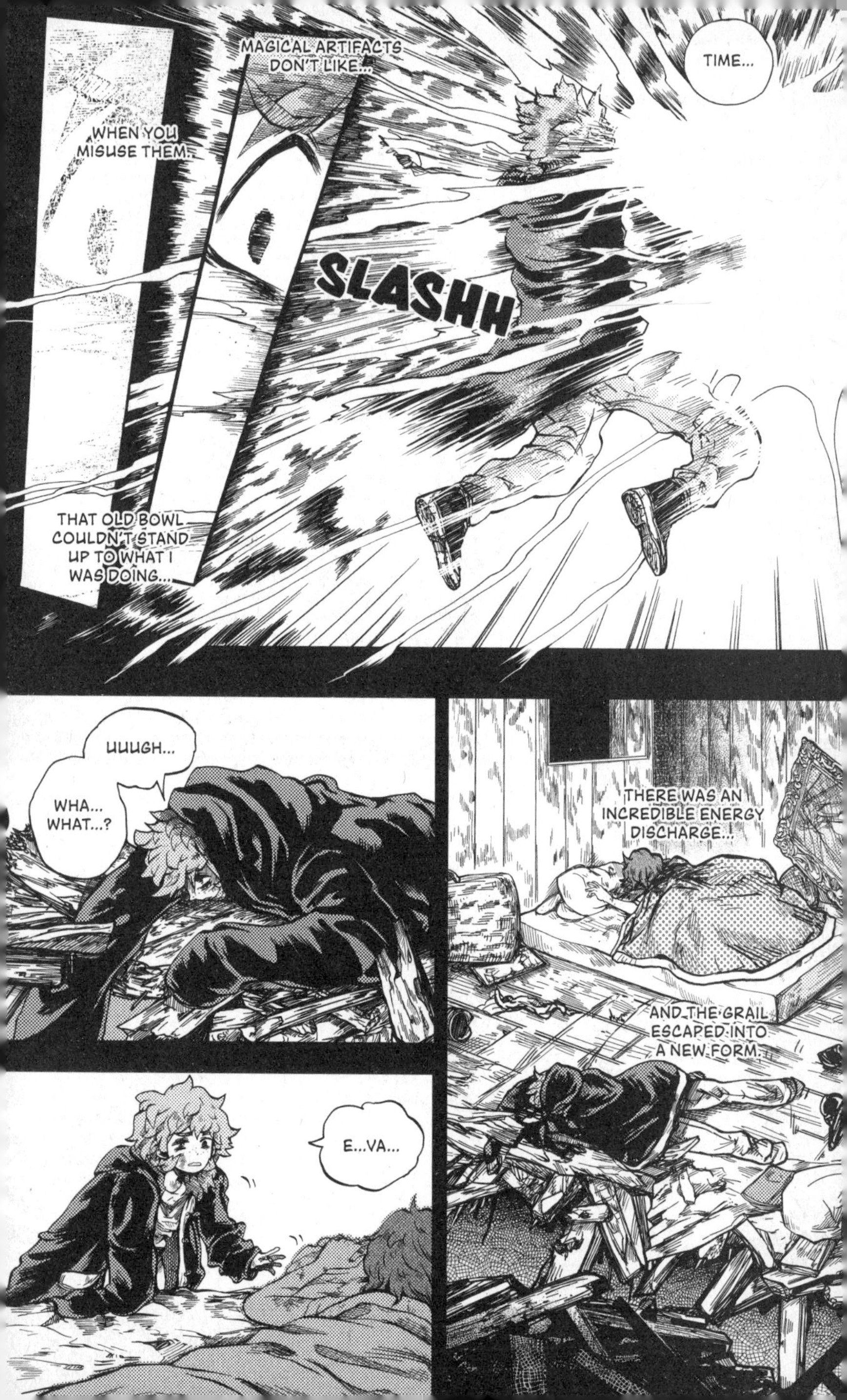
TIME...
MAGICAL ARTIFACTS DON'T LIKE...
WHEN YOU MISUSE THEM.
SLASHH
THAT OLD BOWL COULDN'T STAND UP TO WHAT I WAS DOING...
THERE WAS AN INCREDIBLE ENERGY DISCHARGE...
AND THE GRAIL ESCAPED INTO A NEW FORM.
UUUGH...
WHA... WHAT...?
E...VA...

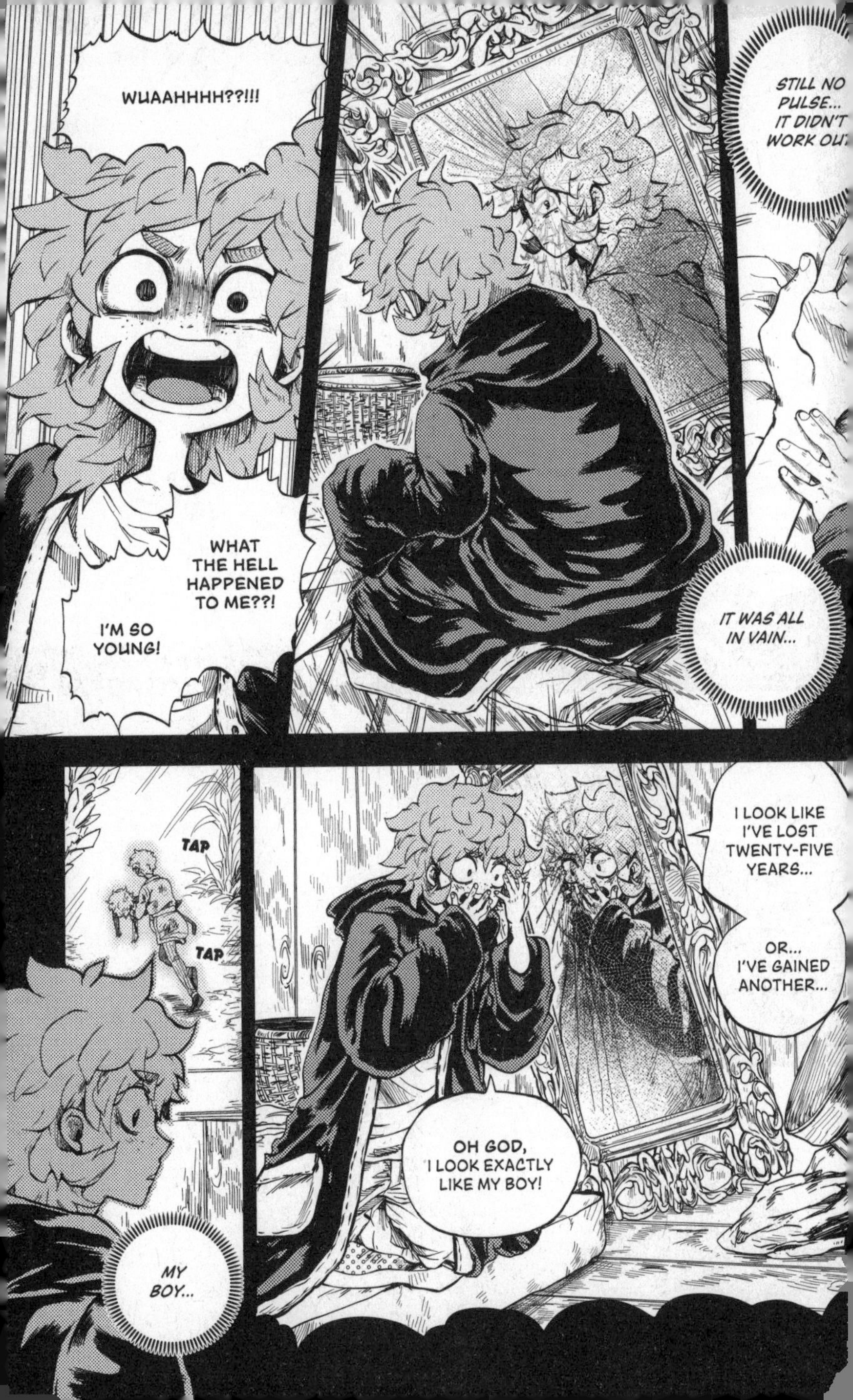
STILL NO PULSE... IT DIDN'T WORK OUT
IT WAS ALL IN VAIN...
WUAAHHHH??!!!
WHAT THE HELL HAPPENED TO ME??!
I'M SO YOUNG!
I LOOK LIKE I'VE LOST TWENTY-FIVE YEARS...
OR... I'VE GAINED ANOTHER...
OH GOD, I LOOK EXACTLY LIKE MY BOY!
TAP
TAP
MY BOY...

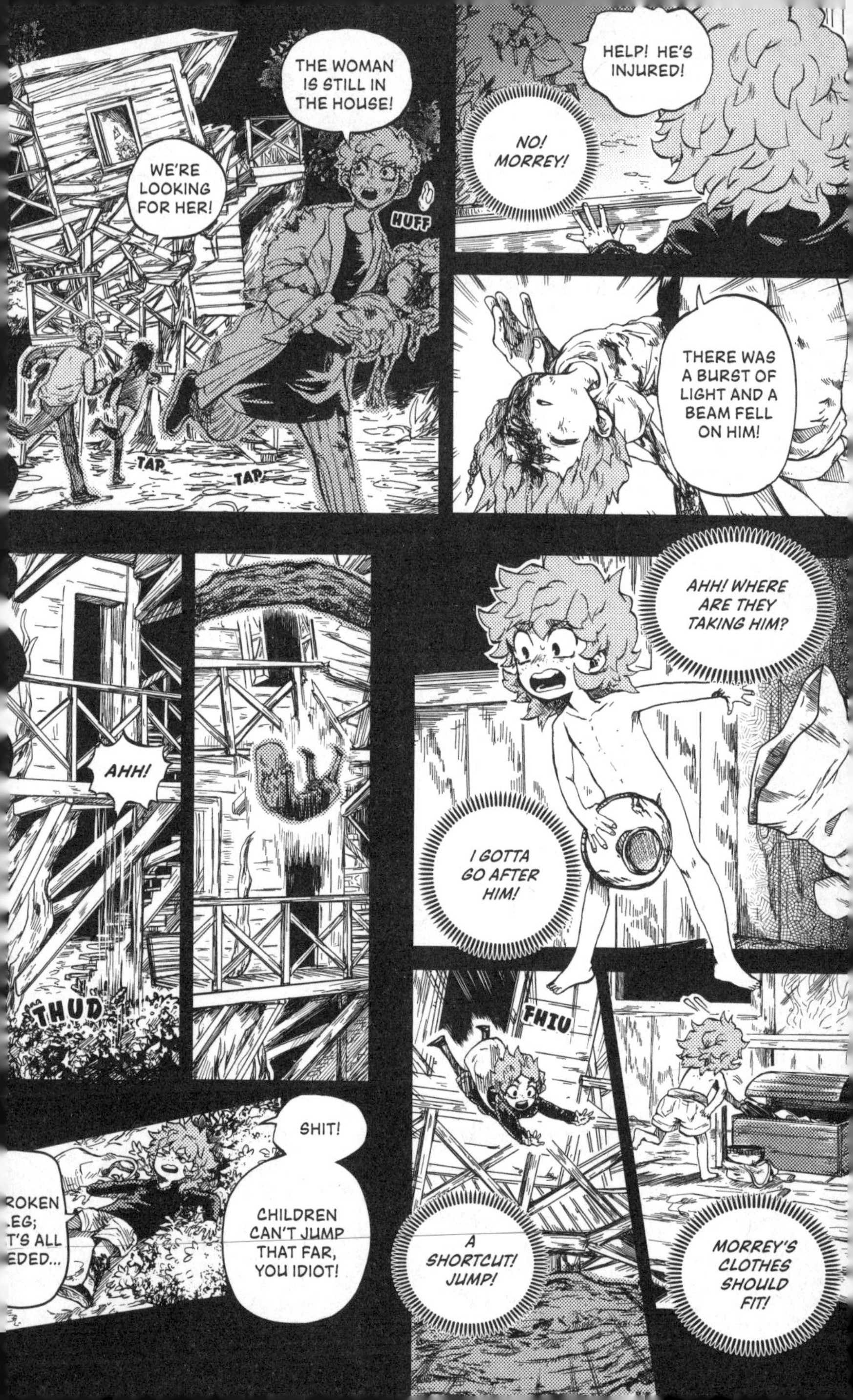
HELP! HE'S INJURED!
NO! MORREY!
THERE WAS A BURST OF LIGHT AND A BEAM FELL ON HIM!
THE WOMAN IS STILL IN THE HOUSE!
WE'RE LOOKING FOR HER!
HUFF
TAP
TAP
AHH! WHERE ARE THEY TAKING HIM?
I GOTTA GO AFTER HIM!
MORREY'S CLOTHES SHOULD FIT!
FHIU
A SHORTCUT! JUMP!
AHH!
THUD
SHIT!
CHILDREN CAN'T JUMP THAT FAR, YOU IDIOT!
ROKEN LEG; T'S ALL EDED...

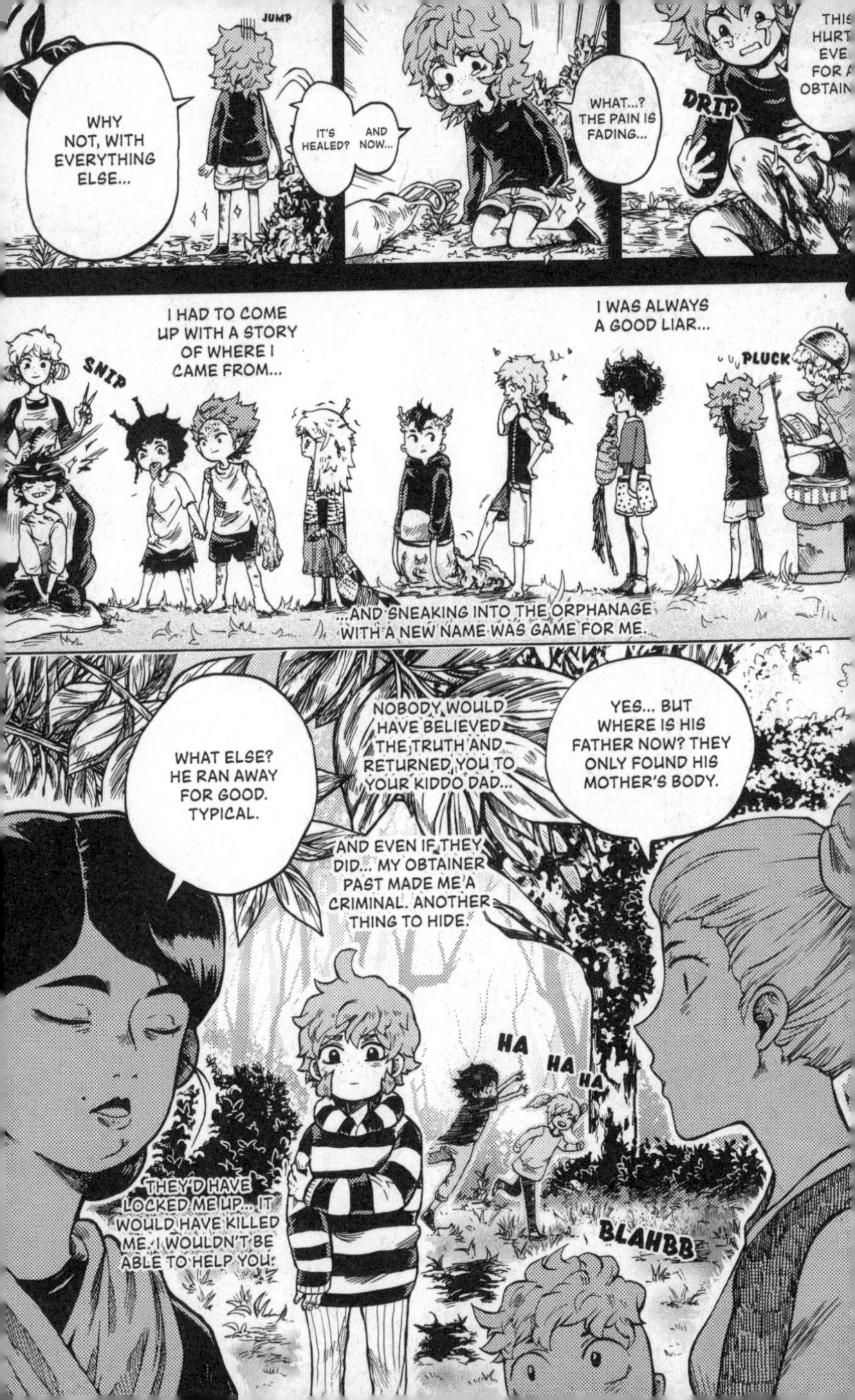
THIS HURT EVE FOR A OBTAIN
DRIP
WHAT...? THE PAIN IS FADING...
JUMP
IT'S HEALED? AND NOW...
WHY NOT, WITH EVERYTHING ELSE...
PLUCK
I WAS ALWAYS A GOOD LIAR...
I HAD TO COME UP WITH A STORY OF WHERE I CAME FROM...
SNIP
...AND SNEAKING INTO THE ORPHANAGE WITH A NEW NAME WAS GAME FOR ME.
YES... BUT WHERE IS HIS FATHER NOW? THEY ONLY FOUND HIS MOTHER'S BODY.
NOBODY WOULD HAVE BELIEVED THE TRUTH AND RETURNED YOU TO YOUR KIDDO DAD...
WHAT ELSE? HE RAN AWAY FOR GOOD. TYPICAL.
AND EVEN IF THEY DID... MY OBTAINER PAST MADE ME A CRIMINAL. ANOTHER THING TO HIDE.
HA HA HA
THEY'D HAVE LOCKED ME UP... IT WOULD HAVE KILLED ME. I WOULDN'T BE ABLE TO HELP YOU.
BLAHBB

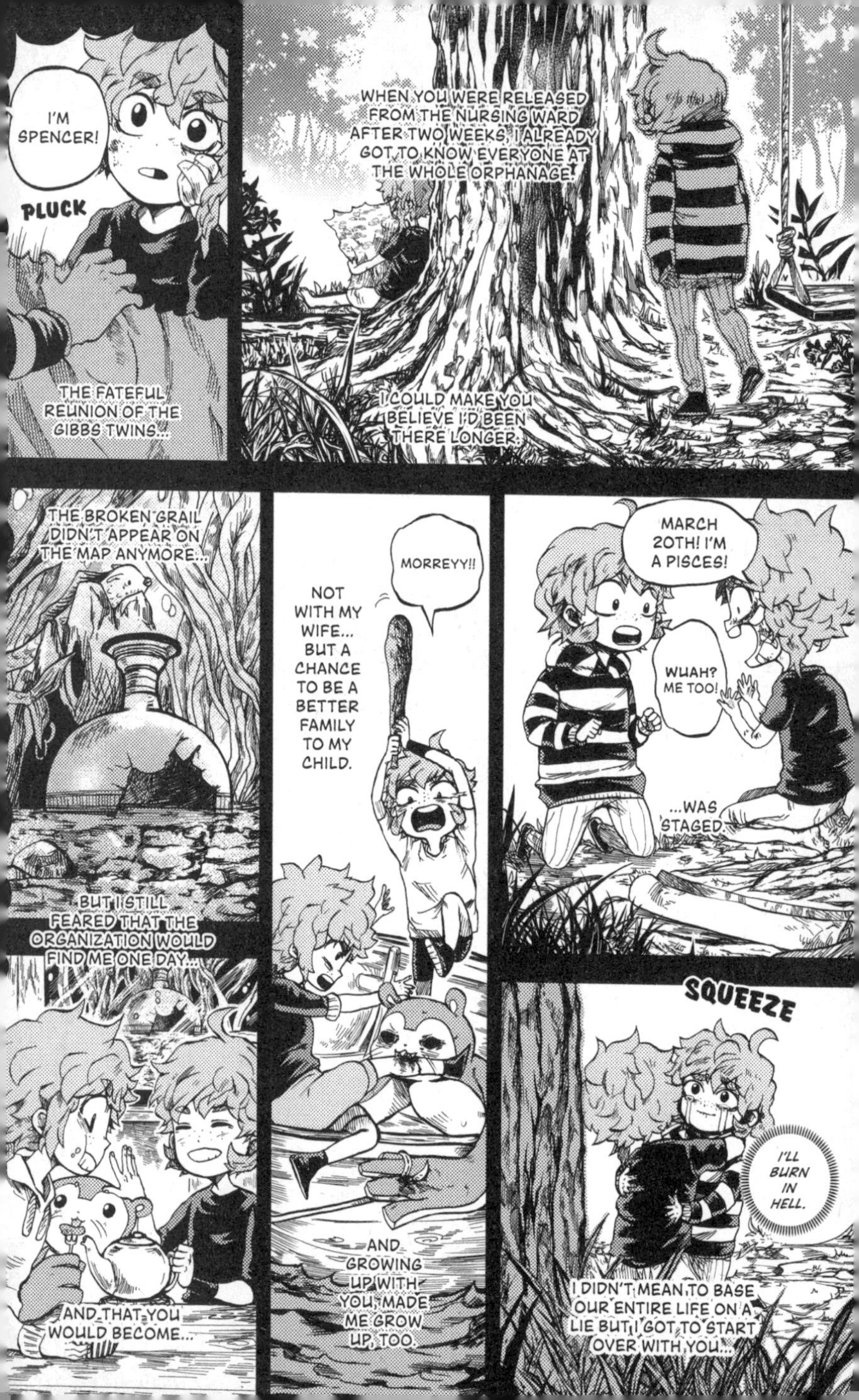
WHEN YOU WERE RELEASED FROM THE NURSING WARD AFTER TWO WEEKS, I ALREADY GOT TO KNOW EVERYONE AT THE WHOLE ORPHANAGE!
I COULD MAKE YOU BELIEVE I'D BEEN THERE LONGER.
I'M SPENCER!
PLUCK
THE FATEFUL REUNION OF THE GIBBS TWINS...
MARCH 20TH! I'M A PISCES!
WUAH? ME TOO!
...WAS STAGED.
SQUEEZE
I'LL BURN IN HELL.
I DIDN'T MEAN TO BASE OUR ENTIRE LIFE ON A LIE BUT I GOT TO START OVER WITH YOU...
MORREYY!!
NOT WITH MY WIFE... BUT A CHANCE TO BE A BETTER FAMILY TO MY CHILD.
AND GROWING UP WITH YOU MADE ME GROW UP, TOO.
THE BROKEN GRAIL DIDN'T APPEAR ON THE MAP ANYMORE...
BUT I STILL FEARED THAT THE ORGANIZATION WOULD FIND ME ONE DAY...
AND THAT YOU WOULD BECOME...

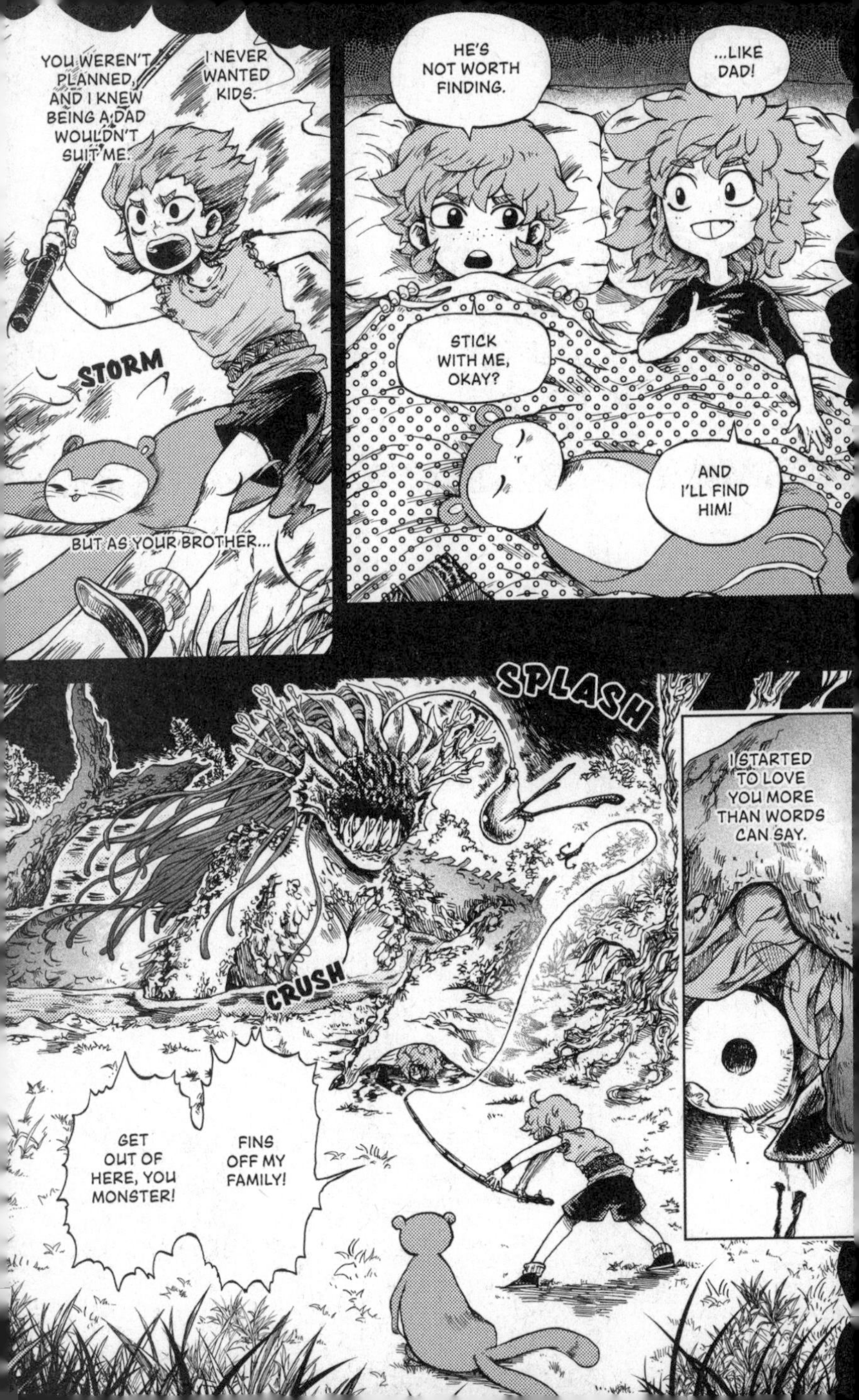
...LIKE DAD!
HE'S NOT WORTH FINDING.
STICK WITH ME, OKAY?
AND I'LL FIND HIM!
I NEVER WANTED KIDS.
YOU WEREN'T PLANNED, AND I KNEW BEING A DAD WOULDN'T SUIT ME.
STORM
BUT AS YOUR BROTHER...
I STARTED TO LOVE YOU MORE THAN WORDS CAN SAY.
SPLASH
CRUSH
FINS OFF MY FAMILY!
GET OUT OF HERE, YOU MONSTER!

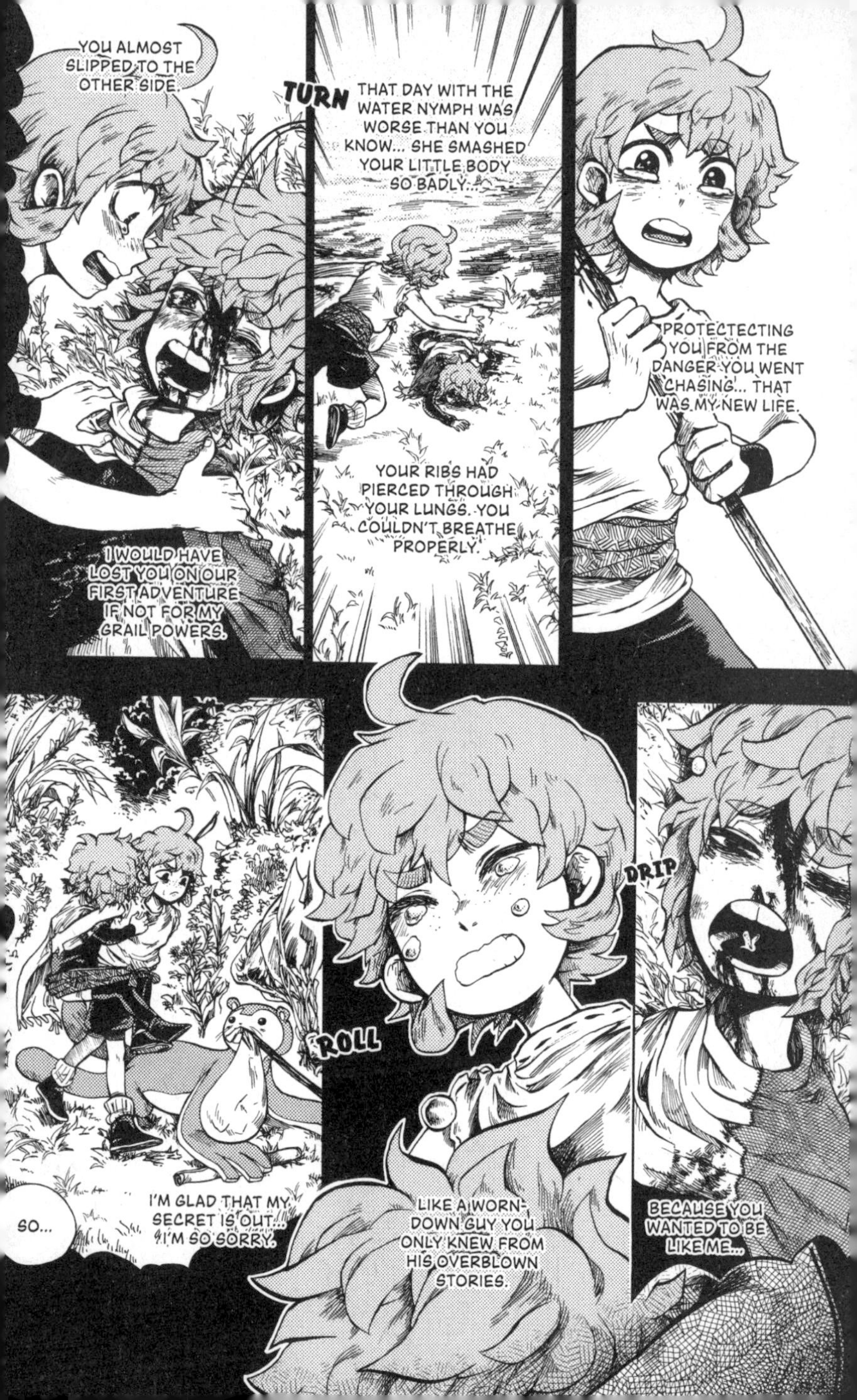
PROTECTECTING YOU FROM THE DANGER YOU WENT CHASING... THAT WAS MY NEW LIFE.
TURN
THAT DAY WITH THE WATER NYMPH WAS WORSE THAN YOU KNOW... SHE SMASHED YOUR LITTLE BODY SO BADLY...
YOUR RIBS HAD PIERCED THROUGH YOUR LUNGS. YOU COULDN'T BREATHE PROPERLY.
YOU ALMOST SLIPPED TO THE OTHER SIDE.
I WOULD HAVE LOST YOU ON OUR FIRST ADVENTURE IF NOT FOR MY GRAIL POWERS.
DRIP
BECAUSE YOU WANTED TO BE LIKE ME...
ROLL
LIKE A WORN-DOWN GUY YOU ONLY KNEW FROM HIS OVERBLOWN STORIES.
I'M GLAD THAT MY SECRET IS OUT... I'M SO SORRY.
SO...

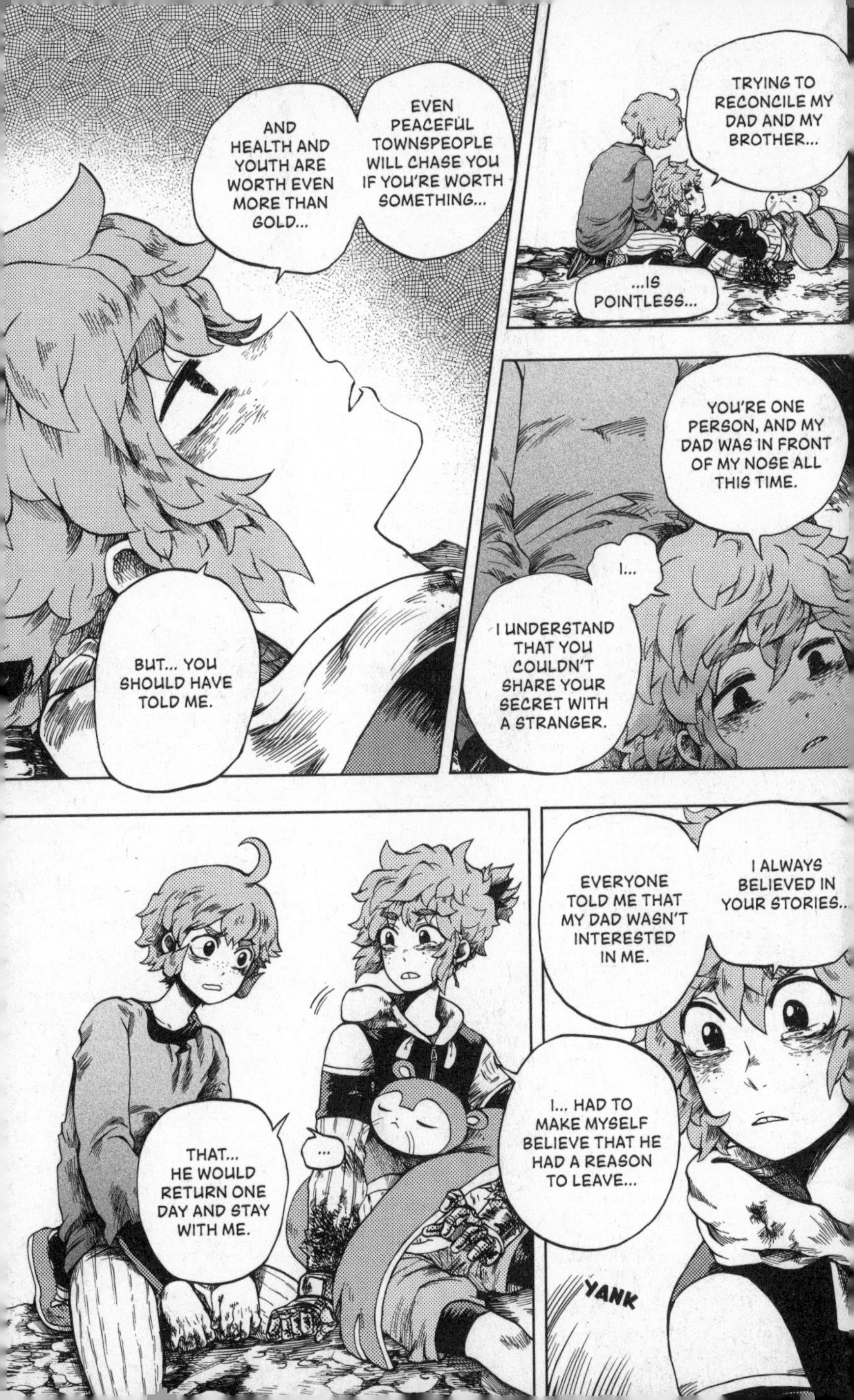
TRYING TO RECONCILE MY DAD AND MY BROTHER...
...IS POINTLESS...
YOU'RE ONE PERSON, AND MY DAD WAS IN FRONT OF MY NOSE ALL THIS TIME.
I...
I UNDERSTAND THAT YOU COULDN'T SHARE YOUR SECRET WITH A STRANGER.
EVEN PEACEFUL TOWNSPEOPLE WILL CHASE YOU IF YOU'RE WORTH SOMETHING...
AND HEALTH AND YOUTH ARE WORTH EVEN MORE THAN GOLD...
BUT... YOU SHOULD HAVE TOLD ME.
I ALWAYS BELIEVED IN YOUR STORIES...
EVERYONE TOLD ME THAT MY DAD WASN'T INTERESTED IN ME.
I... HAD TO MAKE MYSELF BELIEVE THAT HE HAD A REASON TO LEAVE...
YANK
THAT... HE WOULD RETURN ONE DAY AND STAY WITH ME.
...

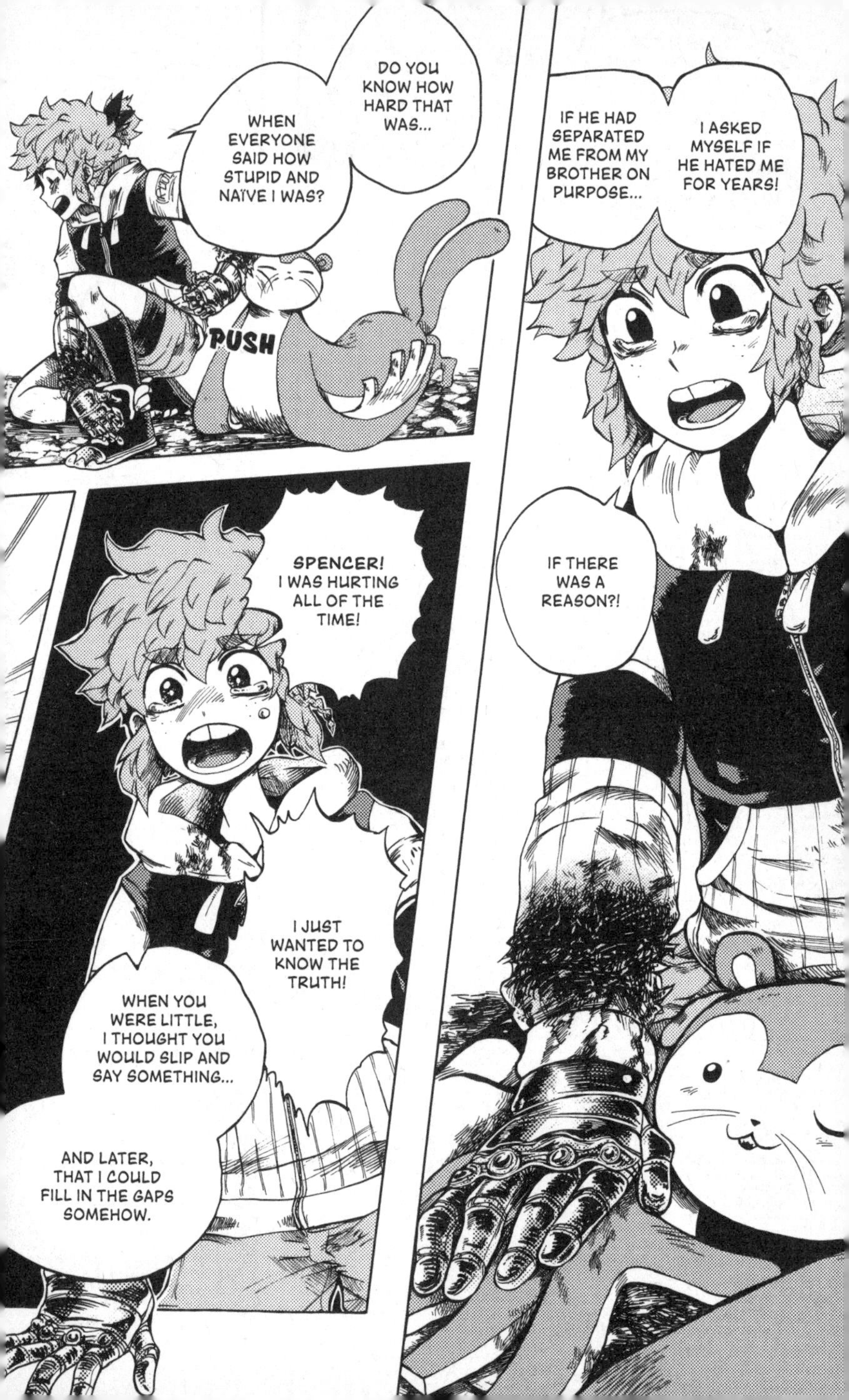
I ASKED MYSELF IF HE HATED ME FOR YEARS!
IF HE HAD SEPARATED ME FROM MY BROTHER ON PURPOSE...
IF THERE WAS A REASON?!
DO YOU KNOW HOW HARD THAT WAS...
WHEN EVERYONE SAID HOW STUPID AND NAÏVE I WAS?
PUSH
SPENCER! I WAS HURTING ALL OF THE TIME!
I JUST WANTED TO KNOW THE TRUTH!
WHEN YOU WERE LITTLE, I THOUGHT YOU WOULD SLIP AND SAY SOMETHING...
AND LATER, THAT I COULD FILL IN THE GAPS SOMEHOW.

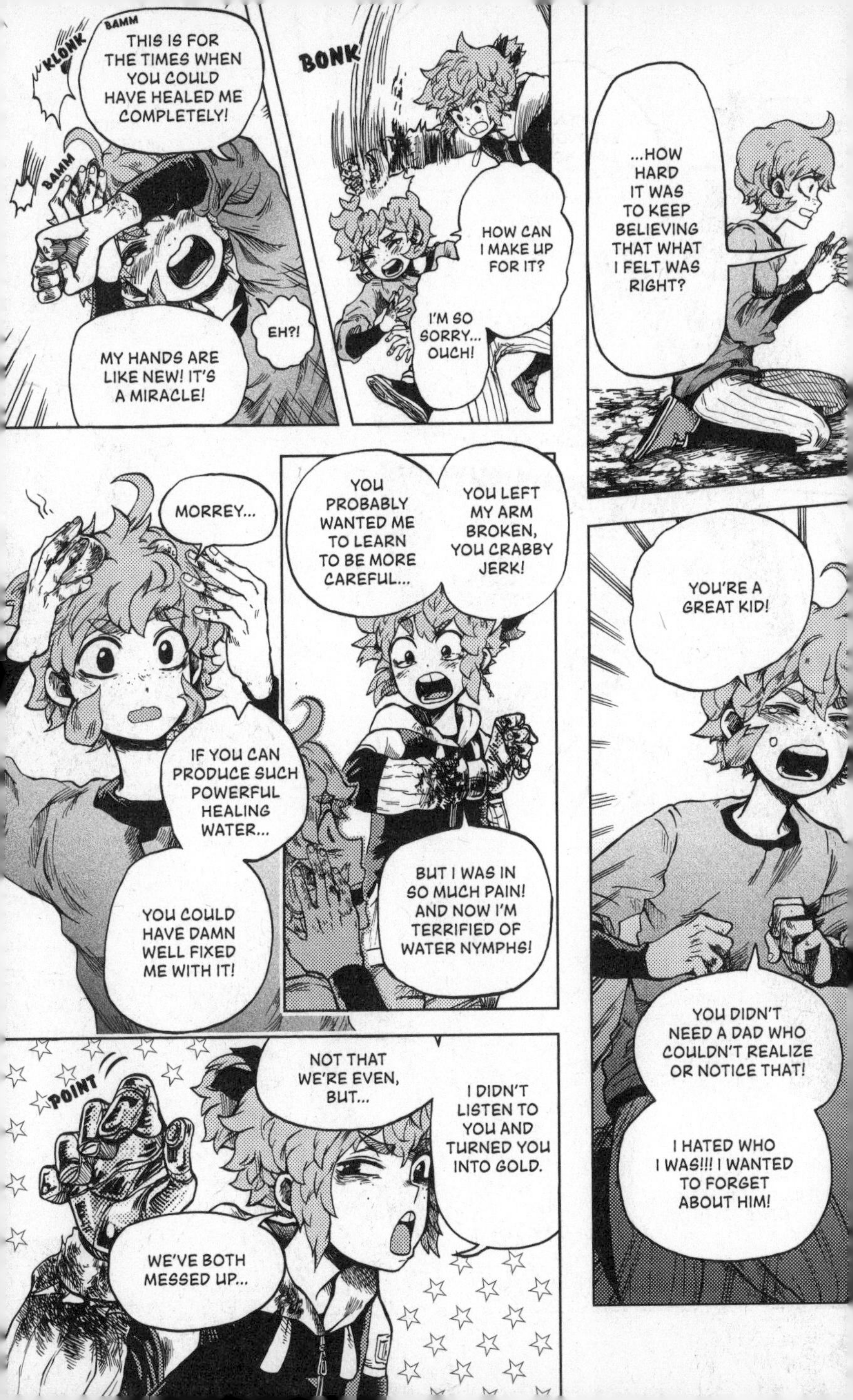
...HOW HARD IT WAS TO KEEP BELIEVING THAT WHAT I FELT WAS RIGHT?
BONK
HOW CAN I MAKE UP FOR IT?
I'M SO SORRY... OUCH!
BAMM
THIS IS FOR THE TIMES WHEN YOU COULD HAVE HEALED ME COMPLETELY!
KLONK
BAMM
EH?!
MY HANDS ARE LIKE NEW! IT'S A MIRACLE!
YOU'RE A GREAT KID!
YOU DIDN'T NEED A DAD WHO COULDN'T REALIZE OR NOTICE THAT!
I HATED WHO I WAS!!! I WANTED TO FORGET ABOUT HIM!
YOU LEFT MY ARM BROKEN, YOU CRABBY JERK!
YOU PROBABLY WANTED ME TO LEARN TO BE MORE CAREFUL...
BUT I WAS IN SO MUCH PAIN! AND NOW I'M TERRIFIED OF WATER NYMPHS!
MORREY...
IF YOU CAN PRODUCE SUCH POWERFUL HEALING WATER...
YOU COULD HAVE DAMN WELL FIXED ME WITH IT!
I DIDN'T LISTEN TO YOU AND TURNED YOU INTO GOLD.
NOT THAT WE'RE EVEN, BUT...
POINT
WE'VE BOTH MESSED UP...

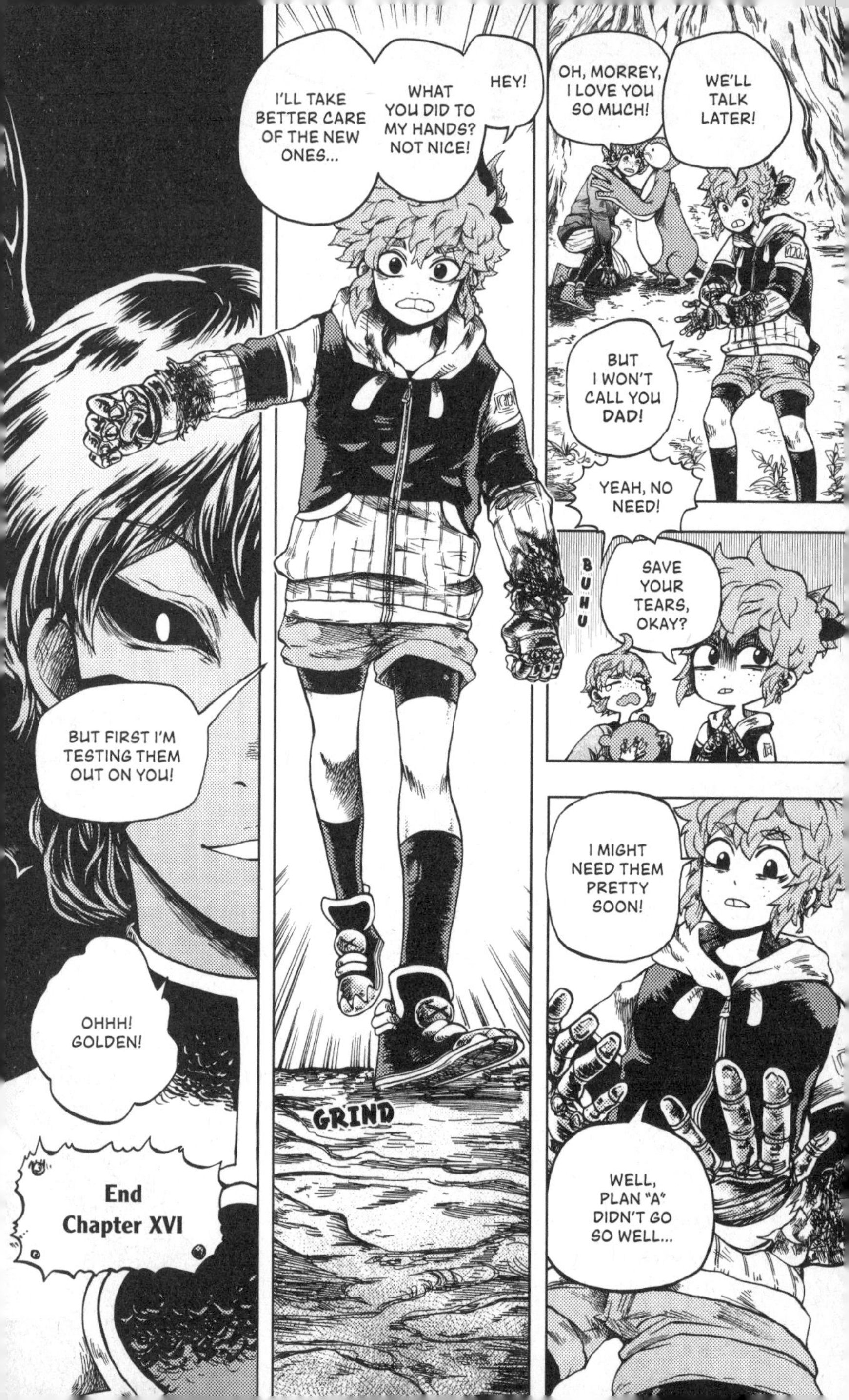
WE'LL TALK LATER!
OH, MORREY, I LOVE YOU SO MUCH!
BUT I WON'T CALL YOU DAD!
YEAH, NO NEED!
SAVE YOUR TEARS, OKAY?
BUHU
I MIGHT NEED THEM PRETTY SOON!
WELL, PLAN "A" DIDN'T GO SO WELL...
HEY!
WHAT YOU DID TO MY HANDS? NOT NICE!
I'LL TAKE BETTER CARE OF THE NEW ONES...
GRIND
BUT FIRST I'M TESTING THEM OUT ON YOU!
OHHH! GOLDEN!
End Chapter XVI

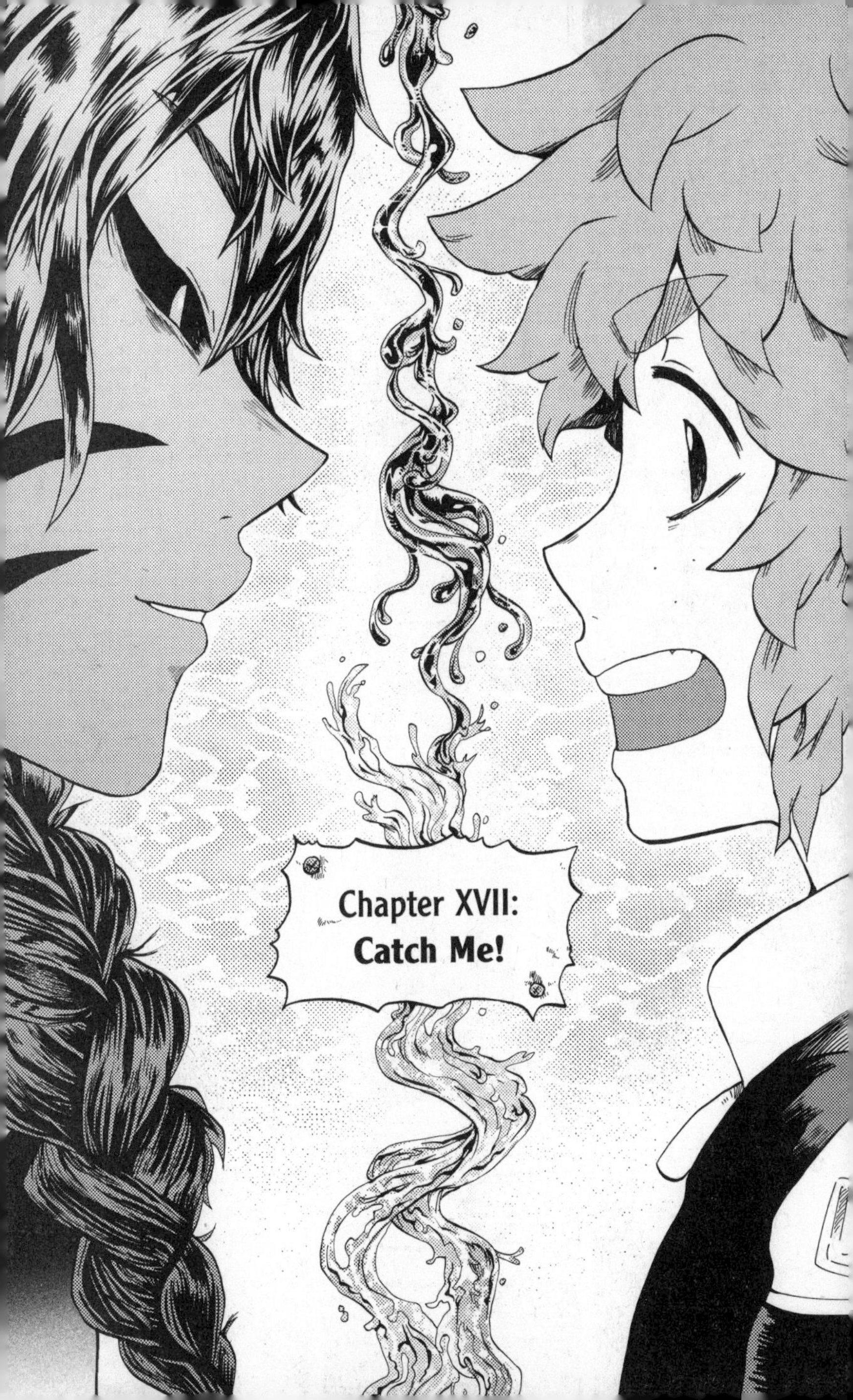
Chapter XVII:
Catch Me!

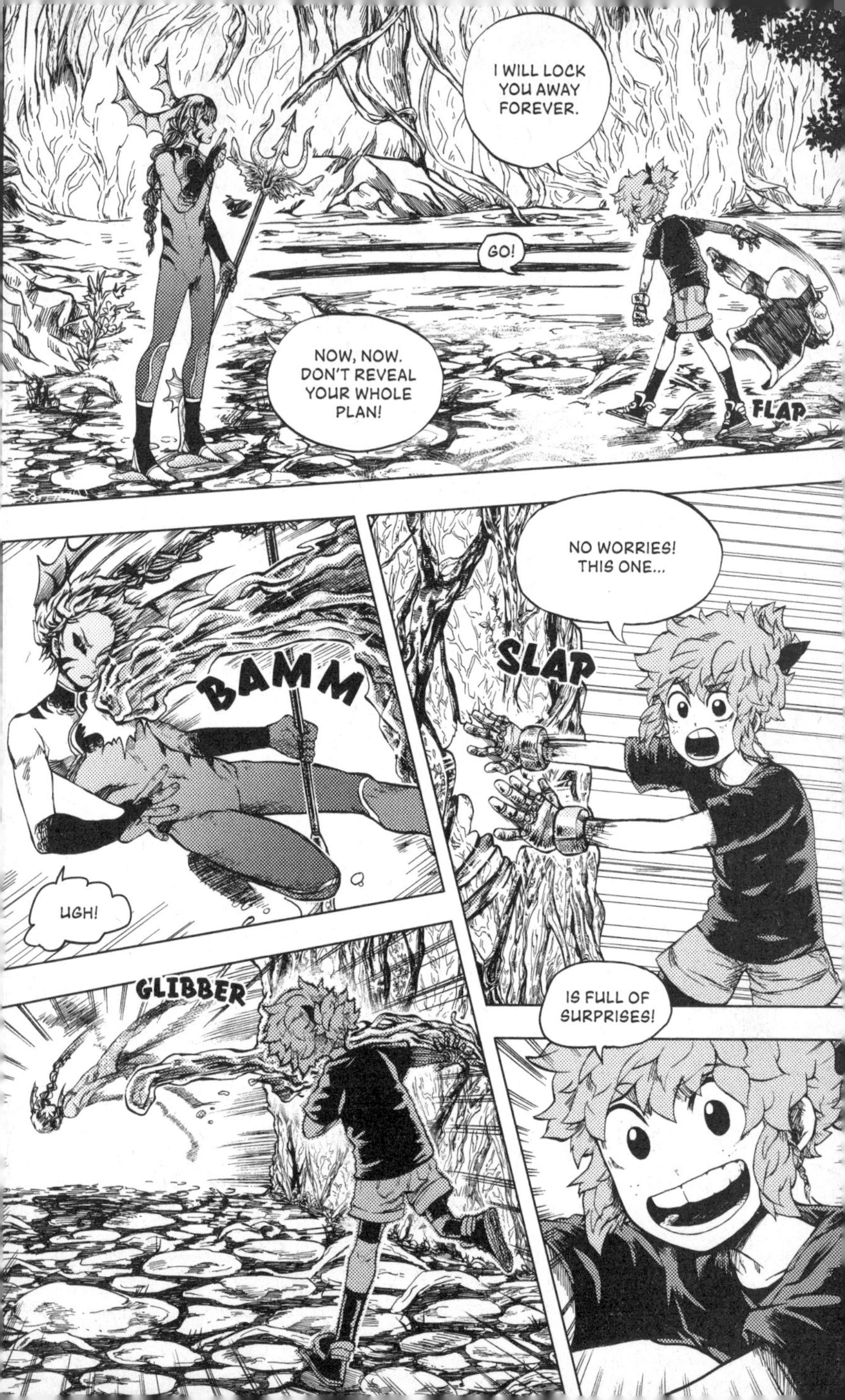
I WILL LOCK YOU AWAY FOREVER.
GO!
FLAP
NOW, NOW. DON'T REVEAL YOUR WHOLE PLAN!
NO WORRIES! THIS ONE...
SLAP
BAMM
UGH!
IS FULL OF SURPRISES!
GLIBBER

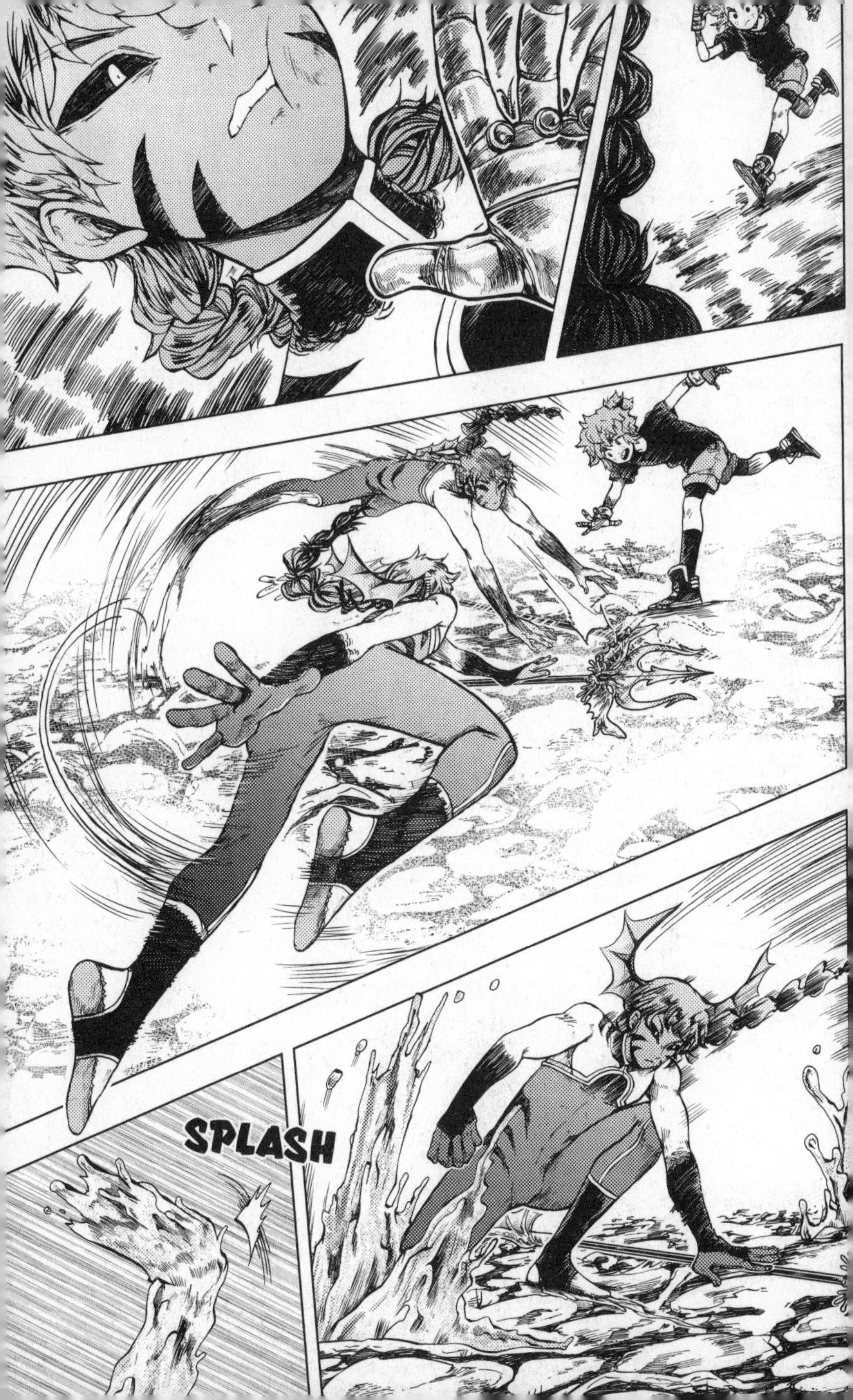
SPLASH

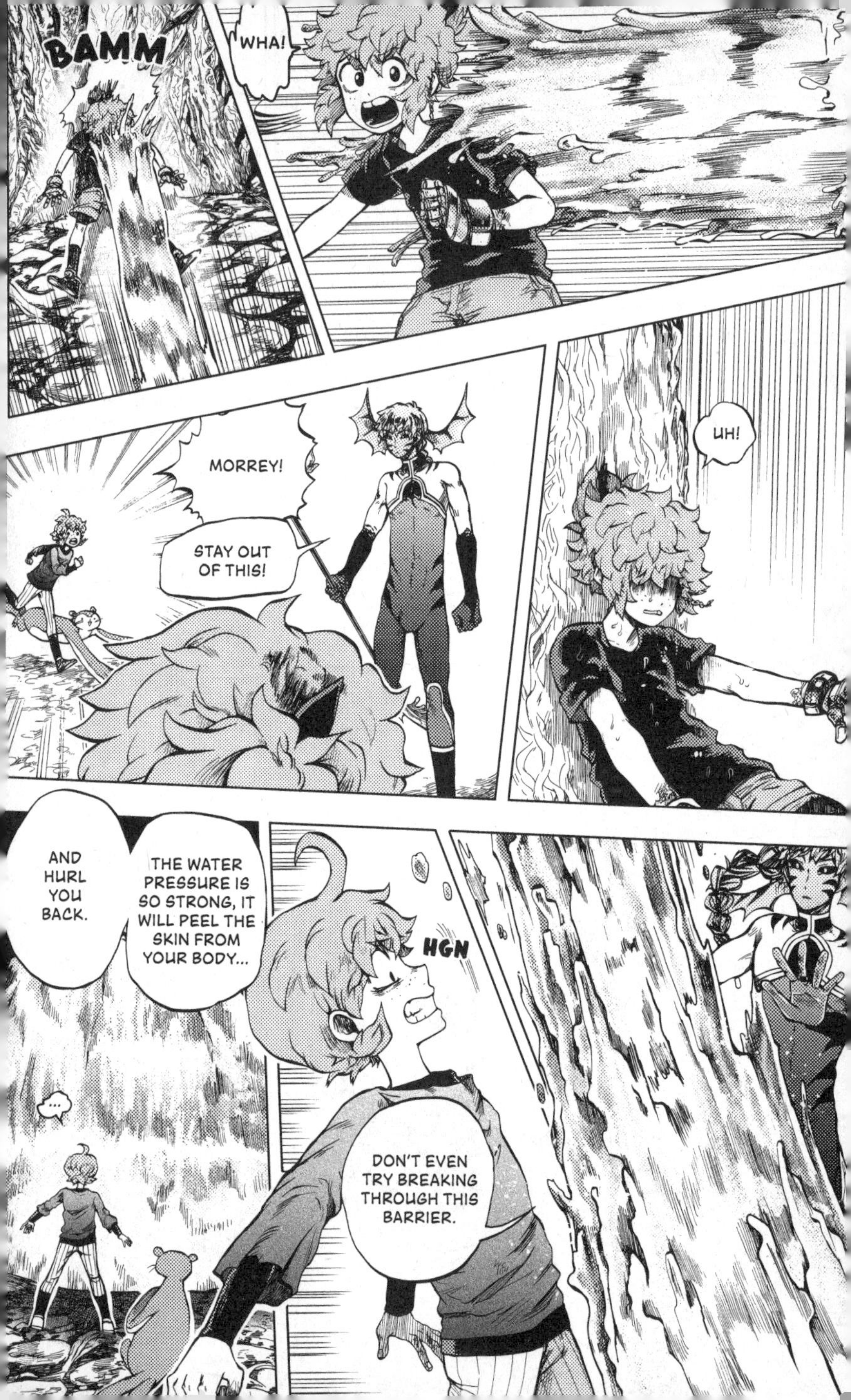
WHA!
BAMM
UH!
MORREY!
STAY OUT OF THIS!
DON'T EVEN TRY BREAKING THROUGH THIS BARRIER.
THE WATER PRESSURE IS SO STRONG, IT WILL PEEL THE SKIN FROM YOUR BODY...
AND HURL YOU BACK.
HGN
...

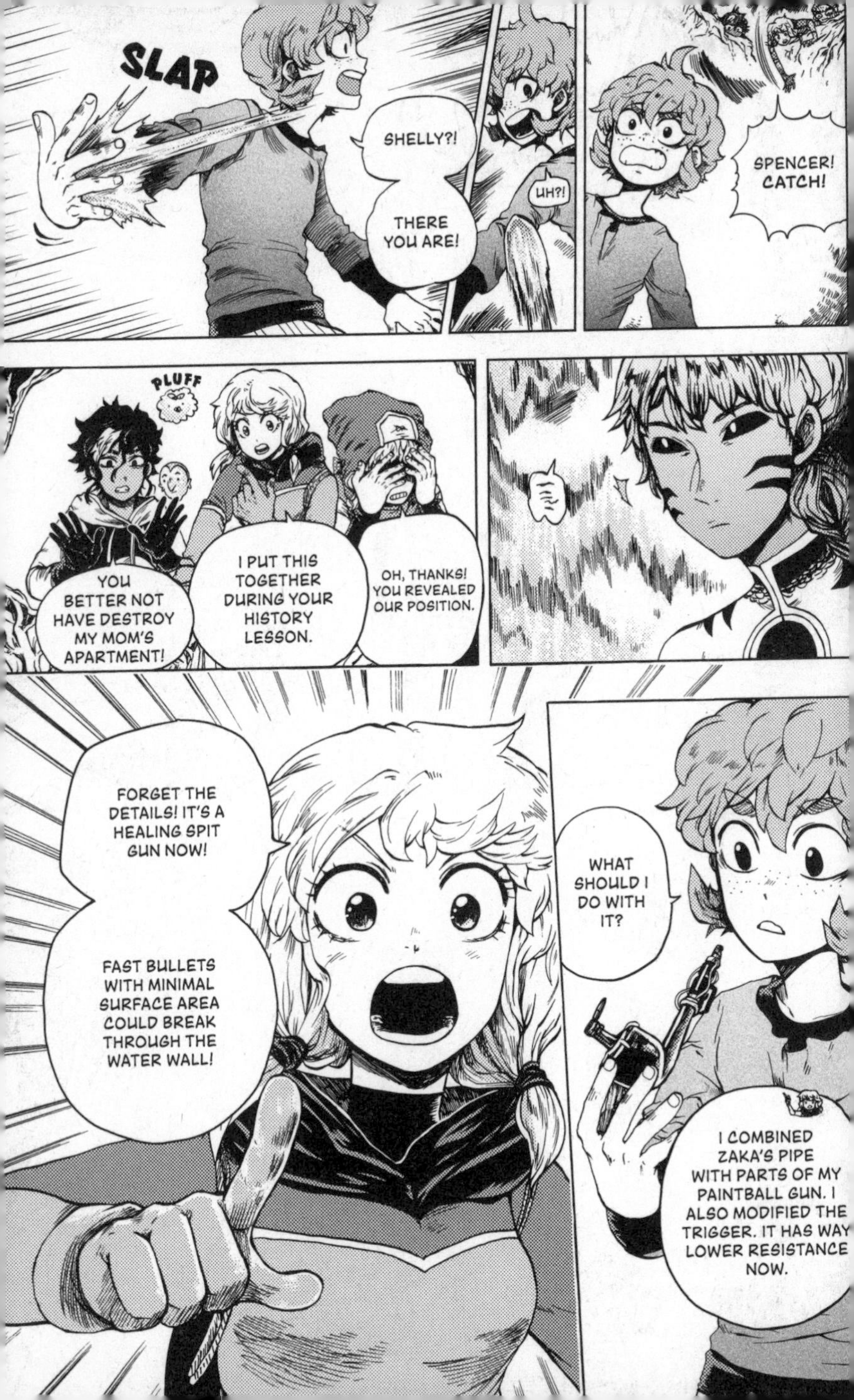
SPENCER! CATCH!
UH?!
SLAP
SHELLY?!
THERE YOU ARE!
PLUFF
OH, THANKS! YOU REVEALED OUR POSITION.
I PUT THIS TOGETHER DURING YOUR HISTORY LESSON.
YOU BETTER NOT HAVE DESTROY MY MOM'S APARTMENT!
WHAT SHOULD I DO WITH IT?
I COMBINED ZAKA'S PIPE WITH PARTS OF MY PAINTBALL GUN. I ALSO MODIFIED THE TRIGGER. IT HAS WAY LOWER RESISTANCE NOW.
FORGET THE DETAILS! IT'S A HEALING SPIT GUN NOW!
FAST BULLETS WITH MINIMAL SURFACE AREA COULD BREAK THROUGH THE WATER WALL!

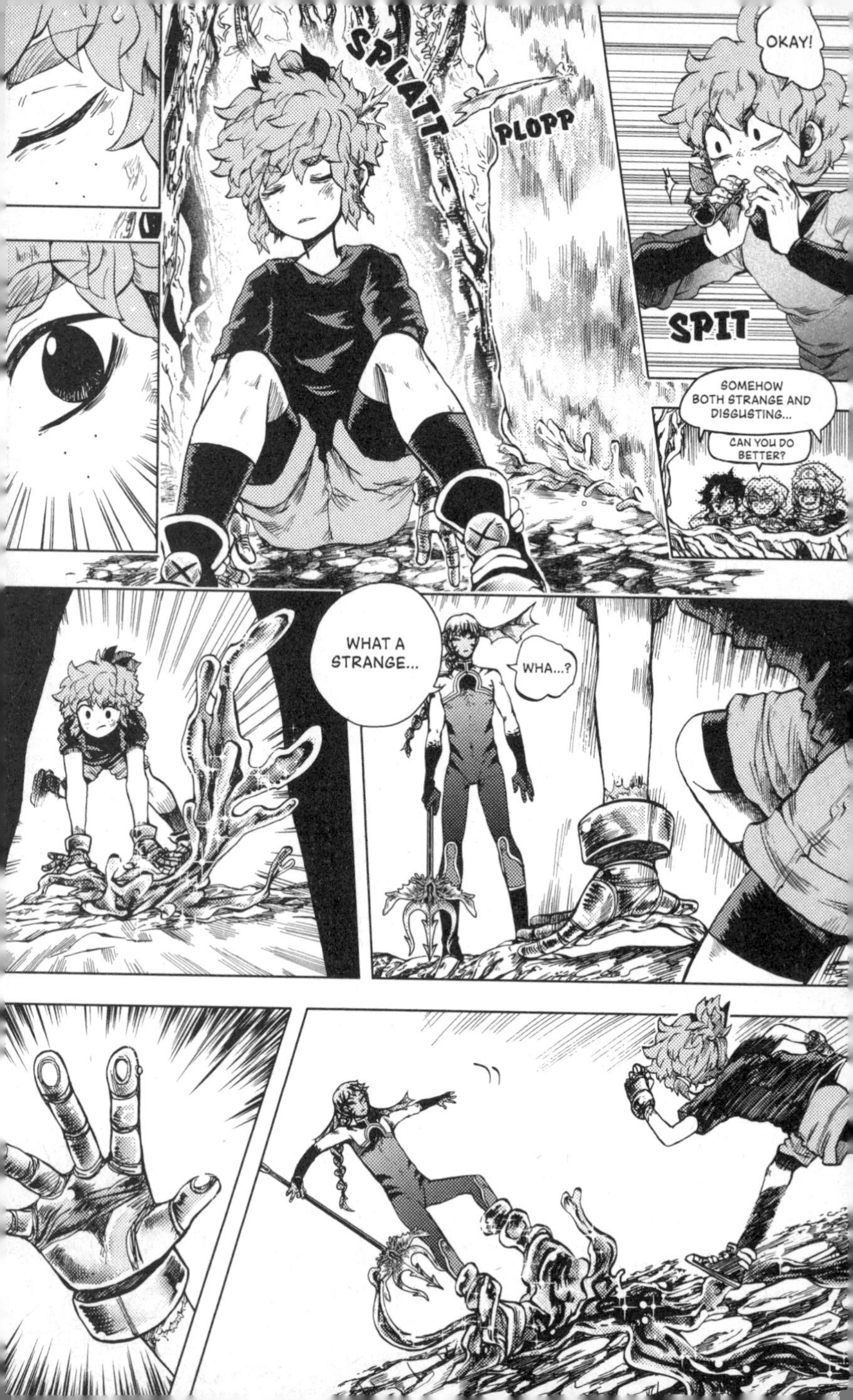
OKAY!
SPIT
SOMEHOW BOTH STRANGE AND DISGUSTING...
CAN YOU DO BETTER?
SPLATT
PLOPP
WHAT A STRANGE...
WHA...?

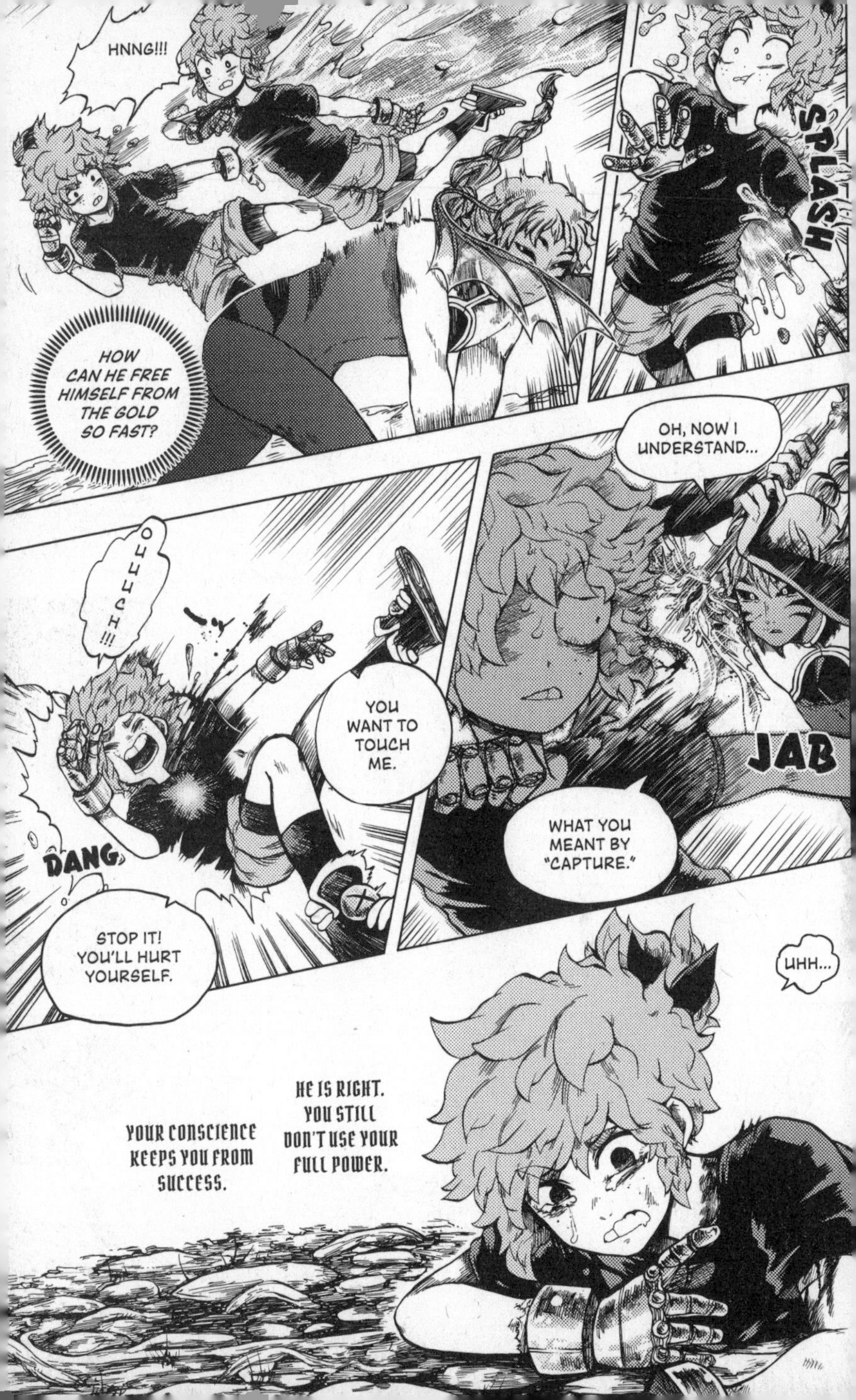
SPLASH
HNNG!!!
HOW CAN HE FREE HIMSELF FROM THE GOLD SO FAST?
OH, NOW I UNDERSTAND...
JAB
WHAT YOU MEANT BY "CAPTURE."
OUUUCH!!!
YOU WANT TO TOUCH ME.
DANG
STOP IT! YOU'LL HURT YOURSELF.
UHH...
HE IS RIGHT. YOU STILL DON'T USE YOUR FULL POWER.
YOUR CONSCIENCE KEEPS YOU FROM SUCCESS.

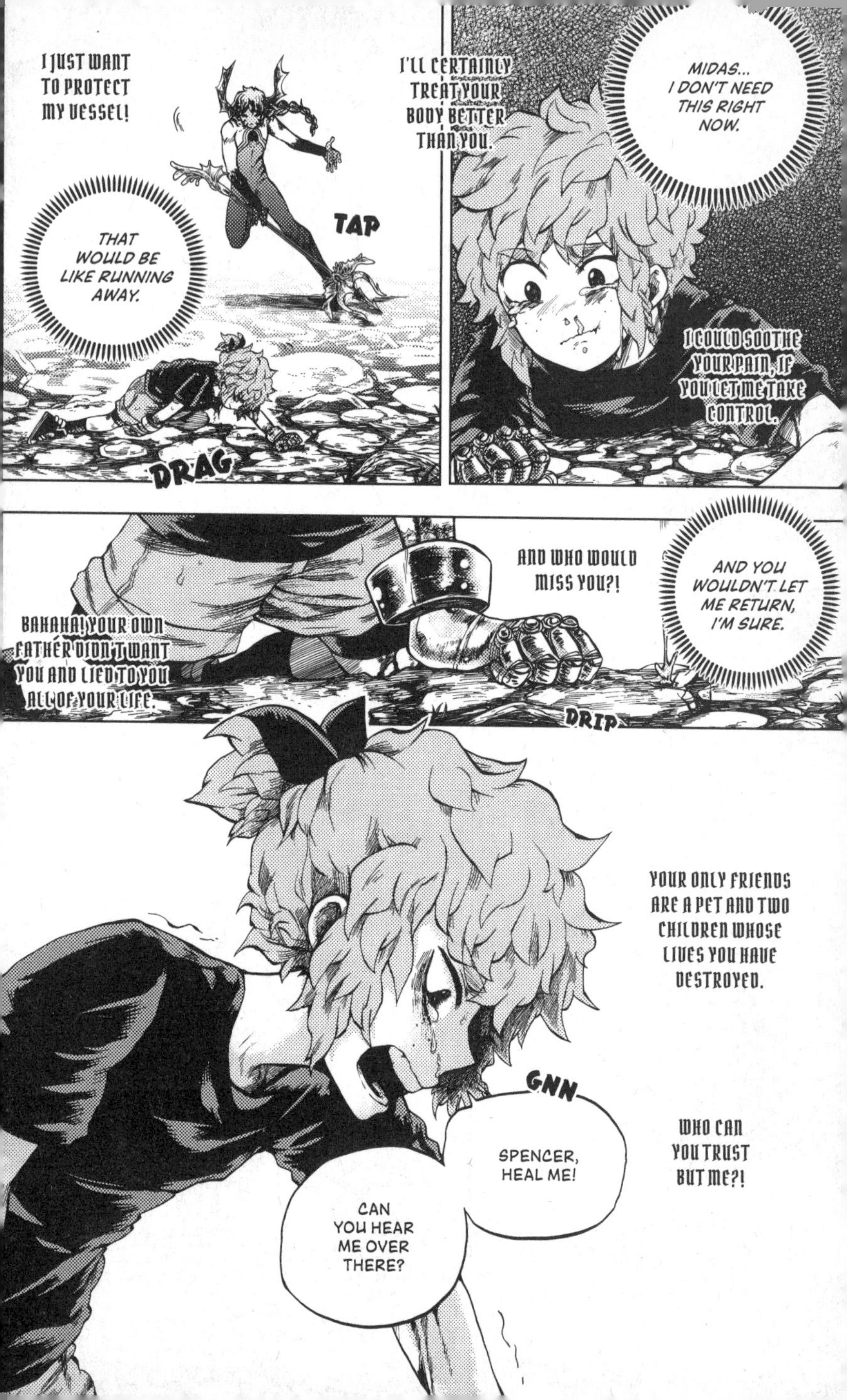
MIDAS... I DON'T NEED THIS RIGHT NOW.
I COULD SOOTHE YOUR PAIN, IF YOU LET ME TAKE CONTROL.
I'LL CERTAINLY TREAT YOUR BODY BETTER THAN YOU.
I JUST WANT TO PROTECT MY VESSEL!
TAP
THAT WOULD BE LIKE RUNNING AWAY.
DRAG
AND YOU WOULDN'T LET ME RETURN, I'M SURE.
AND WHO WOULD MISS YOU?!
BAHAHA! YOUR OWN FATHER DIDN'T WANT YOU AND LIED TO YOU ALL OF YOUR LIFE.
DRIP
YOUR ONLY FRIENDS ARE A PET AND TWO CHILDREN WHOSE LIVES YOU HAVE DESTROYED.
WHO CAN YOU TRUST BUT ME?!
GNN
SPENCER, HEAL ME!
CAN YOU HEAR ME OVER THERE?

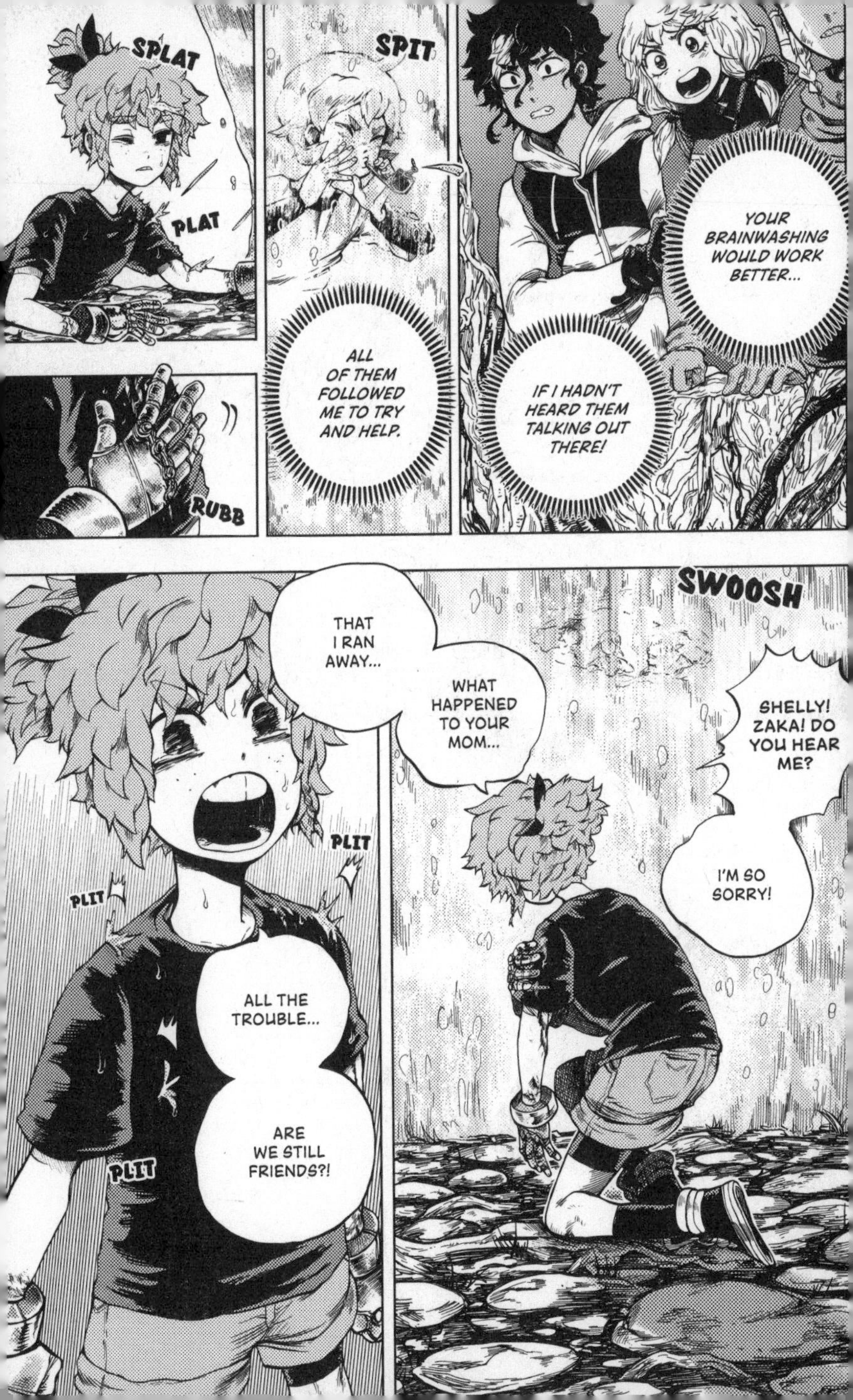
YOUR BRAINWASHING WOULD WORK BETTER...
IF I HADN'T HEARD THEM TALKING OUT THERE!
SPIT
ALL OF THEM FOLLOWED ME TO TRY AND HELP.
SPLAT
PLAT
RUBB
SWOOSH
SHELLY! ZAKA! DO YOU HEAR ME?
I'M SO SORRY!
THAT I RAN AWAY...
WHAT HAPPENED TO YOUR MOM...
PLIT
PLIT
ALL THE TROUBLE...
ARE WE STILL FRIENDS?!
PLIT

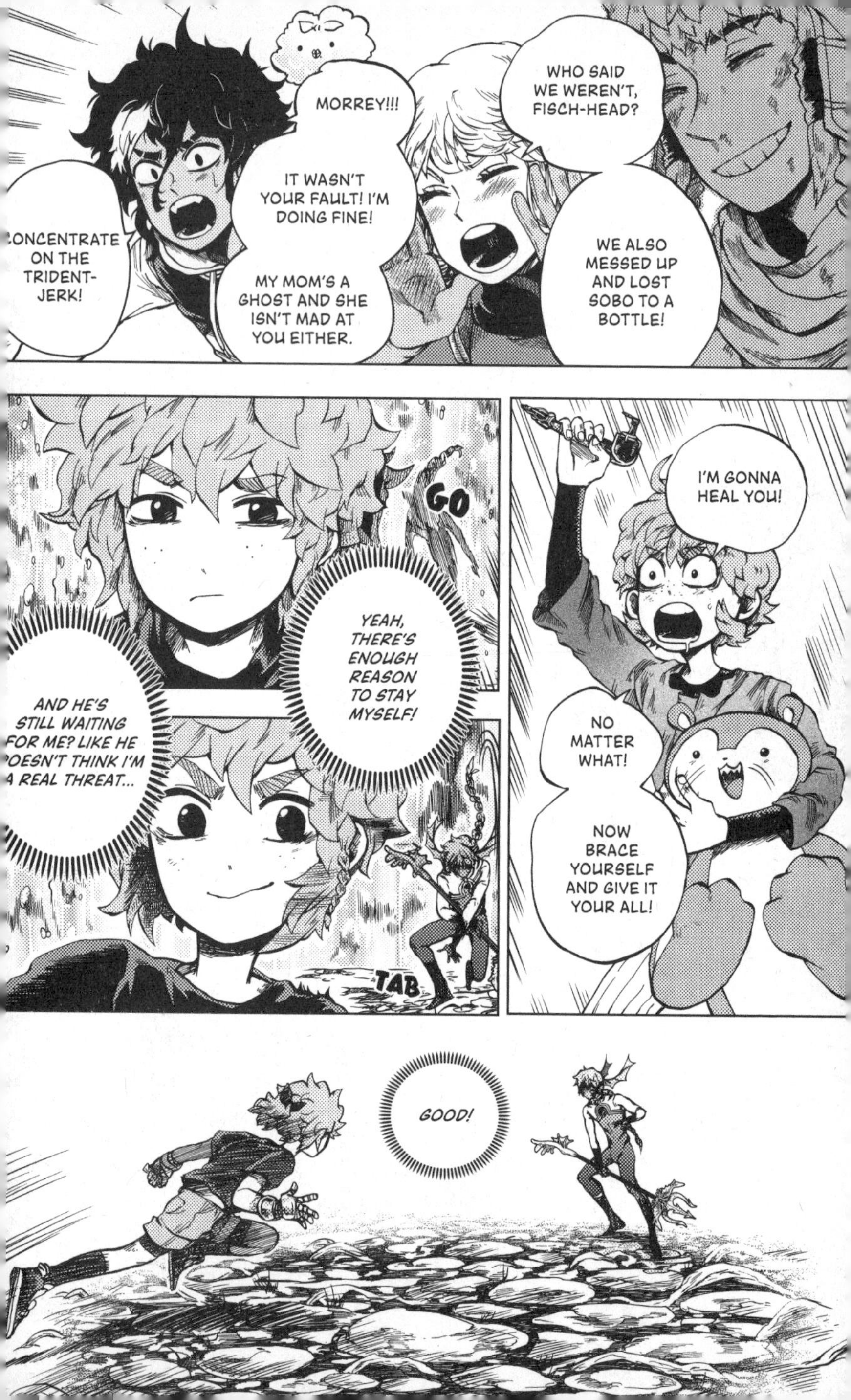
WHO SAID WE WEREN'T, FISCH-HEAD?
WE ALSO MESSED UP AND LOST SOBO TO A BOTTLE!
MORREY!!!
IT WASN'T YOUR FAULT! I'M DOING FINE!
MY MOM'S A GHOST AND SHE ISN'T MAD AT YOU EITHER.
CONCENTRATE ON THE TRIDENT-JERK!
I'M GONNA HEAL YOU!
NO MATTER WHAT!
NOW BRACE YOURSELF AND GIVE IT YOUR ALL!
GO
YEAH, THERE'S ENOUGH REASON TO STAY MYSELF!
AND HE'S STILL WAITING FOR ME? LIKE HE OESN'T THINK I'M A REAL THREAT...
TAB
GOOD!

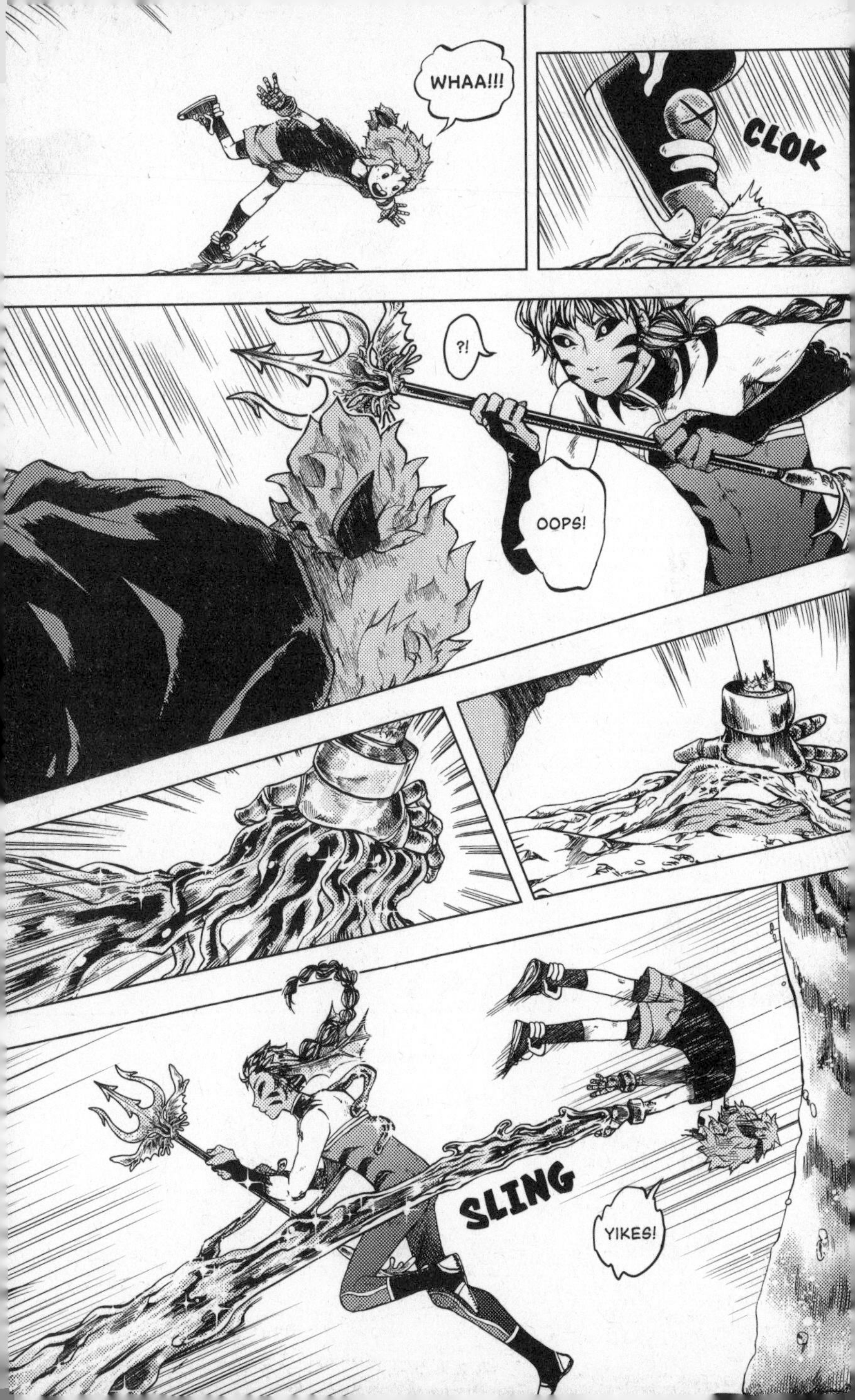
CLOK
WHAA!!!
?!
OOPS!
SLING
YIKES!

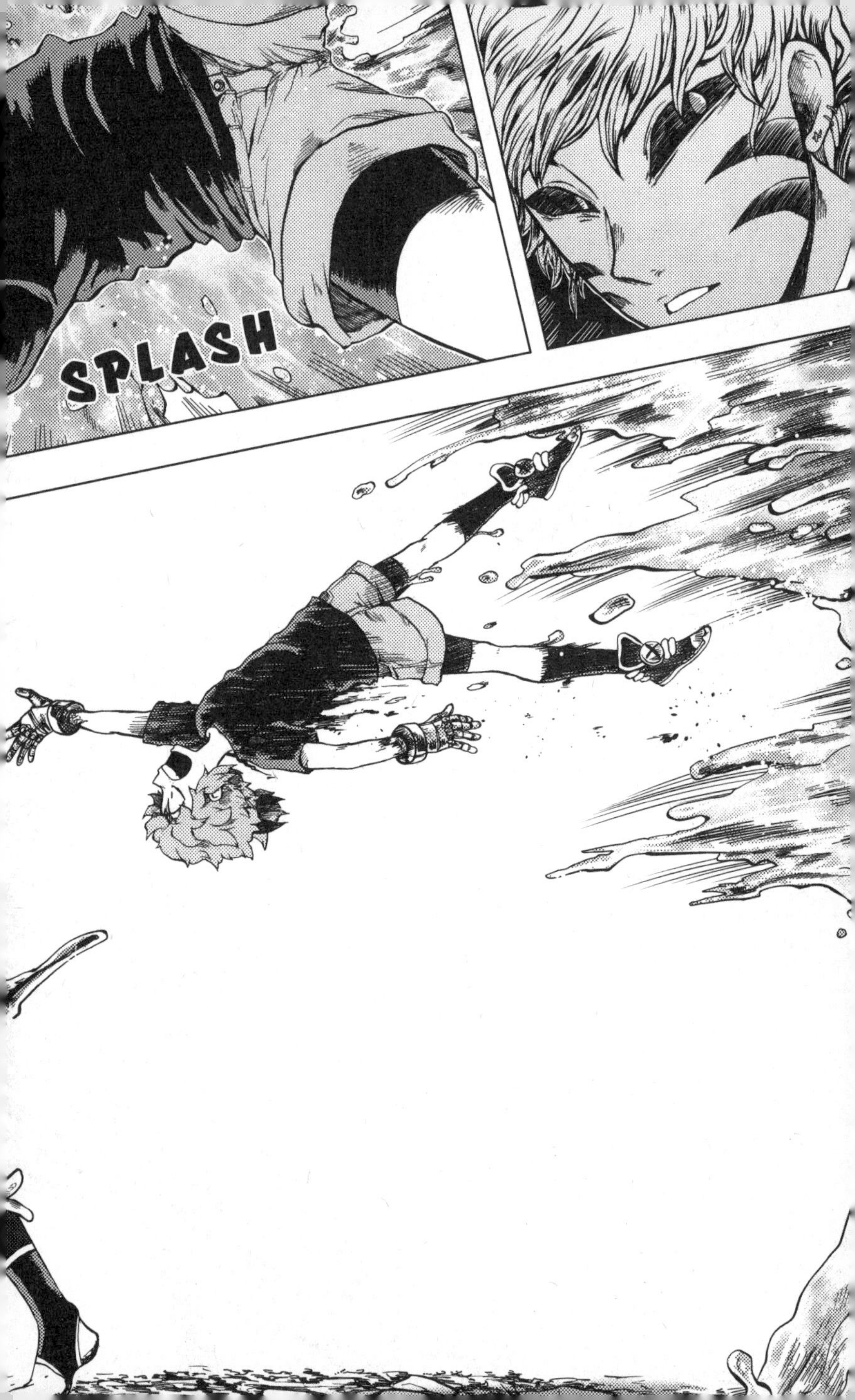
SPLASH

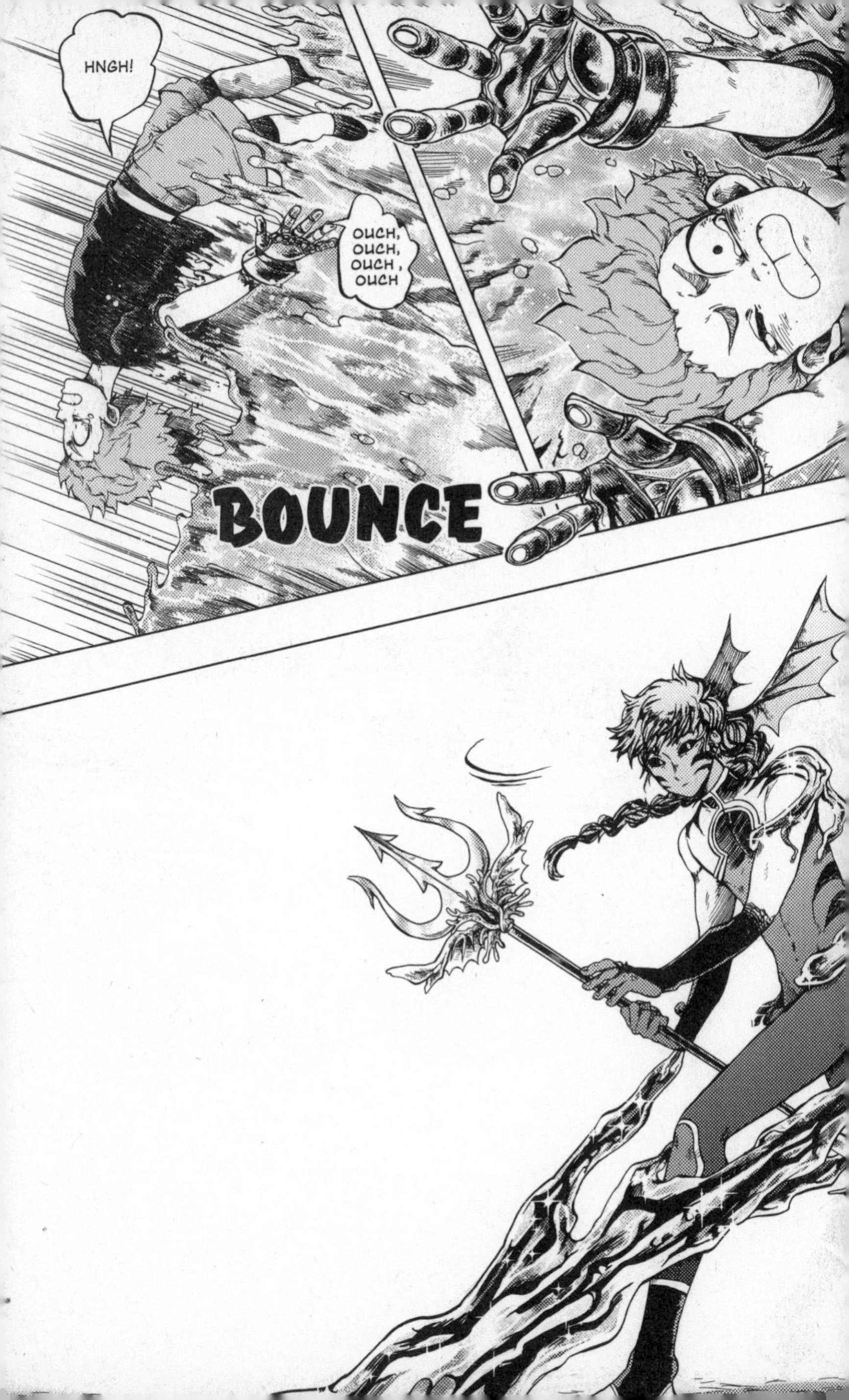
OUCH, OUCH, OUCH, OUCH
HNGH!
BOUNCE

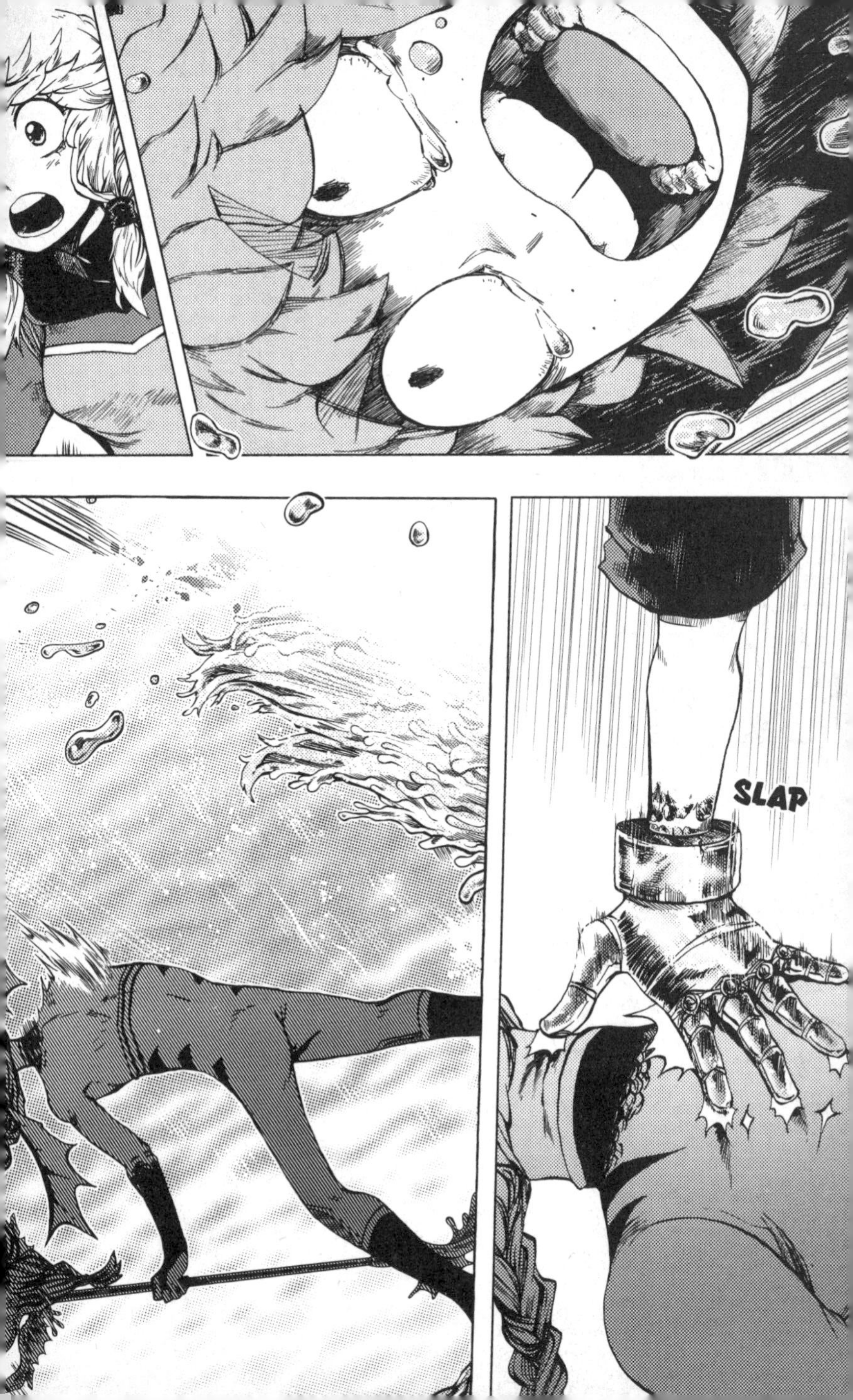
SLAP

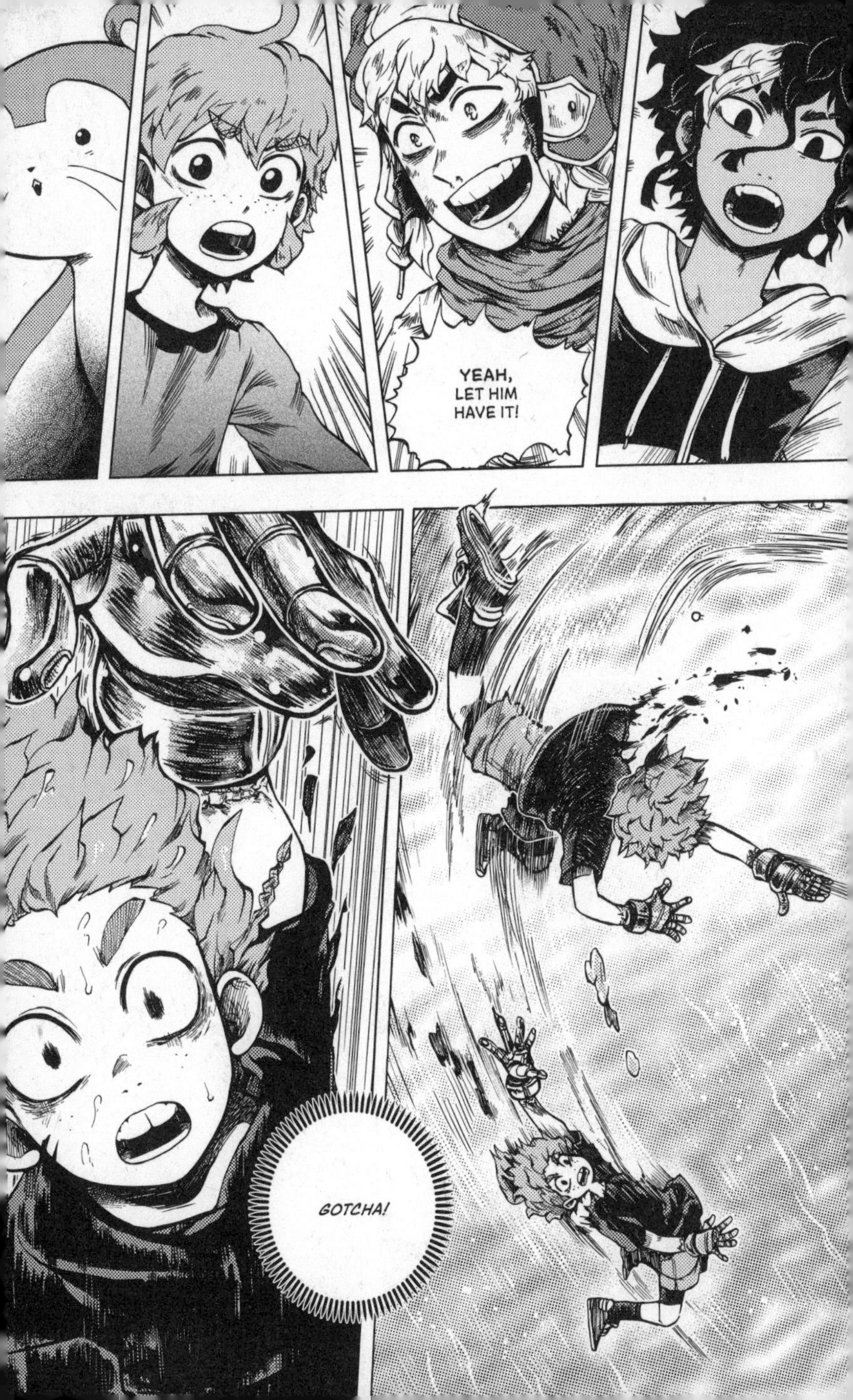
YEAH, LET HIM HAVE IT!
GOTCHA!

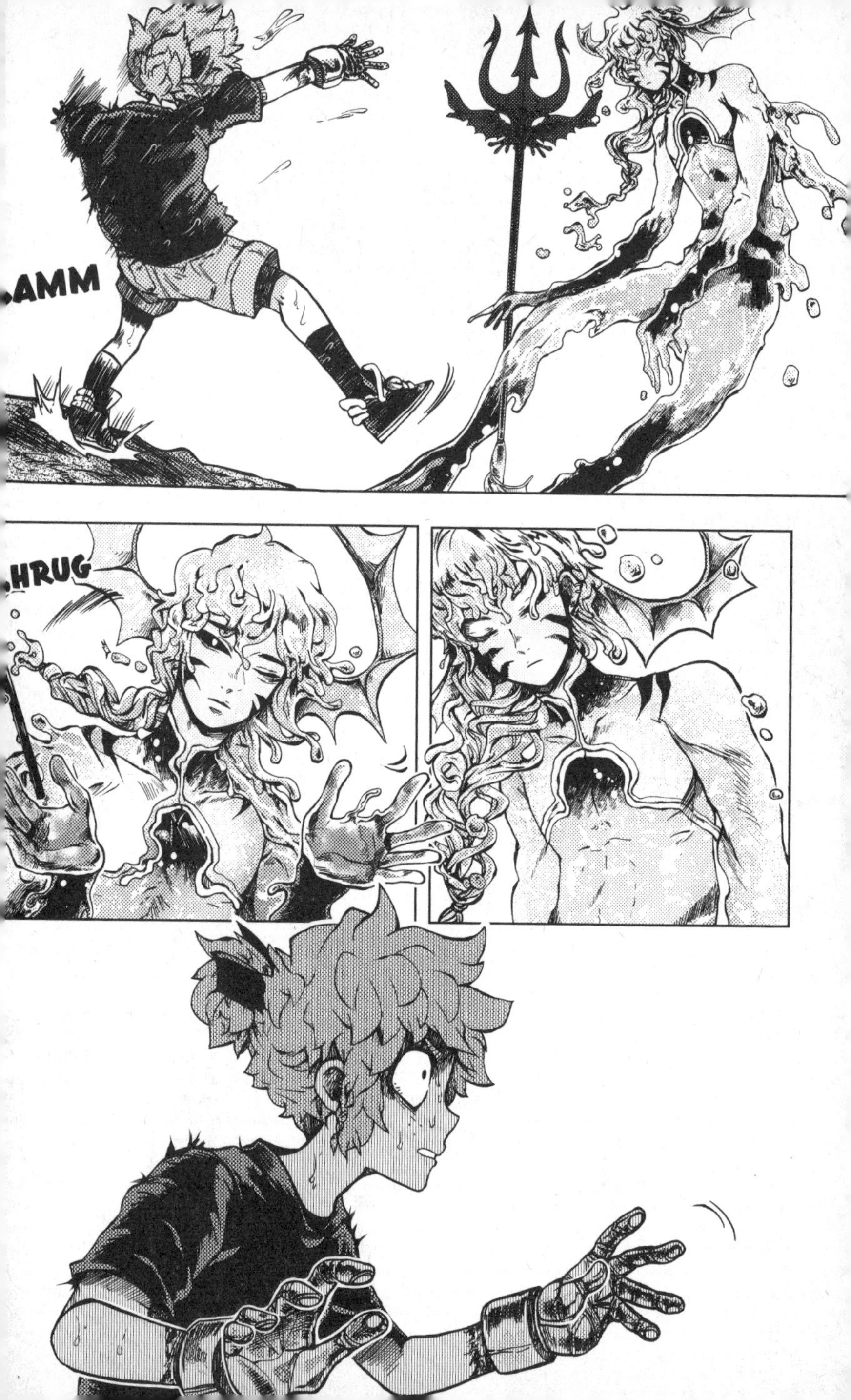
AMM
HRUG

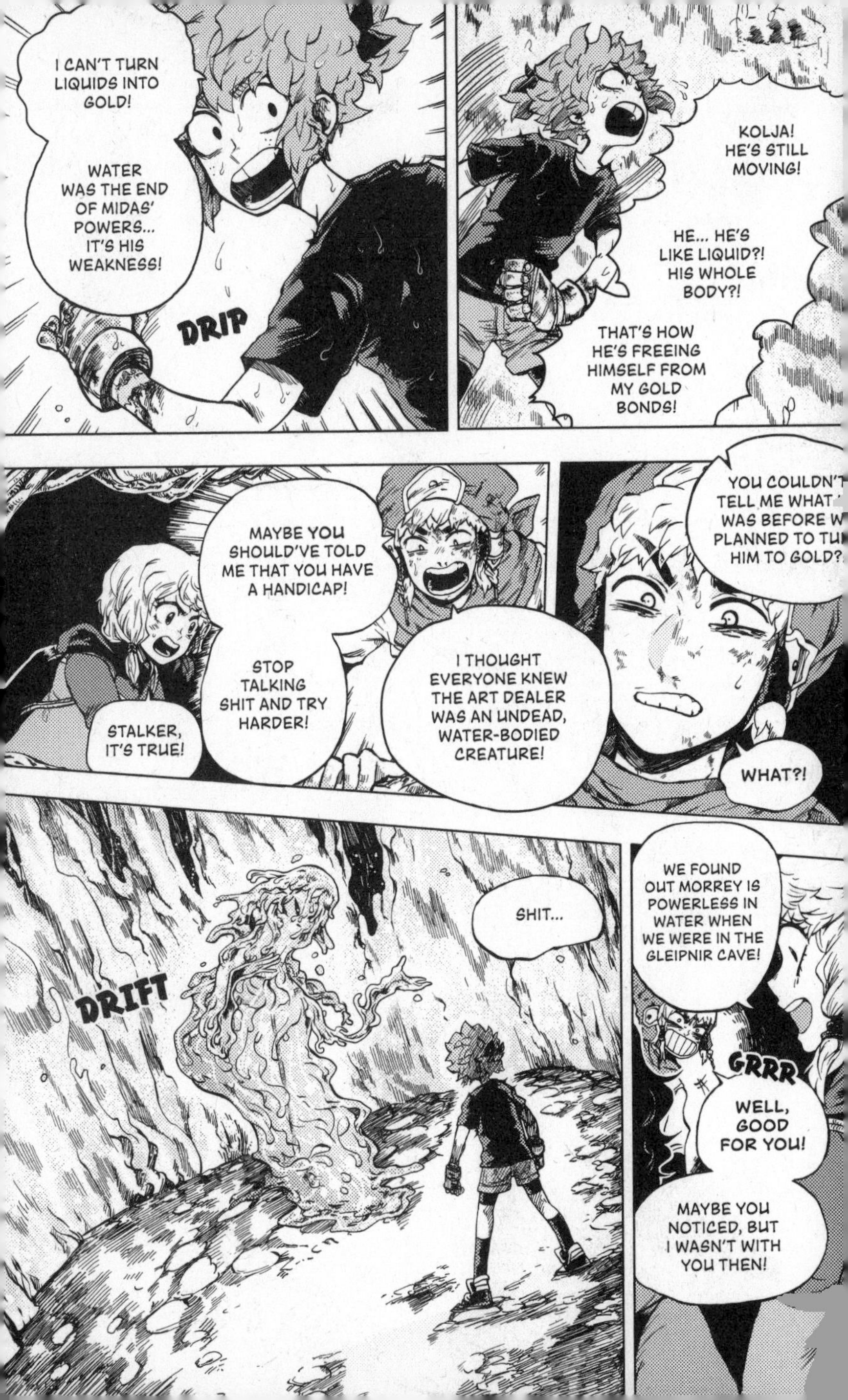
KOLJA! HE'S STILL MOVING!
HE... HE'S LIKE LIQUID?! HIS WHOLE BODY?!
THAT'S HOW HE'S FREEING HIMSELF FROM MY GOLD BONDS!
I CAN'T TURN LIQUIDS INTO GOLD!
WATER WAS THE END OF MIDAS' POWERS... IT'S HIS WEAKNESS!
DRIP
YOU COULDN'T TELL ME WHAT WAS BEFORE W PLANNED TO TU HIM TO GOLD?
I THOUGHT EVERYONE KNEW THE ART DEALER WAS AN UNDEAD, WATER-BODIED CREATURE!
WHAT?!
MAYBE YOU SHOULD'VE TOLD ME THAT YOU HAVE A HANDICAP!
STOP TALKING SHIT AND TRY HARDER!
STALKER, IT'S TRUE!
WE FOUND OUT MORREY IS POWERLESS IN WATER WHEN WE WERE IN THE GLEIPNIR CAVE!
GRRR
WELL, GOOD FOR YOU!
MAYBE YOU NOTICED, BUT I WASN'T WITH YOU THEN!
SHIT...
DRIFT

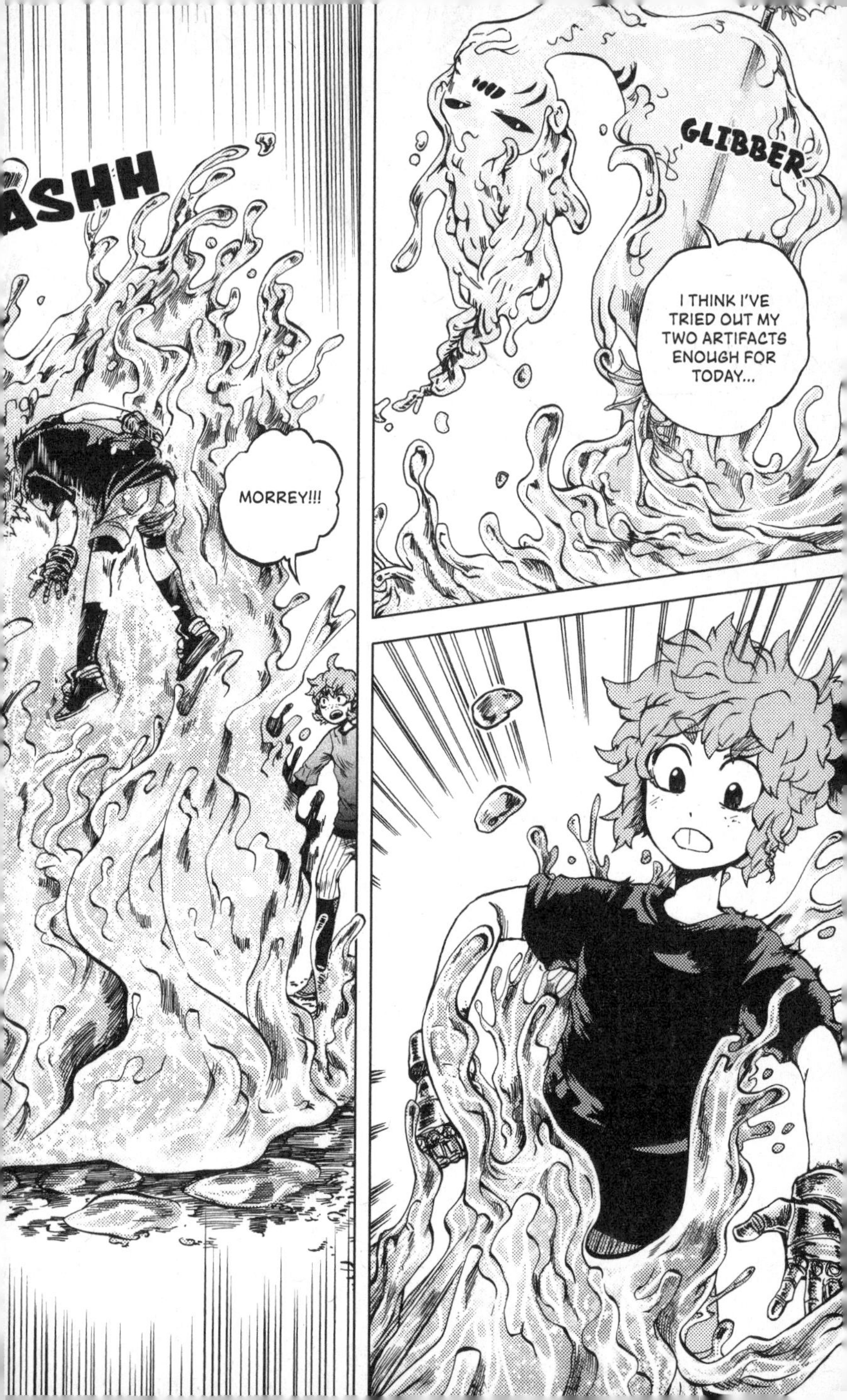
GLIBBER
I THINK I'VE TRIED OUT MY TWO ARTIFACTS ENOUGH FOR TODAY...
ASHH
MORREY!!!

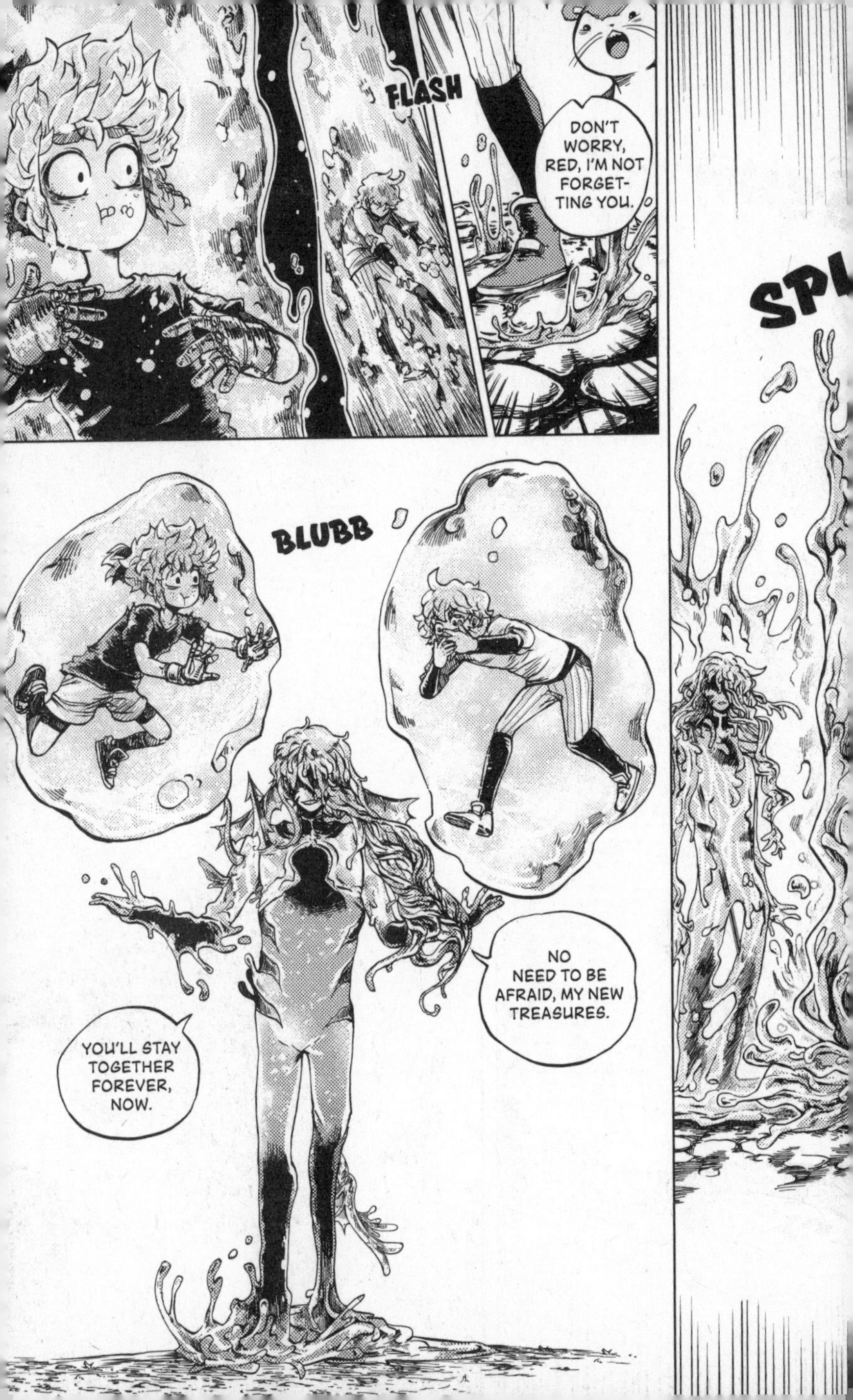
SPL
DON'T WORRY, RED, I'M NOT FORGET-TING YOU.
FLASH
BLUBB
NO NEED TO BE AFRAID, MY NEW TREASURES.
YOU'LL STAY TOGETHER FOREVER, NOW.

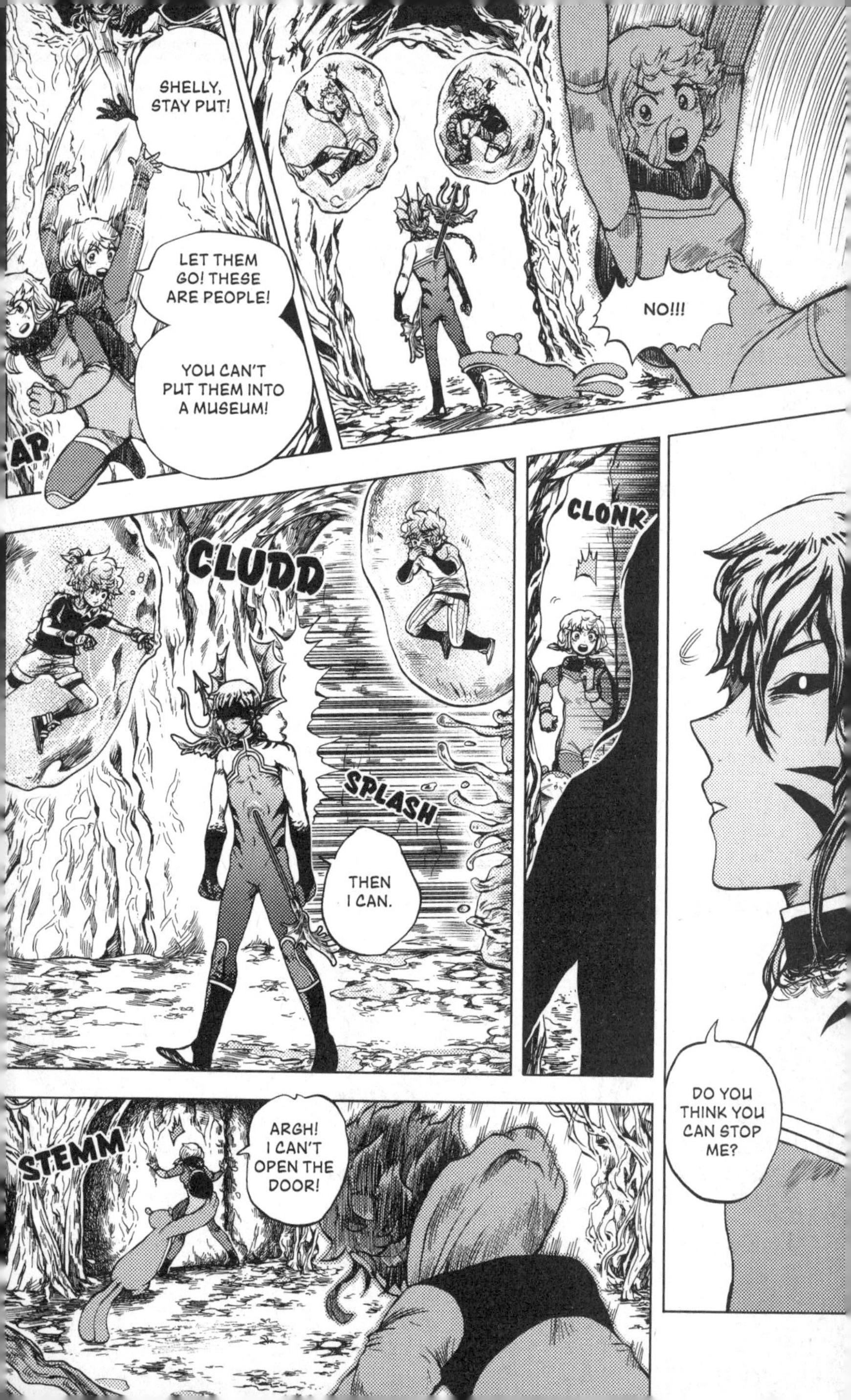
NO!!!
SHELLY, STAY PUT!
LET THEM GO! THESE ARE PEOPLE!
YOU CAN'T PUT THEM INTO A MUSEUM!
AP
DO YOU THINK YOU CAN STOP ME?
CLONK
CLUDD
SPLASH
THEN I CAN.
ARGH! I CAN'T OPEN THE DOOR!
STEMM

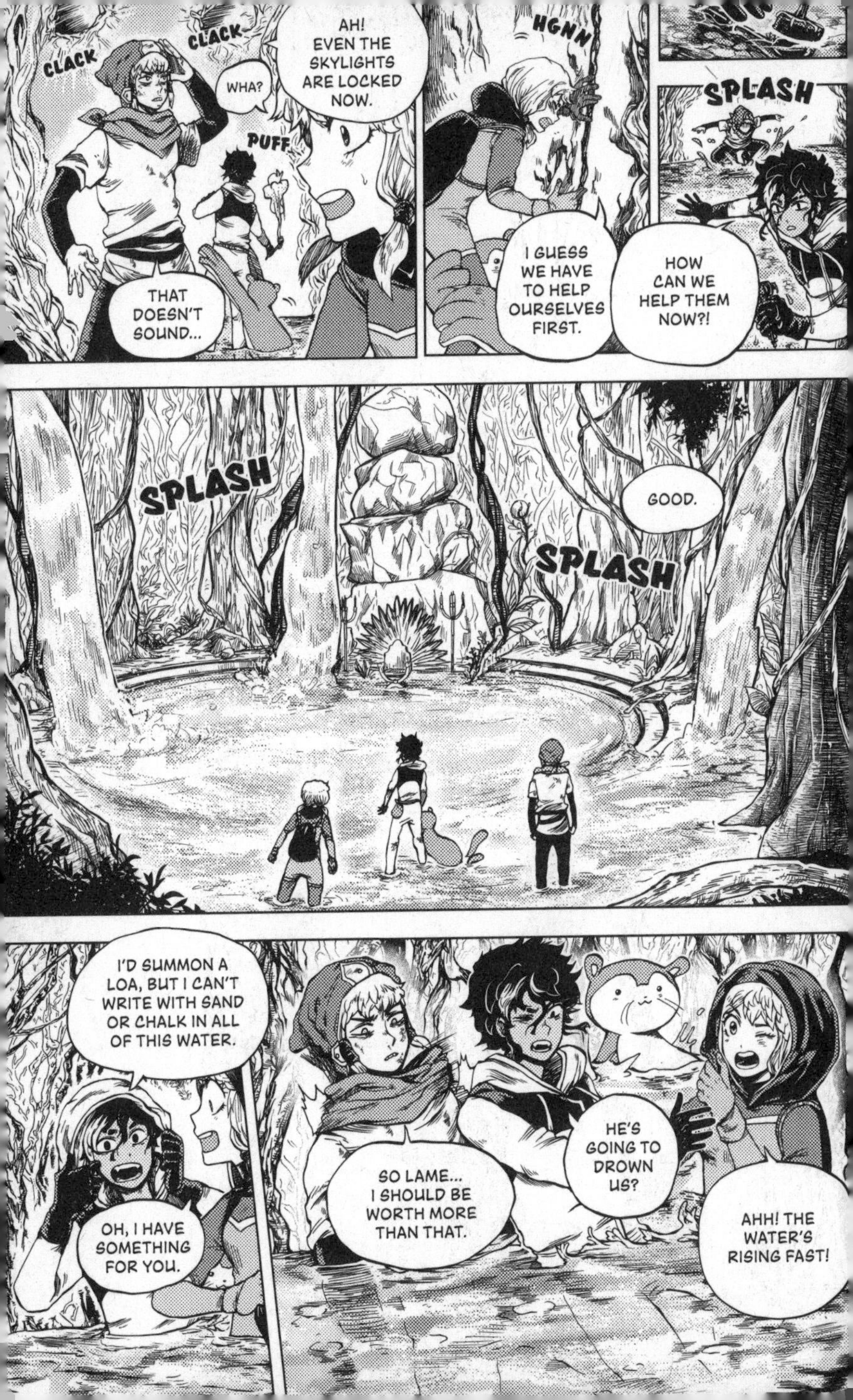
SPLASH
HOW CAN WE HELP THEM NOW?!
HGNN
I GUESS WE HAVE TO HELP OURSELVES FIRST.
AH! EVEN THE SKYLIGHTS ARE LOCKED NOW.
CLACK
WHA?
CLACK
PUFF
THAT DOESN'T SOUND...
GOOD.
SPLASH
SPLASH
AHH! THE WATER'S RISING FAST!
HE'S GOING TO DROWN US?
SO LAME... I SHOULD BE WORTH MORE THAN THAT.
I'D SUMMON A LOA, BUT I CAN'T WRITE WITH SAND OR CHALK IN ALL OF THIS WATER.
OH, I HAVE SOMETHING FOR YOU.

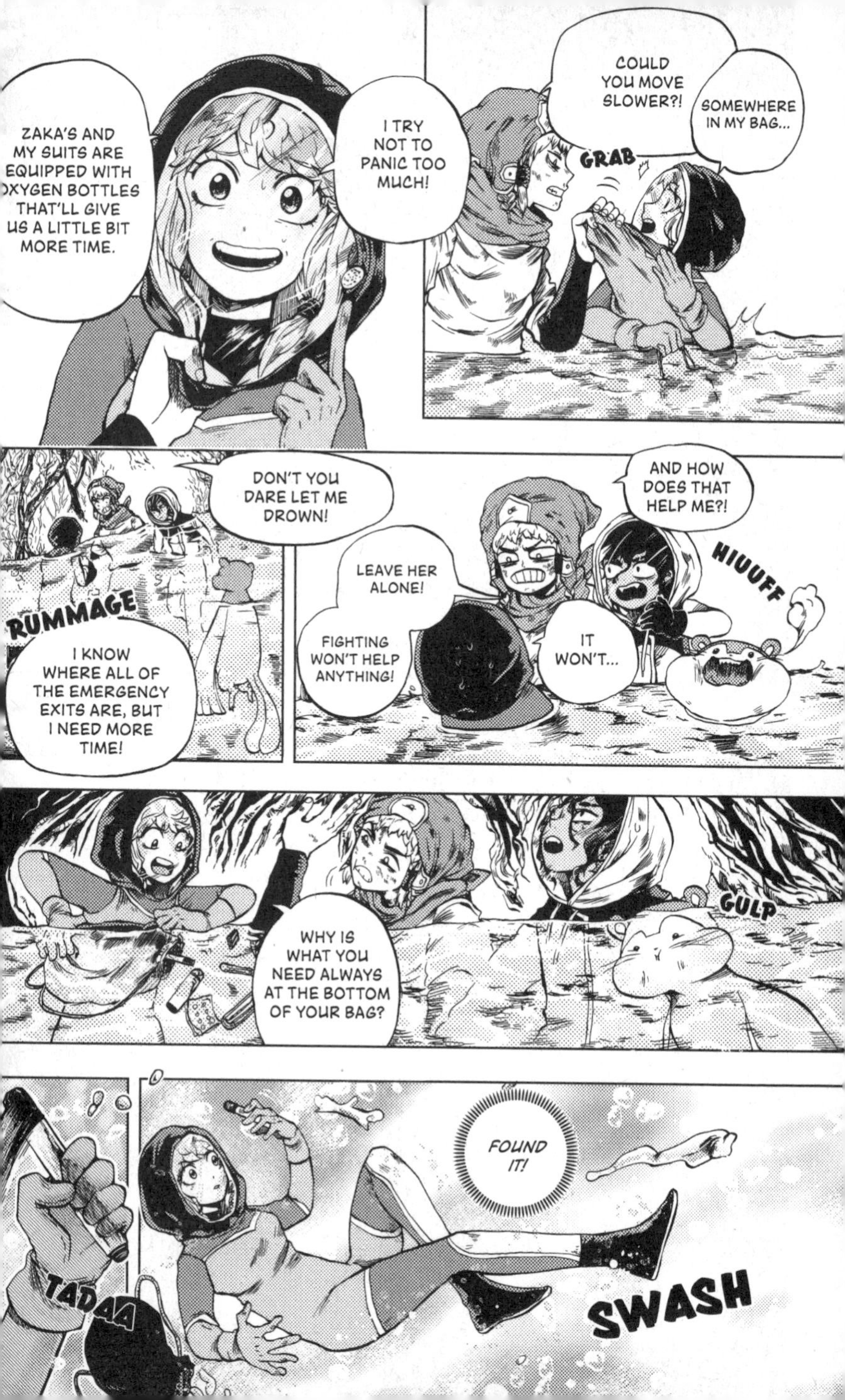

COULD YOU MOVE SLOWER?!
SOMEWHERE IN MY BAG...
GRAB
I TRY NOT TO PANIC TOO MUCH!
ZAKA'S AND MY SUITS ARE EQUIPPED WITH OXYGEN BOTTLES THAT'LL GIVE US A LITTLE BIT MORE TIME.
AND HOW DOES THAT HELP ME?!
HIUUFF
LEAVE HER ALONE!
IT WON'T...
FIGHTING WON'T HELP ANYTHING!
DON'T YOU DARE LET ME DROWN!
RUMMAGE
I KNOW WHERE ALL OF THE EMERGENCY EXITS ARE, BUT I NEED MORE TIME!
GULP
WHY IS WHAT YOU NEED ALWAYS AT THE BOTTOM OF YOUR BAG?
FOUND IT!
SWASH
TADAA

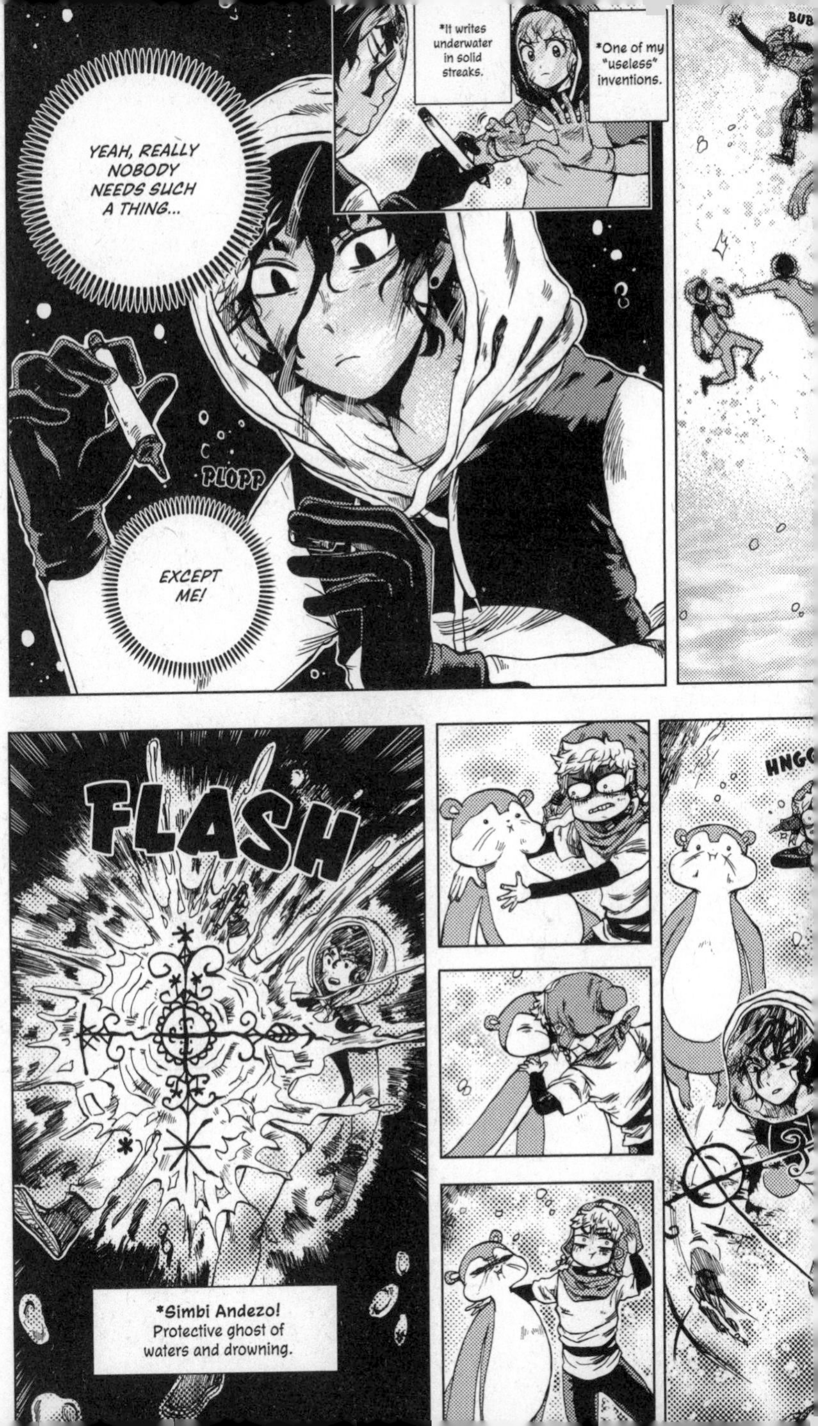
BUB
*One of my "useless" inventions.
*It writes underwater in solid streaks.
YEAH, REALLY NOBODY NEEDS SUCH A THING...
PLOPP
EXCEPT ME!
HNG
FLASH
*Simbi Andezo! Protective ghost of waters and drowning.

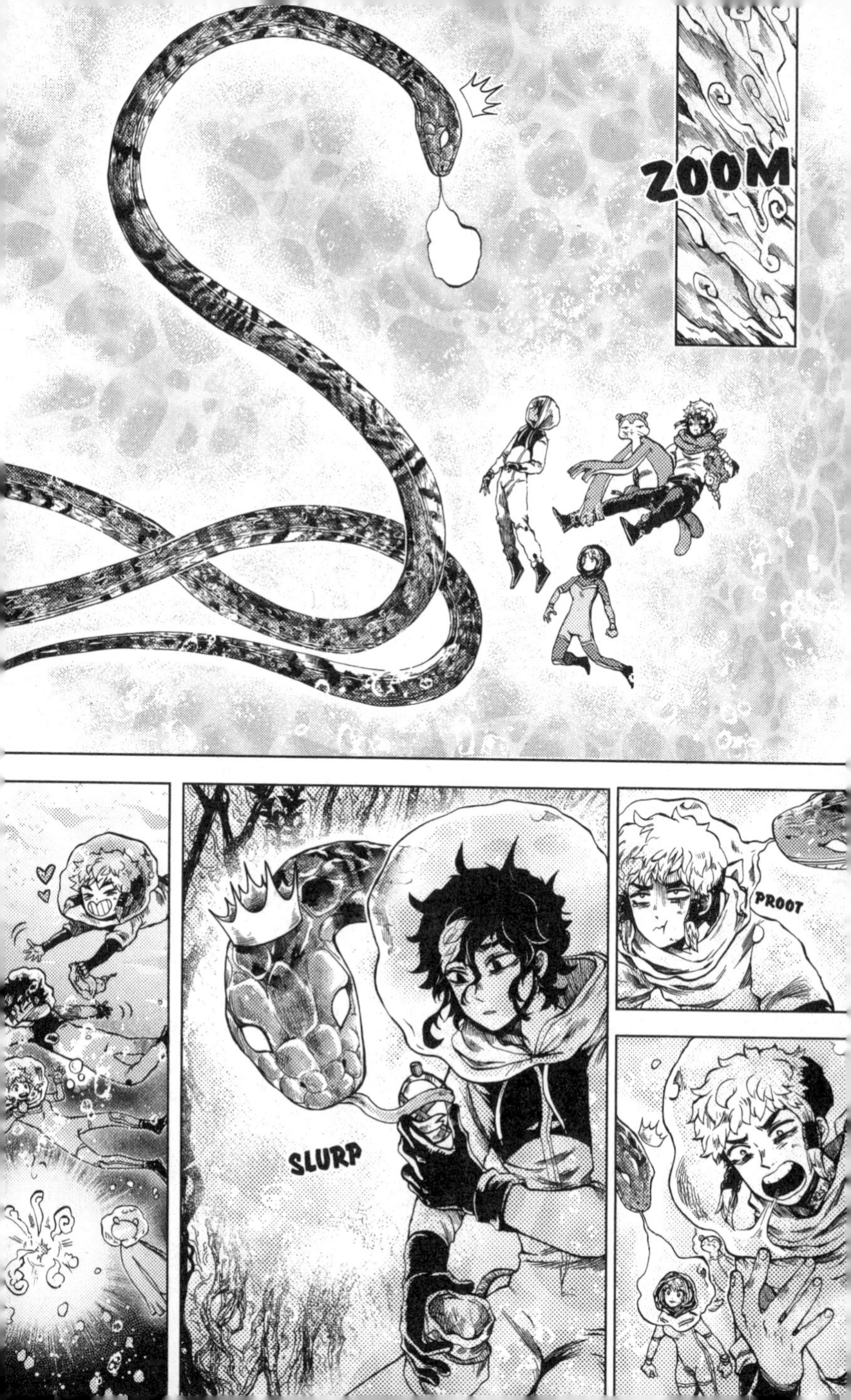
ZOOM
PROOT
SLURP

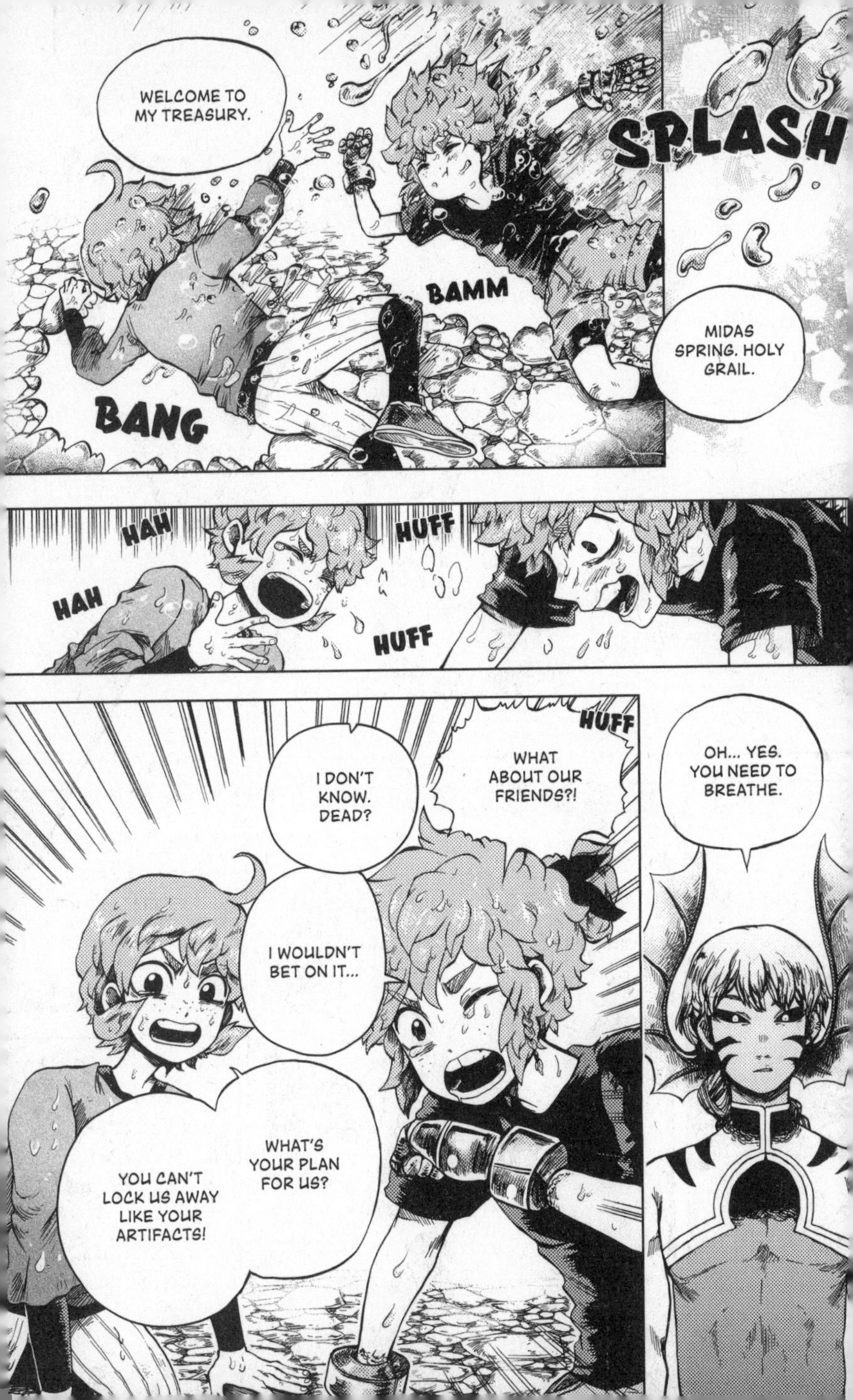
SPLASH
MIDAS SPRING. HOLY GRAIL.
WELCOME TO MY TREASURY.
BAMM
BANG
HUFF
HAH
HUFF
HAH
OH... YES. YOU NEED TO BREATHE.
HUFF
WHAT ABOUT OUR FRIENDS?!
I DON'T KNOW. DEAD?
I WOULDN'T BET ON IT...
WHAT'S YOUR PLAN FOR US?
YOU CAN'T LOCK US AWAY LIKE YOUR ARTIFACTS!

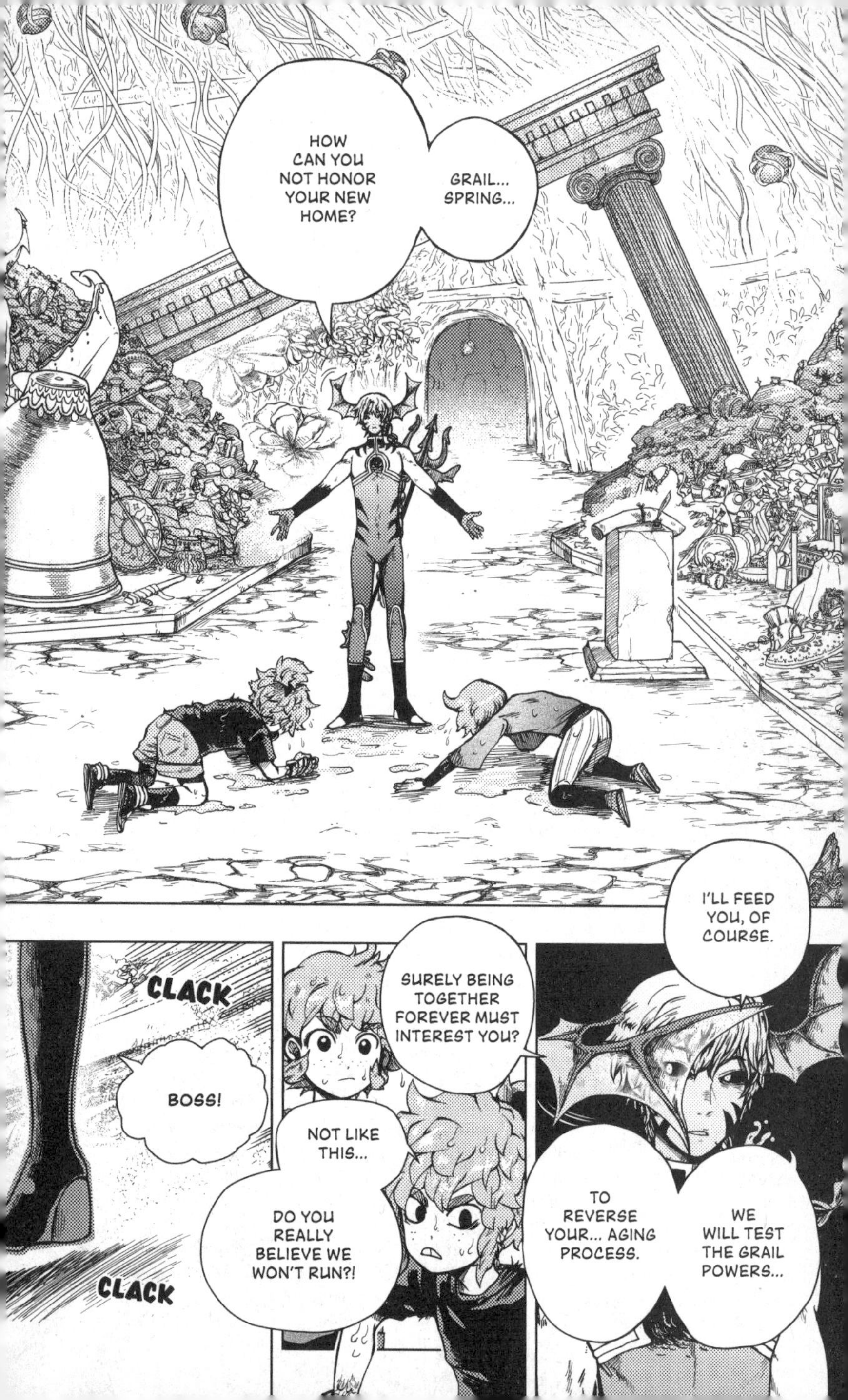
GRAIL... SPRING...
HOW CAN YOU NOT HONOR YOUR NEW HOME?
I'LL FEED YOU, OF COURSE.
SURELY BEING TOGETHER FOREVER MUST INTEREST YOU?
WE WILL TEST THE GRAIL POWERS...
TO REVERSE YOUR... AGING PROCESS.
NOT LIKE THIS...
DO YOU REALLY BELIEVE WE WON'T RUN?!
CLACK
BOSS!
CLACK

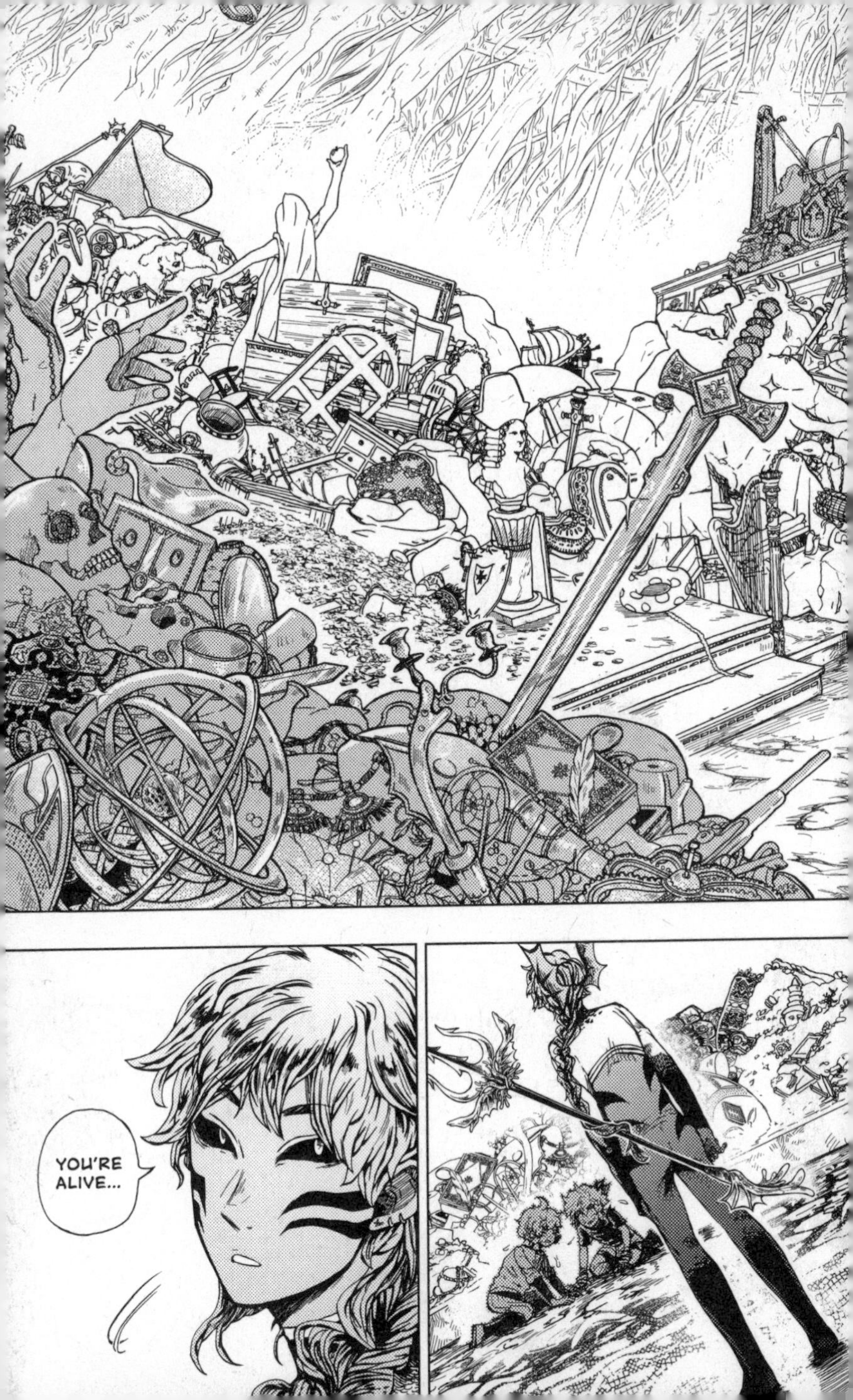
YOU'RE ALIVE...

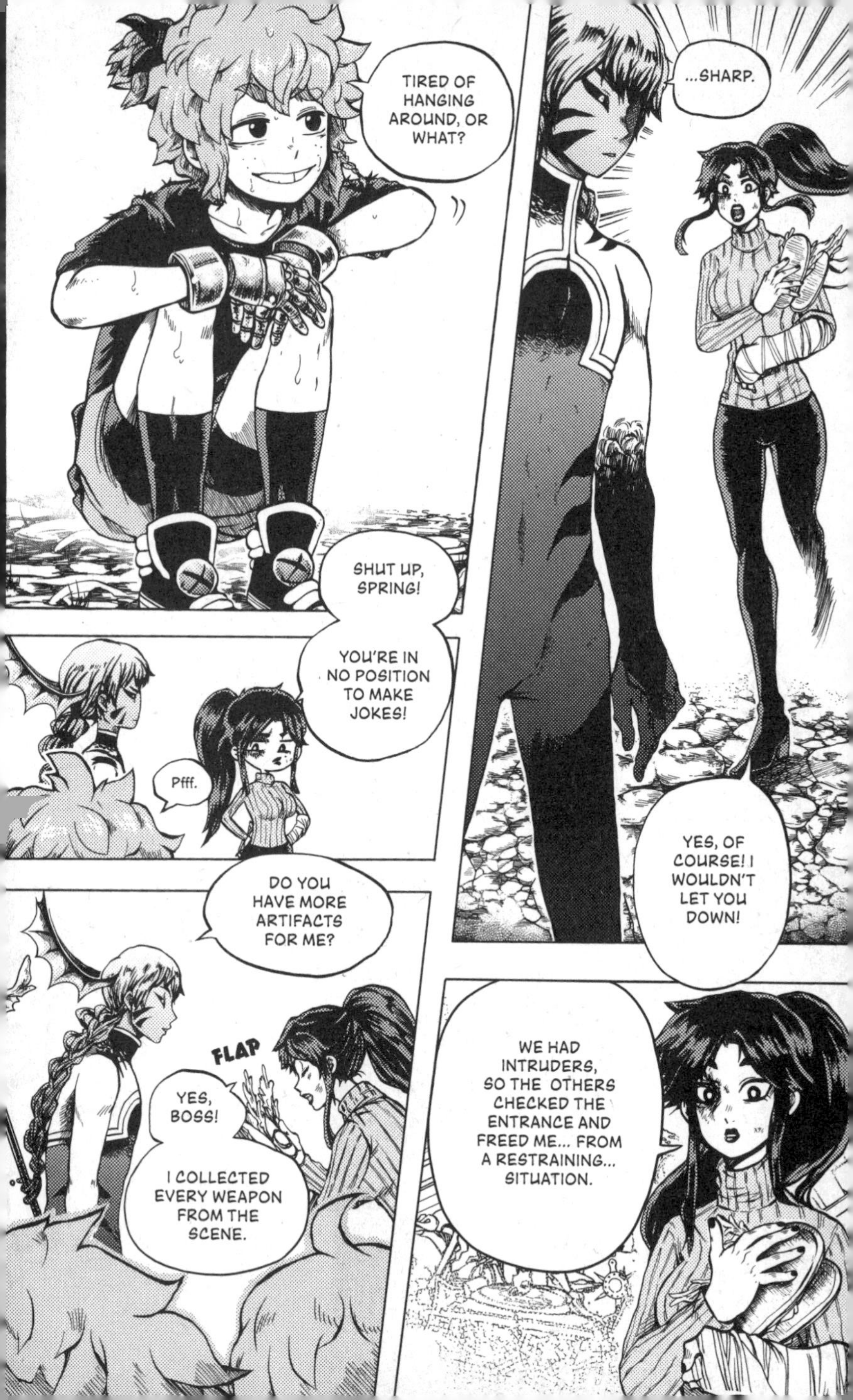
...SHARP.
YES, OF COURSE! I WOULDN'T LET YOU DOWN!
TIRED OF HANGING AROUND, OR WHAT?
SHUT UP, SPRING!
YOU'RE IN NO POSITION TO MAKE JOKES!
Pfff.
WE HAD INTRUDERS, SO THE OTHERS CHECKED THE ENTRANCE AND FREED ME... FROM A RESTRAINING... SITUATION.
DO YOU HAVE MORE ARTIFACTS FOR ME?
FLAP
YES, BOSS!
I COLLECTED EVERY WEAPON FROM THE SCENE.

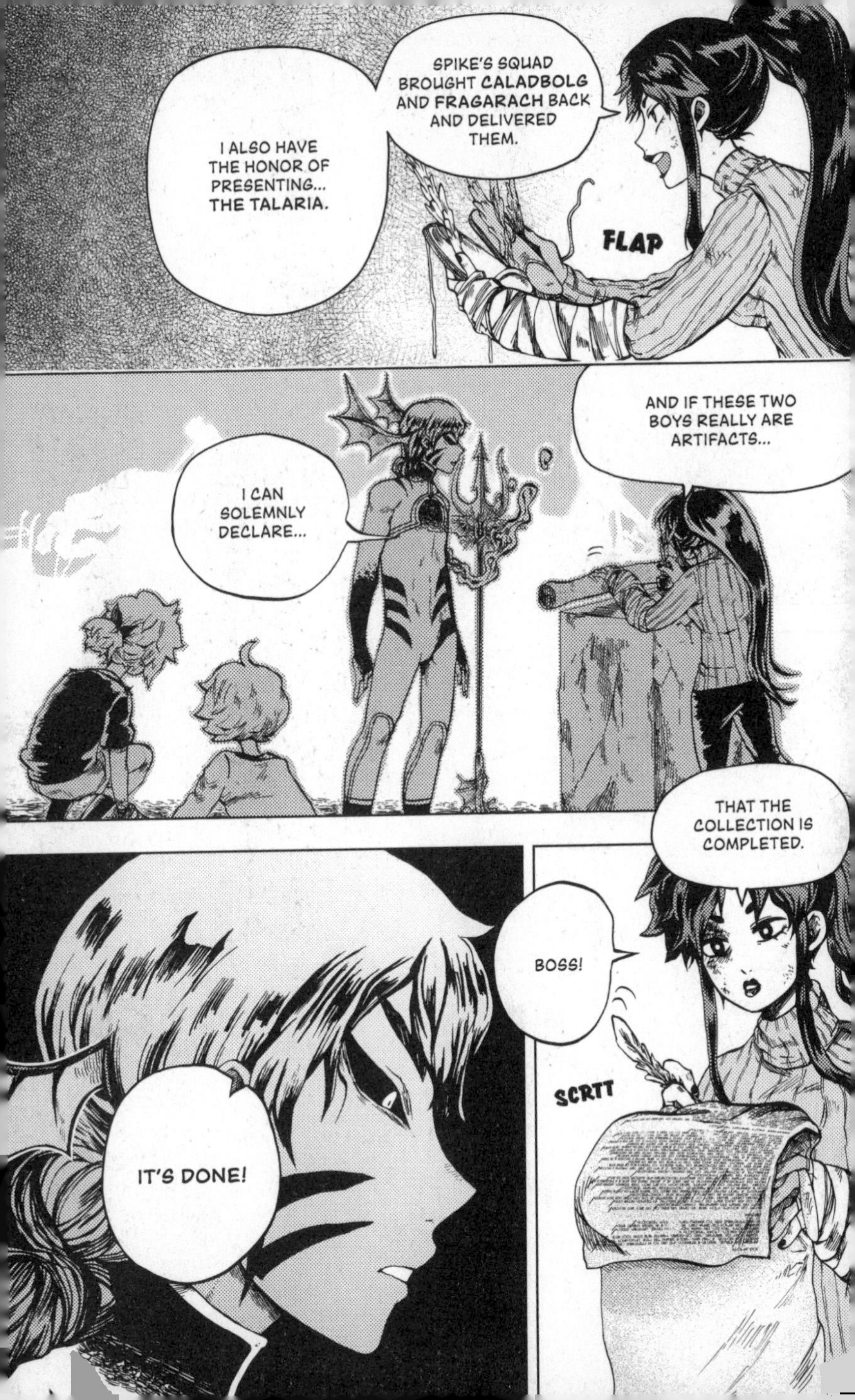
SPIKE'S SQUAD BROUGHT CALADBOLG AND FRAGARACH BACK AND DELIVERED THEM.
I ALSO HAVE THE HONOR OF PRESENTING... THE TALARIA.
FLAP
AND IF THESE TWO BOYS REALLY ARE ARTIFACTS...
I CAN SOLEMNLY DECLARE...
THAT THE COLLECTION IS COMPLETED.
BOSS!
SCRTT
IT'S DONE!

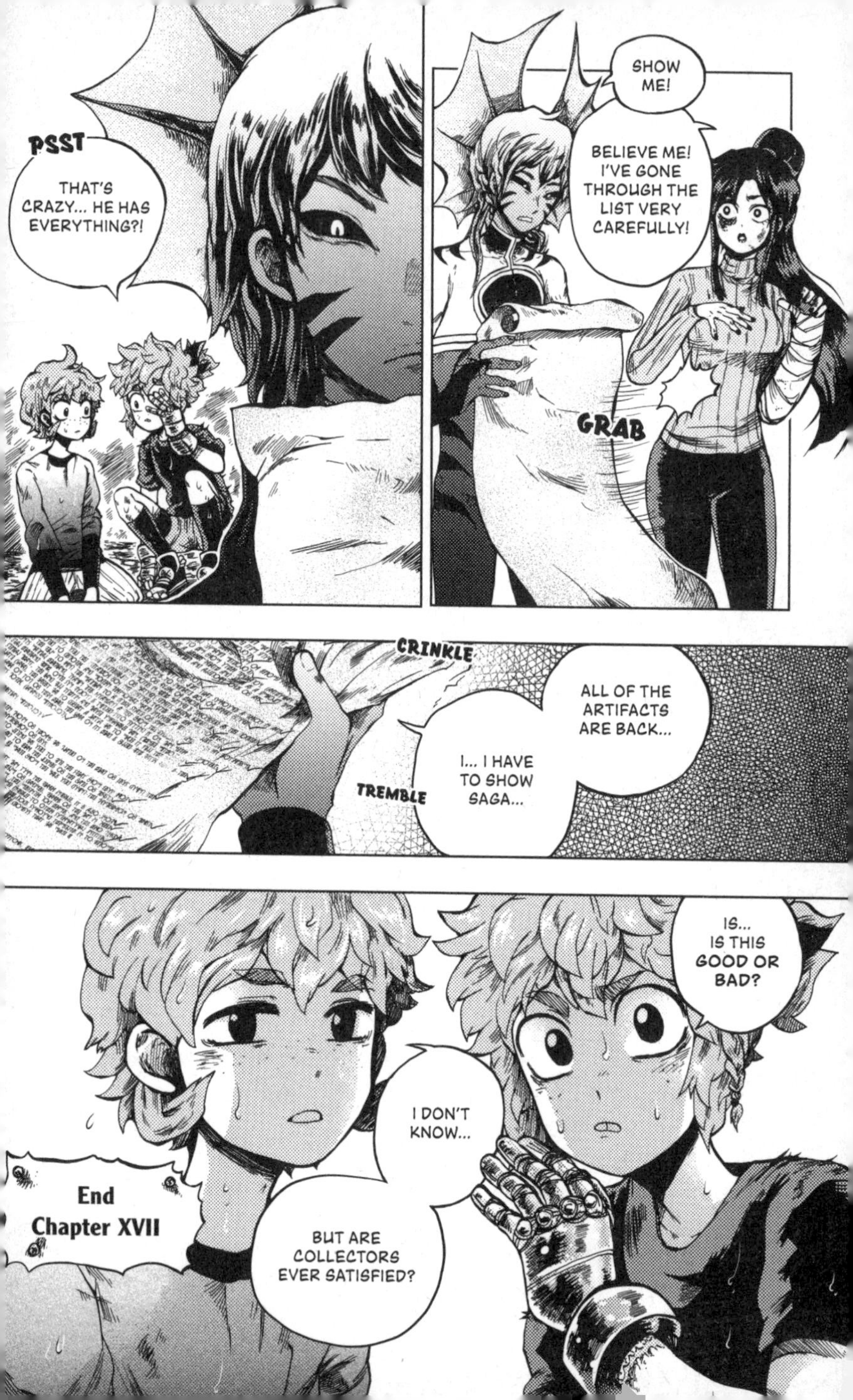
SHOW ME!
BELIEVE ME! I'VE GONE THROUGH THE LIST VERY CAREFULLY!
GRAB
PSST
THAT'S CRAZY... HE HAS EVERYTHING?!
CRINKLE
ALL OF THE ARTIFACTS ARE BACK...
I... I HAVE TO SHOW SAGA...
TREMBLE
IS... IS THIS GOOD OR BAD?
I DON'T KNOW...
End Chapter XVII
BUT ARE COLLECTORS EVER SATISFIED?

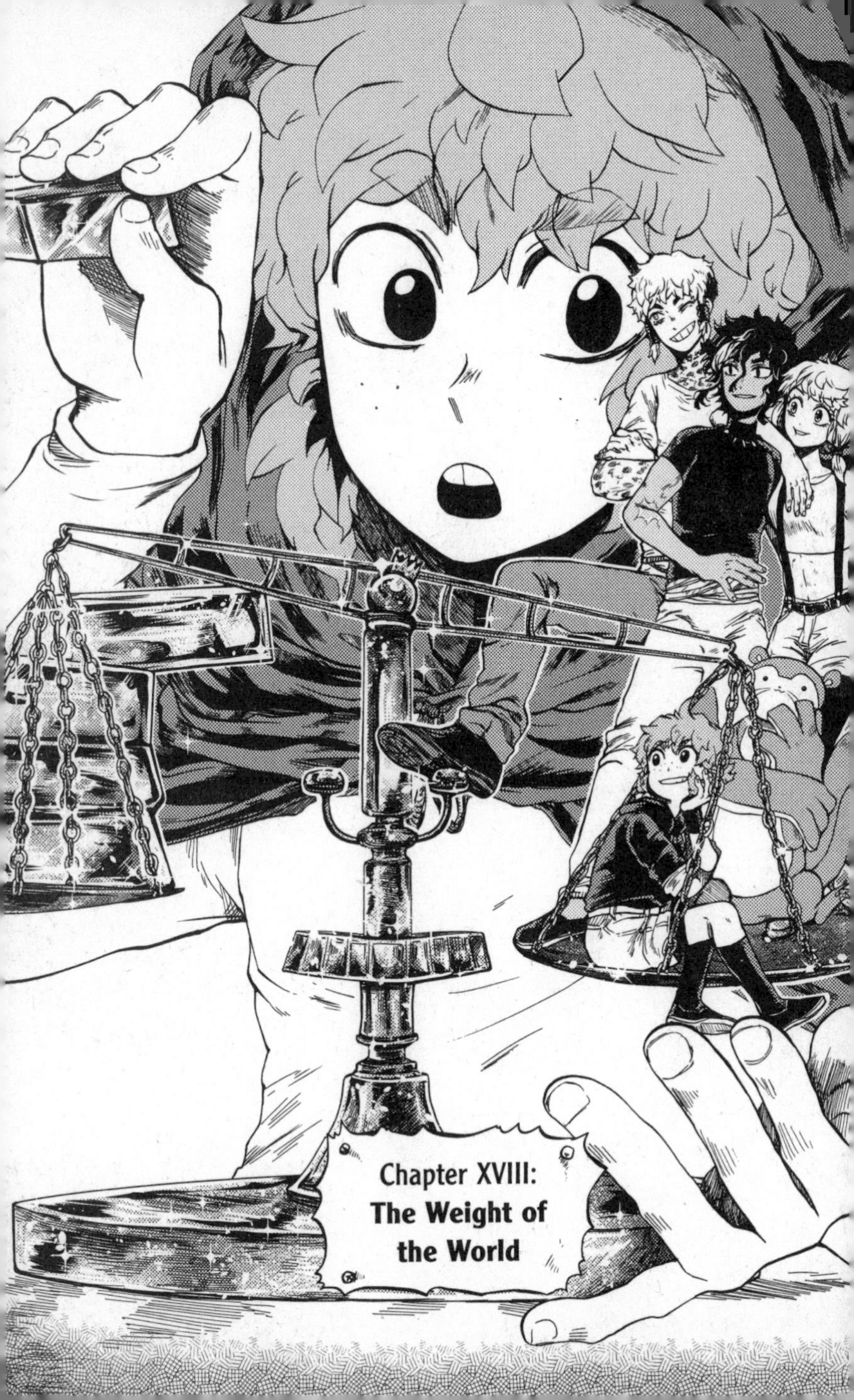
Chapter XVIII:
The Weight of the World

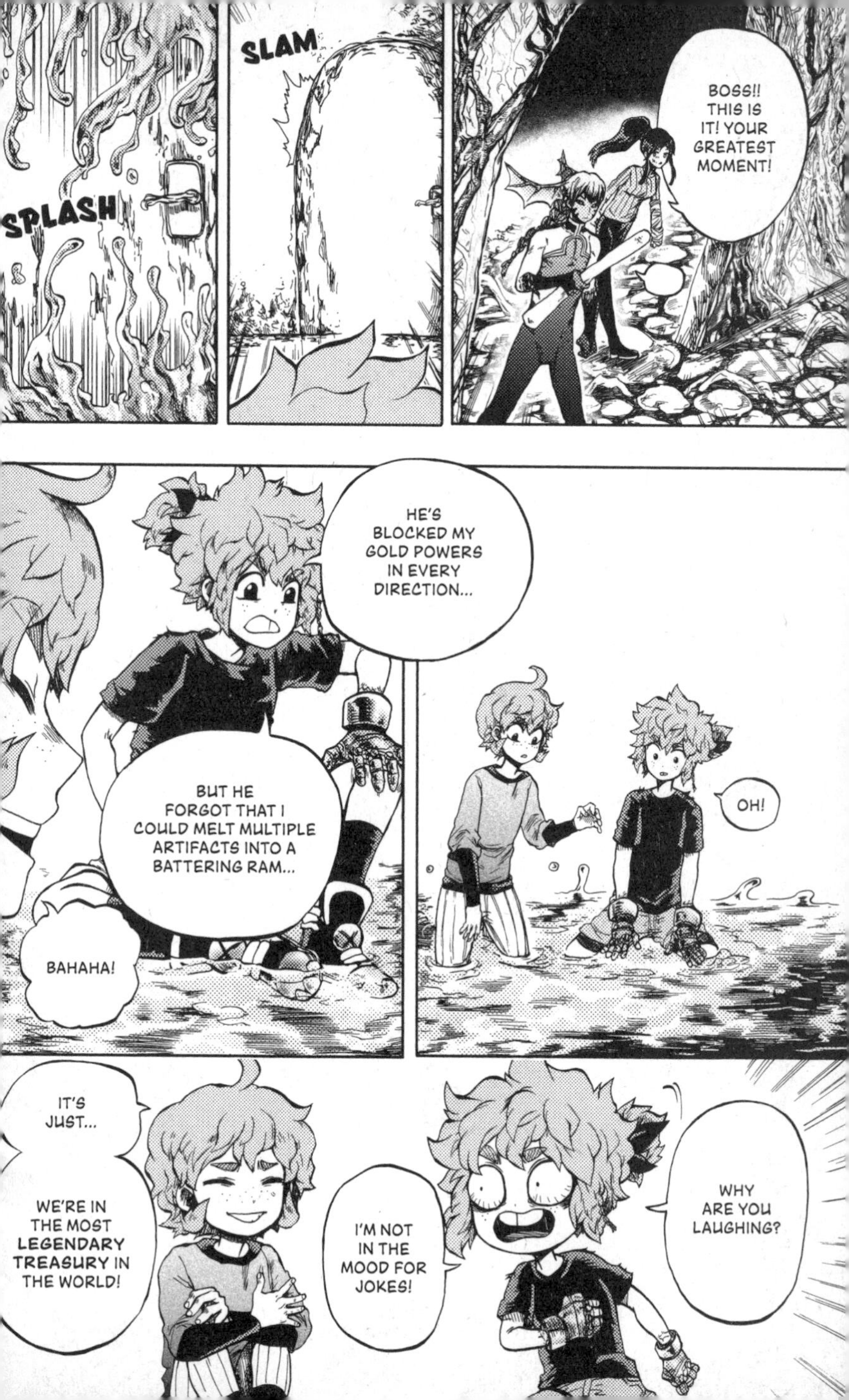
BOSS!! THIS IS IT! YOUR GREATEST MOMENT!
SLAM
SPLASH
HE'S BLOCKED MY GOLD POWERS IN EVERY DIRECTION...
BUT HE FORGOT THAT I COULD MELT MULTIPLE ARTIFACTS INTO A BATTERING RAM...
BAHAHA!
OH!
WHY ARE YOU LAUGHING?
I'M NOT IN THE MOOD FOR JOKES!
IT'S JUST...
WE'RE IN THE MOST **LEGENDARY TREASURY** IN THE WORLD!

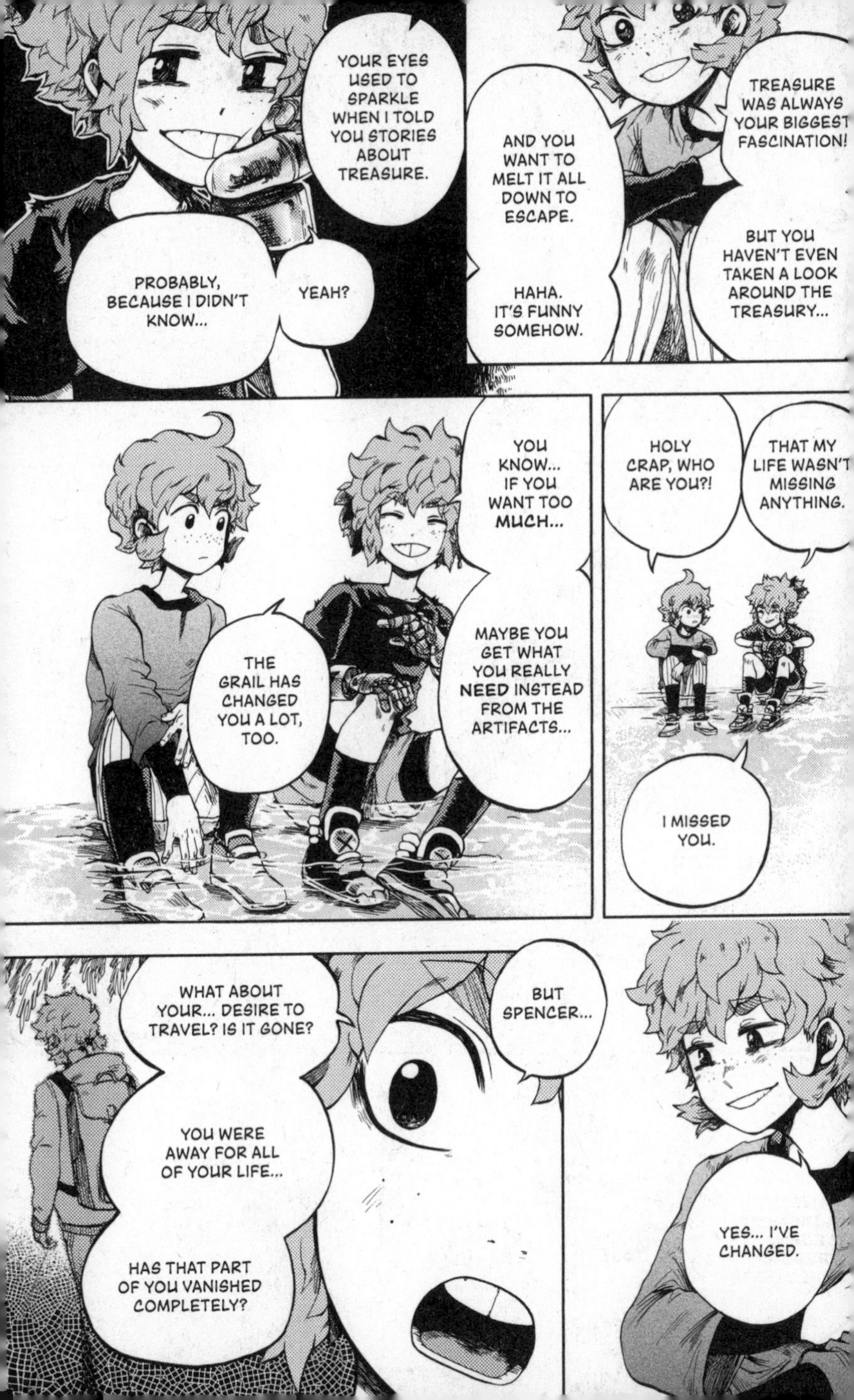
TREASURE WAS ALWAYS YOUR BIGGEST FASCINATION!
BUT YOU HAVEN'T EVEN TAKEN A LOOK AROUND THE TREASURY...
AND YOU WANT TO MELT IT ALL DOWN TO ESCAPE.
HAHA. IT'S FUNNY SOMEHOW.
YOUR EYES USED TO SPARKLE WHEN I TOLD YOU STORIES ABOUT TREASURE.
YEAH?
PROBABLY, BECAUSE I DIDN'T KNOW...
THAT MY LIFE WASN'T MISSING ANYTHING.
HOLY CRAP, WHO ARE YOU?!
I MISSED YOU.
YOU KNOW... IF YOU WANT TOO MUCH...
MAYBE YOU GET WHAT YOU REALLY NEED INSTEAD FROM THE ARTIFACTS...
THE GRAIL HAS CHANGED YOU A LOT, TOO.
YES... I'VE CHANGED.
BUT SPENCER...
WHAT ABOUT YOUR... DESIRE TO TRAVEL? IS IT GONE?
YOU WERE AWAY FOR ALL OF YOUR LIFE...
HAS THAT PART OF YOU VANISHED COMPLETELY?

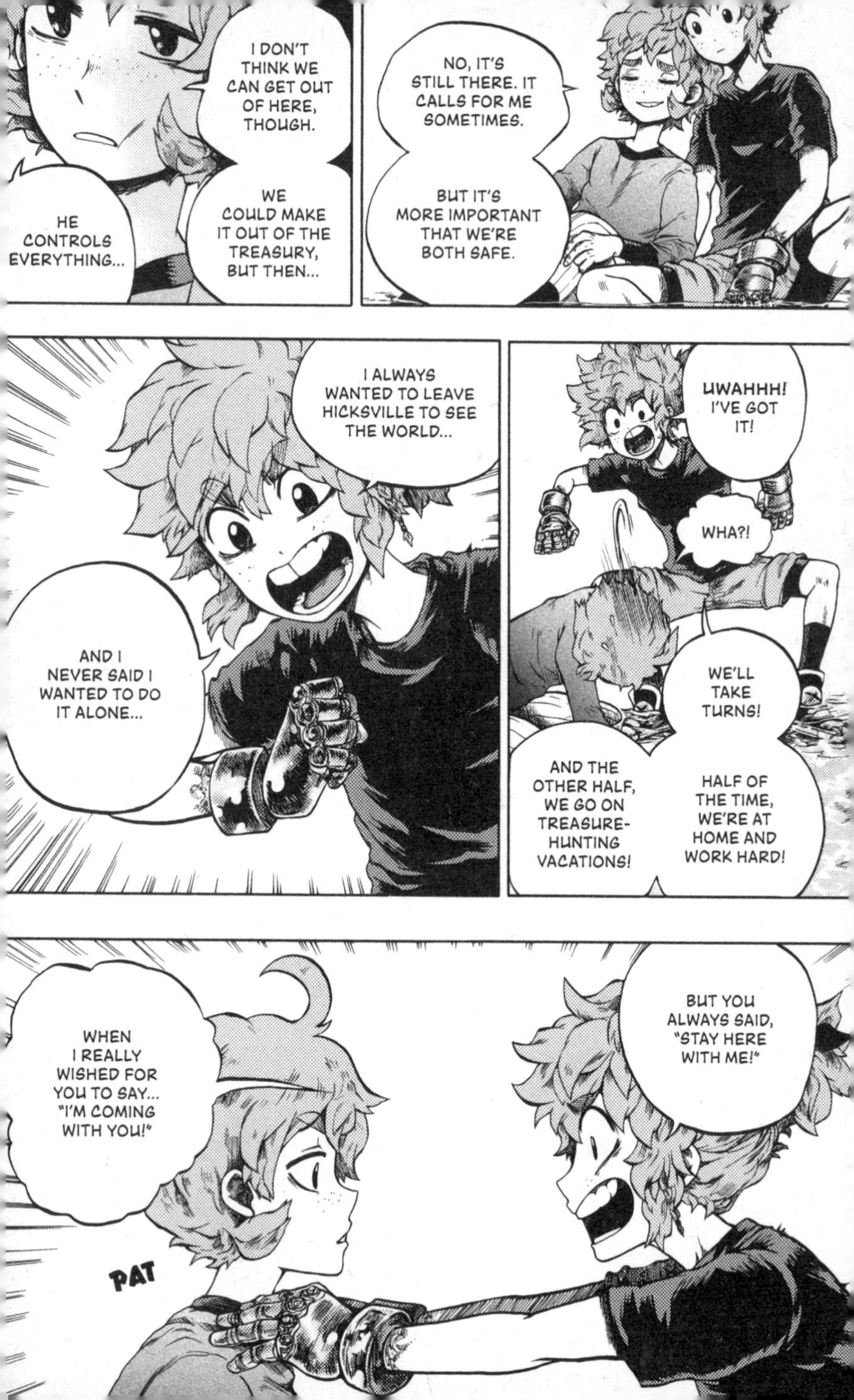
NO, IT'S STILL THERE. IT CALLS FOR ME SOMETIMES.
BUT IT'S MORE IMPORTANT THAT WE'RE BOTH SAFE.
I DON'T THINK WE CAN GET OUT OF HERE, THOUGH.
WE COULD MAKE IT OUT OF THE TREASURY, BUT THEN...
HE CONTROLS EVERYTHING...
UWAHHH! I'VE GOT IT!
WHA?!
WE'LL TAKE TURNS!
HALF OF THE TIME, WE'RE AT HOME AND WORK HARD!
AND THE OTHER HALF, WE GO ON TREASURE-HUNTING VACATIONS!
I ALWAYS WANTED TO LEAVE HICKSVILLE TO SEE THE WORLD...
AND I NEVER SAID I WANTED TO DO IT ALONE...
BUT YOU ALWAYS SAID, "STAY HERE WITH ME!"
WHEN I REALLY WISHED FOR YOU TO SAY... "I'M COMING WITH YOU!"
PAT

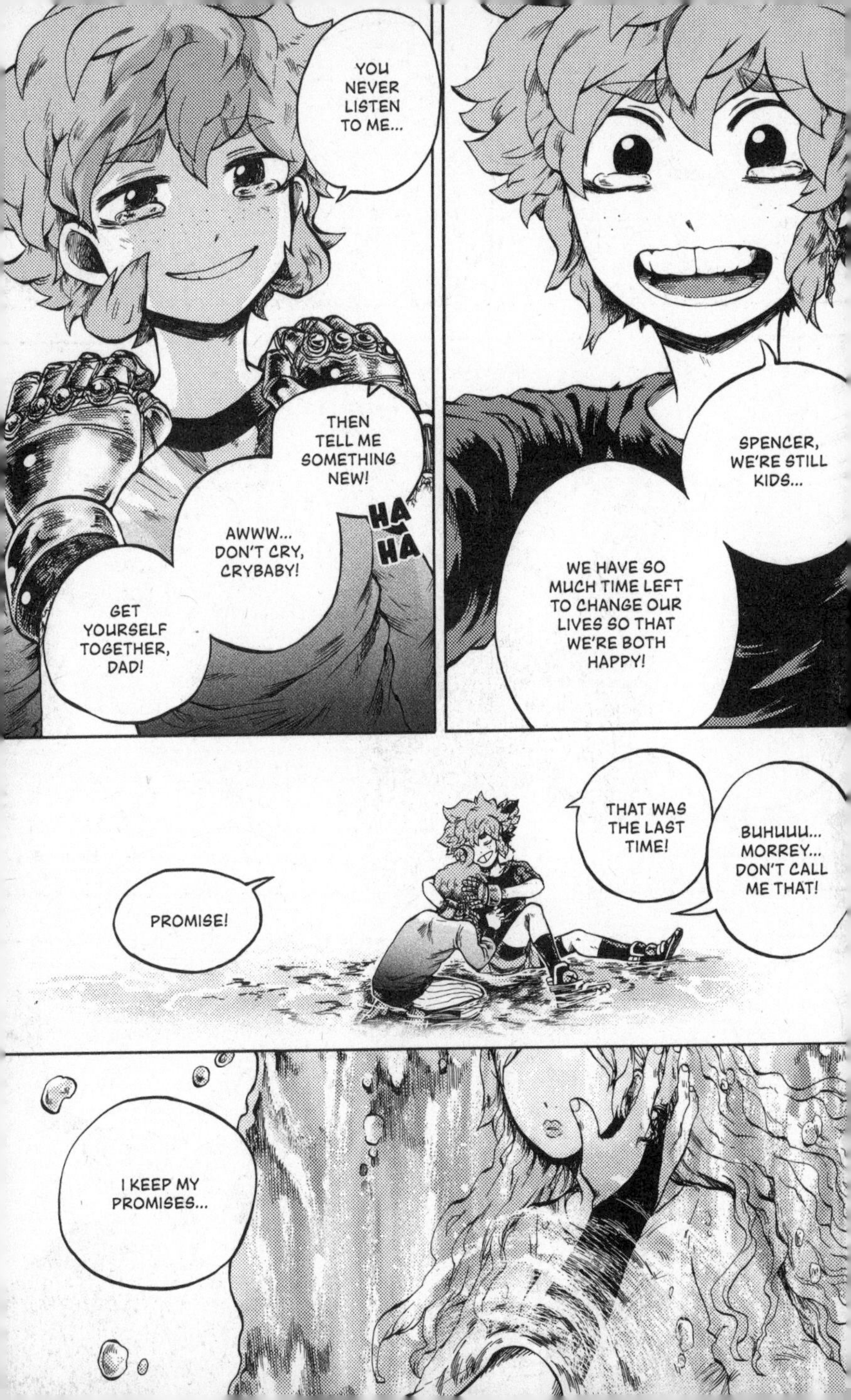
SPENCER, WE'RE STILL KIDS...
WE HAVE SO MUCH TIME LEFT TO CHANGE OUR LIVES SO THAT WE'RE BOTH HAPPY!
YOU NEVER LISTEN TO ME...
THEN TELL ME SOMETHING NEW!
HA HA
AWWW... DON'T CRY, CRYBABY!
GET YOURSELF TOGETHER, DAD!
BUHUUU... MORREY... DON'T CALL ME THAT!
THAT WAS THE LAST TIME!
PROMISE!
I KEEP MY PROMISES...

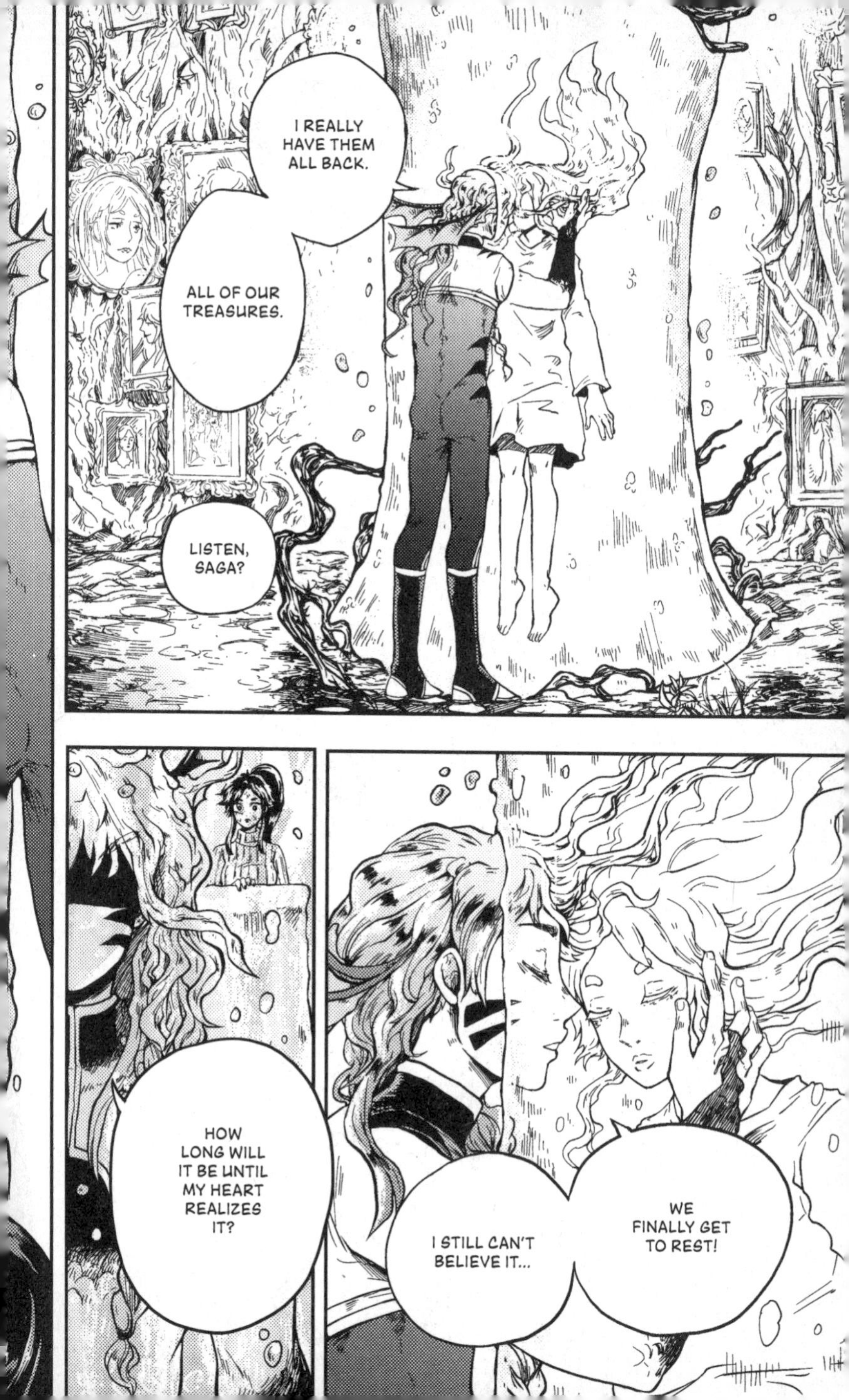
I REALLY HAVE THEM ALL BACK.
ALL OF OUR TREASURES.
LISTEN, SAGA?
WE FINALLY GET TO REST!
I STILL CAN'T BELIEVE IT...
HOW LONG WILL IT BE UNTIL MY HEART REALIZES IT?

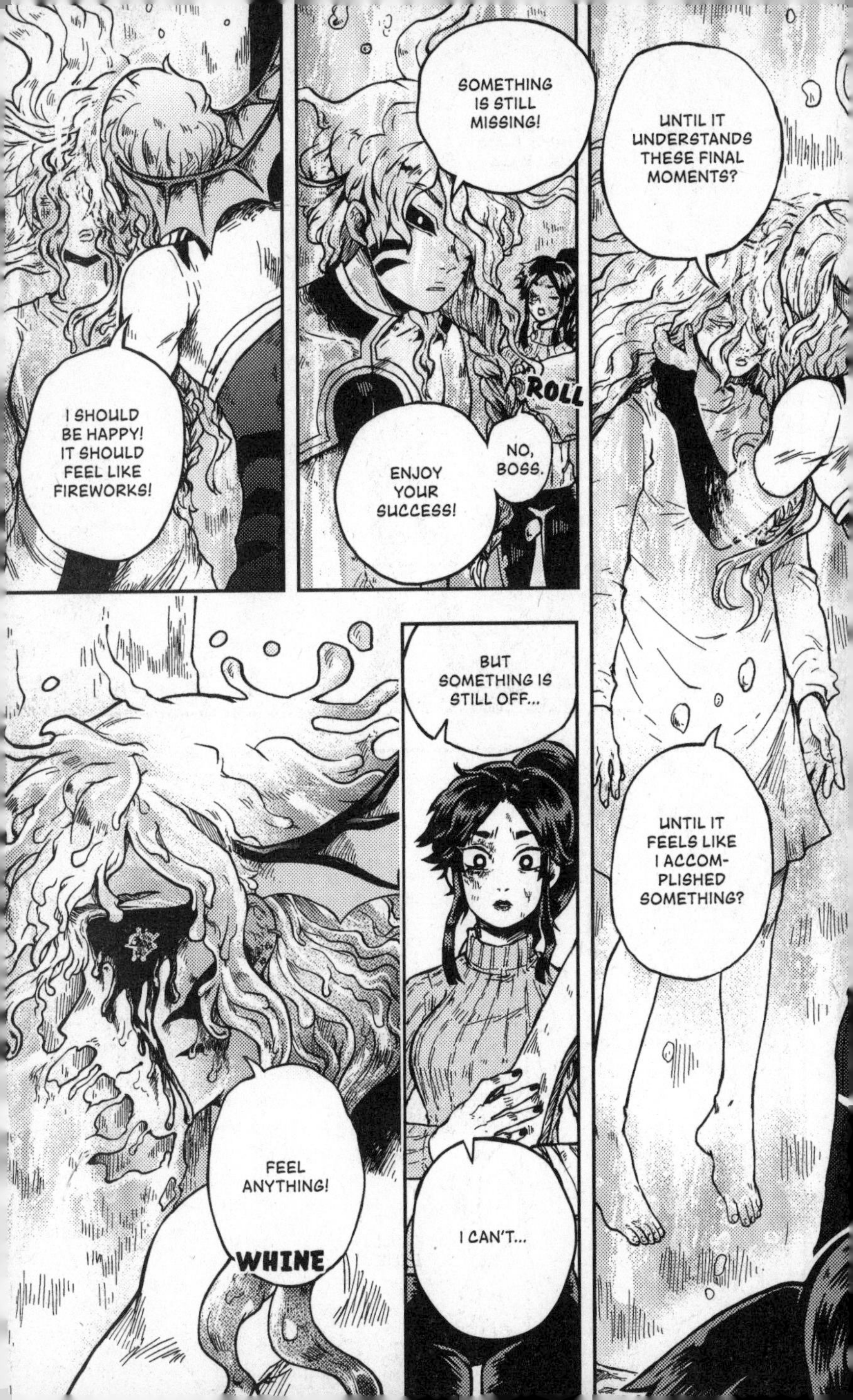
UNTIL IT UNDERSTANDS THESE FINAL MOMENTS?
UNTIL IT FEELS LIKE I ACCOM-PLISHED SOMETHING?
SOMETHING IS STILL MISSING!
ROLL
NO, BOSS.
ENJOY YOUR SUCCESS!
I SHOULD BE HAPPY! IT SHOULD FEEL LIKE FIREWORKS!
BUT SOMETHING IS STILL OFF...
I CAN'T...
FEEL ANYTHING!
WHINE

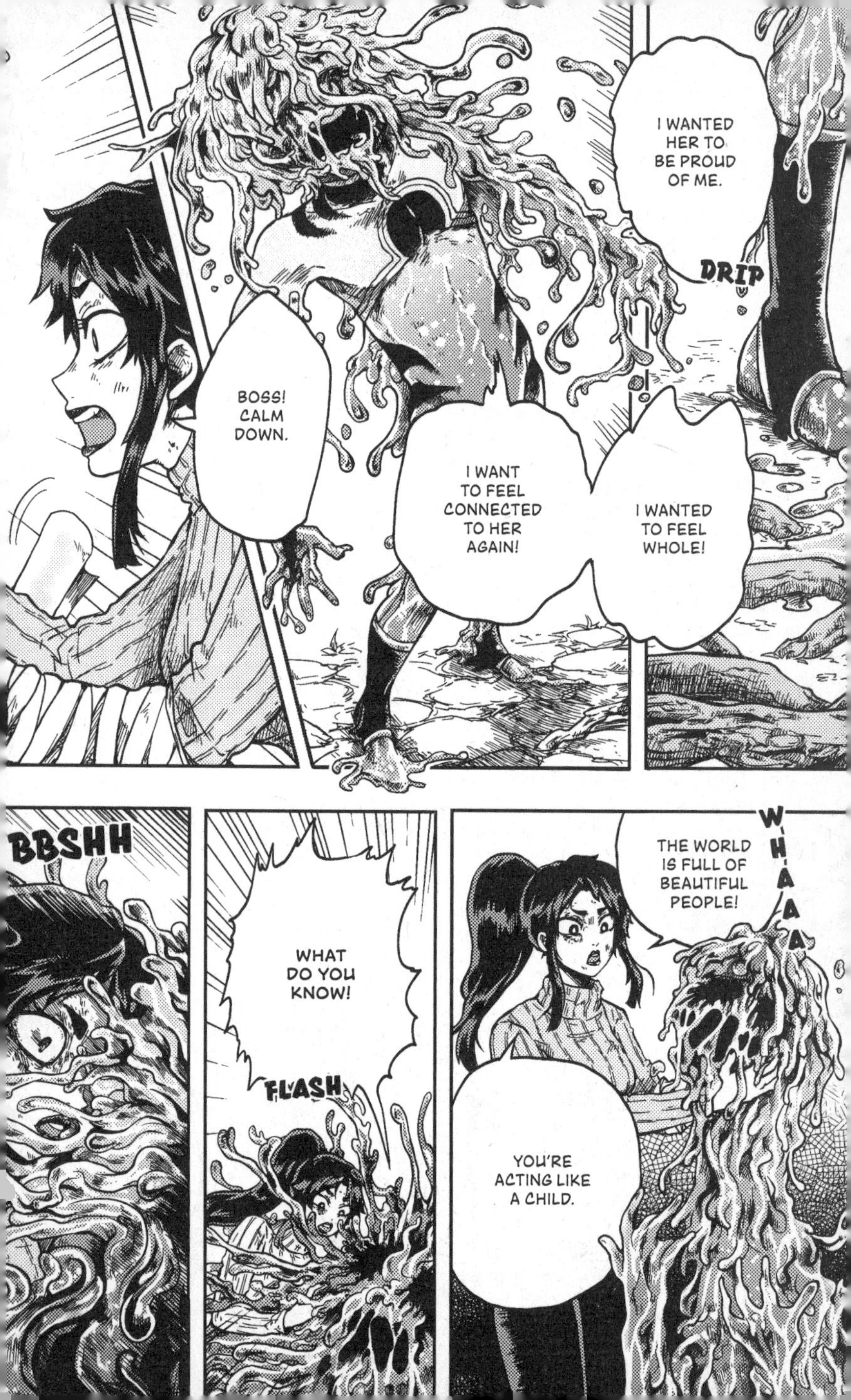
I WANTED HER TO BE PROUD OF ME.
DRIP
I WANTED TO FEEL WHOLE!
I WANT TO FEEL CONNECTED TO HER AGAIN!
BOSS! CALM DOWN.
THE WORLD IS FULL OF BEAUTIFUL PEOPLE!
WHAAAA
YOU'RE ACTING LIKE A CHILD.
WHAT DO YOU KNOW!
FLASH
BBSHH

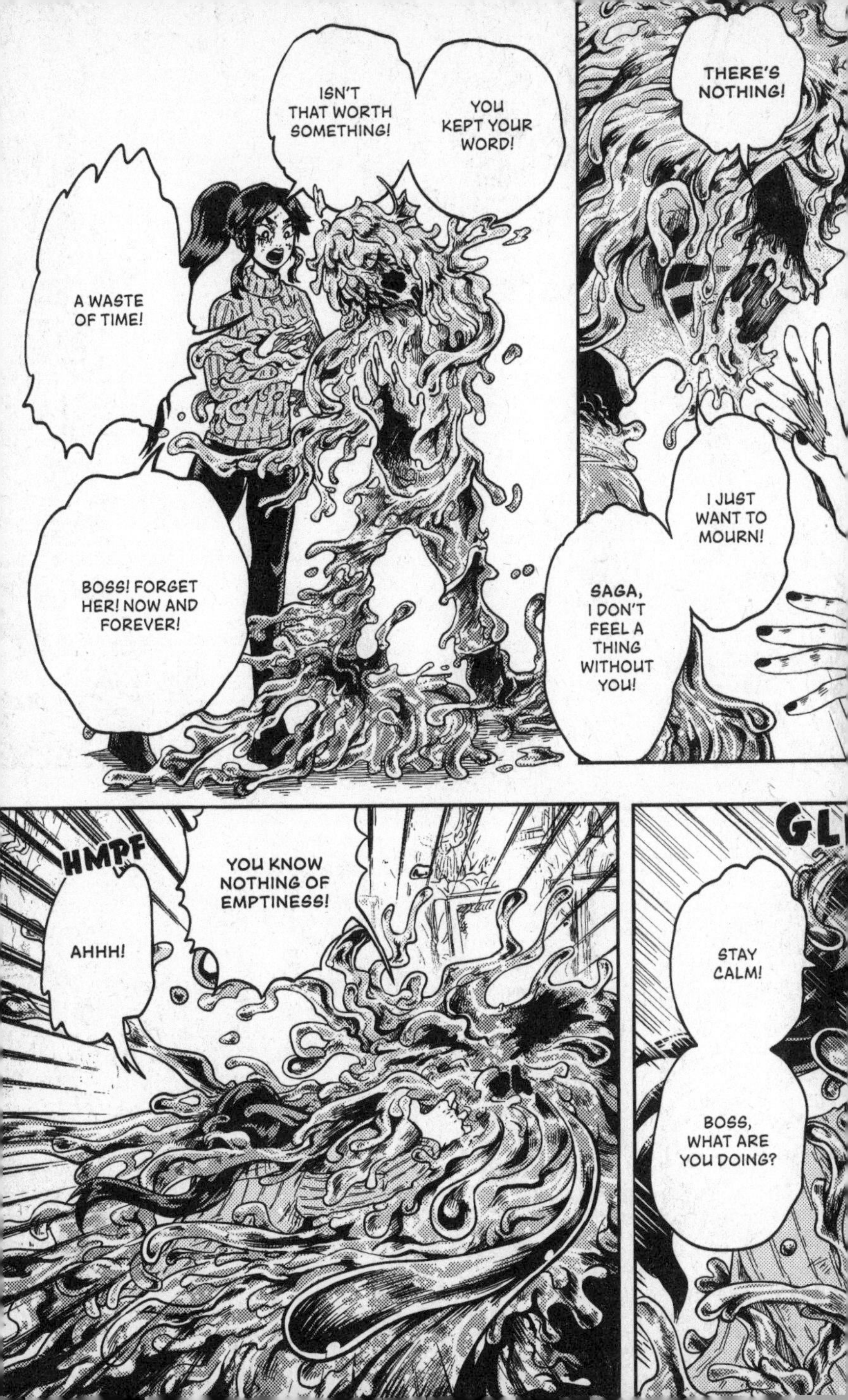
THERE'S NOTHING!
I JUST WANT TO MOURN!
SAGA, I DON'T FEEL A THING WITHOUT YOU!
YOU KEPT YOUR WORD!
ISN'T THAT WORTH SOMETHING!
A WASTE OF TIME!
BOSS! FORGET HER! NOW AND FOREVER!
GL
STAY CALM!
BOSS, WHAT ARE YOU DOING?
YOU KNOW NOTHING OF EMPTINESS!
HMPF
AHHH!

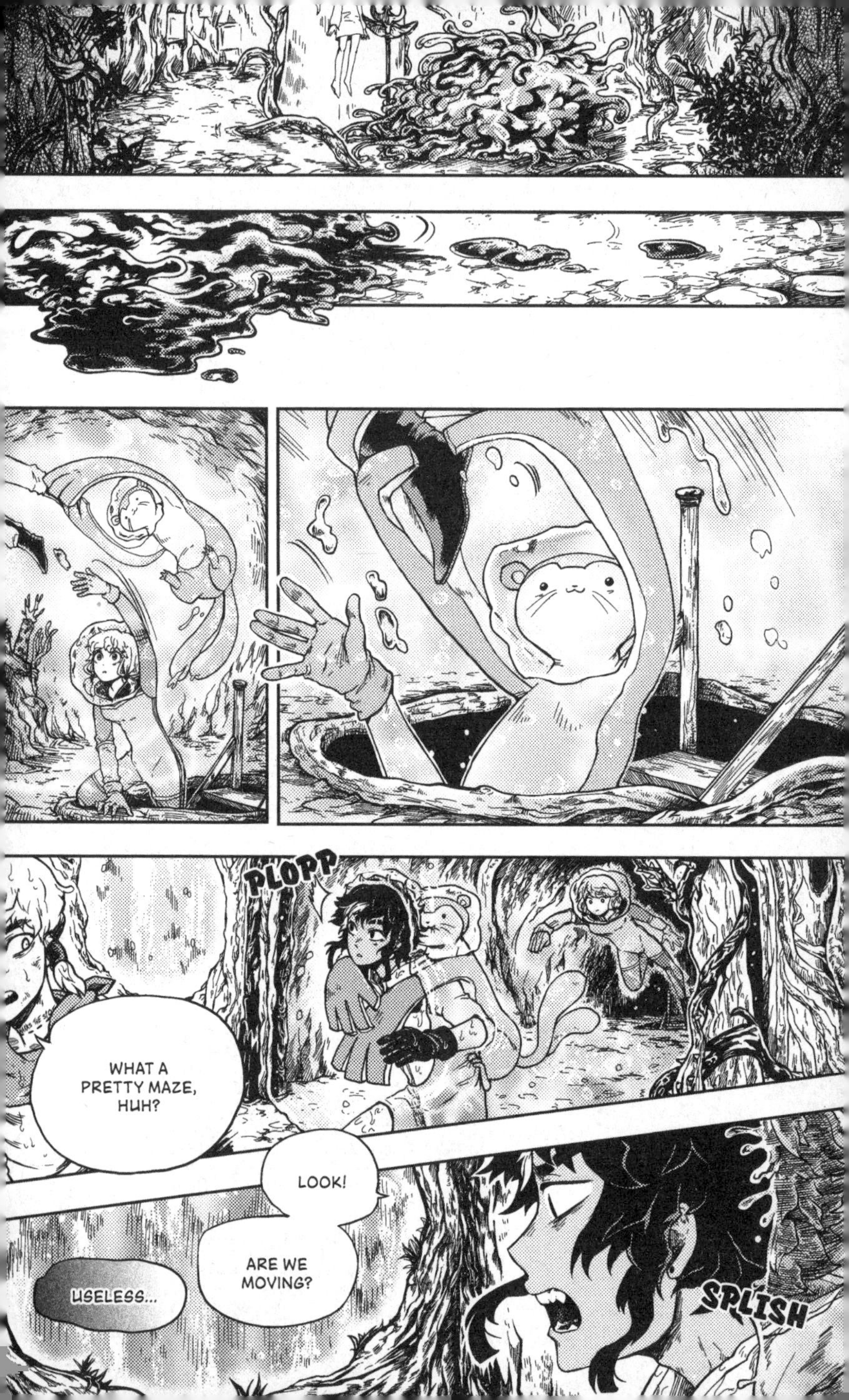
PLOPP
WHAT A PRETTY MAZE, HUH?
SPLISH
LOOK!
ARE WE MOVING?
USELESS...

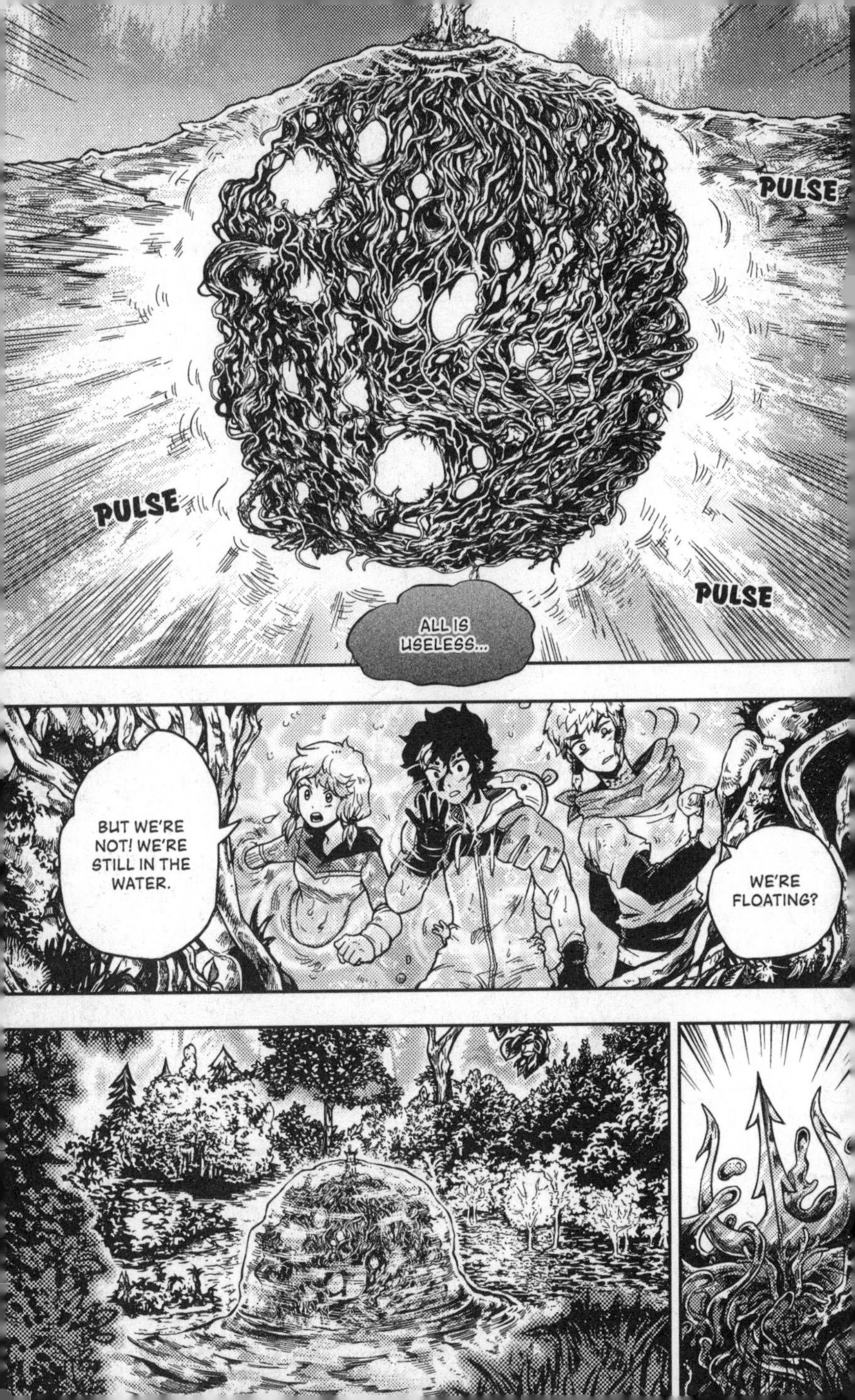
PULSE
PULSE
PULSE
ALL IS USELESS...
WE'RE FLOATING?
BUT WE'RE NOT! WE'RE STILL IN THE WATER.

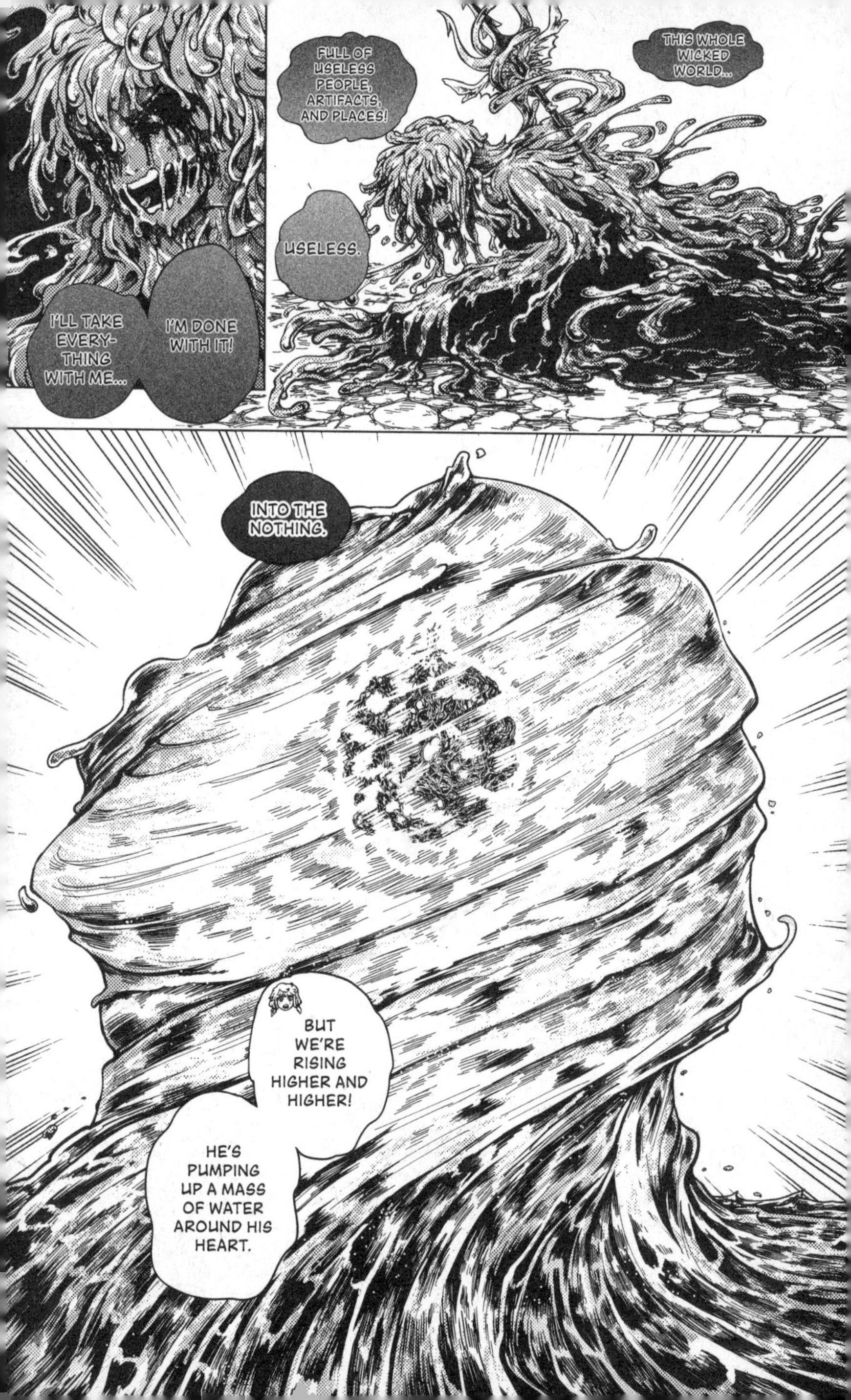
THIS WHOLE WICKED WORLD...
FULL OF USELESS PEOPLE, ARTIFACTS, AND PLACES!
USELESS.
I'M DONE WITH IT!
I'LL TAKE EVERY-THING WITH ME...
INTO THE NOTHING.
BUT WE'RE RISING HIGHER AND HIGHER!
HE'S PUMPING UP A MASS OF WATER AROUND HIS HEART.

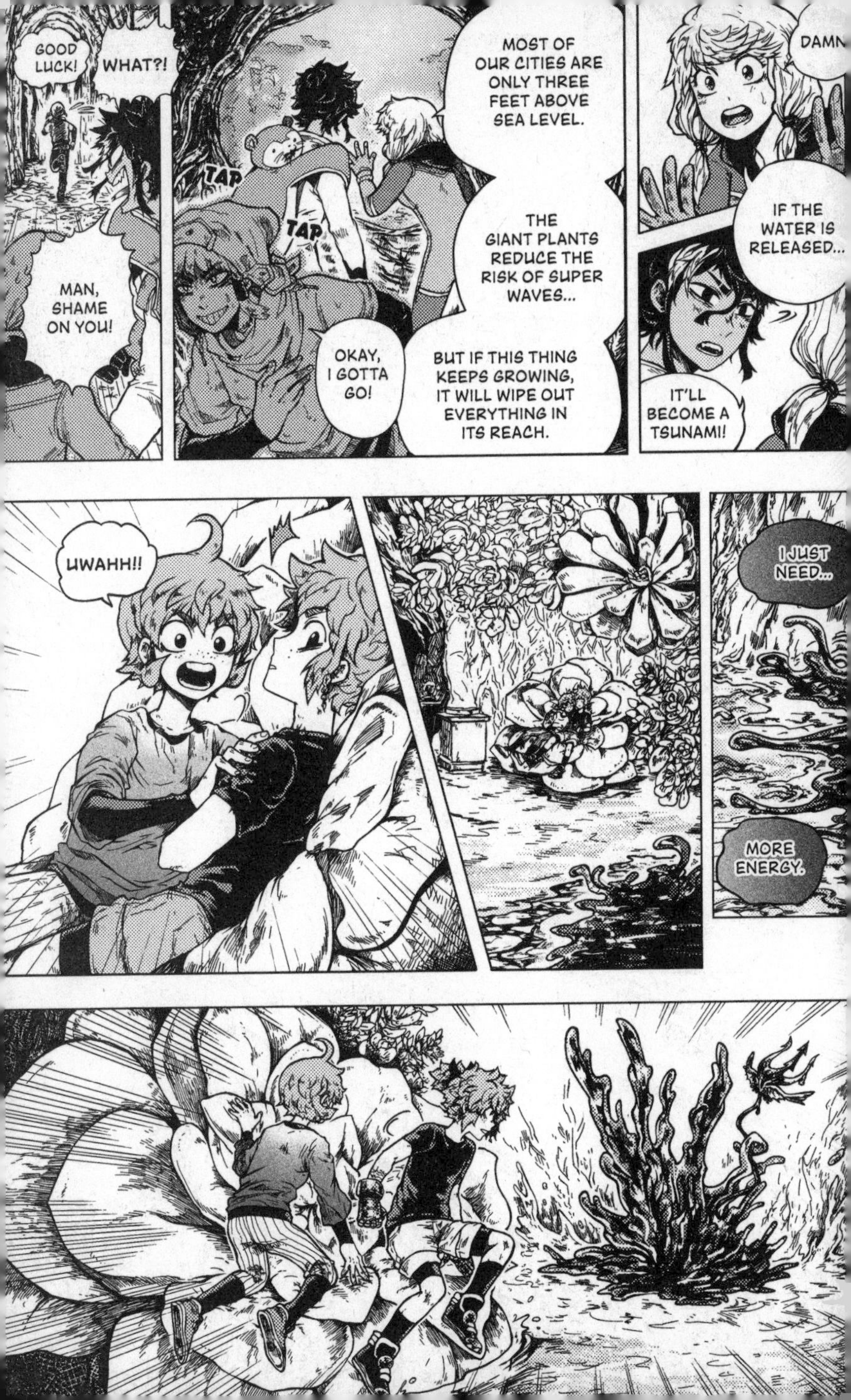
DAMN
IF THE WATER IS RELEASED...
IT'LL BECOME A TSUNAMI!
MOST OF OUR CITIES ARE ONLY THREE FEET ABOVE SEA LEVEL.
THE GIANT PLANTS REDUCE THE RISK OF SUPER WAVES...
BUT IF THIS THING KEEPS GROWING, IT WILL WIPE OUT EVERYTHING IN ITS REACH.
TAP
TAP
OKAY, I GOTTA GO!
GOOD LUCK!
WHAT?!
MAN, SHAME ON YOU!
I JUST NEED...
MORE ENERGY.
UWAHH!!

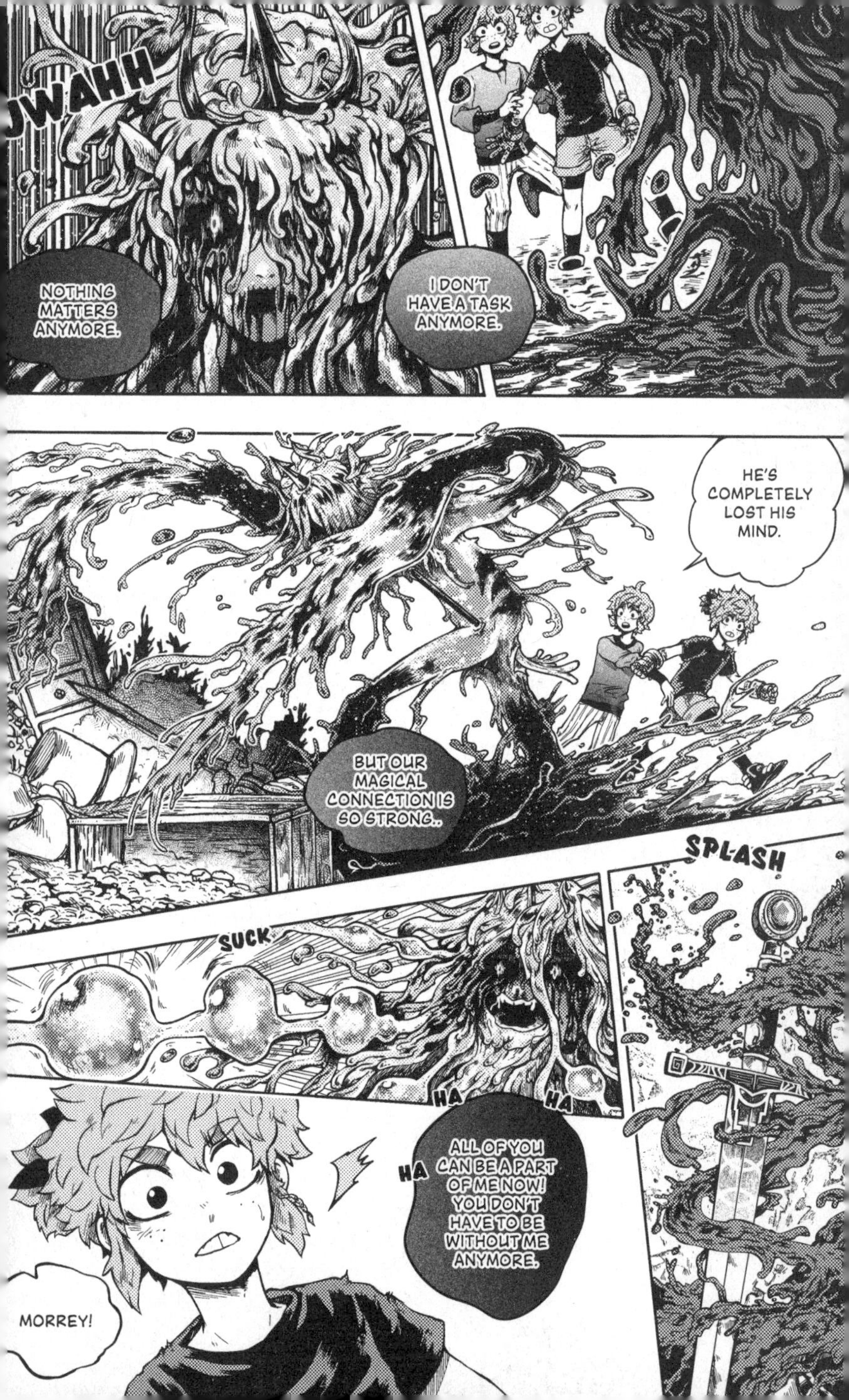
JWAHH
I DON'T HAVE A TASK ANYMORE.
NOTHING MATTERS ANYMORE.
HE'S COMPLETELY LOST HIS MIND.
BUT OUR MAGICAL CONNECTION IS SO STRONG..
SPLASH
SUCK
HA
HA
HA
ALL OF YOU CAN BE A PART OF ME NOW! YOU DON'T HAVE TO BE WITHOUT ME ANYMORE.
MORREY!

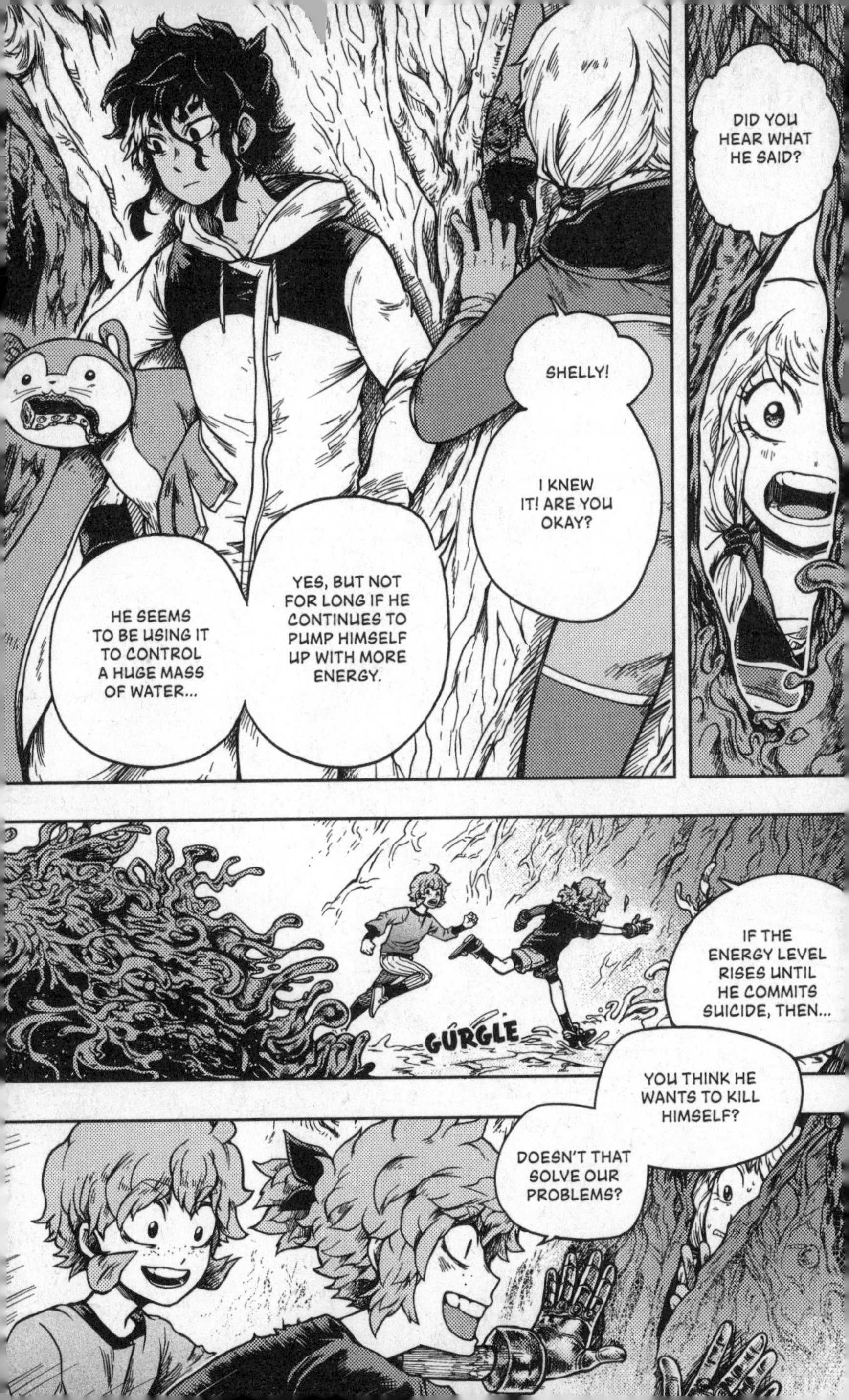
DID YOU HEAR WHAT HE SAID?
SHELLY!
I KNEW IT! ARE YOU OKAY?
YES, BUT NOT FOR LONG IF HE CONTINUES TO PUMP HIMSELF UP WITH MORE ENERGY.
HE SEEMS TO BE USING IT TO CONTROL A HUGE MASS OF WATER...
IF THE ENERGY LEVEL RISES UNTIL HE COMMITS SUICIDE, THEN...
GÚRGLE
YOU THINK HE WANTS TO KILL HIMSELF?
DOESN'T THAT SOLVE OUR PROBLEMS?

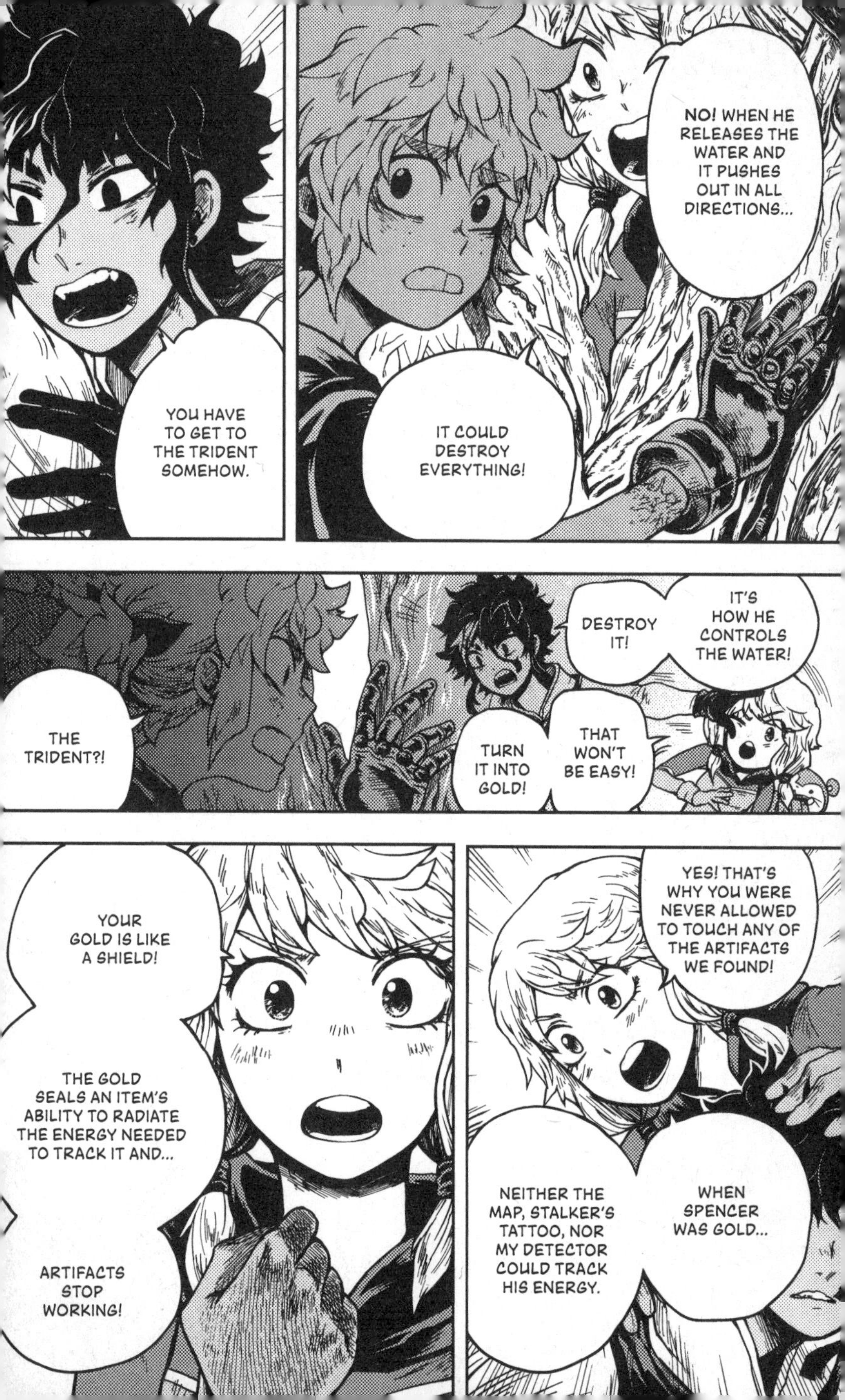
NO! WHEN HE RELEASES THE WATER AND IT PUSHES OUT IN ALL DIRECTIONS...
IT COULD DESTROY EVERYTHING!
YOU HAVE TO GET TO THE TRIDENT SOMEHOW.
IT'S HOW HE CONTROLS THE WATER!
DESTROY IT!
THAT WON'T BE EASY!
TURN IT INTO GOLD!
THE TRIDENT?!
YES! THAT'S WHY YOU WERE NEVER ALLOWED TO TOUCH ANY OF THE ARTIFACTS WE FOUND!
WHEN SPENCER WAS GOLD...
NEITHER THE MAP, STALKER'S TATTOO, NOR MY DETECTOR COULD TRACK HIS ENERGY.
YOUR GOLD IS LIKE A SHIELD!
THE GOLD SEALS AN ITEM'S ABILITY TO RADIATE THE ENERGY NEEDED TO TRACK IT AND...
ARTIFACTS STOP WORKING!

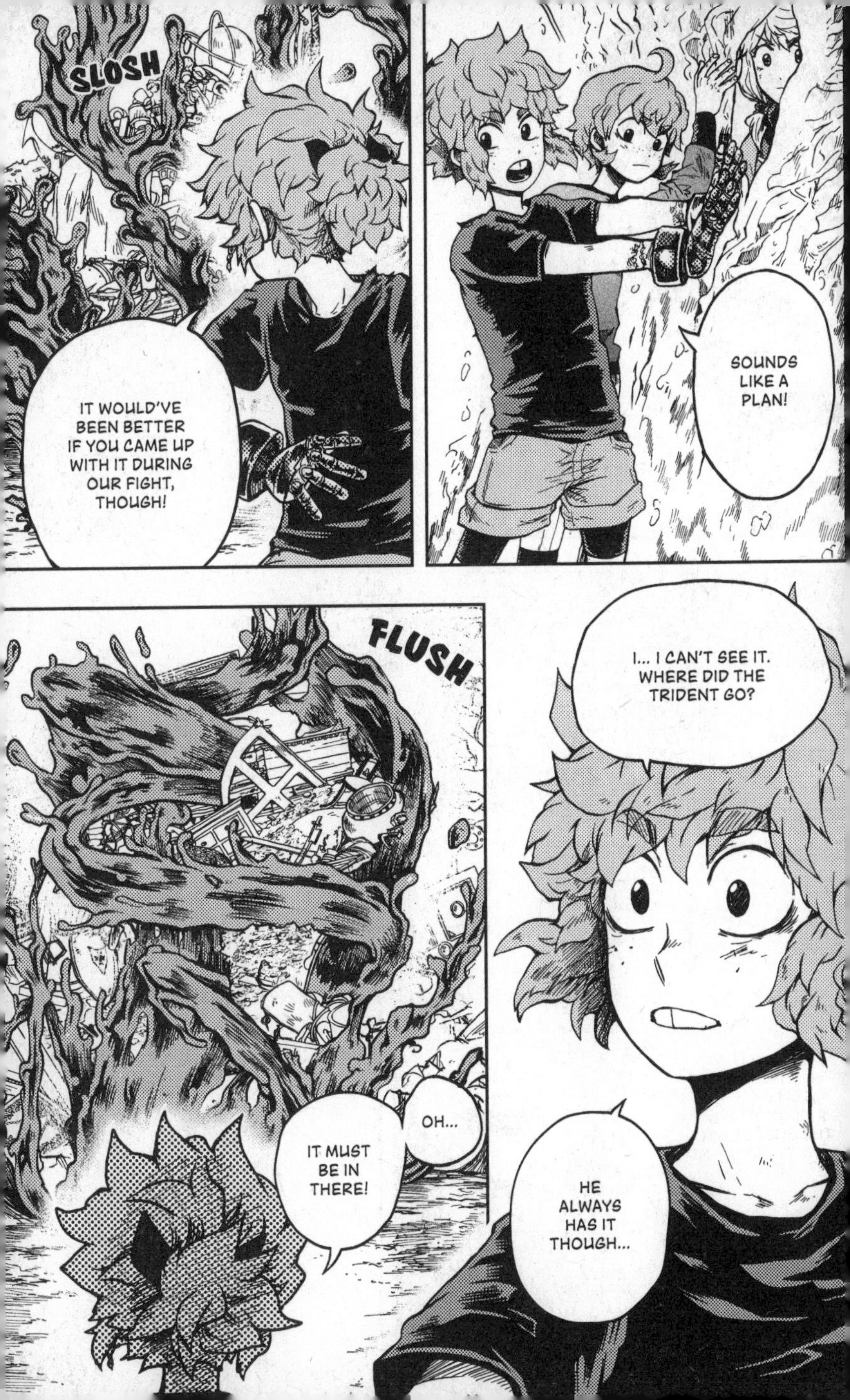
SOUNDS LIKE A PLAN!
SLOSH
IT WOULD'VE BEEN BETTER IF YOU CAME UP WITH IT DURING OUR FIGHT, THOUGH!
I... I CAN'T SEE IT. WHERE DID THE TRIDENT GO?
HE ALWAYS HAS IT THOUGH...
FLUSH
OH...
IT MUST BE IN THERE!

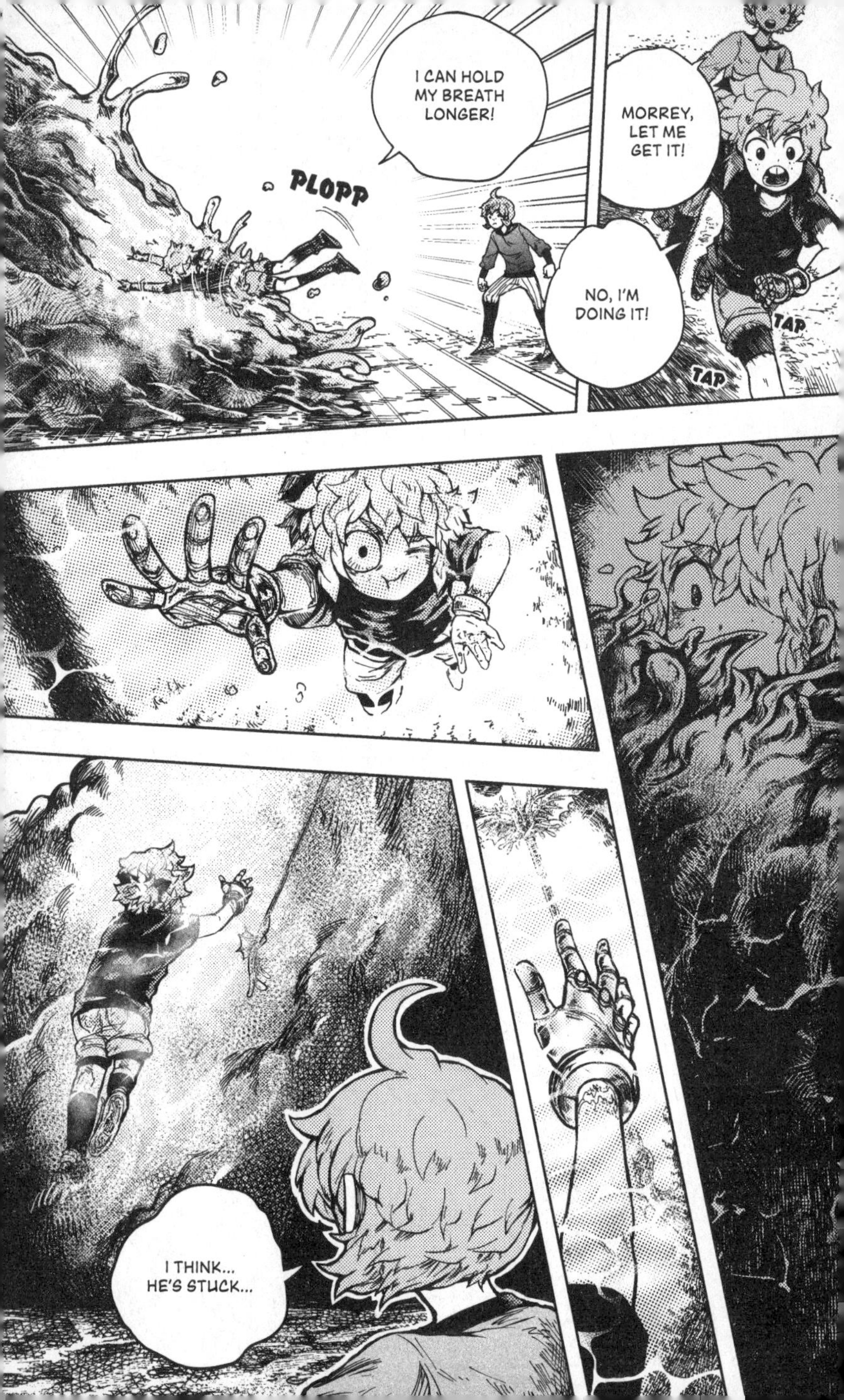
MORREY, LET ME GET IT!
NO, I'M DOING IT!
TAP
TAP
I CAN HOLD MY BREATH LONGER!
PLOPP
I THINK... HE'S STUCK...

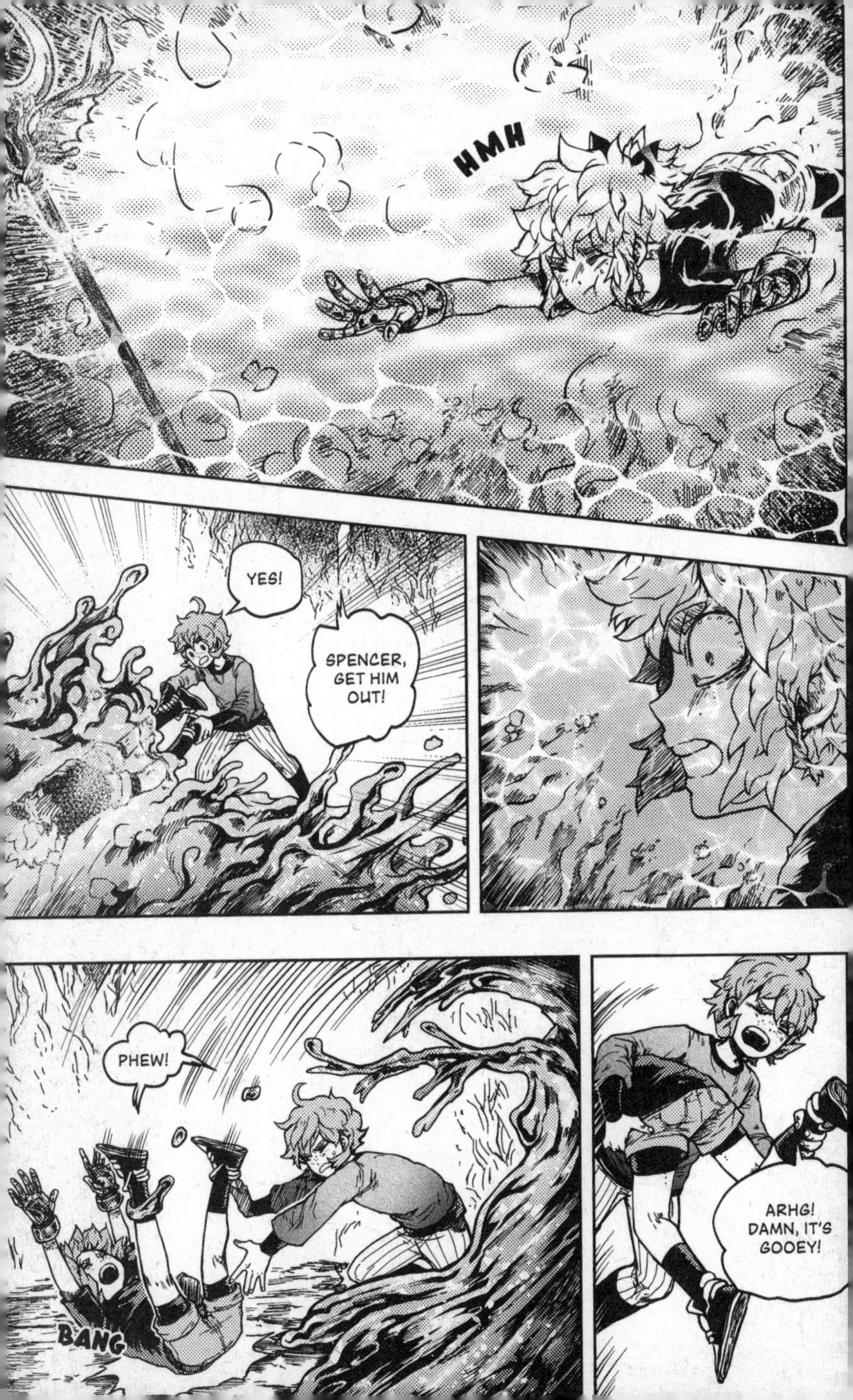
HMH
SPENCER, GET HIM OUT!
YES!
ARHG! DAMN, IT'S GOOEY!
PHEW!
BANG

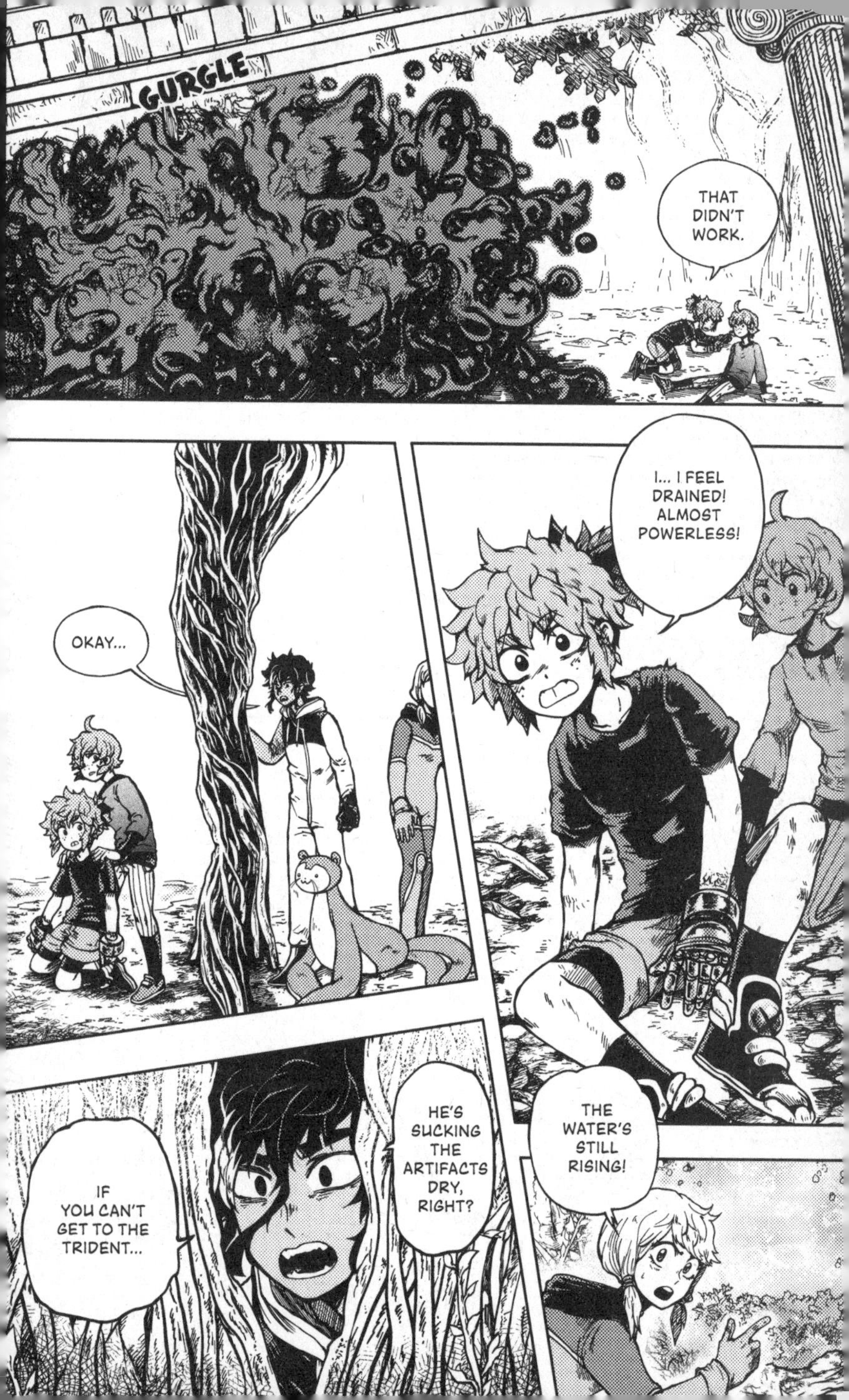
GURGLE
THAT DIDN'T WORK.
I... I FEEL DRAINED! ALMOST POWERLESS!
OKAY...
THE WATER'S STILL RISING!
HE'S SUCKING THE ARTIFACTS DRY, RIGHT?
IF YOU CAN'T GET TO THE TRIDENT...

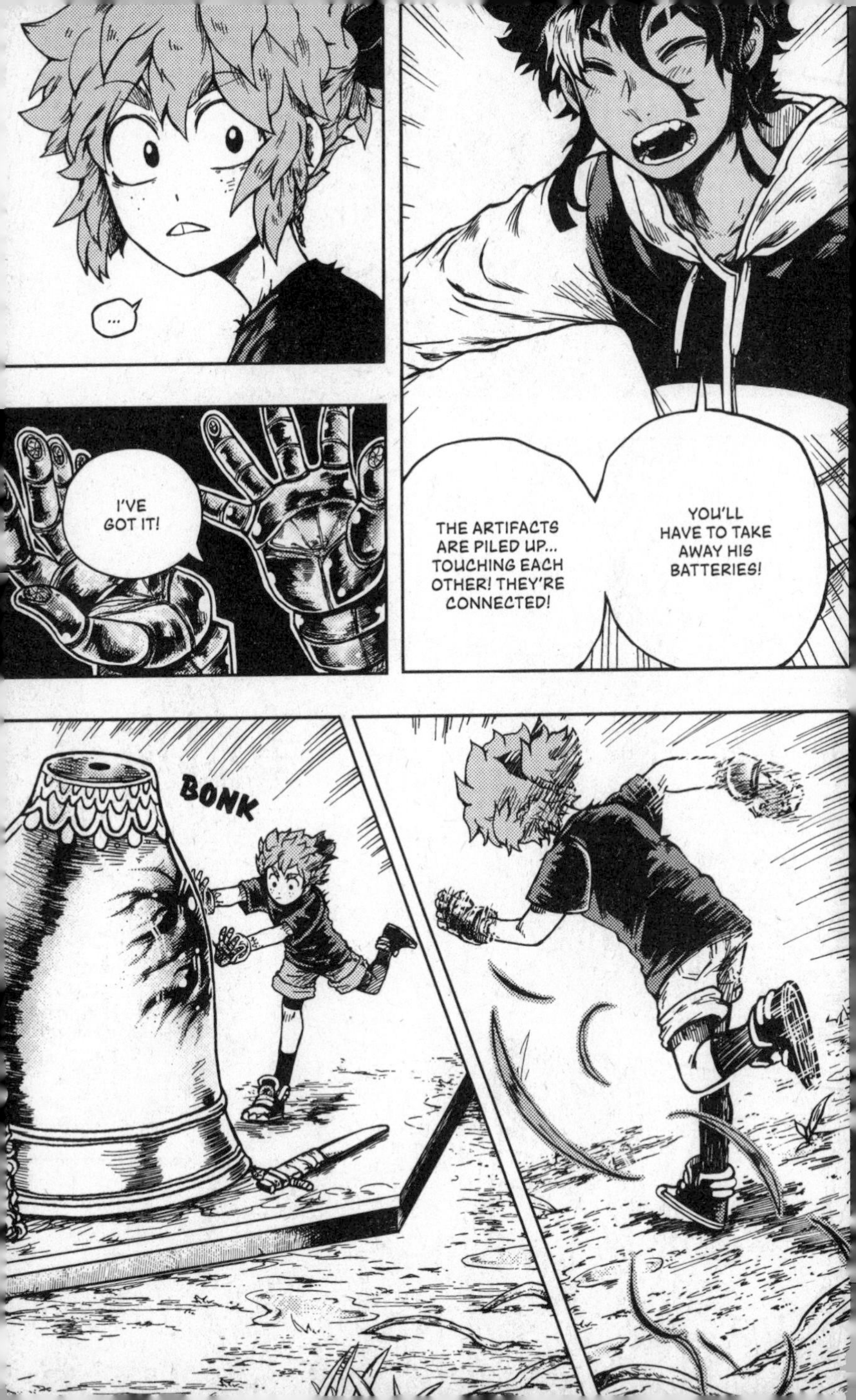
YOU'LL HAVE TO TAKE AWAY HIS BATTERIES!
THE ARTIFACTS ARE PILED UP... TOUCHING EACH OTHER! THEY'RE CONNECTED!
...
I'VE GOT IT!
BONK

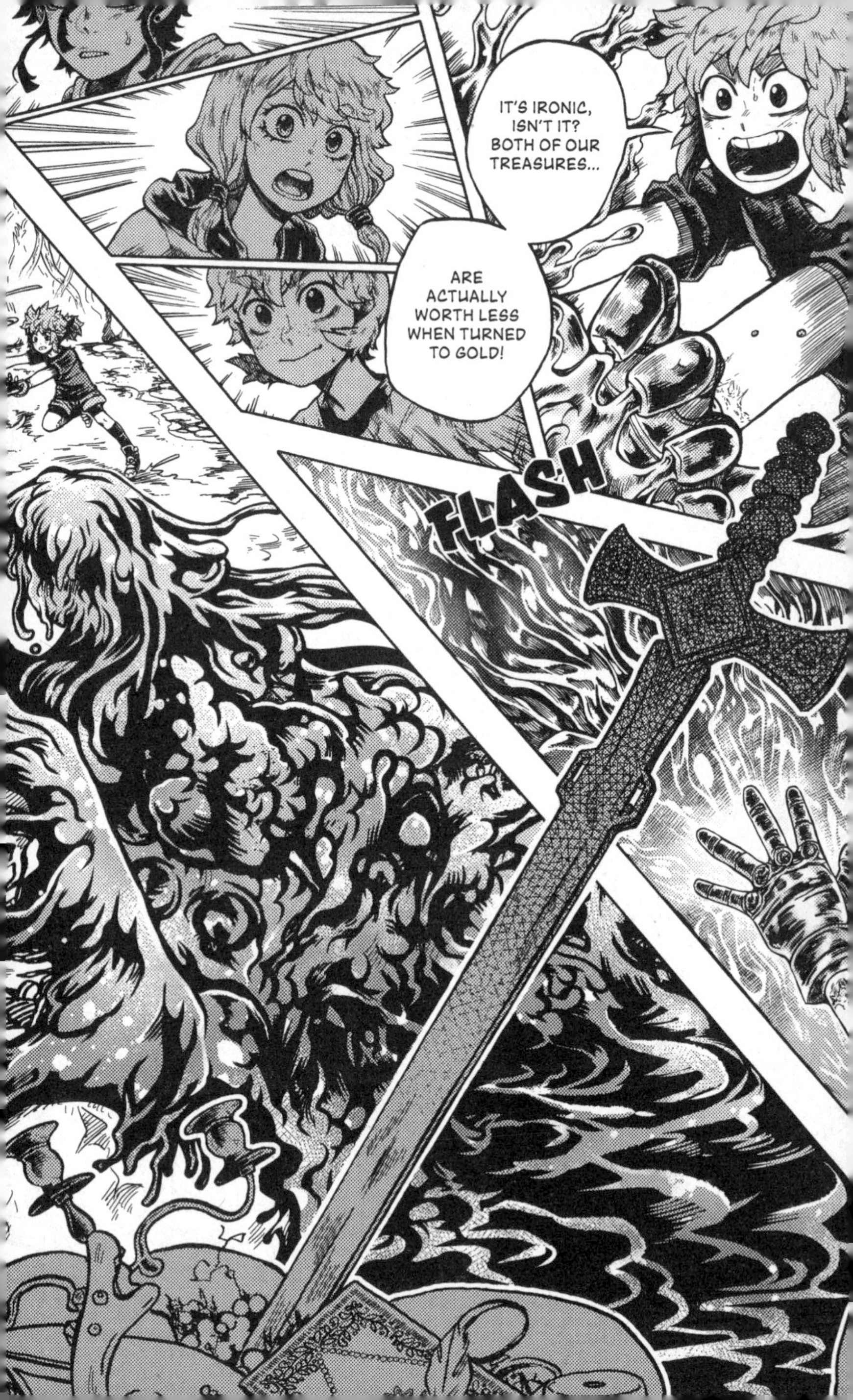
IT'S IRONIC, ISN'T IT? BOTH OF OUR TREASURES...
ARE ACTUALLY WORTH LESS WHEN TURNED TO GOLD!
FLASH

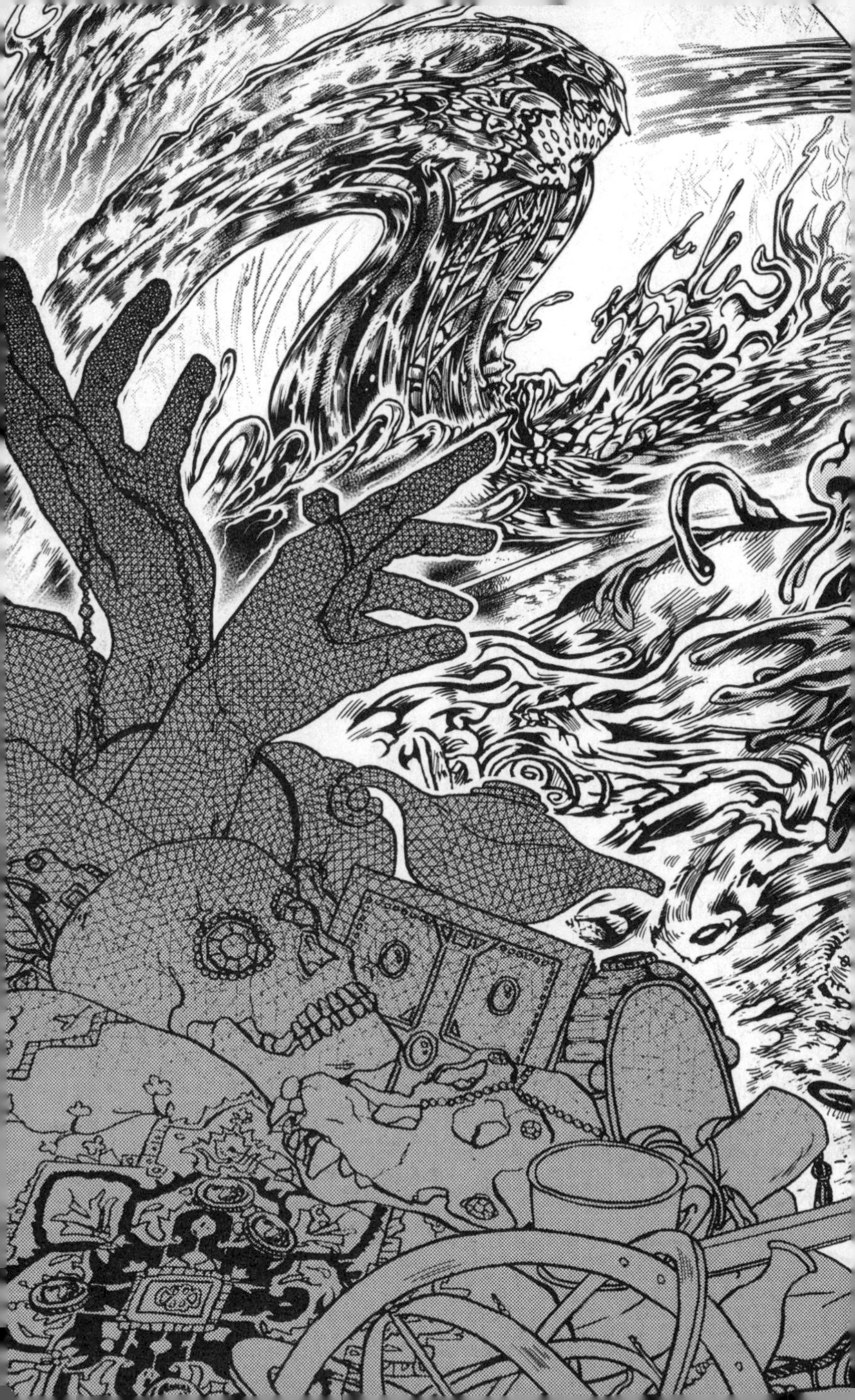

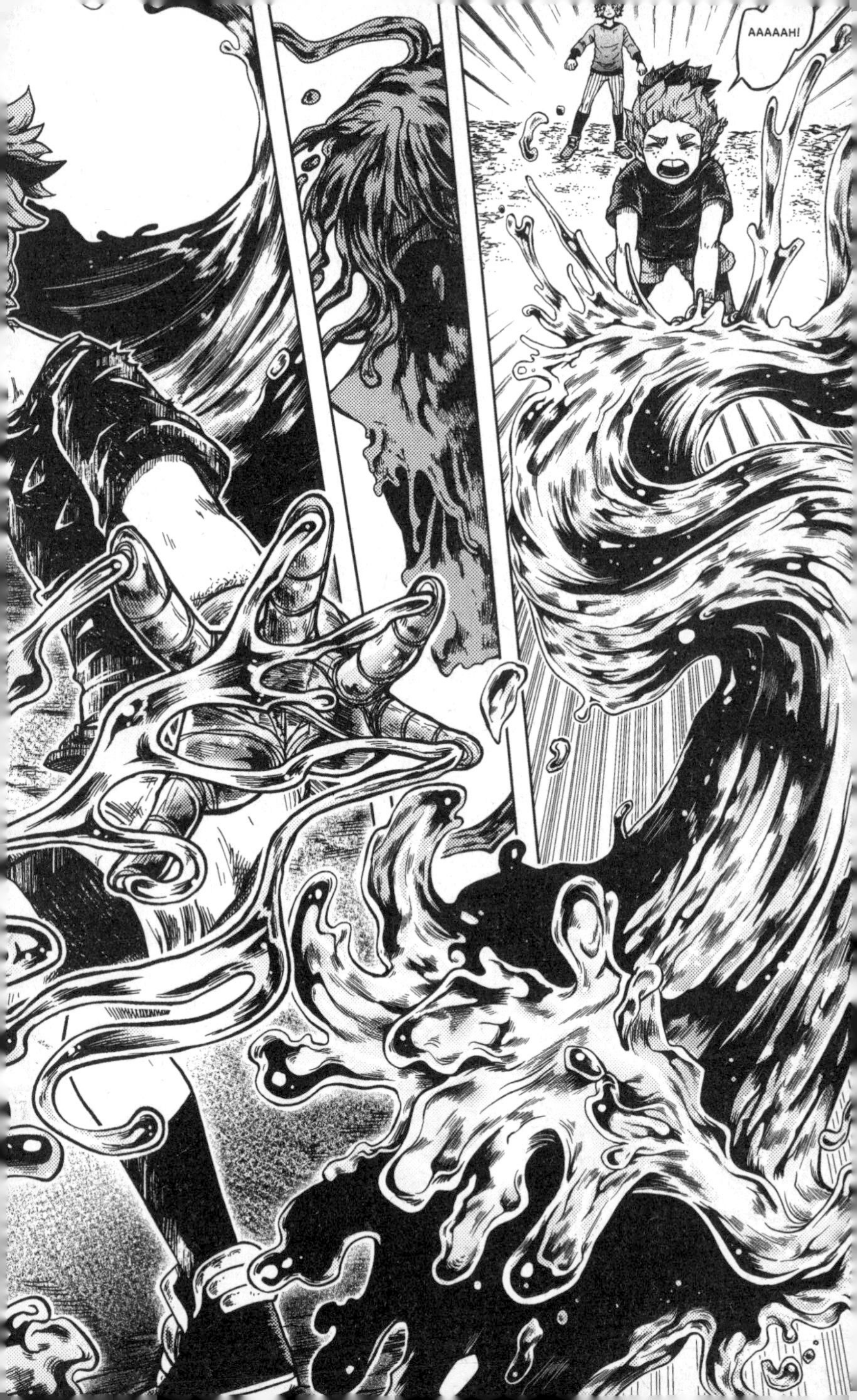
AAAAAH!

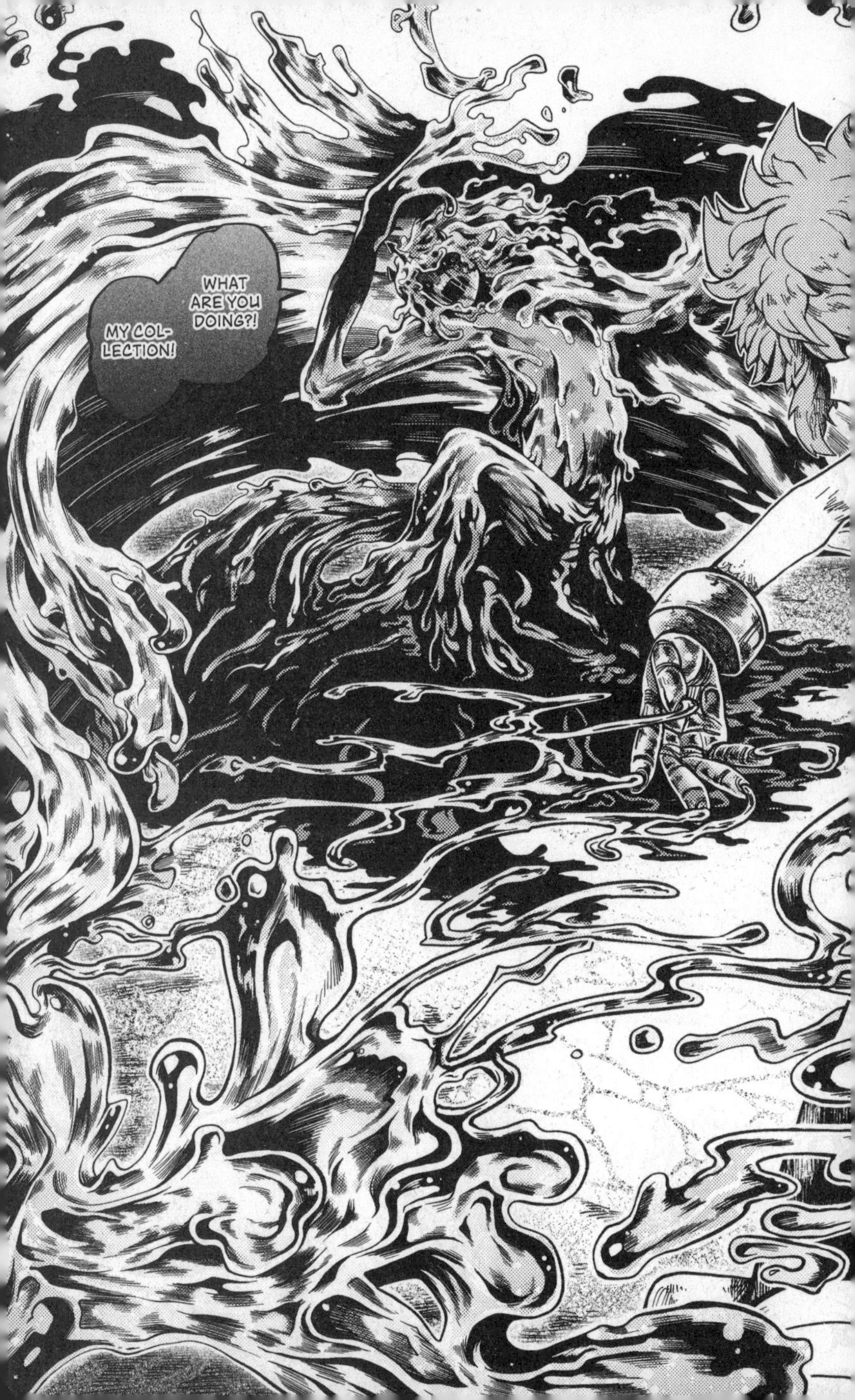
WHAT ARE YOU DOING?!
MY COL-LECTION!

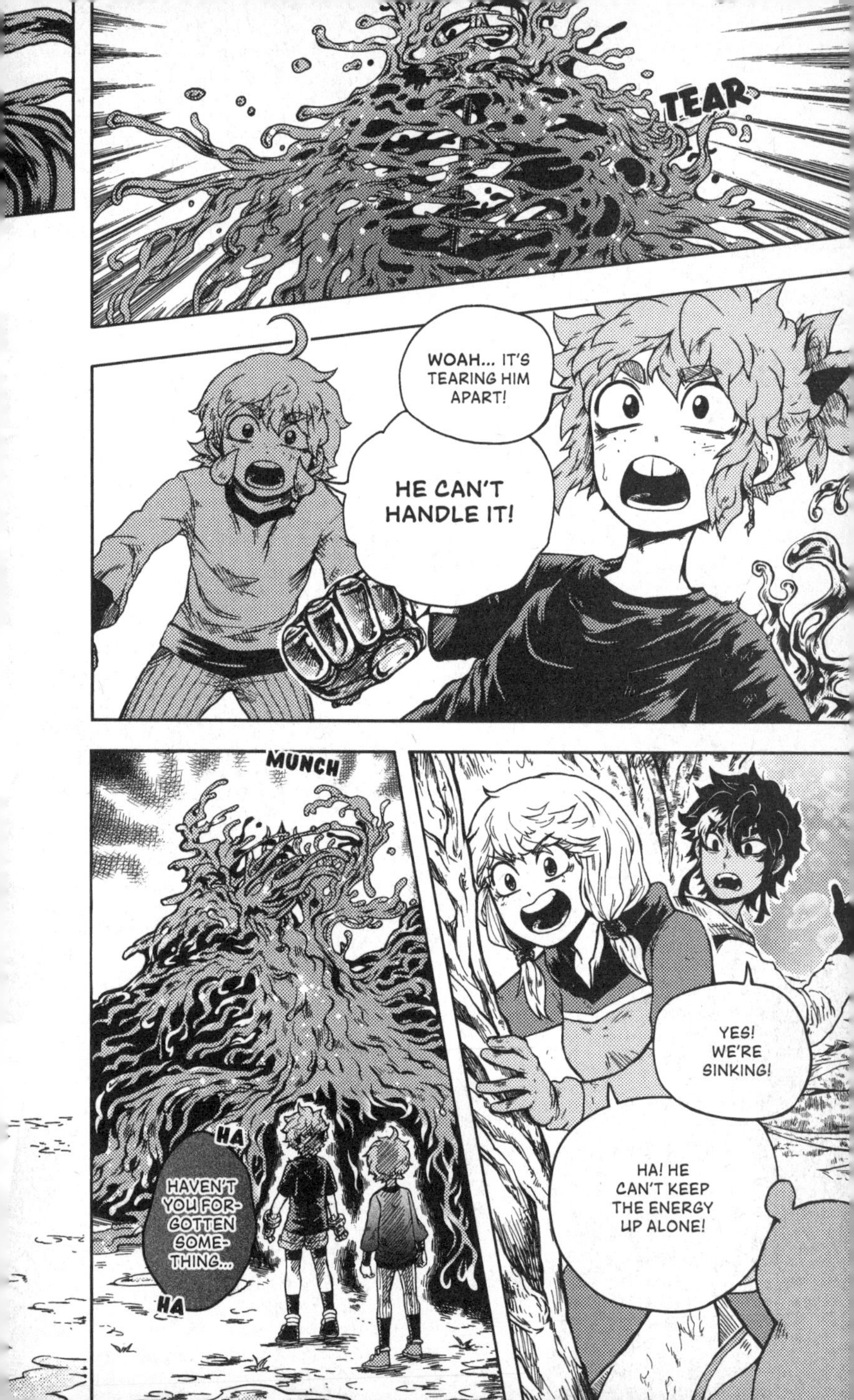
TEAR
WOAH... IT'S TEARING HIM APART!
HE CAN'T HANDLE IT!
YES! WE'RE SINKING!
HA! HE CAN'T KEEP THE ENERGY UP ALONE!
MUNCH
HA
HAVEN'T YOU FOR-GOTTEN SOME-THING...
HA

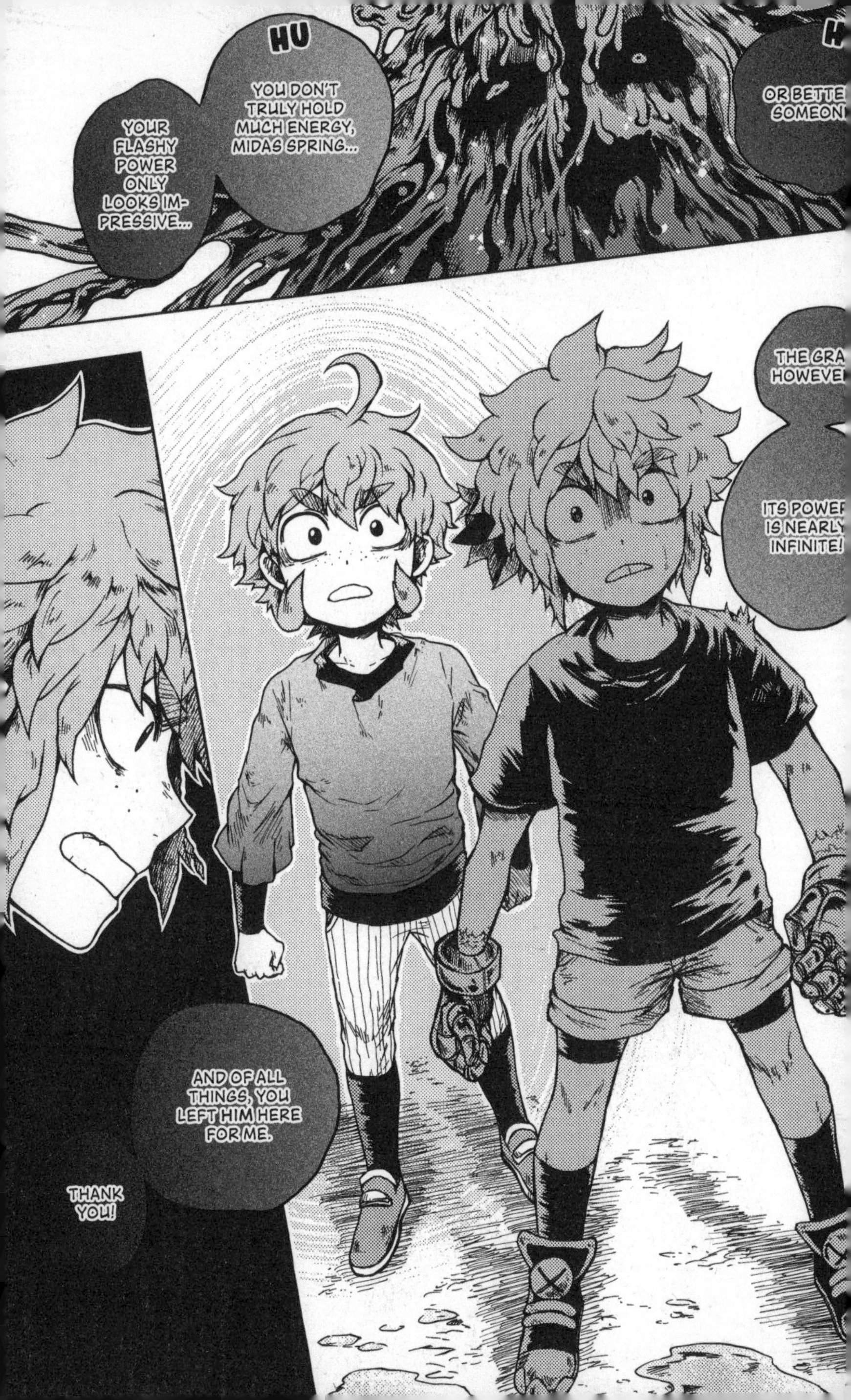
OR BETTE
SOMEON
HU
YOU DON'T TRULY HOLD MUCH ENERGY, MIDAS SPRING...
YOUR FLASHY POWER ONLY LOOKS IM-PRESSIVE...
THE GRA
HOWEVE
ITS POWEF IS NEARLY INFINITE!
AND OF ALL THINGS, YOU LEFT HIM HERE FOR ME.
THANK YOU!

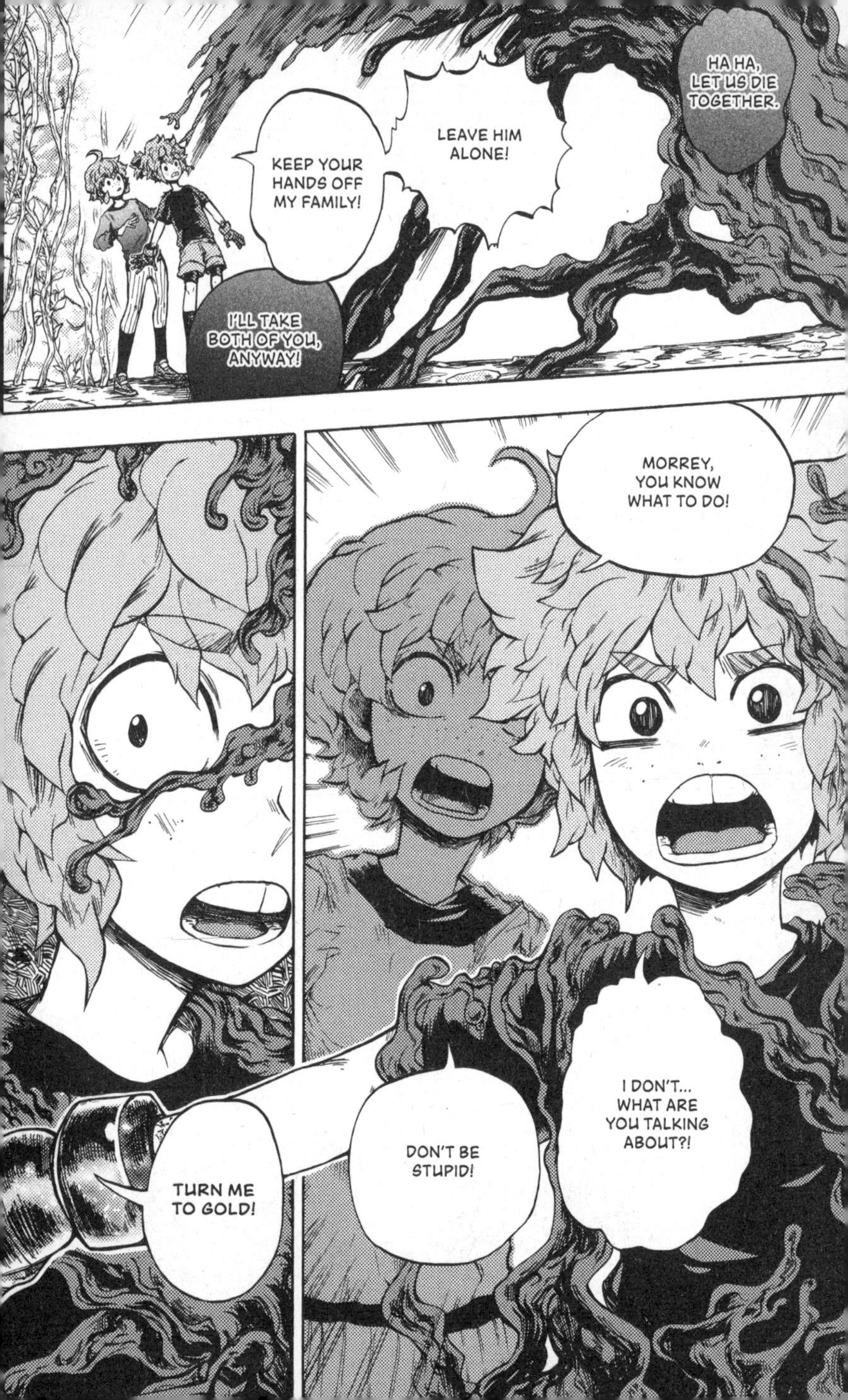
HA HA, LET US DIE TOGETHER.
LEAVE HIM ALONE!
KEEP YOUR HANDS OFF MY FAMILY!
I'LL TAKE BOTH OF YOU, ANYWAY!
MORREY, YOU KNOW WHAT TO DO!
I DON'T... WHAT ARE YOU TALKING ABOUT?!
DON'T BE STUPID!
TURN ME TO GOLD!

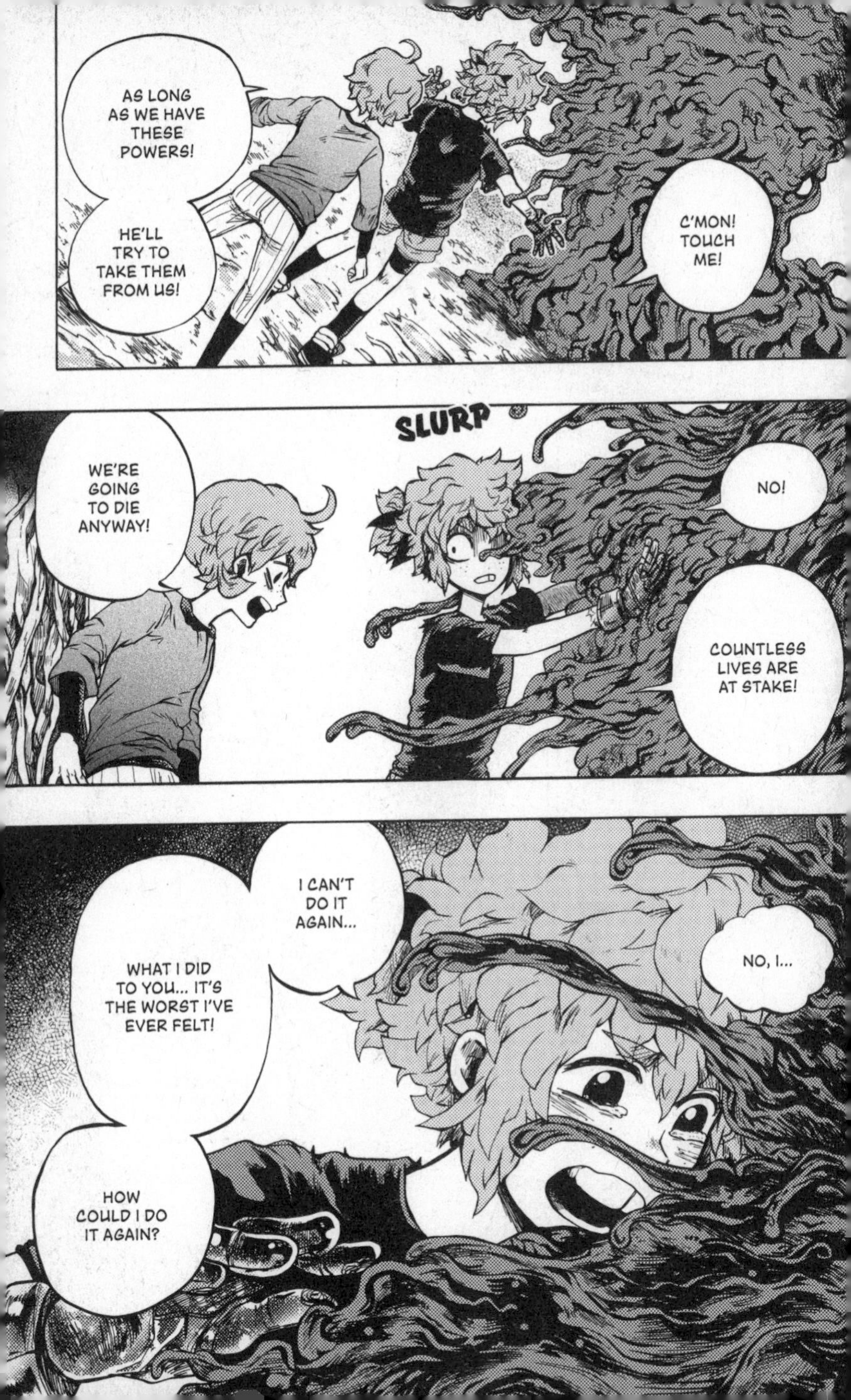
C'MON! TOUCH ME!
AS LONG AS WE HAVE THESE POWERS!
HE'LL TRY TO TAKE THEM FROM US!
SLURP
NO!
COUNTLESS LIVES ARE AT STAKE!
WE'RE GOING TO DIE ANYWAY!
NO, I...
I CAN'T DO IT AGAIN...
WHAT I DID TO YOU... IT'S THE WORST I'VE EVER FELT!
HOW COULD I DO IT AGAIN?

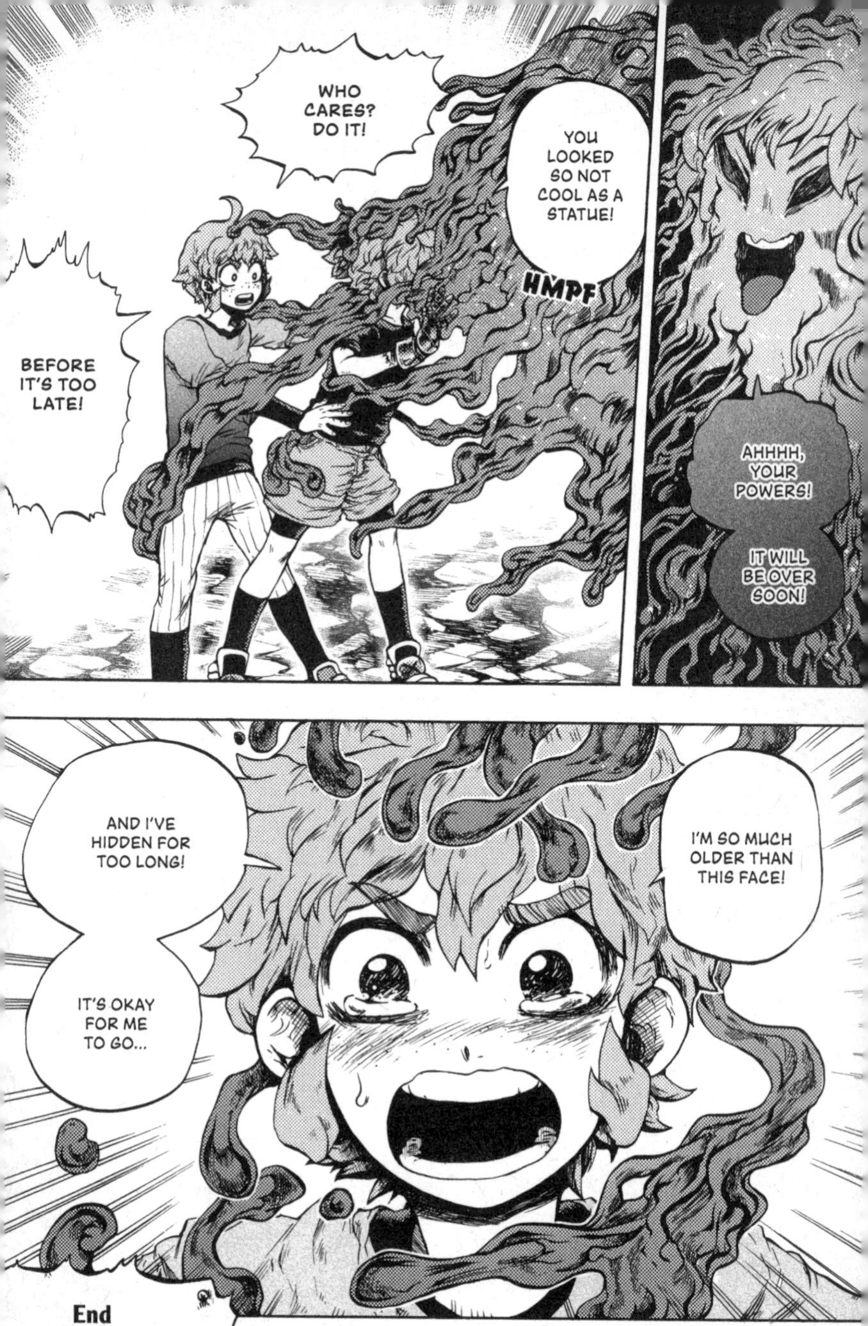
AHHHH, YOUR POWERS!
IT WILL BE OVER SOON!
YOU LOOKED SO NOT COOL AS A STATUE!
HMPF
WHO CARES? DO IT!
BEFORE IT'S TOO LATE!
I'M SO MUCH OLDER THAN THIS FACE!
AND I'VE HIDDEN FOR TOO LONG!
IT'S OKAY FOR ME TO GO...

End Chapter XVIII

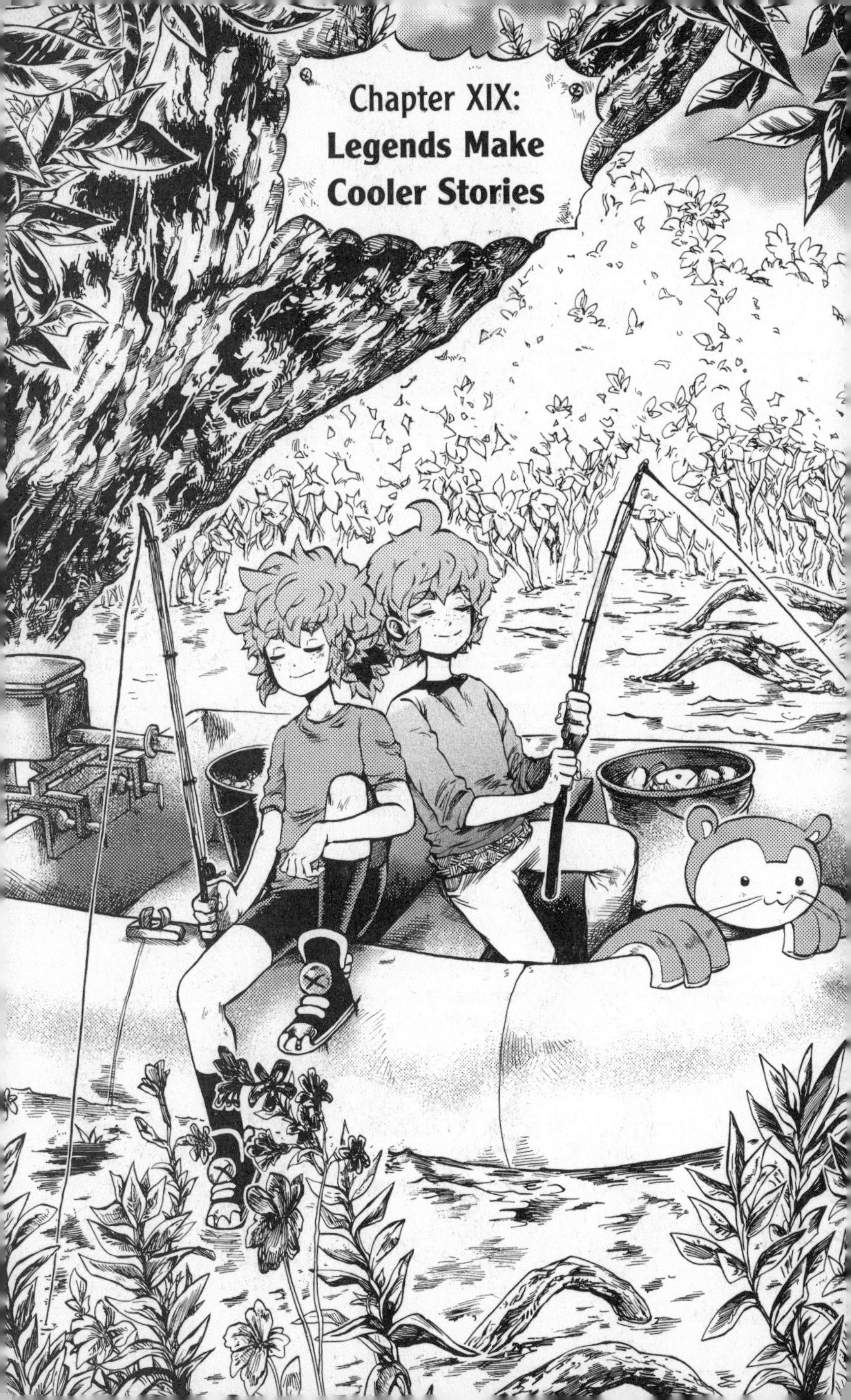
Chapter XIX:
Legends Make
Cooler Stories

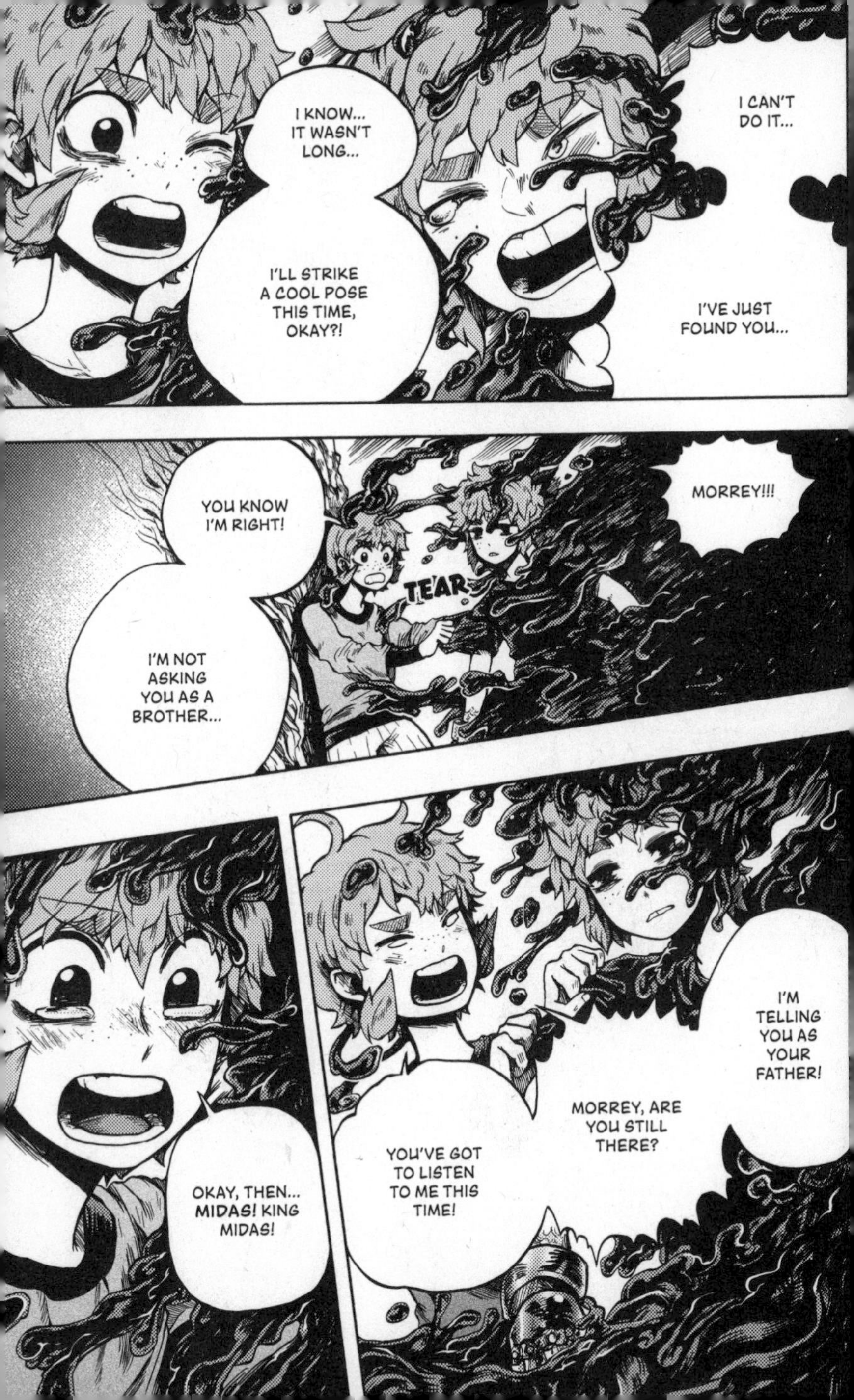
I CAN'T DO IT...
I'VE JUST FOUND YOU...
I KNOW... IT WASN'T LONG...
I'LL STRIKE A COOL POSE THIS TIME, OKAY?!
MORREY!!!
YOU KNOW I'M RIGHT!
TEAR
I'M NOT ASKING YOU AS A BROTHER...
I'M TELLING YOU AS YOUR FATHER!
MORREY, ARE YOU STILL THERE?
YOU'VE GOT TO LISTEN TO ME THIS TIME!
OKAY, THEN... MIDAS! KING MIDAS!

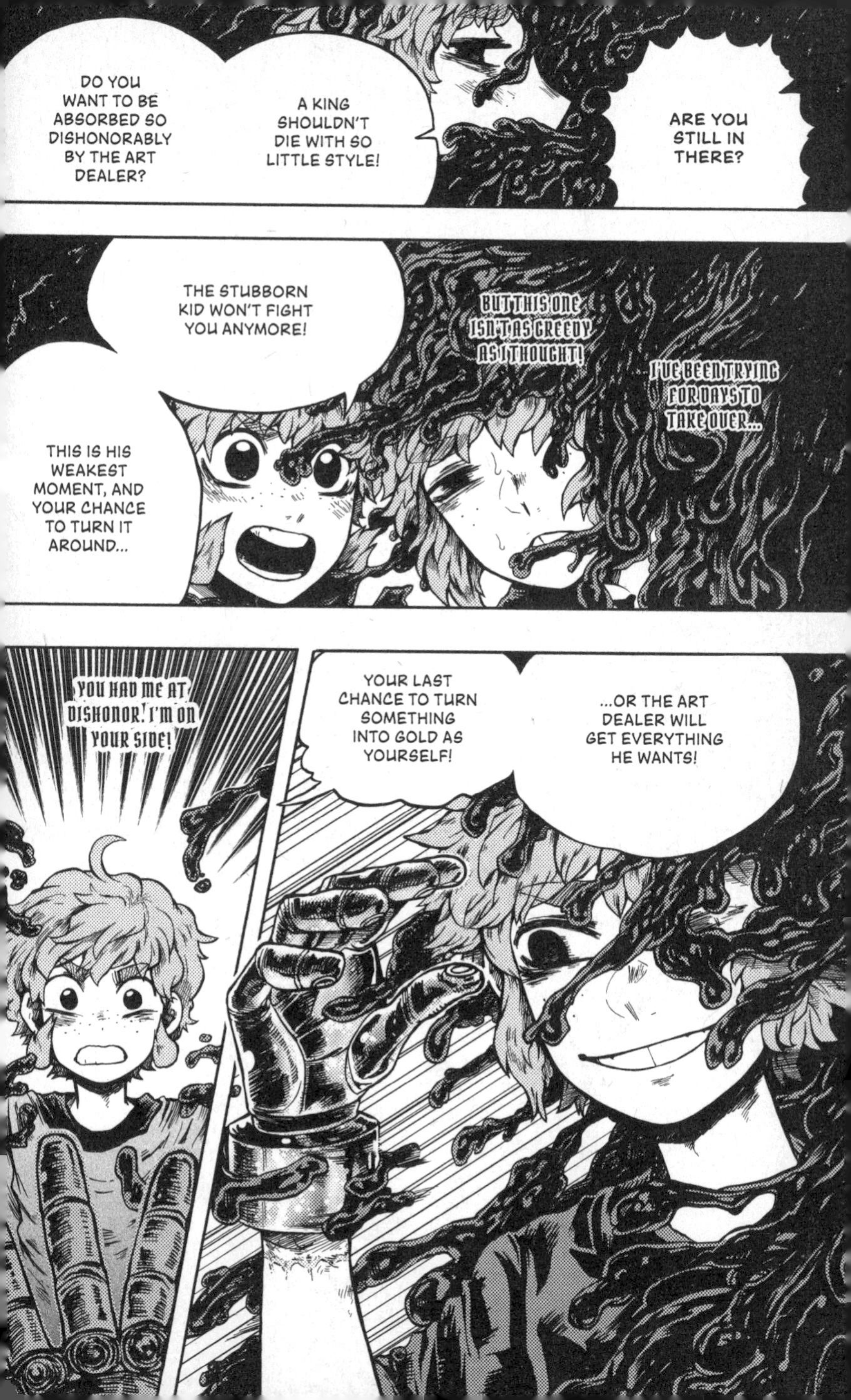
ARE YOU STILL IN THERE?
A KING SHOULDN'T DIE WITH SO LITTLE STYLE!
DO YOU WANT TO BE ABSORBED SO DISHONORABLY BY THE ART DEALER?
BUT THIS ONE ISN'T AS GREEDY AS I THOUGHT!
I'VE BEEN TRYING FOR DAYS TO TAKE OVER...
THE STUBBORN KID WON'T FIGHT YOU ANYMORE!
THIS IS HIS WEAKEST MOMENT, AND YOUR CHANCE TO TURN IT AROUND...
YOUR LAST CHANCE TO TURN SOMETHING INTO GOLD AS YOURSELF!
...OR THE ART DEALER WILL GET EVERYTHING HE WANTS!
YOU HAD ME AT DISHONOR! I'M ON YOUR SIDE!

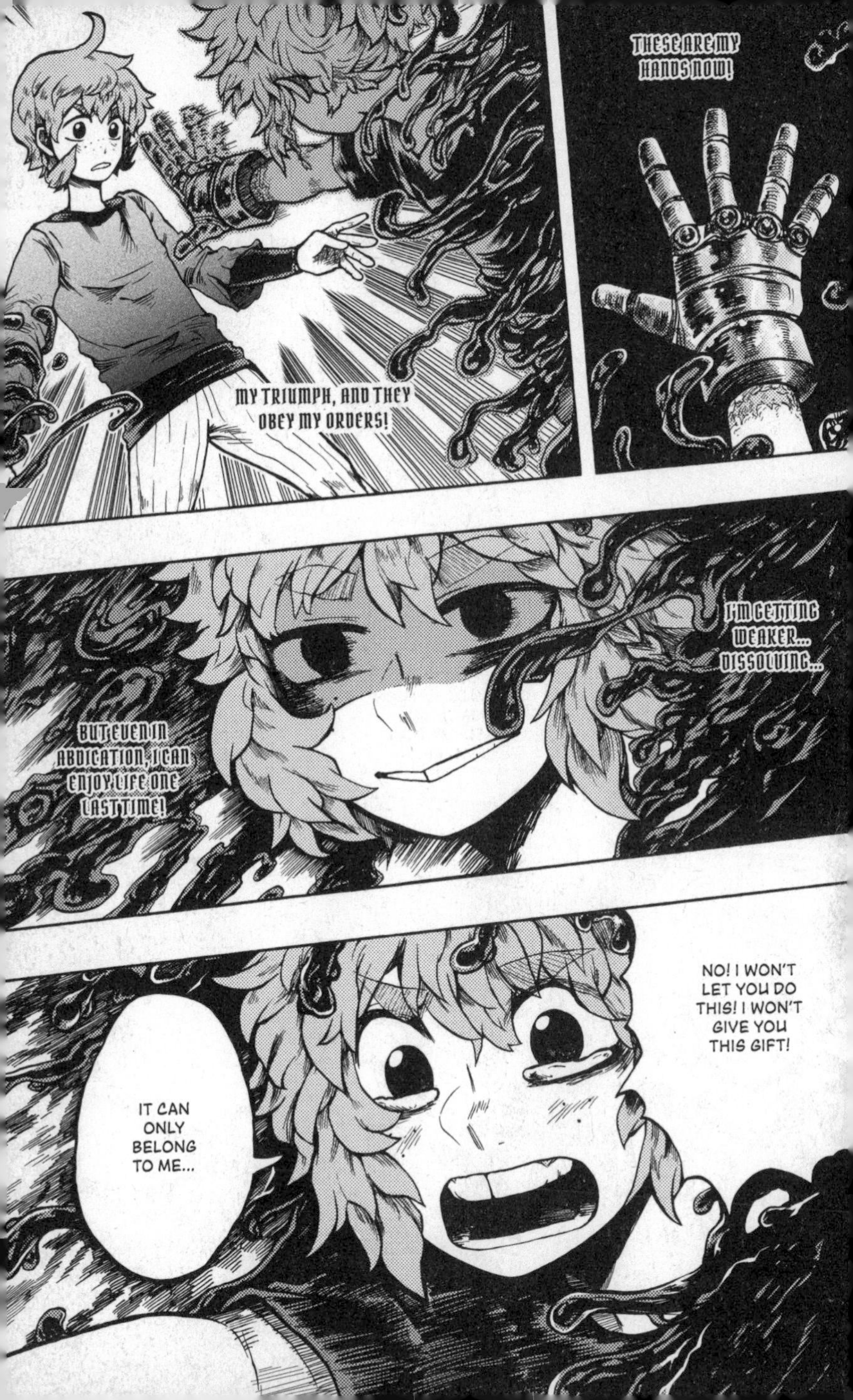
THESE ARE MY HANDS NOW!
MY TRIUMPH, AND THEY OBEY MY ORDERS!
I'M GETTING WEAKER... DISSOLVING...
BUT EVEN IN ABDICATION, I CAN ENJOY LIFE ONE LAST TIME!
NO! I WON'T LET YOU DO THIS! I WON'T GIVE YOU THIS GIFT!
IT CAN ONLY BELONG TO ME...

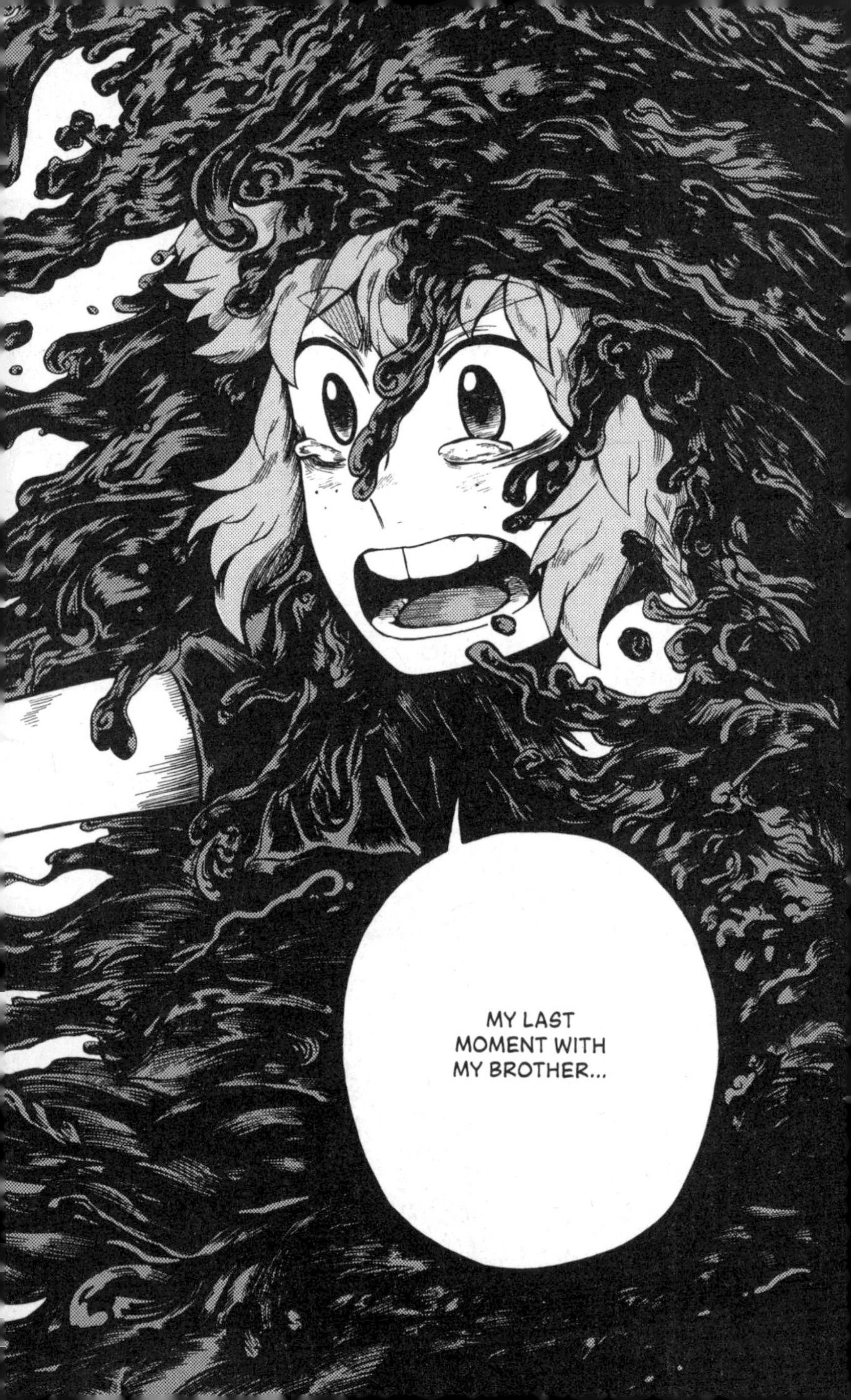
MY LAST
MOMENT WITH
MY BROTHER...

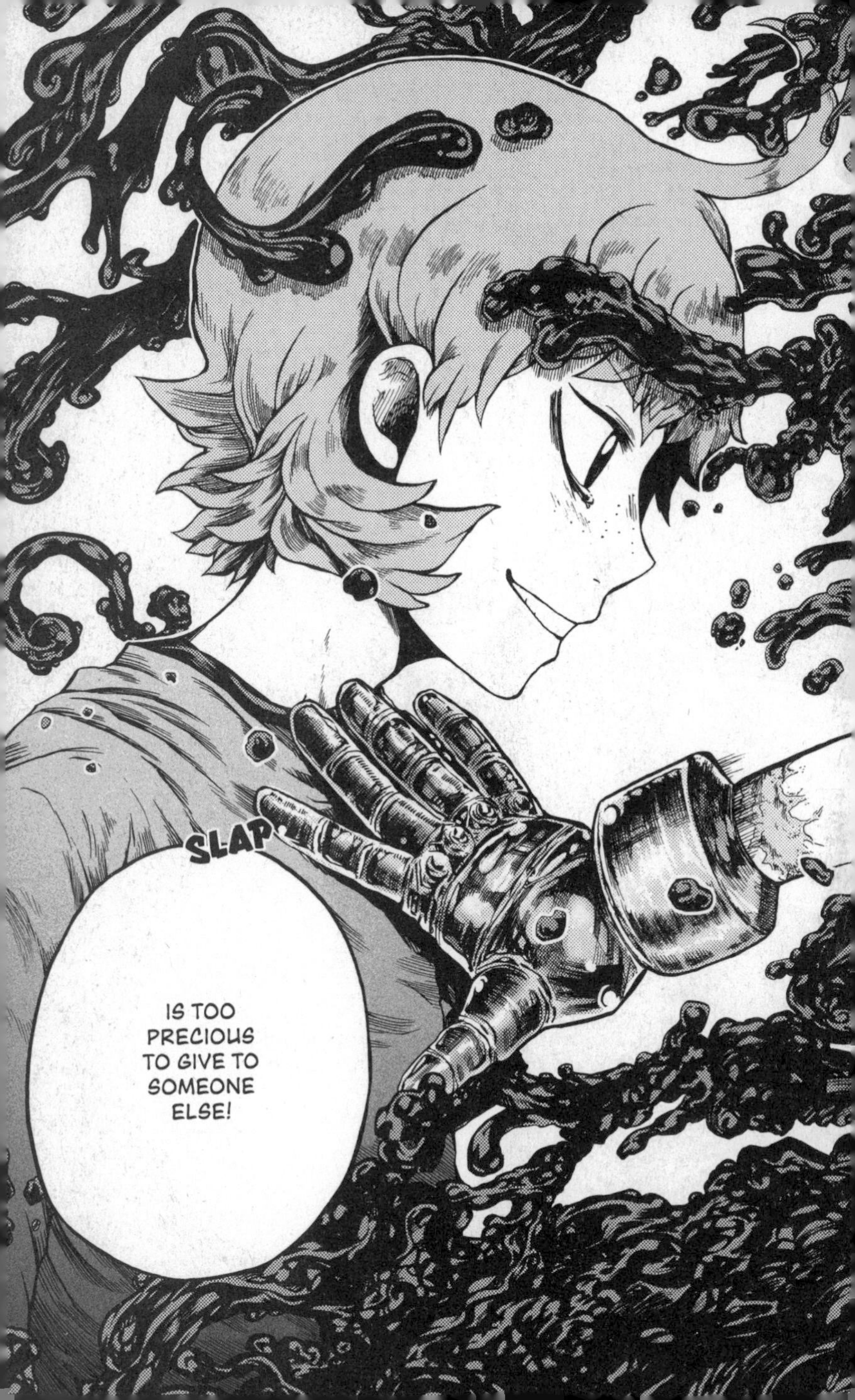
SLAP
IS TOO PRECIOUS TO GIVE TO SOMEONE ELSE!

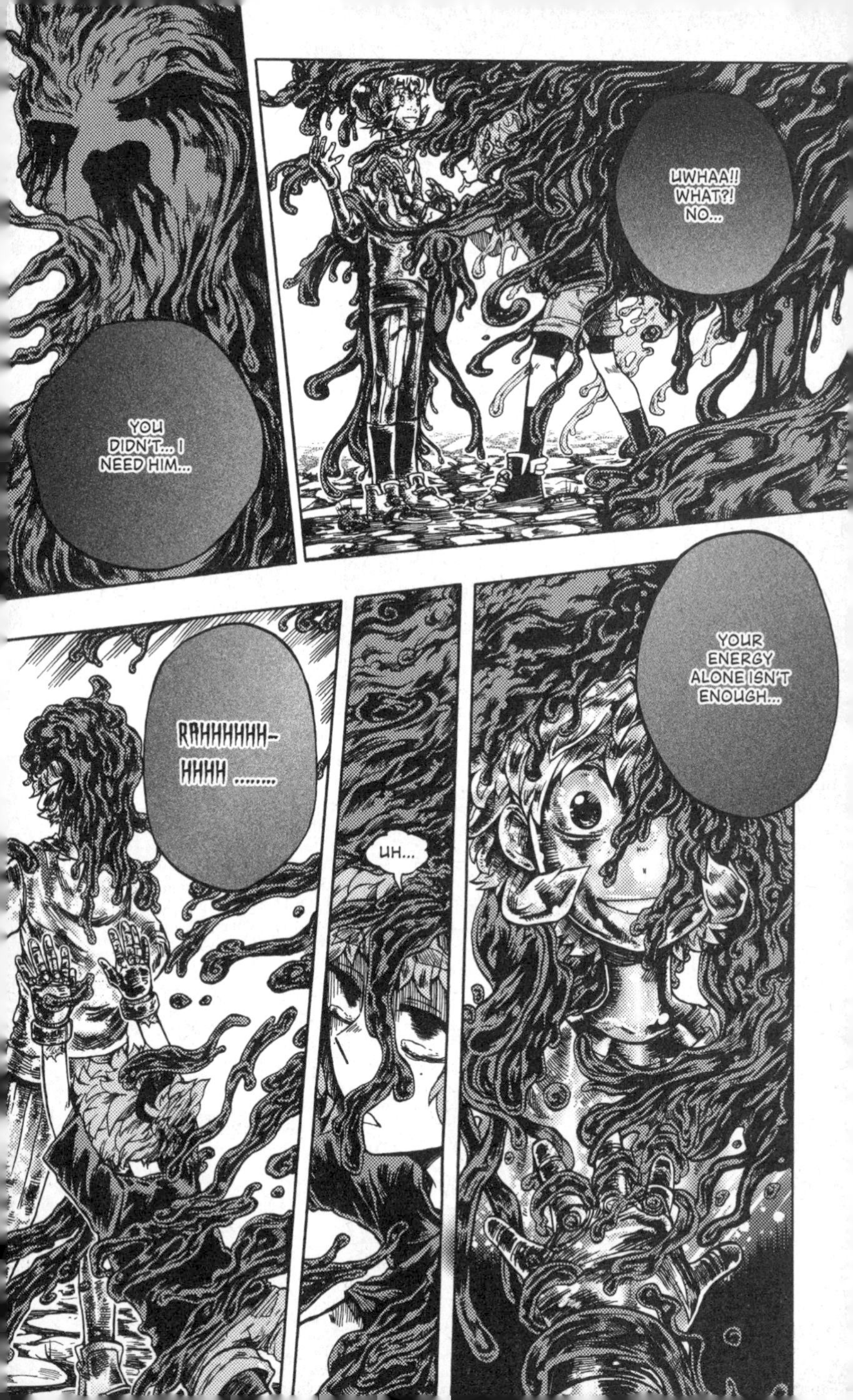
UWHAA!! WHAT?! NO...
YOU DIDN'T... I NEED HIM...
YOUR ENERGY ALONE ISN'T ENOUGH...
UH...
RAHHHHHHH-HHHH ....

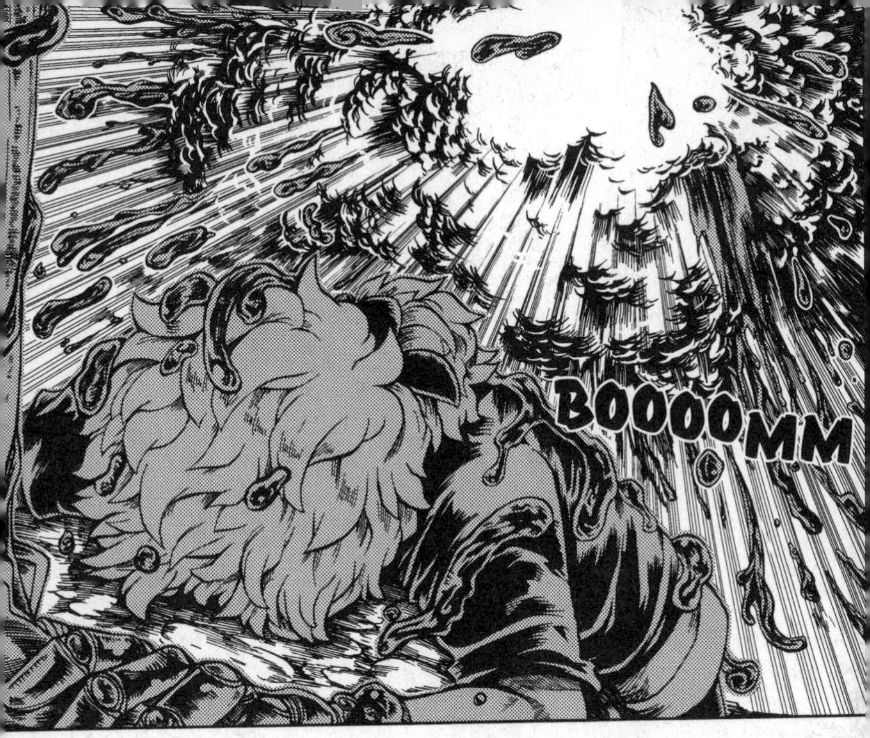
BOOOOMM
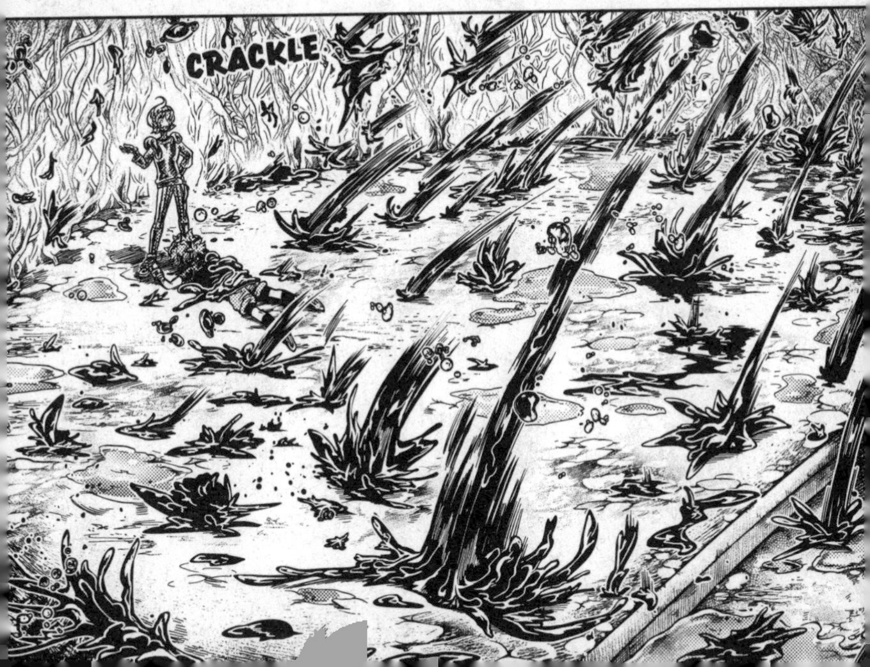
CRACKLE

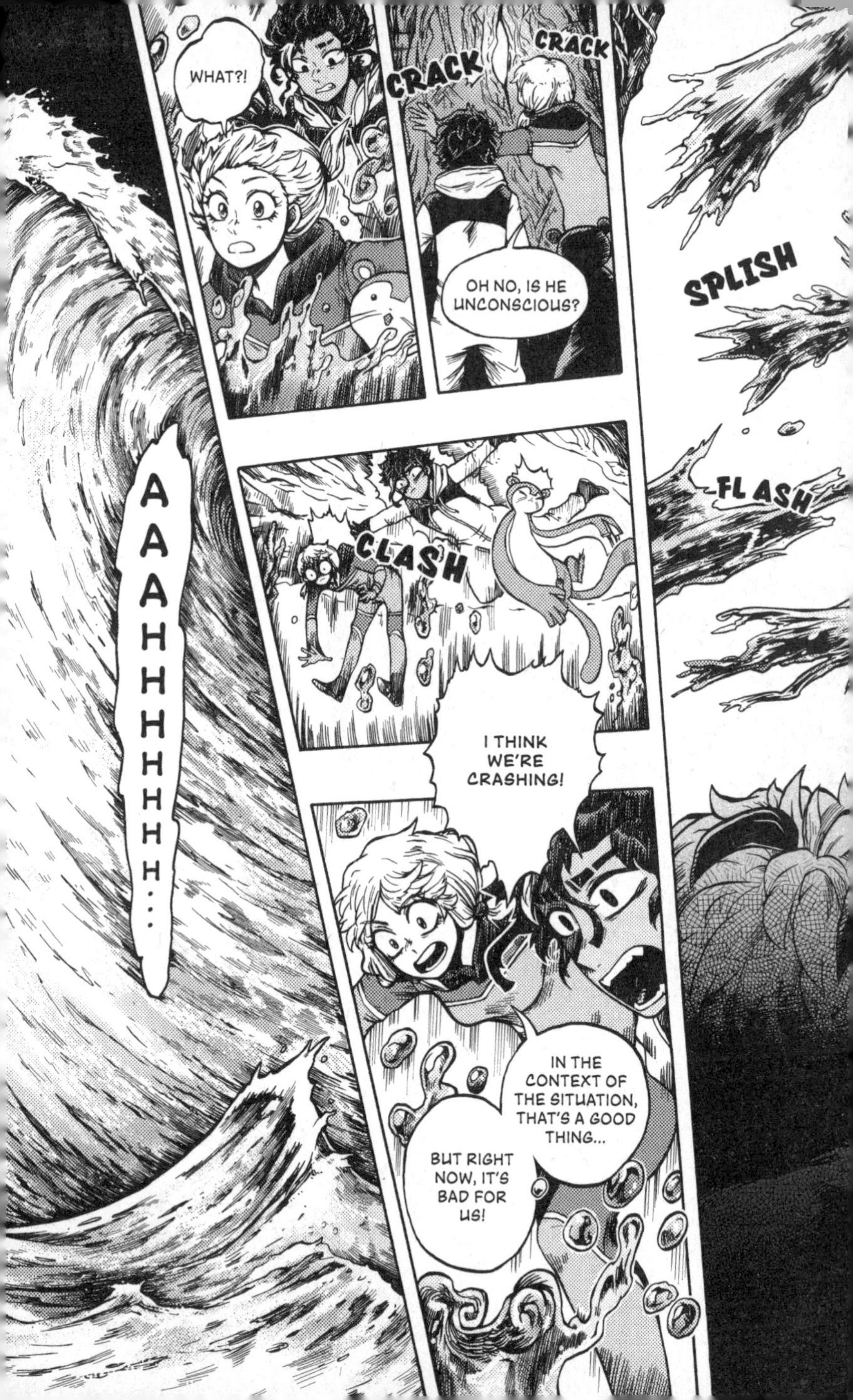
CRACK
CRACK
OH NO, IS HE UNCONSCIOUS?
WHAT?!
SPLISH
FLASH
CLASH
I THINK WE'RE CRASHING!
IN THE CONTEXT OF THE SITUATION, THAT'S A GOOD THING...
BUT RIGHT NOW, IT'S BAD FOR US!
AAAHHHHHHH...

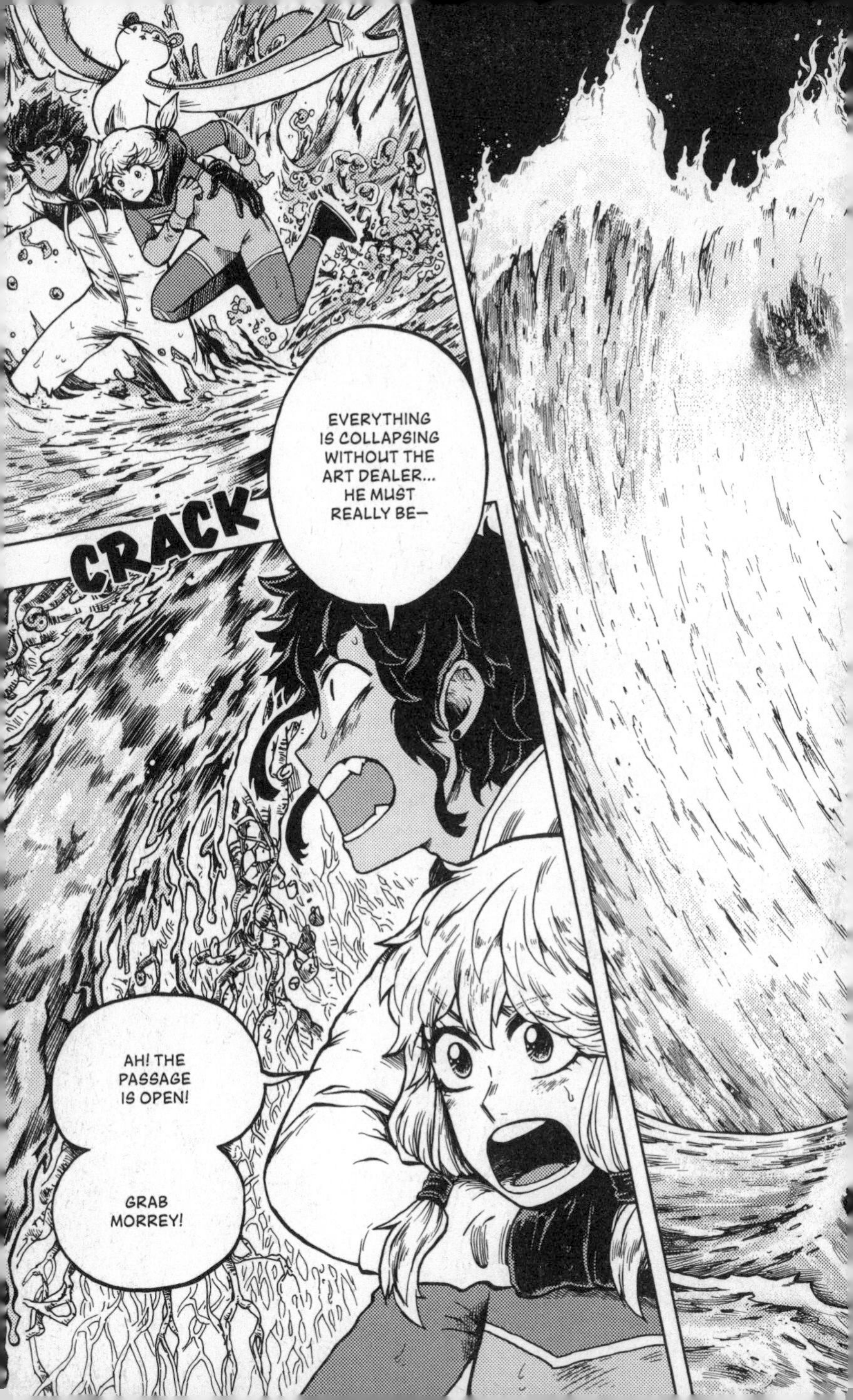
CRACK
EVERYTHING IS COLLAPSING WITHOUT THE ART DEALER... HE MUST REALLY BE—
AH! THE PASSAGE IS OPEN!
GRAB MORREY!

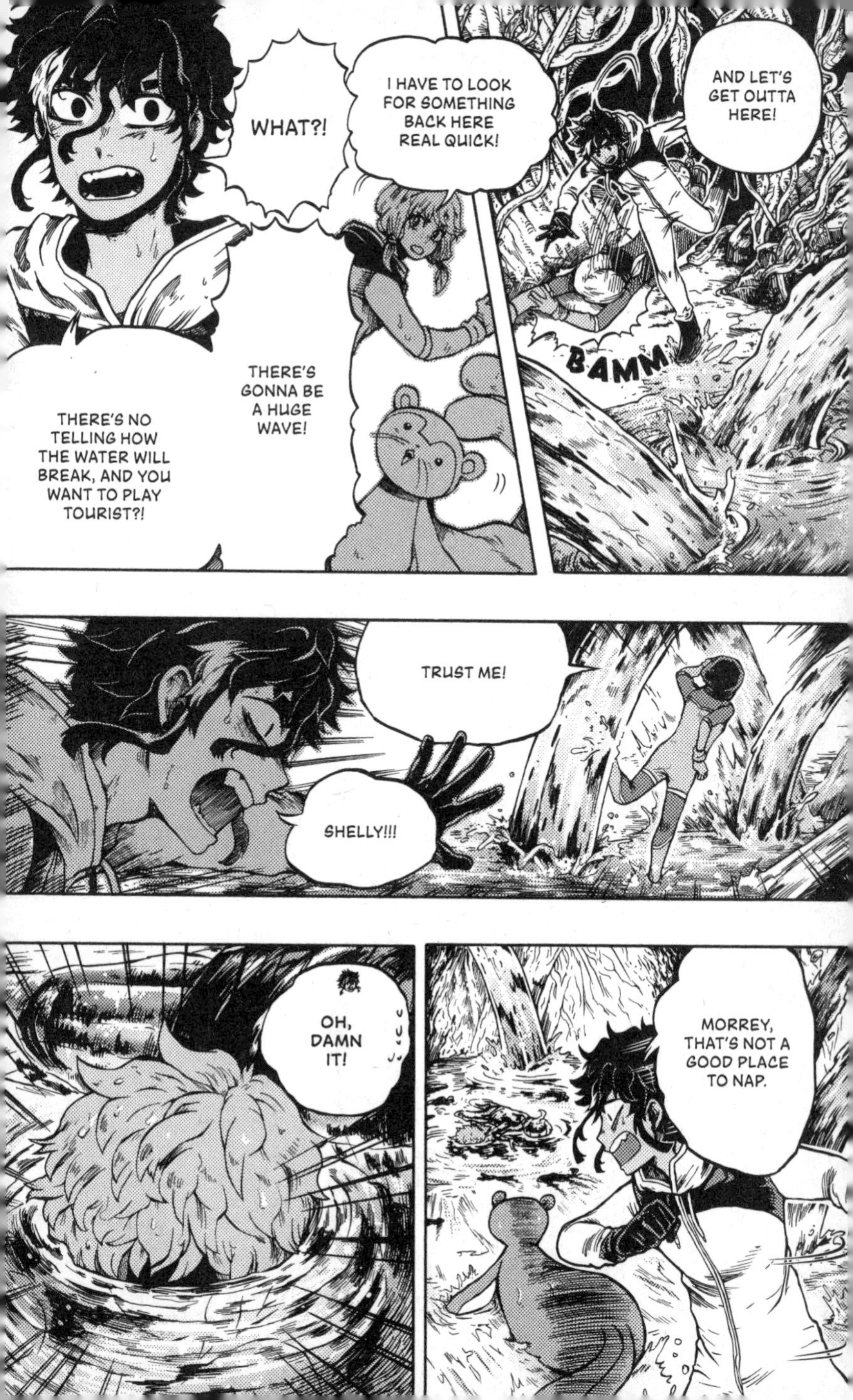
AND LET'S GET OUTTA HERE!
BAMM
I HAVE TO LOOK FOR SOMETHING BACK HERE REAL QUICK!
WHAT?!
THERE'S GONNA BE A HUGE WAVE!
THERE'S NO TELLING HOW THE WATER WILL BREAK, AND YOU WANT TO PLAY TOURIST?!
TRUST ME!
SHELLY!!!
MORREY, THAT'S NOT A GOOD PLACE TO NAP.
OH, DAMN IT!

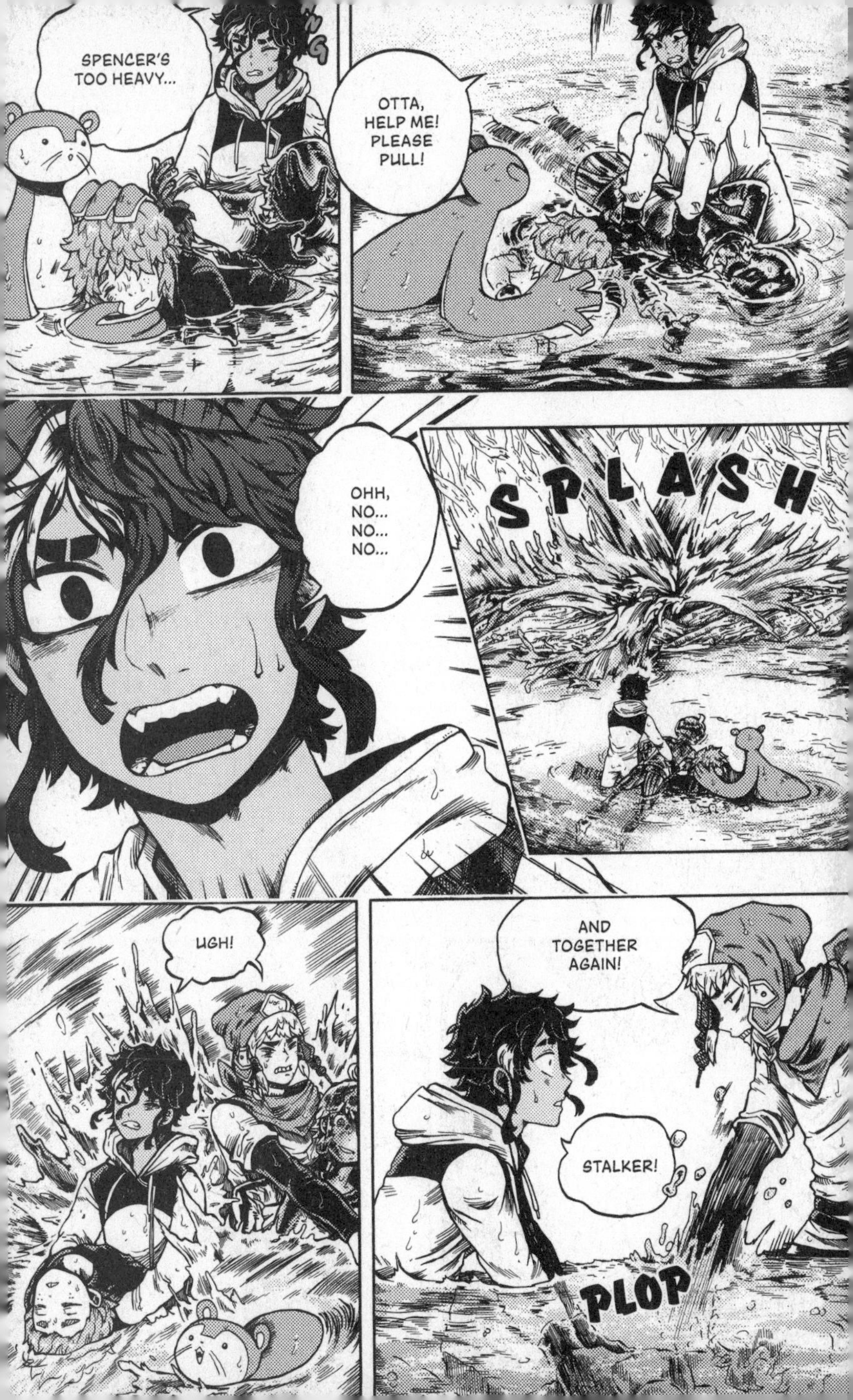
OTTA, HELP ME! PLEASE PULL!
SPENCER'S TOO HEAVY...
SPLASH
OHH, NO... NO... NO...
AND TOGETHER AGAIN!
STALKER!
PLOP
UGH!

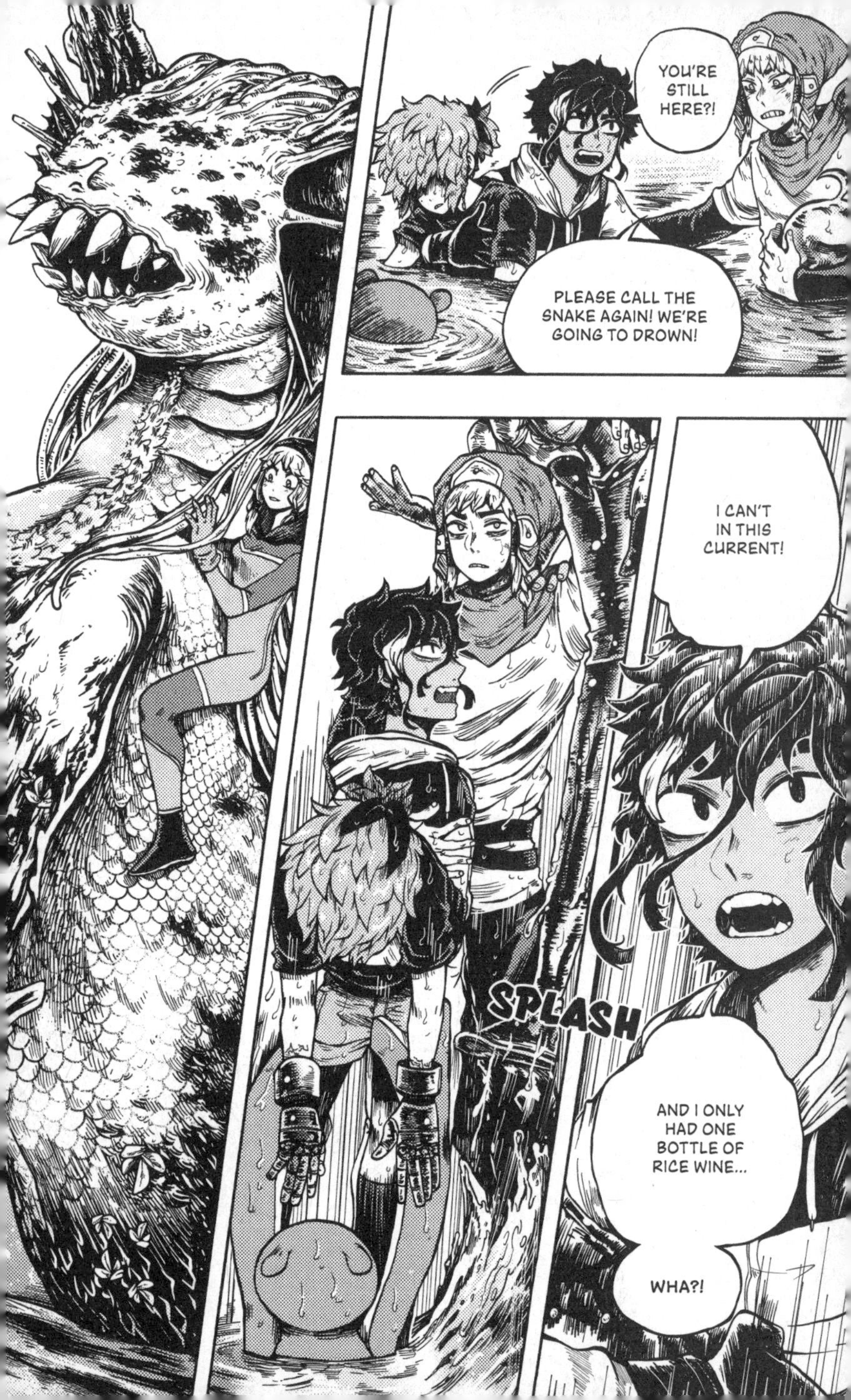
YOU'RE STILL HERE?!
PLEASE CALL THE SNAKE AGAIN! WE'RE GOING TO DROWN!
I CAN'T IN THIS CURRENT!
AND I ONLY HAD ONE BOTTLE OF RICE WINE...
WHA?!
SPLASH

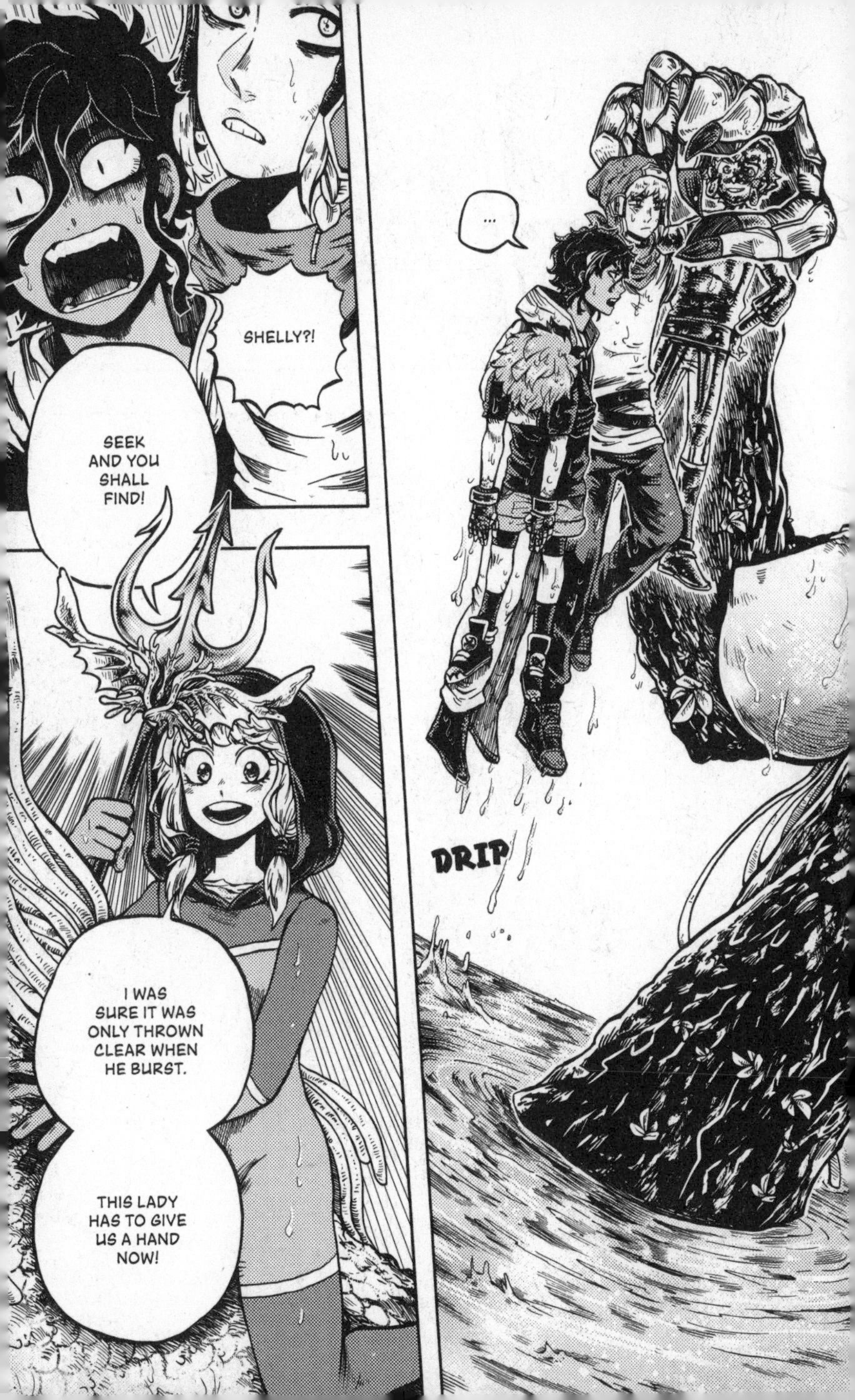
...
DRIP
SHELLY?!
SEEK AND YOU SHALL FIND!
I WAS SURE IT WAS ONLY THROWN CLEAR WHEN HE BURST.
THIS LADY HAS TO GIVE US A HAND NOW!

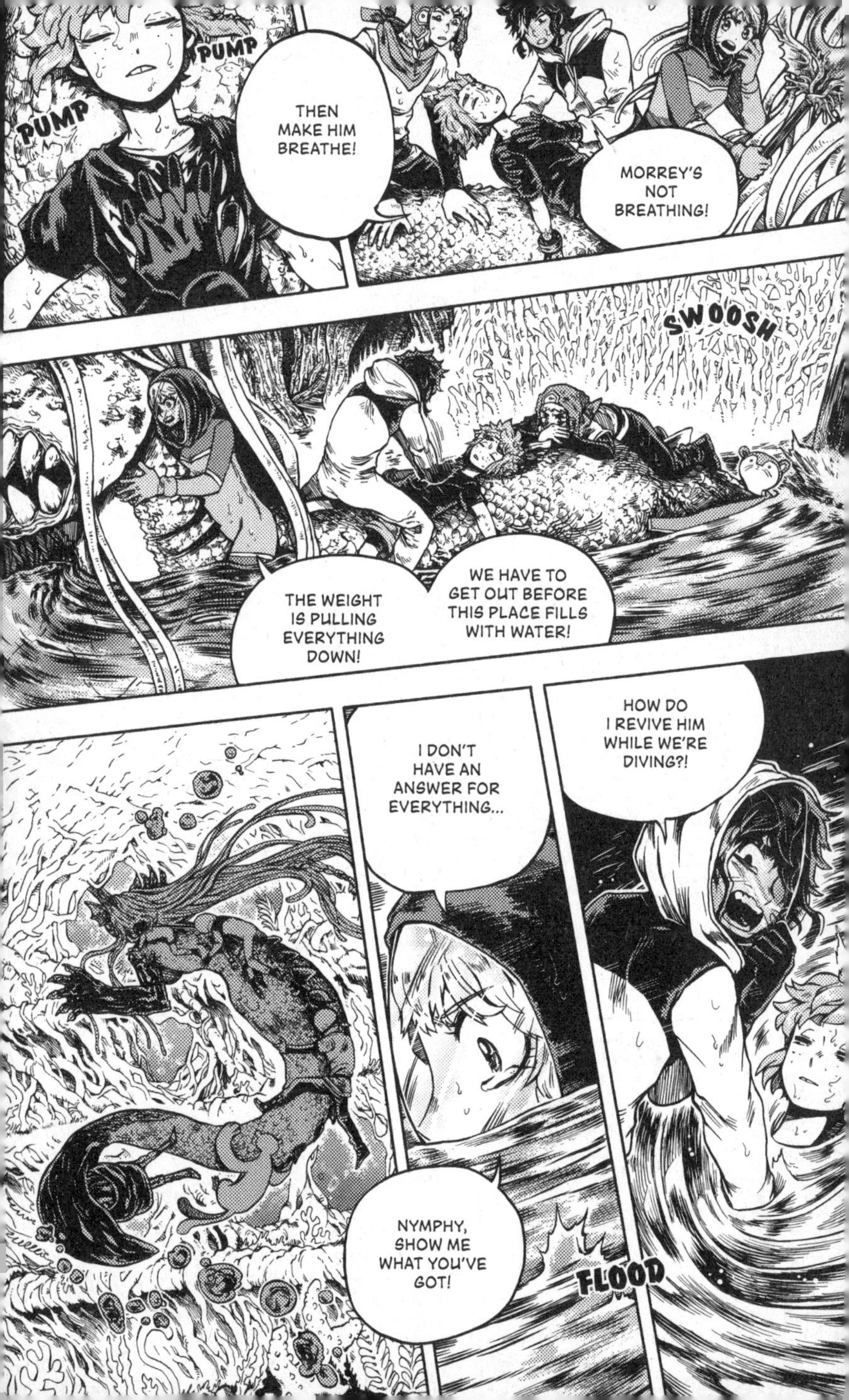
MORREY'S NOT BREATHING!
THEN MAKE HIM BREATHE!
PUMP
PUMP
SWOOSH
WE HAVE TO GET OUT BEFORE THIS PLACE FILLS WITH WATER!
THE WEIGHT IS PULLING EVERYTHING DOWN!
HOW DO I REVIVE HIM WHILE WE'RE DIVING?!
I DON'T HAVE AN ANSWER FOR EVERYTHING...
NYMPHY, SHOW ME WHAT YOU'VE GOT!
FLOOD

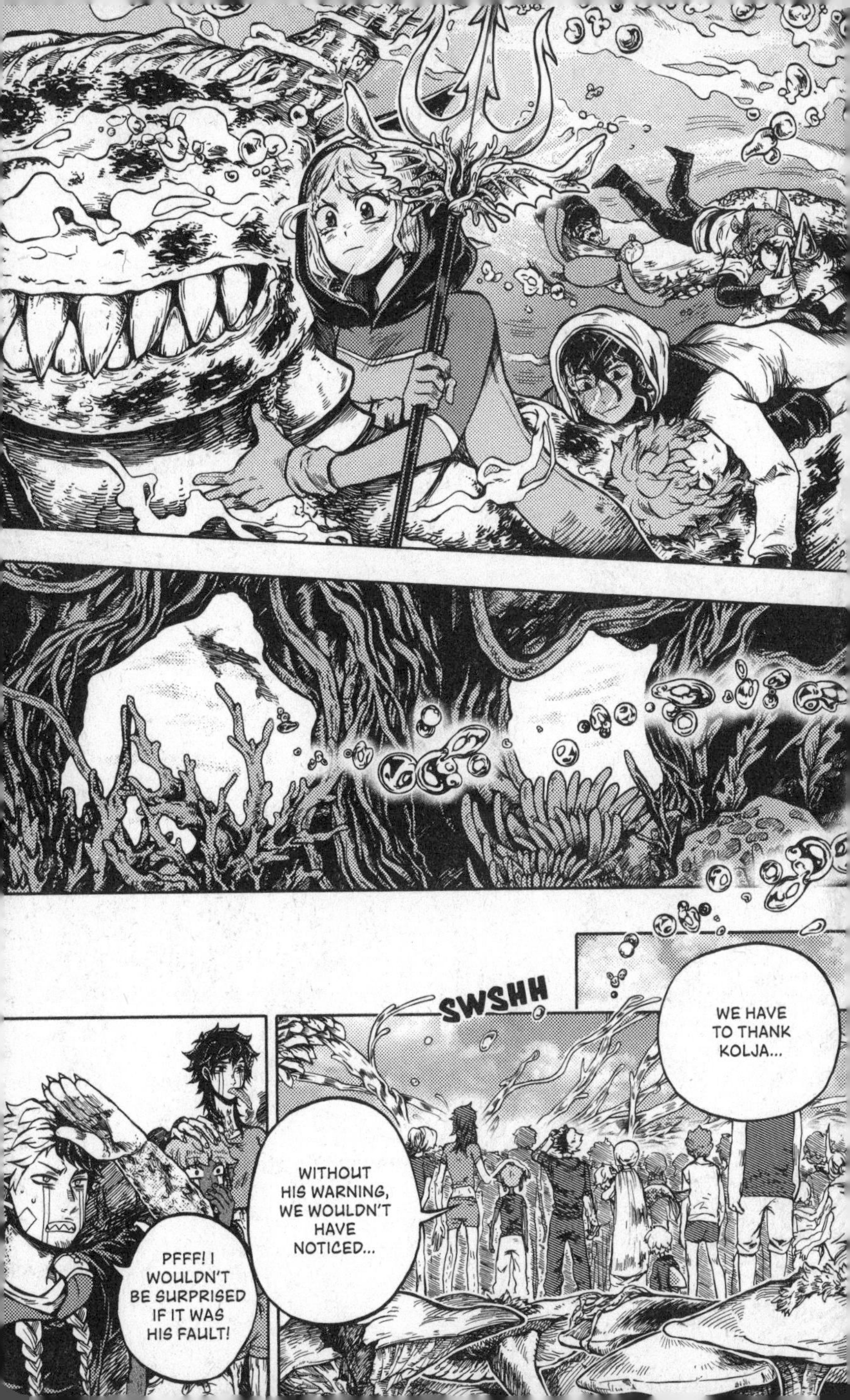
WE HAVE TO THANK KOLJA...
SWSHH
WITHOUT HIS WARNING, WE WOULDN'T HAVE NOTICED...
PFFF! I WOULDN'T BE SURPRISED IF IT WAS HIS FAULT!

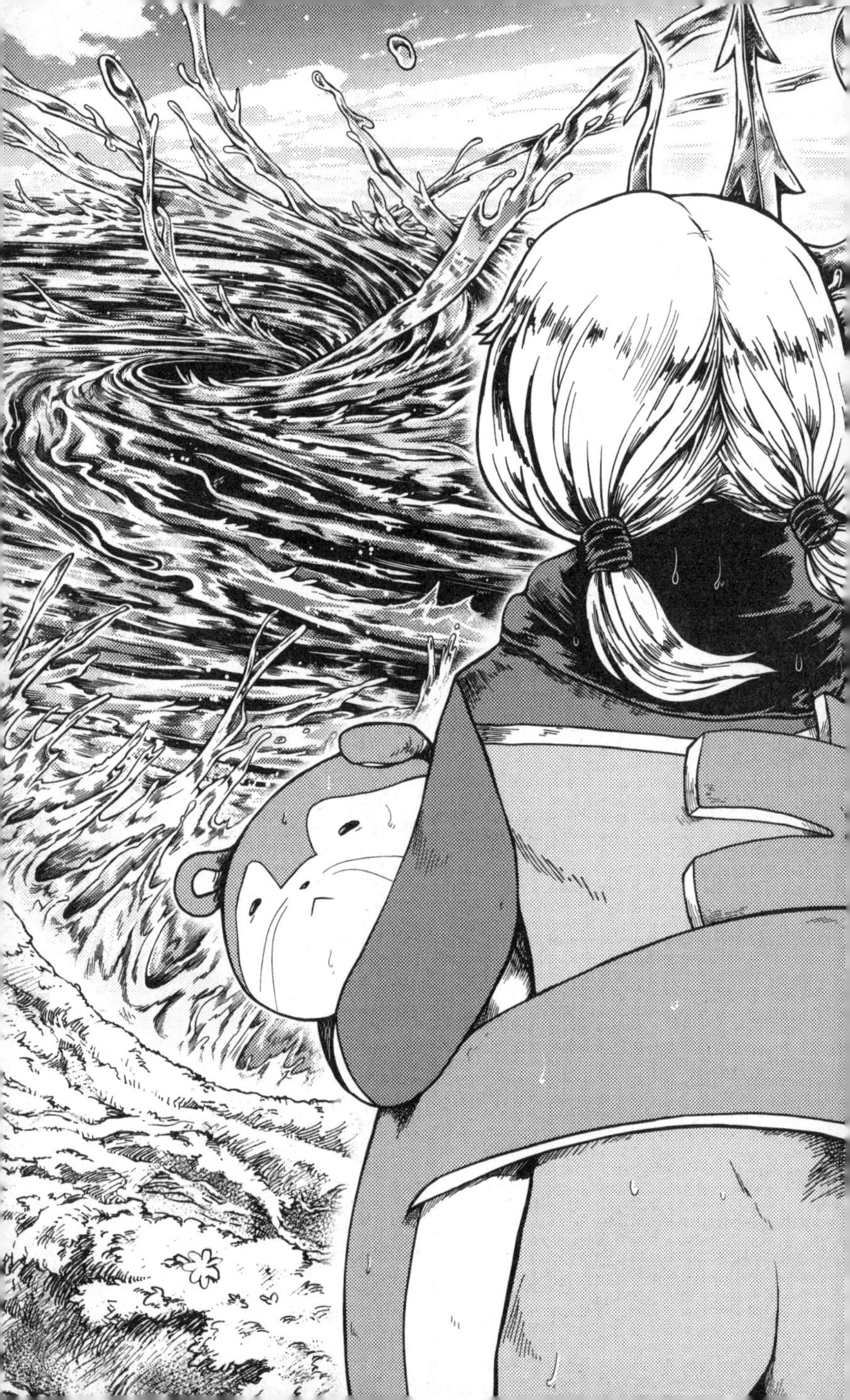

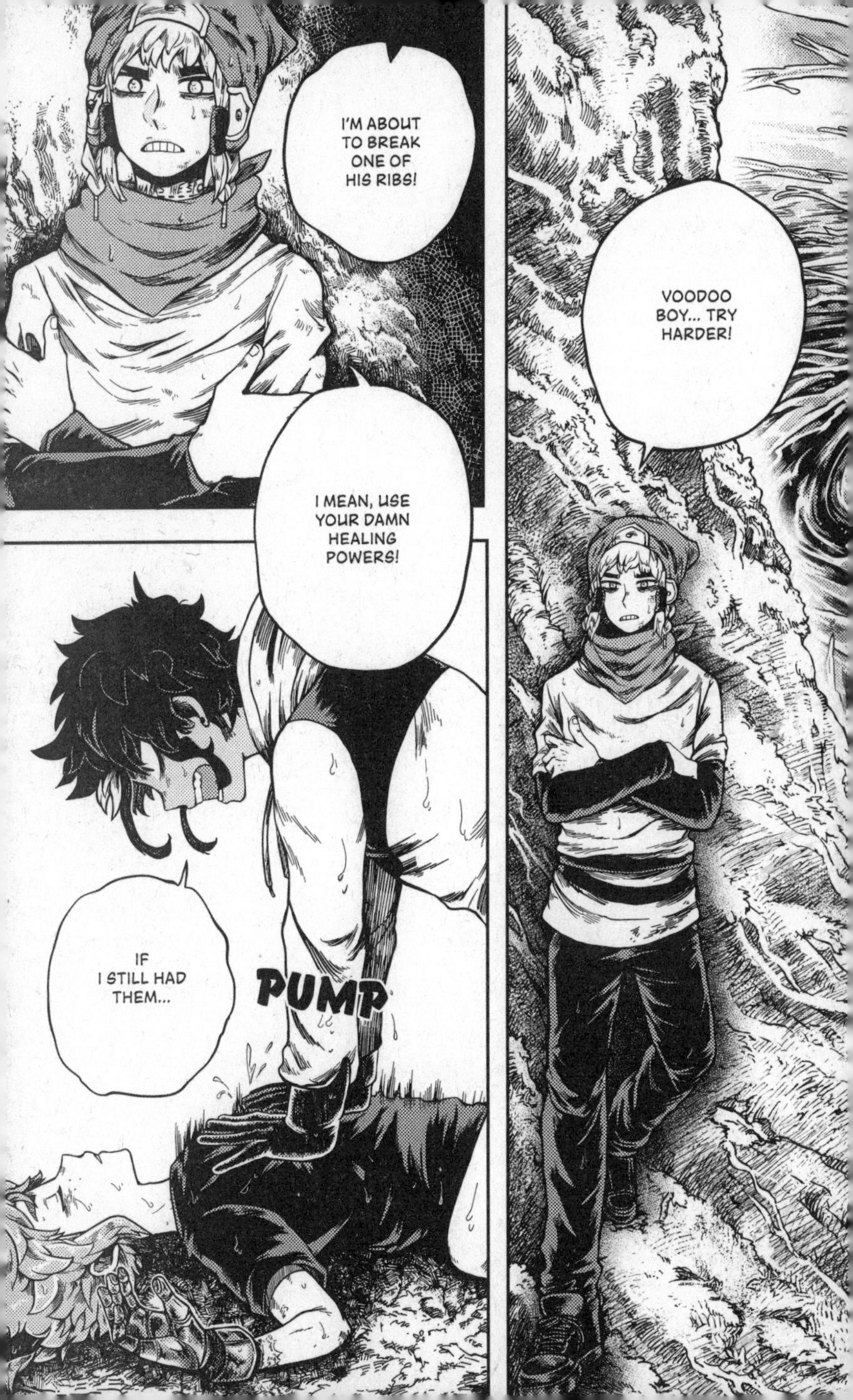
VOODOO BOY... TRY HARDER!
I'M ABOUT TO BREAK ONE OF HIS RIBS!
I MEAN, USE YOUR DAMN HEALING POWERS!
IF I STILL HAD THEM...
PUMP

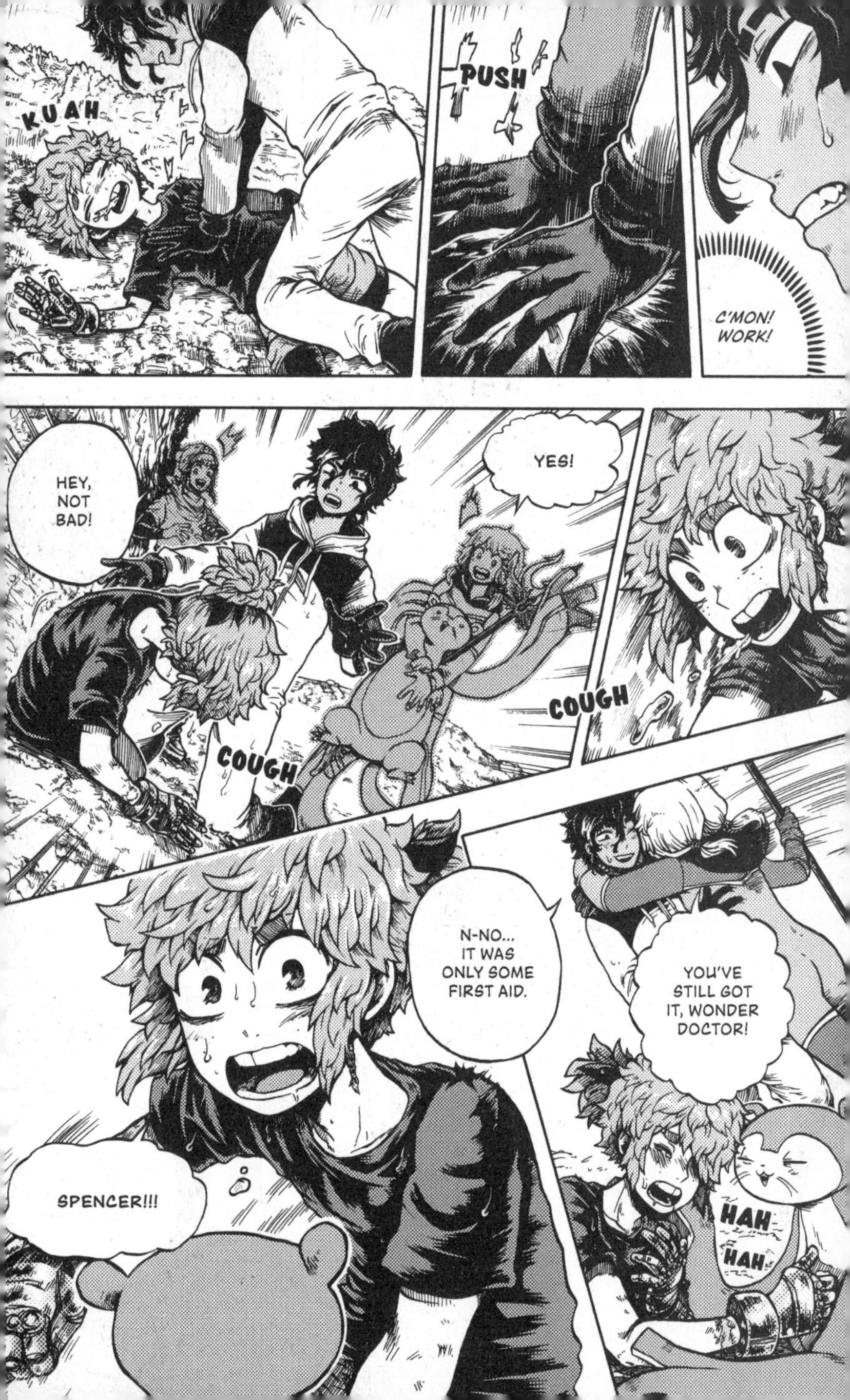
C'MON! WORK!
PUSH
KUAH
COUGH
YES!
HEY, NOT BAD!
COUGH
YOU'VE STILL GOT IT, WONDER DOCTOR!
HAH HAH
N-NO... IT WAS ONLY SOME FIRST AID.
SPENCER!!!

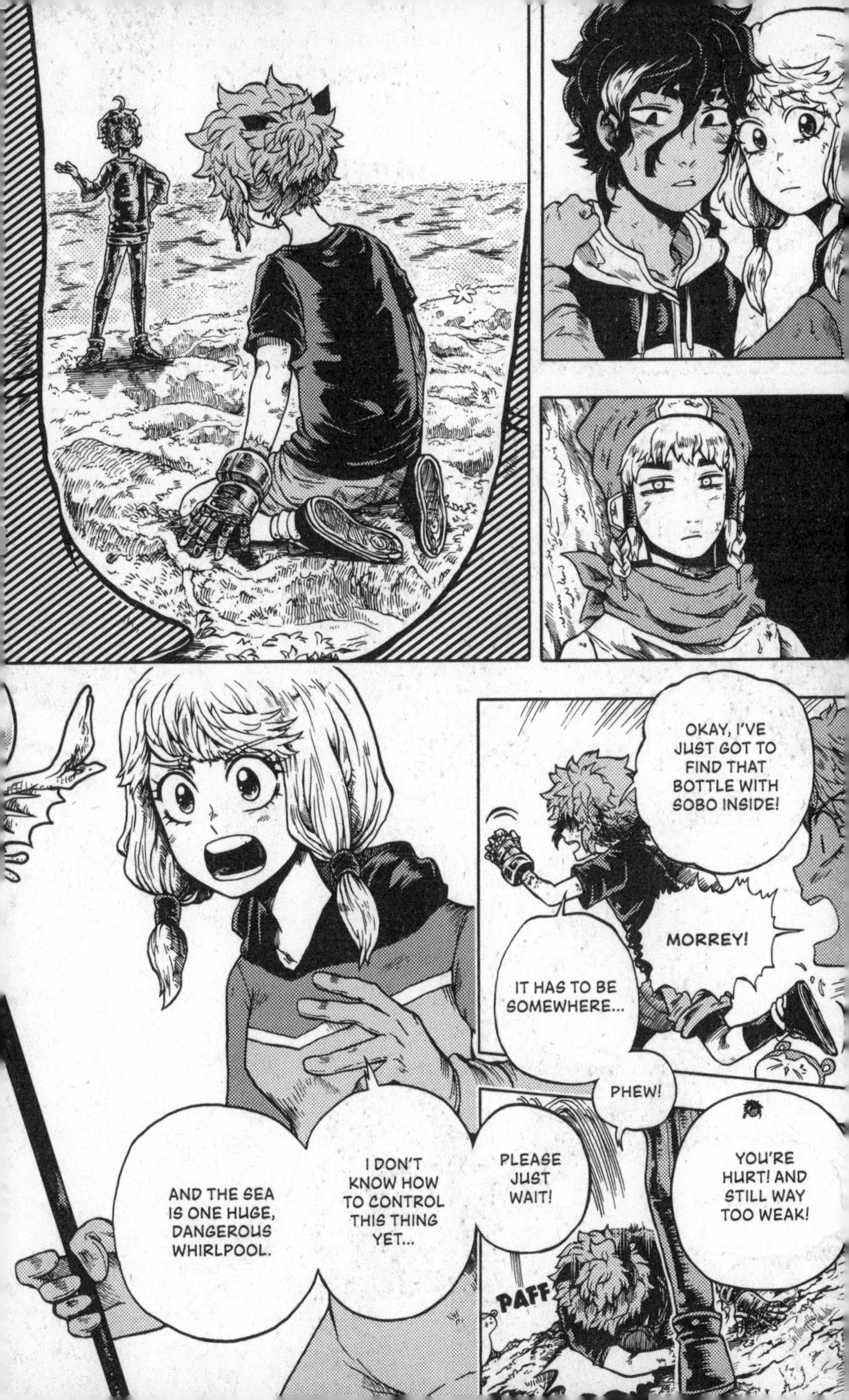
OKAY, I'VE JUST GOT TO FIND THAT BOTTLE WITH SOBO INSIDE!
MORREY!
IT HAS TO BE SOMEWHERE...
PHEW!
YOU'RE HURT! AND STILL WAY TOO WEAK!
PAFF
PLEASE JUST WAIT!
I DON'T KNOW HOW TO CONTROL THIS THING YET...
AND THE SEA IS ONE HUGE, DANGEROUS WHIRLPOOL.

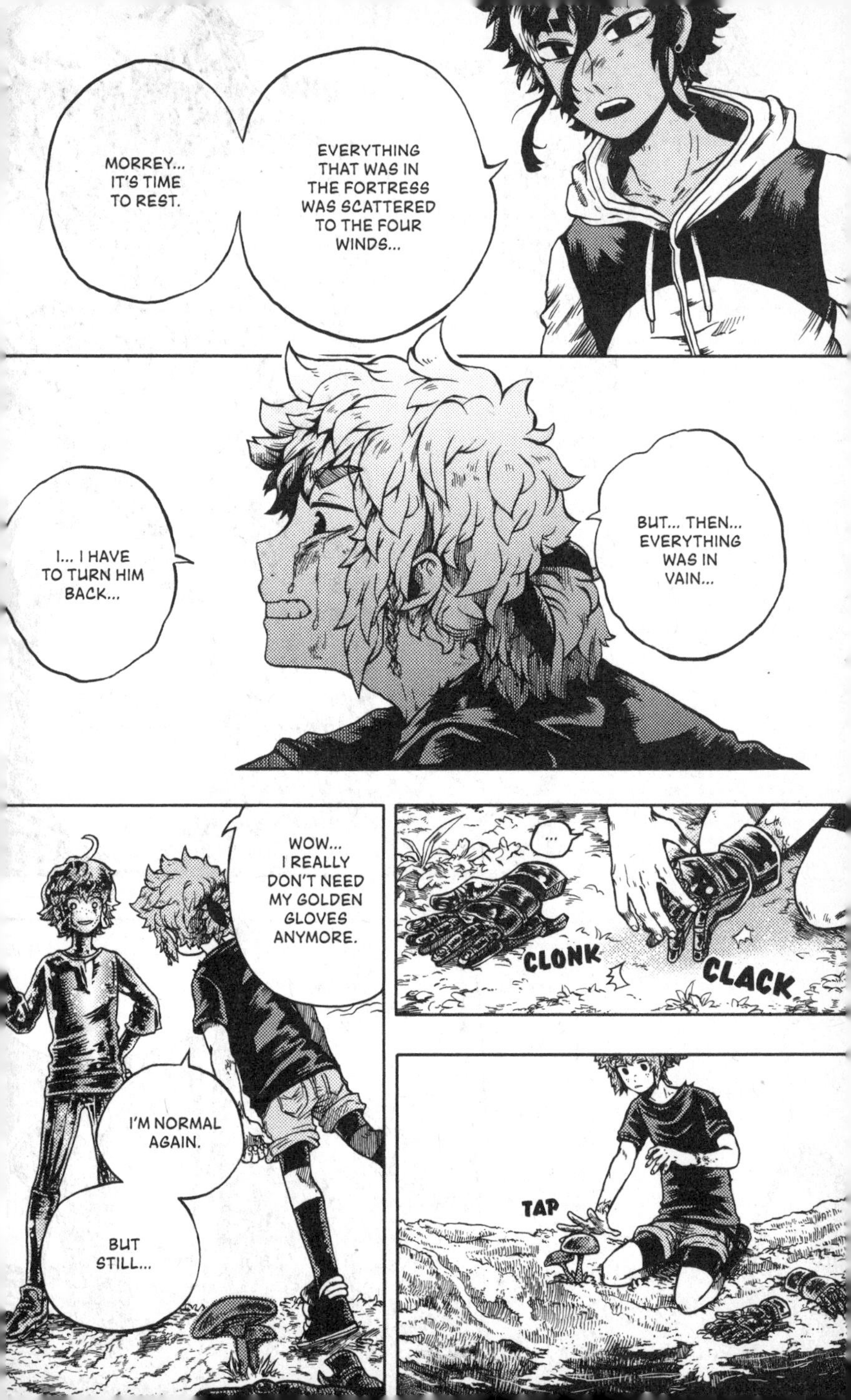
EVERYTHING THAT WAS IN THE FORTRESS WAS SCATTERED TO THE FOUR WINDS...
MORREY... IT'S TIME TO REST.
BUT... THEN... EVERYTHING WAS IN VAIN...
I... I HAVE TO TURN HIM BACK...
...
CLONK
CLACK
TAP
WOW... I REALLY DON'T NEED MY GOLDEN GLOVES ANYMORE.
I'M NORMAL AGAIN.
BUT STILL...

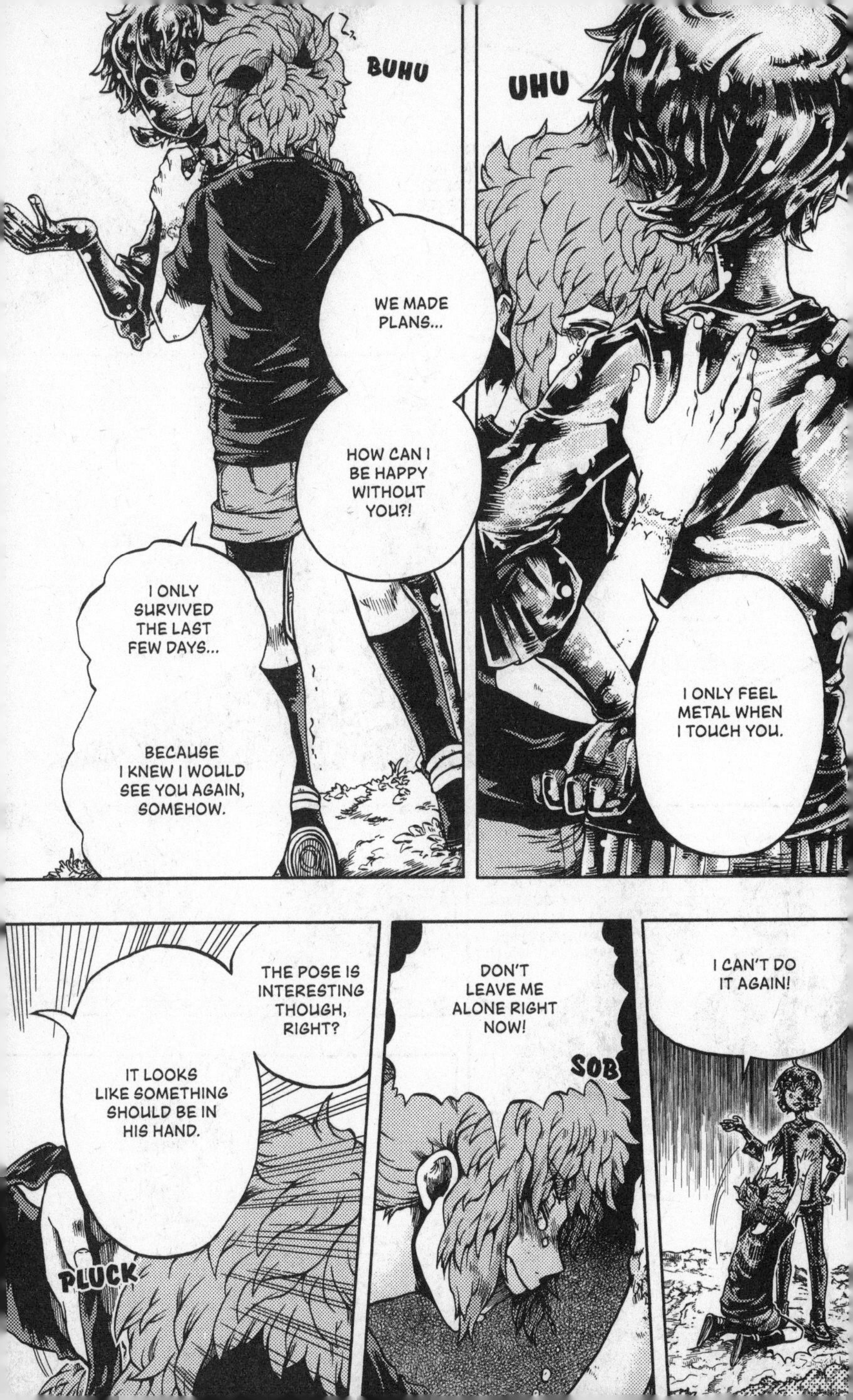
UHU
I ONLY FEEL METAL WHEN I TOUCH YOU.
BUHU
WE MADE PLANS...
HOW CAN I BE HAPPY WITHOUT YOU?!
I ONLY SURVIVED THE LAST FEW DAYS...
BECAUSE I KNEW I WOULD SEE YOU AGAIN, SOMEHOW.
I CAN'T DO IT AGAIN!
DON'T LEAVE ME ALONE RIGHT NOW!
SOB
THE POSE IS INTERESTING THOUGH, RIGHT?
IT LOOKS LIKE SOMETHING SHOULD BE IN HIS HAND.
PLUCK

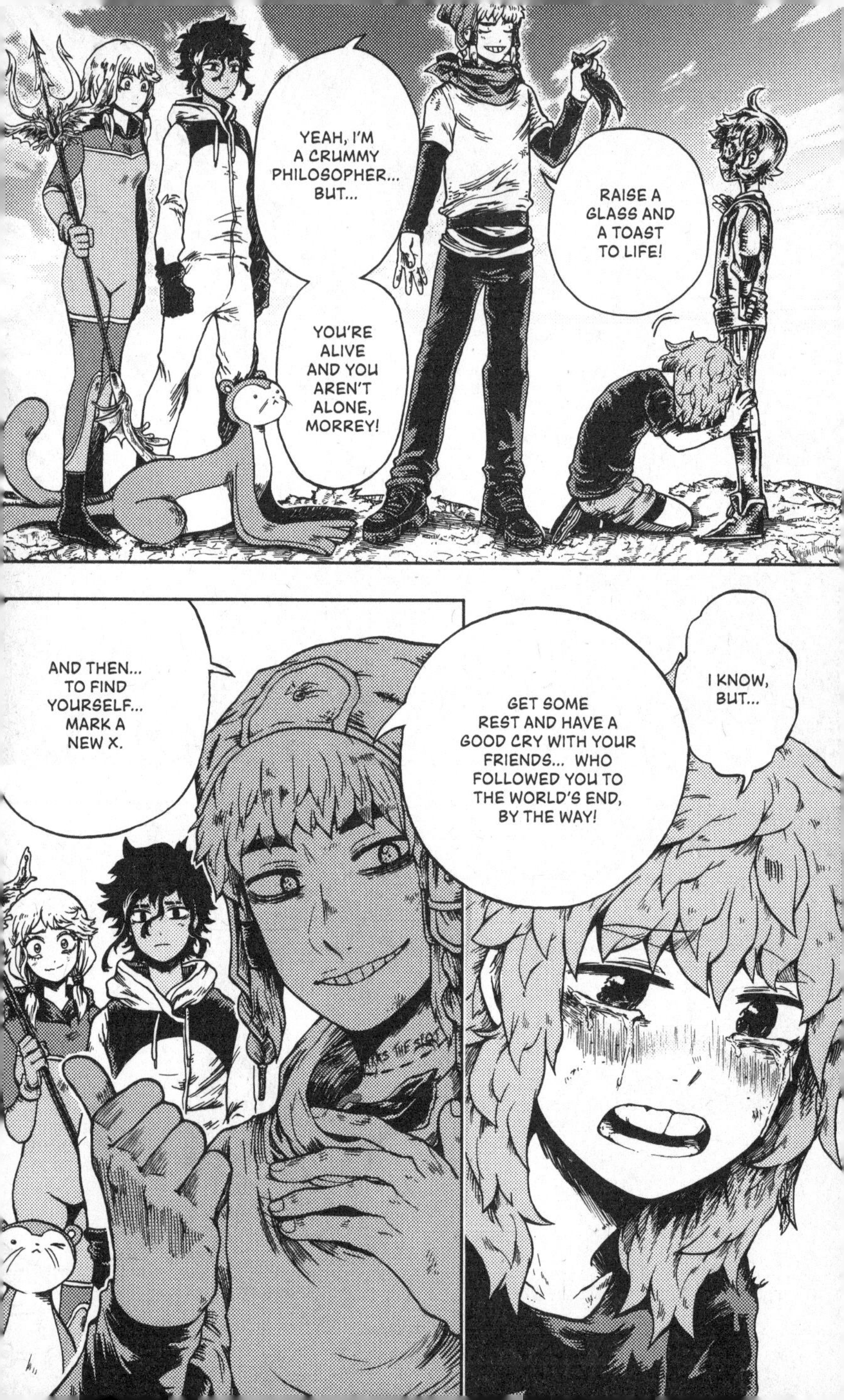
YEAH, I'M A CRUMMY PHILOSOPHER... BUT...
YOU'RE ALIVE AND YOU AREN'T ALONE, MORREY!
RAISE A GLASS AND A TOAST TO LIFE!
I KNOW, BUT...
GET SOME REST AND HAVE A GOOD CRY WITH YOUR FRIENDS... WHO FOLLOWED YOU TO THE WORLD'S END, BY THE WAY!
AND THEN... TO FIND YOURSELF... MARK A NEW X.

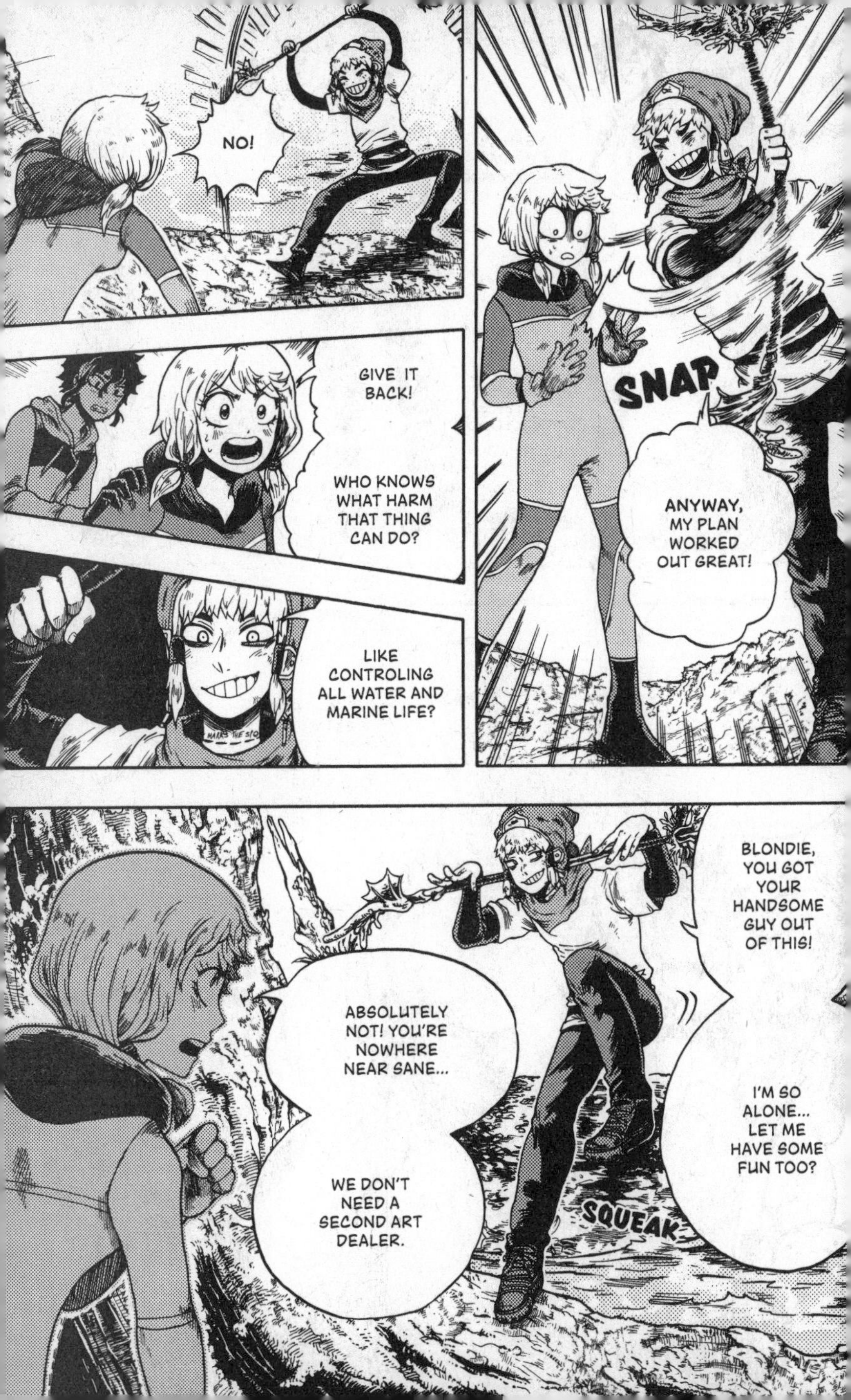
SNAP
ANYWAY, MY PLAN WORKED OUT GREAT!
NO!
GIVE IT BACK!
WHO KNOWS WHAT HARM THAT THING CAN DO?
LIKE CONTROLING ALL WATER AND MARINE LIFE?
BLONDIE, YOU GOT YOUR HANDSOME GUY OUT OF THIS!
I'M SO ALONE... LET ME HAVE SOME FUN TOO?
SQUEAK
ABSOLUTELY NOT! YOU'RE NOWHERE NEAR SANE...
WE DON'T NEED A SECOND ART DEALER.

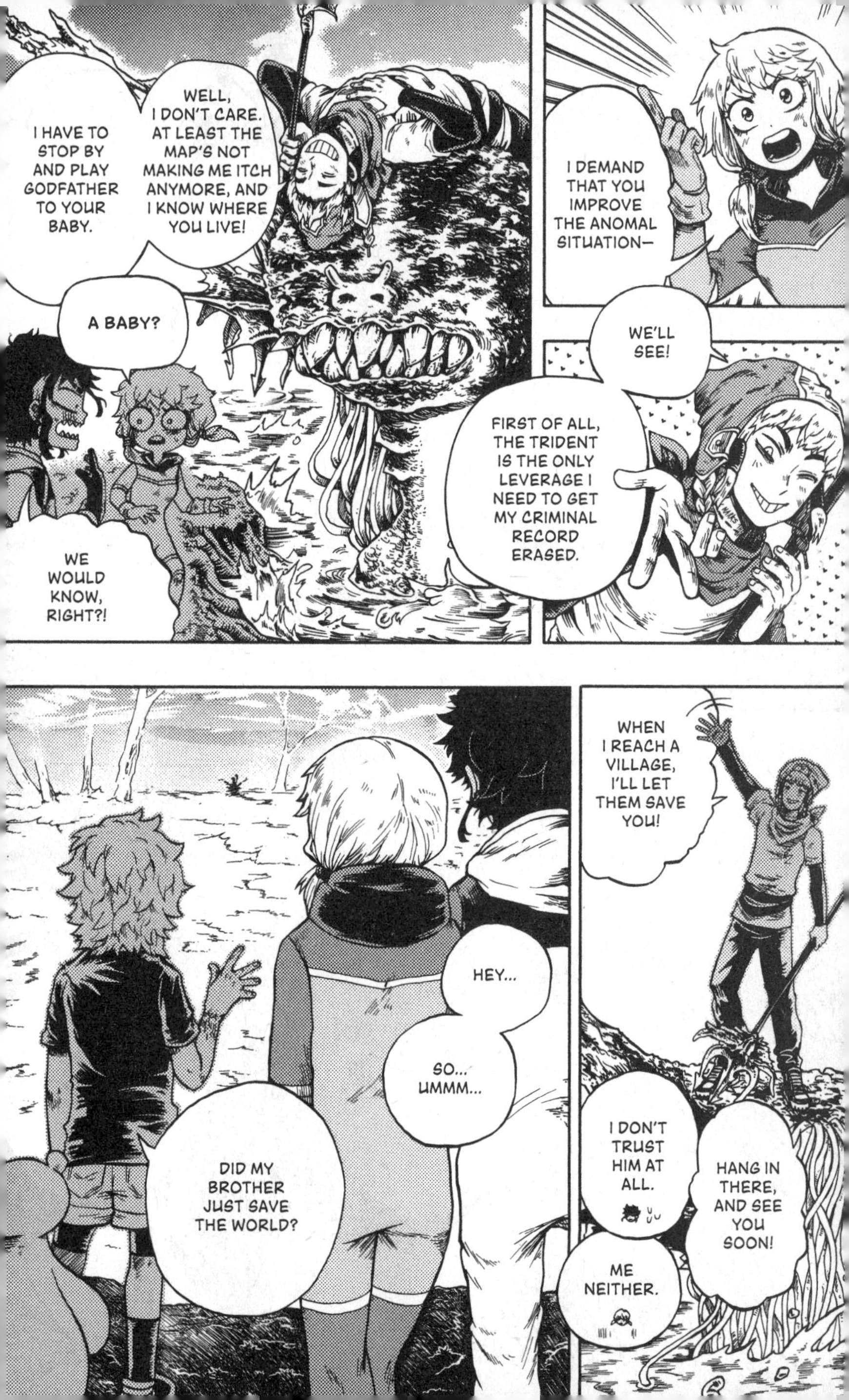
I DEMAND THAT YOU IMPROVE THE ANOMAL SITUATION—
WE'LL SEE!
FIRST OF ALL, THE TRIDENT IS THE ONLY LEVERAGE I NEED TO GET MY CRIMINAL RECORD ERASED.
WELL, I DON'T CARE. AT LEAST THE MAP'S NOT MAKING ME ITCH ANYMORE, AND I KNOW WHERE YOU LIVE!
I HAVE TO STOP BY AND PLAY GODFATHER TO YOUR BABY.
A BABY?
WE WOULD KNOW, RIGHT?!
WHEN I REACH A VILLAGE, I'LL LET THEM SAVE YOU!
HANG IN THERE, AND SEE YOU SOON!
I DON'T TRUST HIM AT ALL.
ME NEITHER.
HEY...
SO... UMMM...
DID MY BROTHER JUST SAVE THE WORLD?

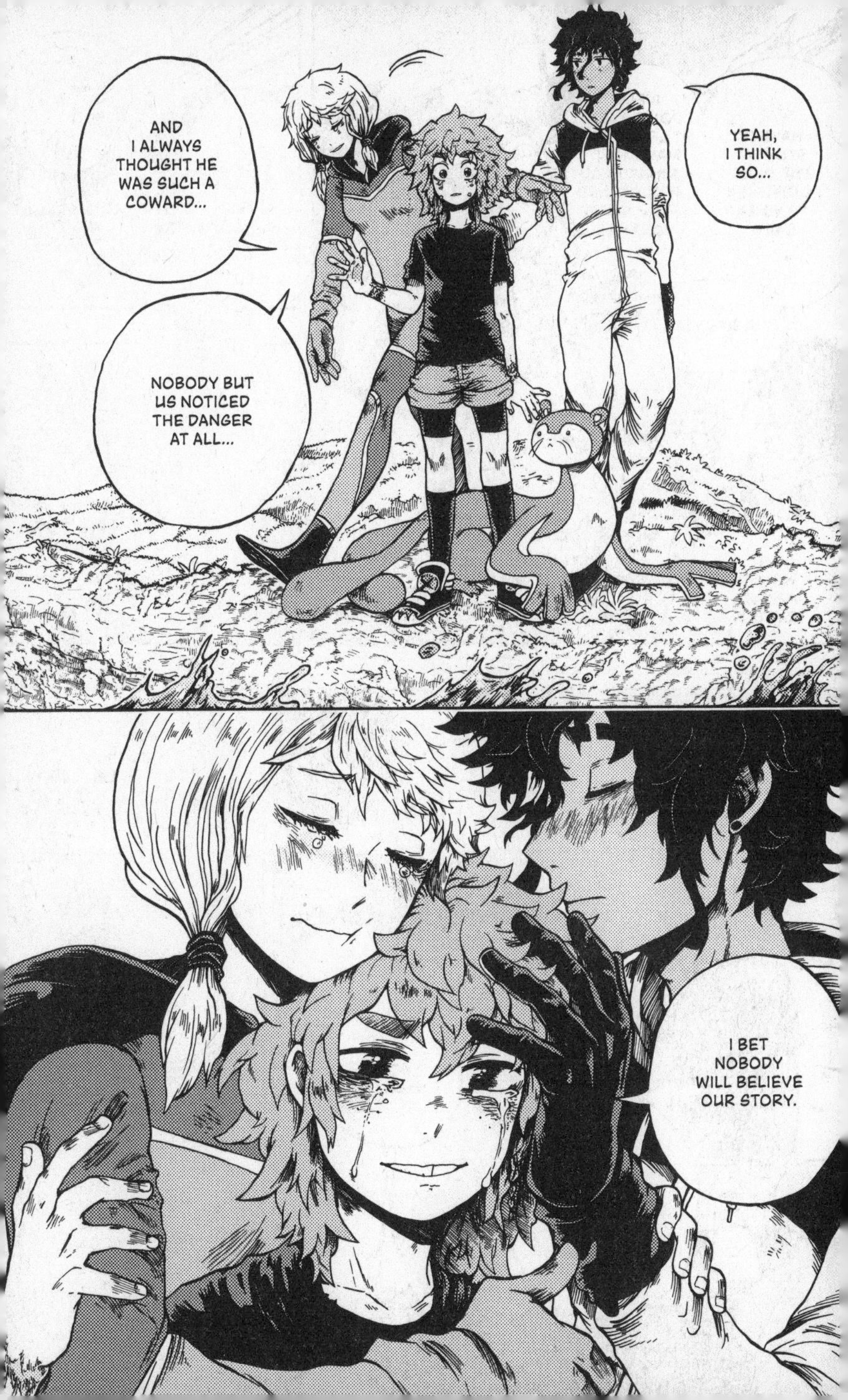
YEAH, I THINK SO...
AND I ALWAYS THOUGHT HE WAS SUCH A COWARD...
NOBODY BUT US NOTICED THE DANGER AT ALL...
I BET NOBODY WILL BELIEVE OUR STORY.

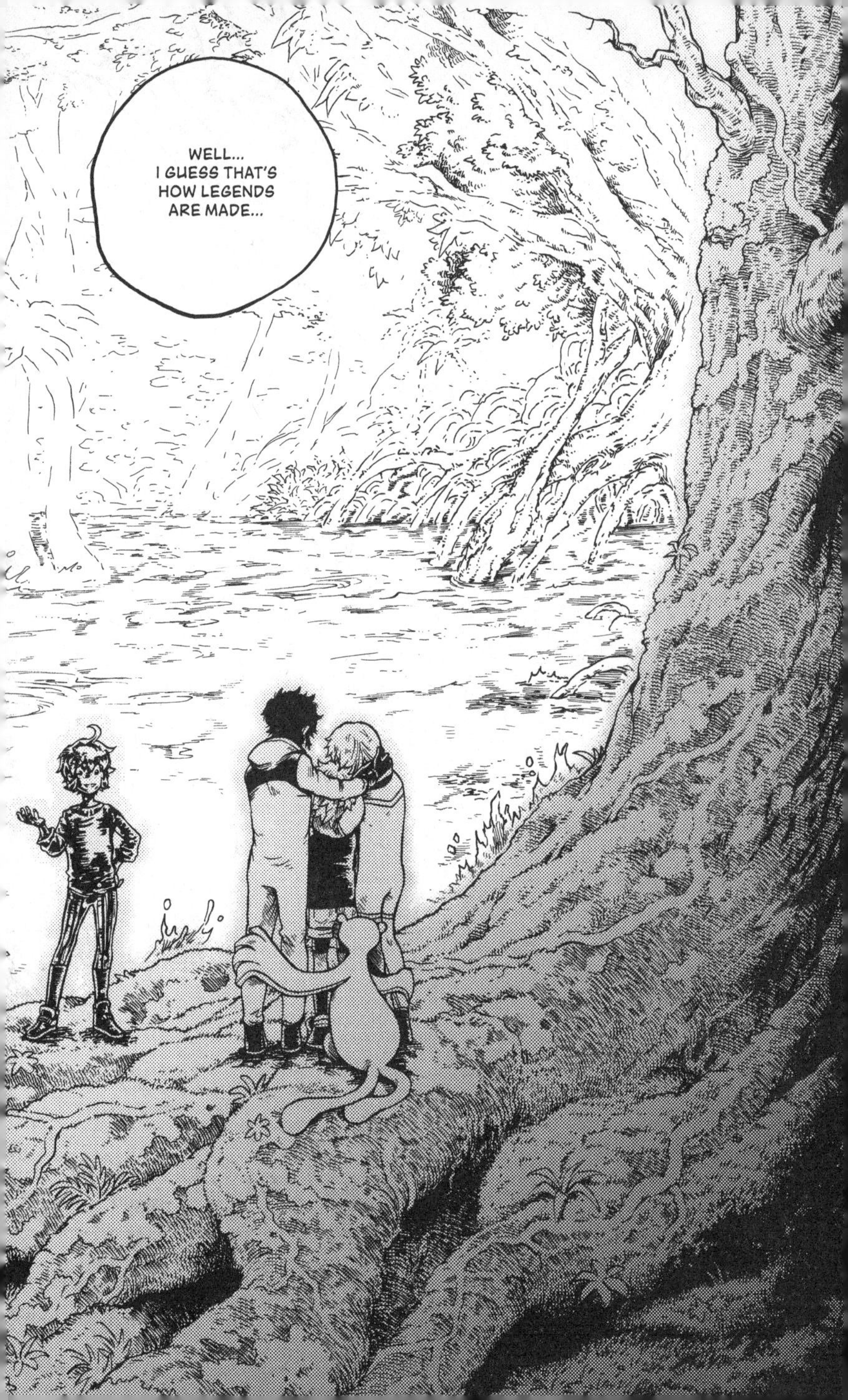
WELL... I GUESS THAT'S HOW LEGENDS ARE MADE...

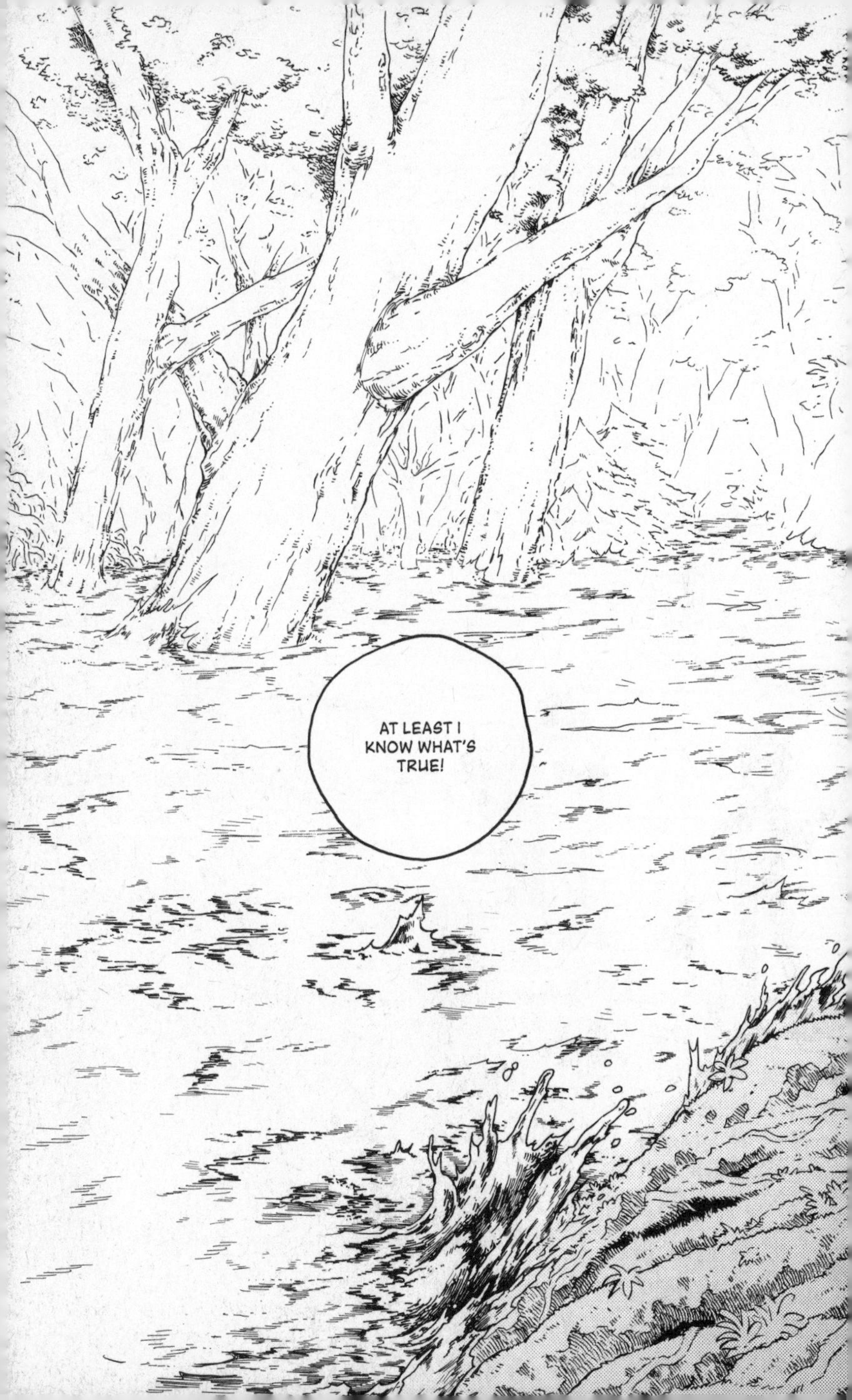
AT LEAST I KNOW WHAT'S TRUE!

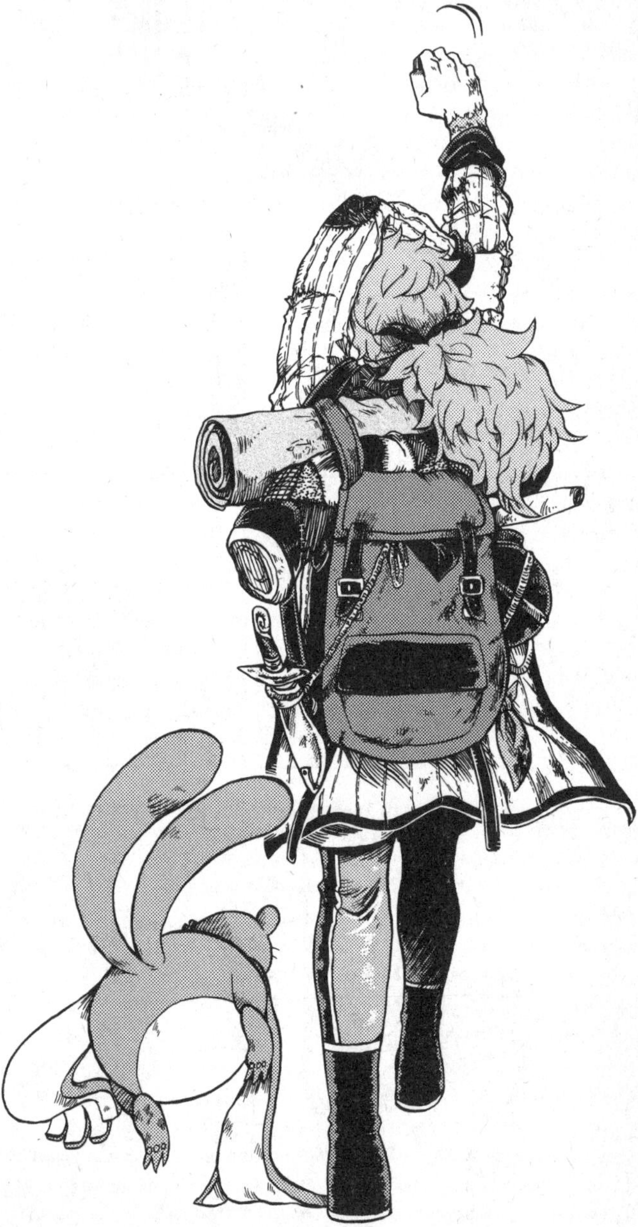

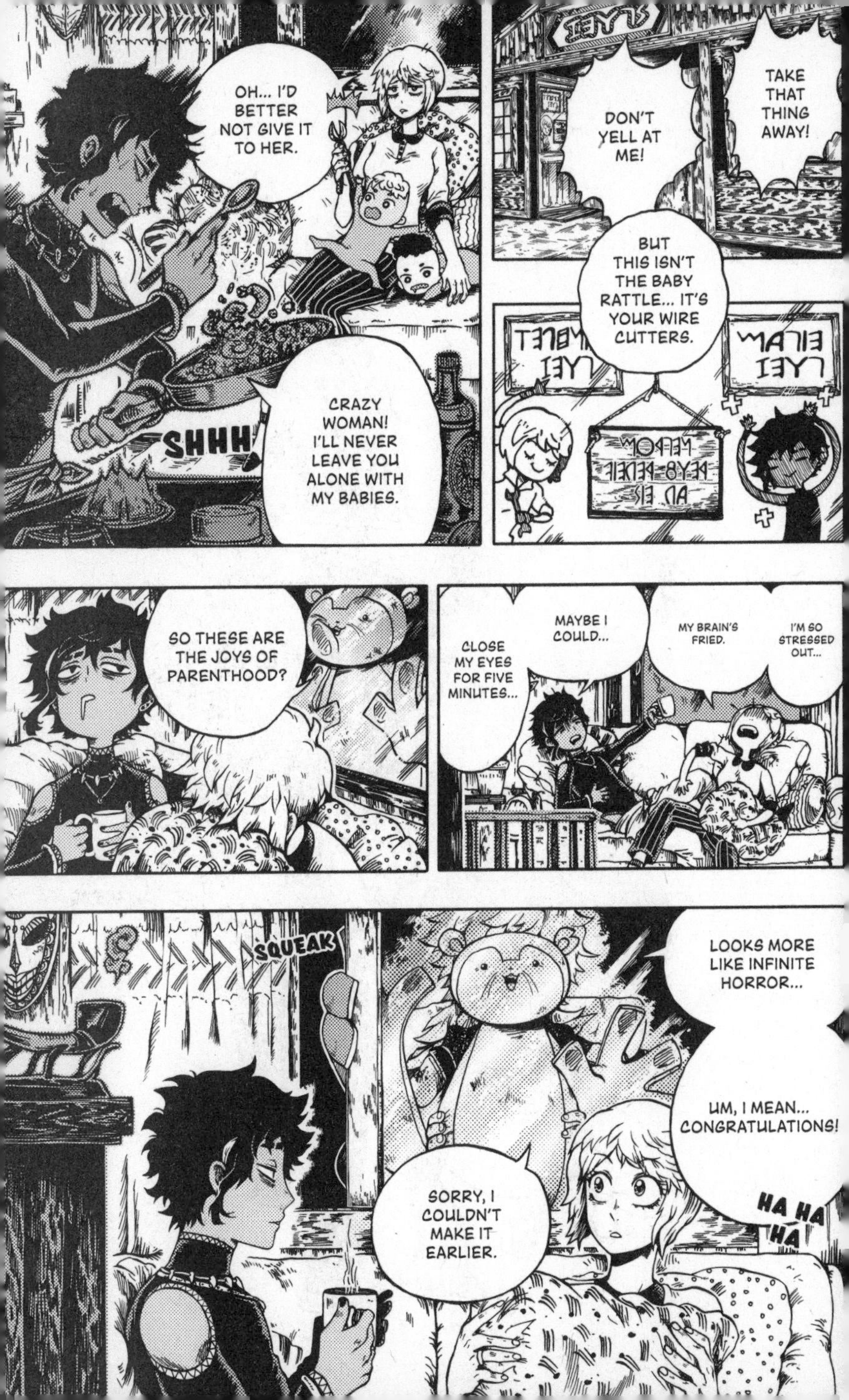
TAKE THAT THING AWAY!
DON'T YELL AT ME!
BUT THIS ISN'T THE BABY RATTLE... IT'S YOUR WIRE CUTTERS.
OH... I'D BETTER NOT GIVE IT TO HER.
SHHH
CRAZY WOMAN! I'LL NEVER LEAVE YOU ALONE WITH MY BABIES.
I'M SO STRESSED OUT...
MY BRAIN'S FRIED.
MAYBE I COULD...
CLOSE MY EYES FOR FIVE MINUTES...
SO THESE ARE THE JOYS OF PARENTHOOD?
LOOKS MORE LIKE INFINITE HORROR...
UM, I MEAN... CONGRATULATIONS!
HA HA HA
SQUEAK
SORRY, I COULDN'T MAKE IT EARLIER.

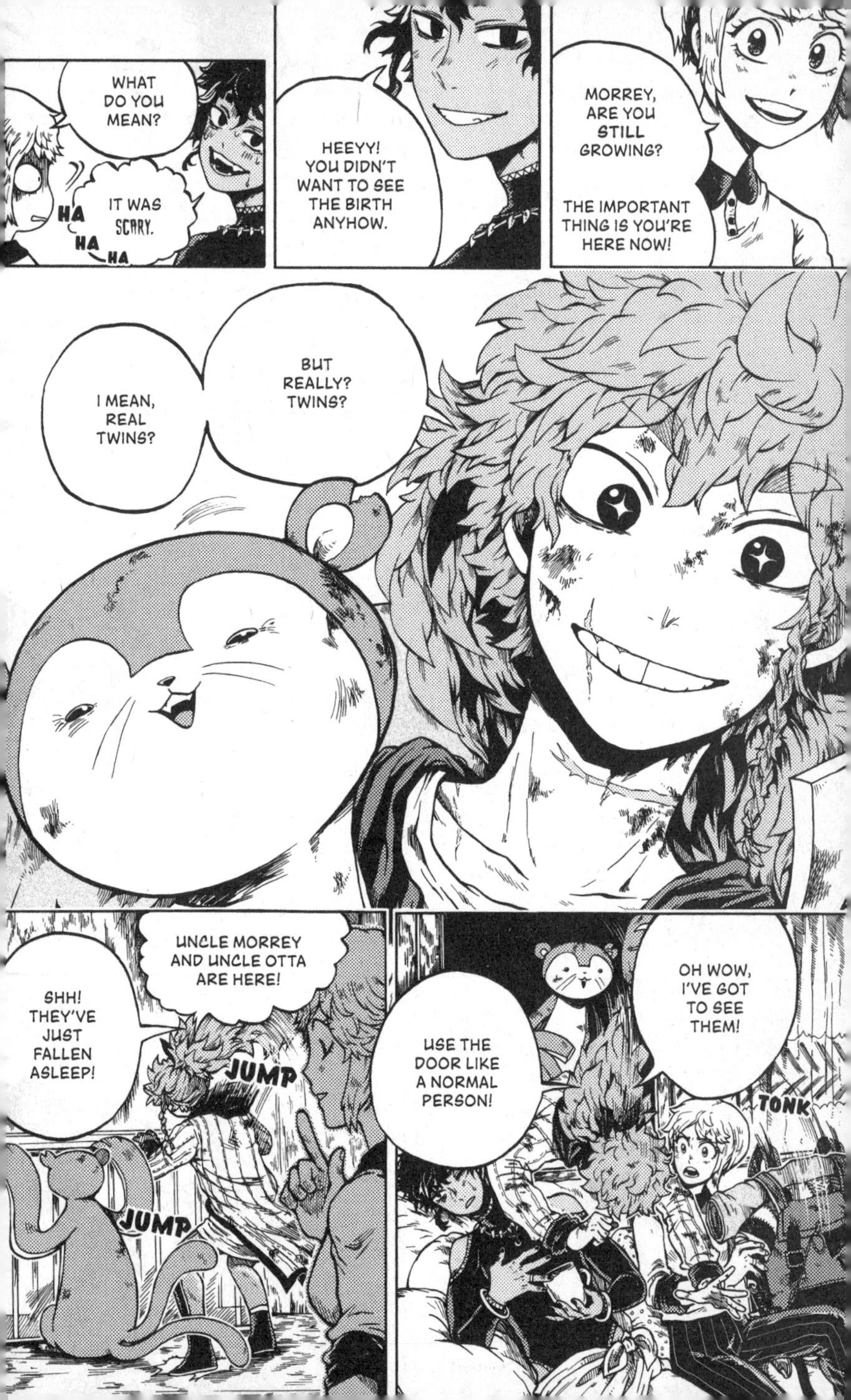
MORREY, ARE YOU STILL GROWING?
THE IMPORTANT THING IS YOU'RE HERE NOW!
HEEYY! YOU DIDN'T WANT TO SEE THE BIRTH ANYHOW.
WHAT DO YOU MEAN?
IT WAS SCARY.
HA HA HA
BUT REALLY? TWINS?
I MEAN, REAL TWINS?
OH WOW, I'VE GOT TO SEE THEM!
TONK
USE THE DOOR LIKE A NORMAL PERSON!
UNCLE MORREY AND UNCLE OTTA ARE HERE!
SHH! THEY'VE JUST FALLEN ASLEEP!
JUMP
JUMP

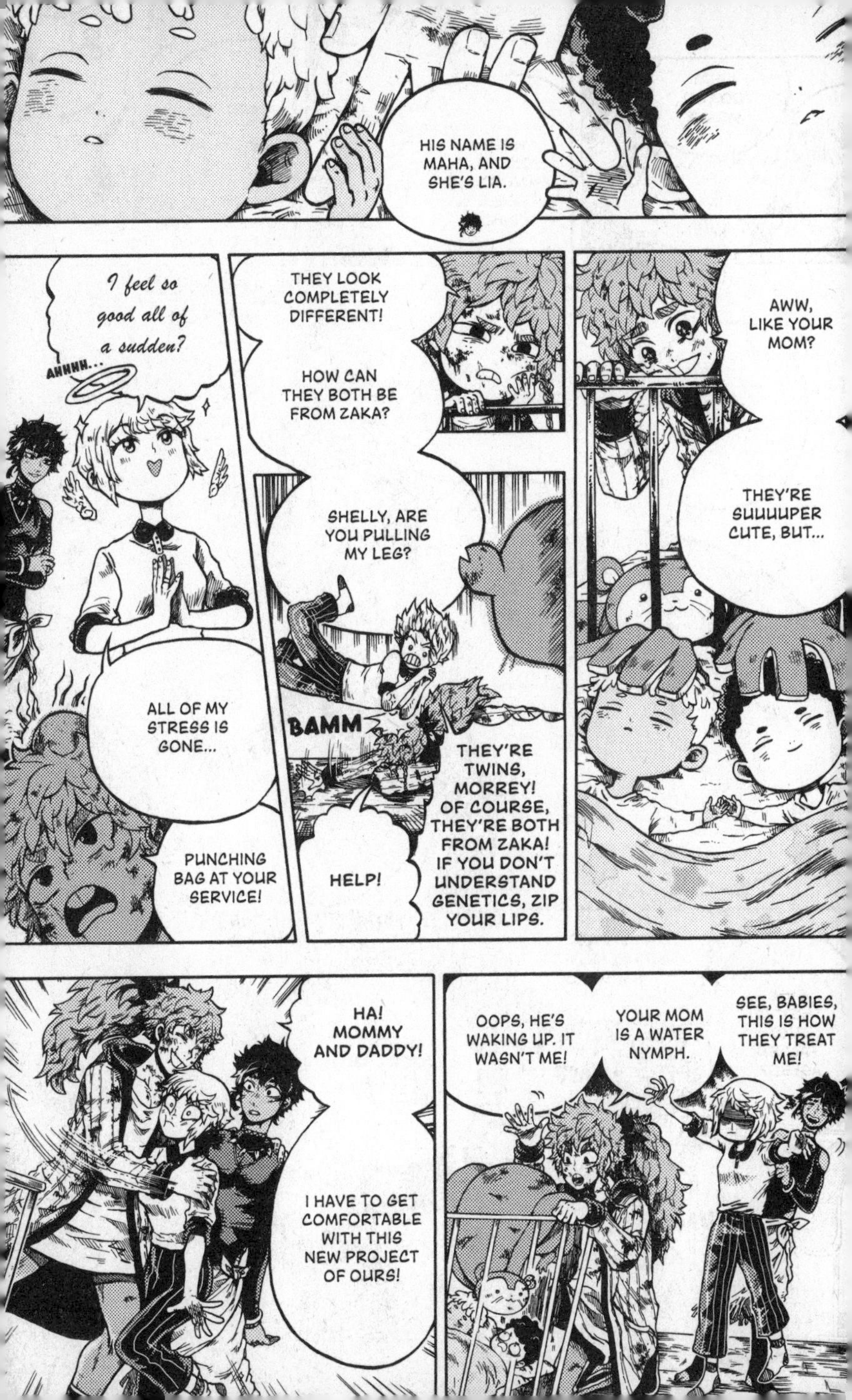
HIS NAME IS MAHA, AND SHE'S LIA.
AWW, LIKE YOUR MOM?
THEY'RE SUUUUPER CUTE, BUT...
THEY LOOK COMPLETELY DIFFERENT!
HOW CAN THEY BOTH BE FROM ZAKA?
SHELLY, ARE YOU PULLING MY LEG?
BAMM
THEY'RE TWINS, MORREY! OF COURSE, THEY'RE BOTH FROM ZAKA! IF YOU DON'T UNDERSTAND GENETICS, ZIP YOUR LIPS.
HELP!
I feel so good all of a sudden?
AHHHH...
ALL OF MY STRESS IS GONE...
PUNCHING BAG AT YOUR SERVICE!
SEE, BABIES, THIS IS HOW THEY TREAT ME!
YOUR MOM IS A WATER NYMPH.
OOPS, HE'S WAKING UP. IT WASN'T ME!
HA! MOMMY AND DADDY!
I HAVE TO GET COMFORTABLE WITH THIS NEW PROJECT OF OURS!

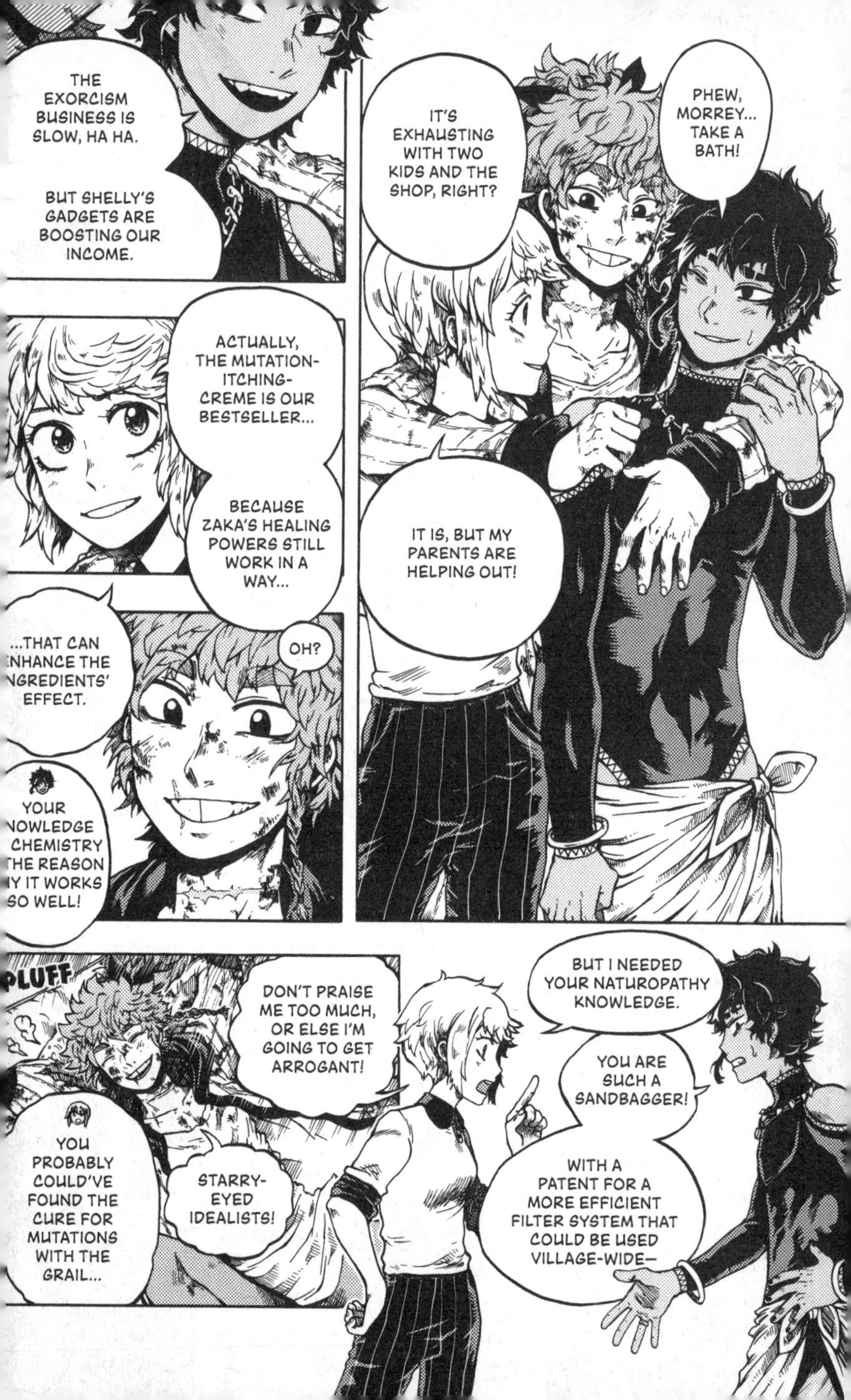
PHEW, MORREY... TAKE A BATH!
IT'S EXHAUSTING WITH TWO KIDS AND THE SHOP, RIGHT?
IT IS, BUT MY PARENTS ARE HELPING OUT!
THE EXORCISM BUSINESS IS SLOW, HA HA.
BUT SHELLY'S GADGETS ARE BOOSTING OUR INCOME.
ACTUALLY, THE MUTATION-ITCHING-CREME IS OUR BESTSELLER...
BECAUSE ZAKA'S HEALING POWERS STILL WORK IN A WAY...
...THAT CAN NHANCE THE NGREDIENTS' EFFECT.
OH?
YOUR NOWLEDGE CHEMISTRY THE REASON Y IT WORKS SO WELL!
BUT I NEEDED YOUR NATUROPATHY KNOWLEDGE.
YOU ARE SUCH A SANDBAGGER!
WITH A PATENT FOR A MORE EFFICIENT FILTER SYSTEM THAT COULD BE USED VILLAGE-WIDE–
PLUFF
DON'T PRAISE ME TOO MUCH, OR ELSE I'M GOING TO GET ARROGANT!
YOU PROBABLY COULD'VE FOUND THE CURE FOR MUTATIONS WITH THE GRAIL...
STARRY-EYED IDEALISTS!

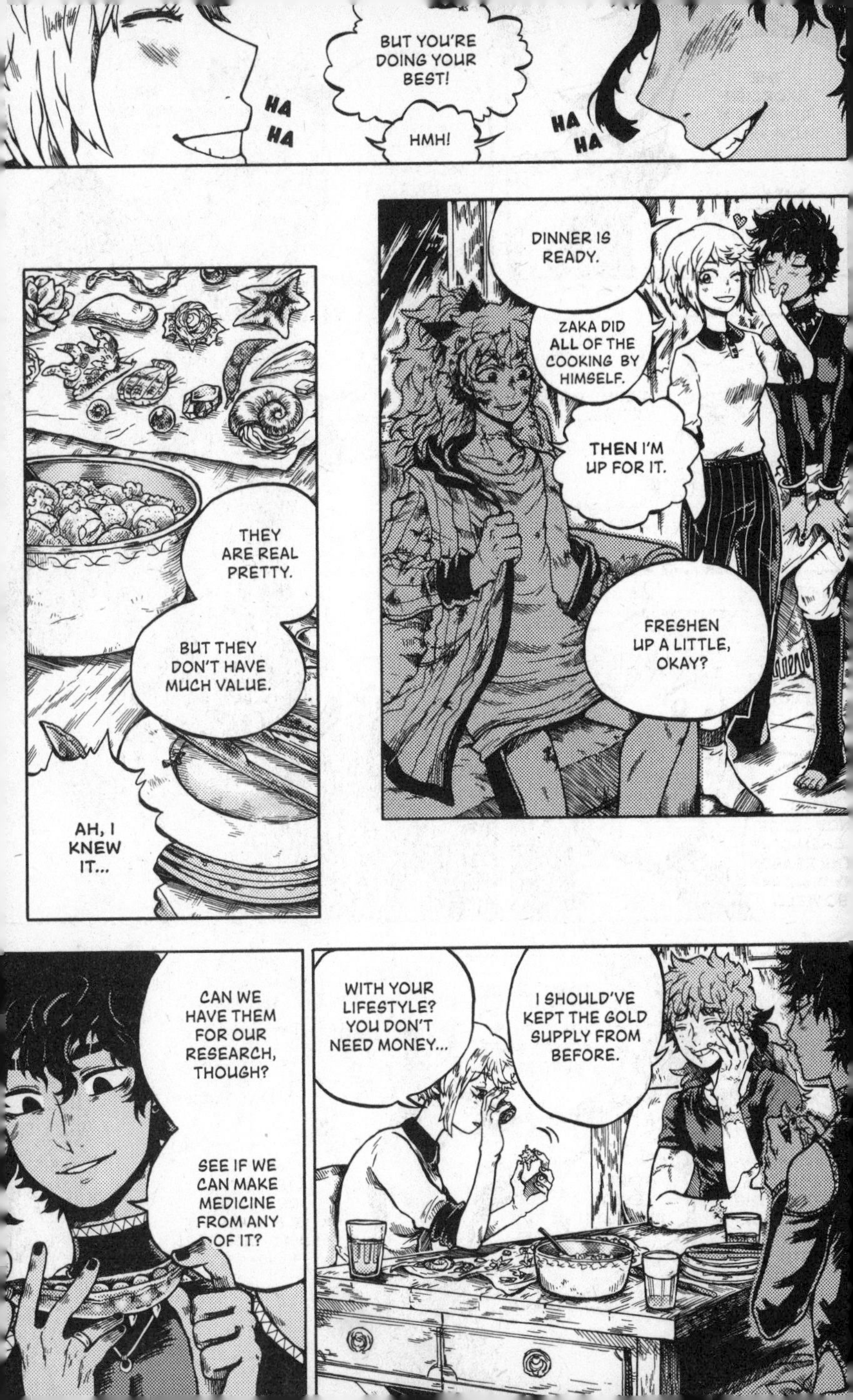
BUT YOU'RE DOING YOUR BEST!
HA HA
HMH!
HA HA
DINNER IS READY.
ZAKA DID ALL OF THE COOKING BY HIMSELF.
THEN I'M UP FOR IT.
FRESHEN UP A LITTLE, OKAY?
THEY ARE REAL PRETTY.
BUT THEY DON'T HAVE MUCH VALUE.
AH, I KNEW IT...
I SHOULD'VE KEPT THE GOLD SUPPLY FROM BEFORE.
WITH YOUR LIFESTYLE? YOU DON'T NEED MONEY...
CAN WE HAVE THEM FOR OUR RESEARCH, THOUGH?
SEE IF WE CAN MAKE MEDICINE FROM ANY OF IT?

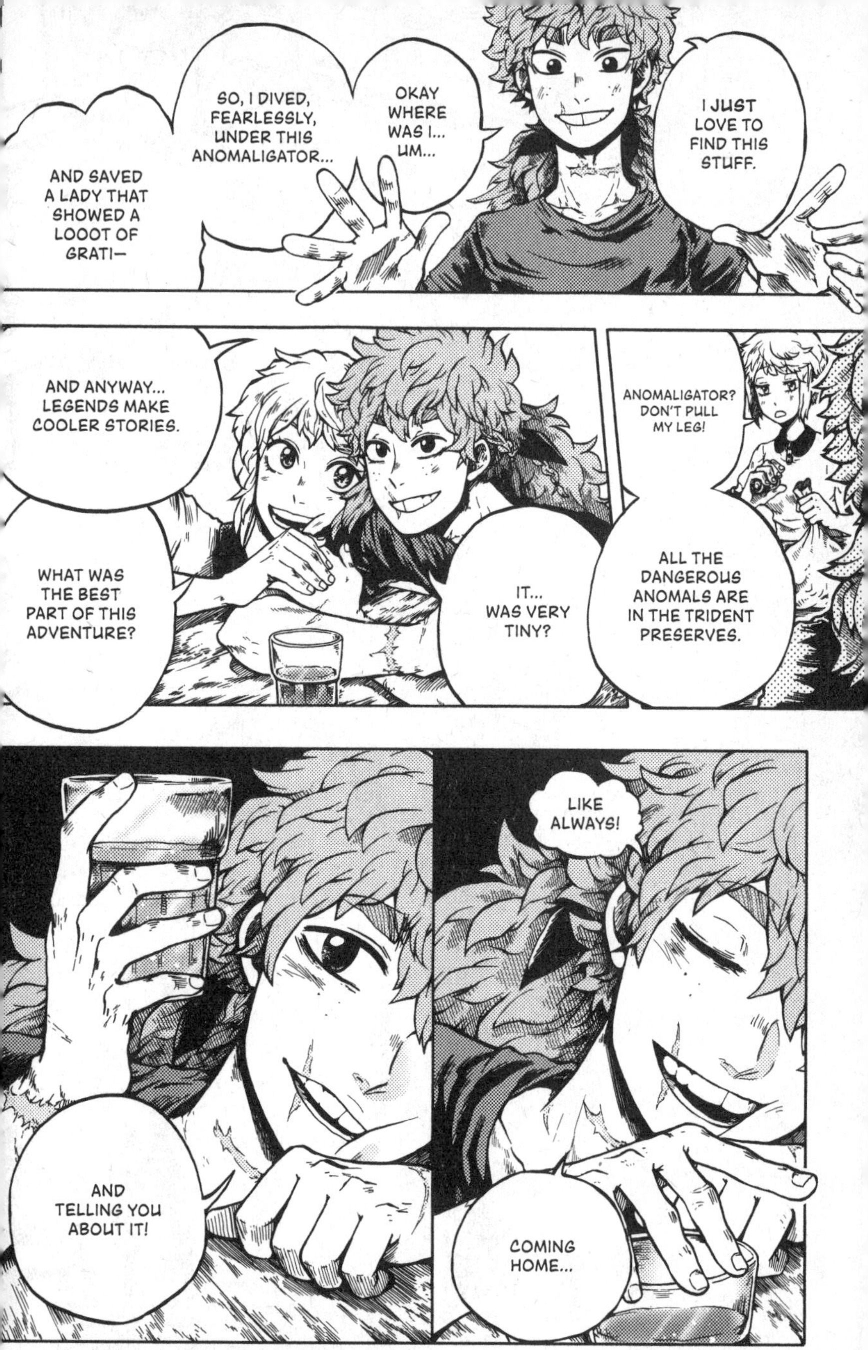

I JUST LOVE TO FIND THIS STUFF.
OKAY WHERE WAS I... UM...
SO, I DIVED, FEARLESSLY, UNDER THIS ANOMALIGATOR...
AND SAVED A LADY THAT SHOWED A LOOOT OF GRATI—
ANOMALIGATOR? DON'T PULL MY LEG!
ALL THE DANGEROUS ANOMALS ARE IN THE TRIDENT PRESERVES.
IT... WAS VERY TINY?
AND ANYWAY... LEGENDS MAKE COOLER STORIES.
WHAT WAS THE BEST PART OF THIS ADVENTURE?
LIKE ALWAYS!
COMING HOME...
AND TELLING YOU ABOUT IT!

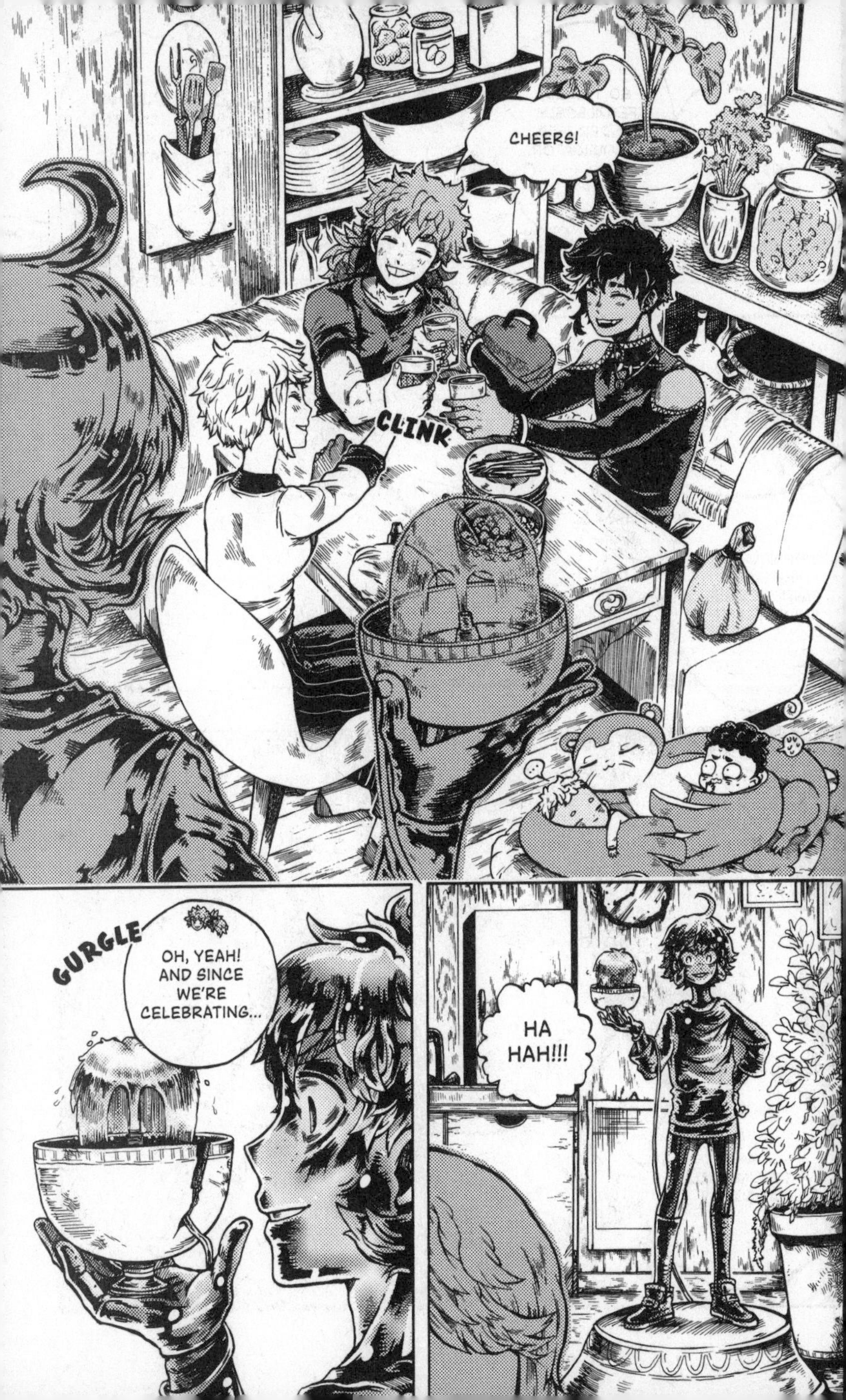
CHEERS!
CLINK
HA HAH!!!
GURGLE
OH, YEAH! AND SINCE WE'RE CELEBRATING...

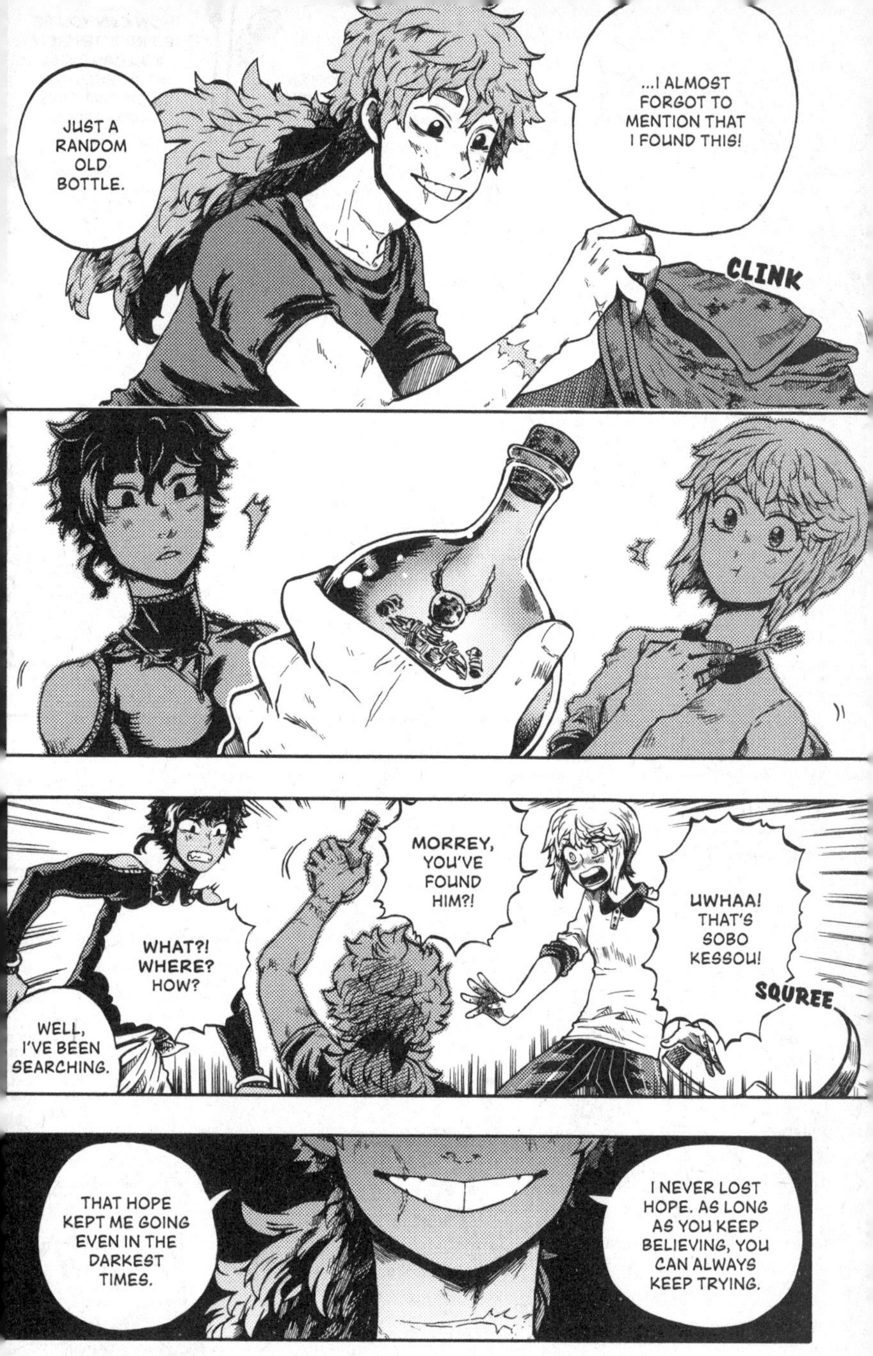
...I ALMOST FORGOT TO MENTION THAT I FOUND THIS!
CLINK
JUST A RANDOM OLD BOTTLE.
UWHAA! THAT'S SOBO KESSOU!
SQUREE
MORREY, YOU'VE FOUND HIM?!
WHAT?! WHERE? HOW?
WELL, I'VE BEEN SEARCHING.
I NEVER LOST HOPE. AS LONG AS YOU KEEP BELIEVING, YOU CAN ALWAYS KEEP TRYING.
THAT HOPE KEPT ME GOING EVEN IN THE DARKEST TIMES.

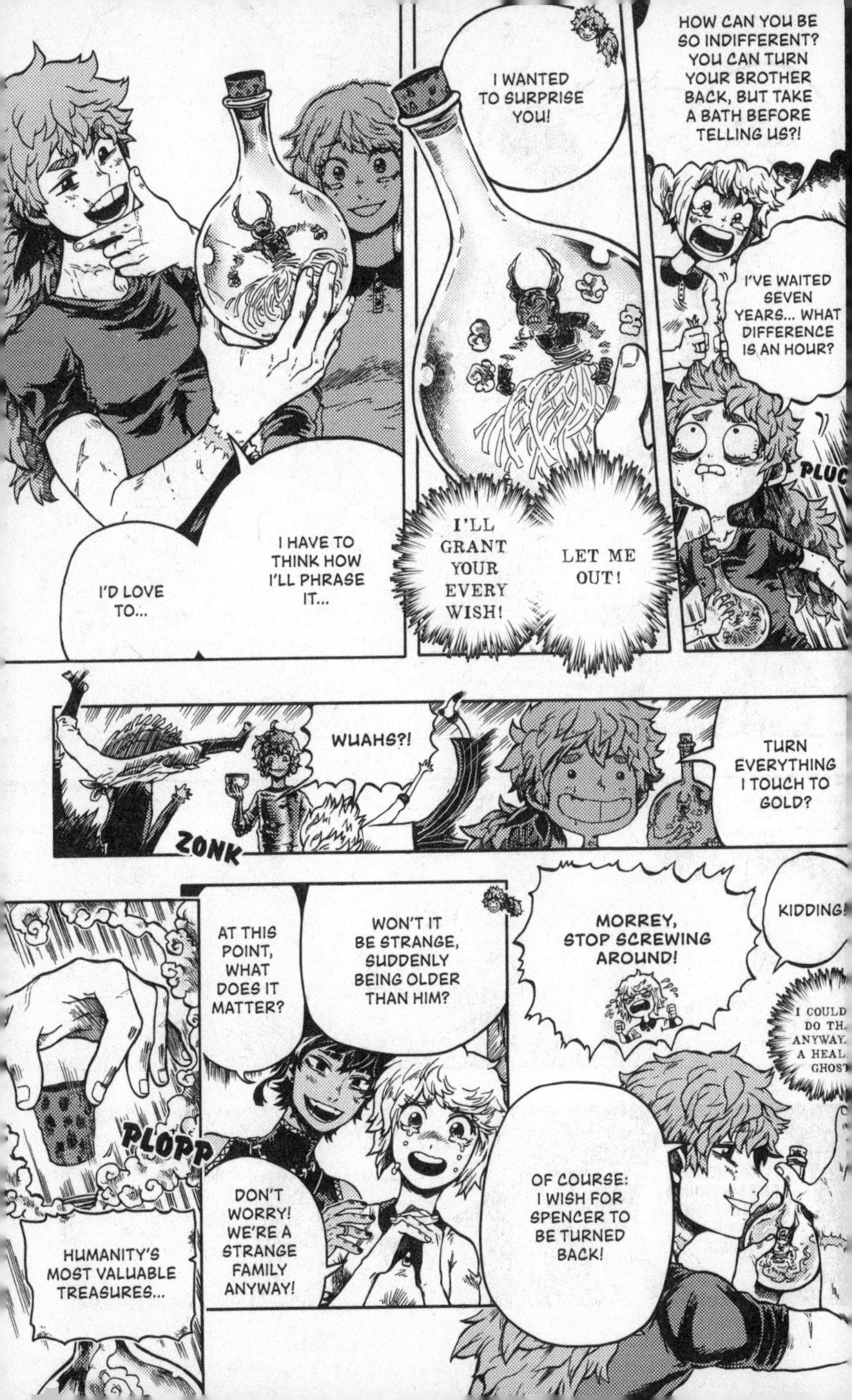
HOW CAN YOU BE SO INDIFFERENT? YOU CAN TURN YOUR BROTHER BACK, BUT TAKE A BATH BEFORE TELLING US?!
I'VE WAITED SEVEN YEARS... WHAT DIFFERENCE IS AN HOUR?
I WANTED TO SURPRISE YOU!
LET ME OUT!
I'LL GRANT YOUR EVERY WISH!
I HAVE TO THINK HOW I'LL PHRASE IT...
I'D LOVE TO...
TURN EVERYTHING I TOUCH TO GOLD?
WUAHS?!
ZONK
KIDDING!
MORREY, STOP SCREWING AROUND!
OF COURSE: I WISH FOR SPENCER TO BE TURNED BACK!
WON'T IT BE STRANGE, SUDDENLY BEING OLDER THAN HIM?
AT THIS POINT, WHAT DOES IT MATTER?
DON'T WORRY! WE'RE A STRANGE FAMILY ANYWAY!
PLOPP
HUMANITY'S MOST VALUABLE TREASURES...

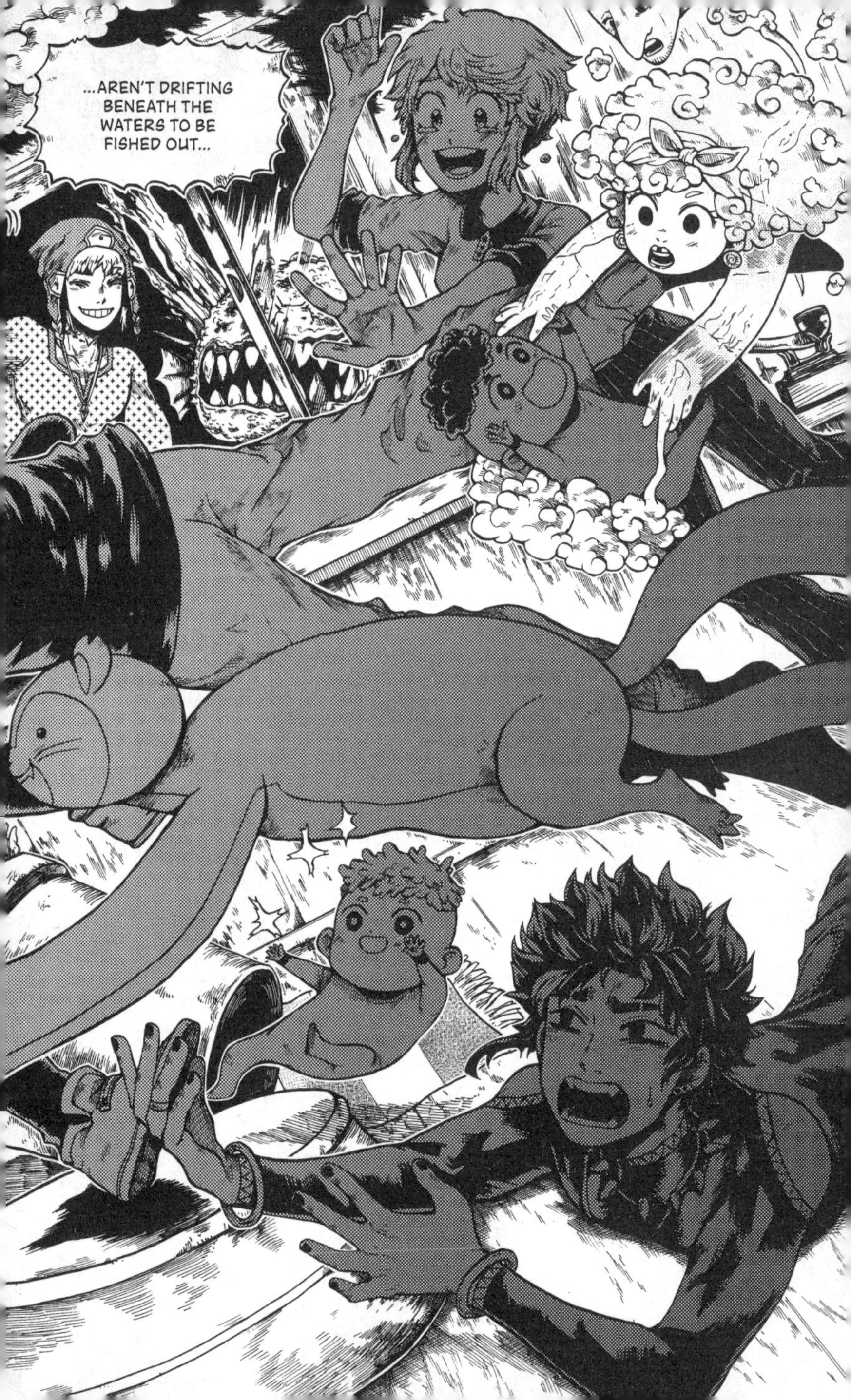
...AREN'T DRIFTING BENEATH THE WATERS TO BE FISHED OUT...

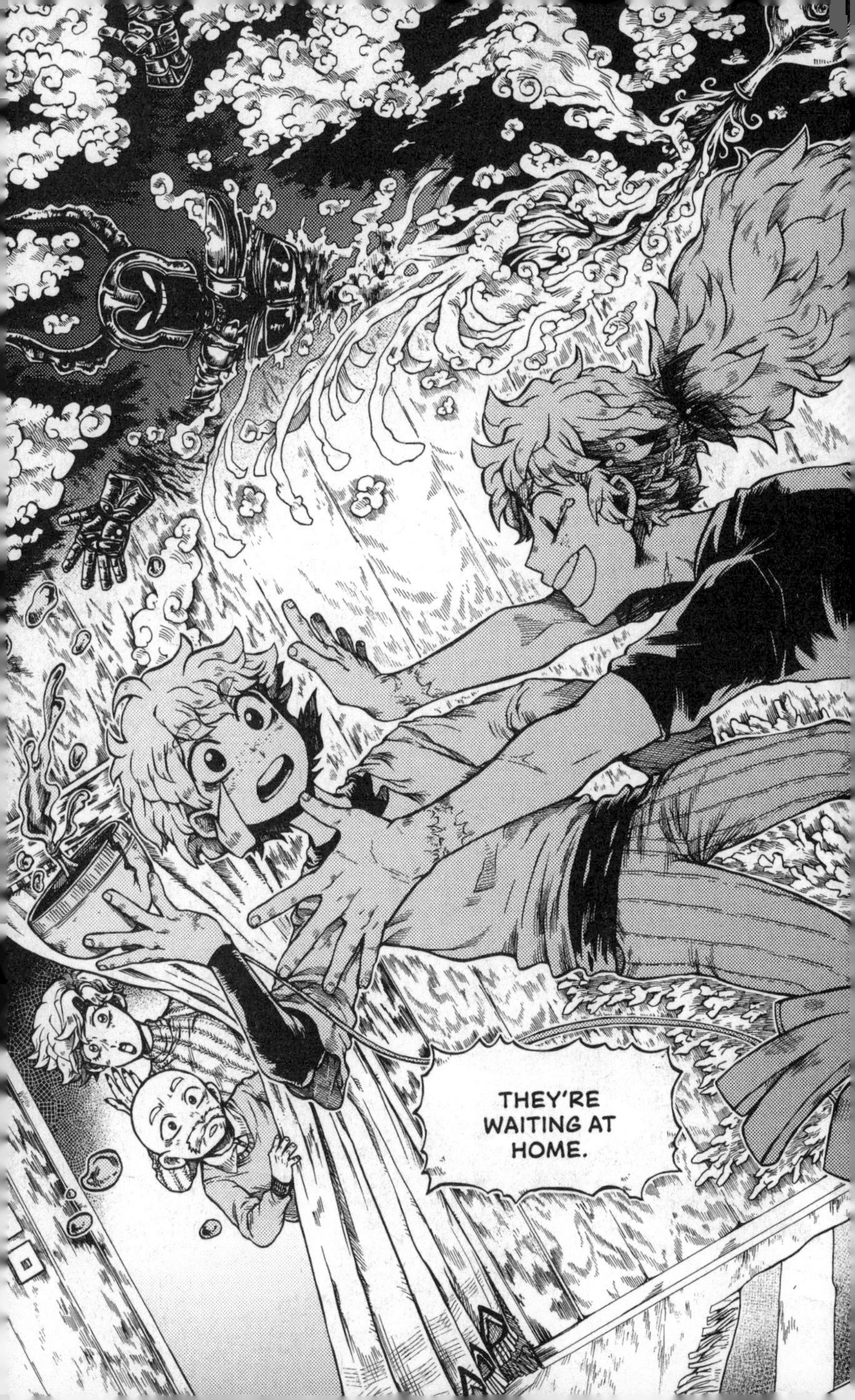
THEY'RE
WAITING AT
HOME.

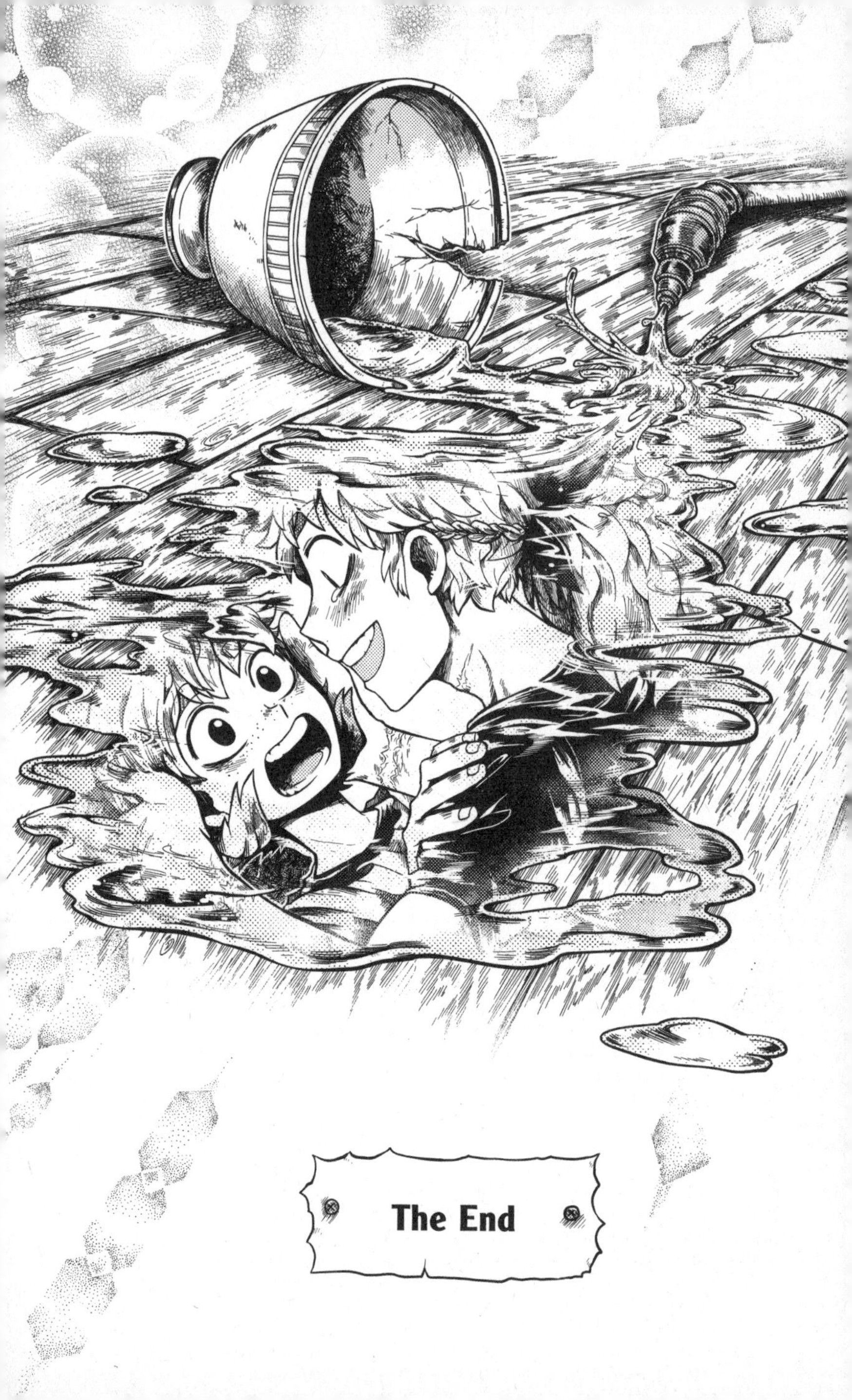
The End

GOLDFISCH

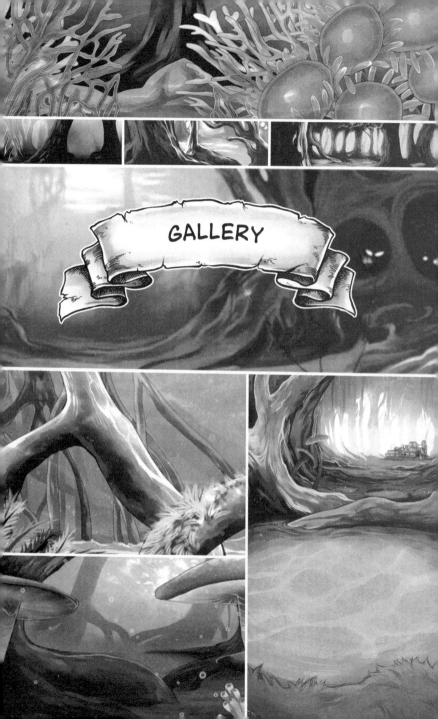

GALLERY

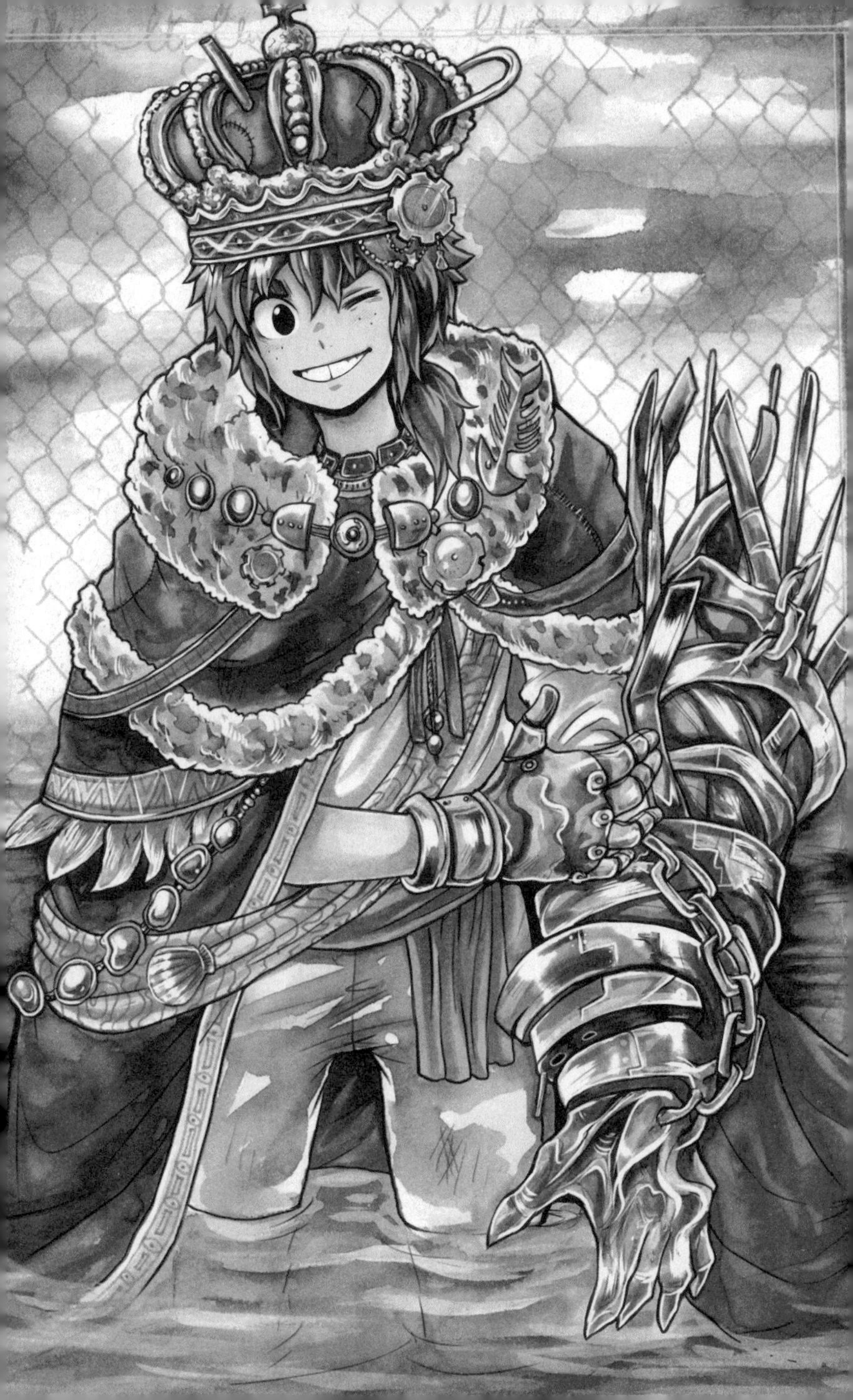

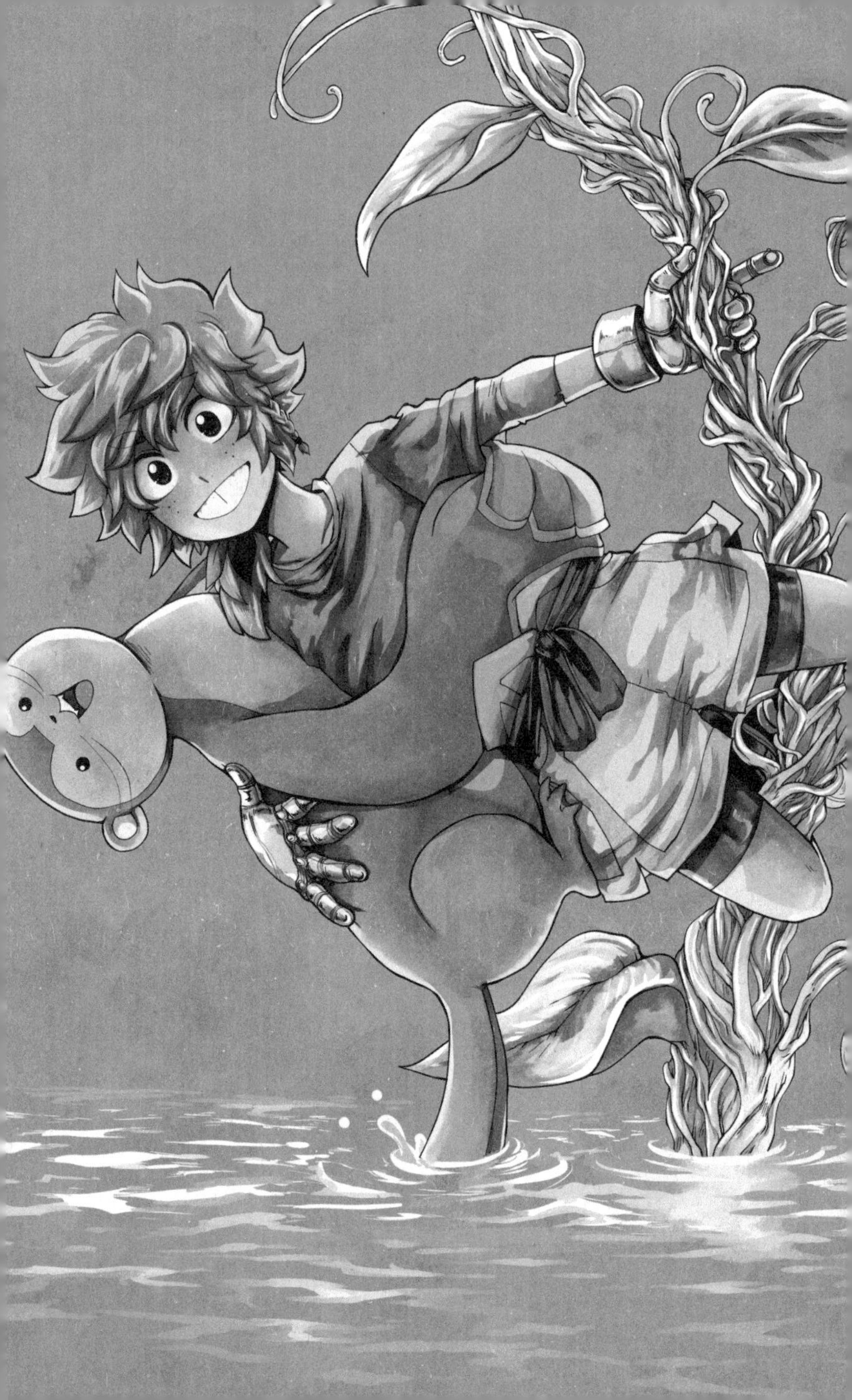

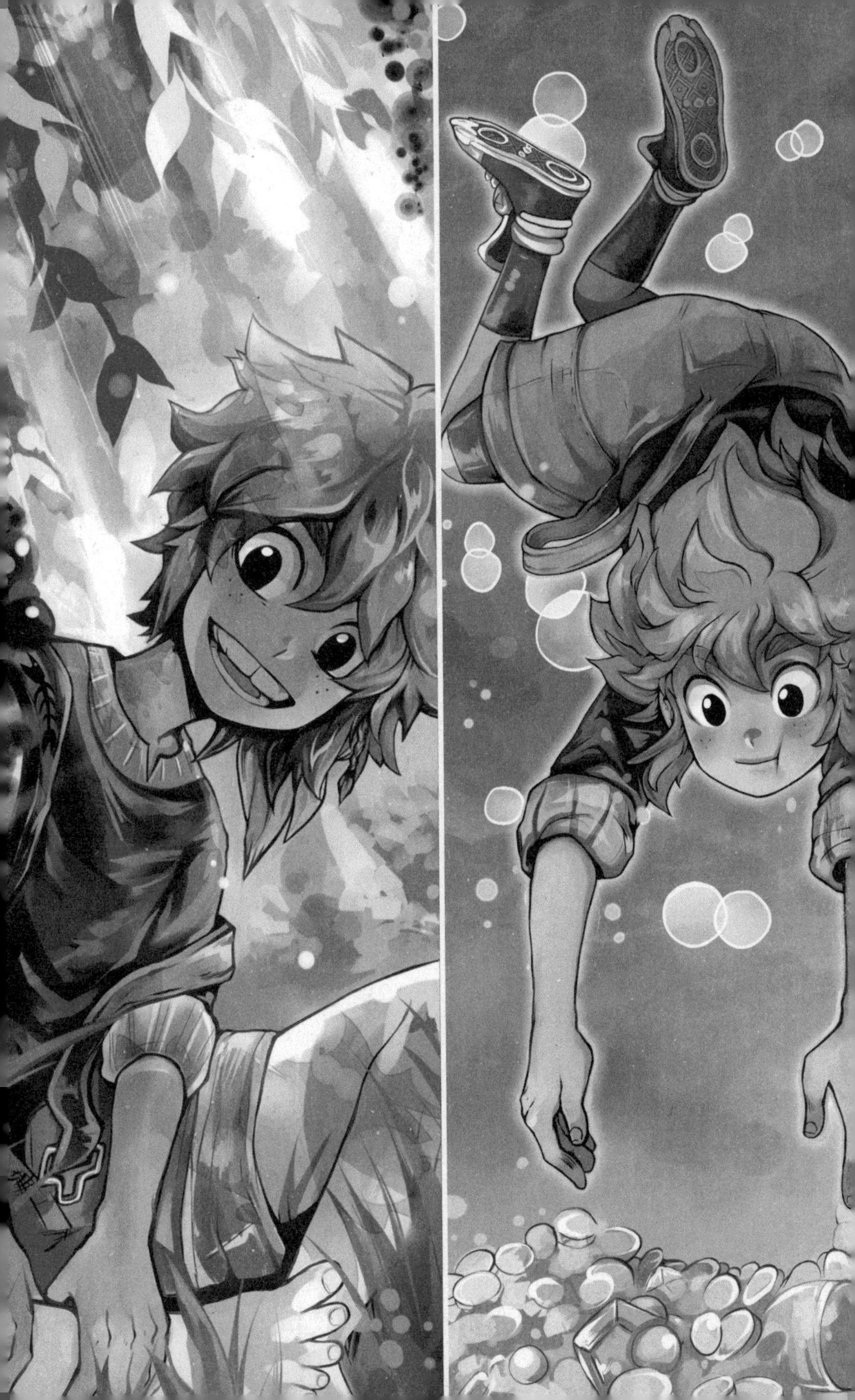

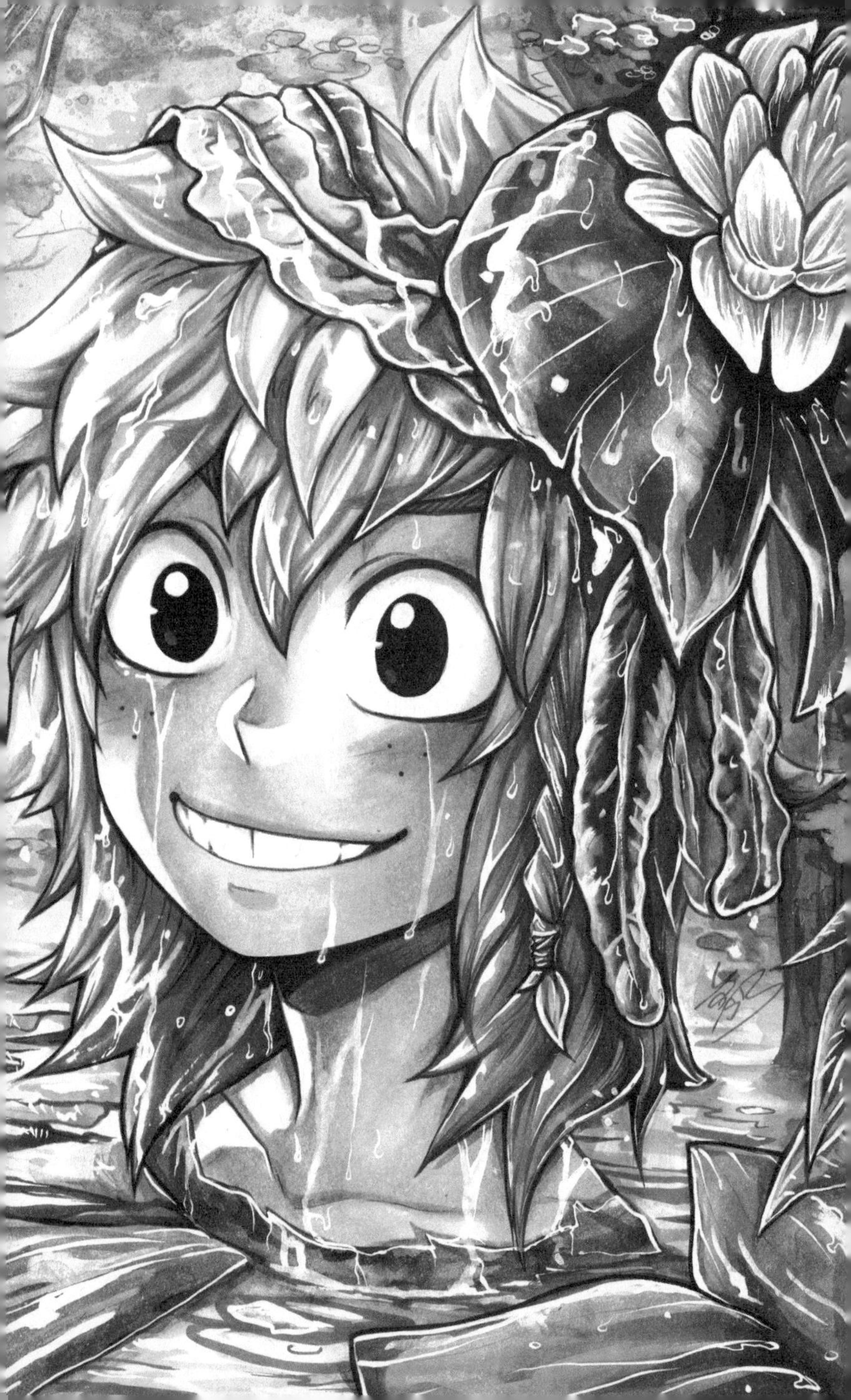

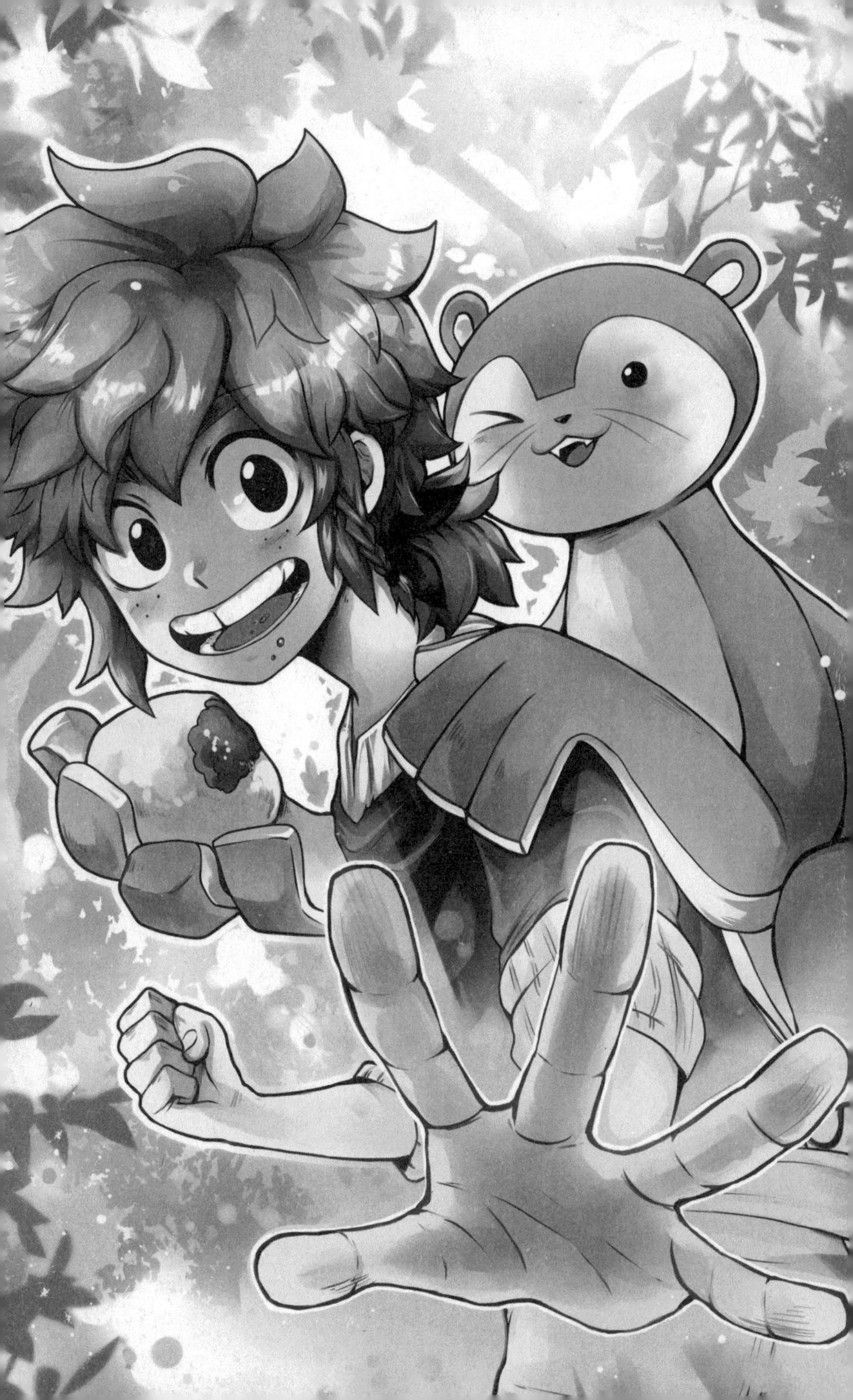

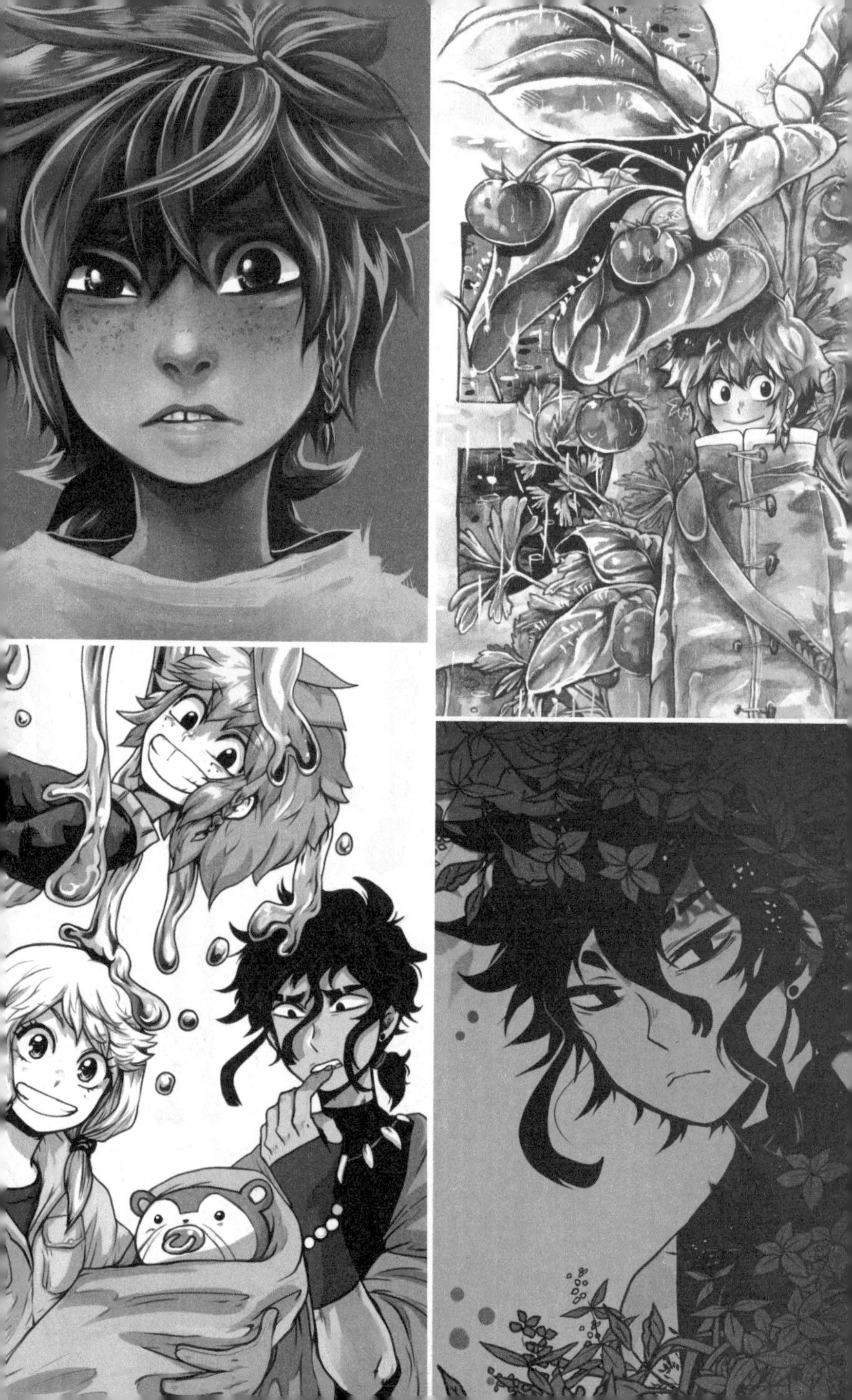

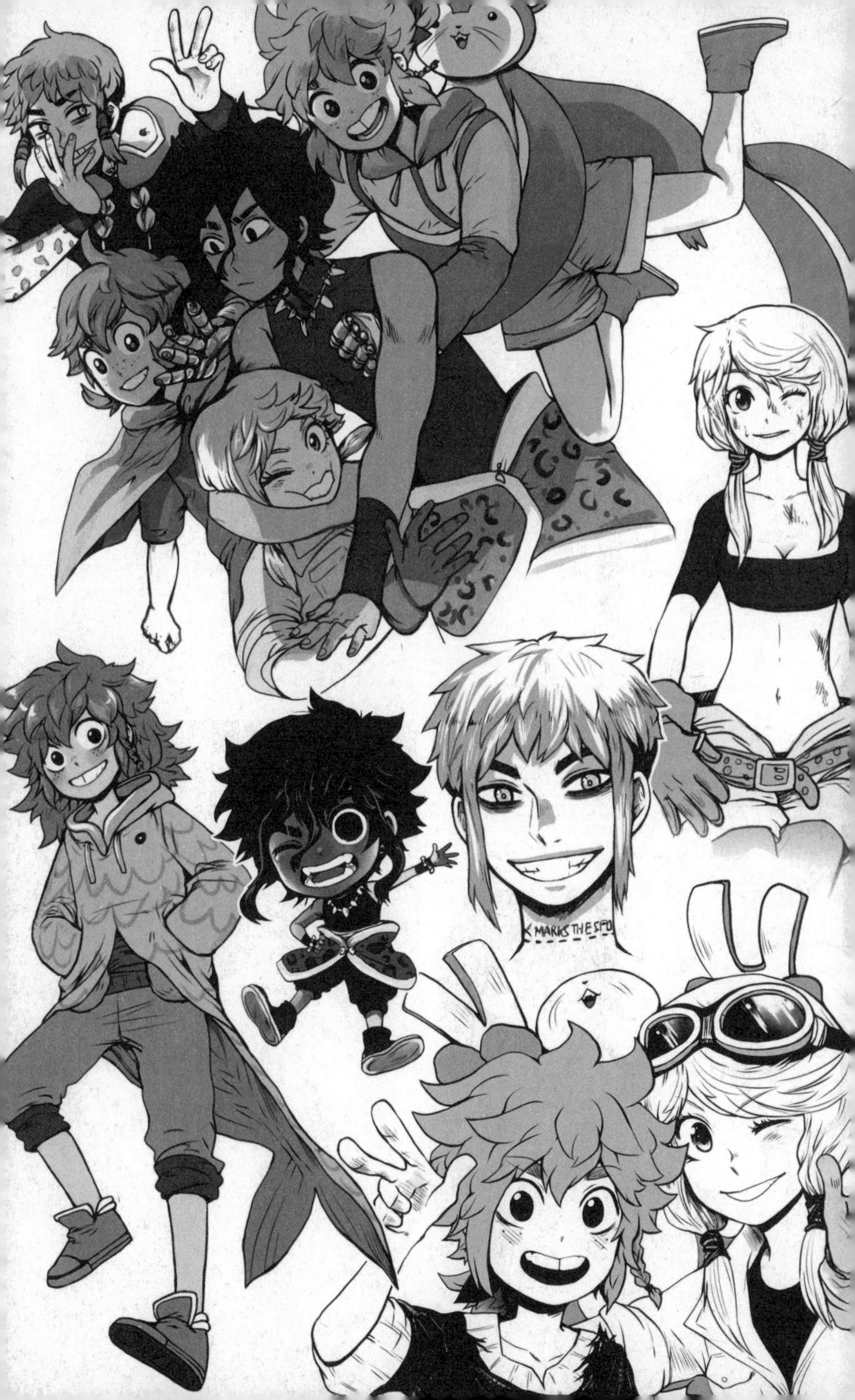
X MARKS THE SPO

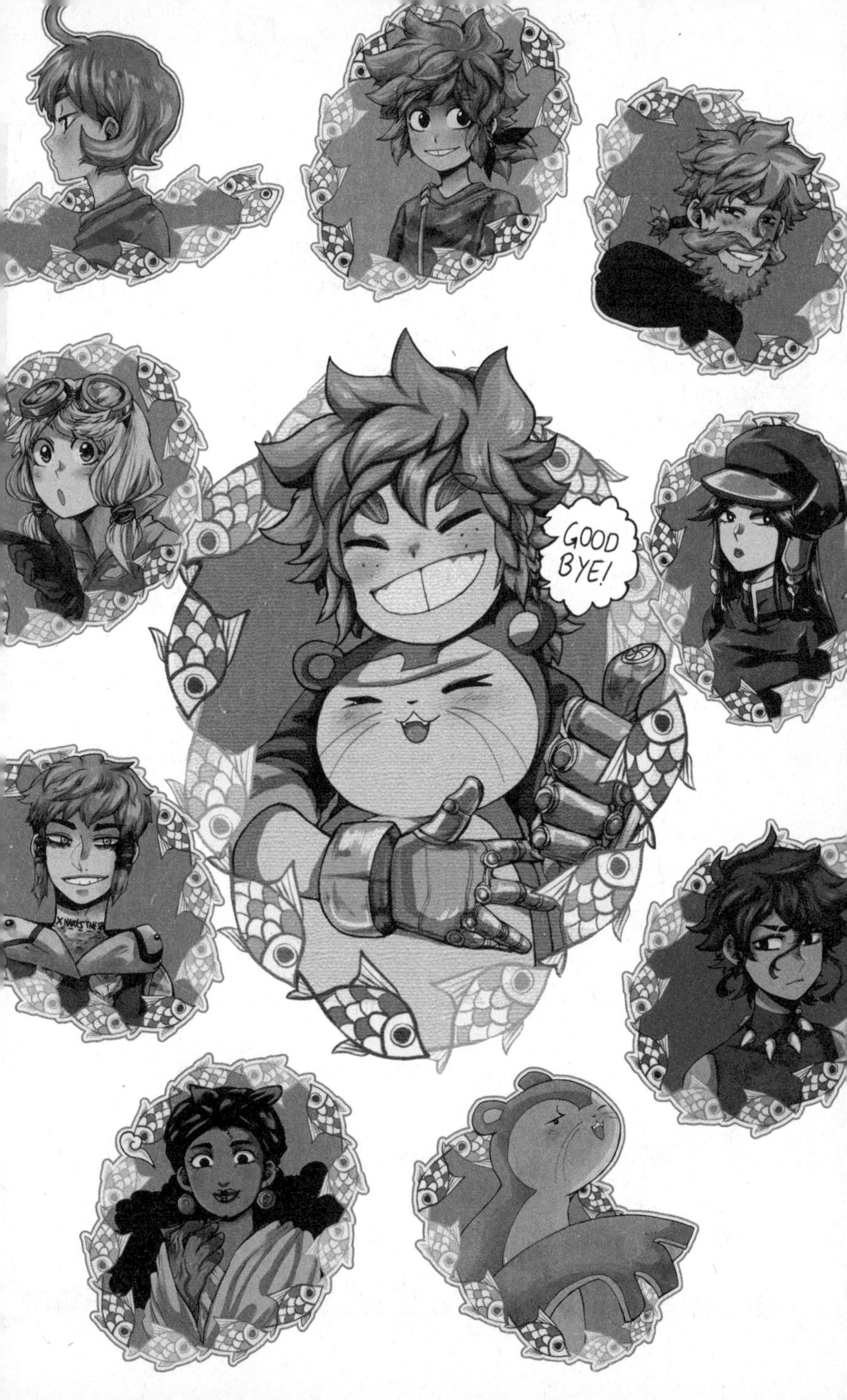
GOOD BYE!

AFTERWORD

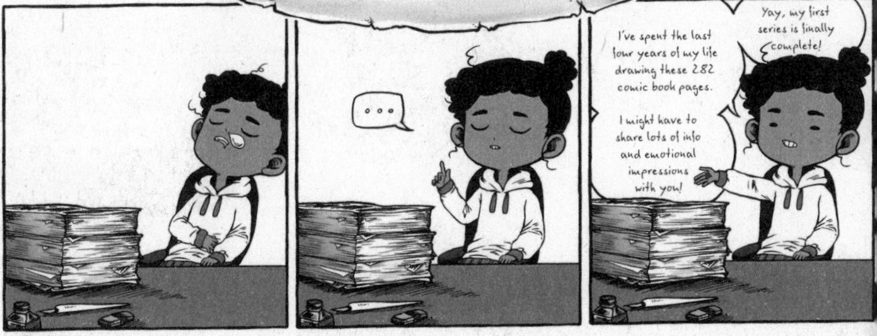

Yay, my first series is finally complete!
I've spent the last four years of my life drawing these 282 comic book pages.
I might have to share lots of info and emotional impressions with you!
...

HEY, READERS! THAT'S IT FOR *GOLDFISCH*...

THIS WORLD STILL HAS ROOM FOR MORE STORIES (E.G. ZAKA AND SHELLY'S KIDS VS. PARANORMAL PHENOMENA) BUT I'VE ACTUALLY TOLD MY STORY.

IN THE FIRST VOLUME, I MENTIONED HOW WELL-PREPARED I HAD BEEN BUT THEN MY PLOT STRUCTURE DISSOLVED A LITTLE TOWARDS THE END AND I LEFT SOME PLOT HOLES THAT I TRIED TO FIX. I HAD NO IDEA HOW I SHOULD PUT ALL OF THIS INTO A BOOK. INSTEAD OF SIX CHAPTERS, I HAVE DRAWN SEVEN AND A HALF AND THEREFORE PRODUCED A THICKER VOLUME. NEVERTHELESS, I HAD TO SQUEEZE LOTS OF PANELS PER PAGE OR FIT IN MULTIPLE DETAILED ACTIONS. THE DENSITY AND SPEED OF THE ENTIRE SERIES WEREN'T AS GOOD AS POSSIBLE, BUT I LEARNED A LOT. I HOPE I CAN USE WHAT I LEARNED ABOUT COMICS AND MYSELF IN MY LIFE. MAYBE YOU'LL SEE US AGAIN?

I APOLOGIZE FOR THE DELAY IN PRODUCTION FOR VOLUME THREE, BUT SERIOUS HEALTH ISSUES MADE ME SLOW DOWN AND TAKE A YEAR OFF. I HOPE YOU CAN SEE MY BLOOD, SWEAT, AND TEARS DRIPPING OUT OF THE BOOK. I GAVE IT MY ALL TO INCREASE THE QUALITY OF THE ARTWORK. I'M GLAD YOU'RE FINALLY HOLDING THIS VOLUME IN YOUR HANDS. I ALSO HOPE THAT YOU WILL SPOT SOME GOOD SCENES, LOVE THE CHARACTERS, AND BE WELL-ENTERTAINED.

MORREY AND HIS CREW HAVE BECOME A PART OF ME. I TRY NOT TO BE MELANCHOLY LEAVING THEM TO THEMSELVES, THOUGH. I KNOW THEY WILL HAVE ANYTHING BUT A BORING LIFE IF UNOBSERVED, HAHA!

IF YOU WANT TO WRITE ME FEEDBACK, PLEASE DON'T HESITATE TO EMAIL ME AT NANAYAA@GMX.DE. REVIEWS ON AMAZON OR GOODREADS ARE ALSO WELCOME!

LOTS OF LOVE,
NANA

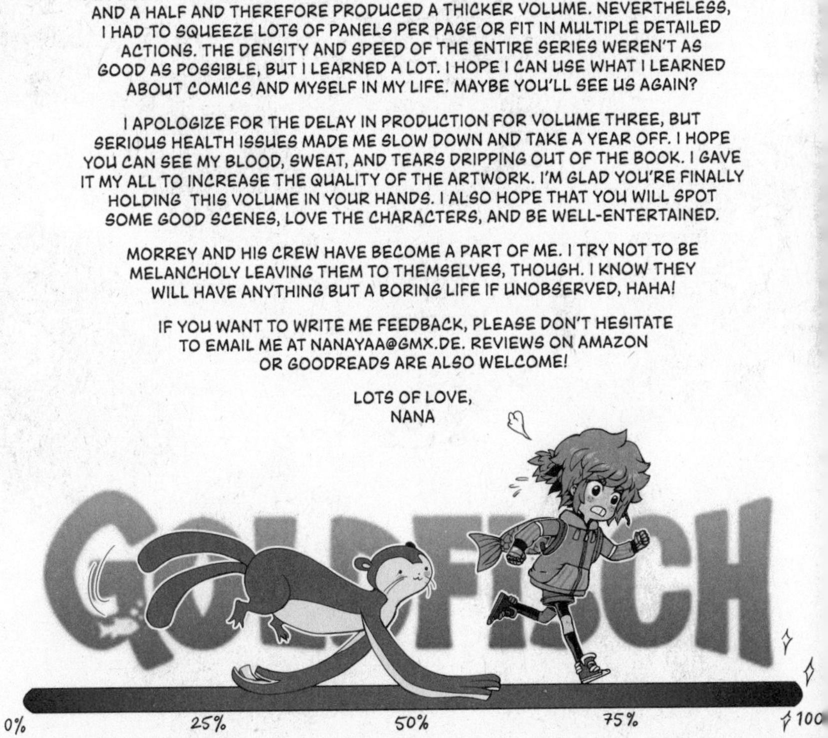

GOLDFISCH
0%
25%
50%
75%
100

ACKNOWLEDGEMENTS

Finally, thank you so much to:

TOKYOPOP USA for the English release, and NOBI NOBI for the French release

TOKYOPOP for the additional product ideas and events

All readers and buyers of this manga, for your support, feedback, and all the patience.

Anna, Izzy, Def, Melanie, Kim, and USA for the ink and help with some backgrounds

Jolly for three volumes of time, effort, and workload on the screentones assistance on all Goldfisch pages

(seriously, you deserve much gratitude)

Yannick and Oliva, for the editorial support

Also very helpful: Coffee, warming pain relief gel, eyedrops, and the German health care system

My family and friends for their emotional support in hard times

Xenia for copying the storyboard lines

HEY FOLKS, IT'S ME AGAIN, JOLLY!

WHAT CAN I SAY. WE DID IT! I'M SO RELIEVED. I'VE BEEN HELPING NANA FOR A WHILE (AND STILL WITH LOTS OF PLEASURE!). *GOLDFISCH, VOLUME 3* REALLY PUT US TO THE TEST LIKE NO PROJECT BEFORE (PRACTICALLY A STORY ABOUT DUES AND EXPERIENCE).

DESPITE THE PRESSURE AND THE CONDITIONS, WE HAVE CREATED AN AMAZING MANGA. WE COULD INCREASE THE QUALITY A GREAT DEAL AND I'M SO, SOOOOO PROUD OF MY "BOSS" FOR MAKING ME A PART OF IT... A PERSONAL NOTE TO NANA: THANK YOU A THOUSAND TIMES FOR ALLOWING ME TO ASSIST YOU. IT WAS A REAL HONOR. ♡

AND, OF COURSE, THANK YOU SO MUCH FOR YOUR SUPPORT AND THE PURCHASE OF *GOLDFISCH 3*. PLEASE FOLLOW NANA'S OTHER PROJECTS (FOLLOWING HER ON SOCIAL MEDIA IS BEST)! :D

KISSIES ON THE HEAD!

JOLLYGRUMP

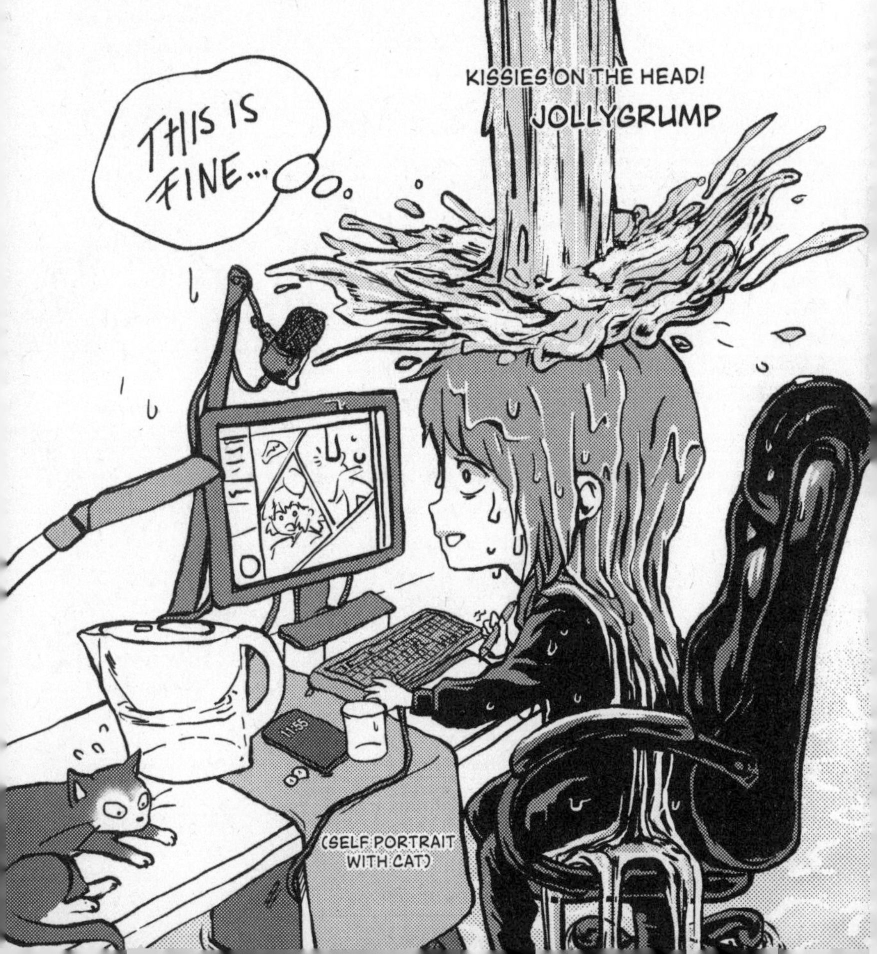
THIS IS FINE...
(SELF PORTRAIT WITH CAT)

COVER DRAFTS

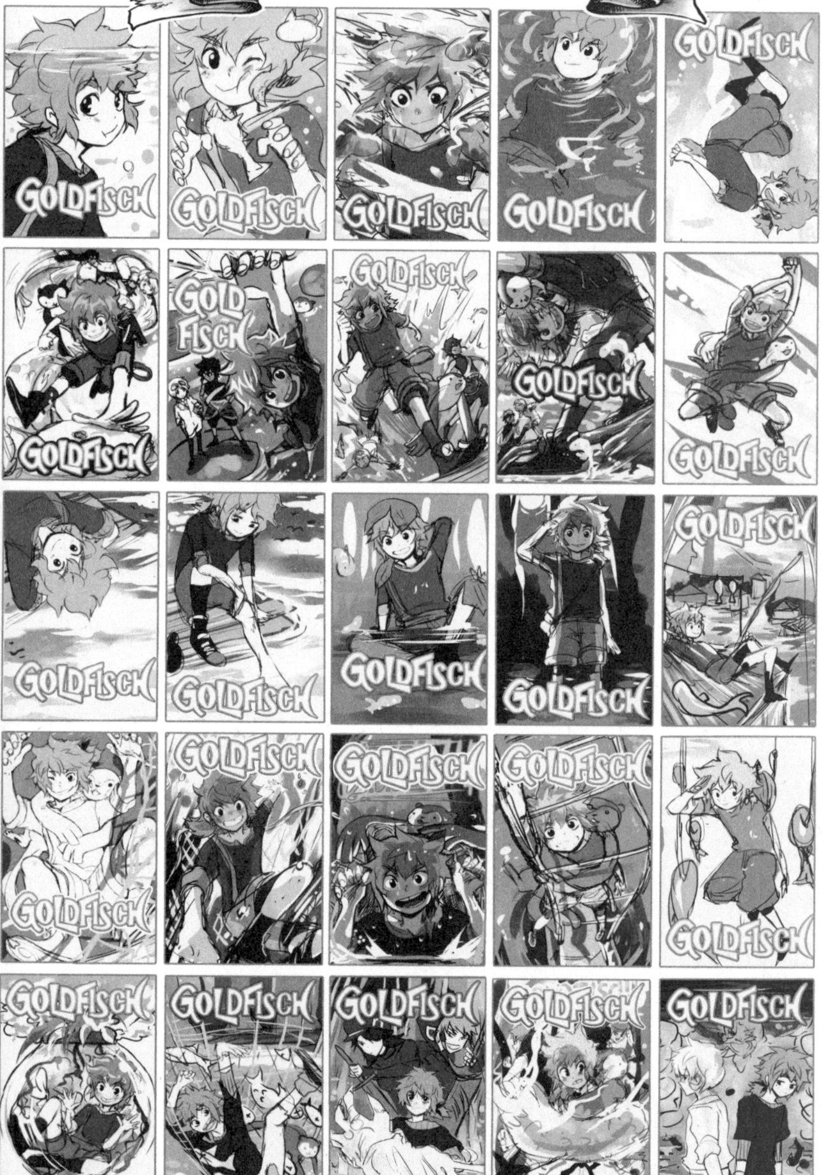
GOLDFISCH
GOLDFISCH
GOLDFISCH
GOLDFISCH
GOLDFISCH
GOLDFISCH
GOLDFISCH
GOLDFISCH
GOLD FISCH
GOLDFISCH
GOLDFISCH
GOLDFISCH
GOLDFISCH
GOLDFISCH
GOLDFISCH
GOLDFISCH
GOLDFISCH
GOLDFISCH
GOLDFISCH
GOLDFISCH
GOLDFISCH
3
GOLDFISCH
2
GOLDFISCH
2
GOLDFISCH
1
GOLDFISCH

GOLDFISCH

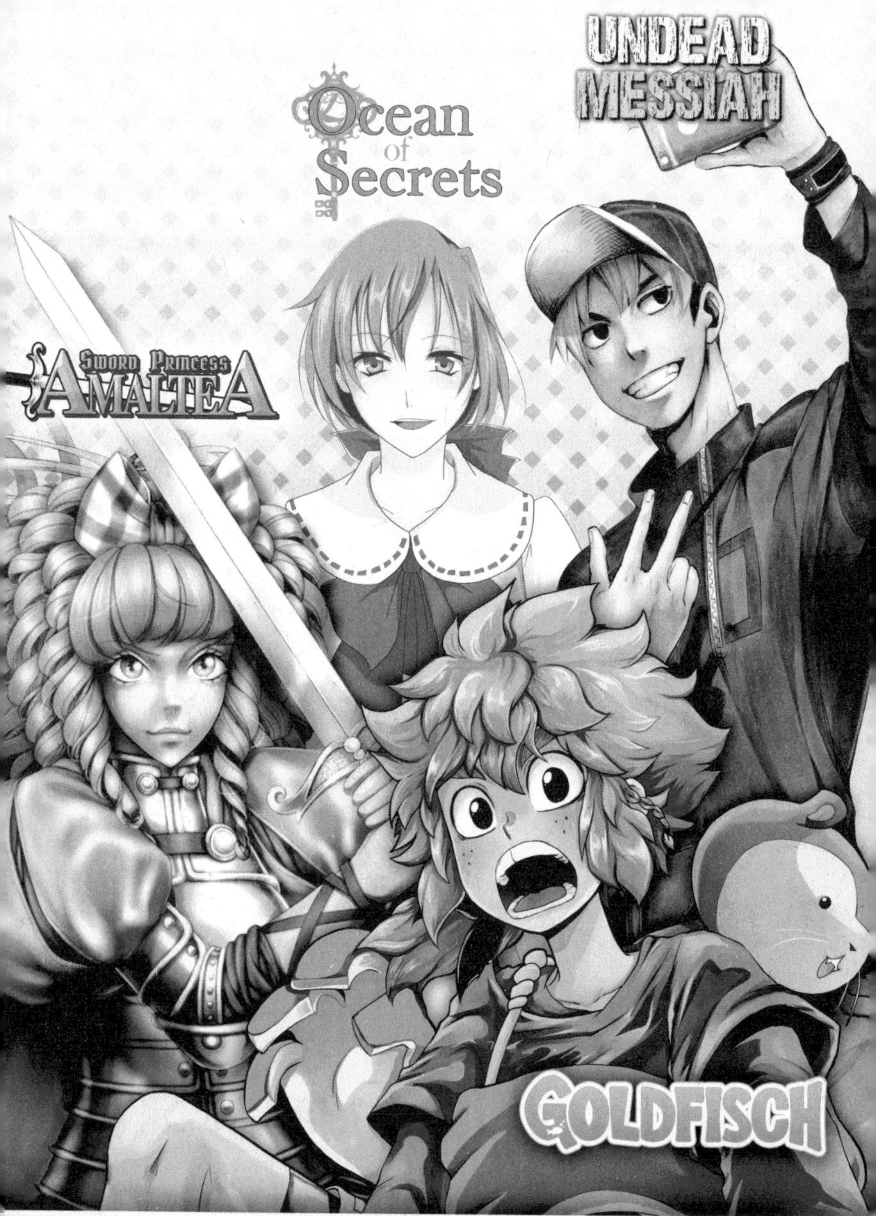
UNDEAD MESSIAH
Ocean of Secrets
SWORD PRINCESS AMALTEA
GOLDFISCH

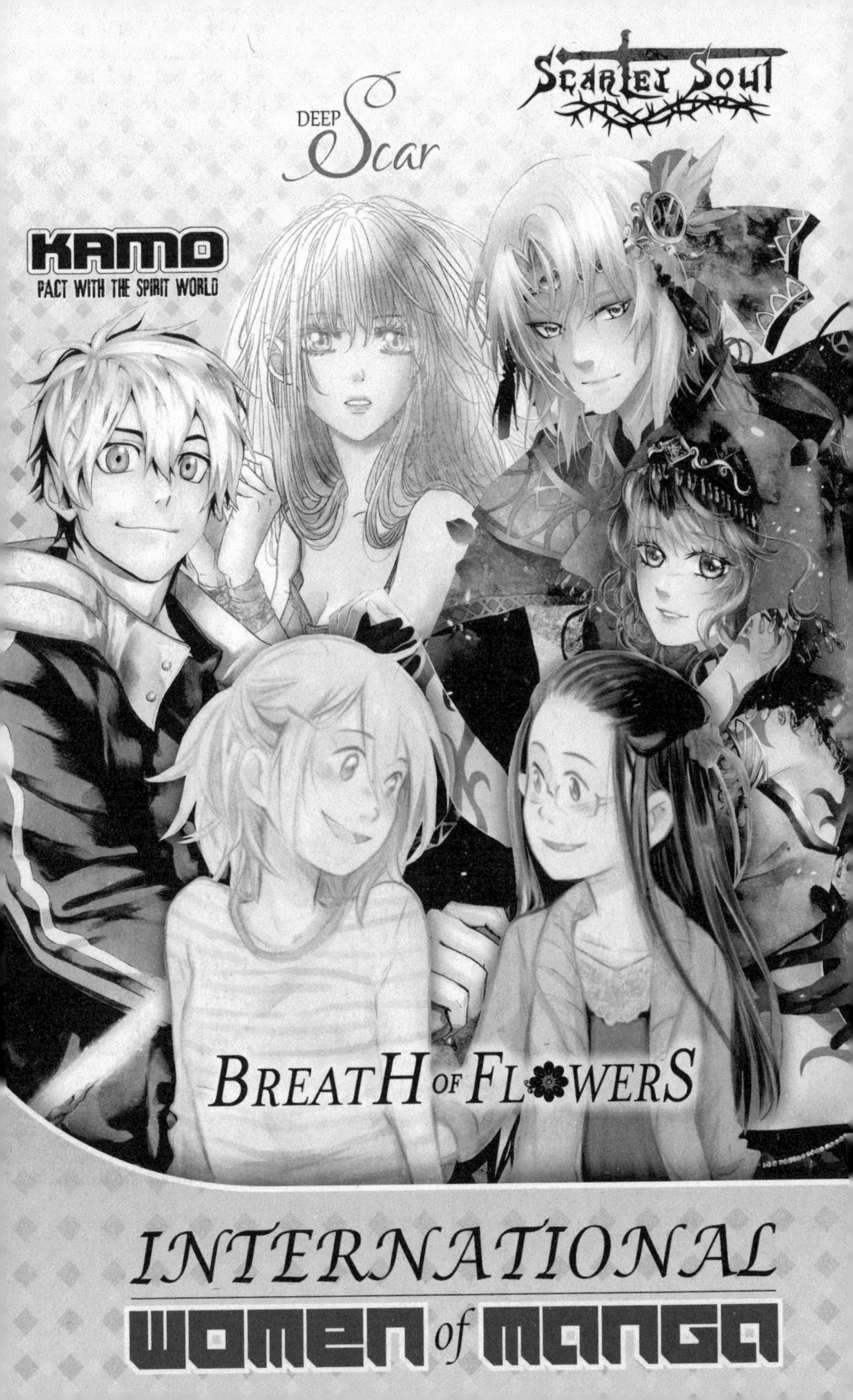
Scarlet Soul
DEEP Scar
KAMO
PACT WITH THE SPIRIT WORLD
BREATH OF FLOWERS
INTERNATIONAL
WOMEN of MANGA

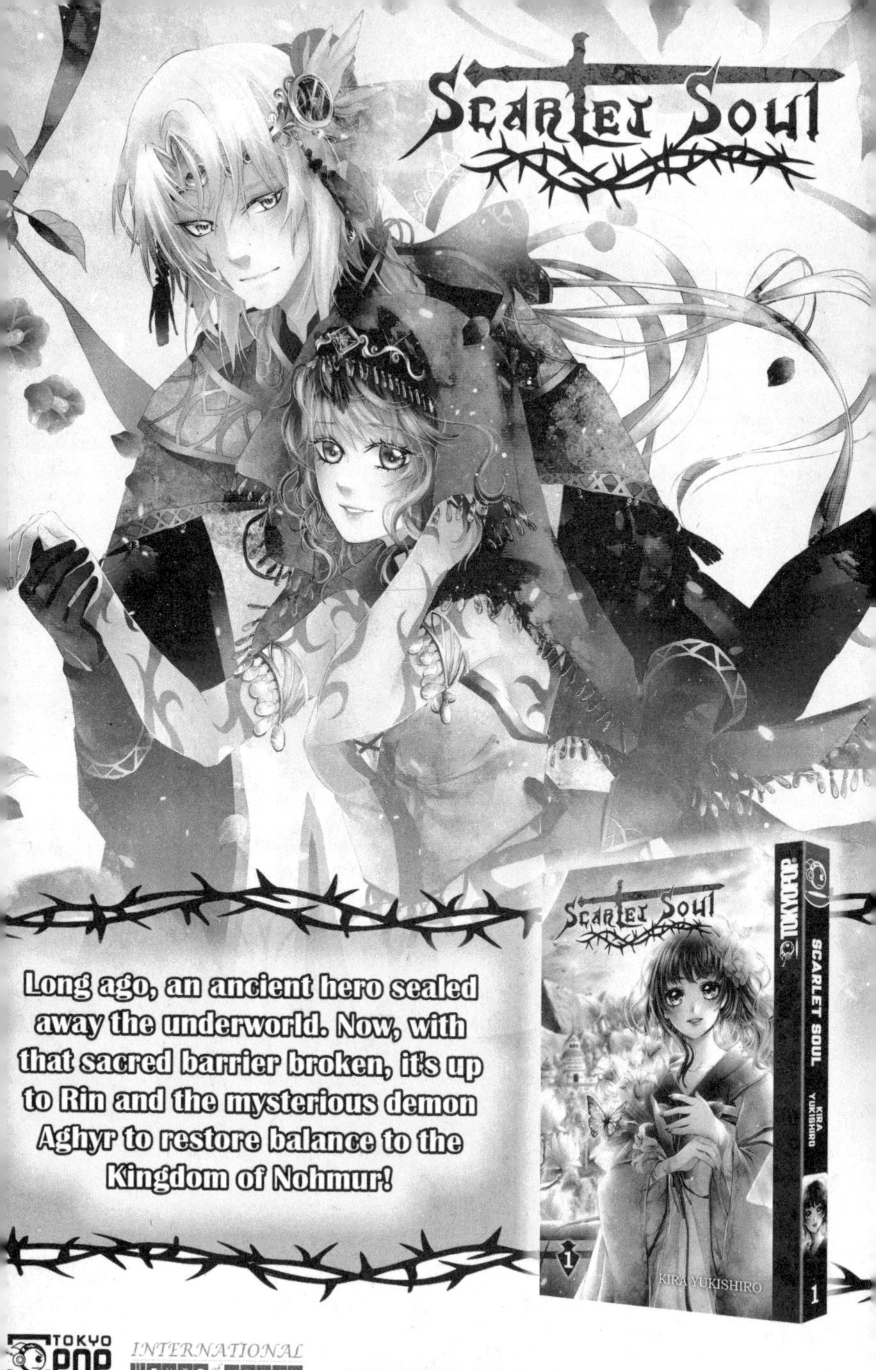
SCARLET SOUL
Long ago, an ancient hero sealed away the underworld. Now, with that sacred barrier broken, it's up to Rin and the mysterious demon Aghyr to restore balance to the Kingdom of Nohmur!
SCARLET SOUL
1
KIRA YUKISHIRO
TOKYOPOP
SCARLET SOUL
KIRA YUKISHIRO
1
TOKYO POP
INTERNATIONAL
women of manga

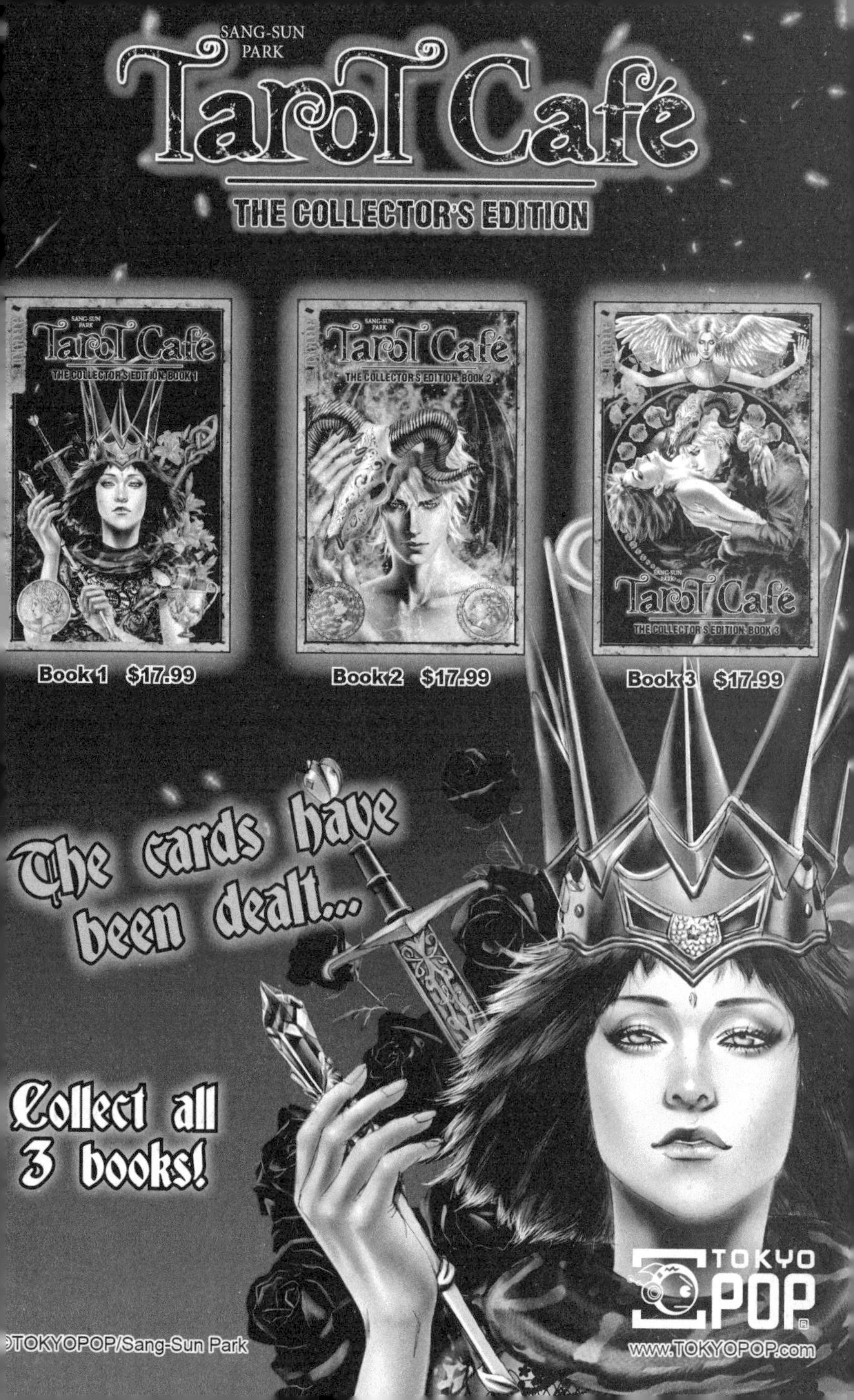
SANG-SUN PARK
Tarot Café
THE COLLECTOR'S EDITION
Book 1 $17.99
Book 2 $17.99
Book 3 $17.99
The cards have been dealt...
Collect all 3 books!
©TOKYOPOP/Sang-Sun Park
TOKYOPOP
www.TOKYOPOP.com

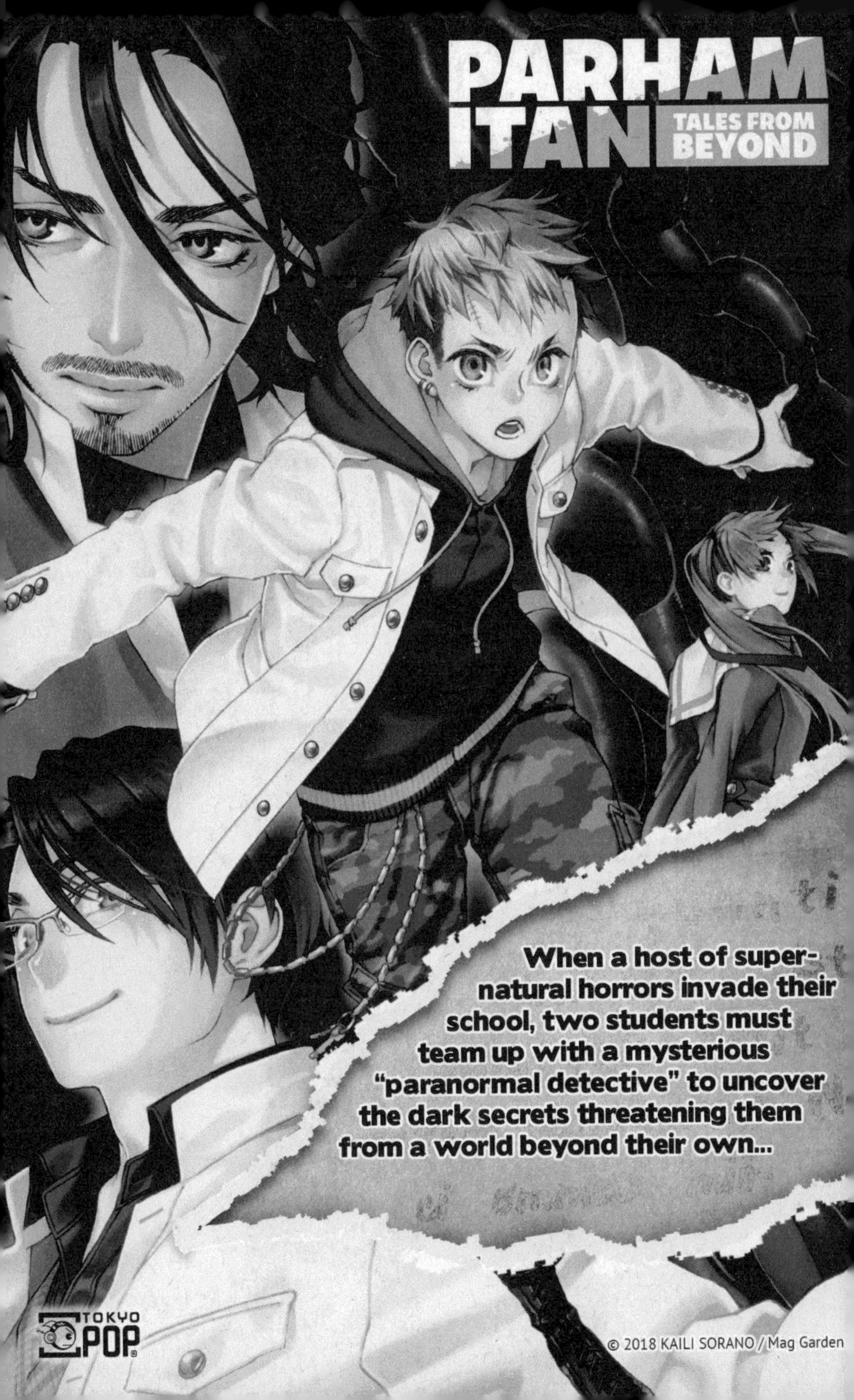
PARHAM ITAN
TALES FROM BEYOND
When a host of super-natural horrors invade their school, two students must team up with a mysterious "paranormal detective" to uncover the dark secrets threatening them from a world beyond their own...
TOKYO POP
© 2018 KAILI SORANO / Mag Garden

THE AUTHOR

At the age of 17, Nana Yaa (born, 1991) won the German manga competition MangaMagie. The German TV host Stefan Raab invited her as an interview partner and guest on his show "TVTOTAL" in 2008. As one of the most productive manga artists in the German manga scene, she has published numerous Doujinshi and short stories and, after contributing to the anthologies of the independent publisher Schwarzer Turm, her first extensive piece of work, Patina, was published by Comicstars Droemer Knauer. Her slice-of-life drama MCS was awarded Doujinshi of the Year in 2016. Nana Yaa lives and works in Neuss, Germany, and holds a BA in Communication Design. If she's not at her drawing board or creating new stories, she's playing RPGs, drinking cocktails with her friends, or spending time with her dog.